LARGE-MOUTHED BLACK BASS, *Micropterus salmoides* (Lacépède)

STATE OF ILLINOIS
DEPARTMENT OF REGISTRATION AND EDUCATION
FRANCIS W. SHEPARDSON, DIRECTOR

DIVISION OF THE
NATURAL HISTORY SURVEY

THE FISHES OF ILLINOIS

BY

STEPHEN ALFRED FORBES, PH.D., LL.D.
AND
ROBERT EARL RICHARDSON, A.M.

SECOND EDITION, 1920

PUBLISHED BY
AUTHORITY OF THE STATE OF ILLINOIS

State of Illinois

NATURAL HISTORY SURVEY DIVISION

Stephen A. Forbes, Chief

BOARD OF NATURAL RESOURCES AND CONSERVATION

Willian Trelease	Biology
John M. Coulter	Forestry
Rollin D. Salisbury	Geology
William A. Noyes	Chemistry
John W. Alvord	Engineering
Kendric C. Babcock	University of Illinois
Francis W. Shepardson	Director

Frank O. Lowden, Governor

Springfield, Ill.
Illinois State Journal Co., State Printers
1 9 2 0

18048—2000

CONTENTS*

*For species whose page numbers are preceded by a star (*) there are distribution maps in the atlas accompanying this report.

List of Color Illustrations

INTRODUCTION

It is the purpose of the present volume to furnish to those interested in Illinois fishes a reliable guide to a knowledge of the species, a careful account of their local and general distribution and of their relations to their environment, a correct idea of the function and relative importance of the different species in the general system of aquatic life, and a fairly full summary of their habits and utilities so far as these are now known. To this end the species have, with very few exceptions, been described anew from the specimens of our collection, with due use, however, of descriptions already extant; analytical keys have been made, adapted, or selected, with special reference to the Illinois species; and our data of geographical and local distribution and of ecological situation and relationship have been analyzed, to a considerable extent, by statistical methods.

The collections and field observations of Illinois fishes upon which this report is based were begun by the senior author in 1876, and were continued by him and by a considerable list of assistants, at rather irregular intervals, to 1903. With the establishment of the Illinois Biological Station on the Illinois River at Havana in 1894, field work in ichthyology became more nearly continuous than had previously been possible. An especially interesting study was made at Havana during the winter and spring of 1898 and 1899 by Mr. Wallace Craig, an assistant of the State Laboratory, to whom was assigned the duty of making systematic collections at fixed points by the uniform use of identical apparatus at each, determining, counting, and recording all the species obtained in each situation. It was the object of this investigation to apply, in the field of ichthyology, the quantitative method which had been used with distinguished success in the study of the plankton of the Illinois River and adjacent waters at the Havana Station. During the summer of 1899 field work was transferred to Meredosia with Mr. H. A. Surface in charge, and later it was taken up by Mr. Thomas Large at Meredosia and Ottawa, to which latter place the station equipment was transferred in 1901. Extensive wagon-trips were made from time to time through various parts of the state for a study of the fishes of the smaller streams, the most important of them in 1899 by Mr. Large, to whom we are indebted for the field determination of many of our specimens and for numerous descriptive notes on the waters and situations visited.

Valuable collections have sometimes been obtained, especially from western Illinois, by arrangement with high-school teachers, who have fished the streams of their neighborhoods in accordance with our instructions, and in consideration of our return of a named series of specimens to their schools.

Our field apparatus consisted mainly of seines of various size and mesh, from the smallest and finest minnow seines to those long enough and deep enough for use in our largest rivers. For collections from weedy ponds and from creeks, and especially from swift waters or from streams where a shore landing was difficult, we have depended largely on the so-called "Baird seine," a close-meshed minnow seine of medium length with a wide-mouthed, deep, conical bag of netting in its center. Trammel-nets have been very serviceable in waters through which a seine could not be drawn, especially in those encumbered by brush or filled with water-plants. Set-nets or pound-nets of various size and mesh, both with and without wings, have brought us much material, especially of the larger and more abundant species. For our knowledge of these, however, we have depended largely upon an inspection of fish markets and an examination of the catches of commercial fishermen, with whom we have, indeed, made frequent trips to their fishing grounds.

More than 200,000 specimens of our 150 species have been thus collected and preserved, under about 1,800 accessions numbers representing differences of date, location, or situation, and from more than 450 localities, fairly well distributed through ninety-three of the one hundred and two counties of the state. These collections bore, as a rule, permanent labels showing the date, place, and body of water from which they came, and, in the majority of cases, some particulars concerning the apparatus used and the more notable features of the situation. This has made possible a statistical analysis of the data of relative abundance of the different species under varying conditions, geographical, local, and ecological, and also of the frequencies of joint or associate occurrence of the various species, one with another, in each class of situation or in each place. The results of statistical comparisons of this kind have been used to some extent in this report, especially in the chapter on geographical and ecological distribution, and in the detailed discussions of the leading families, genera, and species.

A knowledge of the food and feeding activities of fishes is fundamental to any fair understanding of their place and function in the general system of life, and especially to any just appreciation of their importance to man. Unfortunately, our definite knowledge of this field is very limited, and for most of the statements made concerning the food, feeding habits, and alimentary structures of fishes, we have had to draw upon the papers of the senior author, published in volumes I. and II. of the Bulletin of the Illinois State Laboratory of Natural History, and based upon studies made between the years 1878 and 1888.

In the details of the classification we have followed, with little variation, Jordan and Evermann's catalogue of "The Fishes of North and Middle America," published as Bulletin 47 of the U. S. National Museum, but our arrangement of orders and families is that proposed by Boulenger, in Volume VII. of the Cambridge Natural History, and followed in the main by Jordan in his "Guide to the Study of Fishes."

It has not been our purpose to enter into the synonymy except so far as was necessary to connect the specific names here used with both the more general publications in this field and the more special papers on the fishes of Illinois. We have in all cases referred to the original description of the species, and have, with few exceptions, made reference also, using the abbreviations indicated, to the following books and articles:

Gunther: Catalogue of the Fishes in the British Museum. (Abbreviation, G.)

Jordan and Gilbert: Synopsis of the Fishes of North America. (J. & G.)

Jordan: Manual of the Vertebrates of the Northern United States. 8th edition, 1888. (M. V.)

Jordan and Evermann. The Fishes of North and Middle America. (J. & E.)

Boulenger: Catalogue of the Perciform Fishes in the British Museum. (B.)

Nelson: A Partial Catalogue of the Fishes of Illinois. Bull. Ill. State Lab. Nat. Hist., Vol. I., No. 1. (N.)

Jordan: A Catalogue of the Fishes of Illinois. Bull. Ill. State Lab. Nat. Hist., Vol. I., No. 2. (J.)

Forbes: A Catalogue of the Native Fishes of Illinois. Rep. Ill. State Fish Comm., 1884. (F.)

Forbes: Various papers on the food of fishes. Bull. Ill. State Lab. Nat. Hist., Vols. I. and II. (F. F.)

Large: A List of the Native Fishes of Illinois, with Keys. Rep. Ill. State Fish Comm., 1900–02. (L.)

Richardson: A Review of the Sunfishes of the current Genera *Apomotis*, *Lepomis*, and *Eupomotis*, with particular Reference to the Species found in Illinois. Bull. Ill. State Lab. Nat. Hist., Vol. VII., Art. III. (R.)

Besides the assistants already mentioned, especial acknowledgments are due to Mr. H. Garman, assistant in the State Laboratory and collector of much of our material during the early years of the work; to Mr. A. J. Woolman, who, in 1903, made and recorded measurements of many specimens of the commoner species, and who, by his studies of the osteology of the *Catostomidæ* opened the way to improved generic definitions of *Ictiobus* and *Carpiodes*; and to Mrs. Lydia M. (Hart) Green and Miss Charlotte M. Pinkerton, who made, under the supervision of the field ichthyologist, the colored drawings by which this report is illustrated. Professor Frank Smith, Dr. C. A. Kofoid, Mr. C. A. Hart, Mr. J. E. Hallinen, and Mr. E. B. Forbes have, during their several periods of service on the State Laboratory staff, added considerably to our knowledge of the fishes of the state.

It is impracticable to give the names of all outside the staff of the State Laboratory who have been, from time to time, of material assistance in the long course of this work, but this list of acknowledgments would be seriously deficient without particular mention of Dr. S. E. Meek, of the Field Museum, and Dr. Barton W. Evermann, of the U. S. Fish Commission, both of whom have been especially obliging in passing judgment on sets of specimens of difficult determination, and in scrutinizing the tables of geographical distribution printed in the introductory part of this report. It is a pleasure to acknowledge also our indebtedness to a considerable number of careful and observant fishermen who have told us much of the habits and behavior of our best-known fishes. To Messrs. John A. Shulte, of Havana, J. P. Baur, of the U. S. fisheries station at Meredosia, David Yeck, of Meredosia, W. J. & H. L. Ashlock, of Alton, and Miles Newberry, of Havana, we owe many facts concerning the life and economy of our fishes which we should not otherwise have obtained.

More than to any other, the Director is indebted to Mr. R. E. Richardson—his colleague during three years in the preparation of this report—for indispensable service in the field, the laboratory, and the library, and especially for the accumulation and organization of material of all descriptions, for his critical study of the collections, all of which were finally handled by him, and for the preparation or revision of nearly all the technical descriptions printed in this volume.

S. A. Forbes,
Director of Laboratory.

Urbana, August 1, 1908.

THE TOPOGRAPHY AND HYDROGRAPHY OF ILLINOIS*

BY CHARLES W. ROLFE, M. S.

The State of Illinois may be described as a great plain sloping gently towards the south, the northernmost fifth of which is underlaid by rocks of Silurian age, while the surface rocks of the remaining four-fifths are the limestones, sandstones, and shales of the Mississippian and Pennsylvanian, with small areas of Ordovician, Silurian, and Devonian.

The highest portion of this plain lies in the northern part of Jo Daviess and Stephenson counties, where the general surface has an elevation of something over 1,000 feet, and mounds rise more than 200 feet above this level. The highest point is Charles Mound, near the Wisconsin line, which is 1,241 feet above the sea. From this point the surface slopes rather rapidly to the east and south, declining to an average altitude of about 800 feet in Lake county and of 700 feet in Whiteside county. South of Whiteside county the surface levels across the state from east to west are essentially the same wherever the line is drawn, but southward the surface slopes gradually until an average level of 400 feet is reached just north of the Ozark ridge. This ridge is an eastern extension of the Ozark Mountain range, whose highest peaks in Illinois are Williams Hill, in Pope county, which reaches an elevation of 1,065 feet, and Bald Knob, in Union county, 985 feet high. The average altitude of the ridge is from 750 to 800 feet. South of it the surface slopes rapidly to the low valley of the Cache River, the general altitude of which does not exceed 325 to 350 feet. The lowest point in the state is at Cairo, where low water on the Ohio River is 268.58 feet above the sea.

While the general surface of the state is unusually level,

*The general system of the hydrography of the state is so largely a consequence of its surface geology that it can be clearly understood only by way of its geological antecedents and relations. For this reason Professor C. W. Rolfe, for many years head of the Department of Geology in the University of Illinois, was asked to prepare this chapter. With his discussion has been incorporated, with his approval, some additional matter relating especially to the waters themselves, compiled from field notes of the State Laboratory, and from more general sources.—S. A. FORBES.

this does not mean that it presents no marked variations. Few of the 102 counties in the state have a difference of less than 150 feet between their highest and lowest points, while variations of 300 to 400 feet are often found. These differences, however, are not due to variations in the general level, but to the presence of deep preglacial valleys or of moraines, and often of both.

For the present discussion the surface of the state may be divided as follows:

1. The northwestern unglaciated area.
2. The areas of the Iowan and the Illinoisan drift.
3. The area of the Wisconsin drift.
4. The unglaciated southern area.

THE NORTHWESTERN UNGLACIATED AREA

It is believed that at one time the entire northern fifth of the state was covered by rocks of the Trenton, Maquoketa, and Niagara formations, these following each other from below upward in the order named, and each covering the entire area. This portion of the state became dry land at the close of the Silurian and was not again submerged, except possibly in small areas and for brief periods; consequently during the millions of years which elapsed between its emergence from the ocean and the advent of the first ice-sheet it was subjected to large erosion in spite of its low relief. At some time during this long period a low arch was raised across its northwestern corner, and here erosion became much more effective than on the less elevated parts.

The streams of that time cut for themselves cañons 250 to 300 feet deep, extending entirely through the Niagara and Maquoketa, but found their base level at or near the surface of the Galena. An extensive peneplain was formed at this level, covering most of the area now included in the nine counties which lie farthest west. At various points over this peneplain, mostly in its northern and western parts, fragments of the denuded strata were left in the form of mounds which now rise above the general surface. Later the base level was lowered and the rivers began again to deepen their channels, and they have continued this process until now they flow in trenches cut in the rock often to a depth of 300 to 400 feet below the general level. With the mounds rising above the general surface and with the deep channels in which the rivers flow, the topography of the country is extremely broken for that of the Mississippi

Valley. Much of the irregularity shown in Jo Daviess county, however, was produced during and since the glacial period, for the ice-sheet which advanced on the state from the north was divided in southern Wisconsin and left this part of our state untouched.

THE AREAS OF IOWAN AND ILLINOISAN DRIFT

Before describing these areas it is well to call attention to the fact that the preglacial drainage of the entire state seems to have been from northeast to southwest, and that while most of these early stream beds were completely filled by the drift from the ice-sheets, some of them were so large and deep that they were not entirely filled throughout their length, and now control the general direction of our larger streams. Probably, however, no one of them follows a preglacial channel throughout its entire length, and nearly all of the smaller streams flow in postglacial channels, the courses of which have been largely determined by moraines.

Coming now to the areas mentioned in the last heading, it is believed that all of that part of the state which lies north of the Ozark ridge, with the exception of the extreme northwest corner, was covered by one or more of the earlier ice-sheets, and that, when these retreated, they left behind them a thick sheet of drift which filled the smaller channels completely, and some portions of the larger ones as well. Upon the general surface thus formed they also laid down ridges of drift which extended across the country, forming effective dams to the drainage. These dams, which are called moraines, varied in height from a few feet to a hundred or more, and from a few rods to one or several miles in width. They were generally concentric, and so lay nearly parallel to each other. When they were far apart they inclosed large areas which had no outlets, and, filled by rains, formed extensive lakes; but when they were close together the intervening lakes were necessarily smaller and more numerous. The water supply of the time greatly exceeded evaporation, and so these basins were soon filled to the brim and overflowed at the lowest points of the moraines which surrounded them. These openings gradually deepened. Ultimately, by the lowering of their outlets, and also by filling with deposits, the lakes were converted into marshy plains or prairies.

During the time in which the lakes were in existence nothing prevented the growth of vegetation on the confining moraines, and so these areas gradually came to be covered with belts of timber, between which were the lakes or marshes which afterward became prairies.

As the lakes gradually became marshy, the water, flowing from one to the other through the concentric moraines, sought the lowest channels and formed continuous streams. Since certain of the preglacial channels were not completely filled with drift throughout their entire lengths they offered depressions here and there, and the streams followed their course for considerable distances, so that in the end the general direction of the stream was often largely controlled by these valleys.

As time went on these main streams threw off branches behind the moraines which in their turn divided and subdivided, each little branch pushing its channel back towards the nearest slough. In this way a complete drainage system was gradually established, but the courses of the larger branches, and many of the smaller as well, were largely controlled by the moraines behind which they were developed. Gradually, and long before the drainage system was complete, those branches which were pushing backward toward the moraines united with the flood-water streams which flowed down their sides and began to eat into the moraines themselves, thus dividing them into series of isolated hills and short ridges which we now find scattered all over this area. In some cases they removed the moraines entirely. Only a few of these old morainic systems have been studied and are shown on the accompanying map (III.), but many others are known to exist.

The above is, in brief, the history of this area, and indicates in a general way how its streams and surface features were formed. As the drift was deposited on an irregular surface its depth varied greatly, and in many places the streams have cut entirely through it, alternately crossing the divides and channels of former streams, and consequently flowing now on rock and now on mud beds.

With the establishment of a drainage system, erosion of the prairies began, and every storm since that time has carried away portions of the black prairie soil, until now, in many places, it has nearly or entirely disappeared, leaving the gray to brown, more or less acid, subsoil at the surface. In the lake beds, which were protected from erosion, the black soil has been retained and, in some places, even thick beds of peat have been formed. Some lakes were so situated that streams flowing into them brought quantities of sediment. The coarser particles, or sands, were deposited as soon as the velocity was checked, but the water in the lake was kept in motion sufficiently rapid so that the finer sediment was not dropped, but carried away. In this manner the beds of the lakes were covered with thick layers of sand. When drainage was established, this sand, then left dry, was heaped by the wind into dunes and hills. Illustrations of this may be found in the Winnebago swamps, the sandy areas of Mason, Kankakee, and Tazewell counties, and in many other places.

After an interval covering thousands, perhaps tens of thousands, of years following the retreat of the earlier ice-sheets, the northeastern portion of the state was again covered by ice. As this ice melted, its outwash deposited here and there over the older drift a layer of fine but well-assorted material called loess. After the ice had disappeared and the climate had become less humid, this loess was rearranged by the wind and quite probably received additions of similar wind-borne material from the western plains. We speak of it as having been derived from the Iowan and Wisconsin glaciers, but it is quite certain that at least some of these deposits were formed during the retreat of the Illinoisan ice, and rearranged and redistributed by wind during the great drouth which covered part of the interval between the earlier and later invasions. Most of the loess in this state is formed in a broad belt following roughly the course of the Mississippi and its larger tributaries.

All the elements whose origin is here indicated enter into the surface of the area now under discussion at various points. The exact location of many of them will be mentioned in connection with the description of the various river systems.

THE AREA OF THE WISCONSIN DRIFT

As stated above, long after the retreat of the earlier glaciers the northeastern corner of the state was invaded by a new ice-sheet called the Wisconsin glacier. It covered this portion of the state as far south as Paris and Shelbyville, leaving, when it retired, a prominent moraine which runs through these places and then turns northward, passing near Decatur, Clinton, Pekin, Princeton, Sycamore, and Harvard, as shown on the accompanying map (III.). This ridge is known as the Shelbyville or Mattoon moraine. In its retreat this glacier left a series of concentric moraines with intervening lake-beds, the larger of which are well shown on the map.

Another fact, also partially indicated on the map, is that the drainage system in the part of the state north and east of the Shelbyville moraine is not nearly so well developed as in the older Illinoisan drift area, and consequently the streams do not have so many branches. As the streams break through the Shelbyville moraine, they often change the direction of their courses entirely, thus forming curious curves. This is doubtless due to the fact that as the Wisconsin drift sheet is superimposed on the Illinoisan drift, the beds of the streams developed on the surface of the latter are continued under the former, while the streams on the Wisconsin have no relation to them. When the Wisconsin streams broke through their confining moraines, they had to find their way to the most accessible Illinoisan stream as best they could.

The present condition of the area of the Wisconsin drift with its almost unbroken moraines, its black level prairies, peat bogs, lake beds, shallow streams, and incomplete drainage is believed to represent faithfully the condition of the Illinoisan area at an earlier period in its history, and this correspondence enables us to interpret many topographic relations in this area which would not otherwise be apparent. For instance, the control which the moraines of the Wisconsin area exercise on the direction of its streams, the position and size of its lakes, and the location and form of the tracts of black prairie soil are very evident, and it is believed like control would be just as evident in the Illinoisan area if the fragments of its moraines were carefully studied and mapped so that they could be restored and their influence shown. All that has been said about the early history of the Illinoisan area applies as well to the Wisconsin. The only material differences between them are due to age and consequent degree of development.

THE UNGLACIATED SOUTHERN AREA

A natural division of this area would be into mountain ridge and coastal plain. Regarding the first, little need be mentioned beyond the facts that it is a true mountain in structure, although its altitude is low (about 400 feet, on an average, above the general level); that it is composed almost entirely of limestones and sandstones of Mississipian; and that it presents on its southern slope the only approach to volcanic phenomena in the state. That portion of the state south of the Ozarks forms part of the coastal plain which borders the Atlantic and Gulf coasts. It has all the peculiarities of this plain, since it is level, sandy, and covered with residual soils. It is almost entirely drained by the Cache and Big Bay rivers, principally the former, whose current, owing to a reef across the channel near Ullin, is very sluggish.

THE RIVER SYSTEMS

With these general principles in mind we come to a more detailed description of the drainage basins of the principal streams. Nearly the entire surface of the state is drained by two sets of streams, viz: the Rock, Illinois, Kaskaskia, and Big Muddy rivers, direct tributaries of the Mississippi, whose general direction is southwest; and the Saline, Little Wabash, Embarras, and Vermilion, tributaries of the Wabash and through it of the Ohio and Mississippi, whose general direction is southeast. The drainage basins of these streams will now be described in order.

Rock River System

The Rock River system drains a part of southern Wisconsin and most of the northwestern corner of Illinois. Its basin covers an area of almost 10,820 square miles—5,510 in Wisconsin and 5,310 in Illinois (Leverett). This drainage basin is 40 to 50 miles wide in Wisconsin, but near the state-line it reaches a width of about 80 miles. It narrows again in Illinois to 40 miles, and then to 25 miles. Its length is about 175 miles. The outline thus formed is comparable to that of a pear, the stem toward Rock Island. The country in this area is an undulating semi-prairie region. Large expanses of unbroken prairie, groves and some more extensive bodies of timber, swamps, and lakes, are all to be found within its limits. Almost all of the basin lying within Wisconsin is covered with drift from the Wisconsin glacier, but near Janesville Rock River breaks through the "Kettle Moraine" of the Green Bay lobe of this glacier. South of this the basin lies in drift of Iowan and Illinoisan age. Although the exact boundaries of these drift areas are not as yet definitely determined, the western border of the Iowan drift probably extends but a few miles west of Rock River at any point, and for a short distance below Rockford it follows nearly the course of the river. The section of the basin lying in the Wisconsin drift is characterized by extensive swamps and numerous small lakes, the drainage being almost entirely independent of preglacial lines and consequently imperfectly developed. The overflow from the swamps is gathered into little meandering streams which have cut only small channels in the soil. The rest of the basin is older country—undulating, well-drained, and forming excellent farm-land except along Green River, where there are many swamps and sand-hills.

ROCK RIVER

Rock River is, of course, the principal river in the system. It rises in Dodge county, Wisconsin, in what was formerly Lake Horicon, but is now drained and has become an extensive marsh. The lake, which existed until 1868, although a body of water formed by an artificial dam, yet occupied the site of an ancient lake caused by the body of drift which formed a natural barrier to the passage of the water. Gradually this was eroded and the lake drained, probably through the same passage which now forms the channel of Rock River past the village of Horicon. A dam 200 feet in length, erected at this point, would raise the water 10 feet and restore the old lake to a large extent (10th Census). Leaving Horicon, the river runs through the eastern part of its basin until opposite Oconomowoc, where it turns abruptly northwest to Watertown. Here it suddenly bends again to the southwest, following this direction until it reaches the Illinois state-line near the center of its basin. From here it winds and curves toward the southwest, following at first the center of the basin, but finally running decidedly nearer its western boundary line. It empties its waters into the Mississippi near Rock Island.

Throughout its course Rock River is a bright, clear, swiftly flowing stream, affording some of the most magnificent water-powers in the country. Dams have been built at numerous places and are extensively used for milling and manufacturing purposes. Although its tributaries, especially at times of freshets, pour their muddy, yellow sediments into its clear waters, Rock River still retains its remarkable clearness almost to its mouth. Here, however, the water is generally quite turbid in consequence of the sewage and other contaminations which are poured into it.

The river is nearly 300 miles long—almost one half lying in Wisconsin. The altitude of its source is 875 feet, and of its mouth 536 feet, making a total descent of almost 340 feet. The average slope is 1.2 feet per mile. Its most rapid section is in Wisconsin, from the mouth of the Catfish to that of the Pecatonica, where for 30 miles the average slope is 1.9 feet per mile; and the next is from Oregon to Sterling and Rock Falls, in which distance of 36 miles the average slope is 1.31 feet per mile. Locally there are more sudden descents than these—as at the Sterling rapids, where there is a fall of 15 feet. The average low-water flow of Rock River is 3,900 cubic feet per second, and the average yearly flow is 9,944 cubic feet. The average yearly flow is 35 per cent. of the annual precipitation, and the ordinary low-water flow is about .36 cubic feet per second per square mile (10th Census).

There are 10 large lakes tributary to Rock River. These are all in Wisconsin and have a total area of 80 square miles. Among them are Lakes Koshkonong, Mendota, Monona, and Beaver Dam. Lake Koshkonong, in southwestern Jefferson county, is an expansion of Rock River 2 miles wide and 10 miles long, with its foot 6 miles above the mouth of the Catfish River. A large dam has been erected across its outlet and is controlled in the interests of the water-power below. To this and the dams of several other smaller tributary lakes is very largely due the maintenance of a comparatively uniform flow in dry and severely cold seasons.

In Wisconsin the banks of Rock River are quite low and rolling, but at Janesville the river enters a wide preglacial valley which it follows to a point a little below Rockford, Ill. The stream then turns abruptly westward while the valley continues southward toward the Illinois River, the valley of which it enters at Hennepin. This changing of the river course is doubtless due to the Wisconsin moraine which was left across its path when the glacier retreated. The water then found an easier outlet through the preglacial channels of some of its former tributaries. The valley averages about 3 miles in width, although in places it reaches a width of 5 miles. Most of the way the river follows the western edge of the valley, although just above Rockford it crosses to the eastern side and then back again. Thus, the eastern banks are usually low while those on the west are high and steep, in some places rising 75 feet above the water. When the stream turns westward below Rockford, it runs for 50 miles through a narrow valley to a point a few miles below Dixon. For a large part of this distance it flows through the preglacial channels spoken of above. Through this part of its course the stream maintains a width of 500 feet, but its valley varies in width from 1,000 feet to fully 1 mile (Leverett). It forms long undulating curves, except at Grand Detour, where it doubles upon itself in short, abrupt bends. The face of the country along the river is rough, broken, and timbered. The prairie extends to the water's edge in only a few places. The bluffs approaching closely to the river are bold, rocky, and precipitous, rising abruptly at times to a height of 125 feet. The little streams on either side have cut deep ravines in the banks, often exposing the several formations of the Ordovician. The result is certainly very picturesque and somewhat awe-inspiring. Below Dixon the bluffs gradually recede and grow lower until, at Sterling, Rock River begins to flow through a sandy plain known as the Green River basin, a plain which lies 25–40 feet above the stream. Here the course of the river is entirely independent of preglacial lines, and its current is broad and swift. The bluffs of the Mississippi strike Rock River at Milan and for several miles above this point they rise on either side abruptly, in some places towering 150 feet above the water. They then break away and the river flows in an alluvial plain of good farming land. This plain is about 5 miles wide. Near the mouth of Rock River there are several small islands which divert the river into three channels. Two of these branches meet again near Milan, flowing into the Mississippi two and a half miles distant, while the southern stream, known as Kickapoo slough, pursues a winding course southward and westward, opening into the Mississippi a few miles south of the mouth of Rock River.

The upper Rock River is a clear, quiet-flowing stream with sandy bottom. Lower in its course the bed becomes more often rocky and the current quickens. Naturally, the water, unless roiled by freshets, keeps its bright, clear character until well down near the mouth. Its tributaries, however, at times pour in a flood of stained and muddy water, making the lower portion a turbid stream, while, of late, sewage and other contamination have done much to impair the original brilliancy of the water. Yet, as Illinois rivers go, it must even now be considered a clear stream, while the bold bluffs and out-cropping rocks along its banks make it one of the most picturesque rivers in the state.

The principal branches of Rock River are Pecatonica, Kishwaukee, and Green rivers.

PECATONICA RIVER

Pecatonica River rises in Iowa county, Wisconsin, in the driftless area, and flows south, entering Illinois in the northwest corner of Stephenson county. It then flows in a course a little south of west to Freeport, where it turns westward, entering Winnebago county near the center of its western boundary. Another turn is then made, to the north and east, the stream finally emptying into Rock River at Rockton. The Pecatonica is about 150 miles long, over half of this distance lying in Wisconsin. Its drainage basin covers 2,225 square miles, of which 780 are in Illinois. Its discharge in ordinary low water is about 940 cubic feet per second, and the average flow for the year is estimated to be over 2,300 cubic feet per second. Almost all of that portion of the basin lying in Wisconsin is included in the driftless area, the river entering the Illinoisan drift just above the Illinois state-line. It flows through this drift until, at a point 10 miles above its mouth, it enters the Iowan drift. For 10 or 15 miles above this point, however, it follows closely the northern boundary of this drift. The country which the Pecatonica drains is rolling, partly timber and partly prairie.

The Indian name of the river (spelled Peeka-ton-oke on the old maps) is said by some authors to mean "muddy," and by others to mean "crooked." The river, especially in its lower portion, would fit either or both. The fall of the river averages only about half a foot per mile, and throughout its course it curves and winds about, not abruptly but in long undulating turns, through its rich alluvial bottoms, which in some places spread out to a width of 3 miles. Its earthen banks are low and rounded, and covered with heavy timber.

KISHWAUKEE RIVER

Kishwaukee River is formed by two branches which unite about 12 miles above its mouth. The northern branch rises in the Wisconsin moraine in central McHenry county, and the southern in the same moraine in southern DeKalb county. Each of these branches is about 50 miles long, the whole system draining about 1,644 square miles. The lower part of the river lies in drift of the Iowan age, while the upper parts are in that of the Wisconsin age. The northern branch falls about 25 feet in the first 3 miles, and below this the descent averages two and a half to three feet per mile. The southern branch is a little swifter, with an average fall of about 4 feet per mile. The waters of this river are very clear compared with those of the Pecatonica. The banks of the river are not precipitous, although rising 40 to 50 feet high at some points. The entire river valley is low, undulating, semi-prairie country, more or less wooded.

GREEN RIVER

Green River and its basin are quite distinct in their character from the other tributaries of Rock River and their basins. The drainage basin of Green River covers about 1,000 square miles all of which lies on a lake-plain of sand and gravel outwash from the Wisconsin glacier, the river following for most of its course the northern boundary line of the Wisconsin terminal moraine. The surface soil consists of peat, underlaid by sand and gravel. Through this the streams have found difficulty in making their way, unable to cut definite channels through it down to base level. The country consequently remains very imperfectly drained, and the waters gathering between the sand-hills have formed great peat marshes and bogs. Much is being done in late years, however, toward reclaiming these swamps by means of extensive tiling and ditching. The following description represents the condition of this region before this work was so far advanced as it is at present.

Green River is about 93 miles long, extending from eastern Lee county southwest across the corner of Bureau county and then west through Henry county to its northwest corner, there emptying into Rock River. Its headwaters are found in the elevated moraine forming the border of the Wisconsin drift in Southeastern Lee county, and stand 950 to 1,000 feet above tide. The eastern stream descends rapidly, 25 feet in a mile, to the sandy plain outside the moraine. There it soon enters the Inlet swamps lying about 775 feet above tide. These swamps are 10 miles long and 2 to 5 miles wide. Through them the stream has no definite channel but seems to be entirely lost. They are mostly covered with a dense prairie grass among whose roots a thin sheet of water is concealed in the wet seasons of the year. Towards the center the water is deeper and patches of cattails and rushes abound. From the western edge of this area, two to three miles southeast of Lee Center, the surplus waters of the swamps are gathered into a stream with a well-defined channel. This leads westward for 15 miles to another wet area, the Winnebago swamps, making a descent of about 3 feet per mile. These swamps are very similar to the Inlet swamps but much larger. Hills of sand rise in chains and clusters from the midst of them. These hills were originally heaped up by the winds from the sands of the old lake-bed. Some of them are 40–50 feet high and are covered with a scattering and stunted growth of trees. The intervening swamps are fringed with bands of thick-growing swamp grass on a miry, mucky soil. Within these are inner fringes of dense cane-like rushes and cattails growing so thick and tall that it is almost impossible to penetrate them. Then come stretches of clear water with hard sand bottoms. In the next 25 miles, to the crossing of the Bureau-Henry county line, the stream has a poorly defined channel, meandering about through a series of marshes among sand-hills but making a descent of 60 feet. In the remaining 35 to 40 miles to its mouth, the stream falls about 40 feet and maintains a well-defined channel. In the lower 18 to 20 miles, below Geneseo, it has excavated a valley fully 20 feet in average depth and nearly half a mile in width. In this section of its course its uplands are far less sandy.

Along the whole course of Green River, there are no bold bluffs except at Lee Center, where some low outcrops of Galena dolomite are quarried.

The Northwestern Area

The waters of extreme northwestern Illinois differ sufficiently in condition and surroundings from those of the smaller tributaries of the Mississippi farther south to warrant their separate discussion in this report. The surface drained by them is the southernmost part of a tract known to geologists as the Wisconsin driftless area, a region not covered by ice during the glacial period, and consequently wholly destitute of glacial drift. Because of its prolonged exposure to erosion its streams have reached the limit of their development, and run usually through deep valleys with rather a swift current, mostly unobstructed by rapids or falls. As a consequence of this perfect drainage and rapid flow, the surface waters quickly escape to the Mississippi; but as the streams are fed to a considerable extent by springs flowing from the limestone rocks, they rarely are completely dry. There are no lakes, swamps, or other reservoirs for the sedimentation of the surface waters, and the streams are consequently easily roiled by storms, in the intervals of which, however, the water is comparatively clear.

This driftless area of northwestern Illinois contains about 1,030 square miles, and includes all of Jo Daviess county, two thirds of Carroll county, and a part of Stephenson. The surface is rolling and somewhat broken, with a general elevation varying between 700 and 1,000 feet, but rising in mounds and flat-topped hills to the highest point in the state, an elevation known as Charles Mound, in Jo Daviess county, 1,241 feet above the level of the sea. The surface rock of this district is mainly Galena-Platteville, with Maquoketa shales and Niagara limestone capping the higher hills.

The principal streams of this region are Galena River to the north and Apple and Plum rivers farther south. Many additional smaller streams run down from the hills and bluffs to open directly into the Mississippi.

GALENA RIVER

Galena River, called Fever River on many maps, rises chiefly in Lafayette county, Wisconsin, which state contains also nearly 135 of the 197 square miles of its drainage basin. It runs with a rather rapid course through the hilly country of western Jo Daviess county, often over a rocky bed, becoming comparatively broad and sluggish as it crosses the Mississippi bottoms west of the town of Galena to empty into the Mississippi River.

APPLE RIVER

Apple River rises in Lafayette county, Wisconsin, and flows southeast, then southwest and finally south, emptying into the Mississippi in northern Carroll county, Illinois. It has a length of about 45 miles and drains an area of 270 square miles. It crosses the state-line at an elevation of about 950 feet, while its mouth has an altitude of only 588 feet. In Jo Daviess county, the upper channel of the river is narrow and the banks are steep and 150 to 200 feet high. In the lower part, the valley becomes broader and the banks recede until, in Carroll county, the river enters the broad bottom-lands of the Mississippi.

Except for the headwaters of the eastern branch, the entire basin lies in the driftless area and therefore maintains its preglacial course. It has, however, received a marked accession of drainage because of the blocking of a preglacial tributary of the Pecatonica. This diversion occurs just below Melville, and for about 3 miles below this point the stream is in a gorge but little wider than its bed. The small preglacial Apple River is then entered. Outcrops of the Niagara formation occur frequently along the bluffs.

PLUM RIVER

Plum River rises in the northeast corner of Carroll county, and, following a westerly and southerly direction through many windings and abrupt turns, finally empties into the Mississippi in the center of the western boundary of Carroll county. It rises at an altitude of 900 feet but descends to 800 feet in the first 3 miles, to 700 feet in the next two and one half miles, and to 590 feet in the remaining 32 miles of its course. The banks are often 150 feet high, and in some places are very abrupt, while at other points a narrow valley of one eighth to one fourth of a mile intervenes. It is 33 miles long, and drains an area of 307 square miles.

The Mississippi Bluff Drainage

Under this head are included all of the small streams of western Illinois directly tributary to the Mississippi below those of the northwestern area. Those here briefly described are Edwards River, Pope creek, Henderson River, Bear creek, Bay creek, and Cahokia River. The character of a multitude of others may be sufficiently inferred from those of this list. The area drained by these western streams includes two strips of land bordering the Mississippi, one above and the other two below the Illinois basin. It consists of the eastern Mississippi bottoms, varying in width from one to ten miles, and of high bluffs rising from 150 to 250 feet above the river, usually of loess, but occasionally with precipitous rock exposures. Many of the streams rise beyond this range of bluffs on the western prairies.

EDWARDS RIVER.

Edwards River rises in southeastern Henry county, in two branches, and flows westward through this and Mercer county. In the western part of the latter it turns southward for a short distance before emptying into the Mississippi about one and one half miles below New Boston. Below the junction of its two headwater streams the course of the river is remarkably straight and it has few tributaries. This is due to the fact that its basin lies in a narrow and shallow valley between two ridges having a general east-west direction, and so the river drains only this narrow strip. Pope creek, which flows parallel with it on the south, lies in another such valley. Edwards River rises at an altitude of 800 feet, falls 50 feet in its first one and one half miles, and another 50 feet in the next 18 miles. The mouth is about 520 feet above sea-level. The stream has a length of 67 miles, draining an area of 446 square miles.

POPE CREEK

Pope creek rises in northern Knox county and flows westward, emptying into the Mississippi almost opposite the mouth of Iowa River. It rises at an altitude of 750 feet, but its mouth lies at 520 feet. Its length is about 50 miles, and its drainage area is 167 square miles. The bluffs bordering the river are abrupt and often reach a height of 75 to 125 feet.

HENDERSON RIVER

Henderson River rises in two forks, one in the northwest corner of Knox county and the other in Warren county, and flows westward and southward, emptying into the Mississippi at the center of the western border of Henderson county. It drains much of northern Henderson, northern Warren, and part of Knox county, and, although having a total length of scarcely 77 miles, it furnishes drainage through its numerous branches for an area of fully 500 square miles. It rises at an elevation of 800 feet, and descends 100 feet in its first 10 miles, but below this the fall is gradual, the altitude at its mouth being 520 feet.

BEAR CREEK

Bear creek drains the southwestern part of Hancock county and the northern part of Adams—a possible area of 518 square miles. The main branch rises in southern Hancock county and flows south and west 48 miles, emptying into the Mississippi opposite Canton, Mo. The source of this stream is at an elevation of 670 feet, while the mouth has an altitude of 460 feet.

BAY CREEK

Bay creek drains a large part of Pike county and a little of northern Calhoun. It rises in northern Pike county and flows southeastward toward the Illinois River, following a sag between two Illinoisan drift ridges, and nearly reaching the Illinois opposite the village of Bedford. It then curves to the southwest, passes through a gap in the rocky ridge, which to the north and south constitutes the divide between the Mississippi and the Illinois, and enters the Mississippi opposite the town of Louisiana, Mo. The deflection to the west is due to the ridge of Illinoisan drift which follows the east border of the stream and prevents it from entering the Illinois valley. The river has a length of about 50 miles, rising at an altitude of 850 feet, draining 222 square miles, but falling 100 feet in its first two miles, and below this averaging a fall of nearly 7 feet to the mile until it enters the Mississippi flats. The mouth is at an altitude of about 430 feet.

CAHOKIA RIVER

Cahokia River rises in western Montgomery county, crosses southern Macoupin county, and flows south and west, emptying into the Mississippi near East St. Louis. It is about 50 miles long and drains an area of 360 square miles, rising at an altitude of 640 feet, but falling 120 feet in the first 6 miles. Below this it descends to 425 feet at Wanda, the point at which it crosses the Mississippi bluffs and enters the bottom-lands of that river. The mouth of the stream has an elevation of about 400 feet. The banks above Wanda are steep and abrupt, rising 100 feet or more on either side of the water.

ILLINOIS RIVER SYSTEM

The Illinois and its branches drain an area of 28,100 square miles, distributed among three states. Of this area, 24,940 square miles are in Illinois, extending in a broad band, 267 miles long and averaging 100 miles in width, directly across the center of the state in a northeast-southwest direction. From the upper extremity of this band are two projections: one north into Wisconsin, covering 1,020 square miles in that state; the other east into Indiana, covering 3,140 square miles of its northern portion. This eastern projection forms the basin of the Kankakee River, while the northern one includes the basins of the Fox and Des Plaines rivers. It is the union of the drainage of these two projections which may be considered as the origin of the Illinois, this name being applied to the river from the point of junction of the Kankakee and the Des Plaines in eastern Grundy county, Illinois. The Illinois flows westward for about 55 miles, turns rather abruptly southwest a little north of Hennepin and follows this direction until it empties into the Mississippi at the southern end of Calhoun county. The river may readily be divided into two parts: the upper Illinois, consisting of that portion of the river above the turn at Hennepin; and the lower Illinois, below this point. The lower part of the river occupies a preglacial valley, the southward continuation of the preglacial valley occupied by Rock River in southern Wisconsin and northern Illinois. The upper Illinois, however, flows through an interglacial and postglacial valley, the old "Chicago outlet." This outlet was the line of southwestward discharge from the basin of Lake Michigan across the low divides near Chicago and thence down the Des Plaines and Illinois to the Mississippi. It has a depth ranging from 20 to 70 feet, the excavation being almost entirely in beds of drift except for about 15 miles between Lemont and Joliet and 40 miles between Morris and Peru, where rock strata have been eroded. Throughout its entire length the bluffs are steep like river banks, and the deposits made by side streams on the edge of the valley are very meager—a feature which indicates that the stream had great volume, probably filling the channel from bluff to bluff, and a current sufficiently strong to carry nearly all of the detritus brought into it by the side streams.

Since the Illinois is formed by the union of the Des Plaines and the Kankakee, it may be best to describe those streams first.

DES PLAINES RIVER

The Des Plaines drains a narrow intermorainic strip extending north and south a distance of 90 miles from Kenosha county, Wisconsin, to the head of the Illinois in eastern Grundy county, Illinois. The whole drainage basin covers an area of about 1,366 square miles, its greatest width being scarcely 25 miles. This region all lies within the Wisconsin drift, between two rather large moraines to the east and west of it, and containing many smaller moraines which have prevented the formation of good natural drainage-lines. The land is, consequently, very imperfectly drained, and contains numerous small lakes and marshes, although this condition has been much changed by extensive systems of tiling. A series of measurements by the U. S. Geological Survey gives for the average discharge 1,100 cubic feet per second. The water of the northern section is moderately clear, but becomes more turbid and polluted lower down. The bottom of the river and its tributaries is largely sand and gravel, with rock in its portions of swiftest descent.

The Des Plaines has its source in an extended marshy valley

in Kenosha county, Wisconsin. This valley is so nearly level that at times it is very difficult to tell which way the water flows. It stands 112 feet above Lake Michigan (Leverett) and drains northward into Root River as well as southward into the Des Plaines. The Des Plaines flows nearly parallel with the shore of Lake Michigan to a point about 10 miles southwest of Chicago. It then turns southwest for 40 miles, to its junction with the Kankakee. The course of the upper Des Plaines is governed by the moraines along the banks of Lake Michigan, following these more or less in their curves. At Summit it enters into the "Chicago outlet." At flood stages the upper Des Plaines still discharges into Lake Michigan through a portion of this old outlet which is known as "Mud Lake" and South Chicago River. Probably the entire discharge, until recent years, has been into the lake instead of down the "Chicago outlet," thus forming a system entirely distinct from the lower Des Plaines. In the upper portion of the river the fall averages only a little over 1 foot per mile, and its branches are almost all short and small on account of the moraines. The banks, especially on the west, are quite high, in some places reaching a height of 50 feet, but they are not abrupt.

In the 40 miles from Summit to the mouth of the river, the valley averages about 1 mile in width and consists of a rather shallow trough cut out of limestone. This is covered with a thin bed of drift, and the banks of the river are consequently low. Just below Summit there are 12 miles which are almost level, so that the land on each side of the river is poorly drained and swampy. Below this the river widens into Goose Lake, three and a half miles long and one third of a mile wide, through which it makes a descent of about 10 feet. The bed of the river narrows again, and just above Lockport it begins to descend very rapidly, dropping about 70 feet in 8 miles. Below this are two lakes—one, known as Lake Joliet, 2½ miles below Joliet, and the other, Lake Dupage, near the mouth of the Dupage River, the two being three miles apart, and the river falling about 13 feet in the interval (Leverett). In the half mile from Lake Dupage to the junction of the Des Plaines with the Kankakee another descent of two and a half feet is made. The only true flood-plain bottoms lie within the seven miles between Lake Joliet and the head of the Illinois. These are within the range of backwater from the Kankakee, but are overflowed only in case of floods from that stream, having been built up to about the average high-water level. A canal, 100 miles long, called the Illinois and Michigan canal, starts from Lake Michigan at Chicago, and, cutting through the low summit, enters the Des Plaines valley. It crosses the river at Joliet, and then follows along the right bank of this river and of the Illinois to Peru, where it enters the latter river.

The principal branch of the Des Plaines is the Dupage River, which rises in southern Lake county, and, flowing southward, empties into the Des Plaines only 4 miles above its junction with the Kankakee. It is about 50 miles in length, and drains about 366 square miles of intermorainic country. It is a swiftly moving stream, the last 11 miles of its course having a fall of 80 feet. Its banks are generally low and rolling.

KANKAKEE RIVER

Kankakee River rises in a large marsh about three miles southwest of South Bend, St. Joseph county, Ind. It flows in a southwesterly direction to the southern boundary line of La Porte county, and then more westerly, crossing the Indiana-Illinois state-line in southern Lake county, Indiana. It then flows a little south of west to within a few miles of Kankakee, where it receives the Iroquois from the south. Thence it proceeds almost due northwest to near the northeast corner of Grundy county, where it unites with the Des Plaines to form the Illinois.

The Kankakee is about 140 miles long; 85 miles lying in Indiana. Its drainage basin covers about 5,300 square miles, of which 3,140 square miles are in Indiana. This basin has its northern limits in the Valparaiso morainic system, and all of the important northern tributaries find their sources in the same system. Its southern limits, in the portion below the mouth of the Iroquois, are found in the Marseilles moraine. The Iroquois rises in a somewhat distinct area, draining basins south of the Iroquois and Marseilles moraines and passing through a gap in the latter moraine to enter the Kankakee. The eastern limits of the Kankakee basin are mainly in the Maxinkuckee moraine of the Saginaw lobe.

Probably the whole of the Kankakee basin was formerly an old lake, called now by geologists Lake Kankakee, and, at the same time that the old "Chicago outlet" was full, it may have been a line of discharge for the St. Joseph River, now a tributary to Lake Michigan, carrying also a large amount of glacial drainage from the Saginaw and Lake Michigan lobes.

The basin of the Kankakee is generally level, but near the state-line, at Momence, occurs the first limestone outcrop in the bed of the river. This ledge or arch has so prevented the wearing down of the bed that a very large part of the drainage area in Indiana is one vast swamp. From its source to the state-line there is a direct distance of only 75 miles, but within this distance the stream makes 2,000 bends and flows a total length of 240 miles. The difference in level between its source and the state-line is but 97.3 feet, showing a fall of but 1.3 feet to the mile. (Indiana Geological Survey.) The winding of the river reduces the fall to only 5 inches to the mile. Above its junction with the Yellow River the amount of water is insufficient to form a well-defined channel. The water has an almost imperceptible flow, and in many places wild rice, rushes, lily-pads, and aquatic grasses so choke the channel as to cause the flooding of the marshes during summer freshets. Below this point, however, there is quite a definite open channel, although the small tributaries are usually lost in the marsh before reaching the main stream. On the immediate border of the river there is a strip ranging in width from one fourth to one and one half miles which is heavily timbered. The only other timber is found on so-called islands whose surfaces rise 10 to 20 feet above the general level of the marsh. The open marsh is covered with a rank growth of wild grasses, bulrushes, sedges, reeds, wild rice, and other semiaquatic vegetation. Between the woodland bordering the river-bank and the marsh, as well as around the margin of most of the islands, there are dense thickets of elbow-brush, willows, etc. In 1882 there were almost 500,000 acres of marsh land within the valley of the Kankakee. It resembled an immense sponge, slowly absorbing the water during the wet season and as slowly giving it forth during the dry, so that the flow throughout the year was quite regular and uniform in amount. At present, on account of the drainage of a large part of this marsh, the water flows off much sooner after it falls, and consequently the river is higher during the autumn and spring floods and lower at other seasons than formerly. In general the soil of the marsh is a dark, sandy loam, very rich in organic matter. It is very porous, but has the power to take up and retain large quantities of water.

In the 14 miles below Momence, Ill., to its junction with the Iroquois, there is a descent of 25 feet. In the 33.5 miles from the mouth of the Iroquois to the head of the Illinois, the

Kankakee falls 103 feet, or an average of 3 feet to the mile. There are rapids near Altorf and at Wilmington, where sudden descents of 20 feet are made. In Indiana, as stated above, the bed of the river is composed mainly of sand and fine gravel, but at Momence it begins to flow over limestone, and from that point to its mouth it has a rock bottom, affording good foundations for dams for utilizing water-power and for purposes of navigation. The inner valley of the river is but little wider than the stream, and outside this there is a broad bottom averaging about 2 miles in width.

IROQUOIS RIVER

Iroquois River is the chief tributary of the Kankakee in this state. It rises in Jasper county, Indiana, flows southwest until it reaches the center of Iroquois county, Illinois, and then turns north, emptying into the Kankakee at Waldron, Kankakee county. It is about 87 miles long and has a watershed of 2,175 square miles, much of which is imperfectly drained. Fully 935 square miles, or nearly half the basin, lies in Indiana. This part is of the same type as the Kankakee basin, marshy and sandy. Just before the river reaches Watseka, Illinois, it crosses the Iroquois moraine, and then traverses what was probably once a temporary lake-bed. Sand banks, like those along the Kankakee, follow its valley.

It is a much slower stream than the Kankakee in Illinois. For the first 12 miles in this state it falls only about two and a half feet per mile. Below Watseka it descends still more gradually, falling only 10 feet in the first 20 miles and another 10 feet in the last 9 miles of its course. The Iroquois is about half the size of the Kankakee above its junction. Although it rises in the swamp region, it drains a much greater proportion of dry prairie land than the Kankakee, and therefore is, comparatively, a "flashy" stream. Its freshets rise sooner, and they pass off before those of the main river. In the region around Gilman, in the western part of the basin, are many artesian wells which add materially to the flow of the river in ordinary low water.

ILLINOIS RIVER

Measured by its relation to their industrial and civic interests, the Illinois is by far the most important river to the citizens of this state. Larger streams flow along our boundaries, but none affects so closely the welfare of so many of our people. Indeed, from its peculiar position and its relation to other waters, it has always been an especially important stream. To the early explorers, traders, and missionaries, as well as to the aborigines before them, it furnished, together with the Des Plaines and the Chicago portage, one of the most frequently traveled waterways through the interior of the country, and the settlements along its banks were among the earliest in the state. At a later period it became a useful commercial highway, a function which it now seems certain to resume, at no distant day, on a scale of national importance. Its yield of fishery products is greater than that of all the other waters of the state combined,* and it serves an indispensable purpose to the City of Chicago and to the principal towns upon its banks in conveying away their liquid wastes, which it renders harmless by decomposition and useful by converting them more or less directly into a food supply for fishes.

The Illinois may be regarded as in many respects a typical stream of the central prairies of the Mississippi Valley, peculiar now, however, in the enormous amount of sewage which it carries—mainly received from Chicago by way of the drainage canal—together with the large amount of refuse from distilleries and cattle-yards along its course. It flows, in most of its length, down the bed of an ancient outlet of Lake Michigan, by which the waters of that lake were conveyed to the Mississippi River. Within this bed it has excavated its own present channel, with its present bottom-lands or "first bottoms," subject to overflow at high water. Its second bottoms, above the reach of high water, are the flood-plain of the former outlet of the lake. This ancient channel varies in width from 1½ to 6 miles, or, if the flood-plain of the older river be also included, to a maximum width of 20 miles, the bluffs on either side ranging in altitude from 450 to 800 feet. The highest points of these bluffs are near Peoria, and near the mouth of the river in Calhoun county. The watersheds bounding the river basin range in height from 700 to 1,000 feet above the sea, the average elevation being 600 or 700 feet.

The length of the Illinois from its origin in the junction of the Kankakee and the Des Plaines is approximately 273 miles; or, if its longest tributary, the Kankakee, be added, the total is 413 miles. The length of the stream itself is 28 per cent. greater than that of a straight line from its origin to its mouth—an unusually small percentage for the tributaries of the Mississippi. It takes,

*In 1899 the total value of the product of the fisheries of Illinois was $616,452, and that of the fisheries of the Illinois River was $382,372.

in other words, an uncommonly direct course. The area of its basin is approximately 29,000 square miles, 28,100 of which lie within Illinois, 1,020 square miles in Wisconsin, and 3,140 in Indiana. Its basin thus comprises about three sevenths of the area of the state. It extends diagonally across the center of Illinois from the northeast to the southwest as a broad belt about a hundred miles in width, the upper end of which expands in a Y-shaped area to embrace the southwest part of Lake Michigan. The northern arm of the "Y" is formed by the basin of the Des Plaines, and the eastern arm by the more extensive basin of the Kankakee. From its origin, fifty miles southwest of Chicago, it runs almost due west some sixty miles to a point not far above Hennepin, where it turns abruptly towards the left, flowing southwest by south a hundred and sixty-five miles (two hundred and five by river) to its union with the Mississippi, twenty-five miles above St. Louis. Its bottom-lands have an average width of 3.1 miles, from Utica to the mouth of the river. The immediate banks of the stream are usually higher than the adjacent surfaces, and the same may be said of its tributary streams where they flow through the bottoms of the Illinois. Bayous, lagoons, marshes, and temporary ponds occur along the course of the river, especially in its central portion from Hennepin to Meredosia, all subject to invasion or obliteration by the river in times of flood, but filled, at low water, either from springs or from the general drainage of their basins. Spring-fed lakes are rather common along the eastern side of the river, from Pekin to its mouth, deriving their waters from the rainfall collected by the second bottoms, at whose margin they usually lie.

This large area of marshes, lagoons, and lakes affects the life of the river in many important ways. The flood-plain serves as a storage area for the waters of overflow, greatly delaying the run-off at times of flood. This delay is still further prolonged, in many years, by high water in the Mississippi, which often extends far up the Illinois—in a few instances as much as a hundred miles. As a result of these conditions the average volume of water in the stream throughout the year is greatly increased, and a wider range and breeding ground and a greater food supply are afforded to the fishes of the stream.

The fall in the Illinois River is but slight—an average of .267 of a foot per mile of its total length. Fifty and seven tenths feet of this fall occur in the first forty-two miles of its course, and from Utica to the mouth of the river the total fall is but 31 feet, or an average of .137 of a foot to the mile. The effect of this slight fall is seen in the sluggish current of the Illinois, which ranges from .4 of a mile per hour at the lowest water to 1.737 miles when at twelve feet above low-water mark. The usual rate of flow for ordinary stages varies, however, from 1¼ to 2½ miles per hour. The difference between low-water and high-water conditions is immense in many ways, especially because of the great expansion of water surface resulting from slight changes in level. The annual range in river levels, as recorded at Copperas Creek dam, in the twenty-one years from 1879 to 1899 inclusive, varied from 8.9 feet in 1894 to 17.7 feet in 1882. It is estimated that the area and volume of the river are not far from a hundred times as great at the highest water as at the lowest, and the conditions of aquatic life are thus enormously affected. The contrasts presented by the Illinois River at high water and at low water respectively are graphically set forth by Kofoid in his report on the plankton work of the Natural History Survey, published in Volume VI. of the State Laboratory Bulletin.

"A trip by boat," he says, "across the submerged bottom-lands from the Quiver shore [on the east bank, 2½ miles above Havana] to the western bluff in the latter part of May would be far more enlightening than any description that might be given. As we leave the sandy shore of Quiver we traverse the clear, cold, and spring-fed water along the eastern bank with its rapidly growing carpet of *Ceratophyllum* [hornwort], and in a few rods note the increasing turbidity, rising temperature, and richer plankton of the water which has moved down from the more or less open and slightly submerged bottom to the north. As we cross the muddy bank of Quiver ridge and enter the main channel of the river we find rougher water, caused by the wind which usually sweeps up or down the stream with considerable force between the bordering forests. The water also appears much more turbid by reason of silt and plankton, and no trace of vegetation is to be seen save occasional masses of floating *Ceratophyllum* or isolated plants of *Lemna*, *Wolffia*, or *Spirodela* [duckweeds]. Huge masses of cattle-yard refuse, veritable floating gardens, may also at times be seen moving down the channel or stranded in some eddy along shore. As we plunge into the willow thicket on the western shore we have to pick our way through the accumulated drift lodged in the shoals or caught by the trunks of the trees or the submerged underbrush. The surface of the water is one mat of logs, brush, sticks, bark, and fragments of floating vegetation.

with its interstices filled with *Lemnaceæ* [duckweed] dotted with the black statoblasts of *Plumatella.* From this dark labyrinth we emerge to the muddy but quiet waters of Seeb's Lake with its treacherous bottom of soft black ooze. We next enter a wider stretch of more open territory with scattered willows and maples and a rank growth of semiaquatic vegetation, principally *Polygonums* [heart-weed]. The water is clearer and of a brownish tinge (from the diatoms), while mats of algæ adhere to the leaves and stems of the emerging plants. A flock of startled waterfowl leave their feeding grounds as we pass into the wide expanse of Flag Lake. We push our way through patches of lily-pads and beds of lotus, past the submerged domes of muskrat houses built of last year's rushes, and thread our way, through devious channels, among the fresh green flags and rushes just emerging from the water. Open patches of water here and there mark the areas occupied by the "moss" or *Ceratophyllum,* as yet at some depth below the surface. The *Lemnaceæ* are everywhere lodged in mats and windrows, and, amidst their green, one occasionally catches sight of a bright cluster of *Azolla.* The water is clear and brownish save where our movements stir the treacherous and mobile bottom. We now enter a second time the partially wooded country, and cross the submerged ridge to the sandy eastern shore of Thompson's Lake. This ridge is covered by submerged vegetation which has as yet attained but little growth. The "breaks" of the startled fish show that we have invaded favorite feeding grounds. The waters are evidently moving towards the river, and they bear the rich plankton of Thompson's Lake, while their turbidity is doubtless increased by the movements of the fish. Schools of young fry can be seen feeding upon the plankton in the warm and quiet waters. Thompson's Lake, the largest expanse of water in the neighborhood, is wont to be rough in windy weather, but if the day be still we can see the rich aquatic vegetation which fringes its margin and lies in scattered masses toward its southern end. Its waters seem somewhat turbid, but more from plankton than from silt, though the deep soft mud which forms much of its bottom is easily stirred. The slender transparent limnetic young of the gizzard-shad may be seen swimming near the surface. There is a perceptible drift to the south in the open lake, though this current is deflected by the elevated banks of Spoon River towards the Illinois River, crossing the lower bottom-lands above this region. If we push on through the fringing willows at the south we find a series of open places locally known as "ponds." The warm still waters are turbid in places from the movements of fish, and at times we see the compact schools of young dogfish (*Amia calva*) and, if we are late enough in the season, the myriads of young black, tadpole-like catfish (*Ameiurus*), likewise in schools, while young carp (*Cyprinus carpio*) are everywhere. The new vegetation is already springing from the decaying and matted stems of the preceding summer. Turning back towards the river we pass through the heavy timber where the still brown water, cool and clear, overlies the decaying leaves and vegetation of last season's growth, now coated with the flood deposits of the winter. Emerging again upon the river channel, we may find a turbid yellow flood pouring out from Spoon River, bringing down its load of drift and earth, and marking its course down the stream as far as the eye can see.

* * * * * * *

"Contrast with the extent and variety of conditions at flood the limitations placed upon the stream at low water. Instead of an unbroken expanse of four or more miles we find now a stream only 500 feet in width, while the adjacent territory is dry land save where the sloughs, marshes, and lakes remain as reservoirs. Quiver Lake is now much reduced in width, and it may be choked with vegetation except in a narrow channel where the clear water shows little or no current. A half mile below we find the river water rushing in a narrow "cut-off" across the ridge of black alluvium into the lower end of the lake. The wooded banks which separate the river from Quiver and Seeb's lakes are now crowded with a rank growth of weeds and vines. The latter "lake" is reduced to a shallow stagnant arm of the river, whose warm turbid waters are foul with dead mollusks, and whose reeking mud-flats beneath the August sun shine green and red with a scum of *Euglena*. As we pick our way through the tangle of rank vegetation we come upon Flag Lake, now a sea of rushes. The discharge from this marsh to the river ceased in the early summer, and its margins are even now dry, with gaping cracks. Beyond the marsh we pass to the shore of Thompson's Lake to find its southern end choked with vegetation, though the greater part to the north is open water. The woodland and open ground to the south are now pastures and fields of waving corn. The only outlet to this large body of water, now somewhat reduced in area but warm, turbid, and rich in plankton, is a tortuous slough six miles to the north. The discharge, however, is in any case but slight, the lake being, indeed, not infrequently the recipient of river water. Spoon River still pours a sluggish but constant stream into the river, but save for a waterbloom of livid green (*Euglena*) its waters yield but little plankton. Thus, of all the wide area contributing to the plankton of the channel at high water there now remain only Thompson's and Quiver lakes and Spoon River, each much diminished in volume, but all diversified in character.

"Returning now to the river itself we find a gently sloping bank of black mud, baked and cracked by the sun's heat, extending towards the softer deposit at the water's margin. A low growth of grasses, sedges, and weeds springs up as the water recedes. The river margin does not often have much aquatic vegetation. In low-water years, such as 1894 and 1895, a considerable fringe is formed along the shore, but this is quickly cleaned out on the seining grounds, which occupy a large part of the shore, as soon as the fishing season opens in July. In years of normal high-water the vegetation rarely gets much of a foothold along the shores, even at low-water stages. Save for the few sandy banks where springs abound, such as those below Havana along the eastern bluff, there is little, at least in the La Grange pool, to vary this monotony of mud banks and fringing willows. The backwaters have been reduced to the lakes, sloughs, bayous, and marshes which abound everywhere in the bottom-lands. Many of these, as, for example, Phelps and Flag lakes, have ceased in their reduced condition to contribute to the river. Others, like Thompson's Lake, maintain a connection with the river by means of a long and tortuous bayou or slough through which the current flows in or out as the relative levels of the two fluctuate. This lake receives but little water from a few springs and creeks along the bluffs, and like many others in the bottom-lands serves only as a reservoir from which the water is slowly drawn off as the river falls, but when once the lower stages are reached its contributions cease. Still others, like Quiver and Matanzas, maintain direct and open connection with the river, and since they receive tributary streams they continue to feed the river, but in reduced volume. Though the number of tributary areas is thus much reduced at low-water stages, the individual peculiarities of the tributary waters in the bottom-lands become more pronounced. As each one loses its connection with the general flood it becomes a separate unit of environment, with its local differences in those factors which determine the character of the plankton developing in its waters. The resulting contributions may thus differ greatly in amount and component organisms, and accordingly tend to diversify the river plankton of low water to a degree even more marked than that of high water.

"With the confinement of the river waters to the channel goes a marked condensation of the sewage, which, under conditions of uninterrupted low water, leads at times to an excessive development of the plankton, or, if the river is closed by ice, to stagnation conditions. But few years, however, offer such opportunites; for, as a rule, in most low-water periods sudden and heavy rains are wont to occur, which flush the stream, wash away the sewage and plankton-laden waters, and store anew the reservoir lakes without causing any considerable overflow. After each catastrophe of this sort the decline of the flood affords a new and favorable opportunity for the development of the plankton."*

The effects of change of temperature, of differences of turbidity, of chemical conditions of the waters of the stream, and the like, are discussed at length in Dr. Kofoid's report.†

As a framework to this sketch of the Illinois River and the waters of the Illinois basin generally, an outline of its geological surroundings is essential. From its source to Peoria the river flows through a district covered by the Wisconsin drift. From Peoria to southern Pike county the outlines of its western border are covered by the Illinois drift capped by loess. From thence southward they are nearly free from glacial drift, but are heavily coated with loess, while those on the east have a moderate covering of Illinois drift capped by loess. Within the Wisconsin drift the marshes, bogs, and lakes are of small extent, but the drainage lines are, on the whole, rather imperfectly developed.

The portion of the basin lying in the Illinoisan is much better drained. There are almost no marshes or swamps in it, except those in the bottoms of the river itself, but there are numerous shallow valleys which are poorly drained.

The Illinois, as stated before, follows the old "Chicago outlet" as far as its curve near Hennepin. In the 41 miles from the junction of the Des Plaines and the Kankakee down to Utica, where apparently a small preglacial tributary of the Illinois is entered, the course of the present Illinois is independent

*Bull. Ill. State Lab. Nat. Hist., Vol VI., Art. II., pp. 151–156.
†Loc. cit., pp. 168-252.

of preglacial drainage lines. Almost midway of its westward course it crosses the Marseilles moraine. This, no doubt, for a considerable period held a lake in the basin at the head of the river, the Morris basin, but was eventually cut down to the bed of this basin. From the Marseilles moraine, westward, the channel found no prominent drift barriers to remove, but has been compelled to cut down 50 to 75 feet into the rock in opening an outlet from the Morris basin into the valley of the lower Illinois (Leverett).

The part of the "Chicago outlet" lying within the Morris basin has an average width of 4 to 5 miles. A low bluff, formed on the northern border of the basin, has a height of 15 to 20 feet, but on the southern border there is no bluff, that side being heavily coated with deposits of sand. Below Morris the width of the outlet averages only about one and a half miles. The excavation is largely in soft St. Peter sandstone, there being nearly continuous rock bluffs to a height of 60 to 75 feet above the level of the bed of the outlet. In some places, as at Starved Rock, the bluffs reach a height of 126 feet. Buffalo Rock stands out in the valley, a big rocky island.

In the 41 miles to the foot of the rapids near Utica the stream falls 47 feet, or slightly more than 1 foot to the mile (Leverett). This fall is far from regular, there being a series of rock rapids separated by pools.

In the Morris basin the shale bottom has been eroded in places by the current and the hollows have been filled with sand, but from the Morris basin to the bend of the river the rock floor is swept clean.

The old preglacial valley through which the lower Illinois flows, and where rock bed lies many feet below the bottom of the present river, seems to have been so imperfectly filled by glacial deposits that throughout nearly its entire length the stream is re-established in its old course. The valley ranges in width from two and a half to fully fifteen miles. Its greatest width is reached just above the mouth of the Sangamon. The valley is also very broad at the bend of the Illinois. The narrowest portions are a short section near Peoria, where it passes through the Shelbyville moraine, and a section embracing the lower 60 miles, where it traverses the Mississipian and the Silurian limestones.

The Illinois River bottom-lands are covered with patches of timber, sand banks, mud-flats, and meadows. A good deal of this area is too low and marshy for cultivation, full of swamps, bogs, bayous, and lagoons, many of the latter being parts of old channels of the stream which have been cut off and filled up at both ends as a consequence of local changes in the course of the stream; but where the elevation is sufficient the soil is a rich sandy loam. An example of this is found in the "Crow Meadows" in Marshall county. This tract of land is a broad tableland or second bottom extending from the north line of the county down to Sparland, widening near Henry to eight or nine miles between the river and the low bluff-line on the west. It is beyond the reach of inundations, and is of unsurpassed fertility, although it contains much sand. The bluffs rise on each side of the bottom-lands very abruptly in most places, and to a height reaching at times 125 to 150 feet, cut into sharp ridges by the valleys of the small streams that drain the adjacent regions. They are all thickly timbered.

The current of the Illinois from La Salle to its mouth is not sufficient to carry off the material brought in from the upper portion of the stream, and therefore it is in the process of silting up. During the interglacial period when the land-slope was much less, this part of the river became so filled that now the rock bottom lies about 100 feet below the present bed of the river.

The principal tributaries of the Illinois are the Fox, Vermilion, Mackinaw, Sangamon, and Spoon rivers, and Macoupin, Crooked, and Apple creeks.

FOX RIVER

Fox River rises in Waukesha county, Wisconsin, a little northwest of Milwaukee. It flows south and southwest, emptying into the Illinois River at Ottawa, Ill. Its drainage basin is about 130 miles in length and averages 20 miles in width, covering an area of about 2,580 square miles, of which 1,020 lie in Wisconsin. The length of the river is about 172 miles.

The low-water discharge is estimated to be 526 cubic feet per second, or 0.195 cubic feet per second per square mile. It is claimed that the stream has fallen off one-half in its low-water volume since the clearing and cultivating of the land and the draining of the swamps.

The drainage basin of the Fox lies entirely within the limits of the Wisconsin glaciation, and is an undulating prairie land with more or less woodland and some swamps. In this region the morainic ridges lie very close together and are often interlaced, thus making cups or kettles within which lakes were formed. Some of these lakes have been drained so thoroughly that they have become small prairies, while in other places they have been unable to cut down their outlets sufficiently. We have, consequently, a series ranging from quiet land-locked ponds with gravel bottoms to marshes differing but little from the ordinary wet prairie or slough, peat bogs, and the dry prairie land. The bed of the swamps is generally more or less peaty, varying in composition from ordinary black swamp muck to true peat. A few of the lakes are from four to seven miles in length and a mile or more in breadth, while the others usually cover only one or two square miles, or even less. These numerous lakelets, ponds, marshes, and bogs furnish, in their aggregate, a considerable storage for flood waters, and the volume of the stream is consequently comparatively uniform and its changes of level are relatively slow. The water of the upper reaches of the river are usually clear except in times of flood, but the lower part of the stream is often very impure. Though much of the river bed below Elgin is in rock, the tributaries often bring large amounts of sediment, and various manufactories along the river discharge a large amount of refuse into the stream, and it has, of late years, become so foul that nearly all fish except carp and other filth-enduring species have been drowned out.

For a distance of nearly 75 miles from its source Fox River drains only a narrow strip among the morainic ridges of the composite belt, its course being determined by a moraine lying on either side. In this portion of its course its fall amounts to only a few inches to the mile, and its bed expands at frequent intervals into lakes and marshes between which are short stretches having narrow and well-defined channels. The river, here, has no valley, but the stream averages 150 to 200 feet in width, flowing between gravel and clay banks. In some places it runs close to the bluff, while in others a low flood-plain intervenes. Its tributaries in this section are very small, all occupying deep parallel valleys running in an east and west direction and only turning southward when they reach the lowlands bordering the river. All of the lakes lie along the line of these intermorainic valleys. Among those tributary to Fox River are Lake Geneva, Muskego, and Pewaukee. Fox Lake is simply a widening of the river-bed.

From the vicinity of Elgin to Yorkville the bed of the river is alternately rock and mud. This is due to the fact that the present course of the river lies almost at right angles to a series of preglacial valleys which were cut by streams then emptying into Lake Michigan. The present river consequently cuts alternately through the divides and valleys of these old rivers. Probably much of the underground drainage now follows these old channels to the lake.

In its passage through Kane and Kendall counties, the fall of the river is about 3 feet per mile, but in La Salle county it increases to about 5 feet per mile, making a descent of nearly 125 feet in the lower 25 miles of its course. Near Elgin it begins a rapid descent to the low plain that lies on the outer border of the Marseilles moraine and follows this to its mouth. The stream here, for a few miles, has cut to a depth of nearly 100 feet, but in its passage through the plain its bed is sunk to a depth of only 40 to 50 feet except for a few miles near its mouth, where it cuts 125 feet to enter the Illinois. Its channel, even in the lower 75 miles, has a breadth of only about one eighth of a mile.

VERMILION RIVER

Vermilion River of the Illinois (not of the Wabash), about 90 miles in length, drains an area covering about 1,320 square miles. This is a plain of till about 20 miles wide, which lies immediately south and west of the Marseilles moraine in Ford, Livingston, and La Salle counties. The river rises by several branches in the Bloomington morainic system in southeastern Livingston and Ford counties, the main stream following the western or outer border of the inner range of the system from its source to its mouth, and thus flowing in a northwestward direction and emptying into the Illinois near La Salle. The plain descends with the river, so that for 50 miles scarcely any valley is formed though there is a descent of nearly 100 feet. In the last 40 miles, from Pontiac to the banks of the Illinois, it has scarcely 20 feet of slope, and was apparently occupied by a shallow lake until a stream had been given time to open a channel from the Illinois back several miles into the plain. There are sandy deposits along the southern border of the plain which tend to confirm this view. In the lower 25 miles the stream corrades rapidly, making a descent of about 150 feet and cutting its valley mainly in rock. The channel is very narrow, steep, and rocky, especially near the mouth of the river, where the walls rise abruptly 150 feet from the water's edge.

A few miles from the mouth, at a bend in the river, a deep

cañon extends off to the east through Deer Park Glen. It is about one fourth of a mile long, with perpendicular walls, and is in the form of an elongated *S*. It terminates abruptly in a cirque, open at the top and about 150 feet in diameter at the bottom, with a fine spring of soft water bubbling up at its base. In the wet season there is a waterfall of 25 feet which enters it through a narrow chasm at the head. The walls of the cirque are about 175 feet high.

The stream is not of much value as a water-power on account of the unsteadiness of its flow. It has no marshy gathering ground, and the formations in its basin are mainly compact till which yields but little water in seasons of drought.

MACKINAW RIVER

Mackinaw River rises in eastern McLean county. It flows westward through the northern part of this county and across the southern end of Woodford, then turning southwest into Tazewell county. From the center of this county it bends again to the west, following this direction for about 15 miles, when it turns north and east, emptying into the Illinois a little below Pekin. It is about 110 miles long, and drains an area of about 1,200 square miles (Leverett).

The upper part of the river lies inside the main ridges of the Bloomington morainic system, and drains a plain which lies 300 to 350 feet above the Illinois. This section of the Mackinaw is about 40 miles in length, most of its course being along the southern border of the basin. In the first mile it descends 40 feet, but below this its fall averages about 3 feet to the mile.

In its middle course the stream crosses the Bloomington and Shelbyville morainic systems and the narrow plain separating them. The width of the valley increases from about one fourth of a mile in the inner part of the Bloomington belt to about one half of a mile at the outer part, and to nearly a mile in its passage across the Shelbyville moraine. Its fall is still rapid, about 3 feet per mile. There are few tributaries, only a small area being drained.

In its lower course the Mackinaw River winds about in a shallow channel, across the Illinois valley for a distance of nearly 20 miles, making a descent of 75 feet.

This stream is one of the most variable in the state in the quantity of water it carries, since it is subject to great floods in wet seasons and becomes nearly dry in seasons of drought.

This variableness is due to several causes. The principal ones are its rapid fall, its compact drift-beds, and the absence of headwater marshes.

SPOON RIVER

Spoon River rises in southern Bureau county. It flows southwest for almost 100 miles, nearly paralleling the Illinois River. It then turns abruptly southeastward and in 25 miles joins the Illinois opposite Havana, about 40 miles below the mouth of the Mackinaw. It drains about 1,820 square miles. All of this area except a little in the headwater portion, lies outside the limits of the Wisconsin drift, occupying a region covered by the Illinoisan drift upon which there is a capping of loess. The headwaters lie on the western slope of the Bloomington and Shelbyville morainic systems. The course of the main stream, and also of several of its tributaries, appears to have been determined largely by preglacial drainage lines, but they are not entirely coincident with these lines.

Its valley is cut mainly in drift, but exposes rock at many points along the base of the bluffs. The valley is very narrow except for a few miles before it reaches the Illinois River bluffs, where it widens out to 2 to 3 miles. In the first mile of its course it makes a descent of 70 feet. The fall gradually decreases until, in the last 80 miles, it descends only 2 or 3 feet per mile.

The river receives several tributaries from both the east and the west, each of which has a length of 15 to 20 miles or more. These tributaries are widely branching, and the entire watershed displays a perfection of drainage such as does not occur within the limits of the Wisconsin drift. Originally the entire basin was about half timber and half prairie. The prairies are all small, covering only a few square miles each, and separated by the strips of timber which line the many streams.

Spoon River is subject to great variations in its water stages on account of its rapid run-off, due to the rapid descent of the river-bed and the generally well-drained surface of the basin. In seasons of drought, springs along the valley afford a considerable supply of water, but the low-water discharge is less than 200 cubic feet per second (Leverett). The current of the Spoon River is so much stronger than that of the Illinois at the point where it empties into it, that a delta has been formed at its mouth.

SANGAMON RIVER

The Sangamon River has the largest watershed of any of the tributaries of the Illinois. Its drainage basin, covering an area of 5,390 square miles (Leverett), includes extensive plains which are now inadequately drained, but which may by extensive tiling be drained into the river.

The Sangamon rises in eastern McLean county, flowing southeast for about 10 miles into Champaign county, and thence south and west until, in Sangamon county, it takes a northwestward course. In northern Menard county it unites with Salt creek and, flowing westward, soon empties into the Illinois. The length of the river is about 200 miles. Its source is in the Bloomington morainic system at an altitude of about 850 feet. The mouth has an altitude of 429 feet, making a total descent of about 420 feet. In the first 10 miles it makes a descent of 120 feet, thus leaving about 300 feet of fall for the remaining 170 miles of its course. The fall is far from regular, there being sections, often several miles in length, in which it is slight, between which are sections with more rapid fall.

The river flows for its first 90 miles within the limits of the Wisconsin drift, but leaves this a few miles west of Decatur. In these 90 miles it receives no tributaries of importance, its immediate watershed being only 15 to 20 miles wide.

That part of the river valley lying outside of the Wisconsin drift, although generally shallow, is much wider than the portion within the limits of that drift sheet, and bears evidence of having been opened prior to the Wisconsin stage of glaciation. The river and its branches are bordered throughout most of their length by strips of timber about half a mile wide on either side.

The river is subject to great variations in volume, there being in the annual flood-stages a rise sufficient to overflow banks 8 to 12 feet in height. At such times, being a swift stream, it probably discharges not less than 15,000 cubic feet per second, and in extreme floods the discharge probably exceeds 20,000 cubic feet per second. Formerly the flow of the river was more or less regular. This was due to the fact that the portion of the basin lying within the Shelbyville moraine was filled with swamps which absorbed the water as it fell and then gave it forth very gradually. Now, however, a very complete system of tile drainage carries off this water very quickly, and so leaves the river subject to low stages for a large part of the year.

The principal branch of the Sangamon is Salt creek.

SALT CREEK

Salt creek is formed by the union of North and South Salt creeks. North Salt creek has its source between two large ridges of the Bloomington morainic system in southeastern McLean county near the source of the Sangamon. It passes southward through the outer ridge and across the undulating plain south of it, to its junction with the south fork. South Salt creek heads on the outer border of the Bloomington moraine, and flows southwestward across a gently undulating plain to a point 5 miles east of Clinton, where the two streams unite to form Salt creek. Above their junction each stream has a length of 25 to 30 miles. The south branch in its first 2 miles has a fall of 50 feet, and below this a fall averaging 10 feet to every three or four miles. The north branch falls 80 feet in its first 4 miles, with a fall below this averaging 10 feet to every two miles. From their junction the united streams pass westward through the Shelbyville moraine, entering the outer border plain at Kenney, eight miles southwest of Clinton. The general course of the creek continues westward to its junction with the Sangamon 50 miles below. It is 92 miles long, draining an area of 1,940 square miles.

It receives Lake Fork creek from the south about 5 miles above Lincoln, Kickapoo creek from the north about 4 miles below Lincoln, and Sugar creek, also from the north, about 12 miles farther down.

The valley of Salt creek is much broader below the mouth of Lake Fork than above and it seems probable that a larger stream occupied Lake Fork valley prior to the Wisconsin invasion than that which occupied Salt creek valley. The latter appears to be almost wholly a post-Wisconsin stream as far down as its junction with Lake Fork.

Below the junction the stream averages a fall of 10 feet to every three or four miles, but in the lower two miles the bed has a fall of 20 feet. The bed and banks of Salt creek, like those of the Sangamon, are without rock.

CROOKED CREEK

Crooked creek is the last western tributary of the Illinois. It rises in Hancock county and flows in an irregular course, southeast, into the Illinois River at a point 14 miles below the mouth of the Sangamon. The stream is about 60 miles long and drains an area of 1,350 square miles (Leverett). Its watershed lies immediately southwest of that of Spoon River. It extends on the northwest nearly to the bluffs of the Mississippi, there being one tributary in northern Hancock county, from which the Mississippi bluff is distant less than five miles. No important tributaries enter from the west, but several creeks lead into it from the east which have lengths of 15 to 20 miles or more. These eastern tributaries present a remarkable parallelism, and take a nearly uniform direction about S. 65° W. One of them, known as East Crooked creek, occupies a valley which continues beyond this watershed in a direct course to the Mississippi and is thought to have been formed by a subglacial stream. Shallow channels may also have been opened by the same agency along the other eastern tributaries and have occasioned their remarkably direct and parallel courses (Leverett).

The whole of the drainage basin lies in the Illinoisan drift and is very similar in character to the basin of the Spoon River. For a few miles near its mouth the course of Crooked creek has been determined by a preglacial drainage line, but elsewhere the drainage appears to be nearly independent of preglacial lines. A portion of the divide between the Spoon River watershed and the Crooked creek watershed follows a low till ridge.

In the first 14 miles of its course Crooked creek falls 100 feet, but the fall gradually decreases until in the last 20 miles it is only 10 feet. The bluffs of the river, especially in the lower part, are high and abrupt, rising to a height of 100 feet from the water's edge for a large part of the distance. In only a few places are bottom-lands found. They are short and never more than one half of a mile in width. Limestone outcrops are found all along the banks of the river.

APPLE CREEK

Apple creek has a drainage area of about 435 square miles, which includes southeastern Morgan county, northern Greene county, and northwestern Macoupin county. It rises in Morgan county and flows southwestward to its mouth. Its basin has a length of about 40 miles, and the greatest width is about 15 miles. The river is about 53 miles long.

The entire basin lies within the Illinoisan drift. The lower course of the river seems to be along the line of a preglacial valley, but the headwater portion and also a majority of the tributaries show little dependence upon preglacial lines. The drift is comparatively thin over much of the basin, and the streams have cut down into the underlying rocks at many points. The country near the river is hilly and much broken, the valleys of the streams having been excavated to a depth of 100 to 200 feet below the general level of the uplands.

Throughout its course Apple creek is a swiftly flowing stream. In the first 11 miles of its course it drops 100 feet. For the rest of the distance the fall averages about 5 feet to the mile.

MACOUPIN CREEK

Macoupin creek rises in northern Montgomery county and flows southwest into the Illinois. It drains an area of nearly 1,000 square miles (Leverett), consisting of the greater portion of Macoupin county and parts of Montgomery, Greene, and Jersey counties. Its watershed is broad in the middle and tapers toward either end, giving it a broadly ovate outline. The whole of the basin lies within the Illinoisan drift area. With the exception of the headwater portion, above Carlinville, the main stream apparently has its course determined by a preglacial line, there being a broad depression, deeply filled with drift, through which the creek takes its course. The tributary streams appear to be largely independent of preglacial lines.

The basin is composed of gently rolling or nearly level prairies, which occupy the highlands between the streams and cover fully one third of the area, and of heavy belts of timber which skirt the streams. The soil is of a black, peaty character on the level prairies, becomes chocolate-brown on the more rolling surfaces, and degenerates into a light ash-gray near the streams.

The creek is about 90 miles long, and drains 989 square miles. Its fall is varied, some parts, as the lower 17 miles, having a fall of only one and one half feet to the mile, and other parts much more, as the four and one half miles just above this, the fall in this distance being 30 feet. Above this point the average fall is about 2 feet to the mile. The banks are high, in some places rising to 100 feet. In a few places the banks recede from the water's edge, leaving bottom-lands one half to one and one half miles in width.

KASKASKIA RIVER SYSTEM.

The Kaskaskia River system drains a large part of southern Illinois, its drainage basin covering an area of 5,830 square miles. It is about 212 miles long, the narrow upper end reaching within 40 miles of the state of Indiana. The upper third of the basin lies in Wisconsin drift, and the other two thirds in the Illinoisan. The basin is composed of level or undulating country having black soil in the northern part and chocolate to light gray soil in the southern, underlaid by yellow to white clay. Heavy timber lands skirt the rivers, between which lie the prairies. In the southern parts great drift mounds, usually topped with timber, rise often from the midst of the prairies.

KASKASKIA RIVER

Kaskaskia River rises in Champaign county in the Champaign morainic system and flows southwest, emptying into the Mississippi in Randolph county, near Chester, at an altitude of 342 feet. Its descent is generally gradual, the most rapid section of its course being its passage through Moultrie county, where it makes a descent of 55 feet in about 18 miles, or 3 feet to the mile. In the headwater portion there is a fall of only 110 feet in the first 50 miles. In places there are pools several miles in length, the most conspicuous of these being in St. Clair county, where in a distance of 20 miles the fall is scarcely 10 feet.

The upper 80 miles lies in the Wisconsin drift, the stream emerging from the Shelbyville moraine near Shelbyville. In its headwater portion the channel of the stream is narrow and shallow to the inner border of the Shelbyville moraine. The banks are muddy as far as Sullivan, but sandy below this. The drainage of this section of the basin was originally very imperfect, and its undeveloped streams were often little more than series of swales and sloughs. Ditches and tile drains have greatly changed these conditions, however, and the run-off is now fairly prompt and complete. In crossing the moraine the Kaskaskia valley has an average depth of nearly 75 feet, and four miles northeast of Shelbyville the bluffs attain a height of 130 feet, although the channel is so narrow that it is not much more than a trench. The valley continues narrow for a few miles after entering the Illinoisan drift, but widens below the mouth of Robinson creek. This stream seems to follow the lower course of a drainage line (probably interglacial), whose former headwater portion has been concealed by the Shelbyville drift sheet. Its valley has a breadth of nearly half a mile, and the Kaskaskia retains this breadth below the mouth of the creek, increasing to three fourths of a mile in southern Shelby county. These bottoms are generally 14 to 16 feet above the ordinary stage of water, with sometimes a second bottom a few feet higher. During the wet seasons the river often covers the first bottom to a depth of several feet. The hills on each side of the river are from 60 to 70 feet in height. On entering Fayette county, the river opens into a broad preglacial valley whose course farther north is buried under drift. The valley has a width of about 3 miles near Vandalia, but reaches a greater width farther south. It is so masked by drift that it presents the appearance of a broad shallow basin rather than a river valley. It continues nearly to the mouth of the river, where the width contracts abruptly to about a mile upon entering the subcarboniferous limestone which there borders the Mississippi Valley. The bottom-lands are subject to annual overflow, and are still covered with a heavy growth of timber.

The stream is subject to great variations in volume as the compact clay subsoil promotes a rapid run-off and furnishes but little water in seasons of drought; consequently, in summer and fall, the river dwindles to a very small size. At times it may be crossed dry-shod at Vandalia, where it is 60 to 70 feet wide. A rise of 20 feet in its lower course is not rare in flood time, and its flood-plain has been built nearly to that height above the stream-bed.

The two principal tributaries of the Kaskaskia are from the west—Shoal creek and Silver creek.

SHOAL CREEK

Shoal creek drains an area of 947 square miles, or one sixth of the entire basin of the Kaskaskia River (Leverett). This area includes most of Montgomery and Bond counties and western Clinton county. Shoal creek is made up of three branches known as West, Middle, and East Shoal creeks. West and Middle creeks unite to form the West fork, by the union of which with East creek, twenty miles below, the main stream is formed. From the rise of its branches to its mouth in the Kaskaskia this stream has a total length of 79 miles. The watershed has a distinct southward slope, the altitude at the headwaters being 700 to 750 feet, and at the mouth only 400 feet.

The three branches have each formed a channel 50 to 75 feet or more in depth and nearly one fourth of a mile in average width in their passage through southern Montgomery county, and a similar depth is maintained as far down as the junction of the East and West forks near Greenville. Below this point the valley is more shallow, and the stream soon enters the Kaskaskia basin, where its bed is but little lower than the basin plain.

East Shoal creek is bordered closely on the east throughout its entire length by a series of drift knolls and ridges (broken Illinoisan moraines). Shoal creek passes through a break in this system of ridges just below the junction of the East and West forks, beyond which its course is largely independent of drift ridges. Middle Shoal creek winds about among prominent drift knolls near Hillsboro, and West Shoal creek is deflected eastward by a ridge of drift at its junction with Middle Shoal creek. The courses of these streams seem to be mainly independent of preglacial lines but largely determined by Illinoisan moraines. East Shoal creek touches the line of a deep preglacial valley near Greenville, but above that point it has opened a new course, in places trenching into the rock. Even the lower course seems to be largely independent of any preglacial line of drainage.

SILVER CREEK

Silver creek rises in the southeastern corner of Macoupin county, flowing almost due south through eastern Madison and St. Clair counties and emptying into the Kaskaskia opposite New Athens. It has a length of about 60 miles, draining an area of 500 square miles. The basin averages only about 10 miles in width.

At its source the river has an altitude of about 650 feet. In its first 4 miles it falls 50 feet and in the next 16 miles a descent of 100 feet is made. In the lower part the fall is much less, being only 70 feet in the remaining 43 miles.

In its southern half the watershed is diversified by drift ridges and knolls which rise in some cases to a height of 75 feet or more above the border districts. These for a few miles in southeastern Madison county constitute the east border of the watershed, but just south of the line of Madison and St. Clair counties the stream passes through the main belt of ridges, and it has but few prominent ridges and knolls on its east below that point. At its mouth the stream has an elvation of only 370 feet, and the surrounding country, aside from the knolls, stands scarcely 400 feet above tide. Silver creek seems to be largely dependent in the direction of its course on glacial influences. It cuts into the rock at numerous points along its course, and its immediate bluffs stand at the general level of the bordering uplands.

Big Muddy River System

Big Muddy River system drains an area of 2,390 square miles lying in an elliptical shape, with a major axis about 70 miles long running almost north and south, and a minor axis about 50 miles long. This drainage basin includes the greater part of Williamson, Franklin, Jefferson, Perry, and Jackson counties, the southeastern portion of Washington county, and the southern part of Marion county, which forms the extreme southwestern part of the district covered by the Illinoisan drift sheet, lying in the low section just north of the Ozark ridge. The lower 20 miles of the river flows through the Mississippi bottoms. With the exception of the ridge on the southern border, which stands 600 to 800 feet above tide, the basin has few points rising above 550 feet, the average level being 400 to 500 feet. The immediate borders of the main valley fall below 400 feet and the mouth of the stream at low water in the Mississippi is but 320 feet. The country is made up of gray prairies intersected by rivers whose bottom-lands are below the general level. These rivers are skirted by timber belts, so that a large portion of the basin is wooded. The bottom-lands also were formerly timbered, but parts have been cleared and put under cultivation. Over the greater portion of the area the drift is very thin, and rock divides separating the preglacial drainage areas are plainly discernible. The basin of the Big Muddy has been subject to long erosion, and consequently the soils are largely made of clays containing little humus and giving acid reactions.

Big Muddy River has the characteristics of an old stream, in a land long exposed to erosion. It has cut its bed down to drainage level, and it runs its crooked course over a broad flood-plain. It rises in northern Jefferson county, and flows south and then west and south, emptying into the Mississippi about 5 miles below Grand Tower, Jackson county. It is about 94 miles long. Beaucoup creek enters from the north 25 to 30 miles from the mouth, and Little Muddy River enters from the same side about 10 miles farther up. These two streams together drain about the same area as the main stream above the junction, and Beaucoup creek drains about one half more area than the Little Muddy. An eastern tributary, Crab Orchard creek, drains about 250 square miles of the district bordering the Ozark ridge.

The river is very sluggish, and its volume is extremely variable. In the first eleven miles it makes a descent of about 100 feet, but below this the fall is not more than a foot to the mile. In times of spring flood its broad stream is overloaded with silt and its bottom a creeping mass, shifting its contour with every change in rate of flow; and during the summer drouths it shrinks to little more than a chain of nearly stagnant pools.

Throughout the greater portion of its course Big Muddy River occupies a preglacial line of drainage and meanders about in broad bottoms which have been filled with drift and alluvium to an elevation of from 500 to 600 feet or more above the rock bottom. Just below Murphysboro the valley becomes constricted to a width of about a mile in its passage through the elevated ridge which there borders the Mississippi. In its course through the Mississippi bottoms its eastern shore hugs the bluff, which rises 200 to 300 feet above the river. On its west are the low, flat flood-plains of the Mississippi. Above Murphysboro the banks are neither abrupt nor high, and they and the bed of the stream are chiefly clay.

At Murphysboro, about 6 miles below the junction of Beaucoup creek, where the stream is about 160 feet wide, the water has sometimes risen 30 feet, flooding the surrounding flats. Backwater from the Mississippi is felt at that point. The river is very properly named, as it carries great quantities of alluvium which the current is constantly shifting from one place to another.

The Wabash System

The Wabash basin, which covers the greater part of Indiana, includes also about 8,770 square miles of eastern Illinois, drained by the Big Vermilion, the Embarras, and the Little Wabash rivers, and by several smaller streams in the southeastern part of the state. The greater part of its surface lies at an elevation varying between 300 and 700 feet, with the highlands around its headwaters and the region of the Shelbyville moraine rising approximately 100 feet higher. This moraine marks the southern limit of the Wisconsin glaciation, beyond which lies the lower Illinoisan. It divides the Wabash valley in Illinois into two distinctly different regions, the northern of which has the characteristics of a comparatively recent glaciation, and the southern those of a glaciated area long exposed to erosion. In the northern part the streams are few, and their branches are few and comparatively short. The uplands were poorly drained originally, and contained many marshes, sometimes very large, and many shallow lakes. The soil here is deep, black, rich in organic matter, slightly alkaline in reaction, porous, and rather coarsely granulated. In the southern section the soil has been washed and eroded for thousands of years, leaving it as an extremely fine-grained, slightly acid residue, from which most of the organic matter has disappeared. The streams of this long-exposed southern area have developed themselves freely in comparatively deep channels, through which their currents have a sluggish flow, and have lengthened their branches back to the uplands, which are thus effectually drained by natural processes. The large streams, especially in their lower courses, have formed extensive bottom-lands liable to overflow, and, owing to the thorough natural drainage of the country, the waters recede to a very low level during times of drought.

Hydrographic conditions in the Wisconsin glaciation have been greatly changed within comparatively recent years by large drainage operations, carried on at public expense under the operation of state law. Swamps, marshes, and lakes have virtually disappeared, and their places have been taken by rich and highly cultivated farms. Much less change has been made in the lower Wabash Valley as a consequence of human occupancy, but the original rather general covering of both lowland and upland forest has been mainly removed, with the effect to expose the surface to more rapid erosion than heretofore, and to increase the extremes of flood and low water.

WABASH RIVER

Wabash River was given, by the earliest explorers, the name of Ouabouskigou, said to mean "white water" in one of the Indian tongues, and it bears this Indian name on the maps of both Joliet and Marquette. This was later contracted by the French to Ouabache, the spelling of which has since been simply anglicized. The earlier explorers regarded the lower Ohio and the Wabash as forming one stream, to which they gave the latter name, while the upper Ohio bore either its present name or that of "la Belle Rivière."

The Wabash forms, for 198 miles, the boundary between Indiana and Illinois, lying in this part of its course in a preglacial valley, the former bed of a very much larger stream. This valley, five or six miles across in its upper part, is filled with drift which buries the old stream bed to a depth of 60 or 70 feet, and is bounded by bluffs rising from 100 to 200 feet above the river. The Illinois section of the Wabash has a comparatively sluggish current, its fall being less than eight inches to the mile.

Two, and in some places three, different levels are distinguishable in the Wabash valley to-day. The bottom-lands of the river subject to overflow at ordinary high water are from twelve to fifteen feet above the stream, and at about the same height above these are the second bottoms, covered with water only by exceptional floods; and in some places a terrace level may be traced half-way up the bordering bluff. The river flows for the most part along the western side of its valley, occasionally, indeed, quite close to the bluffs, leaving the bottoms largely on the Indiana side of the stream. The bed of the river is often rocky and the current locally swift, and rapids greatly interfered in early days with the use of the stream for transportation purposes. The waters of the Wabash are, like those of the Illinois and the Kaskaskia, commonly brown and opaque with suspended silt, never clearing even at the lowest stages; and the same is true of most of its tributary streams, especially those of the lower Illinoisan glaciation.

VERMILION RIVER

Vermilion River drains an area of about 1,435 square miles in Ford, Champaign, and Vermilion counties in Illinois, and a small section of Fountain and Warren counties in Indiana. It rises only a few miles from the source of a river of the same name which flows northwest into the Illinois, to distinguish it from which it is often called the Wabash-Vermilion or the Big Vermilion. Its course is generally south and east, and it empties into the Wabash 10 miles beyond the Indiana line. It has a length of about 81 miles, and a fall of 320 feet. Its source is in the midst of the Bloomington morainic system at an elevation of 800 feet. It flows thence southward between two ridges, known as the Roberts and Melvin ridges, and passes through the latter ridge, falling 70 feet in this distance of 17½ miles. At this point it receives a tributary of about the same length from the west, which is known as the West branch of the Middle Fork. This branch also rises at an elevation of 800 feet and drains a sag or narrow plain between the Melvin ridge and the outer moraine of the Bloomington system. From this union the stream takes a southeastward course across the northeast corner of Champaign county and into Vermilion county as far as Potomac, where it turns abruptly southward and passes through the outer ridge of the Bloomington moraine. A few miles farther south it receives its larger western tributary, the Salt Fork, and the united stream then flows east for about 6 miles to Danville, takes again a southeast course, and follows this direction to its mouth.

Salt Fork rises in western Champaign county at an altitude of 740 feet and flows south and then east for a distance of 50 miles. It drains a plain in eastern Champaign and western Vermilion counties, lying between the Bloomington and Champaign morainic systems.

North Fork rises in northern Vermilion county at an elevation of 720 feet and flows southward for a distance of 37 miles, emptying into the Vermilion at Danville. It drains only a small area among the ridges of the Bloomington system.

The entire drainage system of the Vermilion is independent of preglacial lines, the drift over this region being so deep as to cover completely the old rock divides. The river and its branches have narrow valleys, and in the upper courses the banks are only from 10 to 50 feet high, and generally bordered by scattered patches of timber. In the lower parts the streams are skirted with strips of woodland from one to four miles in width, and the banks are steep and high. Bed-rock is not exposed in the upper portions, but at and below Danville the river has cut into the Pennsylvanian to a considerable depth.

Generally speaking, the headwaters of all these streams were originally prairie swales, lying in shallow valleys or in broad depressions of an otherwise plain surface. Here they were often choked with weeds in summer, and were very muddy in times of flood, but in their lower courses they often cut deeply into the drift, or even into the underlying rock, forming deep and narrow valleys, sometimes with decidedly gorge-like effect. In comparison with most Illinois streams, however, the waters of the Big Vermilion are in general fairly clear, and the bottoms relatively clean, forming a transition from the typical prairie streams to those characteristic of the adjacent Alleghany plateau.

LITTLE VERMILION RIVER

The Little Vermilion River rises in the southeastern corner of Champaign county and flows southeast, east, northeast, and southwest, a distance of about 60 miles, emptying into the Wabash River in Vermilion county, Indiana. Of this length 45 miles lie in Illinois. It drains a narrow strip covered by the Champaign till-sheet lying between two moraines, the northern of which completely separates the drainage basin of the Little Vermilion from that of the Vermilion proper. Its total drainage area is 213 square miles, 179 of which are in Illinois. It rises at an altitude of 710 feet, and falls 30 feet in its first 4 miles. In the next 9 miles a descent of only 10 feet is made, below which a fall of 50 feet occurs in 4 miles. The descent then becomes more gradual and the stream crosses the state-line at an elevation of about 500 feet. In its upper part it is little more than a prairie drain, but it becomes of more importance farther down, where the banks are 75 to 100 feet high and lined with strips of timber 1 to 3 miles in width.

EMBARRAS RIVER

Embarras River, 132 miles long, drains an area of about 2,400 square miles in eastern Illinois. Its source is in the Champaign morainic system, immediately south of the city of Champaign. For about 20 miles it flows between the outer and the main ridges of the Champaign system, then cuts through the outer ridge in northern Douglas county. Thence it bears southeast, for about 10 miles, to a small till ridge correlated with the Cerro Gordo moraine, crossing this in southeastern Douglas county. Its course is then slightly west of south for 25 miles, at which point it leaves the Shelbyville or earliest Wisconsin sheet of drift, continuing southward 25 to 30 miles farther, to the neighborhood of Newton, where it changes to the southeastward and maintains this course to its mouth, a distance of 50 miles.

The river rises at an altitude of 750 feet, while its mouth lies only 395 feet above tide, making a total descent of 355 feet, or an average descent of two and a third feet to the mile. In the last 53 miles, however, the fall is scarcely more than a foot to the mile.

The upper part of the river, lying within the Wisconsin drift, drains only a narrow strip and has but few tributaries. This section of its basin is mostly prairie with woodlands skirting the larger streams, and the soil is a deep, black, and very fertile loam.

Upon emerging from the Wisconsin drift, the river enters at once a much broader valley which appears to have been excavated prior to the Wisconsin stage of glaciation, for the valley gravels connected with the Shelbyville moraine head down the river bottom in a way to indicate the existence of this valley at the time of their deposition. The valley increases in width from one mile in Cumberland county to 2 miles in Jasper county, and 3 to 5 miles in Crawford and Lawrence counties. Below Newton its course is determined largely by a preglacial line of drainage, which possibly extends up the valley as far as the vicinity of Greenup, 18 miles above Newton. In this section of the basin strips of timber-land border the streams, and the bottoms are somewhat swampy and subject to overflow, but are generally sufficiently dry to admit of some cultivation when cleared. In Lawrence county, between the Embarras and the Wabash rivers, there is an extensive marsh, known as Purgatory swamp, about 10 miles long and from 2 to 4 miles in width. The banks of the river are 50 feet high in Cumberland and Jasper counties, but much lower near its mouth, although the uplands lie 50 to 100 feet above the watercourses.

The interesting contrast between the upper and the lower courses of this stream, in respect to the number of its tributaries, the extent of its flood-plain, and the development of its drainage system generally, is clearly traceable to differences in age between the two glacial areas through which it flows.

LITTLE WABASH RIVER

Little Wabash River, with a length of 160 miles, drains about 3,190 square miles in southeastern Illinois. It lies in an oval basin, much broader in the middle than in its lower and upper parts. It extends, on the west, to the watershed of the Kaskaskia and on the east to the Embarras and Bonpas watersheds. The entire basin lies in the Illinoisan drift, and is made up of rolling prairies lying between the broad belts of woodland which skirt the streams. The difference in level between the creek bottoms and the adjacent highlands does not usually exceed 50 to 75 or 100 feet.

The river rises in southwestern Coles county, and flows south through Shelby and Effingham counties. In northern Clay county it turns southeast for about 50 miles, and then flows alternately southwest and southeast until it empties into the Wabash at the boundary line between Gallatin and White counties, eight miles, in a direct line, from the junction of the Wabash with the Ohio River. The length of the river is about 180 miles. Its source is in the Shelbyville moraine at an elevation of 740 feet, but it descends within 4 miles to 700 feet, to 650 feet in the next 2½ miles, and to 600 feet 12 miles below. Another descent of 100 feet is made in the following 31 miles, while at a point 42 miles below this the 400 feet contour-line is crossed. The mouth of the stream, 104 miles distant, lies 323 feet above tide. Thus the total descent of the river is 317 feet, giving an average fall of about 1.7 feet per mile.

In the first 40 to 50 miles the main stream is largely independent of preglacial lines, and there is consequently little valley. The remainder of its course, however, is determined by a broad preglacial valley except for a short distance below Carmi, where it cuts across a projecting spur of hills leading in from the west. This valley, like others in this region, has been filled in its lower course with drift and alluvium to a level perhaps 100 feet above the rock bottom (Leverett). It is from an eighth to a fourth of a mile wide in Effingham county, but below, reaches a width of one to three miles. At times the river is bordered locally by precipitous bluffs 40 to 50 or even 100 feet in height, while at other points there is a gradually sloping surface from the bottoms up to the level of the adjacent prairie. The river-bottoms are a rich, sandy loam, but are valued little for agriculture on account of the overflow to which they are subject during the annual spring freshets. They are, however, valued for the heavy timber which covers them.

The most important tributary of the Little Wabash is Skillet Fork which enters from the west near Carmi. The length of this stream is about 78 miles, not including the windings of its course, and it has a watershed of nearly 1,080 square miles. It rises in northeast Marion county and flows south and then southeast. Its source is at an elevation of 600 feet, but it has a fall of 100 feet in its first 6 miles and makes another descent of 50 feet in the next 12 miles. During the rest of its course it falls but 100 feet. In the upper, swifter section the precipitous bluffs rise to a height of 60 to 75 feet, and there is little valley; but in the lower part the stream occupies a preglacial valley similar to that occupied by the Little Wabash.

Saline River System

The Saline River system drains into the Ohio that portion of southeastern Illinois which lies immediately north of the Ozark ridge. Its basin covers an area of about 2,000 square miles.

lying entirely within the limits of the Illinoisan drift. Part of the land is quite broken by hills and ledges which range in elevation from 10 to 80 feet above the high-water mark of the streams. A large part of the country, however, is level, and much of the land may be termed "wet," with here and there a not inconsiderable swamp or pond occupying, probably, old waterways. The basin is crossed by "Gold Hill," which extends through Gallatin and Hamilton counties in an east and west direction. This ridge, which attains a height of 343 feet above the high-water mark of the Ohio River, is crossed by the Saline River a few miles below Equality. The soil is light-colored clay loam, and a large part of it is still covered with thick timber.

The river is formed in western Gallatin county by the union of North and South forks, the latter being joined by Middle Fork in the southeastern part of Saline county. From the point of its formation the main stream pursues its course along the base of the Ozark ridge in a southeasterly direction, emptying into the Ohio River in northeast Hardin county. The three forks of the river and their principal tributaries are, in the main, re-established along preglacial lines, and take meandering courses through broad valleys which have been filled to an elevation of 50 to 100 feet or more above their rock bottoms.

The main river is about 16 miles long, and in this distance it makes a descent of only about 35 feet. The banks of the river along its northern border are low, but on the south they rise abruptly and often to a height of 150 feet, especially in the upper half, where the river hugs more closely the base of the ridge. The South Fork is about 49 miles in length. In the first half mile, as it descends the ridge, it falls 50 feet, but the fall gradually diminishes to 50 feet in the last 24 miles. Its total descent is about 300 feet. The banks are rather high, especially along the south, where they rise 50 to 60 feet above the water's edge. Middle Fork is only about 26 miles long, with a fall of about 60 feet. North Fork in the first mile of its course has a fall of about 30 feet. In the remaining 43 miles a descent of about 60 feet is made. The banks of this stream are low and subject to frequent overflow. In southeastern Hamilton county the course of the North Fork is entirely lost for about 3 miles as it crosses a swamp.

The course of the main stream is crooked and the current sluggish, with long stretches of quiet water where soft black ooze can accumulate year after year, and where a typically lacustrine vegetation can grow. Here *Nuphar*, *Nymphæa*, *Potamogeton*, and the limnophilous species of filamentous algæ abound. In dry weather the visible flow may almost cease in places, and in flood a full stream may fill the banks even to overflowing; but it is never quite a rushing muddy torrent, nor ever quite a dry creek with scattered pools floored with gravel or naked clay.

Cache River

Cache River drains the eastern part of Union county, the southwestern half of Johnson county, the northern part of Massac county, and most of Pulask and Alexander counties. The edges of this basin are not clearly defined, but it probably covers an area of about 623 square miles. It lies entirely in the driftless area which covers the southern point of Illinois, just south of the Ozark ridge. The basin is very largely made up of alluvial bottom-lands which border all the streams, and which in southern Alexander county extend entirely across the state from the Cache River to the Mississippi. These bottom-lands are generally flat, and are interspersed with cypress ponds and marshes, being mostly too wet for cultivation without a very thorough system of drainage. They are subject to annual inundations from the floods of the rivers, and are generally covered with timber, now being rapidly removed for lumber. The most elevated portions of these bottom-lands, however, have a light, rich, sandy soil, very productive when cultivated. Farther from the streams, the surface of the country is roughly broken.

The Ohio River may, at one time, have discharged wholly or in part through "Cache valley," which crosses southern Illinois a few miles north of its present course. Its point of connection with Cache valley is immediately north of Metropolis, where for a distance of 4 to 5 miles a clay deposit has accumulated in the line of the old valley. The surface of this clay deposit stands only about 75 feet above the present stream, and is much lower than the surface of the Tertiary deposits on either side. It is not known as yet, whether the channel formerly constituted the sole line of discharge for the Ohio or not. Possibly the river divided its waters between the Cache and its present channel. The bluffs of the powerful stream which excavated the valley of the Ohio extend from the Mississippi half-way across Alexander county, and then turn northeast, leaving a bottom from 3 to 5 miles in width between them and the Cache.

The headwaters of Cache River are in eastern Union county, the river winding first southeast, then south-southwest, south, and east, emptying finally into the Ohio River a few miles below Mound City. It traverses a distance of about 73 miles, beginning at an altitude of 500 feet. It falls 50 feet in a little over 2 miles, 100 feet in the next 15 miles, and only 70 feet in the remainder of its course. Near its head it has a definite channel, but just west of the Union-Johnson county line it enters its first cypress swamp. This, however, is very small, and the bottom-lands again become higher and drier, averaging about half a mile in width for the next nine miles. Then for a distance of about 3 miles there is scarcely any bottom-land, below which the river enters an extensive cypress swamp having a width of 5 miles in some places. A few miles above Collinsburg the bottom again becomes narrow and ledges of sandstone form the bed of the stream, which here is clear and swift. Below this point the water is nearly stagnant, brown in color, and full of drifted logs. The lowlands average about three fourths of a mile in width to near the mouth of Dutchman creek, where they spread out to almost two miles. At the Massac county line, Cache River enters the main swamp region which extends across Pulaski county, and below these swamps the river winds about through wide bottoms to its mouth. The backwater of the Ohio reaches up Cache River hardly as far as Ullin, and floods above this point are more immediately caused by the headwaters of the stream when their discharge is impeded by backwater. The country around the upper Cache is hilly and precipitous, and so in times of freshets it pours immense quantities of water into this lower flat, which then becomes a reservoir. As the waters which the Cache carries come from the Mississippian and cretaceous, they are somewhat different in mineral characteristics from any of the rivers heretofore described.

Big Bay Creek

Big Bay creek drains 275 square miles in eastern Johnson and western Pope counties—an area very similar in character to that drained by the Cache. The stream rises in northwestern Pope county, flows southwest into Johnson county, takes there a southeasterly direction, and empties into the Ohio near Bay

City. It has a length of about 40 miles, with an alt'tude of 750 feet at its source and of 300 feet at its mouth. In the upper 7 miles it falls 300 feet and the banks are steep and abrupt; but below, the river valley expands into a swampy region 3 to 4 miles in width. These swamps connect with those of the Cache River, and often the headwaters of the latter stream find their way to the Big Bay and down it to the Ohio. At other times, high water in the Ohio produces a flow through Big Bay, the swamps, and down the Cache. Much is now being done, through tiling and ditching, to separate completely the basins of the two streams and to make each course distinct. In the lower 8 miles of its course the banks again hug the river closely, and rise on either side to a height of 250 to 300 feet.

The Lake Michigan Drainage

In the northeastern part of the state there is a narrow belt of land from ten to twenty miles in width bordering Lake Michigan and sending its waters into that lake through many small, short streams, only two of which are of sufficient size to received especial mention, namely, the Chicago and the Calumet rivers. Much of this area, including the present site of Chicago, was formerly part of a great glacial lake known to geologists as Lake Chicago, which existed at the same time as the "Chicago Outlet" (see page xxxiv). It discharged its waters southward through this outlet instead of northward as at the present time. This tract of land now lies as a relatively level plain, diversified with old lake-beaches and low glacial moraines. It is very poorly drained and is filled with swamps and lakes.

The small short streams are mostly to be found in Lake county, where they drain a strip from two to four miles in width directly bordering the lake. They rise in the morainic ridge which here extends north and south along the shore at an altitude of about 700 ft., and from its crest they make very rapid and direct descents to the lake.

Chicago River rises in northern Cook county and flows south and east for a distance of 29 miles, emptying into Lake Michigan about a mile and a half north of the Illinois Central station in Chicago, and draining an area of 226 square miles. It rises in a swampy area at an elevation of 630 ft. above tide and makes a descent of 20 ft. in the first two and a half miles of its course. Below this, however, it has almost no fall, the mouth of the stream lying at about 600 ft. above tide. Nine miles from its source Chicago River is joined by a branch from the east. This latter stream rises in Lake county in another swampy intermorainic area at an elevation of 660 ft., and in its length of 12 miles makes a descent of 50 ft. Although the upper courses of this stream and of the main river can not be definitely traced farther up-stream than mentioned above, they seem to drain indirectly a series of marshes lying between moraines extending north and south within those directly bordering Lake Michigan and bounded on the west by the Des Plaines watershed. About one mile from its mouth Chicago River is joined by the South Branch. This river connects with the Des Plaines near Summit and, as stated in the description of the latter river, it has afforded a line of discharge for the upper Des Plaines from the time of the withdrawal of the lake down to historic times. The size and depth of its channel are such as to seem to demand the work of a stream as large as the Des Plaines. Even in quite recent years this river at high-water has been known to overflow into the South Chicago channel and thus to discharge some of its water into Lake Michigan. With the exception of a few miles at the headwaters of North Fork, the entire drainage system lies within the limits of old Lake Chicago. The southward course of the stream outside of the lake bottom is occasioned by till ridges of the Lake Border morainic system, the one on the east preventing direct discharge into Lake Michigan. Within the limits of Lake Chicago the stream follows the slope of the old lake bottom.

Calumet River has its headwaters in the Valparaiso morainic system south of Michigan City, Indiana. Its numerous tributaries also rise in this system, and they and the main stream, on descending from this ridge, flow in the lowland formerly covered by Lake Chicago. Here their courses are controlled to some extent by the lines of sand-dunes formed along the benches of the old lake, and, to a slight extent, by till ridges. The streams have almost no fall, and the section through which they flow is filled with swamps and lakes. The course of the river is meandering, and at times it is almost impossible to determine the direction of the flow of water, as in the swampy region near Blue Island. Lake Calumet, near Pullman, Illinois, is the largest of the many tributary lakes. The mouth of the stream is at South Chicago, Illinois, at an altitude of about 580 ft.

On the General and Interior Distribution of Illinois Fishes

The geography of Illinois is, in its most obvious features, so simple and so monotonous that one naturally expects a similar simplicity and monotony in the geographic distribution of its plants and animals. The plan of its hydrography is as little complicated as the geography of its land areas. Surrounded on more than two thirds of its circumference by three large rivers, the Mississippi, the Ohio, and the Wabash, with Lake Michigan covering a narrow strip at its northeast corner and draining a bordering region of scarcely greater area, its other waters flow southwestward into the Mississippi and southward into the Wabash and the Ohio, all mingling finally opposite its southernmost extremity for their journey to the Gulf. Its principal watersheds are inconspicuous ridges or slightly elevated plains, most of them originally more or less marshy, and the headwaters and tributaries of its various stream systems so approach and intermingle that in times of flood they formed an interlacing network, through which it would seem that a wandering fish might have found its way in almost any direction and to almost any place.

Its climate varies considerably, of course, within the five and a half degrees of its length from north to south, but by nsensible gradations, with no lines of abrupt transition anywhere to set definite boundaries to the range of its aquatic species.

Its surface geology is more diversified than its topography, and its soils, although uniformly fertile throughout most of the state, differ notably in their origin and physical constitution, some of these differences being such as to affect more or less the surface waters and, through them, to influence the conditions of aquatic life. The extreme northwestern and the extreme southern parts of the state are bare of drift; but the surface of all the remainder of the state, excepting a small area above the mouth of the Illinois, has been repeatedly worked over by ice in the course of the successive divisions of the glacial period. The oldest glaciated area, known as the lower Illinoisan glaciation, covers the greater part of southern Illinois and a narrow belt of the southeast part of the central section of the state. Next to this at the northwest, and immediately east of the lower half of the Illinois River, is the middle Illinoisan; above this, in the west-central part of the state, between the Illinois River and the Rock, is the upper Illinoisan; and still farther north, in the Rock River basin, are the Iowan and Preiowan glaciations, reaching northward across the Wisconsin boundary. East of the last three mentioned, and north of the southern Illinois district, the Wisconsin glaciation, the most recent of the series, covers about a fourth of the state. It is to the peculiar features of the lower Illinoisan glaciation especially, that we shall presently be compelled to pay particular attention, because of their evident effect on the distribution of a considerable group of our fishes.

The topographical relations of the state to the surrounding territory are as simple and open as its own interior hydrography, and there is little to suggest the possibility of anything in the least peculiar in the general constitution or the relat ons of its fauna, or anything problematical or especially interesting in the details of the distribution of its native fishes. We shall find reason to believe, however, that this appearance is misleading, and that the subject, studied in detail, contains matter of unusual interest, and presents problems of considerable difficulty, a solution of which will lead us to some novel results.

It is true, however, generally speaking, that the distribution of Illinois fishes reflects, in uniformity and relative monotony, the features of the topography of the state. A few species occurring in Lake Michigan and characteristic of the Great Lakes are, in fact, the only Illinois fishes which are definitely and permanently separated from their fellows in other Illinois waters by what may be called geographical conditions, and these conditions are not physical obstacles to their passage from Lake Michigan to the Illinois River.

Excluding, for the moment, these fishes special to the Great Lakes, we find elsewhere in Illinois a general commingling and overlapping of the fish population of the surrounding territory, the limits to whose range are climatic, local, and ecological, but topographic only in a secondary sense.

THE GENERAL DISTRIBUTION

Most of the 150 species of the native fishes of Illinois range far and wide in all directions beyond its narrow boundaries, thus illustrating the breadth and the simplicity of our geographical affiliations with the surrounding territory; but a considerable number, on the other hand, coming into Illinois from one direction, do not pass beyond it in another, some part of the boundary of the general area of their distribution passing through our state. Several southern fishes go no farther north than Illinois; some northern fishes go no farther south; some eastern species find here their western limit; and a few western species range no farther east. The comparison of these geographical groups whose areas overlap by their borders here in Illinois is a matter of special interest to the student of distribution, because it is in them that we find indicated the more remote affinities of our fish fauna, and from them, if anywhere, we may glean suggestions of its various origins.

It will be convenient for a discussion of this subject to divide the general expanse over which Illinois fishes are distributed, into the following twelve districts: 1, the upper Mississippi Valley, including the Missouri and its tributaries; 2, the lower Mississippi Valley, including the Ohio and its tributaries; 3, the far North, extending northward from the headwaters of the Mississippi, east to the Lake Superior drainage, and west to the Rocky Mountains; 4, the far Northwest, separated from the preceding by the Rocky Mountains range; 5, the Great Lake region; 6, the district of Quebec and New England; 7, the Hudson River district; 8, the north Atlantic drainage, from New England to the Chesapeake Bay; 9, the south Atlantic, from the Chesapeake Bay to Florida; 10, the peninsula of Florida; 11, the east Gulf district, bounded by the Mississippi drainage on the west; and 12, the west Gulf district, bounded by the Mississippi drainage on the east, and extending west and south to include the Rio Grande and its tributaries. The following table shows the recorded distribution of our species over the territory so divided.

TABLE OF THE GENERAL DISTRIBUTION OF ILLINOIS FISHES

	Great Lake Basin	Quebec and New England	Hudson River	North Atlantic	South Atlantic	Florida Peninsula	East Gulf	Lower Miss. and Ohio	Upper Miss. and Mo.	West Gulf and Rio Grande	Far Northwest	Far North
Silvery lamprey (*Ichthyomyzon*)......	+	+	...	...	...	...	...	+	+	...	...	...
Brook lamprey (*Lampetra*)..........	+	...	...	...	...	...	...	+	+	...	...	...
Paddle-fish (*Polyodon*)..............	+	...	...	...	...	...	...	+	+	...	...	...
Lake sturgeon (*Acipenser*)...........	+	+	...	...	...	...	...	+	+	...	...	+
Shovel-nosed sturgeon................	...	...	...	...	...	...	...	+	+	+	...	...
White sturgeon (*P. albus*)...........	...	...	...	...	...	...	...	+	...	...	...	...
Long-nosed gar.....................	+	+	...	+	+	+	+	+	+	+	...	...
Short-nosed gar....................	+	...	...	...	...	+	+	+	+	...	...	...
Alligator-gar......................	...	...	...	...	...	+	...	+	+	+	...	...
Dogfish (*Amia*)....................	+	+	...	...	+	+	+	+	+	...	...	...
Mooneye (*alosoides*)...............	...	...	...	...	...	...	...	+	+	...	...	+
Toothed herring (*tergisus*)..........	+	+	...	...	...	...	...	+	+	...	...	+
Gizzard-shad (*Dorosoma*)............	+	...	...	+	+	+	+	+	+	+	...	...
Skipjack (*chrysochloris*).............	+	...	...	...	...	...	+	+	+	+	...	...
Whitefish..........................	+	+	...	...	...	...	...	...	...	...	...	+
Lake herring.......................	+	+	...	...	...	...	...	...	...	...	...	...
Lake trout.........................	+	+	...	...	...	...	...	...	...	...	+	+
Eel................................	+	+	+	+	+	+	+	+	+	+	...	...
Black-horse (*Cycleptus*).............	...	...	...	...	...	...	...	+	+	+	...	...
Red-mouth buffalo (*cyprinella*).......	...	...	...	...	...	...	...	+	+	...	...	+
Mongrel buffalo (*urus*).............	...	...	...	...	...	...	...	+	+	...	...	...
Small-mouth buffalo (*bubalus*)........	...	...	...	...	...	...	...	+	+	...	...	...

Table of the General Distribution of Illinois Fishes—*continued*

	Great Lake Basin	Quebec and New England	Hudson River	North Atlantic	South Atlantic	Florida Peninsula	East Gulf	Lower Miss. and Ohio	Upper Miss. and Mo.	West Gulf and Rio Grande	Far Northwest	Far North
River carp (*carpio*)	...	...	...	...	...	...	...	+	+	+	...	...
Blunt-nosed carp (*difformis*)	...	...	...	...	...	...	...	+	+	...	...	...
Lake carp (*thompsoni*)	+	+	...	...	...	...	...	...	+	...	...	...
Quillback carp (*velifer*)	+	...	...	...	...	...	...	+	+	+	...	+
Chub-sucker	+	+	+	+	+	+	+	+	+	+	...	...
Striped sucker	+	...	...	+	+	...	+	+	+	+	...	...
Common sucker (*commersonii*)	+	+	+	+	+	...	...	+	+	...	...	+
Hogsucker (*nigricans*)	+	+	...	+	+	...	+	+	+	...	...	...
White-nosed sucker (*anisurum*)	+	+	...	...	+	...	...	+	+	...	...	+
Common red-horse (*aureolum*)	+	+	+	...	...	...	...	+	+	...	...	+
Short-headed red-horse (*breviceps*)	+	...	...	...	...	...	...	+	+	...	...	...
Placopharynx duquesnei	+	...	...	...	...	...	+	+	+	...	...	...
Harelipped sucker (*Lagochila*)	+	...	...	...	...	...	...	+	+	...	...	...
Stone-roller (*Campostoma*)	+	...	...	...	+	...	+	+	+	+	...	...
Red-bellied dace (*Chrosomus*)	+	+	...	+	+	...	...	+	+	...	...	...
Silvery minnow (*H. nuchalis*)	...	...	...	+	+	...	+	+	+	+	...	+
Hybognathus nubila	...	...	...	...	...	...	...	+	+	...	...	...
Black-head minnow (*P. promelas*)	+	+	...	...	...	...	...	+	+	+	...	+
Blunt-nosed minnow (*P. notatus*)	+	+	...	+	...	...	+	+	+	...	...	...
Horned dace (*Semotilus*)	+	+	+	+	+	...	+	+	+	...	...	...
Opsopœodus emiliæ	+	...	...	...	+	...	+	+	+	...	...	...
Golden shiner (*Abramis*)	+	+	+	+	+	+	+	+	+	+	...	...

TABLE OF THE GENERAL DISTRIBUTION OF ILLINOIS FISHES—*continued*

	Great Lake Basin	Quebec and New England	Hudson River	North Atlantic	South Atlantic	Florida Peninsula	East Gulf	Lower Miss. and Ohio	Upper Miss. and Mo.	West Gulf and Rio Grande	Far Northwest	Far North
Bullhead minnow (*Cliola vigilax*)	+	...	...	...	...	...	+	+	+	+	...	...
Notropis anogenus	+	...	...	...	...	...	...	...	+	...	...	...
N. cayuga	+	...	...	...	...	...	...	+	+	...	...	+
N. cayuga atrocaudalis	+	+	...	...	...	...	...	+	...	+	...	...
N. heterodon	+	...	...	...	...	...	...	+	+	...	...	...
Straw-colored minnow (*N. blennius*)	+	+	...	...	...	...	...	+	+	+	...	+
N. phenacobius	...	...	...	...	...	...	...	...	+	...	...	...
N. gilberti	...	...	...	...	...	...	...	...	+	...	...	...
N. illecebrosus	+	...	...	...	...	...	...	+	+	...	...	...
Redfin (*N. lutrensis*)	...	...	...	...	...	...	...	+	+	+	...	...
Spot-tailed minnow (*N. hudsonius*)	+	+	+	+	+	...	...	+	+	...	...	...
Silverfin (*N. whipplii*)	+	+	...	...	...	...	...	+	+	...	...	...
Common shiner (*N. cornutus*)	+	+	+	+	+	...	+	+	+	...	...	+
Notropis pilsbryi	...	...	...	...	...	...	...	+	+	...	...	...
N. jejunus	...	...	...	...	...	...	...	+	+	...	...	+
Shiner (*N. atherinoides*)	+	+	...	...	...	...	...	+	+	...	...	+
Notropis rubrifrons	+	+	...	...	+	...	...	+	+	...	...	...
Blackfin (*N. umbratilis atripes*)	+	...	...	...	+	...	+	+	+	...	...	...
Ericymba buccata	+	...	...	...	...	...	+	+	+	...	...	...
Sucker-mouthed minnow (*Phenacobius*)	...	...	...	...	...	...	...	+	+	+	...	...
Long-nosed dace (*R. cataractæ*)	+	+	...	+	+	...	...	+	+	+	+	+
Black-nosed dace (*R. atronasus*)	+	+	+	+	+	...	...	+	+	...	...	...

TABLE OF THE GENERAL DISTRIBUTION OF ILLINOIS FISHES—*continued*

	Great Lake Basin	Quebec and New England	Hudson River	North Atlantic	South Atlantic	Florida Peninsula	East Gulf	Lower Miss. and Ohio	Upper Miss. and Mo.	West Gulf and Rio Grande	Far Northwest	Far North
Hybopsis hyostomus							+	+	+			
Spotted shiner (*H. dissimilis*)	+							+	+			
Silver chub (*amblops*)	+						+	+	+			
Storer's chub	+							+	+			+
River chub (*kentuckiensis*)	+			+	+		+	+	+			
Flat-headed chub (*Platygobio*)								+	+			+
Blue cat (*furcatus*)								+	+	+		
Ictalurus anguilla								+		+		
Channel-cat (*punctatus*)	+					+	+	+	+	+		+
Great Lake catfish (*lacustris*)	+	+										
Yellow bullhead (*natalis*)	+				+	+	+	+	+	+		
Common bullhead (*nebulosus*)	+	+	+	+	+	+	+	+	+	+		+
Black bullhead (*melas*)	+						+	+	+			
Mud-cat (*Leptops*)							+	+	+	+		
Common stonecat (*N. flavus*)	+			+				+	+			
Tadpole cat (*S. gyrinus*)	+		+	+		+	+	+	+			
Freckled stonecat (*S. nocturnus*)								+	+	+		
Slender stonecat (*S. exilis*)	+							+	+			
Brindled stonecat (*S. miurus*)	+							+	+			
Mud-minnow	+	+		+				+	+			
Grass pike (*Esox vermiculatus*)	+						+	+	+			
Pike (*E. lucius*)	+	+		+				+	+		+	+

Table of the General Distribution of Illinois Fishes—*continued*

	Great Lake Basin	Quebec and New England	Hudson River	North Atlantic	South Atlantic	Florida Peninsula	East Gulf	Lower Miss. and Ohio	Upper Miss. and Mo.	West Gulf and Rio Grande	Far Northwest	Far North
Muskallunge	+	+	...	...	...	...	...	+	+	...	...	+
Menona top-minnow (*F. diaphanus* m.)	+	...	...	...	...	...	...	+	+	...	...	...
Striped top-minnow (*F. dispar*)	+	...	...	...	...	...	+	+	+	...	...	...
Common top-minnow (*F. notatus*)	+	...	...	...	...	...	+	+	+	+	...	...
Viviparous top-minnow (*affinis*)	...	...	...	+	+	+	+	+	+	+	...	...
Chologaster papilliferus	...	...	...	...	...	...	...	...	+	...	...	...
Brook stickleback	+	+	...	...	...	...	...	+	+	...	...	+
Nine-spined stickleback	+	+	+	...	...	...	...	...	...	...	+	+
Trout-perch	+	+	...	+	...	...	...	+	+	...	...	+
Brook silverside	+	...	...	...	+	+	+	+	+	...	...	...
Pirate-perch	+	...	...	+	+	+	+	+	+	...	...	...
Pigmy sunfish (*Elassoma*)	...	...	...	...	+	...	+	+	...	...	...	...
White crappie (*annularis*)	+	...	...	+	+	...	+	+	+	...	...	...
Black crappie (*sparoides*)	+	+	...	+	+	+	+	+	+	...	...	...
Round sunfish	...	...	...	...	+	+	+	+	...	...	...	...
Rock bass	+	+	+	+	+	...	+	+	+	...	...	+
Warmouth (*Chænobryttus*)	+	...	...	...	+	+	+	+	+	+	...	...
Green sunfish (*cyanellus*)	+	...	...	...	...	...	...	+	+	+	...	...
Lepomis ischyrus	...	...	...	...	...	...	...	...	+	...	...	...
L. symmetricus	...	...	...	...	...	...	...	+	...	+	...	...
L. euryorus	+	...	...	...	...	...	...	...	+	...	...	...
Lepomis miniatus	...	...	...	...	...	+	+	+	+	...	...	...

TABLE OF THE GENERAL DISTRIBUTION OF ILLINOIS FISHES—*continued*

	Great Lake Basin	Quebec and New England	Hudson River	North Atlantic	South Atlantic	Florida Peninsula	East Gulf	Lower Miss. and Ohio	Upper Miss. and Mo.	West Gulf and Rio Grande	Far Northwest	Far North
Long-eared sunfish	+	...	...	...	+	+	+	+	+	+	...	...
Orange-spotted sunfish (*humilis*)	...	...	...	...	...	...	...	+	+	+	...	...
Bluegill (*pallidus*)	+	...	...	...	+	+	+	+	+	+	...	...
Eupomotis heros	...	...	...	...	...	...	+	+	...	+	...	...
Pumpkinseed (*gibbosus*)	+	+	+	+	+	...	...	+	+	...	...	...
Small-mouthed black bass	+	+	+	+	+	...	+	+	+	+	...	...
Large-mouthed black bass	+	+	+	+	+	+	+	+	+	+	...	+
Pike-perch (*S. vitreum*)	+	+	...	+	+	...	+	+	+	...	...	+
Sauger (*S. canadense griseum*)	+	+	...	...	...	...	...	...	+	...	...	+
Yellow perch	+	+	+	+	+	...	...	+	+	...	...	+
Log-perch (*P. caprodes*)	+	+	...	+	...	...	+	+	+	+	...	...
Hadropterus evermanni	...	...	...	...	...	...	...	+	+	...	...	...
H. phoxocephalus	+	...	...	...	...	...	...	+	+	...	...	...
Black-sided darter (*H. aspro*)	+	...	...	...	+	...	...	+	+	...	...	+
Hadropterus ouachitæ	...	...	...	...	...	...	...	+	...	...	...	...
H. evides	+	...	...	...	...	...	...	+	+	...	...	...
H. scierus	...	...	...	...	...	...	...	+	...	+	...	...
Cottogaster shumardi	+	...	...	...	...	...	...	+	+	...	...	...
Green-sided darter (*blennioides*)	+	...	...	...	...	...	+	+	+	...	...	...
Johnny darter (*B. nigrum*)	+	+	+	+	+	...	...	+	+	...	...	+
Boleosoma camurum	...	...	...	...	...	...	+	+	+	+	...	...
Crystallaria asprella	+	...	...	...	...	...	...	+	...	...	...	...

TABLE OF THE GENERAL DISTRIBUTION OF ILLINOIS FISHES—*concluded*

	Great Lake Basin	Quebec and New England	Hudson River	North Atlantic	South Atlantic	Florida Peninsula	East Gulf	Lower Miss. and Ohio	Upper Miss. and Mo.	West Gulf and Rio Grande	Far Northwest	Far North
Sand darter (*Ammocrypta*)	+	...	...	...	...	...	...	+	+	+	...	...
Banded darter (*E. zonale*)	+	...	...	...	...	...	+	+	+	...	...	...
Blue-breasted darter (*E. camurum*)	+	...	...	...	...	...	...	+	+	...	...	...
Etheostoma iowæ	...	...	...	...	...	...	...	...	+	...	...	+
E. jessiæ	+	...	...	...	...	...	+	+	+	+	...	...
Rainbow darter (*E. cæruleum*)	+	...	...	+	...	...	...	+	+	+	...	...
Etheostoma obeyense	...	...	...	...	...	...	...	+	...	...	...	...
E. squamiceps	...	...	...	...	...	...	+	+	...	...	...	...
Fan-tailed darter (*E. flabellare*)	+	+	...	+	+	...	...	+	+	...	...	...
Boleichthys fusiformis	+	+	...	+	+	+	...	+	+	+	...	...
Least darter (*Microperca*)	+	...	...	+	...	...	...	+	+	...	...	...
White bass (*Roccus chrysops*)	+	+	...	...	...	...	...	+	+	...	...	...
Yellow bass (*Morone*)	...	...	...	...	...	...	...	+	+	...	...	...
Sheepshead (*Aplodinotus*)	+	+	...	...	...	...	+	+	+	+	...	+
Miller's thumb	+	+	...	+	+	...	+	+	+	...	...	...
Cottus ricei	+	...	...	...	...	...	...	...	...	...	...	...
Uranidea kumlienii	+	...	...	...	...	...	...	...	...	...	...	...
Burbot (*Lota*)	+	+	+	...	...	...	...	+	+	...	...	+
Number of species	108	53	19	40	45	23	56	134	131	47	4	37

Arranged according to the number of Illinois species in each, these districts succeed each other in the following order.

DISTRICTS	No. of species	Per cent. of all Illinois species
Lower Mississippi and Ohio valleys	134	89
Upper Mississippi and Missouri valleys	131	87
The Great Lake basin	108	72
The east Gulf district	56	37
Quebec and New England	53	36
The west Gulf and Rio Grande district	47	31
The south Atlantic district	45	30
The north Atlantic district	40	27
The far North	37	25
The Florida peninsula	23	15
The Hudson drainage	19	13
The far Northwest	4	3

Next to the two Mississippi Valley districts and the Great Lake basin, which average 124 Illinois species, our fishes are most largely represented in the east Gulf and the Quebec and New England districts, averaging 54 Illinois species—the first closely related to the lower Mississippi, and the second a continuation eastward of the Great Lake basin. Then follow the north and south Atlantic and the west Gulf districts, with an average of 43 species; the far North, the Florida peninsula, and the Hudson River districts, with 37 to 19 species; and, finally, the far Northwest, with but 4 Illinois species.

The northern and the southern affiliations of the assemblage of fishes represented in our Illinois collections may be contrasted by comparing the list of Illinois species occurring in either or both of the more northerly divisions—that is, the far North and the Quebec and New England districts—on the one hand, with a list of those found in either or all of the three most southerly districts—that is, the Florida peninsula, the east Gulf, and the west Gulf and Rio Grande—on the other hand. In this northern list of Illinois fishes there are 64 species, and in the southern list there are 77; but 25 of these species are more or less common to both north and south, leaving 39 Illinois fishes distinctively northern in their distribution and 52 distinctively southern. Northern and southern species thus mingle in our territory in unequal proportions, the southern element largely preponderating.

If we look to the further distribution of the northern and southern elements of our fish population, distinguishing northeastern from northwestern species, and southeastern from southwestern, we find that the southeastern species largely outnumber the southwestern in Illinois, and that the northeastern outnumber the northwestern. Thus there are 47 species of the west Gulf and Rio Grande region in this state, and 58 species of the east Gulf and Florida districts.

Further, there are more species known as common to Illinois and the far northeast than there are to Illinois and the southwestern district of the west Gulf and the Rio Grande. Notwithstanding the much greater distance from us of the Quebec and New England district, there are 53 of the fishes of that region known in Illinois to 47 of those of the west Gulf district. The northeastern fishes have, however, been much more carefully collected than the southwestern, and an equal knowledge of both districts might change these relative numbers.

THE INTERIOR DISTRIBUTION

The interior distribution of the fishes of the state may best be exhibited by treating each considerable stream-system as a unit, and comparing the fishes of each such system with all the others. The state may be convenient'y divided into ten such hydrographic districts, as follows:

1. The Galena district, including the streams of the northwestern unglaciated area, most of which empty into the Mississippi through Galena, Apple, and Plum rivers. 2. The Rock River district, extending southward and westward from the northern boundary of the state to the Mississippi at the mouth of the Rock. 3. The Illinois district, including the entire drainage of the Illinois River. 4. The Michigan district, a narrow strip along the borders of Lake Michigan—the Lake Michigan drainage—most of which centers in the Chicago and the Calumet rivers. 5. The Mississippi River, and an irregular strip adjacent not included in any of the more definite river systems and mainly drained by small streams of the bluffs and neighboring highlands. This district is divided by the lower end of the Illinois basin. 6. The Kaskaskia basin. 7. The Illinois drainage of the Wabash, including that stream itself so far as it helps to form the boundary line between Illinois and Indiana. 8. The basin of the Big Muddy River, in the southwestern part of the state. 9. The Saline River basin, in the southeastern

part of the state. 10. The Cairo district, the driftless area of extreme southern Illinois, drained by the Cache River and smaller tributaries of the Ohio. The Ohio itself is included in this last district.

The following list and table gives the details of the distribution of the species in a way to show the number of collections of each species made by us from each district. A cross opposite a species name indicates that the species occurs in the basin mentioned at the head of the column, but that it is not represented by preserved collections affording numerical data.

Interior Distribution of Illinois Fishes by River Systems
Species and Number of Collections of each

	Districts										Sections		
	Galena District	Rock River	Illinois River	Michigan Drainage	Mississippi and Creeks	Kaskaskia	Wabash	Big Muddy	Saline	Cairo District	North	Central	South
Number of species	44	92	128	57	97	69	95	42	55	101	120	123	119
Collections made	13	73	1115	20	57	41	103	10	18	95	269	1083	192
Silvery lamprey	....	1	12	1	+	....	1	....	....	....	+	+	+
Brook lamprey	....	....	....	1	....	....	....	....	....	1	+	0	+
Paddle-fish	....	....	8	....	+	....	+	....	....	1	0	+	+
Lake sturgeon	....	....	+	+	+	....	....	....	....	+	+	+	+
Shovel-nosed sturgeon	....	....	+	....	+	....	+	....	....	+	0	+	+
White sturgeon	....	....	....	....	4	....	....	....	....	....	0	+	0
Long-nosed gar	....	1	20	1	10	1	+	....	....	4	+	+	+
Short-nosed gar	....	1	52	....	4	+	+	....	....	1	+	+	+
Alligator-gar	....	....	+	....	+	....	....	....	....	+	0	+	+
Dogfish	....	....	27	1	3	+	1	....	2	1	+	+	+
Mooneye	....	....	1	....	+	....	....	....	....	+	0	+	+

INTERIOR DISTRIBUTION OF ILLINOIS FISHES BY RIVER SYSTEMS
SPECIES AND NUMBER OF COLLECTIONS OF EACH—*continued*

	Districts										Sections		
	Galena District	Rock River	Illinois River	Michigan Drainage	Mississippi and Creeks	Kaskaskia	Wabash	Big Muddy	Saline	Cairo District	North	Central	South
Toothed herring	....	....	8	1	+	....	....	....	....	7	+	+	+
Gizzard-shad	1	3	89	1	1	7	2	....	....	3	+	+	+
Skipjack	2	1	3	....	2	....	....	....	....	+	+	+	+
Whitefish	....	....	....	+	....	....	....	....	....	....	+	0	0
Lake herring	....	....	....	+	....	....	....	....	....	....	+	0	0
Lake trout	....	....	....	+	....	....	....	....	....	....	+	0	0
Eel	....	....	+	+	+	....	+	....	....	+	+	+	+
Black-horse	....	....	1	....	2	....	....	....	....	....	0	+	+
Red-mouth buffalo	1	1	28	....	9	....	2	....	....	1	+	+	+
Mongrel buffalo	1	....	17	1	1	....	....	....	....	....	+	+	+
Small-mouth buffalo	1	1	46	1	9	....	2	....	....	+	+	+	+
River carp	....	1	11	....	2	1	+	....	1	+	+	+	+
Blunt-nosed carp	1	6	54	....	8	15	21	....	3	3	+	+	+
Lake carp	....	....	10	....	1	....	....	....	....	....	+	+	0
Quillback carp	1	19	39	....	1	1	8	....	1	+	+	+	+
Chub-sucker	....	4	48	....	2	21	47	6	7	10	+	+	+
Striped sucker	1	1	13	1	....	13	16	1	1	3	+	+	+
Common sucker	1	14	69	....	9	5	26	....	3	9	+	+	+
Long-nosed sucker	....	....	....	+	....	....	....	....	....	....	+	0	0
Hogsucker	1	11	61	....	1	9	27	....	....	1	+	+	+
White-nosed sucker	....	2	14	+	1	....	....	....	....	....	+	+	+

Interior Distribution of Illinois Fishes by River Systems
Species and Number of Collections of each—*continued*

	Districts										Sections		
	Galena District	Rock River	Illinois River	Michigan Drainage	Mississippi and Creeks	Kaskaskia	Wabash	Big Muddy	Saline	Cairo District	North	Central	South
Common red-horse	2	13	90	....	5	10	25	....	1	2	+	+	+
Short-headed red-horse	....	4	39	1	3	7	2	....	....	+	+	+	+
Placopharynx duquesnei	....	1	1	....	+	....	1	....	....	+	+	+	+
Harelipped sucker	....	....	....	....	....	....	+	....	....	....	0	0	+
Stone-roller	1	20	99	....	14	9	36	1	1	10	+	+	+
Red-bellied dace	....	4	13	....	2	....	....	....	....	4	+	+	+
Silvery minnow	2	6	86	1	16	10	27	6	11	18	+	+	+
Hybognathus nubila	1	3	....	....	1	....	....	....	....	1	+	+	+
Black-head minnow	....	8	67	....	12	6	5	....	....	+	+	+	+
Blunt-nosed minnow	3	33	162	3	19	31	77	8	13	25	+	+	+
Horned dace	1	9	72	....	16	10	24	4	6	14	+	+	+
Opsopœodus emiliæ	....	3	49	1	1	1	18	3	6	4	+	+	+
Golden shiner	1	18	183	1	8	19	50	7	10	10	+	+	+
Bullhead minnow	1	14	110	....	5	22	38	1	3	2	+	+	+
Notropis anogenus	....	....	2	....	....	....	....	....	....	....	+	0	0
Notropis cayuga	1	4	29	2	5	....	1	....	....	1	+	+	0
N. heterodon	....	5	81	1	1	....	4	....	....	3	+	+	+
Straw-colored minnow	1	22	108	4	9	6	44	....	2	1	+	+	+
Notropis phenacobius	....	....	2	....	....	....	....	....	....	....	+	0	0
N. gilberti	....	3	15	....	10	....	2	....	....	....	+	+	+
N. illecebrosus	....	....	2	....	1	....	17	....	....	+	+	+	+

INTERIOR DISTRIBUTION OF ILLINOIS FISHES BY RIVER SYSTEMS
SPECIES AND NUMBER OF COLLECTIONS OF EACH—*continued*

	Districts										Sections		
	Galena District	Rock River	Illinois River	Michigan Drainage	Mississippi and Creeks	Kaskaskia	Wabash	Big Muddy	Saline	Cairo District	North	Central	South
Spot-tailed minnow	....	4	133	4	4	....	....	....	....	2	+	+	+
Redfin	....	1	142	9	16	4	....	4	1	10	+	+	+
Silverfin	3	34	116	1	8	29	71	2	3	6	+	+	+
Common shiner	1	19	105	....	11	14	22	....	1	12	+	+	+
Notropis pilsbryi	....	....	1	....	....	....	....	....	....	....	+	0	0
N. jejunus	1	5	21	1	10	....	5	....	2	5	+	+	+
Shiner	3	8	82	6	8	4	19	4	6	11	+	+	+
Notropis rubrifrons	2	4	8	....	....	....	....	....	....	....	+	+	0
Blackfin	2	9	67	....	3	25	56	5	11	19	+	+	+
Ericymba buccata	....	....	4	....	....	25	58	....	....	+	0	+	+
Sucker-mouthed minnow	2	15	78	....	13	17	36	1	4	8	+	+	+
Long-nosed dace	....	....	....	....	....	....	....	....	....	1	0	0	+
Black-nosed-dace	....	1	4	....	....	....	....	....	....	1	+	0	+
Hybopsis hyostomus	....	2	1	....	....	....	....	....	....	....	+	+	0
Spotted shiner	....	6	3	....	....	1	1	....	....	....	+	+	+
Silver chub	....	....	2	....	....	10	37	4	2	....	0	+	+
Storer's chub	....	1	7	....	7	....	5	....	4	4	+	+	+
River chub	1	12	90	....	8	10	16	....	....	1	+	+	+
Flat-headed chub	....	....	....	....	....	....	....	....	....	3	0	0	+
Blue cat	....	....	1	....	1	....	....	....	....	2	0	+	+
Ictalurus anguilla	....	....	+	....	+	....	....	....	....	+	0	+	+

Interior Distribution of Illinois Fishes by River Systems
Species and Number of Collections of each—*continued*

	Districts										Sections		
	Galena District	Rock River	Illinois River	Michigan Drainage	Mississippi and Creeks	Kaskaskia	Wabash	Big Muddy	Saline	Cairo District	North	Central	South
Channel-cat	....	17	108	....	7	17	26	2	1	2	+	+	+
Great Lake catfish	....	....	....	+	....	....	....	....	....	....	+	0	0
Yellow bullhead	....	3	82	....	....	10	18	3	4	6	+	+	+
Common bullhead	....	....	42	....	1	1	....	....	....	4	+	+	+
Black bullhead	1	11	144	....	19	15	35	4	6	10	+	+	+
Mud-cat	+	3	22	....	2	1	2	....	....	+	+	+	+
Stonecat	2	3	32	....	1	1	2	....	....	+	+	+	0
Tadpole cat	....	2	132	....	11	14	21	3	8	5	+	+	+
Freckled stonecat	....	....	5	....	1	2	+	....	....	....	0	+	+
Slender stonecat	1	....	1	....	2	....	....	....	....	2	+	+	+
Brindled stonecat	....	....	1	....	....	1	26	....	5	1	0	+	+
Mud-minnow	....	8	18	1	1	....	4	1	1	6	+	+	+
Grass pike	....	5	61	1	4	11	19	7	6	9	+	+	+
Pike	....	2	17	1	1	....	....	....	....	1	+	+	0
Muskallunge	....	....	+	....	....	....	....	....	....	....	+	0	0
Menona top-minnow	....	....	11	7	....	....	+	....	....	....	+	+	0
Striped top-minnow	....	1	75	1	....	....	8	....	....	5	+	+	+
Common top-minnow	1	6	66	....	6	23	58	8	17	27	+	+	+
Viviparous top-minnow	....	....	1	....	1	....	4	1	2	9	0	+	+
Chologaster papilliferus	....	....	....	....	....	....	....	....	....	6	0	0	+
Brook stickleback	....	....	1	2	....	....	....	....	....	....	+	0	0

INTERIOR DISTRIBUTION OF ILLINOIS FISHES BY RIVER SYSTEMS
SPECIES AND NUMBER OF COLLECTIONS OF EACH—*continued*

	Districts										Sections		
	Galena District	Rock River	Illinois River	Michigan Drainage	Mississippi and Creeks	Kaskaskia	Wabash	Big Muddy	Saline	Cairo District	North	Central	South
Nine-spined stickleback	....	....	....	1	....	....	....	....	....	....	+	0	0
Trout-perch	....	....	14	1	....	....	....	....	....	....	+	+	0
Brook silverside	1	6	89	2	2	1	21	....	....	....	+	+	+
Pirate-perch	....	....	54	....	....	9	11	7	11	9	+	+	+
Pigmy sunfish	....	....	....	....	....	....	5	....	....	1	0	0	+
White crappie	2	9	119	2	13	6	14	3	3	6	+	+	+
Black crappie	....	8	130	3	15	8	13	3	1	....	+	+	+
Round sunfish	....	....	1	....	....	....	1	1	2	8	0	0	+
Rock bass	....	4	35	1	3	2	1	1	....	2	+	+	+
Warmouth	....	3	83	....	3	5	10	6	6	11	+	+	+
Green sunfish	2	20	158	....	16	33	57	7	12	15	+	+	+
Lepomis ischyrus	....	1	3	....	....	....	....	....	....	....	+	+	0
L. symmetricus	....	....	2	....	....	....	3	....	....	4	0	+	+
L. euryorus	....	....	1	....	....	....	....	....	....	....	0	+	0
L. miniatus	....	....	24	....	1	....	2	....	....	....	+	+	+
Long-eared sunfish	....	3	37	1	....	27	57	7	8	16	+	+	+
Orange-spotted sunfish	....	5	112	....	22	15	23	2	3	3	+	+	+
Bluegill	2	7	179	1	6	3	18	1	1	6	+	+	+
Eupomotis heros	....	....	....	....	....	....	5	....	....	1	0	0	+
Pumpkinseed	....	4	82	4	2	....	1	....	....	1	+	+	+
Small-mouthed black bass	....	16	69	....	5	2	8	1	....	3	+	+	+

INTERIOR DISTRIBUTION OF ILLINOIS FISHES BY RIVER SYSTEMS
SPECIES AND NUMBER OF COLLECTIONS OF EACH—*continued*

	Districts										Sections		
	Galena District	Rock River	Illinois River	Michigan Drainage	Mississippi and Creeks	Kaskaskia	Wabash	Big Muddy	Saline	Cairo District	North	Central	South
Large-mouthed black bass	....	7	135	4	13	8	33	2	4	12	+	+	+
Pike-perch	....	3	20	1	13	1	+	....	....	....	+	+	+
Sauger	....	1	13	....	3	1	....	....	....	....	+	+	0
Yellow perch	....	+	75	3	6	....	....	....	....	....	+	+	0
Log-perch	....	4	35	3	5	9	8	....	1	2	+	+	+
Hadropterus evermanni	....	....	3	....	....	....	....	....	....	....	0	+	0
H. phoxocephalus	....	12	58	....	3	10	6	....	2	....	+	+	+
Black-sided darter	2	15	70	....	1	22	42	2	7	11	+	+	+
Hadropterus ouachitæ	....	....	....	....	....	....	1	....	....	....	0	0	+
H. evides	....	1	....	....	....	....	....	....	....	....	+	0	0
H. scierus	....	....	1	....	....	....	1	....	....	....	0	+	0
Cottogaster shumardi	....	....	14	....	....	2	1	....	....	....	0	+	+
Green-sided darter	....	....	+	....	....	....	36	....	....	....	0	+	+
Johnny darter	3	22	100	3	10	27	58	1	6	8	+	+	+
Boleosoma camurum	....	1	45	2	2	12	17	7	11	10	+	+	+
Crystallaria asprella	1	3	....	....	2	....	1	....	....	....	+	+	+
Sand darter	....	3	7	....	1	2	16	....	....	....	+	+	+
Banded darter	1	11	21	....	....	....	1	....	....	....	+	+	+
Blue-breasted darter	....	2	6	1	....	....	....	....	....	1	0	+	0
Etheostoma iowæ	....	2	4	1	....	....	....	....	....	1	+	0	+
E. jessiæ	....	4	119	....	5	11	14	2	1	4	+	+	+

INTERIOR DISTRIBUTION OF ILLINOIS FISHES BY RIVER SYSTEMS
SPECIES AND NUMBER OF COLLECTIONS OF EACH—*concluded*

	Districts										Sections		
	Galena District	Rock River	Illinois River	Michigan Drainage	Mississippi and Creeks	Kaskaskia	Wabash	Big Muddy	Saline	Cairo District	North	Central	South
Rainbow darter	2	9	39	....	1	2	29	1	4	13	+	+	+
Etheostoma obeyense	....	....	....	....	....	....	....	....	1	....	0	0	+
E. squamiceps	....	....	....	....	....	1	1	....	1	7	0	+	+
Fan-tailed darter	1	6	11	....	1	1	14	....	....	3	+	+	+
Boleichthys fusiformis	....	1	13	....	....	5	18	3	8	8	+	+	+
Least darter	....	1	10	....	....	....	....	....	....	1	+	0	+
White bass	1	2	36	2	12	....	....	....	....	1	+	+	+
Yellow bass	....	1	95	....	5	....	....	....	....	....	+	+	+
Sheepshead	....	1	53	....	13	....	....	1	1	1	+	+	+
Miller's thumb	....	....	5	....	....	....	....	....	....	6	+	+	+
Cottus ricei	....	....	....	+	....	....	....	....	....	....	+	0	0
Uranidea kumlienii	....	....	....	+	....	....	....	....	....	....	+	0	0
Burbot	....	....	3	1	....	....	....	....	....	....	+	+	0

THE ILLINOIS BASIN AND THE OTHER DISTRICTS COMPARED

The key to the distribution of Illinois fishes within the state is the species list of the Illinois basin. Covering fully one half the area of Illinois, and extending in a broad belt diagonally northeast and southwest across its northern two thirds, this basin contains nearly every variety of stream, lake, pond, and marsh to be found between the Great Lakes on the one hand and the giant flood of the Mississippi on the other, and it is to be expected that its fish population will be highly typical of

Illinois as a whole. It includes, in fact, more than four fifths of the species on our Illinois list, and the special features of the various other basins and areas may best be seen by comparing them with this characteristic central basin as a type.

The following is a list of the species of the Illinois system obtained by us in collections, arranged in the order of the frequency of their appearance in 1,115 collections made from that stream and its tributary waters.

SPECIES OF THE ILLINOIS BASIN, AND NUMBER OF COLLECTIONS CONTAINING EACH

Species	Collections	Species	Collections*
Golden shiner	183	Common red-horse	90
Bluegill	179	Gizzard-shad	89
Blunt-nosed minnow	162	Brook silverside	89
Green sunfish	158	Silvery minnow	86
Black bullhead	144	Warmouth	83
Redfin (*lutrensis*)	142	Shiner	82
Large-mouthed black bass	135	Yellow bullhead	82
Spot-tailed minnow	133	Pumpkinseed	82
Tadpole cat	132	*Notropis heterodon*	81
Black crappie	130	Sucker-mouthed minnow	78
Etheostoma jessiæ	119	Yellow perch	75
White crappie	119	Striped top-minnow	75
Silverfin	116	Horned dace	72
Orange-spotted sunfish	112	Black-sided darter	70
Bullhead minnow	110	Common sucker	69
Straw-colored minnow	108	Small-mouthed black bass	69
Channel-cat	108	Blackfin	67
Common shiner	105	Black-head minnow	67
Johnny darter	100	Common top-minnow	66
Stone-roller	99	Hogsucker	61

*A cross (+) in this column indicates the known occurrence of a species which is not represented in our collections from the Illinois basin.

SPECIES OF THE ILLINOIS BASIN, AND NUMBER OF COLLECTIONS CONTAINING EACH—*continued*

Species	Collections	Species	Collections
Yellow bass	95	Grass pike	61
River chub	90	*Hadropterus phoxocephalus*	58
Blunt-nosed carp	54	Pike	17
Pirate-perch	54	*Notropis gilberti*	15
Sheepshead	53	White-nosed sucker	14
Short-nosed gar	52	Trout-perch	14
Opsopœodus emiliæ	49	*Cottogaster shumardi*	14
Chub-sucker	48	Striped sucker	13
Small-mouth buffalo	46	Red-bellied dace	13
Boleosoma camurum	45	Sauger	13
Common bullhead	42	*Boleichthys fusiformis*	13
Quillback carp	39	Silvery lamprey	12
Rainbow darter	39	Menona top-minnow	11
Short-headed red-horse	39	Fan-tailed darter	11
Long-eared sunfish	37	River carp	11
White bass	36	Least darter	10
Rock bass	35	Lake carp	10
Log-perch	35	Paddle-fish	8
Stonecat	32	Toothed herring	8
Notropis cayuga	29	*Notropis rubrifrons*	8
Red-mouth buffalo	28	Storer's chub	7
Dogfish	27	Sand darter	7
Lepomis miniatus	24	Blue-breasted darter	6
Mud-cat	22	Freckled stonecat	5
Notropis jejunus	21	Miller's thumb	5
Banded darter	21	Black-nosed dace	4
Long-nosed gar	20	*Ericymba buccata*	4
Pike-perch	20	Skipjack	3

SPECIES OF THE ILLINOIS BASIN, AND NUMBER OF COLLECTIONS CONTAINING EACH—*concluded*

Species	Collections	Species	Collections
Mud-minnow	18	Spotted shiner	3
Mongrel buffalo	17	*Lepomis ischyrus*	3
Hadropterus evermanni	3	Brindled stonecat	1
Burbot	3	Slender stonecat	1
Notropis phenacobius	2	Brook stickleback	1
Silver chub	2	Round sunfish	1
Lepomis symmetricus	2	*Lepomis euryorus*	1
Notropis anogenus	2	*Hadropterus scierus*	1
N. illecebrosus	2	Lake sturgeon	+
Viviparous top-minnow	1	Shovel-nosed sturgeon	+
Mooneye	1	Alligator-gar	+
Black-horse	1	Eel	+
Placopharynx duquesnei	1	*Ictalurus anguilla*	+
Notropis pilsbryi	1	Muskallunge	+
Hybopsis hyostomus	1	Green-sided darter	+
Blue cat	1		

Of the twenty-three Illinois species which have not been taken by us in the Illinois River or its tributaries, two are distinctively western fishes, and occur but rarely anywhere within our limits; nine are southern species, few of which have been found as far north as the mouth of the Illinois, and one other is only southern in this state; two are northern species which barely reach our borders; five are typical fishes of the Great Lakes; one has been found by us only in the main Mississippi and the Ohio; one is a subterranean fish of strictly local occurrence; and the two remaining species are very rare in this state.

Further particulars as to the species of these various geographical groups are given in the following classified list.

ILLINOIS SPECIES NOT FOUND IN THE ILLINOIS BASIN

WESTERN (2):
- *Hybognathus nubila*
- Flat-headed chub

NORTHERN (2):
- Long-nosed sucker
- Nine-spined stickleback

SOUTHERN (10):
- Harelipped sucker
- Pigmy sunfish
- Round sunfish
- *Eupomotis heros*
- *Hadropterus ouachitæ*
- *H. evides*
- *Crystallaria asprella*
- *Etheostoma obeyense*
- *E. squamiceps*
- Brindled stonecat

GREAT LAKES (5):
- Whitefish
- Lake herring
- Lake trout
- *Cottus ricei*
- *Uranidea kumlienii*

MAIN MISSISSIPPI (1):
- White sturgeon

SUBTERRANEAN (1):
- *Chologaster papilliferus*

RARE IN ILLINOIS (2):
- Brook lamprey
- Long-nosed dace

As the Illinois basin contains 128 of the 150 species taken by us in the state, it is evident that the other and smaller basins must differ from this negatively rather than positively. Being not only much smaller, but also much less complex than the Illinois district, and offering less variety of situations for fishes as homes and places of resort, they may lack many species which find a fit environment somewhere in the Illinois or its dependent waters, but can contain relatively few not found there as well.

Regarded from this standpoint, the Michigan district is farthest removed from the Illinois ichthyologically, and of its fifty-seven species nine (16 per cent.) are wanting in the Illinois basin. The Cairo district differs much less, eight of its one hundred and one fishes being without representation in our collections from the Illinois system. Next follows the Wabash basin in Illinois, with ninety-five species and a difference from the Illinois basin of 6.1 per cent.; the Galena district, with forty-four species and a difference of 4.6 per cent.; the Saline district, with fifty-five species, and a difference of 3.8 per cent.; and the Mississippi and its marginal area, with ninety-seven species, 3.2 per cent. of which are wanting to the Illinois streams and lakes. The Kaskaskia and the Big Muddy, on the other hand, which are scarcely more than extensions of the Illinois district downward to the southern end of the state, contain virtually no fishes not in the main district, the Kaskaskia but one out of sixty-nine (1.4 per cent.), and the Big Muddy none out of forty-two species. The Rock River district differs from the Illinois by only three species out of ninety-two (3.2 per cent.). These data are presented more compactly in the table following.

DIFFERENCES BETWEEN THE SMALLER DISTRICTS AND THE ILLINOIS BASIN

Districts	Species in district	Species not found in Illinois basin	Ratios of difference
Illinois	128	——	——
Michigan	57	9	.16
Cairo	101	8	.08
Wabash	95	6	.061
Galena	44	2	.046
Saline	55	2	.038
Mississippi	97	3	.032
Rock River	92	3	.032
Kaskaskia	69	1	.014
Big Muddy	42	0	.000

Five species were found in the Illinois system and not in any other—three of them minnows of the genus *Notropis* (*anogenus*, *phenacobius*, and *pilsbryi*), one of them a sunfish (*Lepomis euryorus*), and one of them a darter (*Hadropterus evermanni*). All of these species have been very rare in our collections, occurring only from one to three times each, and it was probable that they would be found, if at all, where the largest number of collections was made.

The Galena district is distinguished from the Illinois basin especially by the presence of a minnow and a darter (*Hybognathus nubila* and *Crystallaria asprella*), the latter southern in its main range, and the former western, not occurring, indeed, farther east than western Illinois. These two fishes appear in the Rock River basin also, together with another distinctively western darter (*Hadropterus evides*). In the Michigan district, besides the five lake fishes already referred to—the whitefish, the lake herring, the lake trout, and two cottoids or miller's thumbs, *Cottus ricei* and *Uranidea kumlienii*—are the brook lamprey, the long-nosed sucker, the Great Lake catfish, and one of the sticklebacks (*Pygosteus pungitius*). All but the lamprey (which is rare in Illinois) are northern species not taken by us in the Illinois valley. The Mississippi district is distinguishe from the Illinois by the presence of the rare white sturgeon (*Parascaphirhynchus albus*), hitherto taken only in the Mississippi itself, and by a southern darter and a western minnow already referred to. In the Kaskaskia district we find another southern darter (*Etheostoma squamiceps*). The six fishes of the Wabash district not found in the Illinois or its tributaries, are all southern species. The Big Muddy list contains no species not found in the Illinois basin; and the Saline River district contains two southern darters (*Etheostoma squamiceps* and *E. obeyense*). And, finally, among the eight species by which the Cairo district differs from the Illinois are three southern and two western species, a cave-fish, and two species of general distribution but rare in Illinois (*Lampetra wilderi* and *Rhinichthys cataractæ*).

Thus, of the twenty-three Illinois fishes not found by us in the waters of the Illinois basin, eight are distinctively southern, six are purely northern, if we include in this number the Great Lake fishes, four are western, one is an extremely local cave-fish, and four are so rare in Illinois that their appearance in any waters is a matter of unusual chance. The limitation upon the range of these imperfectly distributed species is thus climatic and general, and not geographic or local. This state lies on the extreme borders of their proper territory, and they are not found more commonly in our waters because climatic and other general conditions most favorable to their maintenance, here reach the vanishing point.

Lists of Species distinguishing different Districts from the Illinois Basin

GALENA DISTRICT (2):
- *Hybognathus nubila* (Western)
- *Crystallaria asprella* (Southern)

ROCK RIVER DISTRICT (3):
- *Hybognathus nubila* (Western)
- *Hadropterus evides* (Western)
- *Crystallaria asprella* (Southern)

MICHIGAN DISTRICT (9):
- Brook lamprey (rare)
- Long-nosed sucker (Northern)
- Whitefish (Great Lakes)
- Lake herring (Great Lakes)
- Lake trout (Great Lakes)
- Great Lake catfish (Northern)
- Nine-spined stickleback (Northern)
- *Cottus icei* (Great Lakes)
- *Uranidea kumlienii* (Great Lakes)

—7 F

MISSISSIPPI STRIP (3):
- White sturgeon (rare; Mississippi only)
- *Hybognathus nubila* (Western)
- *Crystallaria asprella* (Southern)

KASKASKIA RIVER DISTRICT (1):
- *Etheostoma squamiceps* (Southern)

WABASH DISTRICT (6):
- Harelipped sucker (rare; Southern)
- Pigmy sunfish (Southern)
- *Eupomotis heros* (Southern)
- *Hadropterus ouachitæ* (Southern)
- *Crystallaria asprella* (Southern)
- *Etheostoma squamiceps* (Southern)

SALINE RIVER DISTRICT (2):
- *Etheostoma obeyense* (Southern)
- *E. squamiceps* (Southern)

CAIRO DISTRICT (8):

- Brook lamprey
- *Hybognathus nubila* (Western)
- Long-nosed dace (rare in Illinois)
- Flat-headed chub (Western)
- *Chologaster papilliferus* (subterranean)
- Pigmy sunfish (Southern)
- *Eupomotis heros* (Southern)
- *Etheostoma squamiceps* (Southern)

RELATIONS OF EACH DISTRICT TO ALL THE OTHERS

In the foregoing discussions and analyses the fishes of the various districts have been compared with those of the largest and most central district as a type; but a fuller and more accurate idea of the composition of the fish population of Illinois and of its relations in the various hydrographic divisions of the state may be obtained by a comparison of the species of each of our ten districts successively with those of all the others. This may be done in an exact and uniform manner by determining for each pair of districts the ratio which the number of species common to the pair bears to the whole number of species occurring within the area of both the districts taken together as one. In the Galena district, for example, there are 44 species recorded, and in the Saline River basin there are 55, a total of 99; but as 26 of these species have been found in both these districts, this number has been taken twice in the above addition, and the number of species found by us in the entire area of these two districts is consequently 73. The ichthyological affinity of these two areas is evidently to be measured by the ratio which the number of species common to both bears to the whole number of species found in either or both the areas—in this case, the ratio of 26 to 73, or 36 per cent. That is, 36 per cent. of the fishes found in either of these two districts have been found by us in both of them.

A similar analysis of the data for each of the forty-five pairs which it is possible to make up from our ten hydrographic districts, yields the material for the following table of common species and of ratios of affiliation. This table shows, in the lower left-hand part, the number of species common to each pair of districts, and in the upper right-hand part the ratios which these numbers bear to the number of species occurring in each pair of districts taken as one. The number of species common to any two districts will be found in the lower left-hand part of the table, where the column for one district intersects with the line for the other, and the ratio of affiliation for the same pair of districts will be found in the opposite part of the table at the intersection of the line for the first with the column for the second. A simple inspection of the figures in the latter part shows at once which districts are most alike and which are most unlike in respect to their fish inhabitants. Thus, the Rock and Illinois basins and the Mississippi are the most closely related, according to these data, with affiliation ratios of 68-72 per cent. and an average of 70; and the Michigan, Galena, and Big Muddy districts are the least alike, with ratios of 20-28 per cent. and an average of 23. The two highest single ratios of ichthyological affiliation are those of the Illinois and Mississippi rivers (.72) and of the Big Muddy and Saline (.70).

NUMBER OF SPECIES COMMON TO EACH PAIR OF DISTRICTS, AND RATIOS OF SUCH COMMON NUMBERS TO THE WHOLE NUMBER OF SPECIES IN EACH PAIR

Districts	1. Galena	2. Rock River	3. Illinois R.	4. Michigan	5. Mississippi	6. Kaskaskia	7. Wabash	8. Big Muddy	9. Saline	10. Cairo	Averages
1. Galena	....	45	32	20	41	40	38	28	36	37	.352
2. Rock River	42	....	68	35	69	59	63	40	47	62	.542
3. Illinois River	42	89	....	35	72	53	66	33	41	68	.52
4. Michigan	17	39	48	....	34	25	29	22	23	32	.283
5. Mississippi	41	77	94	39	....	54	61	34	42	66	.525
6. Kaskaskia	32	60	68	25	58	....	66	52	63	53	.517
7. Wabash	38	72	89	34	73	66	....	41	53	63	.534
8. Big Muddy	19	38	42	18	35	38	40	....	70	39	.398
9. Saline River	26	47	53	21	45	48	52	40	....	49	.471
10. Cairo	39	74	93	38	79	59	76	40	51	....	.521
Total species	44	92	128	57	97	69	95	42	55	101	
Number of collections	13	73	1115	20	57	41	103	10	18	95	

The data of this table may be generalized by bringing into comparison the *average* of the ratios of affiliation for each district with those for all the rest, as shown in the column of figures farthest to the right. If the ten districts are arranged in the order of the size of their average ratios, they readily fall into two groups, the first of six districts, with relatively high ratios, and the second of four, with relatively low ratios. The first group comprises the basins of the larger rivers—the Mississippi, the Rock, the Illinois, the Kaskaskia, the Wabash, and the Ohio, each with its more or less complex system of tributaries. The average ratio for this group is 52.7 per cent. The second group is made up of small, widely separated districts, containing only small streams and lakes, except that one of them includes a little of the shallow southwestern border of Lake Michigan. In this group are the northwestern driftless area, the Saline River and its tributaries, the Big Muddy district, and the Michigan district, with an average affiliation ratio of 37.6.

If we average separately, for these groups, the ratios of each district to all the other districts of its group, we obtain for the first and higher group a ratio of mutual affiliation of 63 per cent., and for the lower group a similar ratio of 33 per cent. It is thus made clear that the districts most typical of our Illinois fauna are the first six above mentioned, while those most individual and peculiar—least closely affiliated among themselves and each with all the others—are the Michigan, the Galena, the Saline, and the Big Muddy districts, excepting only the relation of the two last mentioned which, as already said, is unusually close.

THE FISHES OF NORTHERN, CENTRAL, AND SOUTHERN ILLINOIS

If mere difference in latitude, involving a climatic difference within a range of five and a half degrees, limits the distribution of any of our fishes, the fact should appear upon a comparison of the species list of the northern, central, and southern sections of the state, although due caution must, of course, be exercised that other and more local causes are not confused with climatic ones. The division of the state here adopted is shown on Map II. of the accompanying atlas.

The fishes of these three divisions number 119 species for northern, 123 for central, and 119 for southern Illinois, respectively. Fourteen species have been found by us only in the northern division, 9 only in the southern, and 5 only in the central, and 89 species are found in all three sections. Twelve species occur in both northern and central Illinois, but not in southern, 17 in both southern and central Illinois, but not in northern, and 4 in both the northern and southern divisions of the state, but not in the central.

FISHES OF LIMITED DISTRIBUTION IN ILLINOIS

Illinois Distribution	General Distribution
Species Peculiar to Northern Illinois	
Whitefish	Great Lakes
Lake herring	" "
Lake trout	" "
Long-nosed sucker	Northern
Notropis anogenus	"
N. phenacobius	
N. pilsbryi	Southern
Great Lake catfish	Northern
Muskallunge	"
Brook stickleback	"
Nine-spined stickleback	"
Hadropterus evides	Rather general
Cottus ricei	Great Lakes
Uranidea kumlienii	" "
Species Peculiar to Southern Illinois	
Harelipped sucker	Southern
Long-nosed dace	General; rare in Illinois
Flat-headed chub	Western
Chologaster papilliferus	Local; cave
Pigmy sunfish	Southern
Round sunfish	"
Eupomotis heros	"
Hadropterus ouachitæ	"
Etheostoma obeyense	"
Species in Northern and Central Illinois, but not in Southern	
Lake carp	Northern

FISHES OF LIMITED DISTRIBUTION IN ILLINOIS—*concluded*

Illinois Distribution	General Distribution
Notropis cayuga	General
N. rubrifrons	"
Hybopsis hyostomus	"
Stonecat	Northern and southwestern
Pike	Northern
Menona top-minnow	"
Trout-perch	"
Lepomis ischyrus	
Sauger	General
Yellow perch	Northern
Burbot	Great Lakes
Species in Southern and Central Illinois but not in Northern	
Paddle-fish	General
Shovel-nosed sturgeon	"
Alligator-gar	Southern
Mooneye	Northern
Black-horse	General
Ericymba buccata	"
Silver chub	"
Blue cat	Southern
Ictalurus anguilla	"
Freckled stonecat	"
Brindled stonecat	General
Viviparous top-minnow	Southern
Lepomis symmetricus	"
Cottogaster shumardi	General
Green-sided darter	"
Etheostoma squamiceps	Southern

An examination of the general distribution of the species of these sectional lists of Illinois fishes shows, as was to have been expected, that the distinctively northern Illinois fishes are chiefly northern in their outside range, and that those of southern Illinois are mainly southern. Thus, of the 14 especially northern Illinois fishes, 11 are northerly in their general distribution and 1 is southerly; while of the 9 distinctively southern Illinois species, 6 are southerly in their general range, 1 is western, and 1 is a cave-fish local to Illinois. The species found in the northern and central sections of the state and not in the southern are varied in their distribution, 6 of them ranging northward from Illinois, and 4 of them in all directions, while 1 has been thus far found in Illinois only. The central and southern fishes, on the other hand, comprise 7 southern species, 1 of northern and 8 of general range, and 1 whose distribution is not recorded. Including only species whose general area shows that their restricted occurrence in Illinois is a feature of their geographical distribution at large, and excluding fishes special to the Great Lakes, we have twenty-six species whose distribution in this state seems limited by conditions connected with differences in latitude merely—twelve of these species essentially northern and fourteen of them southern.

Especially Northern Species in Illinois (16):

Whitefish
Lake herring
Lake trout
Long-nosed sucker
Lake carp
Notropis anogenus
Great Lake catfish
Mooneye
Pike
Muskallunge
Menona top-minnow
Brook stickleback
Nine-spined stickleback
Trout-perch
Cottus ricei
Uranidea kumlienii

Especially Southern Species in Illinois (14):

Alligator-gar
Blue cat
Ictalurus anguilla
Freckled stonecat
Harelipped sucker
Notropis pilsbyri
Viviparous top-minnow
Pigmy sunfish
Round sunfish
Lepomis symmetricus
Eupomotis heros
Hadropterus ouachitæ
Etheostoma obeyense
E. squamiceps

USE OF LOCALITY MAPS

In the foregoing discussion of the sectional distribution of Illinois fishes no account has been taken of differences in the frequency of the occurrence of the species in the different sections in which they have been found, a single occurrence in southern Illinois, for example, counting for as much as fifty such occurrences in the northern part of the state. That highly interesting and important peculiarities of distribution are concealed by this gross method of comparison is made evident by an examination of the maps of the distribution of our collections of the various species accompanying this report, where the data are presented in a way to show, not the number of collections, it is true, in which each species was represented, but the number and distribution of localities from which the species has been obtained. From such a study of these maps it appears that the northern half or two thirds of this state is more favorable to a considerable number of species than the southern part, since these species have been taken there in a much larger number of localities; and also that a small group of species of wide general distribution has been found by us with surprising frequency in the Wabash drainage in this state as compared with that of adjacent districts.

The preference of certain species for the northern part of Illinois over the southern is clearly illustrated by the distribution maps of the following fifteen species: *Noturus flavus Carpiodes thompsoni*, *Notropis cayuga*, *N. hudsonius*, *N. rubrif, ons*, *Hybopsis dissimilis*, *H. kentuckiensis*, *Fundulus diaphanus*, *Percopsis guttatus*, *Eupomotis gibbosus*, *Stizostedion canadense*, *Perca flavescens*, *Etheostoma zonale*, *Roccus chrysops*, and *Morone interrupta*. With few and slight exceptions, all the species of this varied list, representing eight families and twelve genera, are so definitely lim'ted to the northern half of this state that one gets the impression, as he examines these maps in succession, that some invisible barrier to their southward dispersal exists in the neighborhood of the Sangamon River.

PECULIARITIES OF DISTRIBUTION IN THE LOWER ILLINOISAN GLACIATION

That the distribution of these more northerly species is not limited by the watersheds is shown by the fact that they range across the state indifferently into all the stream systems of northern Illinois. It is not until we compare with our distribution maps a map of the surface geology of the state (Map III.) that we find a plausible explanation of a part, at least, of this peculiar distribution, for all but one of the species above mentioned are wholly excluded from the area of this glaciation, and this excepted species (*Hybopsis dissimilis*) appears in but one locality within the lower glaciation, and that a short distance within its border, on the upper Kaskaskia.

Especially significant in this relation are several cases in which species of this list range southward in the eastern part of the state upon the upper tributaries of the Kaskaskia and the Embarras, for in so doing they simply follow southward the course of the Shelbyville moraine which forms the boundary between the Wisconsin and the lower Illinoisan glaciations in east-central Illinois. The maps for *Noturus flavus*, *Hybopsis dissimilis*, *H. kentuckiensis*, and *Stizostedion canadense* are examples.

That this coincidence of distribution and surface geology points to a true explanation is further shown by the maps for twenty-two other species which range more definitely to the southward than the foregoing twelve, but which nevertheless avoid the southern glaciation more or less completely and to an unmistakable degree. For example, 19 of our 94 collection localities for the hogsucker (*Catostomus nigricans*) lie below the Springfield parallel, but only three of them are in the lower Illinoisan glaciation, and these are barely within its borders. Of our thirty localities for the short-headed red-horse (*Moxostoma breviceps*) only two are in this glaciation, and these are near its boundaries on the Embarras and the Kaskaskia. The very abundant minnow *Campostoma anomalum* was taken by us from one hundred and sixty localities, thirty-one of which are south of the Sangamon and eight of them from the non-glaciated area of the Cairo district, but only one of the entire number is within the lower glaciation, and that is on the upper Kaskaskia just across the limiting moraine. The map for *Notropis cornutus* shows one hundred and sixty-one localities from which collections of this species were made, ninety of them below the Sangamon and twenty-nine in the Cairo district, but only three are in the southern glaciation. Other species testifying to the same effect will be found in the following list of fishes absent from this characteristic southern Illinois district.

Illinois Fishes Rare or wanting in the Lower Illinoisan Glaciation

Short-nosed gar
Common bullhead
Stonecat
Lake carp
Quillback carp
Common sucker
Hogsucker
Short-headed red-horse
Stone-roller
Red-bellied dace
N. rubrifrons
Spotted shiner
Storer's chub
River chub
Pike
Menona top-minnow
Trout-perch
Pumpkinseed
Small-mouthed black bass
Sauger

Notropis cayuga
N. heterodon
Straw-colored minnow
Notropis gilberti
Spot-tailed minnow
Common shiner
Notropis jejunus
Yellow perch
Banded darter
Rainbow darter
Fan-tailed darter
White bass
Yellow bass
Miller's thumb

Fishes Tolerant of the Lower Illinoisan Glaciatio

Dogfish
Channel-cat
Yellow bullhead
Black bullhead
Mud-cat
Tadpole cat
Brindled stonecat
Chub-sucker
Striped sucker
Silvery minnow
Blunt-nosed minnow
Opsopœodus emiliæ
Golden shiner
Bullhead minnow
Silverfin
Shiner
Blackfin
Ericymba buccata
Silver chub
Grass pike
Common top-minnow
Viviparous top-minnow
Pirate-perch
White crappie
Round sunfish
Warmouth
Green sunfish
Long-eared sunfish
Orange-spotted sunfish
Large-mouthed black bass
Black-sided darter
Boleosoma camurum
Sand darter
Etheostoma jessiæ
Boleichthys fusiformis

Among the ninety-eight Illino's species for which distribution maps have been prepared, thirty-four belong clearly to this group of fishes which seem to avoid the conditions common to the flat gray lands of the southern part of the state. Thirty-five species, on the other hand, are distributed over this glaciation in a way to indicate a tolerance of its conditions if not an indifference to them, the data concerning the remainng twenty-nine species being ambiguous or indecisive in this respect.

Two facts concerning the soil and waters of the lower Illinoisan glaciation may be held to account, at least in part, for the failure of certain species of fishes to thrive in its streams. Compared with the other regions of the state, this oldest of our glaciation areas has developed its drainage system to a point such that the rainfall runs off rapidly in a large number of small streams, leaving no marshes or ponds to hold back the waters during periods of dry weather. It is a level country whose streams fill up quickly and run down rapidly, the smaller ones drying up completely during the midsummer drought, which is here more marked than farther north. These variable and temporary creeks are, of course, less favorable to the maintenance of a varied and permanent fish population than the waters of the earlier Illinoisan or the Wisconsin areas.

As a further consequence of its geological antiquity, involving degenerative chemical changes and a long-continued leaching, the soil of this lower glaciation has become an extremely fine-grained, light-colored clay which, when compact, sheds water almost completely, but which washes into the streams as a fine detritus that remains persistently in suspension and renders the waters very urbid for a long time after a rain. Standing pools, indeed, never become even approximately clear. So persistent is this turbidity, due to very finely divided matter in suspension, that the chemists of the Water Survey find it almost impossible to free the water wholly from suspended solids even by repeated filtration. Furthermore, this soil has a definitely acid reaction, to which is due a notable physical difference between the soils of this area and those of the later glaciations west and north of it. A surplus of lime in a soil coagulates or granulates it, causing its ultimate particles to cohere in larger granules, while in an acid soil this effect is entirely wanting. This lack of granulation in a very finely divided soil increases, of course, the permanent muddiness of its waters as compared with those of the areas in which lime in the soil renders it alkaline.

The acidity of this southern soil seems not to be of a kind or amount to affect the surface waters sensibly and directly, since the water samples from this region analyzed by the State Water Survey show a soft water, slightly alkaline, and chemically unobjectionable as a medium for fishes.

CLASSIFICATION AND USE OF ECOLOGICAL DATA

That these conditions are a part, at least, of the cause of the phenomenal distribution of southern Illinois fishes may be shown by a comparison of our ecological data for the fishes of the two lists—one composed of those adapted to the conditions of the lower Illinoisan glaciation and the other of those avoiding them. In the organization of the data of our collections of Illinois fishes, those concerning the character of the water body in which collections were made were classified in a way to show the number of collections of each species taken from each class of situation. By reducing these numbers to ratios of frequency of occurrence, we have a means of exhibiting the preference of species with respect to the situations in which each occurs. *Pimephales notatus*, for example, was found twenty times over a muddy bottom to thirty-four over a bottom of mud and sand, and to forty-six over a bottom of rock and sand. *Aphredoderus sayanus*, on the other hand, was found sixty-two times on a muddy bottom to nineteen times in each of the other situations.

By tabulating data of this description separately for each of the two lists of species referred to—thirty-four species in the one list and thirty-five in the other—and averaging the ratios for each group separately, significant evidence was obtained of the factors which affect the distribution of these fishes.

The species which distribute themselves freely over southern Illinois are those which are generally tolerant of turbid waters, as shown by the fact that 32 per cent. of all our collections of this group came from muddy streams and ponds, 34 per cent. from situations where the bottom was composed largely of rock and sand, and 24 per cent. from a bottom of sand and mud. The species avoiding the central area of southern Illinois, on the other hand, are, as a rule, intolerant of muddy waters, only 10 per cent. of all our data-bearing collections of this group coming from such situations, while 61 per cent. of them were from bottoms of rock and sand, and 29 per cent. from those of sand and mud. It is consequently clear that the suspended detritus of the streams of southern Illinois and the clay and mud of which their banks and bottoms are commonly composed, are an important part, at least, of the cause of the smaller variety of fishes in these waters; and these conditions trace back through the character of the soil to the geological history of the central part of southern Illinois.

FISHES OF THE OHIO AND OF THE MISSISSIPPI DRAINAGE

A comparison and classification of our distribution maps from another point of view enables us further to distinguish two rather definite groups of species coincident in great measure, but not wholly so, with the two groups which we have found in an opposite relation to the lower Illinoisan glaciation. No less than 27 of our species have either an exclusive, or at least a strongly preponderant, distribution in the Mississippi drainage in the western and northern parts of the state, while 8 species, on the other hand, are very definitely preponderant in the Ohio drainage in the southern and eastern parts. Nineteen of the 27 species of the first list are also on the list of species excluded from the region of the lower Illinoisan glaciation, while 6 of the 8 species of the second list are also on that of species distributed freely through this southern Illinois district. We have evidence here of another influence strongly affecting distribution, coincident in part with that already discussed, but independent of it also in part, the two causes, or sets of causes, operating together to determine the actual range of most of the species of limited distribution in this state.

The impression produced by an examination of the two sets of maps for the fishes above mentioned, is that of a small group of species, on the one hand, which enter the state from the south and east by way of the Wabash and the smaller tributaries of the Ohio, and, on the other hand, of a much larger group, most of which have entered the state from the west and north, making their way to its interior mainly by the Illinois and the Rock, but sometimes by the Kaskaskia and the Big Muddy also. Species of the Ohio group sometimes seem to spread into the headwaters of adjacent streams, especially into the branches of the Kaskaskia where these come nearest to the Embarras, and into those of the Big Vermilion of the Illinois which are nearest to the Little Vermilion of the Wabash. Some species, however, remain carefully within the tributaries of the Wabash system.

It seems possible that this appearance of an approach to the state and entrance upon its territory from opposite directions is not altogether deceptive, and that the annual movements of the fishes of the state, up the streams at the time of the spring floods, downwards with the recession of the waters, and still farther downwards, for many species, into deeper water in the winter, may take these two contingents of our fish population in opposite directions, from and towards local centers of population for the species, situated on opposite sides of the state. Whether and where such local centers of population actually exist, is a question which can not be answered definitely for lack of numerical or statistical data in the faunal lists and other literature of geographical distribution for the surrounding states. If they exist, the Wabash fishes would constitute one such system, and those of the Mississippi and its tributaries, another.

If we may speculate still further upon this subject, we may perhaps surmise that a general critical analysis of the fish population of the larger area of which Illinois forms the central part, would enable us to distinguish fairly well-defined districts, each with its characteristic assemblage of prevalent species, so associated and ecologically related as to form a balanced assemblage of species, all so adjusted to each other and so advantageously placed in their environment as to constitute a closed system, which the characteristic species of adjacent areas can not enter, or in which they can not permanently remain.

DSTRIBUTION CHIEFLY IN THE OHIO DRAINAGE

Brindled stonecat	Pirate-perch
Green-sided darter	*Notropis illecebrosus*
Boleichthys fusiformis	*Ericymba buccata*
Chub-sucker	Long-eared sunfish

DISTRIBUTION CHIEFLY IN THE MISSSSIPPI DRAINAGE

Short-nosed gar	White bass
Stonecat	Yellow bass
Lake carp	Common bullhead
Notropis cayuga	Short-headed red-horse
Spot-tailed minnow	Red-bellied dace
Notropis rubrifrons	*Notropis gilberti*
Spotted shiner	Long-nosed gar
Pike	Dogfish
Menona top-minnow	Mongrel buffalo
Trout-perch	Black-head minnow
Pumpkinseed	*Hybognathus nubila*
Sauger	Redfin
Yellow perch	Rock bass
Banded darter	

BOUNDARY BETWEEN NORTHERN AND SOUTHERN SPECIES

Recurring next to the distinction made on another page (ciii) between northern and southern fishes whose areas extend into Ill·nois but not beyond, and comparing the distribution of these groups within the state, as given on Map CIII., we see that northern and southern species meet and mingle in the western part of the state from Meredosia to Pekin on the Illinois, and from Quincy to Dallas City on the Mississippi, but that in eastern Illinois they are separated by a wide interval extending from Cook county to the mouth of the Embarras, in which interval we have never taken any representative of either group.

The distinctively southern species, although most abundant south of the line 28° 30′, nevertheless go up the Waba h to the Embarras, up the Kaskaskia to Shelby county, up the Mississippi to Henderson county, and up the Illinois to Pekin, also following the branches of the Sangamon to Logan county. The northern species, on the other hand, although most abundant above 40° 20′, come down the Illinois to Meredosia, and down the Mississippi to Quincy.

The boundary between the northern and southern species thus appears as a broad belt some fifty miles in width, extending two thirds of the way across the state just about its center, but widening to a distance of one hundred and seventy-five mi es on the eastern boundary.

GENERAL FEATURES OF ECOLOGICAL DISTRIBUTION

In addition to the general distribution of Illinois fishes over the North American continent, their general or partial distribution within the state, and the unevenness of their distribution over the different divisions of the state, hydrographic, climatic, and geological, there are also recognizable differences and inequalities of distribution corresponding to the size of the water bodies in which the species are found, to the nature of the bottom and the consequent clearness and purity of the waters, and to the existence and rate of current or flow in the waters inhabited by them. In this class of divisions, geological distribution merges into ecological relation, the distribution of species being no longer by geological areas, but by ecological situations. In this sense two species may occupy precisely the same territory without ever coming into any effective contact with each other, because they are differently related to certain features of their environment.

As an explanation of the more general facts of distribution requires an analysis and interpretation of continental, terrestrial, and even cosmic agencies affecting it, so an understanding of what we may call the ecological distribution of a species, requires a corresponding analysis of the ecological features of the region. Such an analysis can here be carried but a little way, since the ecological data borne by our collections are only of a very general type; but such as they are, they may, if used with discretion, add definiteness and detail and some degree of statistical precision to our knowledge of this part of the subject

The attention of the reader is called especially to the interesting manner in which our statistics of associate occurrence exhibit the frequent tendency of closely allied species inhabiting the same territory to avoid each other's company, and thus to evade competition with one another, by the choice of different haunts and situations within the area of their common habitation. In consequence of this tendency, we sometimes find widely unlike species more closely and commonly associated in our collections than like, the ecological repulsion of each for its similars bringing dissimilars together in more or less definite associate groups. Apparent examples of this reaction may be found in the body of this report in the discussion of the suckers, the minnows, the catfishes (especially the bullheads), the top-minnows, and the sunfishes.

Ninety-seven of our species have been collected in large enough numbers, and from a sufficient variety of locations, to give us data for comparison with reference to the general character and size of the water bodies which they prefer; 62 species furnish available data concerning the bottom or substratum of these water bodies; and 49 species, data concerning current and rate of flow. The numbers of collections for the various species covered by these figures vary greatly from a minimum of 10 collections of a species to a maximum of 376. Unfortunately, the larger and more important fishes are commonly represented by the smaller numbers of collections, and statements made concerning these are less likely to be found fairly accurate and generally correct than are those concerning the smaller fishes, represented by larger numbers of collections.

One available set of our data may best be presented in tabular form, for such use as the student may wish to make of them; and to this table we add, as an illustration of its use, only a few statements concerning the more conspicuous ecological groups of our Illinois fishes.

By assorting the species according to the size of the ratios of frequency of occurrence for each class of situations distinguished in this table, we may separate those strongly preferring the given situation from those apparently avoiding it. In this way we learn that the species occurring in our collections with disproportionate frequency in the larger rivers of the state are the mud-cat (*Leptops olivaris*), one of the river carp (*carpio*), the toothed herring (*Hiodon tergisus*), and the sheepshead (*Aplodinotus*), among the larger fishes; and a small darter (*Cottogaster shumardi*), the trout-perch (*Percopsis guttatus*), and a minnow (*Hybopsis dissimilis*) among the smaller fishes.

The principal larger fishes of the smaller rivers make a much longer list, comprising the hogsucker, two of the native carp (*velifer* and *difformis*), a species of red-horse (*aureolum*), the rock bass, and the small-mouthed black bass; and the principal smaller species are six darters (*Etheostoma zonale*, *Hadropterus phoxocephalus*, *H. aspro*, *Diplesion blennioides*, *Etheostoma cœruleum*, and *Ammocrypta pellucida*), a stonecat (*Noturus flavus*), and *Hybopsis kentuckiensis*, and four other minnows, all of the genus *Notropis* (*rubrifrons*, *gilberti*, *blennius*, and *cornutus*)—

their ratios running from 70 per cent. for *rubrifrons* to 41 per cent. for *cornutus*.

The species of our list which have from 50 to 100 per cent. of their representatives in creeks, as illustrated by our collections, include three sunfishes (the green sunfish, the round sunfish, and the long-eared sunfish), three suckers (the common sucker, the chub-sucker, and the striped sucker), four darters, ten minnows, and the brindled stonecat.

The larger species found most abundantly in lakes, ponds, and other stagnant waters were the common bullhead, the buffaloes, the yellow perch, the white bass, the yellow bass, the large-mouthed black bass, and five sunfishes (both crappies, the warmouth, the pumpkinseed, and the bluegill); and the smaller kinds were the smallest of our fishes (*Microperca punctulata*), another darter (*Boleichthys fusiformis*), two minnows (*Notropis cayuga* and *N. heterodon*), the mud-minnow, and a killifish (*Fundulus dispar*).

Turning next to the 62 species for which our data of preference or avoidance of a muddy bottom are available, we find 7 species whose ratios of frequency of occurrence in such situations range from 43 to 88 per cent., and which may consequently be called limophagous fishes. These are the warmouth sunfish, the black and the yellow bullheads, the pirate-perch, a single darter (*Boleosoma camurum*), and two minnows, the golden shiner and the common shiner (*Notropis cornutus*).

It is interesting to find, by an examination of our maps, that all these 7 species are freely distributed over the lower Illinoisan glaciation of the southern part of the state, where, as we have already shown, only fishes indifferent to a peculiarly persistent turbidity of the water are likely to occur.

By selecting from this same list of 62 species those with the lowest ratios of frequency over a muddy bottom, we get 13 species (with ratios of 4 to 10 per cent.) which evidently avoid such situations; and these, again, are without exception so distributed that the area of the lower Illinoisan glaciation is almost never entered by them. These are one of the native carp (*velifer*), a species of red-horse (*aureolum*), the small-mouthed black bass, two darters (*Hadropterus phoxocephalus* and *Etheostoma cœruleum*), five minnows (*Campostoma anomalum, Notropis heterodon, Ericymba buccata, Hybopsis kentuckiensis,* and *Notropis blennius*), two stonecats, and the little brook silverside (*Labidesthes*).

A more precise statement and a fuller discussion of the ecological relations of our fishes, including statistics of companionship for the various species, as shown by the frequency of their joint occurrence in collections, must be left for later contributions.

Attention may be profitably called, in conclusion, to the economic significance of the details of distribution of the various species, as influenced both by geographical and ecological conditions, since a proper understanding and application of these facts will prevent wasteful efforts to introduce species where they do not belong and can not thrive. Indeed, the more detailed our knowledge of favorable, and even optimum, conditions for the different species, and the more exact, also, our acquaintance with the relations of each species of fish to its companion species in any associate assemblage, the more intelligent, and hence the more successful, in the long run, will be our efforts to extend the range and multiply the numbers of the more useful species and to lessen the numbers of those especially injurious.

ECOLOGICAL TABLE

ALL ILLINOIS SPECIES WITH AT LEAST TEN AVAILABLE RECORDS EACH*

Jordan and Evermann Nos.	Species	Water (97 species)					Current (49 species)				Bottom (62 species)			
		Available collections	Larger rivers	Smaller rivers	Creeks	Lakes, ponds, etc.	Available collections	Swift to moderate	Sluggish to stagnant	Variable	Available collections	Mud	Rock and sand	Mud and sand
151	Long-nosed gar..........	35	25	19	7	22	....	....	....	....	....	....	....	....
152	Short-nosed gar........	57	28	24	4	25	....	....	....	....	....	....	....	....
155	Dogfish................	37	18	7	6	30	....	....	....	....	....	....	....	....
207	Channel-cat............	171	20	32	27	8	31	68	19	13	75	21	44	35

*The figures of this table, except those in the columns for available collections, are ratios of frequency of the species in our collections, computed with due reference to the comparative numbers of collections of all kinds made in each situation.

ECOLOGICAL TABLE—*continued*

ALL ILLINOIS SPECIES WITH AT LEAST TEN AVAILABLE RECORDS EACH

Jordan and Evermann Nos.	Species	Water (97 species)					Current (49 species)				Bottom (62 species)			
		Available collections	Larger rivers	Smaller rivers	Creeks	Lakes, ponds, etc.	Available collections	Swift to moderate	Sluggish to stagnant	Variable	Available collections	Mud	Rock and sand	Mud and sand
215	Yellow bullhead.........	122	7	6	37	23	14	36	43	21	35	43	34	23
217	Common bullhead.......	48	15	5	4	44	....	....	....	....	....	....	....	....
218	Black bullhead..........	244	8	21	37	26	38	37	53	10	56	54	46	....
221	Mud-cat...............	30	53	21	5	8	....	....	....	....	....	....	....	....
222	Stonecat...............	41	10	53	34	...	15	60	13	26	24	8	58	34
223	Tadpole cat............	193	17	5	23	41	21	48	43	9	45	29	27	44
231	Brindled stonecat.......	30	3	36	60	...	....	....	....	....	13	8	62	30
261	Red-mouth buffalo......	39	13	...	9	48	....	....	....	....	....	....	....	....
262	Mongrel buffalo.........	19	17	...	7	45	....	....	....	....	....	....	....	....
264	Small-mouth buffalo.....	52	14	12	4	49	....	....	....	....	....	....	....	....
265	River carp.............	15	47	...	8	10	....	....	....	....	....	....	....	....
266	Blunt-nosed carp........	102	9	42	30	12	16	50	25	25	47	21	36	43
268	Quillback carp..........	70	10	50	19	5	19	47	32	21	28	4	60	36
289	Common sucker.........	132	3	19	71	1	49	39	47	14	79	13	44	43
294	Hogsucker.............	99	4	63	25	4	71	20	63	17	59	....	54	46
302a	Chub-sucker............	131	9	12	57	14	23	52	48	....	57	32	39	29
303	Striped sucker..........	46	2	31	53	3	....	....	....	....	19	26	32	42
305	White-nosed sucker......	18	7	44	20	6	....	....	....	....	....	....	....	....
314	Common red-horse......	143	9	32	40	4	47	57	28	15	65	6	55	39
319	Short-headed red-horse...	55	13	25	15	22	....	....	....	....	14	14	43	43

ECOLOGICAL TABLE—*continued*

ALL ILLINOIS SPECIES WITH AT LEAST TEN AVAILABLE RECORDS EACH

Jordan and Evermann Nos.	Species	Water (97 species)					Current (49 species)				Bottom (62 species)			
		Available collections	Larger rivers	Smaller rivers	Creeks	Lakes, ponds, etc.	Available collections	Swift to moderate	Sluggish to stagnant	Variable	Available collections	Mud	Rock and sand	Mud and sand
328	Stone-roller	195	3	37	55	1	65	63	23	14	105	7	57	36
334	Red-bellied dace	23	10	...	71	...	....	....	....	....	....	....	....	....
340	Silvery minnow	183	12	36	32	7	30	47	40	13	67	33	40	27
349	Black-head minnow	95	14	30	48	4	12	50	42	8	44	25	41	34
350	Blunt-nosed minnow	376	5	34	43	12	108	50	34	16	202	20	46	34
355	Horned dace	151	4	28	63	2	42	48	36	16	81	17	47	36
391	*Opsopœodus emiliæ*	40	13	6	36	32	....	....	....	....	....	....	....	....
394	Golden shiner	303	12	17	29	32	28	32	57	11	82	44	29	27
398	Bullhead minnow	187	17	31	28	7	36	67	17	16	62	11	44	45
405	*Notropis cayuga*	29	...	13	26	57	13	54	38	8	15	....	27	73
406	*N. heterodon*	92	19	1	19	60	....	....	....	....	14	7	22	71
408	Straw-colored minnow	185	7	44	37	3	63	49	26	25	103	10	50	40
420	*Notropis gilberti*	30	2	49	43	2	....	....	....	....	18	11	45	44
426	*Notropis illecebrosus*	11	...	...	100	...	....	....	....	....	....	....	....	....
428	Spot-tailed minnow	147	28	5	2	39	....	....	....	....	10	20	80	....
432	Redfin	163	24	32	20	14	13	46	38	16	55	27	40	33
448	Silverfin	268	6	39	40	4	65	54	26	20	126	13	56	31
456	Common shiner	178	2	41	50	4	76	45	36	19	102	44	48	8
476	*Notropis jejunus*	51	27	19	13	11	....	....	....	....	12	25	67	8
485	Shiner	206	20	36	15	11	23	57	30	13	48	21	64	14

ECOLOGICAL TABLE—*continued*

ALL ILLINOIS SPECIES WITH AT LEAST TEN AVAILABLE RECORDS EACH

Jordan and Evermann Nos.	Species	Water (97 species)					Current (49 species)				Bottom (62 species)			
		Available collections	Larger rivers	Smaller rivers	Creeks	Lakes, ponds, etc.	Available collections	Swift to moderate	Sluggish to stagnant	Variable	Available collections	Mud	Rock and sand	Mud and sand
489	*Notropis rubrifrons*	13	4	70	26	...	11	45	18	36	11	....	82	18
498a	Blackfin	208	3	32	65	...	69	41	45	14	109	17	43	40
499	*Ericymba buccata*	74	1	18	81	...	14	43	29	28	38	8	63	29
501	Sucker-mouthed minnow	159	5	36	53	1	53	53	24	23	92	15	51	34
528	Spotted shiner	11	50	27	22	...	...	...	...	...	...	...	...	...
533	Silver chub	41	5	29	66	...	13	77	15	7	20	30	55	15
534	Storer's chub	28	21	32	11	10	...	...	...	...	...	...	...	...
536	River chub	129	4	41	51	1	55	53	24	23	74	8	43	49
674	Toothed herring	10	46	...	...	16	...	...	...	...	...	...	...	...
677	Gizzard-shad	105	17	32	7	20	...	...	...	...	22	23	55	22
919	Mud minnow	34	7	24	8	49	...	...	...	...	...	...	...	...
922	Grass pike	111	7	16	34	30	14	36	57	7	29	38	21	41
939	Menona top-minnow	17	...	...	42	49	...	...	...	...	...	...	...	...
966	Striped top-minnow	83	11	...	3	72	...	...	...	...	...	...	...	...
967	Common top-minnow	208	6	25	49	12	34	41	50	9	81	32	42	26
1000	Viviparous top-minnow	17	12	21	32	12	...	...	...	...	...	...	...	...
1145	Trout-perch	15	52	...	4	19	...	...	...	...	...	...	...	...
1147	Pirate-perch	100	18	5	42	21	14	21	72	7	37	62	19	19
1177	Brook silverside	120	13	28	13	36	16	31	44	25	21	10	62	28
1381	White crappie	166	15	19	17	34	14	64	29	7	43	35	49	16

ECOLOGICAL TABLE—*continued*

ALL ILLINOIS SPECIES WITH AT LEAST TEN AVAILABLE RECORDS EACH

Jordan and Evermann Nos.	Species	Water (97 species)					Current (49 species)				Bottom (62 species)			
		Available collections	Larger rivers	Smaller rivers	Creeks	Lakes, ponds, etc.	Available collections	Swift to moderate	Sluggish to stagnant	Variable	Available collections	Mud	Rock and sand	Mud and sand
1382	Black crappie	179	17	16	10	42	....	....	....	....	28	25	50	25
1383	Round sunfish	11	....	....	69	30	....	....	....	....	....	....	....	....
1385	Rock bass	48	7	49	24	13	20	55	15	30	27	....	48	52
1387	Warmouth	122	12	17	12	45	....	....	....	....	17	88	12	....
1391	Green sunfish	313	7	25	52	11	80	39	45	16	156	28	41	31
1397	*Lepomis miniatus*	23	10	....	11	41	....	....	....	....	....	....	....	....
1399	Long-eared sunfish	112	2	12	76	4	17	41	47	12	41	37	63	....
1400	Orange-spotted sunfish	174	12	25	34	20	21	38	38	24	60	30	35	35
1403	Bluegill	214	16	10	7	54	....	....	....	....	24	25	58	17
1408	Pumpkinseed	85	6	17	4	56	....	....	....	....	....	....	....	....
1409	Small-mouthed black bass	100	6	43	23	19	40	55	18	27	50	6	68	26
1410	Large-mouthed black bass	211	8	20	17	40	19	58	26	16	48	19	54	27
1413	Pike-perch	36	16	10	8	33	....	....	....	....	....	....	....	....
1414	Sauger	16	36	....	4	25	....	....	....	....	....	....	....	....
1415	Yellow perch	83	20	7	3	51	....	....	....	....	....	....	....	....
1417	Log-perch	60	10	38	27	19	14	93	7	....	20	....	100	....
1418	*Hadropterus phoxocephalus*	85	7	57	27	3	32	87	13	....	48	6	94	....
1421	Black-sided darter	159	6	42	47	1	49	70	30	....	76	16	84	....
1436	*Cottogaster shumardi*	16	55	....	4	18	....	....	....	....	....	....	....	....
1443	Green-sided darter	24	....	46	53	....	....	....	....	....	....	....	....	....

ECOLOGICAL TABLE—*concluded*

ALL ILLINOIS SPECIES WITH AT LEAST TEN AVAILABLE RECORDS EACH

Jordan and Evermann Nos.	Species	Water (97 species)					Current (49 species)				Bottom (62 species)			
		Available collections	Larger rivers	Smaller rivers	Creeks	Lakes, ponds, etc.	Available collections	Swift to moderate	Sluggish to stagnant	Variable	Available collections	Mud	Rock and sand	Mud and sand
1446	Johnny darter	234	3	25	53	16	71	68	32	....	126	11	89	....
1448	*Boleosoma camurum*	107	9	23	42	17	17	41	59	....	39	60	40	....
1450	Sand darter	19	13	47	39	...	....	....	....	....	....	....	....	....
1461	Banded darter	32	3	74	23	...	18	89	11	....	19	11	89	....
1474	*Etheostoma jessiæ*	158	20	19	16	24	12	83	17	....	31	23	67	....
1477	Rainbow darter	80	3	44	45	1	29	83	17	....	37	8	92	....
1489	*Etheostoma squamiceps*	10	...	35	64	...	....	....	....	....	....	....	....	....
1490	Fan-tailed darter	30	9	...	87	4	....	....	....	....	11	....	100	....
1494	*Boleichthys fusiformis*	56	1	12	24	62	....	....	....	....	21	33	67	....
1497	Least darter	12	...	...	4	95	....	....	....	....	....	....	....	....
1529	White bass	56	28	...	8	46	....	....	....	....	....	....	....	....
1531	Yellow bass	100	20	4	...	52	....	....	....	....	....	....	....	....
1871	Sheepshead	57	29	16	1	27	....	....	....	....	....	....	....	....

GENERAL SUMMARY

The principal conclusions of this chapter may be thus summarized:

1. The 150 native species of Illinois fishes here recognized, are so distributed within and without the state as to indicate an unequal commingling of the faunæ of the surrounding territories, southeastern species preponderating over southwestern, northeastern over northwestern, eastern over western, and southern over northern.

2. The Illinois basin may be taken as typical, in its fish population, of the ichthyology of the whole state—occupying, as it does, a central position, including more than half the area of the state, and containing a great variety of waters and situations fit for the habitation of fishes, and more than four fifths of the species found anywhere in Illinois. The more important fishes of the state not known from this basin are a few distinctively northern species, most of which are peculiar to the Great Lakes, and a few southern species which do not range as far north, in this state, as the mouth of the Illinois. The remainder are very rare in our territory, most of them coming from the west and south, and they are extremely insignificant elements of our fish fauna.

3. If the ten stream systems of the state be brought into comparison one with another, it appears that the six larger areas, containing the largest streams and presenting the greatest variety of situations, are much more closely affiliated ichthyologically than are the four smaller areas. The least closely affiliated with each other and with all the rest are the Michigan district of northeastern Illinois and the Big Muddy basin in the southwest. The closest relations are those between the Illinois, the Rock, and the Mississippi.

4. In the absence, in Illinois, of geographical barriers to the dispersal of fishes, the causes influencing their distribution are climatic, geologic, and ecological. As Illinois extends through 5.5° of latitude, differences of climate between the northern and the southern sections of the state are sufficient to affect, in considerable measure, the distribution of its plant and animal species—differences which, in its ichthyology, express themselves in the presence in northern Illinois, but not in southern, of 17 species of general northward range; and in southern Illinois, but not in northern, of 14 species of general southward range. These two groups of species meet and mingle in the great north and south rivers of the western half of the state, in an area of common occupation about fifty miles in width, from the latitude of Springfield northward, while on the eastern boundary of the state, occupied by small streams of various direction, these groups are separated by an interval of about a hundred and seventy-five miles over which no representative of either group has been taken.

5. Geological limitations to the dispersal of fishes are illustrated by peculiarities of distribution in southern Illinois as

related to the area of the lower Illinoisan glaciation, which 34 species evidently avoid while 35 other species enter upon it freely and inhabit it successfully. A comparison of the ecological relations of these two groups of species as represented by our collection records, shows that they are strongly distinguished by the repugnance of the first group, and the indifference of the second, to waters with a muddy bottom, collections of the first group having been made from such situations in an average ratio more than three times as great as that for the second. The waters of this region, on the other hand, are remarkably and persistently turbid, never clearing themselves spontaneously. This is owing in part to the extremely fine division of the soil, and in part to its generally acid character and the consequent lack of "granulation," or cohesion of its ultimate particles in granules, such as occurs in the alkaline soils of the other geological areas of the state. The surface waters of the district are soft and slightly alkaline, but contain much silica, and much solid matter in suspension which it is extremely difficult to remove completely by any ordinary filtering or precipitation process. The inference is plain that it is to this condition of the waters—due to the geological history of the soil of this region—that the unequal distribution of these fishes is largely to be attributed.

6. In consequence of another clearly recognizable inequality of distribution, partly coincident with the two preceding and partly independent of them, two additional groups may be distinguished; one of 8 species, distributed in this state mainly through the Ohio and Wabash drainage, and the other of 27 species, distributed through the Mississippi and its more northerly tributaries. The general distribution throughout the country at large of each of these two groups of species is quite varied, and offers no hint of a reason for these differences in Illinois Two hypothetical explanations are suggested — the first presupposing different centers of population outside the state, from and towards which these species move, into and out of Illinois streams, with the spring rise, summer recession, and winter cooling of the waters, one of these centers to the west and north, and one to the east and south; and the second presupposing an organization of the fish population into more or less distinct communities of mutually well-adjusted species, each community so adapted to its environment that members of adjacent communities can not successfully intrude upon its territory.

7. An analysis of our statistical data of ecological distribution gives us many instances of a marked difference in preference of situation between nearly related species inhabiting the same area, the effect of which is to break the force of a competition between these species such as would prevail if they were similarly distributed ecologically as well as geographically. Closely related species are, as a consequence, often found much less frequently associated in their common territory than either is with widely unlike species of the same geographical range. Exceptions to this rule are found where similar species occupy adjacent areas of distribution which merely overlap by their borders.

8. A table of the broader ecological relations of 97 species of Illinois fishes is made the basis of a few general statements, but that subject as a whole is reserved for more detailed treatment elsewhere.

Winding in the Haul

Inshore with the Haul

Staking the Cork Line

Loading the Live-box

A seven-thousand-pound Catch of Paddle-fish

The Fisheries of Illinois

Since the state and the nation maintain, in their commissions of fish and fisheries, special agencies for the investigation and promotion of economic ichthyology, the Natural History Survey is not constructively responsible for work in this field. The subject of our fisheries is, however, an essential part of the science of ichthyology broadly considered—a division, indeed, of ichthyological ecology, of which the reciprocal relations and interactions of fishes and men are as legitimate and necessary a part as those of fishes and any other factor of their ecological environment. The economic element has, consequently, been taken into account in our discussion of species and the larger groups, and a brief résumé of its principal features is evidently appropriate to this introduction.

The distinction of Illinois as a fish-producing state is to be found in its relation to the Mississippi River and some of the most important branches of that stream. Bordered by the main river for the whole length of its longest side, by the second largest tributary of the Mississippi for 130 miles of its southeastern boundary, and by the Wabash for 198 miles on the east, the state is also traversed diagonally by the Illinois River, admirably adapted, by its sluggish current, by the many bottomland lakes connected with it at low water, by the extensive breeding-grounds afforded to fishes during the period of the spring overflow, and by the vast abundance of fish food in its waters at all seasons of the year, to support an unusually large and varied fish population. Illinois is consequently far in the lead of all the states of the Mississippi Valley in respect to river-fishery products. It markets a larger value per annum in fishes taken from flowing streams than all the states immediately surrounding it taken together. The total for this state in 1899 was $517,420, and that for Iowa, Missouri, Kentucky, Indiana, and Wisconsin combined was $435,137. Illinois furnishes, indeed, more than one third of the fishes sent to market from all the streams of the Mississippi Valley,—valued in 1899 at $1,473,040. Furthermore, the Illinois River and its tributaries produced in 1899, 72 per cent. of all the fishes taken from the streams of the state, and a fourth of the entire fish product of the Mississippi Valley came in that year from this one stream. The totals for the different Illinois stream systems were as follows: Illinois, $371,110; Mississippi, $118,278; Wabash, $38,065; Ohio, $20,029; Kaskaskia, $3,002; Big Muddy, $1,136.

The Great Lake fisheries in Illinois waters are of insignificant proportions. The total longshore product for Cook and Lake counties during the last census year was $12,500—about $2,000 less than the sum derived from our river turtles alone.

The river fisheries of the state gave employment in 1899 to 2,389 men, and utilized a capital of $225,000. Sixteen steamboats, 200 house-boats, and 1,500 row-boats were used in these fisheries, together with about 45 miles of seines, 10 miles of trammel-nets, half a mile of gill-nets, and 14,000 fyke-nets, pound-nets, and traps. The seines and the fyke-nets together yielded about 80 per cent. of the product, the seines bringing in $251,562 and the fyke-nets $210,054, Set-lines yielded $37,191; trammel-nets, $24,185; traps, $2,707; gill-nets, $1,290; drift-lines, $1,141; pound-nets, $811; and hand-lines, $701.

The dozen most productive kinds of Illinois fishes, according to the statistics of the last census year, were as follows: European carp, $244,322; buffalo, $111,707; catfishes and bullheads, $68,535; sheepshead or drum, $17,729; crappie, $14,419; sunfish, $12,067; black bass, $10,842; suckers and red-horse, $7,845; paddle-fish, $6,210; white, yellow, and rock bass, $5,601; lake and shovel-nosed sturgeon, $3,904; wall-eyed pike, $1,174.

About three dozen of our 150 species of Illinois fishes have a marketable value as food, and a dozen more may be classed as edible, although not popular enough or abundant enough within our limits to have any commercial value as Illinois products. A dozen of the more useful species are of really good quality, and half of these are among the best of the fresh-water fishes. In the following list the edible species are distinguished in classes of graduated importance, according to our judgment of the estimation in which these fishes are generally held. A few species are put in a lower class than their quality would call for because of their infrequent occurrence in our fisheries.

Although the fisheries of the state are not, it must be admitted, commercially of the first importance, they are of sufficient economic interest to make it the duty of all concerned to preserve them carefully and to take all practicable measures for

LIST OF ILLINOIS FOOD FISHES

First class	Second class	Third class	Fourth class
Whitefish	Golden shad (rare)	Paddle-fish	Dogfish
Great Lake trout	Northern mooneye (rare)	Lake sturgeon	Gizzard-shad
Blue cat	Lake herring	Shovel-nosed sturgeon	River carp
Channel-cat	Eel	White-nosed sucker	Lake carp
Mud-cat	Missouri sucker	Common red-horse	Spotted sucker
Common pike	Red-mouth buffalo	Short-headed red-horse	Common sucker
White crappie	Mongrel buffalo	Yellow bullhead	Burbot
Black crappie	Small-mouth buffalo	Common bullhead	
Bluegill	European carp	Black bullhead	
Small-mouthed black bass	Eel cat (*anguilla*) (rare)	Little pickerel	
Large-mouthed black bass	Lake catfish (rare)	Warmouth	
Wall-eyed pike	Rock bass	Sheepshead	
	Blue-spotted sunfish		
	Long-eared sunfish		
	Pumpkinseed		
	Sand-pike		
	Yellow perch		
	White bass		
	Yellow bass		

their improvement and development. Making due allowance for fishes sold in local markets, distributed by peddlers, eaten by those who take them, and not represented, consequently, in published statistics of the trade, it may fairly be said that our Illinois fisheries now yield at the rate of a pound a day, throughout the year, of cheap and desirable food to about 80,000 persons—virtually equivalent to one meal of fish a day for a quarter of a million people. It is encouraging to conclude, from a comparison of available statistics, that we have no reason to believe that the general fishery product of our rivers is now declining, either in value or amount. On the contrary, according to reports of the State Fishermen's Association published from 1897 to 1901, the total value of the Illinois River product increased by 60 per cent. during that interval, being $207,685 for 1897 and $351,753 for 1901. The yield of carp increased in value 69 per cent. during this period; that of buffalo, 88 per cent.; of black bass, 32 per cent.; of catfish and bullpouts, 41 per cent.; of crappie, 47 per cent.; of sunfish and yellow perch, 154 per cent.; and that of striped bass, 27 per cent.,—the only important species then reported as diminishing being the sheepshead, or fresh-water drum, commonly marketed as white perch, the yield of which declined 27½ per cent.*

Comparative Statistics, Fisheries Illinois River, 1897 and 1901

computed from reports of the illinois fishermen's association

	1897	1901
Carp	99,059	167,266
Buffalo	48,139	90,357
Black bass	3,434	4,532
Drum	20,452	14,838
Catfish and bullpouts	26,283	36,933
Spoonbill	....	232

*Unpublished data of shipments from Illinois River points, recently furnished me through the courtesy of Mr. N. H. Cohen, President of the Illinois State Fish Commission, enable me to compare the total product of this river for 1906 and 1907 with that for 1899 as contained in the Report of the United States Commissioner of Fish and Fisheries for the year ending June 30, 1901. Against a total product of the Illinois River of approximately 14½ million pounds in 1899 we have for 1906 16,149,076 pounds, and for 1907 13,218,137 pounds, or an average for the two latter years of 14,683,606 pounds.—S. A. F.

Comparative Statistics, Fisheries Illinois River, 1897 and 1901—*concluded*

	1897	1901
Sunfish and perch	3,080	7,830
Striped bass	3,234	4,117
Crappie	4,004	5,880
Dogfish	....	10,460
	207,685	342,445

A large part of the increased yield is doubtless due, however, to a mere enlargement of fishing operations, illustrated by the data for 1894 and 1899, which show that the number of men employed increased in the interval between these years by 44 per cent. and the capital invested by 44¼ per cent. This favorable condition of our fisheries is doubtless due in part to natural conditions, and evidently also in great measure to state leg slation effectively controlling the times and methods of capture, and providing for the recovery and restoration, to streams suitable for their maintenance, of fishes left stranded on the river bottoms by the retreat of the waters of overflow.

It will be seen from the foregoing that the Illinois River, with its tributary lakes and streams, is by far the most important fishing ground within the boundaries of Illinois, and that this stream and its dependencies are gifts of nature to the state, valuable in many ways, which we should fully appreciate and utilize to the best advantage, allowing no single interest to destroy or overshadow any other. Measures for its utilization as a sewage outlet for great cities and as a commercial highway between the Mississippi and the Great Lakes, and for the reclamation of its enormously fertile bottom-lands, should not be taken without due regard to its importance and promise as a perpetual source of cheap and healthful food to the people of the state and country.

EXPLANATION OF TERMS AND MEASUREMENTS MOST FREQUENTLY USED IN KEYS AND DESCRIPTIONS

1. GENERAL BODY PROPORTIONS

The *length* of the fish is measured from the tip of the snout (muzzle) to the base of the caudal rays (end of last vertebra). It does not include the caudal fin, and does not necessarily include the last scales, which in most scaled fishes encroach more or less on the base of the fin. In fishes with a heterocercal tail the length is measured on the median line to the point where that line crosses the line of insertion of the caudal rays.

The *depth* of the fish is the vertical distance through the body at its deepest part.

The *width* of the fish is taken at the widest part of the body.

The *caudal peduncle*, or tail, is the tapering portion of the body behind the base of the last ray of the anal fin. Its length is taken from a vertical from that point to the base of the mid-caudal rays. The depth of the caudal peduncle is taken at its slenderest part.

The *profile* is the curve from the front of the dorsal fin to the tip of the snout.

2. THE HEAD AND CONTIGUOUS PARTS

The *length of the head*, ordinarily called "head" in descriptions, is measured from the tip of the snout to the extreme hinder margin of the bony portions of the opercle. It includes the opercular spine in percoid fishes.

The *width of the head* is taken at its widest part.

The *interorbital space*, or distance, is the horizontal distance on the top of the head between the eyes.

The *diameter of the eye*, called "eye" in descriptions, is taken lengthwise, the form of the orbit not always being round.

The *nose*, or *snout*, is measured from the tip of the upper jaw to the anterior margin of the orbit.

The *length of the upper jaw*, referred to as "maxillary" in descriptions, is measured from the tip of the upper jaw (premaxillary symphysis) to the posterior end of the maxillary.

The *gill-rakers* are counted both above and below the angle or bend of the gill-arch, the upper number being mentioned first, and rudiments being omitted. The formula 35+60, for example, indicates 35 rakers on the upper and 60 on the lower limb; if the number on the upper limb of the arch is unknown or unessential, it is indicated as "×".

The *teeth*. For explanation of dental formulæ used in description of *Cyprinidæ*, see foot-note, pp. 102-103.

3. THE FINS

Fins may be either *soft* or *spinous*, or may consist partly of *soft rays* and partly of *spines*. The rays of the soft fin or portion are distinguished from spines by their articulated or jointed structure. The peculiar "cross-marks" on the soft ray are, as a rule, easy to make out with the naked eye unless the specimen is very small or the fin rays are covered with thick skin or dark pigment. In cases of doubt the epidermis may be scraped away from a part of the ray or spine and a lens used. In counting the fin rays, rudimentary rays are omitted. Rudimentary rays are those rays, in general, at the beginning of the fin which are unbranched, membraneless, closely appressed the one to the other, and in ordinary cases not more than half the length of the fully developed rays. This limitation does not, however, apply to the so-called "club-shaped" short first dorsal ray of certain *Cyprinidæ* (*Pimephales* and *Cliola* spp.), which is separated from the ray back of it by a well-developed membrane. The last ray of the dorsal and anal fins is often split nearly or quite to the base and appears as two rays, although counted as only one (Fig. 3). In descriptions, Arabic numerals are used to indicate fin rays and Roman numerals to indicate spines. If a fin contains both spines and soft rays in a continuous series, a comma is used to separate the numerals indicating the two portions, "Dorsal X, 13," for example, indicating a single dorsal fin with 10 spines and 13 soft rays. Two separate dorsal fins are indicated by a dash separating the numerals, "Dorsal X–12" and "Dorsal X–I, 12," indicating respectively: first, a single spinous dorsal of 10 spines followed by a separate soft dorsal of 12 rays; and second, a spinous dorsal of 10 spines followed by a separate second dorsal fin consisting of a single spine and 12 soft rays.

The *height* of a fin is measured on the longest ray.

The *length* of a fin is measured along its base.

The *origin* or *insertion* of a fin—identical terms—is that of its first ray, or spine. The *position* of a fin is, technically, the distance from the tip of the snout to the base of its first ray or spine. For example, it may be said of a fish that the "position of the dorsal fin" is contained more, or less, than twice in the fish's length

4. The Scales

The most ready indication of the size of the scales in a fish is furnished by the enumeration of the scales in the lateral line, or, if that is absent, of those in a line along the horizontal axis, as nearly as possible, from the upper corner of the gill-opening to the base of the caudal rays. It is customary in descriptions to include also counts of the scales in oblique series from the middle line of the back to the lateral line and including it; and the number between the lateral line (not including it) and the median line of the belly in front of the anal fin. These counts are expressed in a conventional formula, "Scales 6–42–9," for example, indicating 6 scales in an oblique series above the lateral line, 42 in the lateral line (or in a longitudinal series from the gill-opening to the base of the caudal rays), and 9 in oblique series below the lateral line.

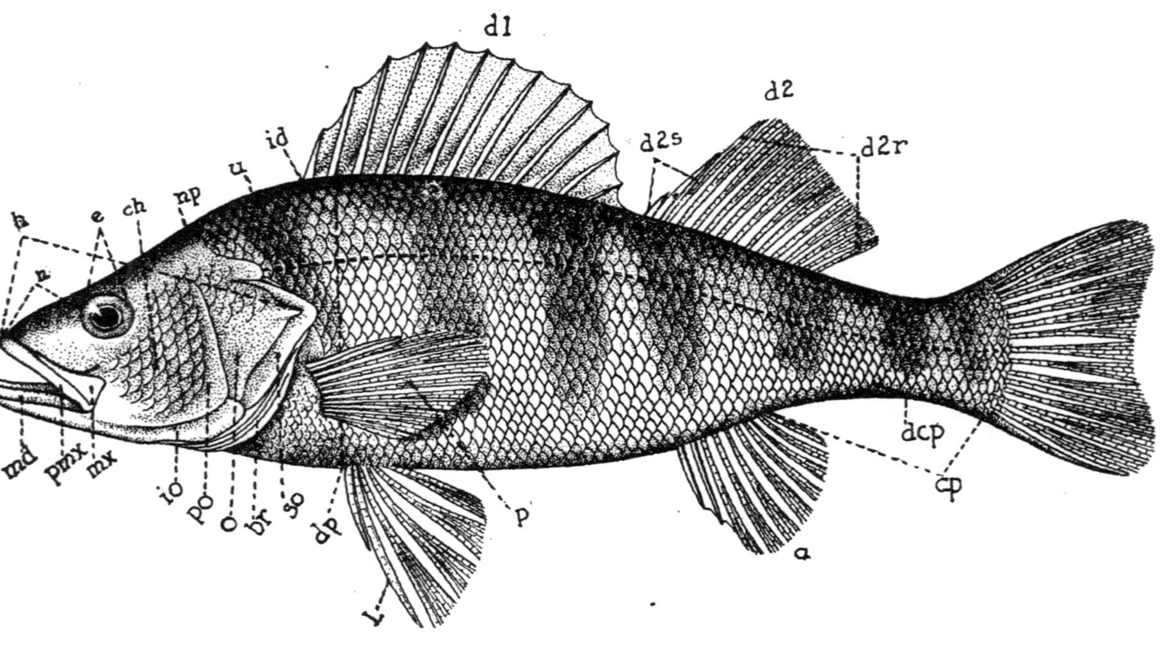

Fig. 1

Common Perch, *Perca flavescens* (Mitchill). External parts referred to in keys and descriptions: *a*, anal fin; *br*, branchiostegal rays; *ch*, cheek; *cp*, length of caudal peduncle; *d1*, spinous dorsal fin; *d2*, soft dorsal fin *d2r*, rays of second dorsal fin; *d2s*, spines of second dorsal fin; *dcp*, depth of caudal peduncle; *dp*, depth (of body); *e*, eye; *id*, insertion of dorsal fin; *io*, interopercle *md*, lower jaw, or mandible; *mx*, ma illary; *n*, nose, or snout; *np*, nape; *o*, opercle; *p*, pectoral fin; *pmx*, premaxillary; *po*, preopercle; *so*, subopercle; *v*, ventral fin.

Glossary of Anatomical and other Technical Terms*

Abdominal ventral fins. Ventrals which are inserted posteriorly, the pelvic bones having no connection with shoulder girdle. (See key to families, b, note, p. 1.)

Acanthopterygian. Spiny rayed. Said of the numerous families of fishes related to the basses and perches, in which part or all of the rays of at least one dorsal fin and the first ray of the ventral fins are of a spinous (unarticulated) character. (See *spine* and *ray*.)

Accessory caudal rays. Short, procurrent rays on the upper and lower (rather than posterior) part of the caudal peduncle.

Accessory pectoral scale. An enlarged scale at the base of the pectoral fin in certain herring-like fishes.

Actinosts. Small bones at the base of the paired fins.

Adipose fin. A fleshy fin-like structure behind the dorsal fin, as in salmons and catfishes. This is sometimes more or less continuous with the caudal fin, being separated from it only by a notch.

Air-bladder. A sac filled with air or other gases, lying beneath the backbone, and either adherent or not to the walls of the visceral cavity. It may be simple (most teleosts) or divided into compartments by constrictions (*Catostomidæ* and *Cyprinidæ*) or of a cellular structure (some *Ganoidei*). It is typically connected with the œsophagus by a duct, which is closed in many recent forms.

Ammocœtes. A name applied to the larval form of lampreys.

Amphicœlian Concave both before and behind. Said of the vertebræ of fishes generally, with the exception of certain forms. (See *opisthocœlian*.)

Anadromous. Running up rivers from the sea to spawn, as do shad and some salmonoids.

Anal. Pertaining to the anus, or vent.

Anal fin. The fin on the median line behind the vent. (Fig. 1, a)

Anal papilla. A protuberance, usually bilobed, in front of the genital pore and behind the vent in darters and sculpins.

Angular. A bony element of the lower jaw.

Antrorse. Directed forward.

Anus. The posterior external opening of the alimentary canal; the vent.

Arterial bulb. (See *conus arteriosus*.)

Articular. A bony element of the lower jaw.

Articulated. Jointed. (See *ray*.)

Auditory ossicles. (See *Weberian ossicles*.)

Barbel. An elongated, feeler-like projection, usually about the mouth, chin, or nose, as in the carp, and in catfishes.

Branchial. Of the gills (*branchiæ*).

Branchiostegals. Bony rays supporting the membranes which close the branchial cavity below. (Fig. 1, br.)

Buccal. Of the mouth.

Caducous. Falling off. Said of certain plate-like scales on the belly of darters.

---

*In the preparation of this glossary, that of Jordan's Manual of the Vertebrates (ed. 8) has been of substantial assistance, and, naturally, some of the definitions will be found to be the same. In addition, however, a good many new terms have been inserted, and many old definitions amended, applied to particular cases, extended to more informative dimensions, or simplified by reference to figures.

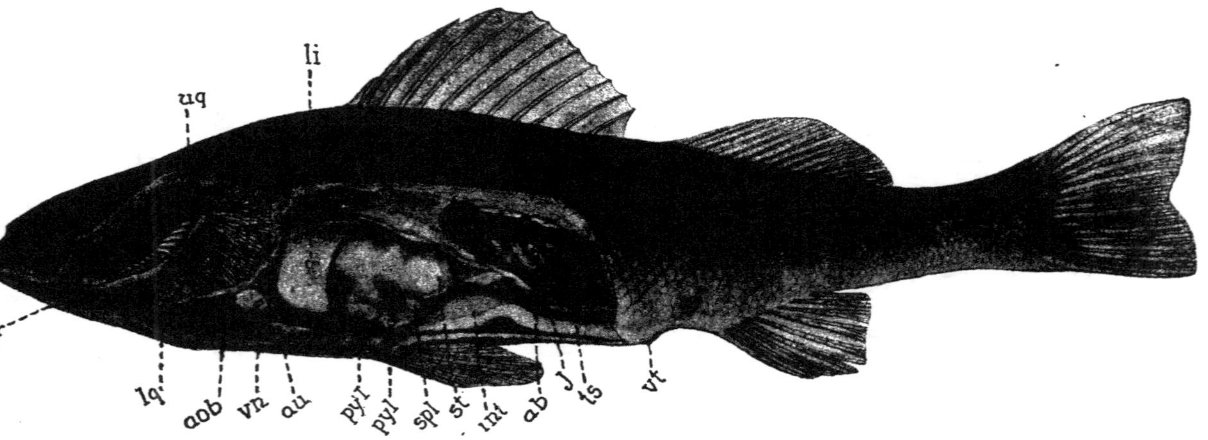

Fig. 2

Dissection of Perch, showing principal features of anatomy: *aob*, *conus arteriosus;* *au*, auricle; *gr*, gill-rakers; *int*, intestine *j*, cavity of air-bladder; *lg*, lower limb (or angle) of gill-arch; *li*, liver; *pyl*, pyloric cæca; *pl*, spleen; *st*, stomach; *ts*, testis; *ug*, upper limb (or angle) of gill-arch; *vn*, ventricle; *vt*, vent.

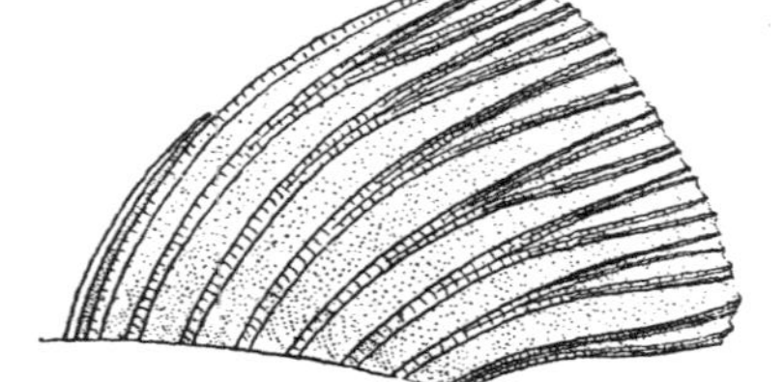

Fig. 3

Dorsal fin of Horned Dace, *Semotilus atromaculatus* (Mitchill), showing difference between rudimentary and developed rays and splitting to base of last ray.

Cæcum. A blind sac, or tubular diverticulum, connected with the alimentary canal. (Fig. 2, pyl.)

Canines. Conical teeth (in jaw) which are larger than the rest, as in the pike-perch.

Cardiform. Said of teeth which are coarse and sharp, like wool-cards.

Carinate. Keeled; having a sharp median ridge. Said of the belly of certain herring-like fishes.

Catadromous. Going down to the sea to spawn, as does the common eel.

Caudal. Pertaining to the tail or caudal fin.

Caudal peduncle. The fleshy (usually tapering) end of the body, between the anal and caudal fins. (Fig. 1, cp.)

Centrum. The body of a vertebra.

Chiasma. The union of the trunks of the optic nerves, in ganoid fishes. In teleostean fishes (recent bony forms) the optic nerves cross or interlace without uniting to form a solid chiasma.

Chin. The space between the two rami of the lower jaw.

Chondrocranium. The rudimentary cartilaginous cranial skeleton, corresponding to the primitive skull of cartilaginous fishes, of which traces remain in recent bony forms.

Clavicle. An element of the shoulder girdle.

Compressed. Flattened from side to side.

Conus arteriosus. A muscular and contractile bulb between the ventricle and the root of the aorta. It is furnished interiorly with one or more transverse rows of pocket-shaped valves to prevent a backward flow of the blood. (Fig. 2, aob.)

Coracoid. (See *hyper-* and *hypo-coracoid.*)

Ctenoid. With the posterior edge pectinated. Said of the scales in most spiny-rayed fishes.

Cycloid. Smooth-edged. Said of the concentrically striated (not ctenoid) scales of typical soft-rayed fishes.

Dentary. An element of the lower jaw, usually bearing teeth.

Dentate. With tooth-like notches.

Depressed. Flattened from above downwards.

Depth. The vertical diameter or distance through, as of the body or head of fishes.

Dorsal. Pertaining to the back.

Dorsal fin. The fin on the back, in front of the adipose fin, if that is present. (Fig. 1, d1, and d2.)

Ectopterygoid. A paired bone of the roof of the mouth. (Fig. 1 and Fig. 56, ecp.)

Emarginate. With a slight, shallow notch at the tip. Said of the caudal fin of fishes. (Fig. 7.)

Entopterygoid. A paired bone of the roof of the mouth, behind the ectopterygoid. (Fig. 56, enp.)

Falcate. Scythe-shaped.

Falciform. (See *falcate.*)

Fauna. The assemblage of animals inhabiting a region.

Filament. Any slender or thread-like structure.

Filamentous. Slender or thread-like; said of certain elongated fin-rays in some fishes.

Fontanelle. An unossified space in the roof of the skull, filled with cartilage or covered with membrane.

Foramen. A hole or opening.

Frontal. One of the anterior bones of the roof of the skull.

Fulcra. Spine-like structures bordering the anterior rays of the fins in ganoid fishes.

Furcate. Forked.

Fusiform. Spindle-shaped. Said of the form of fishes which have the body tapering both anteriorly and posteriorly, and but little or not at all compressed.

Ganoid. A term applied to scales or plates of bone covered by enamel. Those of the gars are examples.

Ganoid fishes. A name applied to the families of sturgeons, paddle-fishes, gars, etc. (See analytical key to the orders of *Teleostomi*, p. 13.)

Gill-arches. The bony axes of the gills. (Fig. 2, ug and lg.)

Gill-membranes. The thin wall of skin, supported by the branchiostegals, and closing the gill-cavity below. (Fig. 8 and 9.)

Gill-rakers. A series of tooth- or filament-like bony appendages placed along the anterior edge of the first gill arches. (Fig. 2, gr.)

Graduated. Becoming progressively longer in one direction. Said of the spines in the fins of certain fishes.

Gular plate. A bony plate imbedded in the skin between the sides of the lower jaw of certain ganoid fishes.

Hœmal spine. The lower spine of a caudal vertebra.

Heterocercal. Unequally lobed. Said of the tail of a fish in which the vertebral column is bent upward posteriorly. (Fig. 4, 5, and 6. See also note under c, of key to families, p. 1.)

Homocercal. Equally lobed. Said of the tail when the backbone stops (at least apparently) at the middle of the base of the caudal fin. (Fig. 7. See *heterocercal.*)

Hyoid. A bone in the floor of the mouth; tongue bone. (Fig. 57, hy.)

Hyomandibular. One of the chain of bones forming the suspensorium of the lower jaw (i. e., connecting it with the skull).

Hypercoracoid. An element of the shoulder girdle.

Hypocoracoid. An element of the shoulder girdle.

Hypural. The expanded last vertebra.

Imbricated. Overlapping, like shingles on a roof.

Infraoral. Below the mouth. Said of the teeth of the mouth disc below the œsophageal opening in lampreys. (Fig. 10.)

Infraorbitals. A chain of small bones below the eye.

Interneurals. The bones to which the dorsal fin rays are attached.

Interopercle. A bone of the lower part of side of head. (Fig. 1, io.)

Interorbital space. The space between the eyes on top of the head.

Isocercal. With the vertebræ becoming progressively smaller backward, as in the codfishes.

Isospondylous. With the anterior vertebræ simple. Said of the herring- and pike-like fishes, which lack the Weberian ossicles found in the suckers, carps, and catfishes. (See Weberian ossicles.)

Isthmus. The fleshy interspace between the gill-openings.

Jugular. Pertaining to the throat. Said of the ventral fins or vent when placed in advance of the attachment of the pectorals.

Keeled. (See *carinate.*)

Larva. The young of an animal, if differing in an important way from the adult.

Lateral line. A series of sensory muciferous tubes along the sides of a fish.

Leptocephalus. A name applied to the larval form of the eel.

Lingual. Pertaining to the tongue.

Lingual teeth. The serrated teeth on the "tongue" (i. e., at the opening of the œsophagus) in lampreys. (Fig. 10.)

Lunate. With a broad and shallow notch.

Mandible. The lower jaw. (Fig. 1, md.)

Maxillary. The posterior element of the lower jaw. (Fig. 1, mx.)

Metapterygoid. One of the chain of bones connecting the lower jaw with the skull.

Molar. With a flattened, grinding surface. Said of teeth.

Muciferous. Producing or containing mucus.

Muscular impressions. The visible diagonal lines or grooves marking externally the intervals between the muscle plates. (See *myotome.*)

Muzzle. The anterior extremity of the head.

Myotome. A muscle plate. (See *muscular impressions.*)

Nape. The part of the neck next to the occiput. (Fig. 1, np.)

Nasal. A bone of the nose.

Neural spine. The upper spine of a vertebra.

Notochord. The embryonic cartilaginous vertebral column, persistent in lampreys, sharks, and rays, and most ganoids.

Nuchal. Pertaining to the nape.

Obsolete. All but disappeared; only faintly apparent.

Occiput. The back of the head.

Ocellus. An eye-like spot.

Opercle. The gill-cover. (Fig. 1, o. See *operculum.*)

Operculum. A bone of the side of the head, forming the major portion of the covering of the gill cavity.

Opercular flap. A backward prolongation of the posterior angle of the opercle. (Fig. 62, 63.)

Opercular gill. A rudimentary gill on the lower inner face of the operculum in gars and sturgeons. It is a true gill, receiving venous blood, in which respect it differs from a pseudobranch. In the gars, in which there is both an opercular gill and an exposed pseudobranch, meeting at an angle on the inner face of the operculum, the opercular gill may be recognized by its inferior position and by the downward and backward direction of its gill-filaments. (See *pseudobranch.*)

Opisthocœlian. Concave behind only; said of the vertebræ of gars, which connect by ball and socket joints, as in reptiles.

Orbit. The bony eye-socket.

Ossicula auditus. (See *Weberian ossicles.*)

Palatine. A paired bone of the roof of the mouth. (Fig. 56, pl.)

Papilla. A small fleshy projection.

Papillose. Covered with papillæ.

Parietal. One of the roofing bones of the skull.

Pectinate. Having teeth like a comb.

Pectoral. Pertaining to the breast.

Pectoral arch. (See *shoulder girdle.*)

Pectoral fins. The anterior or uppermost of the paired fins. (Fig. 1, p.)

Pectoral girdle. (See *shoulder girdle.*)

Pelvic arch, or *girdle.* The bones to which the ventral fins are attached; pubic bones.

Peritoneum. The membranous inner lining of the abdominal cavity.

Pharyngeal bones. Bones representing a fifth gill-arch, behind the gills, opposed to each other, usually in several upper and one lower pairs, as masticatory structures, for which purpose they are, as a rule, armed with teeth. (Fig. 57, lph. and Fig. 56, uph.)

Physostomous. Having the air-bladder connected with the œsophagus by an open duct.

Plectospondylous. Having the anterior vertebræ modified and furnished with Weberian ossicles. (See *Weberian ossicles.*)

Plicate. With wrinkle-like folds.

Postclavicle. An element of the shoulder girdle.

Postfrontal. A roofing bone of the skull.

Post-temporal. The element of the shoulder girdle which connects it with the skull.

Prefrontal. An anterior roofing bone of the skull.

Premaxillary. The paired bone forming the front of the upper jaw. (Fig. 1, pmx.)

Preopercle. A bone of the cheek. (Fig. 1, po.)

Preorbital. A large bone lying in front of the eye.

Procurrent. Coming forward. Said of small accessory caudal rays encroaching on the caudal peduncle in front of the base of the caudal fin.

Protractile. Capable of being drawn forward. Said of premaxillaries which are extensible forward and are separated (when retracted) from the skin of the forehead by a groove.

Pseudobranch. A rudimentary gill-like structure, not functioning as a gill, developed on the upper inner side of the opercle, differing from true gills in the fact that it is supplied with arterial rather than venous blood. The pseudobranch may be exposed in the branchial cavity (as in the perch) or covered entirely by skin or hidden in the spiracular cavity (as in sturgeons and the paddle-fish). (See *spiracle* and *opercular gill.*)

Pterygoids. Paired bones of the roof of the mouth. (See *entopterygoid* and *ectopterygoid.*)

Pubic bones. (See *pelvic girdle.*)

Punctulate. Dotted.

Pyloric cæca. (See *cæcum.*)

Quadrate. One of the chain of bones connecting the lower jaw with the skull.

Ray. An articulated cartilaginous rod supporting the membrane of a fin. (Fig. 1, d2r. See *spine.*)

Retrorse. Turned backward.

Rudimentary. Undeveloped.

Scapular arch. (See *shoulder girdle.*)

Scute. A bony or horny plate.

Shoulder girdle. The framework of bones, in most fishes connected with the skull, to which the pectoral fins are attached, including the post-temporal, clavicle, postclavicle, hypercoracoid, and hypocoracoid.

Soft dorsal. That dorsal fin or portion of it which consists of soft rays only. (Fig. 1, d2r. See *spinous dorsal.*)

Spine. Fin rays which are unbranched and unarticulated, and, as a rule, more or less stiffened and sharpened apically. (Fig. 1, d2s. See *ray.*)

Spinous dorsal. The dorsal fin or portion of it which consists of unbranched, unarticulated spines only. (Fig. 1, d2s. See *soft dorsal.*)

Spiracle. An opening in the head, anterior to and above the opercular opening, representing a primitive gill-cleft, in paddle-fishes and in some sturgeons.

Spiral valve. A spiral infolding of the wall of the intestine in ganoid fishes.

Subopercle. The bone below the opercle. (Fig. 1, so.)

Suborbitals. (See *infraorbitals.*)

Subulate. Awl-shaped.

Supplemental maxillary. A small bone lying on the upper posterior edge of the maxillary.

Supraoccipital. The unpaired bone at the back of the skull, usually with a crest above.

Supraoral. Above the mouth.

Symphysis. The point of junction of the two parts of the lower jaw in front; the tip of the chin.

Symplectic. A bone connecting the hyomandibular and quadrate.

Swim-bladder. (See *air-bladder.*)

Teleost. A name applied to fishes which have the skeleton fully ossified, embracing most recent forms. (See *ganoid.*)

Terete. Cylindrical and tapering.

Tessellated. Marked with checks or squares, as in mosaic work.

Thoracic. Pertaining to the chest or thorax.

Thoracic ventral fins. Ventral fins which are attached far forward, nearly beneath the pectorals, the pelvic bones being connected with the shoulder girdle. (See key to families, bb, note, p. 2.)

Truncate. Cut squarely off.

Vent. The external opening of the alimentary canal; anus.

Ventral. Pertaining to the abdomen.

Ventral fins. The posterior or lower paired fins, corresponding to the posterior limbs in higher vertebrates. (Fig. 1, v.)

Vertebra. A single bone of the spinal column.

Vertical fins. The fins (dorsal, anal, and caudal) on the median line of the body, in contradistinction from the *paired* fins (pectorals and ventrals).

Villiform. Of the form of villi. Said of teeth which are slender and crowded closely together in velvety bands.

Vomer. The anterior bone of the roof of the mouth. (Fig. 56, vo.)

Weberian ossicles. A chain of small bones developed in connection with the modified anterior vertebræ and connecting the air-bladder with the ear in suckers, carps, and catfishes.

KEY TO THE FAMILIES OF ILLINOIS FISHES

a. External gill-openings, seven on each side; nostril single, median; no paired fins; mouth circular, suctorial; no true jaws...... **Petromyzonidæ.** Page 5.

aa. External gill-openings, one on each side, the gills covered by an operculum; nostrils paired; one or two pairs of fins not median; mouth more or less obviously a transverse cleft.

b. Ventral fins, abdominal* or wanting.

c. Tail evidently heterocercal.†

d. Body naked or with 5 series of bony shields.

e. Body naked; mouth horizontal...................... **Polyodontidæ.** Page 15.

ee. Body with 5 series of bony bucklers; mouth inferior.. **Acipenseridæ.** Page 21.

dd. Body with cycloid scales or rhombic (ganoid) plates.

f. Body with rhombic (ganoid) plates; dorsal fin short (of about 10 rays), posterior .... **Lepisosteidæ.** Page 30.

ff. Body covered with cycloid scales; dorsal fin long (of about 50 rays)......... ....**Amiidæ.** Page 37.

cc. Tail not evidently heterocercal.

g. A single soft dorsal fin, without spines, except in scaleless forms and in the carp, which has two pairs of maxillary barbels. (In forms with an adipose fin the ventrals are inserted distinctly nearer the anal than the pectorals.)

h. Vent behind insertion of ventrals when ventrals are present; body eel-shaped in forms without ventrals.

i. Head naked.‡

j. Body more or less completely scaled § (the scales small and sometimes hard to make out in eel-shaped forms); head without barbels or with not more than 2 or 4 (all maxillary).

k. Gill-membranes "free"¶ from isthmus, i. e., split far forward and meeting in an acute angle. (Fig. 8.)

l. No adipose fin; belly narrow, carinated; silvery fishes.

m. Lateral line present.................................... **Hiodontidæ.** Page 42.

mm. Lateral line wanting.

n. Last rays of dorsal fin much elongated; mouth small, low................. .... **Dorosomidæ.** Page 45.

nn. Dorsal fin normal, its last rays not elongated; mouth large, terminal, oblique. .... **Clupeidæ.** Page 47.

---

* In this key understood to mean that the first ventral ray or spine is inserted evidently nearer to the first (soft) rays of the anal than to the angle under the throat formed by a union of free gill-membranes, or (in case the gill-membranes are not free from the isthmus) to a transverse line connecting the lower corners of the opercular openings. Exceptions to the application of this definition are found in some species of *Gasterosteidæ*, *Pœciliidæ*, and *Percopsidæ* which do not come within our range.

† The heterocercal structure of the tail (i. e., the upward bending of the end of the vertebral column) is in all ganoids indicated externally by the obliqueness of the line of insertion of the caudal rays. This line forms a regular crescent, set at right angles with the horizontal axis of the body, in other fishes. In one genus of American ganoids (*Amia*) the line forms an irregular crescent, which is set, however, at a distinctly oblique angle with the horizontal axis. (Fig. 4-7.)

‡ Care must be used here, as the scales are often imbedded, or obscured by mucus. The edges of the scales may be lifted by a needle in these cases.

§ Except in a few forms, not found in Illinois.

¶ See note under **kk**.

ll. An adipose fin.......................................**Salmonidæ.** Page 50.

kk. Gill-membranes more or less broadly joined* to isthmus, not meeting in an acute angle. (Fig. 9.)

o. Ventral fins wanting; body eel-shaped..................**Anguillidæ.** Page 58.

oo. Ventral fins present; body not eel-shaped.

p. Dorsal fin of more than 25 rays, or shorter, and the lips thickened and covered with plicate or papillose skin; pharyngeal teeth numerous and comb-like ....**Catostomidæ.** Page 61.

pp. Dorsal fin of not more than 10 rays; lips usually thin, never plicate or papillose; pharyngeal teeth fewer than 8 on a side, in 1 to 3 rows............. .... **Cyprinidæ.** Page 94.

jj. Body and head naked (except in some tropical forms); head typically furnished with 4 to 8 long barbels (1 pair nasal, 1 pair maxillary, and 2 pairs chin barbels in fresh-water forms of United States)...**Siluridæ.** Page 172.

ii. Head scaly; body completely scaled.

q. Lateral line present; jaws shaped like a duck's bill.....**Esocidæ.** Page 205.

qq. Lateral line wanting.

r. Upper jaw not protractile...............................**Umbridæ.** Page 202.

rr. Upper jaw protractile (i. e., the upper lip separated from the skin of the forehead by an evident groove, which passes wholly across the muzzle). ....**Pœciliidæ.** Page 210.

hh. Vent jugular, in front of pectorals and close behind gill-openings; eyes more or less concealed beneath skin; ventrals ordinarily wanting.......... ....**Amblyopsidæ.** Page 217.

gg. Dorsal fin with either (1) a single spine (occasionally 2), in which case the ventrals are inserted distinctly nearer to the first ray of the pectorals than to the first ray of the anal and an adipose fin is present; or (2) with two or more free spines; or (3) preceded by a separate spinous dorsal finlet of 4 or more spines.

s. Dorsal with a single spine or preceded by 4 or more free spines.

t. No adipose fin; dorsal free, preceded by 4 or more free spines.............. ....**Gasterosteidæ.** Page 221.

tt. An adipose fin; dorsal, anal, and ventral fins each with a weak and rather indistinct spine ....**Percopsidæ.** Page 225.

ss. Dorsal fin preceded by a finlet of 3 to 8 slender spines..**Atherinidæ.** Page 226.

bb. Ventral fins thoracic† or jugular.

u. Ventral rays usually I, 7 (I, 6 or 7); vent in front of pectorals.............. ....**Aphredoderidæ.** Page 228.

uu. Ventral rays I, 3 to I, 5, typically I, 5; vent normal.

v. Chin without barbel.

w. Body scaled.

x. Anal spines 3 to 10.

y. Lateral line wanting......................................**Elassomidæ.** Page 231.

yy. Lateral line present.

z. Dorsal fins confluent, the spinous portion always somewhat lower than the soft portion; in forms with deep notch between dorsal fins, the highest dorsal spine but little more than half the height of the highest soft ray. ....**Centrarchidæ.** Page 232.

zz. Dorsal fins either (1) separate, and the soft and spinous portions about equally high; or (2) barely confluent, with the notch between them very deep and with the highest dorsal spine as high as, or higher than, the highest soft ray (marine forms not included)........**Serranidæ.** Page 318.

---

* In these forms the distance from the tip of the snout to the angle of the gill-membranes or to a transverse line connecting the lower corners of the gill-openings is greater than the distance from the same point to the back of the orbit.

† In all Illinois species of the following families (below **bb**) the ventrals are distinctly nearer to the throat (angle of gill-membranes), or to a transverse line connecting the lower corners of the opercular openings, than to the first anal spine, *except* in the deep-bodied genera of *Centrarchidæ*; in which, however, the ventrals are nearer to the throat than to the first *soft ray* of the anal.

xx. Anal spines 1 or 2, never more than 2.

z^1. Lateral line not extending on rays of caudal fin..........**Percidæ.** Page 269.

z^1z^1. Lateral line extending on rays of caudal fin............**Sciænidæ.** Page 322.

ww. Body naked, or variously armed with scales, prickles, or bony plates, never uniformly scaled.....................................**Cottidæ.** Page 325.

vv. Chin with a median barbel..............................**Gadidæ.** Page 330.

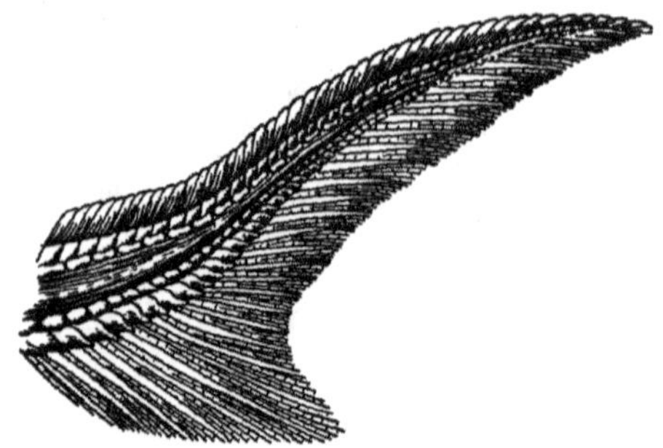

Fig. 4

Heterocercal tail of Sturgeon (*Acipenser*).

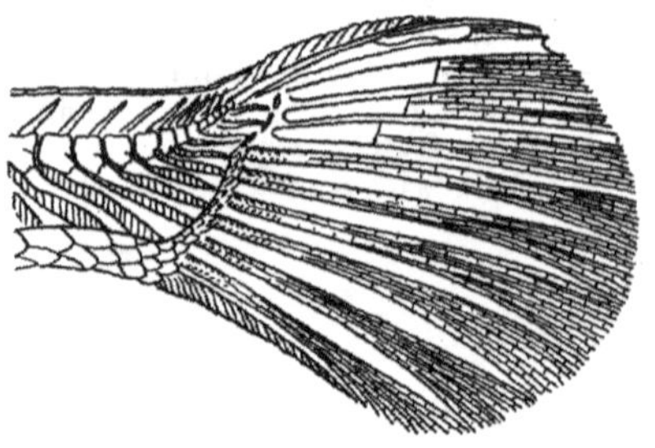

Fig. 5

Heterocercal tail of Garpike (*Lepisosteus*).

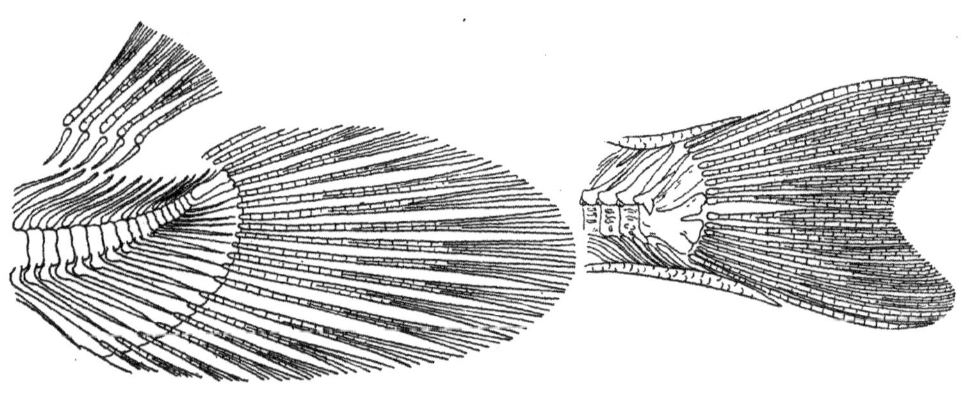

Fig. 6

Heterocercal tail of Dogfish (*Amia*).

Fig. 7

Typical homocercal tail of Pike-perch (*Stizostedion*). (After Jordan and Evermann.)

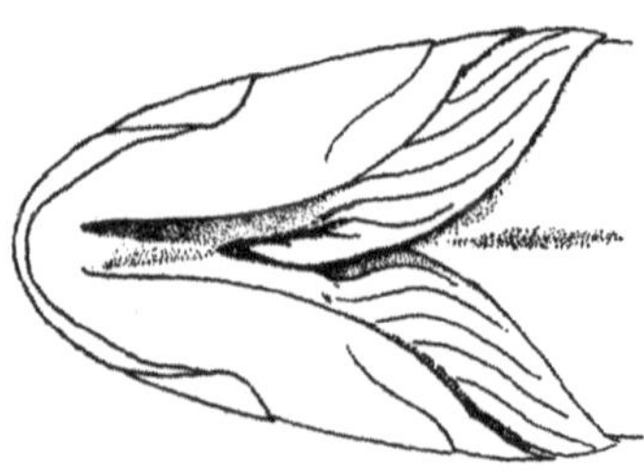

Fig. 8

Ventral view of head of Large-mouthed Black Bass, showing free gill-membrane.

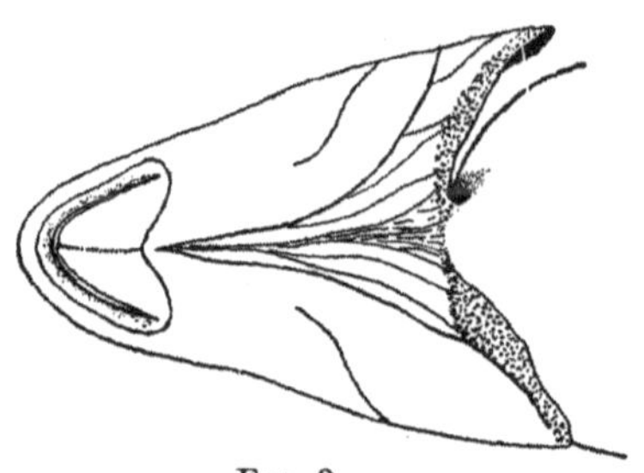

Fig. 9

Ventral view of head of Common Sucker (*Catostomus commersonii*), showing connection of gill-membranes.

Class **MARSIPOBRANCHII**

THE HAGFISHES AND LAMPREYS

Skull imperfectly developed, not separate from the vertebral column; no true jaws, no limbs, no shoulder girdle, no pelvic elements, and no ribs; gills in the form of fixed sacs, purse-shaped, without branchial arches; nostril single. Naked, eel-shaped animals, with a suctorial mouth, inhabiting both fresh and salt water.

Order **HYPEROARTII**

THE LAMPREYS

Nasal duct not penetrating the palate. This order is equivalent to the single family *Petromyzonidæ*, which follows.

Family **PETROMYZONIDÆ**

THE LAMPREYS

Limbless, eel-shaped, naked-skinned vertebrates of parasitic or modified parasitic habit, with a circular suctorial mouth furnished with cusp-like teeth suited for rasping; body subcylindrical forward, vertically flattened behind; skeleton wholly cartilaginous; skull imperfect, continuous with the vertebral column; no shoulder girdle, no pelvic elements, and no ribs; vertical fins with feeble rays, ordinarily continuous around the tail; gills 7 in number on each side, in the form of fixed sacs, and without true branchial arches, being supported by a wicker-like arrangement of cartilages known as the "branchial basket"; gill-openings separate, arranged in a row along each side of neck; nostril single, median, in front of eyes, the nasal tube not penetrating the palate; mouth suctorial, without true jaws; interior of buccal funnel (mouth disk) armed with horny teeth or tooth-like tubercles, these being simple or multicuspid and resting on papillæ; teeth immediately above and below œsophagus (on the so-called "tongue") more or less specialized; heart without arterial bulb; alimentary canal straight, simple, without cæcal appendages, pancreas, or spleen; intestine with a spiral valve; air-bladder wanting; generative outlet peritoneal, the eggs small and falling into the abdominal cavity; young undergoing a metamorphosis, the larvæ being blind and burrowing in the mud or sand.

These remarkable creatures are among the most peculiar in our waters,—peculiar in appearance, in habits and behavior, in structure, in taxonomic relations, in physiological activities, and in relations to nature. They are not true fishes, their primitive skeletal structures, the total absence of limbs and limb-bases, the very highly specialized suctorial mouth by means of which they attach themselves to their victims to devour their flesh and blood, their peculiar and numerous purse-shaped gills, and their single median nostril distinguishing them easily from the true eels and from all other fish-like vertebrates except their marine relatives, the hagfishes. From the hagfishes they are distinguished by having functional eyes in the adult, and by the fact that their single nasal tube does not open into the mouth.

Lampreys are found in the coastal and inland waters of the temperate regions of both hemispheres, most species passing a part of their lives in salt water. A number of kinds, however, live entirely in fresh water, and all spawn in fresh water so far as known. Species of *Petromyzon* are found along the coasts and in the rivers of Europe, West Africa, Japan, and North America, the great sea-lamprey of Europe and America (*P. marinus*) being represented in the interior waters of New York by a land-locked variety. Some four other genera are American, two of these (*Ichthyomyzon* and *Lampetra*) being found in our state or in neighboring waters of the Mississippi Valley and eastern United States.

The common names given to lampreys are numerous. They are called variously, in this country and in England, "lampreys," "lamperns," "lampers," "lamper eels," or even (by misnomer) simply "eels." The name "blood-sucker" is not uncommonly applied to them by our fishermen.

All lampreys are carnivorous, and most species, in feeding, attach themselves to the bodies of fishes by means of the sucking mouth, rasping off the flesh and sucking the blood of their helpless victims, which swim about unable to dislodge them. The ring-muscle of the mouth-disk works all the teeth at once against the selected surface, and both scales and skin are soon bored through. The relentless voracity of these fearful pests of our fresh waters is shown by the deep holes* which they make in the living bodies of their victims, and by their own intestines gorged with blood and flesh. Their hold is probably seldom loosened by any fish, unless by accident. The power of suction exerted by the buccal funnel, without the aid

* For photographs showing the work of lampreys see Surface, Bull. U. S. Fish Comm., 1898, pp. 209-215; and 4th Ann. Rep. Comm. Fish, Game, and For., N. Y., 1898, pp. 191-245.

of the formidable armature of cusps, is such as to require considerable force* to loosen it. Lampreys most frequently attach themselves to the side of a fish under the pectoral fin. Scaleless fishes, such as catfish and spoonbills, and the relatively sluggish soft-rayed and soft-scaled fishes, such as suckers and buffaloes, are much more subject to their attack than the more alert and better protected spiny-rayed fishes. The list† of species infested in Cayuga Lake, New York, by the land-locked marine lamprey (*Petromyzon marinus unicolor*) included practically all the fresh-water species which were not too small. The brown bullhead (*Ameiurus nebulosus*) suffered most severely, and the common fine-scaled sucker (*Catostomus commersonii*) next. Black bass were rarely attacked. The period of the lamprey's most destructive activity was in early spring—February and March.

Whether adult lampreys take any food except the flesh and blood of the fish upon which they prey is not certainly known. A common statement of the earlier writers that they feed on worms, insects, and decaying animal matter, probably rests mainly on hearsay and needs confirmation. Stomachs of Cayuga Lake lampreys examined by Dr. Gage in 1893 and 1898 contained nothing but blood and fragments of muscle. The presence of pieces of various small animals in the stomachs of lampreys, which has been only occasionally reported, is probably due to the complete perforation of the body wall and intestine of the infested fish. The charge sometimes made that lampreys eat the eggs of fishes has not been substantiated.

The breeding habits and development of the brook lampreys of both America (*Lampetra wilderi*) and Europe (*L. planeri*) have been studied in detail by various workers. The females spawn in shallow water, and, as a rule, where there is some current over pebbly or stony bottom near the headwaters of a stream. During the spawning process the females cling with their oval mouths to pebbles or stones, with the body streaming in the current, and are clasped at the nape by the suctorial disks of the males. The young lampreys burrow in the mud as soon as hatched. They are sightless at first, the eyes being

* Recent experiments by Miss Dawson (Biol. Bull., IX., 1905, pp. 1-21, 91-111) have shown that the funnel of a dead brook lamprey (*Lampetra wilderi*) becomes firmly attached to a perfectly smooth surface when merely pressed against it with the fingers. Her experiments also indicate that a lamprey is able to glide about over the surface of its host without loosening its hold.

† H. A. Surface, Fourth Ann. Rep. Comm. Fish, Game, and For., N. Y., 1898, pp. 191-245.

deeply buried beneath the skin. The mouth is toothless, and is not circular, like that of the adult, but the upper lip is of a squarish, hood-like form, and the lower one is much shorter and included within it. The food of the larval lamprey consists of microscopic organisms which are carried into the pharynx by currents of water produced by ciliary action. It is an interesting fact, first ascertained by Alcock*, that during the larval period the epidermis of the European brook lamprey (*L. planeri*) has the power of secreting a digestive ferment which protects the burrowing larva from the injurious action of fungi and bacteria. The length of the larval period is from 3 to 5 years. The period of transformation, during which the eyes move to the surface, the suctorial disk replaces the hood, and the teeth are formed, is 7 or 8 months—September to April according to Gage. It, is not known how long a period of parasitic activity intervenes between this transformation and complete sexual development in typical, parasitic lampreys. That spawning takes place but once and that it is accompanied by serious pathological changes in both parents, from which they recover with difficulty if, indeed, at all, is a belief long generally held. This is known to be true of the small American brook lamprey (*L. wilderi*), in which spawning and death are said to follow so soon after the transformation that the parasitic stage appears to be quite passed over in the life cycle, the adults not taking food of any kind.

The economic importance of lampreys as food for man and as bait, especially in the European countries, has been and is to-day considerable. In the earlier centuries they were highly esteemed as an article of food in England, France, and Germany, the French regarding as an especial delicacy stewed lampreys which had been first drowned in wine. In England to-day both the fresh-water and the marine lampreys hold a place among edible fishes, and in Russia extensive lamprey fisheries were still carried on along the Volga in 1873. Nets and wicker traps are used in the lamprey fisheries. As late as 1880 an extensive fishery was carried on along the lower Connecticut River, though this industry is now practically discontinued. Lampreys pickled and put up in tins may be obtained of our larger American dealers in fishery products, and are said to be of very fine flavor.

* Journ. Anat. and Physiol. norm. path. (2) XIII., pp. 612-637.

KEY TO GENERA OF **PETROMYZONIDÆ** FOUND IN ILLINOIS

a. Supraoral cusps 2 or 3 in number, placed close together; dorsal fin continuous, with a broad notch..**Ichthyomyzon.**

aa. Supraoral cusps spaced wide apart, one at each end of a crescent-shaped plate, which may bear a rudimentary median cusp; dorsal fin with a sharp notch..**Lampetra.**

GENUS **ICHTHYOMYZON** GIRARD

RIVER LAMPREYS

Supraoral plate typically armed with 2 or 3 (sometimes 4) separate teeth, set close together; anterior lingual tooth with a median groove; dorsal fin continuous, with a broad and shallow notch. Small lampreys, confined to the rivers of the Mississippi Valley and eastern United States.

ICHTHYOMYZON CONCOLOR (KIRTLAND)

SILVERY LAMPREY

(PL., p. 16)

Kirtland, '40, Bost. J. Nat. Hist., III, 342 (**Petromyzon argenteus**); id., l. c., 473 (**Ammocœtes**); Girard, '58, Pac. R. R. Surv., 381, 382 (**castaneus** and **hirudo**).

G.,VIII, 507 (**hirudo**); J. and G., 10 (**argenteus**); M. V., 10 and 11 (**Petromyzon castaneus** and **concolor**); J and E., I, 11 (**castaneus** and **concolor**); N., 52 (**argenteus** and **hirudo**); J., 70 (**Ammocœtes argenteus** and **hirudo**); F., 86 (**argenteus**); L., 7 (**concolor** and **castaneus**).

Length 10 inches; depth 9.8 to 13.8 in length; width of body 1.4 to 2 in its depth; distance from last gill-opening to front of dorsal fin 3.3 to 3.8 in length; last gill-opening to vent 1.9 to 2.2; muscular impressions (between last gill-opening and vent) 49 to 55. Color silvery, bluish above, sometimes with bluish spots; a small dusky spot above each gill-opening, usually conspicuous even in the larva. Head (to first gill opening) 6.5 to 8.3 in length; diameter of expanded buccal disk about ⅔ length of head, a double row of fimbriæ about the circumference of the disk, inside of which is a thin flexible lip; eye 6 to 8 in head to first gill-opening; anterior lingual tooth with a median (anterior) groove; supraorals typically bicuspid, occasionally with one, three, or four cusps; infraorals typically 7 to 9, occasionally 10, and in one of our specimens 13; extraorals, when supraorals are bicuspid, as a rule unicuspid, though this character is subject to much variation, instances of as many as 6 or 7 bicuspid extraorals having been noted in specimens with bicuspid supraorals.*

* A study of our 31 specimens of *Ichthyomyzon* shows an amount of intergradation in dental characters that makes impossible the separation of the nominal species *castaneus* (=*concolor*), as is evident from the following tabulation:

Supraorals.	*Infraorals.*	*Extraorals.*	*Specimens.*	
bicuspid	7	all unicuspid (*concolor*)	5	
"	7	1-7 bicuspid	5	
"	8	0 "	3	
"	8	2-7 "	6	
"	9	0 "	4	
"	9	6 "	1	
"	10	2 "	1	
unicuspid	7	0 "	1	
tricuspid	8	0	1	
"	8	3	1	*cas-taneus*
"	9	3	1	
"	10	6	1	
quadricuspid	13	8	1	

Dorsal fin continuous with caudal, with a perceptible depression in front of vent; greatest height of fin about ⅓ distance from vent to end of tail, height at depression about ¾ greatest height anterior to it, and about ⅓ to ⅔ height of posterior portion; the larvæ with the dorsal fin single as in adults.

Our 15 collections of this species are chiefly from the Illinois River at Havana, Meredosia, Ottawa, and Pekin. We have also 1 collection from Green River, 1 from the Wabash at Mt. Carmel, and several specimens from the Mississippi at Alton, and have records of the occurrence of the species at Galena, Cairo, and Quincy. It seems that lampreys are, on the whole, rather rare in our waters. Illinois River fishermen seem to know little of them. Fishes with lampreys attached, or with marks of their previous presence, are not common in the seine catches along the Illinois. At Alton they seem to be more numerous, showing their usual preference for spoonbills, which species is said rarely to be taken at Alton or Grafton without lamprey marks. At Havana also they are commonest on the spoonbills —sometimes two or three fast to a single fish—and next on buffalo-fish and carp.

At Galena and at Cairo lampreys have been seen by one of the State Laboratory assistants, Mr. J. E. Hallinen, attached to large catfish. We may consequently say that, so far as known to us, lampreys are not seriously injurious to the fisheries or the fish population of this state, perhaps because of the scarcity of suitable nesting places in our comparatively sluggish and muddy streams.

This species is found in the Great Lakes and the St. Lawrence River, in the valleys of the Ohio, the Missouri, and the upper Mississippi, and northward to the Assiniboin (*castaneus*).

Genus **LAMPETRA** Gray

BROOK LAMPREYS

Supraoral plate crescent-shaped, with a large bluntish cusp at each end, separated by a wide space, there being rarely a very small median cusp; lingual teeth small, with dentate edges, the median denticle enlarged; dorsal fin with a sharp notch or entirely divided. Small lampreys of the brooks of Europe and North America.

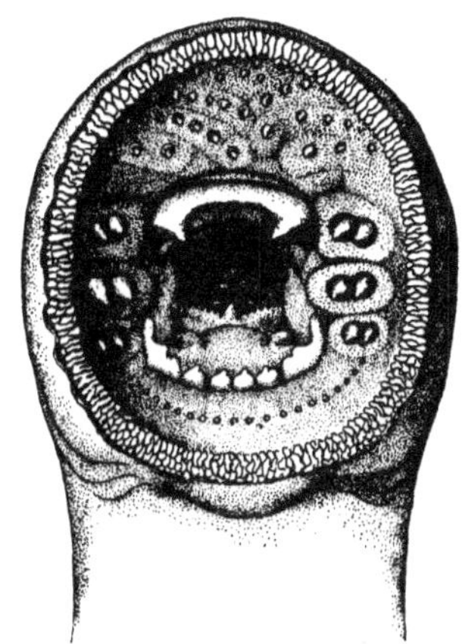

Fig. 10

Oral disk of Brook Lamprey (*Lampetra wilderi* Gage)

LAMPETRA WILDERI Gage

BROOK LAMPREY; SMALL BLACK LAMPREY

Rafinesque, '20, Ichth. Oh., 84 (**Petromyzon nigrum**; name preoccupied); Jordan & Evermann, '96, B. U. S. N. M., 47, I, 13.

G., VIII, 504 (**Petromyzon branchialis**); J. & G., 9 (**Ammocœtes niger**); M. V., 10 (**A. branchialis**); N., 52 (**P. niger**); J., 70 (**A. niger**); F., 86 (**A. niger**); L., 7.

Length 6 to 10 inches; depth 13 to 16 in length; width of body 1.3 to 1.4 in its depth; distance from last gill-opening to front of dorsal 3.4 to 3.5 in length; last gill-opening to vent 1.9 to 2; muscular impressions 70–73. Color bluish black above, silvery below. Head (to first gill-opening) 7.9 to 8.7 in length; diameter of expanded buccal disk less than ½ head; fimbriæ consisting of small and closely set tubercles, not arranged in definite rows, and densest on lower lip; no flexible lip inside fimbriæ; eye 6 to 7 in head; supraoral lamina with a large triangular cusp at each end, separated by an interval nearly twice the width of base of a single cusp; infraorals 6 or 7, a single cusp at each end of the plate larger than those (4 or 5) between; 3 lateral (extraoral) bicuspids on each side of mouth; remaining teeth simple, unicuspid, and rather weakly developed.* Dorsal fin consisting of an anterior and posterior portion, separated in adults by a deep notch (in breeding season) or divided by a narrow space; in larvæ the fin divided by a space equal to the greatest height of the fin; first dorsal about half the height of second.

Males with a long urogenital papilla, whose length in breeding season is equal to the diameter of the eye.

Here described from 5 specimens, one from Lake Michigan (presented by Dr. Jordan), and four from Cayuga Lake, New York (from Dr. Gage). A half dozen larvæ received from an unknown source in the winter of 1903, probably from within Illinois and in answer to circular letters of inquiry concerning lampreys, are doubtless of this species. Its almost total absence from our collections is probably a consequence of its small size and non-parasitic habit.

This species is known from western New York and the Great Lakes to the Ohio and Mississippi rivers and west to Iowa and Kansas.

* It is the belief of Gage ('93) and others that this lamprey is not parasitic in habit.

Class PISCES

FISHES

Skull well developed, separate from the vertebral column; a lower jaw, or both upper and lower jaws, developed; limbs typically present and developed as fins, in rare cases (*Apodes*, etc.) wanting through atrophy; shoulder girdle usually present, rarely obsolete; pelvic bones present (as a rule), absent, or represented by rudiment or vestige.—Bridge, *Cam. Nat. Hist.*, p. 475); gills attached to bony or cartilaginous gill-arches; nostrils paired.

The class Pisces as here defined, includes, in addition to the true fishes (*Teleostomi*), the sharks, skates, and Chimæras (*Elasmobranchii*), and the lung-fishes (*Dipnoi*). To the first-mentioned subclass belong all American fresh-water fishes and fish-like vertebrates above the lampreys. The relation borne to each other by the 10 orders of *Teleostomi* represented in the waters of the central Mississippi Valley may be expressed in the following analytical key.

Key to Orders of TELEOSTOMI

(The definitions following will in some cases not apply to species not occurring in Illinois.)

a. Tail strongly heterocercal throughout life; some fins usually with fulcra; arterial bulb muscular and with numerous valves (not less than 3); optic nerves forming a solid chiasma; air-bladder with a well-developed duct.

b. Skeleton cartilaginous; ventrals with an entire series of basilar segments.

c. Maxillary and interopercle obsolete; skin naked; air-bladder cellular. .... **Selachostomi.**

cc. Maxillary and interopercle present; skin with 5 series of bony shields; air-bladder simple.......... **Chondrostei.**

bb. Skeleton bony; ventrals with basilar segments rudimentary; air-bladder cellular.

d. Vertebrae concavo-convex; maxillary transversely divided into several pieces; scales rhombic enameled plates.......... **Rhomboganoidea.**

dd. Vertebræ double-concave; maxillary not transversely divided; scales cyloid.......... **Cycloganoidea.**

aa. Tail homocercal, diphycercal; arterial bulb thin, with a pair of opposite valves; optic nerves crossing, not forming a solid chiasma; duct to air-bladder slender or obsolete.

e. Ventral fins abdominal, if present, (the pelvic girdle being present and abdominal in forms which lack ventrals); mostly soft-rayed forms.

f. Mesocoracoid present except in eel-shaped forms; air-bladder with open duct when present.

g. Anterior vertebræ not modified, similar to the others, or more elongate, separate and not provided with Weberian ossicles.

h. Body not eel-shaped; vertebræ usually in moderate numbers; ventrals ordinarily present; mesocoracoid present........................**Isospondyli.**

hh. Body eel-shaped; vertebræ very numerous, 100 to 250; no ventral fins; mesocoracoid wanting..**Apodes.**

gg. Anterior (3 or 4) vertebræ modified, coössified and provided with a chain of small bones (Weberian ossicles), connecting the air-bladder with the auditory apparatus in typical forms; mesocoracoid present.

i. Parietals distinct from the supraoccipital; symplectic present; maxillary perfect or (rarely) wanting....................................**Plectospondyli.**

ii. Parietals usually fused with the supraoccipital; symplectic absent, maxillary imperfect, forming the base of a conspicuous barbel...**Nematognathi.**

ff. Mesocoracoid absent; body not eel-shaped.

j. Air-bladder with open duct; no spines in fins; shoulder girdle connected with the skull by a bifid post-temporal..................................**Haplomi.**

jj. Air-bladder with a rudimentary duct or with duct obsolete; dorsal fin with one or two rudimentary spines, with two or more free spines, or preceded by a finlet of four or more spines....**Acanthopteri** (with abdominal ventrals).

k. Air-bladder with rudimentary duct. (Suborder *Salmopercæ.*)

kk. Duct to air-bladder wanting.

l. Dorsal fin preceded by two or more free spines. (Suborder *Hemibranchii.*)

ll. Dorsal fin preceded by a finlet of four or more spines. (Suborder *Percesoces.*)

ee. Ventral fins thoracic or jugular, spines typically, though not always, present in the fins.

m. Pelvic girdle more or less solidly attached to the clavicular arch; spines ordinarily present in the fins......**Acanthopteri** (with thoracic ventrals). Including the great group of scombriform and perciform fishes and their allies.

mm. Pelvic bones loosely attached to the clavicular arch by ligament; fins without spines; tail isocercal, the hippural not expanded..........**Anacanthini.**

ORDER **SELACHOSTOMI**

THE PADDLE-FISHES

Skeleton chiefly cartilaginous; the notochord persistent and the vertebræ imperfectly formed, acentrous; anterior vertebræ single; fins without spines, the ventrals abdominal; a mesocoracoid arch present; a feeble suboperculum and a small rayed operculum; maxillary obsolete; air-bladder cellular, with open duct. Fresh-water fishes of large size, inhabiting rivers of North America and China. The order contains but one family, *Polyodontidæ.*

FAMILY **POLYODONTIDÆ**

THE PADDLE-FISHES

Fishes with smooth* skin, and with the snout prolonged and expanded into a thin flat blade or paddle; notochord persistent; skeleton chiefly cartilaginous, the vertebral column entirely so; the division into vertebræ imperfect; ventral fins abdominal; dorsal and anal fins far back; tail heterocercal, the caudal fin with fulcra; pectorals low; a mesocoracoid arch present; gills 4½; spiracles present; spiracular pseudobranch vestigial or obsolete; no opercular gill; a single broad branchiostegal; a small operculum present; suboperculum feeble and interoperculum obsolete; nostrils double, situated at base of blade; optic nerves forming a solid chiasma; mouth broad, terminal, shark-like, the cleft deep, and overhung by the paddle-shaped snout; border of mouth formed by premaxillaries, the maxillaries being obsolete; two pairs of minute barbels situated on the under side of the rostrum in front of the mouth; jaws and palatines, in younger specimens, with numerous fine deciduous teeth; intestine with a spiral valve; pyloric cæca present, in the form of a broad, branching, leaf-like organ; air-bladder cellular, not bifid, connected by a duct with the œsophagus; arterial bulb with several pairs of valves.

This family is represented by but two genera, each containing a single species. These are *Polyodon spathula,* the paddle-fish of the Mississippi Valley, and *Psephurus gladius,* found in the valley of the Yang-tse-Kiang in China. The latter species is said to reach a length of 20 feet. Fossil *Polyodontidæ* are represented by the head and caudal region of a form

* The upper lobe of the tail has a trace of the primitive rhombic scale-covering.

(*Crossopholis magnicaudatus*) discovered in the Eocene Green Rivers shales of Wyoming by Cope.

The fishes of this family, in addition to their growing economic importance in America, are of exceptional interest to biologists on account of their primitive shark-like* form and characters, and their consequent importance in tracing the descent of the bony fishes.

GENUS **POLYDON** LACÉPÈDE

PADDLE-FISHES

Gill-rakers† exceedingly fine, slender, and numerous; paddle broad and widening forwards; caudal fulcra† of moderate size, 13 to 20 in number. Represented by a single species, confined to the rivers of the Mississippi Valley in North America.

POLYODON SPATHULA (WALBAUM)

PADDLE-FISH; SPOONBILL CAT

Walbaum, 1792, Artedi Pisc., 522 (**Squalus**).
G., VIII, 346 (**folium**); J. & G., 83; M. V., 33; J. & E., I, 101; N., 51 (**folium**); J., 69 (**folium**); F. F., I. 2, 82 (**folium**), II. 7, 464, II. 8, 514, ff; F., 85; L., 7.

Body fusiform, little compressed; large fishes with a smooth skin and an elongate paddle-shaped snout; length 5 to 6 feet; depth 4 to 4½ in length without snout; caudal peduncle slender ,tapered, nearly cylindrical in cross-section, its least depth less than ⅓ depth of body. Color pale to dusky bluish olive; channel specimens (from Mississippi River) regularly lighter in color than those from sloughs. Head large, its total length including spathula and opercular flap 1.5 to 1.7 in length of head and body; eye to back gill-opening about 3 in distance from eye to base of caudal; spathula (from eye) 3.2 to 3.5 in length in adults, 2.3 to 2.8 in younger specimens (1 to 2½ feet); greatest breadth of spathula (near tip) 3.4 to 4.3 in its length, least breadth (near base) 5.3 to 5.4; a pair of minute barbels on under side of rostrum, at a distance in front of mouth about equal to width of rostrum at its base; eye small, about 5½ in interorbital space, situated nearly over tip of mandible and directed obliquely downward and sidewise; mouth very large, shark-like, its cleft equal to ⅔ distance from eye to back of gill-opening; jaws and palate with numerous fine teeth in young specimens; lower lip of spiracle with a small barbel-like lappet; opercular flap greatly elongate and tapering, reaching nearly to front of dorsal fin in half-grown specimens and almost or quite to the ventral fins in adults; gill-membranes connected,

* The American paddle-fish (*Polyodon spathula*) was originally described by Walbaum (1792) as a species of shark; and Rafinesque, who described the species under at least three different names, was misled once into an elaborate description of it under the name *Proceros* "a singular new genus of sharks."

† These characters separate *Polyodon* from *Psephurus*, the paddle-fish of China.

Brook Lamprey. *Lampetra wilderi* Gage

Paddle-fish, *Polyodon spathula* (Walbaum)

free from isthmus; gill-rakers long and slender and exceedingly numerous, in a double series on each arch. Dorsal fin posterior, nearly over anal, its insertion behind base of ventrals, on a raised fleshy base; dorsal rays 50 to 65; caudal heterocercal, but scarcely unequally furcate, the upper lobe with 13 to 20 well-developed fulcra; anal rays about 60. Body scaleless; tip of caudal peduncle and sides of upper caudal lobe with small elongate rhombic plates; margins of gill-openings, under flap, with numerous corneous shagreen-like denticles; a continuous lateral line of ramifying tubes from eye along upper part of head to base of caudal fin; upper and under side of paddle, top and sides of head, and opercular flap much sprinkled with sensory pits, distributed in small circular patches.

This is, on the whole, the most remarkable of our fresh-water fishes. Its large, paddle-shaped snout, of no very obvious use, and regarded by Kofoid as "an expanded sense organ" merely; its enormous mouth with weak and slender-boned jaws, very finely toothed in the young, but smooth and toothless in the adult; the elaborate straining apparatus borne on its gill-arches; and its dependence, although one of our largest species, on the semi-microscopic animals and plants of the plankton as the most important element of its food, give it a unique place in the classification and the economy of the fish population of our larger rivers.

It is found in the bayous, lowland streams, and rivers channels of the Mississippi Valley, northward to Minnesota and Wisconsin, and southward as far as Louisiana and Texas. It is not found in the basin of the Great Lakes, and is rare in any except the larger water bodies of its range. It is represented in our collections rather sparingly, coming only from the central and southern regions of Illinois (Ohio R., at Cairo, and Illinois R., at Meredosia and Havana). It is abundant in the bayous of the Mississippi about Alton. It is rather rare now in the Illinois River above Meredosia, though it was formerly abundant throughout the year as far north as Havana, where it is now taken only in spring. Its entrance to the upper Illinois is generally thought to be obstructed by the dams.

The paddle-fish grows to a great size. The largest on record, reported by Drs. Jordan and Evermann from Lake Manitou, Indiana, weighed 163 ℔. Mr. Wm. C. Harris records an example, from Lake Tippecanoe, Indiana, which was 6 ft. 2 in. in length, and 4 ft. in greatest circumference, and weighed 150 ℔. It is not ordinarily taken heavier than 30 to 50 ℔.

Various names in addition to those here used have been applied to this fish, the commonest of which are spoonbill, shovel-fish or shovel-cat, duck-bill cat, and spade-fish. Perhaps the earliest mention of the paddle-fish is by Pére Marquette (1673–1677), who described it as a remarkable fish, resembling a trout with a large mouth. "Near its nose * * is a large bone shaped like a woman's busk, three fingers wide and a cubit long, at the end of which is a disk as wide as one's hand." —*Jesuit Relations*, LIX., p. 111. Edition Thwaites.

Although the paddle-fish frequents waters with a muddy bottom, the relatively minute size of many of the objects on which it feeds, the absence of mud from its intestine, and its seeming preference for animal food, indicate that it is not only able to gather large quantities of very minute objects from among the weeds and from the muddy bottom, *without filling itself with mud*, but that it can separate the *Entomostraca* from the algæ among which they swim.

The facts concerning the food of this fish were first ascertained and published by the senior author in 1878,* and were studied again more extensively by him in 1888.† The paddle-fish is generally supposed by fishermen to live on the slime and mud of the river bottom, an idea confirmed at first sight by the general appearance of the contents of the alimentary canal, which are commonly a dark brownish semi-fluid mass resembling mud, but which, when placed under a microscope, are seen to be made up largely of countless myriads of *Entomostraca* of nearly every form known to occur in our waters. Mixed with these in varying proportion, often, indeed, predominating, are soft-bodied aquatic insect larvæ, chiefly those of day-flies, dragon-flies, and gnats (*Chironomus*), and a smaller percentage of adult aquatic insects, amphipod crustaceans, leeches, and water-worms (*Naidæ*), to which are added, in some cases, considerable quantities of aquatic vegetation, largely algæ, but including likewise fragments of various aquatic plants. In the food of eight specimens, obtained from Peoria, Pekin, and Henry, on the Illinois, from the Ohio at Cairo, and from the Mississippi at Quincy, in six years between 1877 and 1887, no fishes or mollusks were found; but insects and crustaceans—the latter mainly *Entomostraca*—made by far the larger part of the food, the insects being taken by all the specimens and in nearly twice the ratio of the crustaceans, neuropterous larvæ of day-flies (*Hexagenia*) alone amounting to 47 per cent. As these are com-

* Bull. Ill. State Lab. Nat. Hist., Vol. I., p. 82.

† Ibid., Vol. II., pp. 464-467.

monly creeping over the mud or swimming near the bottom, it is likely that this fish is usually a bottom feeder. One of our specimens contained nothing but insect food, the ephemerid larvæ above mentioned amounting to 85 per cent. of it. In another, 30 per cent. of the food was algæ belonging to the genus *Nostoc*; in still another, *Entomostraca* made 80 per cent. of the food, and in a second specimen, 95 per cent.

An explanation of the peculiar feeding habits of this species is to be found in its no less remarkable alimentary structures. The very remarkable straining apparatus borne by the gills, the immense mouth-opening, and the equally large gill-slits, provide for the rapid passage of enormous quantities of water through the gill-chamber, and for the thorough straining out of all contents available for food. The absence of any raptatorial teeth or crushing apparatus in its large and feeble jaws or in its throat makes it impossible for the paddle-fish to capture other fishes or to break the shells of mollusks, and it is dependent consequently on the stores of insect and crustacean life most commonly reserved for young or half-grown fishes. It thus becomes a rival, for food, of all the other species in our waters, living continuously upon objects which all of them must have for at least a part of their lives.

By observing its feeding operations while in confinement, Dr. C. A. Kofoid learned that "in swimming the mouth is held wide open, without the rhythmical respiratory movements common in most fishes, though it is occasionally closed energetically. The plankton is thus strained from the water by the long gill-rakers, and *Polyodon* is a living plankton-net. The fish was never observed to use the bill to stir up the bottom, or in any mechanical way. It quickly perceives plankton or ground fish added to the water of the tank, and, when feeding, circles repeatedly over the same path, at times dragging the lower fins upon the bottom."

In swimming slowly by the use of its caudal fin, its head and paddle are thrown alternately to the right and left, the tip of the paddle thus covering a considerable space on each side of the line along which it is swimming.

Little is known of the breeding habits of the paddle-fish. The young have been much sought by zoologists, but up to the present time none under 6 or 8 inches in length have been authentically reported. Females full of nearly ripe roe have been seen by different observers in this latitude in the latter part of

May, but the attempt to find their spawning beds has thus far failed. Dr. Kofoid reported a 30-℔ female taken moving *down stream* at Meredosia May 5, 1899, which had evidently completed spawning, the large ovary being flabby and spent. On the other hand, a male weighing 25℔, taken in Meredosia Bay, had the testes large and full of milt. It is a common belief of the fishermen that these fishes spawn in deep water, though the reasons for this view are not conclusive.

Dr. Evermann has recorded the paddle-fish's habit of swimming near the surface of the water during the spring run—a fact which is known to some fishermen*, and is taken advantage of by them in their fishing operations. At other seasons the paddle-fish is taken occasionally with set-lines.

Although long used and esteemed by the negroes of the South, it has not had, until recently, any commercial value. Small specimens weighing from 5 to 25 ℔, are now regularly sold, without head, fins, or tail, under the name of "boneless cat." It is said that the flesh resembles that of the larger catfishes, though perhaps inferior in quality. The fish is valued chiefly, however, for the roe, which is made into a good quality of caviar and sold for a high price. The caviar industry is chiefly carried on along the lower Mississippi River, in Mississippi and Tennessee. The paddle-fish catch of Illinois was in 1894 reported at 135,756 ℔, valued at $2,658; and in 1899 at 195,174 ℔, with a value of $6,210. The total production of the Mississippi Valley varies annually from 1,000,000 to 2,500,000 ℔, about 10,000 ℔ of this now being made each year into caviar.

* Mr. H. L. Ashlock, of Alton, says that he always fishes the upper portion of the water for spoonbills, and gets them when the other fishermen can get none, since few of them seem to know of this peculiar habit of the species.

Order **CHONDROSTEI**

THE STURGEONS

Skeleton chiefly cartilaginous, the vertebral column entirely so; vertebræ simple, acentrous, the notochord being persistent; fins without spines; ventral fins abdominal; a mesocoracoid arch present; opercular series represented by an operculum only; maxillary present; air-bladder simple, with a well-developed duct. Large fishes of the seas and fresh waters of northern regions. A single living family.

Family **ACIPENSERIDÆ**

THE STURGEONS

Elongate, subcylindrical fishes, with the head covered with bony plates united by sutures, and with the body armed with 5 longitudinal rows of bony bucklers; skin of sides between bucklers roughened more or less with small irregular plates or spine-tipped ossicles; skeleton chiefly cartilaginous, the notochord persistent and the vertebræ imperfectly developed; ventral fins abdominal, behind middle of body; dorsal and anal fins posterior; tail heterocercal, its upper lobe covered with rhombic scales; pectorals placed low; gills 4; spiracles developed in some species; an accessory opercular gill; spiracular pseudobranch small or obsolete; no branchiostegals; an operculum and an interoperculum present; no suboperculum or preoperculum; nostrils double, in front of eye; lateral line present, concealed, traversing the interior of the lateral bucklers; eyes small; optic nerves forming a chiasma; mouth inferior, protractile, with thickened papillose lips; four barbels in a transverse series on lower side of snout in front of mouth; no teeth except in very young; stomach without blind sac; rectum with a spiral valve; pancreas divided into pyloric appendages; air-bladder simple, connected with œsophagus by a duct; arterial bulb with several pairs of valves.

Sturgeons are widely distributed in the seas, estuaries, and rivers of Europe, Asia, and America, south of the arctic circle, most species being anadromous—that is, living part of the time in salt water and ascending rivers to spawn, as do the salmon and the shad. About 10 species of the genus *Acipenser* are found along the coasts and in the seas and rivers of Europe and Asia, being most abundant in the Black Sea, the Azov, and the Caspian. Five species are found in North America, two on the Atlantic coast, two on the Pacific coast, and one in the Great Lake region—one of the Atlantic species (*A. sturio*) frequenting the coasts of both Europe and America. The shovel-nosed sturgeons are represented in the waters of the Mississippi Valley by two species. Three species of the genus *Pseudoscaphirhynchus*, resembling more or less the American shovel-nosed forms, are confined to small tributaries of the Aral in Tartary. Fossil *Acipenseridæ* are little known, though numerous scutes have been described from Tertiary formations of Europe and America. Some species of sturgeon reach an immense size, specimens of the great Russian sturgeon (*A. huso*) having been taken weighing more than 3,000 ℔. *A. rubicundus*, of the North American Great Lakes, reaches a length of four to six feet. The smallest of the species of *Acipenser*, the sterlet (*A. ruthenus*) of Europe, reaches three feet in length.

Sturgeons are bottom feeders, using their hard beaks to stir up the mud in their search for food. Stomachs of sturgeon have been found to contain worms, mollusks, insect larvæ, small fishes, and aquatic plants. In feeding, the mouth is protruded downwards, spout-like, and thrust into the mud. The sensitive barbels and papillose lips doubtless assist in locating objects of food, although the intestines are generally more or less filled with mud, swallowed with the organisms it contains. Schools of sturgeon have been observed in clear water along the coasts digging up the soft bottom of shallows with their snouts, in search, no doubt, of mollusks and other organisms. Sturgeons are ordinarily captured with gill-nets and set-lines, though seines and pound-nets, set for other fish, are said to take them in considerable numbers.

Their breeding season is in spring, as a rule from the first to the last of May. The eggs of all species very quickly become glutinous and adhere to sticks, weeds, and other objects. The incubation period of the Atlantic sturgeon is about 7 days in water at 62° to 65° Fahr. The young live on the yolk alone up to a length of ¾ inch, and from that size to 5 inches they feed on rhizopods, algæ, *Infusoria*, and minute larvæ.

The flesh of all sturgeon, excepting the small shovel-nosed forms of Asia, is used as food, and from the eggs of the larger kinds caviar is prepared. If eaten fresh the flesh, except of young specimens, is usually found to be rather coarse and beefy, and in consequence sturgeon are as a rule smoked or boiled in vinegar before being sold Smoked sturgeon is now considered scarcely inferior to halibut, and the demand for it is increasing. The consumption of smoked sturgeon in the United States was given in 1898 as about 4,000,000 ℔ annually. The smoked flesh usually keeps only from one to two weeks. It is not kept in cold storage because of its tendency to mold. Sturgeon is canned on a small scale, and the roe, preserved in brine and sold in tight packages under the name of *caviar*, is an expensive food product highly relished by many. The method of preparing caviar is simple, the first essential being to work the eggs lose from the membranous tissue in which they are embedded. When once separated they are mixed with Luneburg salt, with a small addition of one of the ordinary preservatives. The eggs are then sieved and drained for 12 to 20 hours, after which they are ready for packing. Caviar is usually packed in small oaken kegs, although it is also sealed in small tins for the retail trade. The Russian output amounts to about 8,000,000 ℔ annually, most of it prepared on the Volga and the Caspian. The American product is about 300,000 ℔ annually (1898), about ¾ of it being exported. Sturgeon bladders are used in the manufacture of isinglass, and oil is made from the offal and softer parts. Sturgeon skin has been somewhat used of late for an ornamental leather. The skin is exceptionally durable and has been used for laces for mill-belts.

Owing to their great commerical importance, the artificial propagation of sturgeon has long been a subject of more or less nterest in this country and in Europe. Up to the present time, however, although the artificial fertilization of the eggs and the successful hatching of the young has been accomplished experimentally*, it has not been practiced on a large scale anywhere, the difficulty of obtaining ripe roe and milt at the same time, the adhesiveness of the eggs and their tendency to mold, and the difficulty of finding food for the young (which live on microscopic organisms), having proved serious obstacles. It has, however, been the opinion of all who have investigated the subject that if artificial culture were once undertaken, these difficulties would soon be greatly diminished. It may be said that the number of eggs produced by the Atlantic sturgeon is from 1,000,000 to 2,500,000 to a single adult female—a fact of much importance to its artificial culture.

* The eggs were fertilized dry by Dean (Bull. U. S. Fish Comm., 1893, p. 335), and then put into water and allowed to adhere in a single layer to a sheet of cloth stretched over a frame. They were hatched out in the current of the river, the loss by fungus being only 5 per cent. Artificial propagation was tried by the Germans in 1888 with fair success, and in America by Ryder (1889), who lost most of his eggs. Some success has been more recently obtained by the Russian government, operating on the Ural.

Key to Illinois Genera of ACIPENSERIDÆ

a. Spiracles present; caudal peduncle short, roundish, and incompletely armored; snout not shovel-shaped.......................................**Acipenser.**

aa. Spiracles wanting; caudal peduncle long, flattened, and completely armored; snout broad and shovel-shaped.

b. Ribs 10 or 11; gill-rakers 2- to 5-pointed; belly and breast wholly covered with subrhombic plates.................................**Scaphirhynchus.**

bb. Ribs 20 or 21; gill-rakers 2- or 3-pointed; belly and breast naked............ **Parascaphirhynchus.**

Genus ACIPENSER Linnæus

THE STURGEONS

Snout not shovel-shaped; caudal peduncle short, roundish, and incompletely armored; lower lip developed only at corners (2-lobed); spiracles and pseudobranchs present; gill-rakers lance-shaped; air-bladder well developed. Large fishes, numerous in all northern rivers and seas.

ACIPENSER RUBICUNDUS Le Sueur

LAKE STURGEON; ROCK STURGEON; RED STURGEON

(Pl., p. 36)

Le Sueur, '18, Trans. Amer. Phil. Soc., 388.

G., VIII, 338-339, 341 (**rubicundus, maculosus,** and **liopeltis**); J. & G., 87; M. V., 34; J. & E., I, 106; N., 51 (**maculosus** and **rubicundus**); J., 69 (**maculosus** and **rubicundus**); F., 85; L., 7.

Body elongate, rather slender, nearly cylindrical; depth 7 to 7.8 in length; size large, reaching a length of 6 feet and a weight of 100 ℔. Color dark olive above, sides paler or reddish, often with irregular blackish spots; color changing with age, the young drab and the adults green or red. Head 3.1 to 3.8 in length; snout narrow, subconic, strongly convex above, flat below, its length 2 to 2.4 in head (usually less than 2.3); interorbital space 3.2 to 4 in head; eye small, 3.3 to 4.2 in interorbital distance; width of mouth about ¾ greatest width of snout; lips 2-lobed, the lobes of the lower lip separated by a wide smooth space; barbels of nearly equal length, weakly pectinate on their outer edges; distance between two inner barbels greater than between each inner and outer; gill-membranes united to isthmus; gill-rakers 27+6, lance-shaped*, the surface of the arch between outer and inner rows of rakers rather broad and covered with fine papillæ. Dorsal fin with 35–36 rays, its insertion over tips of reflexed ventrals; anal rays 25–28; upper caudal lobe considerably longer than lower, but not produced into a filament as in the shovel-nosed sturgeons; caudal fulcra numerous. Dorsal scutes 12–16, lateral 32–43, ventral 8–10; skin of breast and belly and of sides between scutes more or less densely covered with small rough spinule-

* A single bifid raker was observed on the upper part of the first arch in one specimen.

or tubercle-like ossifications;* sides of upper caudal lobe sheathed with small rhombic plates.

This species, which is confined to inland waters, was formerly abundant throughout the Great Lake region and the Mississippi Valley. Lake sturgeon have of late years been steadily decreasing, and are now only rarely taken in the Mississippi on our own borders, and are seldom caught in the Illinois. Fishermen at Alton now see but five or six in a year that weigh over 10 ℔, whereas fifteen years ago forty or fifty large ones, weighing from 50 to 100 ℔, were taken each season.

The lake sturgeon is said to inhabit comparatively shoal waters in the lakes, ascending streams in the spring to spawn. The most extensive study of their habits has been made by Milner, who found their food, in the Great Lakes, to consist almost entirely of fresh-water snails (*Gasteropoda*). Crawfishes and insect larvæ are also eaten by them, and the eggs of fishes have been occasionally found in their stomachs, though not in quantity sufficient to justify the charge of destructive spawn-eating sometimes made. Lake sturgeon taken in the vicinity of grain elevators have been found with stomachs well filled with corn or wheat. They spawn early in June, generally preferring rocky ledges near the shores. While their spawn is probably subject to the depredations of other fishes, the young are well protected, after reaching two or three inches in length, by their spine-tipped bucklers. Adult sturgeons are much subject to attack by lampreys.

Previous to 1870 the flesh of the lake sturgeon was scarcely used. Fishermen generally made no use of them at all, and by many they were considered a nuisance and ruthlessly destroyed. In the following decade, however, several firms began the business of smoking lake sturgeon and manufacturing caviar, isinglass, and oil from the eggs, air-bladders, and viscera. Smoked lake sturgeon is now considered a superior article, and lake caviar is ranked as the best produced in the United States—selling (in 1898) for eighty cents a pound, while the Delaware product brought only sixty cents, and the South Atlantic fifty cents (Gill).

* Younger specimens are much rougher than adults; in a young sturgeon 10 inches long taken at Ottawa, Ill., each lateral scute has a peculiar flexuose keel or ridge in place of the characteristic central spine; and the ventral plates are similarly keeled. We have small specimens in addition which are perfectly normal in the character mentioned.

The artificial propagation of lake sturgeon was seriously considered by the United States Government in 1898, when a hatchery would have been established on Lake Erie or Ontario if a location had been found where spawning females and ripe males were plentiful enough to justify it. The Michigan Fish Commission hatched and planted 450,000 young sturgeons in the Detroit River in 1893, 130,000 in 1894.

The sturgeon fisheries of the Illinois lake shore, at Chicago, South Chicago, and Waukegan, were formerly of considerable importance, the catch at those three points in 1885 amounting to 101,362 ℔, or nearly as much as was obtained in 1899 from the whole of Lake Michigan. The quantity taken in 1899 was negligible, finding no place in the statistics. The decrease in Lake Michigan in the two decades ending 1899 is shown by the following totals:

1880	3,839,600 ℔.
1885	1,406,678 "
1890	946,897 "
1893	311,780 "
1899	108,279 "

We find no early statistics of the sturgeon fisheries of the Illinois and Mississippi rivers, though it is generally known that they have decreased greatly in the past 30 years. The quantity of lake sturgeon taken from the Illinois River in 1894 was 2,145 ℔, while the Mississippi on our borders the same year furnished 37,366 ℔. In 1899 the Illinois River product had fallen to 635 ℔, and in 1903 no lake sturgeon at all were reported from the Illinois. The total product of the interior waters of the United States, exclusive of the Great Lakes, in 1894 was 1,494,022 ℔, falling in 1899 to 234,145, and in 1903 to 142,059 ℔.

Genus **SCAPHIRHYNCHUS** Heckel

SHOVEL-NOSED STURGEONS

Snout broad and shovel-shaped; caudal peduncle long and flattened and completely armored; lower lip well developed, with 4 lappet-bearing papillose lobes; spiracles wanting; pseudobranchs rudimentary; gill-rakers 2- to 5-pointed; ribs 10 or 11; air-bladder 5 in length of head and body. Fresh-water fishes of the Mississippi Valley. One species known.

White Sturgeon, *Parascaphirhynchus albus* Forbes & Richardson

Shovel-nosed Sturgeon, *Scaphirhynchus platorhynchus* (Rafinesque)

SCAPHIRHYNCHUS PLATORHYNCHUS (Rafinesque)

SHOVEL-NOSED STURGEON

(Pl., p. 26)

Rafinesque, '20, Ichth. Oh., 80 **(Acipenser).**

G., VIII, 345 **(cataphractus)**; J. & G., 88 **(Scaphirhynchops)**; M. V., 34; J. & E., I, 107; N., 51 **(Scaphirhynchops)**; J., 69 **(Scaphirhynchops)**; F., 85 **(Schaphirhynchops)**; **L., 8.**

Body comparatively elongate; depth 6.7 to 11.7 in length; distance from gill-opening to front of dorsal fin 2.1 to 2.2 in length without caudal; length 2 to 3 ft.* Color pale olive, darker above, where the color is often a yellowish brown; belly whitish. Head 3.5 to 3.8 in length of head and body; rostrum comparatively short and wide, its greatest width 1.3 to 1.6 in its length; interorbital space 3.3 to 3.7 in head; eye 5.3 to 8.3 (usually less than 7) in interorbital space; mouth wide, 1.6 to 1.9 in greatest width of rostrum; labial papillæ well developed; barbels flattened, the anterior edge furnished with one, and the posterior edge with two rows of branched fringe-like pectinations; inner barbels 1.1 to 1.4 in length of outer; gill-membranes meeting at the isthmus in a rather shallow and usually quite obtuse angle, the membranes foreshortened, as a rule falling short of the notch in the pectoral shields; gill-rakers 12+5, 2- to 5-pointed on the lower half of arch, the upper surface of which is a narrow edge, scarcely separating the outer and inner rows of rakers. Dorsal rays 28 or 29, length of base of fin 12 to 14.3 in length of head and body; anal rays 17 or 18, ventral 21 or 22, pectoral 43 or 44; caudal filament very much elongated in younger specimens. Dorsal scutes 17 or 18, lateral 42 to 47 (usually 42–44), ventral 11 to 13; spines of dorsal and lateral scutes falling considerably short of their posterior edge; area on body between dorsal and lateral and between lateral and ventral series of scutes entirely covered with small, irregularly shaped scale-like plates; belly and breast completely armored, the plates subrhombic in form, becoming much smaller forward.

This fish is fairly common in the Mississippi, Ohio, and Missouri rivers, and in the other larger streams of the Mississippi Valley, being more abundant southward. Little is known of its habits. It spawns between April and June, probably ascending smaller streams for that purpose. The stomachs of two specimens studied by us were found to contain considerable quantities of a greenish gnat larva (*Ceratopogon*), a small number of nymphs of May-flies (*Hexagenia*), a single dragon-fly nymph (*Libellula pulchella*), which occurs on bottom mud in comparatively shallow water, and a few caddis-fly larvæ (*Phryganeidæ*).

* Of 41 males and 21 females recently examined by Dr. Evermann (Rep. U. S. Fish Comm., 1901, pp. 285-286) the average length and weight for females was 25.4 inches and 3.24 ℔, the largest female being but 29.5 inches long and weighing 4.75 ℔, while males averaged 21.7 inches and 1.89 ℔, the longest being 27 inches. These measurements are considerably under those usually assigned in the literature, and it seems probable that the species rarely reaches a length greater than 3 feet.

The flesh of the shovel-nosed sturgeon is now regularly marketed, being cut into steaks or smoked. At Louisville, where this fish is abundant and is taken in seines, the eggs are mixed with those of the paddle-fish and used for caviar. The shovel-nosed sturgeon fishery of the Mississippi and its tributaries yields now about 700,000 ℔ annually. The catch in the Mississippi on our border varies from 50,000 to 100,000 ℔. The Illinois River catch was 18,000 ℔ in 1899, but has since rapidly declined, and this fish is seldom taken now so far north as Havana.

GENUS **PARASCAPHIRHYNCHUS** FORBES & RICHARDSON

WHITE STURGEON

Snout broad and shovel-shaped; caudal peduncle long and flattened and completely armored; lips as in *Scaphirhynchus;* spiracles wanting; pseudobranchiæ obsolescent; gill-rakers 2- or 3-pointed; ribs 20 or 21; air-bladder 8 in length of head and body. Mississippi and Missouri rivers. One species.

PARASCAPHIRHYNCHUS ALBUS FORBES & RICHARDSON

WHITE STURGEON*

(PL., p. 26)

Forbes & Richardson, '05, Bull. Ill. State Lab. Nat. Hist., VII, 37-44.

Body comparatively short; depth 7.5 to 9 in length of head and body; distance from gill-cavity to front of dorsal fin 2.5 in length; length 3 to 4 ft.† Color very light, the upper parts bluish gray in life, the lower parts of the sides and belly shading from very light gray to almost milky white. Head longer and somewhat more depressed than in *S. platorhynchus*, 2.9 to 3.2 in length; width of rostrum 2.5 to 2.9 in its length, the snout narrower and more pointed than in *Scaphirhynchus*; interorbital space 3.7 to 4.2 in head; eye very small, 8.3 to 10 in distance between orbits; mouth larger than in *Scaphirhynchus*, its width 1.4 to 1.6 in the greatest width of the rostrum; papillæ of the four clusters of the lower lip reduced to a few flattened scallops at the hinder margin of the lappet; barbels doubly pectinated on the anterior edge, the posterior pectinations obsolete or wanting, the inner barbels 1.7 to 2.9 in length of outer; gill-membranes meeting in a full and deep and rather sharp angle, the membranes continued backward on each side so as to cover the anterior fourth of the pectoral shields; gill-rakers 10

* This fish is distinguished as the "white sturgeon" by the Mississippi River fishermen who are acquainted with it, the common shovel-nose (*Scaphirhynchus platorhynchus*), which is of a yellowish brown color, being known by them usually as the "switch-tail," in allusion to its long caudal filament.

† Our largest specimen of this species measures 43½ inches from tip of snout to base of caudal, its weight being 9¾ ℔. Mr. H. L. Ashlock, of Alton, says that he has seen specimens 4½ feet in length, with an estimated weight of 15 to 25 ℔.

or 11, + 3, 2- or 3-pointed on lower half of arch, the two rows of each arch separated by a broad smooth surface. Dorsal rays 35 to 43, the base of the fin 11.8 to 12.8 in length of head and body; anal rays 20 to 23, ventral 23 to 26, pectoral 43 to 49; caudal filament scarcely developed. Dorsal scutes 16 to 19, lateral 41 to 47, ventral 10 to 13; spines of dorsal and lateral scutes usually not far from even with their posterior margin; area between dorsal and lateral and between lateral and ventral series of scutes more or less densely covered with small denticulated ossifications, diminishing in size and abundance from above downward; some imperfectly formed plates along base of dorsal row of shields as far forward as the backward reach of the pectorals, these plates becoming more numerous and larger farther back, where they are continuous with those which roof the caudal peduncle; belly wholly naked to front of ventrals; breast with a few bony points similar to those on the lower part of the sides.

This species is known to us at present only from the Mississippi River at Grafton and Alton, Illinois. It is rare in the catches at those places, only one in three hundred of the shovel-nosed sturgeons taken belonging to this species. It is said by Mr. H. L. Ashlock, who first brought the fish to our notice, to be somewhat commoner in the lower Missouri. The spawning season is between June 1 and August 1. The sexual differences are unknown, all our seven specimens being males. The fish is said by Mr. Ashlock to prefer swifter water than the common shovel-nose. The stomachs of the seven types were nearly empty, and the greatly comminuted matter which they contained was wholly unidentifiable.

ORDER **RHOMBOGANOIDEA**

THE GARPIKES

Skeleton chiefly bony; vertebræ separate, simple, with the centra well ossified and opisthocœlous, i. e., connected by ball and socket joints, the concavity of each vertebra being behind; fins without spines; ventral fins abdominal; a cartilaginous mesocoracoid; opercular skeleton complete; maxillary transversely divided into several pieces; air-bladder cellular, lung-like, opening into the dorsal side of the œsophagus. Fresh-water fishes of North America. A single living family.

FAMILY **LEPISOSTEIDÆ**

THE GARPIKES

Elongate, subcylindrical fishes with beak-like jaws, and with the external bones of the head hard and rugose; body covered with hard, rhombic ganoid plates, imbricated in oblique series; skeleton bony; fins with fulcra; dorsal posterior, nearly opposite anal; tail heterocercal, in the young produced as a filament beyond the caudal fin; gills 4, a slit behind the fourth; no spiracles; an accessory opercular gill (hyoidean hemibranch); pseudobranch exposed, meeting the hemibranch at an angle on the inner side of the opercle; branchiostegals 3; opercular skeleton complete; nostrils near end of upper jaw; lateral line developed; optic nerves forming a chiasma; premaxillaries forming most of border of upper jaw; maxillary transversely divided into several pieces; both jaws with 2 (or 3) series of conical teeth, the outer smaller; vomer, palatines, and pharyngeals with small rasp-like denticles; tongue toothless, emarginate, free at tip; stomach not cæcal; pyloric appendages numerous; spiral valve of intestine rudimentary; air-bladder cellular, lung-like, somewhat functional as a lung, opening into the dorsal side of the œsophagus; arterial bulb with several pairs of valves.

Garpikes are abundant throughout the Mississippi, Rio Grande, Great Lake, and Appalachian regions, as well as farther southward along the Mexican and Central American coasts and in the fresh waters of Cuba. They are unknown (except as fossils) outside of the limits of the range given, being, as are *Amia* (the dogfish) and *Polyodon* (the paddle-fish), one of the characteristic features of the American fauna. But one living genus is known. Fossil garpikes of the genus *Lepisosteus* and of a related genus (*Clastes*) have been found in the Eocene of Europe and America.

The gars are voracious fishes, feeding to a considerable extent on the young of other species. They have no appreciable commercial value, and are treated as a nuisance and a pest by all interested in the fisheries.

GENUS **LEPISOSTEUS** LACÉPÈDE

GARPIKES

Characters of the genus included in description preceding.

KEY TO THE SPECIES OF **LEPISOSTEUS** FOUND IN ILLINOIS.

a. Large teeth in upper jaw in a single row on each side; size moderate, length seldom exceeding four feet.

b. Beak long and slender, its least width about 20 in its length, its length 2.6 to 3.4 in distance from eye to caudal; length caudal peduncle 1⅓ to 1½ (or even twice) greatest depth of body..............................**osseus.**

bb. Beak shorter and broader, its least width about 5½ in its length, its length 3.6 to 6 in distance from eye to caudal; length caudal peduncle normally not greater than greatest depth of body........................**platostomus.**

aa. Large teeth in upper jaw in two rows on each side; size very large, length 6 to 10 feet; beak short and broad, variable, its least width 3 to 5 in its length..**tristœchus.**

LEPISOSTEUS OSSEUS (LINNÆUS)

LONG-NOSED GAR; BILLFISH

(PL., p. 35; MAP V)

Linnæus, 1758, Syst. Nat., Ed. 10, 313 (**Esox**).

G., VIII, 330 (**Lepidosteus**); J. & G., 91 (**Lepidosteus**); M. V., 35; J. & E., I, 109; N., 51 (**Lepidosteus**); J., 68 (**Lepidosteus**); F., 85 (**Lepidosteus**); F. F., II. 7, 464; L., 8.

Size large, length over 4 feet; depth 10 to 13 in length including beak, 9 to 10 in distance from eye to base of caudal; length of caudal peduncle as a rule 1⅓ to 1½ times, sometimes as much as twice, greatest depth of body.* Color pale olive, silvery below; vertical fins and posterior part of body with round black spots, more distinct in the young; very young with a blackish lateral band, typically narrow and not extending on belly as in *L. platostomus*. Head (including beak) 2.7 to 3.1 in length; beak long and narrow, its greatest width about 6, its least width about 20 in its length; length of beak 2.65 to 3.40 in distance from eye to caudal; eye large, circular, 1.6 to 2.3 in interorbital space. Dorsal rays 8 or 9 (usually 8); anal rays 8 (sometimes 9); length of pectoral 8 to 9 in distance from eye to caudal. Scales 8 or 9, 60–63; 6 or 7; lateral line complete.

* We have found this the most reliable single character for separation of the very young of this species and the next.

This voracious, active, and well-protected fish is a notable winner in the long struggle for existence which its species has maintained, but it is a wholly worthless and destructive nuisance in its relations to mankind. It is the enemy of practically all the other fishes in our waters, and so far as it eats anything but fishes, it subtracts from the food supply of the more valuable kinds. It has, in fact, all the vices and none of the virtues of a predaceous fish. On the other hand, it is preyed upon by nothing that swims, and is so well adapted to the varied features and vicissitudes of its habitat that it is proof against any but the most extraordinary occurrences.

From its long cylindrical shape and its activity when alarmed, it is not as likely to be held by the fishermen's nets as most other fishes of its weight, and it consequently survives on our fishing grounds in very disproportionate numbers, and diminishes their average productiveness in no small degree.

It is distributed throughout the Mississippi Valley and Great Lake region and southward into Texas and Mexico. It is abundant also along the Atlantic slope as far north as New Jersey. It is scarce in the smaller streams and is generally more abundant southward. It grows to a length of five or six feet, and is so variable in form and color that local differences have given rise to a considerable number of scientific synonyms. In Illinois it is abundant and widely distributed, occurring in all parts of the state, including Lake Michigan. Our 35 collections were made from 14 localities, from Cairo to Chicago and the Rock River valley. It was taken in 9 of our collections from large rivers; in 2 of those from small rivers; in 4 from creeks; and in 15 from lakes, ponds, and sloughs.

The long-nosed gar frequents quiet waters, being especially abundant in those more or less stagnant. It occurs on both muddy and sandy bottoms, but has an apparent liking for logs and piles of brush. Although never moving together in schools, gars tend to assemble in large numbers within limited areas. In winter they frequently become so benumbed as to be almost insensible to their surroundings. They are of a sleepy habit and often lie motionless for a long time, returning persistently to the same place when disturbed. They frequently come to the surface, and thrusting their bills out of the water, open and close their jaws with a snap. This is the act of "breaking" so familiar to all fishermen, its purpose being to renew the air in the cellular swim-bladder. In "breaking" the gar turns partly over on one side, emitting a large bubble of air, after which it swallows and then sinks again below the surface. This habit is discontinued in cold weather, however, and from October to April gars do not come to the surface to breathe.

The gar is a voracious feeder and is especially destructive to minnows and the young of other fishes. The stomachs of specimens examined by Dr. Dean contained practically nothing but small soft-rayed fishes, less than 3½ inches long. Eleven small minnows were taken from the stomach of one male 24 inches long, and 16 from the stomach and pharynx of another 27 inches long. No perch or sunfish were found. Sixteen minute minnows have been taken by us from the stomach of a single specimen 2 inches long, while other young specimens examined, had filled themselves with water-fleas (*Scapholeberis mucronata*). The gar approaches its prey stealthily, and its attack is instantaneous and usually successful. Young gars have been observed to approach and seize minnows sidewise afterwards struggling for some time to get them into proper position for swallowing—as is the habit of lizards and alligators. The abundance* and destructiveness of gars in particular localities have recently led to serious efforts at extermination, and pound-nets have been found quite useful for this purpose.†

The long-nosed gar spawns in this latitude between the middle of May and the middle of June, the time at Havana, Illinois, being ordinarily from June 1 to 12 It is known to spawn in shoal water, usually in grass and weeds, but Captain Schulte, of Havana, has seen gars spawning about the stone piles of railroad bridges under construction at Havana. Young gars were reared by Dr. Mark, who found that they could be maintained entirely on the larvæ of mosquitoes. They are extremely interesting, and even beautiful, little animals, each marked with a broad black lateral band; and they are especially noticeable for the evanescent lance-shaped upper lobe to the caudal fin. They may often be seen swimming singly in shallow water along the margins of streams in June and July. Their earliest food is apparently *Entomostraca*, but they begin at a surprisingly early age their life work of keeping down the fish population of the waters they inhabit. A specimen only an inch and a quarter long, examined by us, had taken a minute fish, and another two

* It is stated by Dr. Dean that garpikes have been known to occur in such numbers in South Carolina as to fill the shad nets and interrupt the shad fishery for many days.

† By their use, Chautauqua Lake, N. Y., was practically freed from gars in 1896-97.

inches long and only an eighth of an inch in depth had filled itself with no fewer than sixteen very young minnows.

Gars are of practically no commercial value. Rafinesque says that their flesh may be eaten and describes the method of skinning—by splitting in a zigzag line between the bony plates. Dr. Dean has seen gars, with the bill cut off and the skin removed, exposed for sale in the markets at Washington, D. C. They are, however, almost universally thrown away by fishermen, and by most their destruction is rightly sought by all means that offer. Gar skins have been used to a small extent in the arts, for covering picture frames, purses, and fancy boxes, the rhombic plates being very hard* and taking a fine polish. A very few skins are saved for this purpose each year.

LEPISOSTEUS PLATOSTOMUS Rafinesque

SHORT-NOSED GAR

(Map VI)

Rafinesque, '20, Ichth. Oh., 72.
G., VIII, 329 (**platystomus**); J. & G., 91 (**platystomus**); M. V., 36 (**platystomus**); J. & E., I, 110; N., 51 (**platystomus**); J., 69 (**platystomus**); F., 85 (**platystomus**); F. F., II. 7, 464 (**platystomus**); L., 8.

Length 2 to 3 feet; depth 8 to 10 in length including beak, 6.7 to 8.2 (usually less than 7.5)in distance from eye to base of caudal; length of caudal peduncle normally equal to greatest depth of body. Color dark olive-green above, lighter toward lateral line; sides lustrous olive-buff, shading to light olive-yellow toward tail; belly white, the scales edged with fine dark dots; an evident dark spot and usually two or three fainter ones on caudal peduncle; fins olive-buff, dorsal, caudal, and anal each with several more or less distinct roundish black spots (more distinct in young); iris crossed by a dusky band which also crosses the opercle and is continuous with a broad but faint lateral band; coloration of very young (1 to 3 inches) generally much darker than in the preceding species, the black side stripe broad and extended more or less completely to belly. Head (including beak) 3 to 3.9 in length; beak comparatively short and broad, its greatest width about 2⅓ and its least width about 5½ in its length; length of beak contained 3.6 to 5.3 times in distance from eye to caudal; eye 2 to 2.4 in interorbital space. Dorsal rays 8; anal 8 (occasionally 9); length of pectorals 7 to 8 in distance from eye to caudal. Scales 9 or 10, 60–64, 6 or 7; a specimen (Ac. No. 24416) 3 inches long with lateral pores forming an open groove on posterior half of body.

The short-nosed gar is generally common throughout the Mississippi Valley, being most abundant, as is the preceding species, in the southern part of its range. It is distributed in

* It is said that breastplates formerly made from gar skins by Caribbean savages would turn a knife, spear, or hatchet. (Rep. U. S. Fish Comm., 1902.)

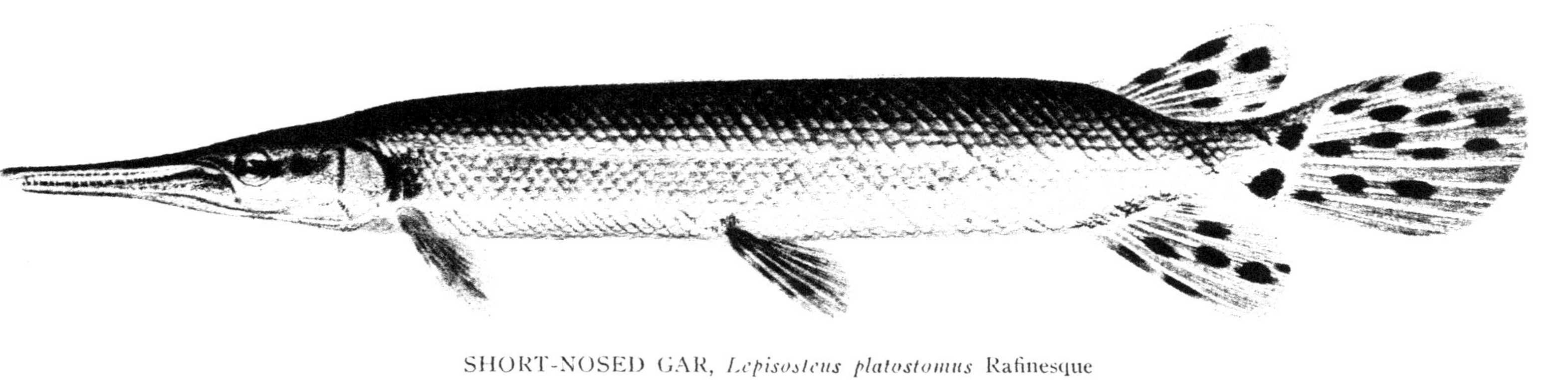

SHORT-NOSED GAR, *Lepisosteus platostomus* Rafinesque

BROOK LAMPREY, *Lampetra wilderi* Jordan & Evermann

Ammocoetes stage

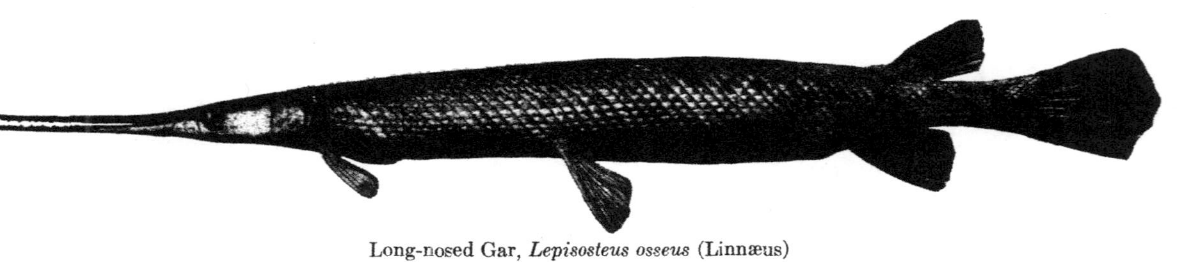

Long-nosed Gar, *Lepisosteus osseus* (Linnæus)

Alligator-gar, *Lepisosteus tristoechus* (Bloch & Schneider)

Illinois about as *L. osseus*, occurring in 57 collections, from Rock River, the Illinois, the Mississippi, and the Ohio. It is locally known by Illinois River fishermen as the "duck-bill gar," though the name "short-billed gar" is commoner.

The spawning season at Havana in 1898 was May, while in 1899 it continued until August. Females with spent ovaries were taken as early as May 10 by Dr. Kofoid in 1899. The habits of this gar are not otherwise known to be different from those of the preceding species.

LEPISOSTEUS TRISTŒCHUS (Bloch & Schneider)

ALLIGATOR-GAR

Bloch & Schneider, 1801, Syst. Ichth., 395 (**Esox**).
G., VIII, 329 (**viridis**); J. & G., 92 (**Litholepis**); M. V., 36; J. & E., I, 111; N., 51 (**adamanteus**); J., 69 (**Litholepis spathula**); F., 84 (**Litholepis**); L., 8.

Length 5 to 8 feet; depth in length 8, in distance from eye to caudal 7; length of caudal peduncle rather less than depth of body. Color greenish, paler below, adult usually without spots. Head (including beak) 3.7 in length; beak typically somewhat shorter and broader than in *L. platostomus*, its length about 5.3 in distance from eye to caudal, its least width about 4½ in its length. Dorsal rays 8; anal 8. Lateral line 56; transverse series 22. Description based on a mounted specimen 6 feet 6½ inches in length to base of caudal, owned by Mr. Sherman Reubel, Grafton Ill. Specimen 7 ft. 2 in. long in State Museum at Springfield. Specimen 5 ft. 6 in. long in University of Illinois Museum.

The home of the alligator-gar is in the streams of the Gulf of Mexico, from Mexico to Cuba. It ascends the Mississippi above St. Louis, and has occasionally been taken in the lower Illinois River. It is said by Dr. Jordan to reach a length of 20 feet.

Little is definitely known of the habits of this species. Many stories have been told of its gigantic size and ferocious and uncanny habits, some of them doubtless more or ess fanciful. A picturesque and valuable account of the habits of the alligator-gar by Geo. P. Dunbar, a Southern naturalist, may be consulted in the *American Naturalist* for May, 1882, pp. 383-385. Its size and strength are such that the ordinary apparatus of the river fisherman will not hold it unless it chances to be caught at some unusual disadvantage, and it is consequently rather rarely seen. Its powers of destruction must be enormous, and it seems to take, in the fresh waters of the country, the place filled by sharks in the high seas It was formerly made into oil, by the people of Arkansas, for use as a lotion to prevent attack by the buffalo-gnat. Dr. Meek saw numbers of this species in the markets at Tampico, Mexico, where it was regarded as a good food-fish.

LAKE STURGEON, *Acipenser rubicundus* Le Sueur

DOGFISH (Male), *Amia calva* Linnæus

ORDER **CYCLOGANOIDEA**

Skeleton bony; vertebræ amphicœlous, as usual among fishes, the anterior ones not modified; fins without spines; ventrals abdominal; a mesocoracoid; opercular skeleton complete; maxillary bordering mouth, not transversely segmented; air-bladder cellular, lung-like, opening into œsophagus. Fresh-water fishes of the United States and Canada. A single living genus and family.

FAMILY **AMIIDÆ**

THE BOWFINS

Oblong, subcylindrical fishes, compressed posteriorly, and with the head bluntish and its external bones corrugated and very hard, scarcely covered by skin; body covered with cycloid scales; skeleton bony; fins without spines or fulcra; dorsal fin long and low; tail slightly heterocercal; gills 4, a slit behind the fourth; no spiracles; no pseudobranch and no opercular gill; branchiostegals 10 to 12; opercular skeleton complete; throat with two peculiar comb-like appendages of uncertain function; nostrils double, the anterior with a short barbel; lateral line developed; optic nerves forming a chiasma; jaws equal, the lower U-shaped, with a bony gular plate between the rami; premaxillary not protractile; jaws and palatines with strong conical teeth; vomer and pterygoids with bands of small teeth; stomach with blind sac; no pyloric cæca; intestine with a rudimentary spiral valve; air-bladder cellular, bifid in front, lung-like, connected by a glottis with the pharynx, and capable of assisting in respiration.

These fishes are remarkable for the simultaneous occurrence of primitive ganoid characters—the cellular air-bladder, spiral valve, gular plate, etc.—along with marked features of resemblance to the modern isospondylous forms (herring and their allies). The species next described is the sole surviving representative of a once large family, chiefly represented to-day by numerous fossils. The *Amiidæ* first appeared in the Upper Jurassic of France and Bavaria (genus *Megalurus*), and fossilized remains of *Amia* occur in the Eocene of northern Europe and North America. The latter genus apparently became extinct in Europe at the close of the Lower Miocene.

Genus **AMIA** Linnæus

DOGFISH; BOWFINS

Characters of the genus included in description preceding.

AMIA CALVA Linnæus

DOGFISH; BOWFIN; GRINDLE

(Pl. p. 36; Map VII)

Linnæus, 1766, Syst. Nat., Ed. 12, 500.
G., VIII, 325; J. & G., 94; M. V., 37; J. & E., I, 113; N., 51; J., 68; F., 84; F. F., II, 7, 463; L., 8.

Length 1½ to 2 feet, females larger than males; body oblong, compressed posteriorly, back scarcely elevated; depth 4.6 to 6.2 in length; caudal peduncle deep and compressed, its depth 1.6 to 1.8 in its length. Color dark olive, somewhat lustrous above, lighter on sides and below, the mingling of lighter yellowish with darker olive areas giving the fish a more or less reticulated appearance; belly cream-colored; dorsal fin dark olive-buff, with two narrow longitudinal bands of darker olive crossing it, the first near base and second near free margin, a light space intervening between the two dark bands; caudal light olive with irregular darker vertical bars; at base of upper caudal rays in males a dense black spot* of elliptical outline with a yellowish to bright orange border; anal, ventral, and pectoral fins a brilliant apple-green, base and tips often tinged with orange; females in spring color are in general tones similar to males, but lack the caudal ocellus, the green lower fins, and the yellowish tints on the fins and sides of belly, their lower fins being dull olive-buff and the belly white; young specimens are lighter, bright apple-green, with dorsal and caudal tipped with a narrow black edging, and nose, eye, cheek, and opercle crossed by a narrow dusky stripe. Head subconic, depressed above, 3.5 to 4.3 in length; width of head 1.6 to 1.8 in its length; interorbital space 3.2 to 3.8 in length of head; eye small, 8.8 to 10.3 in head, 2.4 to .3 in interorbital; nose bluntly rounded, 3.2 to 4.3 in head; a pair of short nasal barbels, whose length is less than eye, cupped at tips; mouth large, maxillary reaching far back of eye, 2 to 2.2 in head. Dorsal fin with base twice the length of the head, the rays 47 to 51, height of dorsal less than ⅓ length of head; anal rays 9–10; caudal fin rounded (masked heterocercal); ventrals short of anal; pectorals very short, 1.7 to 1.9 in head. Scales "polygono-cycloid," 9 or 10, 66–68, 11 or 12; lateral line complete.

This species is abundant and widely distributed throughout the Great Lake region and the Mississippi Valley, principally in sluggish waters. In Illinois it is abundant in sloughs and lakes adjoining the Mississippi and the Illinois, and is found in the larger and more sluggish streams of the southern part of the state. It is not so abundant northward. Eight of

*A faint candal ocellus, apt to be overlooked, is present in females.

our 37 collections came from large rivers, 14 from lakes, ponds, and sloughs, and but 4 from creeks.

The usual local name of this species is "dogfish" in the Great Lake region and the upper Mississippi Valley. It is known eastward and southward oftener as "bowfin," or "grindle," the latter becoming "grinnel" in southern Illinois. It has been found by our collectors offered for sale by hucksters as "prairie-bass" in southern Illinois. The name "mudfish" is sometimes used eastward, and that of mud-jack, locally in Illinois. It is of general distribution in rivers, lakes, and swamps, but is most abundant in weedy waters. It seems to prefer rather shallow water, where, according to Dr. Reighard, it feeds principally at night, retreating to somewhat deeper water during the day. Dr. Ayres* found it in winter in Oconomowoc Lake, Wisconsin, in closely huddled schools in gravelly pockets among water weeds, so close together that two at a time could be impaled on a fish spear. In the early spring of 1894, when a rise in the Illinois River loosened and lifted the icy covering of the stream, a belt of open water between the ice and the shore was thickly packed, in places, with dogfish, so sluggish with the cold that they could be caught with the bare hands. In spring and summer these fishes are frequently seen to come to the surface to breathe, the exhalation being indicated by the escape of bubbles of air.

The teeth of the dogfish are sharp and strong and it is exceedingly voracious and savage, feeding upon any animals that come within its reach—chiefly fish, crawfish, and mollusks.

The food of 21 specimens, taken from all parts of the state in various months from April to September, was entirely animal—about a third of it fishes, among which were recognized minnows and buffalo-fish. About a fourth consisted of small mollusks, and nearly 40 per cent. of it of crawfishes. Insects, although commonly present, occurred in only insignificant ratio. Dr. Dean found scraps of meat and a lump of raw potato in the stomach of one of these fishes, but the latter was undigested. Charles Hallock (quoted by Dr. Goode)† says that an *Amia* has been known to bite a two-pound fish in two at a single snap.

The breeding period‡ of the dogfish is from April 1 to June 1 or July 1, varying with the season and the latitude. It

* Quoted by Whitman & Eycleshymer.

† Nat. Hist. Aq. An., p. 569.

‡ April 19 to June 1, estimate of average for four years (Reighard); April-May (Whitman & Eycleshymer).

spawned at Havana in 1898 between May 1 and 15, and in 1899 until July 31. Dr. Kofoid took freshly spent females June 14, 1899. Its nests were found by Dr. Reighard* in quiet bays or inlets, usually well grown with vegetation, places with stumps, roots, and logs seeming to be selected as a rule. The male builds the nest, usually at night, and probably unassisted by the female. For this purpose the vegetation is rubbed or bitten off and the loose rubbish brushed away with the tail and fins, leaving a bed of soft rootlets or of sand or gravel for the eggs. Spawning takes place more frequently at night than by day, the male guarding the nest after the eggs are laid. The eggs hatch in 8 to 10 days, according to temperature, and the young remain in the nest about 9 days, attaching themselves to rootlets by the adhesive organ on the snout, or lying on their sides in the bottom of the nest. After they leave the nest the male accompanies and defends the young, which move in a compact school until they reach a length of about 4 inches. The young, like those of the gar, have at first a lance-shaped temporary caudal fin, beneath which the permanent caudal develops, at first as an inferior lobe.

This fish is very little esteemed as food, the flesh being soft and pasty. It is said to vary in quality, however, according to the waters from which it is taken. The negroes of the South eat it with great relish (Goode), and it is often eaten also in Southern Indiana and southern Illinois by the whites. It is thrown away as a rule at Alton (Ashlock), but is saved by practically all of the Illinois River fishermen, by whom it is shipped to the cities, both east and west. Some large shipments from Havana have been made to New York City markets. The Illinois River furnishes very nearly the total product marketed in the United States. In 1903 a catch of 1,097,050 lb, valued at $10,972, was taken from this river and its tributaries, the Mississippi and minor tributaries furnishing the same year only 8,200 lb.

This species is as gamy as voracious, and is extremely tenacious of life, being "one of the hardest fighters that ever took the hook." Charles Hallock, as quoted by Goode, says that it will take frogs, minnows, and sometimes even the spoon, while Dr. Dean is authority for the statement that trolling for bowfish is becoming a favorite sport of some eastern anglers. The young, of about 6 inches length, are said by Hallock to

* The following account of breeding habits is mainly taken from Reighard ('00 and '01).

make excellent bait for pickerel and pike, living for hours on the hook. They can be kept "in a rain barrel all summer without change of water."

The hardiness of this fish and its willing endurance of conditions fatal to most species give it a predominance in our waters, which, combined with its numbers, activity, voracity, and wide range of food, make it, on the whole, a dangerous and destructive enemy to our fisheries. The time will doubtless come when thoroughgoing measures will be taken to keep down to the lowest practicable limit the dogfish and the gars—as useless and destructive in our productive waters as wolves and foxes formerly were in our pastures and poultry-yards.

Order **ISOSPONDYLI**

HERRING-, SHAD-, AND SALMON-LIKE FISHES

Skeleton bony; anterior vertebræ simple, without Weberian ossicles; dorsal and anal fins without spines; ventrals abdominal; an adipose fin present in some families; pectoral arch suspended from the skull; mesocoracoid arch well developed, as in the *Plectospondyli* and the ganoids, forming a bridge between the hypercoracoid and the hypocoracoid; opercle well developed; maxillary distinct, forming part of the margin of the upper jaw; air-bladder, if present, with an open duct; gills 4, a slit behind the fourth, as normally in bony fishes.

A large and widely distributed group, including most of the marine soft-rayed fishes, excepting deep-sea forms and a limited number of fresh-water species. Families numerous; 4 represented in Illinois. Members of some families possess strong ganoid affinities, a gular plate and two transverse series of arterial valves occurring in *Albula*. Fossil remains abundant.

Key to Families of **ISOSPONDYLI** found in Illinois

a. No adipose fin; belly narrow, carinated; silvery fishes.
b. Lateral line present.. **Hiodontidæ.**
bb. Lateral line wanting.
c. Last rays of dorsal much elongated; mouth small, low............ **Dorosomidæ.**
cc. Dorsal fin normal, its last rays not elongate (elongate in some marine forms); mouth large, terminal, oblique.................................. **Clupeidæ.**
aa. An adipose fin; belly not carinated............................ **Salmonidæ.**

Family **HIODONTIDÆ**

THE MOONEYES

Body rather deep and much compressed, covered with silvery cycloid scales; head naked; belly not serrate; lateral line developed; skeleton bony; vertebræ about 60, the anterior not modified, ventral fins abdominal; dorsal fin rather posterior; no adipose fin; caudal forked; mesocoracoid present; gill-membranes free from isthmus; branchiostegals 8 to 10; pseudobranchiæ obsolete; gill-rakers few, short, and thick; adipose eyelid little developed; mouth terminal, oblique; premaxillary not protractile; maxillary small, articulated to end of premaxillary and forming lateral margin of upper jaw; sides of lower jaw fitting within the upper so that the dentaries shut against the palatines; premaxillaries, maxillaries, and dentaries, vomer, palatines, sphenoid, pterygoids, and tongue with small cardiform teeth; stomach horseshoe-shaped, without blind sac; one pyloric cæcum; air-bladder large, with open duct; no oviducts, the eggs falling into the abdominal cavity before exclusion.

Fresh waters of North America; a single genus known. The species are of little value as food.

Genus **HIODON** Le Sueur

MOONEYES

Characters of genus included above. Three species; two found in Illinois.

Key to the Species of **HIODON** found in Illinois

a. Belly in front of ventrals carinated; dorsal with 9 developed rays, inserted behind ventrals; eye less than interorbital space....................**alosoides.**

aa. Belly in front of ventrals not carinated; dorsal with 11 or 12 developed rays, inserted in front of ventrals; eye greater than interorbital space....**tergisus.**

HIODON ALOSOIDES (Rafinesque)

NORTHERN MOONEYE

Rafinesque, 1819, J. Phys., 421 (**Amphiodon alveoides, misprint**).
J. & G., 259 (**Hyodon**); M. V., 69; J. & E., I, 413; F., 74 (**Hyodon**); L., 20.

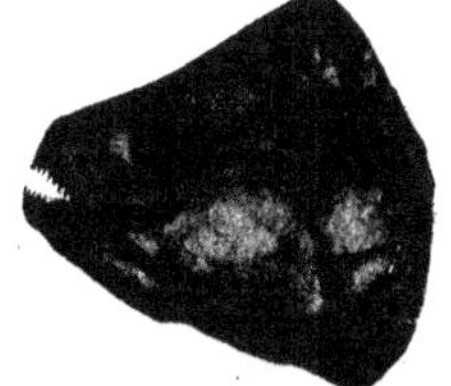

Fig. 11

Length 12 inches; body greatly compressed, greatest width often 3 in adults; depth in length 3.3 to 3.7; depth caudal peduncle 1.1 to 1.4 in its length. Color bluish above; sides and belly silvery with more or less golden luster forward and bluish to pinkish farther back. Head 4.5 to 4.9; width head 1.9 to 2.1 in its length; interorbital space 3.6 to 4 in head; eye 3.6 to 4; nose 4.9 to 5.9, more noticeably upturned than in the next species; mouth large, maxillary reaching past middle of orbit, 1.9 to 2.1 in head. Dorsal fin with 9 developed rays, inserted behind front of anal; anal rays 31; ventrals very short, about 1¾ in head; pectorals longer than in the next species, 1.1 to 1.2 in head. Scales 6, 56–58, 7 or 8; lateral line complete.

This rather large and handsome silver-coated fish is now too rare in Illinois to have any especial significance in our waters.

Some years ago it was much more abundant than now in the Mississippi and the Ohio, as many as a thousand pounds at a time having been caught, according to Mr. Ashlock, from the former river near Alton and the latter at Cairo. This species ranges from the Ohio through the Great Lake region to the Saskatchewan, becoming especially abundant in Manitoba and other parts of British America. Our nine collections came from the Illinois River at Meredosia and Havana, excepting one, which was from the Ohio at Cairo. It is found only in our largest streams, and is commonest in rather swift open water. It is readily caught when plentiful by minnow bait, and is a very gamy fish, although of little value as food. It lives mainly on both terrestrial and aquatic insects, mollusks, and small minnows. It is said by Illinois fishermen to be frequently seen pursuing its minnow prey at evening in the vicinity of their boats.

HIODON TERGISUS Le Sueur

TOOTHED HERRING; MOONEYE

Le Sueur, 1818, J. Ac. Nat. Sci. Phila., I, 366.
G., VII, 375 (**Hyodon**); J. & G., 260 (**Hyodon**); M. V., 69; J. & E., I, 413; N. 44 (**Hyodon**); J., 54 (**Hyodon**); F., 74 (**Hyodon**); F. F., I. 2, 79, II. 7, 440; L., 20.

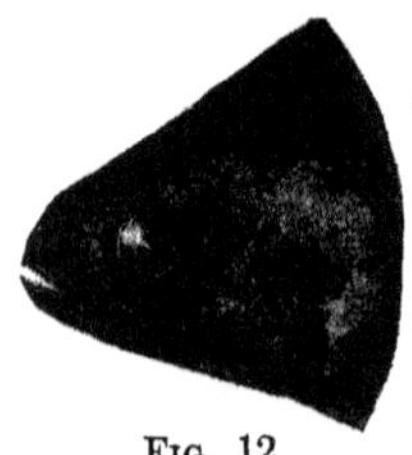

Fig. 12

Length 10 or 12 inches; body somewhat less compressed than in the last species, greatest width not over $2\frac{1}{2}$ in depth; depth in length 3 to 3.3; depth caudal peduncle 1.4 in its length. Color pale olive-buff above with faint steel-blue luster; sides silvery, lustrous, white at the ventral edge. Head 4 to 4.4 in length; width head 2 to 2.1; interorbital space 3.9 to 4; eye 2.8 to 3.6 in head; nose 4. to 5.5; mouth slightly smaller than in the last, maxillary falling short of middle of orbit, 2.1 to 2.5 in head. Dorsal fin with 11 or 12 developed rays, inserted in front of anal. Scales 5 or 6, 55, 7; lateral line complete.

The toothed herring—a name given this species by way of contrast with the "thread-herring" or gizzard-shad (*Dorosoma*)—has been taken by us only some half dozen times in Illinois, and then only in the Rock and Illinois rivers. It ranges from the Ohio River north and west to the Lake of the Woods, the Assiniboin, and the Saskatchewan. It is very abundant in Lake Erie and the Ohio, where large numbers are sometimes caught with the seine. It feeds on insects and their larvæ, mollusks, and small minnows. It is a vigorous biter, and gamy

TOOTHED HERRING, *Hiodon tergisus* Le Sueur

GRASS PIKE, *Esox vermiculatus* Le Sueur

on the hook. Dr. Estes says that it will rise to the fly, coming up for it, testing it, and getting away again almost before the angler can strike. It seems not to be valued as food, and is too rare in our waters to have any commercial importance.

Family **DOROSOMIDÆ**

THE GIZZARD-SHAD

Body short and deep and much compressed, covered with thin cycloid scales; head naked; belly sharp-edged, armed with bony serratures; no lateral line; skelton bony; vertebræ 49; anterior vertebræ not modified; ventral fins abdominal; dorsal about midway of body, its last ray prolonged and filiform; no adipose fin; pectorals and ventrals with an accessory scale; caudal forked; mesocoracoid present; gill-membranes free from isthmus; branchiostegals about 6; gill-rakers slender and exceedingly numerous; pseudobranchiæ large; adipose eyelid present; mouth rather inferior, oblique; premaxillary non-protractile; maxillary with supplemental bone, narrow and short, forming but a small portion of the lateral margin of the upper jaw; no teeth; stomach short, muscular, like the gizzard of a fowl.

Coasts and rivers of warm regions; two genera in American waters. Thin-bodied, bony fishes, of little value as food.

Genus **DOROSOMA** Rafinesque

GIZZARD-SHAD

Characters of genus included above. Lower Mississippi Valley and streams of Gulf coast as far south as Yucatan. A single species found in the waters of Illinois.

DOROSOMA CEPEDIANUM (Le Sueur)

GIZZARD-SHAD; HICKORY-SHAD

(Pl., p. 46; Map VIII)

Le Sueur, 1818, Journ. Acad. Nat. Sci. Phila., I, 361 (**Megalops**).
G., VII, 409 (**Chatoëssus**); J. & G., 271; M. V., 74; J. & E., I, 416; N., 44 (**notatum**); J., 55; F., 73; F. F., I. 2, 79 (**var. heterurum**); II. 7, 437, II. 8, 528, ff; L. 20.

Length usually not over 12 inches*; body deep and considerably compressed, depth 2.6 to 2.9 in length; greatest width 3½ in depth in adults; caudal peduncle short and deep, its depth in its length 1.1 to 1.3 Color silvery, bluish above, with reddish and brassy reflections; a large dark spot behind opercle in the young; fins more or less dusky. Head deep posteriorly

* Specimens 15 to 18 inches, weighing about 3 pounds, occasionally taken from the Mississippi at Alton. (H. L. Ashlock.)

and tapering forward, 3.7 to 4.3 in length; width of head 1.9 to 2.2 in its length; interorbital greater than eye, 3.6 to 4.3 in head; eye 3.4 to 4.8 in head; nose shorter than eye, 4.9 to 6.1 in head; mouth small, more or less inferior, extending little back of front of eye; maxillary 3.4 to 4.2 in head; lower jaw shorter than upper. Dorsal fin about midway between muzzle and base of caudal, slightly behind ventrals, of 12 rays; last dorsal ray greatly elongated, extending past middle of anal; anal rays 30 or 31; pectorals 1.2 to 1.5 in head; ventrals half way to front of anal in adults. Scales 56 to 57, transverse series 23; no lateral line; ventral scutes 19 (before ventrals), 12 or 13 (behind ventrals).

This immensely abundant species, although little esteemed as a food fish, is one of the most useful in our waters because of the almost exhaustless food supply which it offers to all the game fishes of our larger streams and lowland lakes. Living itself mainly upon food derived from the muddy bottoms of our very muddy rivers and lakes, it serves as a means of converting this mere waste of nature into the flesh of our most highly valued fishes.

For this service it is especially adapted by the possession of a very effective straining apparatus in its gills, by means of which it separates the finest particles of silt from objects large enough to serve it as food, and by the extraordinary development of its digestive surface in a long and convoluted small intestine, thickly beset with finger-like villi within, and with tubular cæca without, each of which is closed at its outer end and pours into the intestine through its inner opening the digestive juices which it is the function of these organs to secrete. The thick-walled muscular stomach, resembling the gizzard of a bird—whence its name of gizzard-shad—is another adaptation to a kind of food not available to most other fishes.

It occurs throughout the Mississippi Valley, in brackish waters along the Atlantic and the Gulf as far as Mexico, and in the streams and lakes of the Mississippi Valley. In Illinois the gizzard-shad inhabits all our larger rivers, together with the lakes connected with them, sometimes ascending smaller tributaries during the season of the spawning migration, and it has also made its way, by means of canals, into lakes Erie and Michigan. In summer it is a rather active fish, sometimes darting rapidly about in all directions and often leaping out of the water. When surrounded by the seine, it is likely to escape in schools by skipping lightly over the cork line. In winter it withdraws largely to the deeper waters, where it hibernates in a benumbed condition.

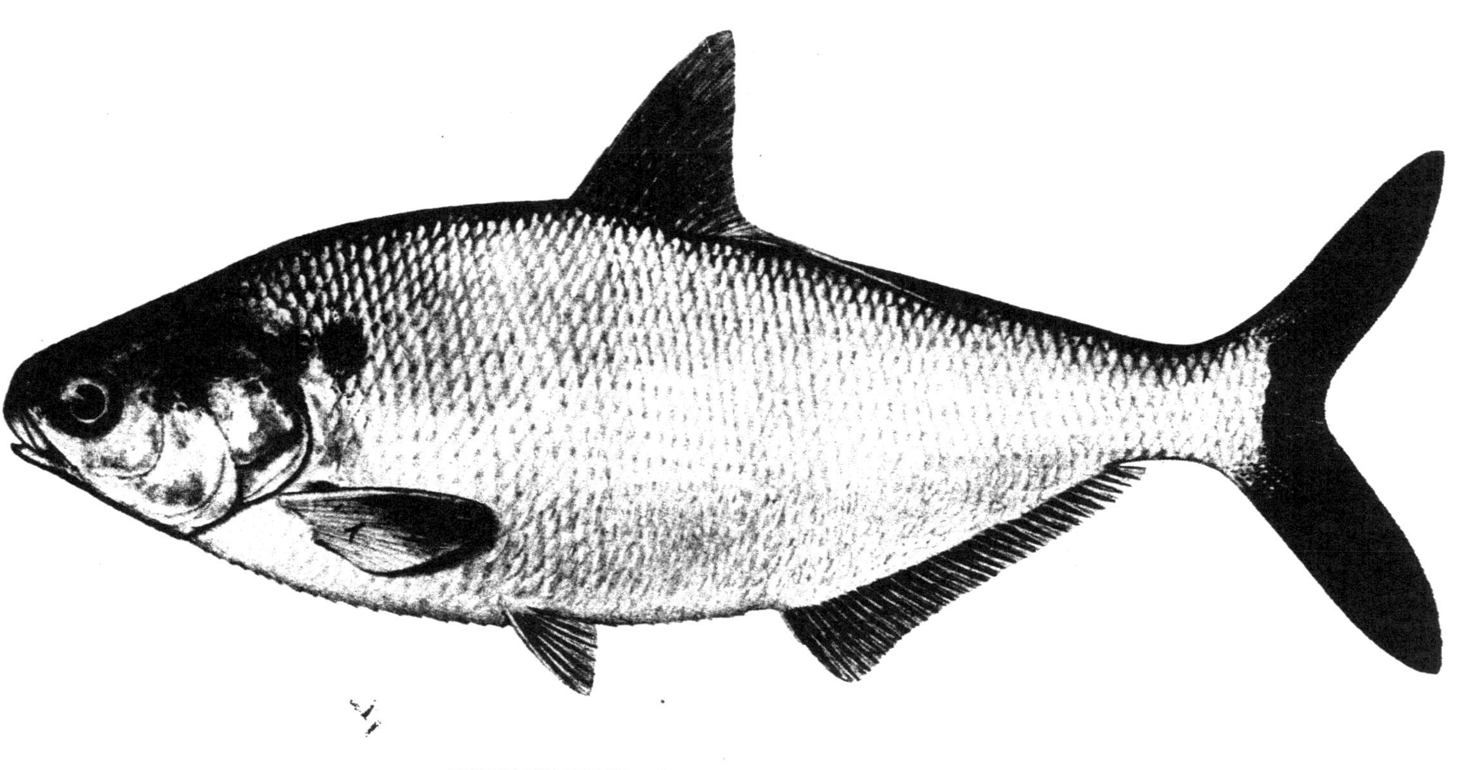

GIZZARD-SHAD, *Dorosoma cepedianum* (Le Sueur)

We have found gravid females, and males running with milt, in the central part of the Illinois River in May, and have seen specimens in February in so sluggish a condition, that they were easily dipped up with a net.

The young are extremely different from the adult, slender and minnow-like in shape, and with a row of fine teeth on the upper jaw, although the mouth of the adult is entirely toothless and smooth. The internal structure of the young also differs remarkably from that of the full-grown fish, especially in the much greater simplicity of the digestive apparatus, the intestine, in specimens not more than an inch long, passing almost directly back from the stomach to the vent. The food of the young consists, like that of most of our young fishes, almost wholly of small crustaceans and insect larvæ—the animal plankton of our waters. That of larger specimens, on the other hand, is very uniform in character, comprising quantities of mud, with which the intestine is commonly packed from end to end, mixed with many minute plants, and much vegetable debris. Occasionally in the vicinity of distilleries, this fish feeds, like the buffalo-fish, on distillery slops, and sometimes one will find univalve mollusks, aquatic insects, and the like, sparsely represented in the food. Half-grown specimens often contain larger quantities of the plankton organisms than are found in the food of the adult.

The flesh is coarse and not delicate in flavor, but still is not unpalatable, and is eaten by some. In the Great Lake region this species is often caught and offered for sale under the name of "lake shad." It is seldom used in Illinois, however, but is systematically picked out of the catch and thrown away by the fishermen, who regard it as a nuisance rather than a benefit, commonly ignoring its value as food for the species we most prize.

Family **CLUPEIDÆ**

THE HERRINGS

Body oblong or elongate, more or less compressed, covered with cycloid or pectinated scales; head naked; belly rounded, or compressed and serrated; lateral line wanting; skeleton osseous; vertebræ 40 to 56, anterior ones not modified; ventral fins abdominal; dorsal median or somewhat posterior; no adipose fin; caudal forked; mesocoracoid present; gill-membranes free from isthmus; gill-rakers slender; branchiostegals usually few (6 to 15); pseudobranchiæ present; adipose eyelid present or wanting; mouth terminal, oblique; premaxillaries not protractile; maxillaries composed each of about 3 pieces, forming lateral margin of upper jaw; teeth usually small or wanting, variously arranged; air-bladder large, with open duct.

Species numerous (about 150 known), abundant and widely distributed in all seas, usually swimming in immense schools. Many species ascend fresh waters in spring to spawn and a few are permanent residents in fresh water. Two genera are found in streams tributary to the Atlantic and the Gulf and in the Mississippi Valley.

Key to the Genera of CLUPEIDÆ found in Illinois

a. Premaxillaries meeting at a large angle, so that the tip of the upper jaw does not appear to be notched; cheeks longer than deep; teeth feeble... **Pomolobus.**

aa. Premaxillaries meeting in front at a very acute angle, so that the emarginate front of the upper jaw receives the slender tip of the lower; fore part of cheeks very deep, deeper than long; jaws toothless.................... **Alosa**

Genus POMOLOBUS Rafinesque

ALEWIVES

Body rather elongate, more or less compressed; belly sharp-edged, strongly serrated before and behind ventrals; mouth terminal, oblique; jaws about equal, the upper somewhat notched at tip; mandible shutting within maxillaries; teeth feeble, variously placed; dorsal short, nearly median, its posterior ray not prolonged in a filament; scales thin, cycloid. Species numerous, mostly anadromous, inhabiting both northern and tropical seas; one species found in fresh waters of the Mississippi Valley.

POMOLOBUS CHRYSOCHLORIS Rafinesque

GOLDEN SHAD; SKIPJACK; BLUE HERRING

Rafinesque, 1820, Ichth. Oh., 39.

J. & G., 266 (**Clupea**); M. V., 73 (**Clupea**); J. & E., I, 425; N., 44 (misspelled); J., 55; F., 73 (**Clupea**); F. F., II. 7, 439; L., 20.

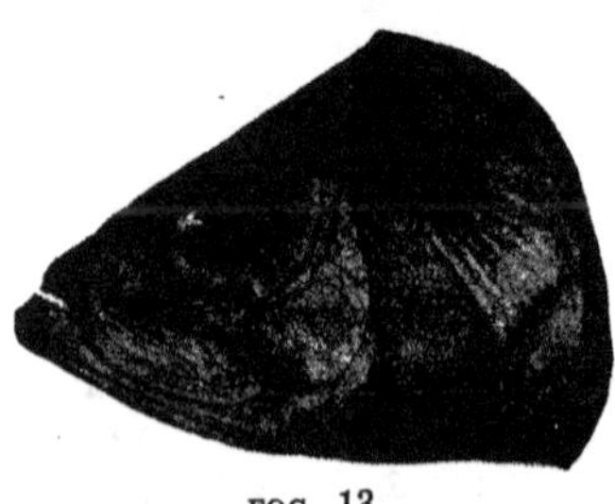

FOG. 13

Length 15 inches; body elongate, compressed, greatest width somewhat less than 2½ in dep'h in adults; depth 3.6 to 4.3; depth caudal peduncle 1.4 to 1.6 in its length. Color silvery to greenish with bluish and golden reflections; back light olive-gray with strong bluish luster; sides light olive-green, shading to silvery white, with golden luster; belly opaque milk-white; no dark spot behind opercle. Head pointed, 3.7 to 4 in length; width head 2.3 to 2.6 in its length; interorbital space 5.8 to 6.3 in head, less than eye; eye 4.5 to 5.9 in head; adipose eyelid present; nose 4.3 to 5.2 in head, mouth large, terminal, opening very high, lower jaw strongly projecting; maxillary past middle of orbit, 2.2 to 2.4 in head; teeth feeble, a few on premaxillary and sometimes some on lower jaw. Dorsal fin nearer muzzle than base of caudal, inserted in front of ventrals, its rays 16; anal rays 18; pectorals 1.7 in head in adults, little more than ½ to ventrals; ventrals less than half way to anal in adults; pectorals with a double accessory scale above and with scaly sheath below base; accessory ventral scale present. Scales 52–54, transverse series 14 or 15; ventral scutes 20+13.

The golden shad, or skipjack, is a beautiful, symmetrical fish, shading from green to silvery, with rich golden reflections. It ranges along the Gulf coast from Pensacola on the east to Galveston on the south and west, and up the Mississippi and Ohio rivers to Pittsburg and the larger streams of Kansas. It is not a common fish in Illinois, and occurs but seven times in our collections, all from Mississippi, Rock, and Illinois River localities. It appears at Alton in small numbers in September, two pounds being about the maximum weight. It is an active fish, frequently leaping from the water in sport or in pursuit of its prey—whence its name of skipjack. It is a predaceous species, the young feeding on insects, and the adults on other fishes.

Genus **ALOSA** Cuvier

SHAD

Body quite deep and compressed; head deep, the cheeks deeper than long; jaws toothless; upper jaw with a sharp, deep notch at tip, the premaxillaries meeting at a very acute angle; dorsa much nearer snout than base of caudal; other characters as in *Pomolobus*, to which *Alosa* is closely allied. North Atlantic and Gulf of Mexico, ascending rivers in spring; species 4 or 5, 3 of them found in the Mississippi and its larger tributaries north about to the latitude of St. Louis.

ALOSA OHIENSIS Evermann

OHIO SHAD

Evermann, Rep. U. S. Fish Comm., 1901, p. 277.

Length 18 inches; body very long, slender, and much compressed; dorsal and ventral outlines very gently and evenly arched; depth 3.6; caudal peduncle very long, the distance from base of caudal to dorsal fin equaling distance from that point to preopercle. Head 4.5 in length; eye 5.5; mouth large; maxillary 2.1 in head, broad, reaching posterior border of eye; lower jaw slightly projecting; gill-rakers 26+49=75. Dorsal rays 18; anal 18.

Ohio River at Louisville, whence the types were obtained by Dr. Evermann in 1897 and 1898.

Family **SALMONIDÆ**

THE SALMON FAMILY

Body oblong or elongate, covered with cycloid scales; head naked; lateral line present; skeleton bony; anterior vertebræ not modified; ventral fins abdominal; dorsal fin about median; adipose fin present; caudal forked; mesocoracoid present; gill-membranes free from isthmus; branchiostegals 10 to 20; pseudobranchiæ present; gill-rakers various; mouth terminal; maxillary forming lateral margin of upper jaw; a supplemental maxillary present; premaxillaries not protractile; teeth various, sometimes wanting; stomach siphonal; pyloric cæca numerous; air-bladder large, with open duct; ova large, falling into abdominal cavity before exclusion.

Fresh waters and seas of northern regions of Europe, Asia, and America; many species anadromous; genera, 10; species about 70; 5 genera found in fresh waters of the United States and Canada.

Most of the species are of moderate or large size, and are prized for their food qualities. Among them also are numbered the choicest of all fresh-water game fishes. They are the best adapted of all fishes to the purposes of artificial culture, which in recent years has aided materially in keeping up their fisheries. The fact that the eggs can be transported long distances in ice without injury has made possible the introduction of American and British forms into some of the temperate regions of the southern hemisphere.

Key to the Genera of **SALMONIDÆ** found in Lake Michigan and Adjacent Waters

a. Mouth not deeply cleft, the mandible articulating with the quadrate bone under or before the eye; dentition more or less feeble or incomplete; scales moderate, 60 to 95 in lateral line.

b. Mouth rather small; lower jaw usually included and overhung by the more or less projecting snout; premaxillaries broad, with the cutting edge nearly vertical or directed backward; gill-rakers on long limb of first arch usually fewer than 30 and rather short.................................**Coregonus.**

bb. Mouth larger, the lower jaw usually more or less projecting beyond upper; premaxillaries rather narrow, with the cutting edge nearly horizontal and directed forward; gill-rakers on long limb of first arch usually more than 35, long and slender..**Argyrosomus.**

aa. Mouth deeply cleft, the lower jaw articulating with the quadrate bone behind the eyes; strong teeth on jaws, vomer, palatines, and tongue; scales very small, 175 to 230 in lateral line.

c. Vomer with a raised crest, extending backward from the head of the bone, free from its shaft, and armed with strong teeth; hyoid bone with a broad band of strong teeth; species grayish-spotted, without bright colors...... **Cristivomer.**

cc. Vomer without raised crest, only the head being toothed; hyoid bone with very weak teeth or none; species red-spotted, the lower fins with bright edgings .... **Salvelinus.**

Genus **COREGONUS** (Artedi) Linnæus

WHITEFISHES

Body more or less elongate, compressed; head conic, the snouth projecting; lower jaw usually included; premaxillaries broad, with the cutting edge nearly vertical; jaws toothless or nearly so; gill-rakers usually rather short; dorsal fin about median, of 11 to 14 rays; caudal deeply forked; scales thin, cycloid; air-bladder very large; pyloric cæca about 100; vertebræ 56 to 60. Clear lakes of northern Europe, Asia, and America. Species about 15, of which 3 are found in the Great Lake region.

Key to Species of **COREGONUS** found in Lake Michigan

a. Gill-rakers 17 to 20 on lower limb of first arch; maxillary about 4 in head, about reaching pupil; body considerably compressed, the back arched in front of dorsal fin.. **clupeiformis.**

aa. Gill-rakers 11 or 12 on lower limb of first arch; maxillary 4.8 to 5.5 in head, not reaching eye; body long, slender, and roundish, not much elevated or compressed .... **quadrilateralis.**

COREGONUS CLUPEIFORMIS (Mitchill)

COMMON WHITEFISH

Mitchill, Amer. Month. Mag., II, 1818, 321 (**Salmo**).
J. & G., 299; M. V., 77; J. & E., I, 465; N., 44 (**Argyrosomus**); J., 54; F. F., I. 6, 95; F., 73; L., 20.

Length 2 feet or more; body oblong, compressed, back always more or less elevated, becoming notably so in the adult; depth in length 3 to 4. Color olivaceous above; sides white, not silvery; lower fins sometimes dusky. Head 5, comparatively small and short; interorbital space 3.4 in head; eye 4 to 5; nose 3.8 in head; tip of snout on level of lower edge of pupil; mouth small, maxillary reaching past front of orbit, about 4 in head; lower jaw included; gill-rakers .5 diameter of eye, usually about 10+17 to 19. Dorsal rays 11; anal 11. Scales 8–74–9; lateral line continuous.

This is a northern species, occurring in vast abundance in all the Great Lakes and in some of their tributary waters, and ranging north to the Arctic Ocean. It was formerly abundant in southwestern Lake Michigan within the limits of the State of

Illinois, but is now taken from that part of the lake, if at all, in very small numbers only. It is still much the most important food species occurring within our territory, but reckless fishing has reduced it to insignificance as an Illinois fish. The long-shore fishery in this state, which as late as 1885 produced over eighty thousand pounds per annum, yielded only some two hundred pounds in 1899. Indeed, the total catch of the several species of whitefish (*Coregonus*) in the Great Lakes, now gives us only five million to eight million pounds a year as compared with eighteen million pounds in 1885 and twenty-one million pounds in 1879.

The record weight of a single whitefish is twenty-three pounds—the weight of a specimen taken at White Fish Point, Lake Superior. Its mean weight in northern Lake Michigan is four or five pounds, and fishes weighing as much as fifteen pounds are now very rare.

This is probably, on the whole, the favorite food-fish of our inland waters In the words of Sir John Richardson, "Though it is a fat fish, instead of producing satiety it becomes more agreeable to the palate, and I know from experience that, though deprived of bread and vegetables, one may live wholly upon this fish for months, or even years, without tiring." It is mainly eaten fresh, but it is also smoked or salted in considerable quantities.

This species spends most of its time, as a rule, in the deeper and cooler parts of the lakes which it inhabits, coming towards the shore and sometimes entering streams in October and November as the spawning season approaches. In many lakes there is a migration movement from deep to shallow water in early summer also. The whitefish spawns during October, November, and December, in depths varying from eight to fifteen fathoms, beginning, it is said, when the water reaches about 40° F. It is most active on its spawning grounds in the evening and at night, each female depositing several hundred eggs at a time, and the total number averaging about ten thousand for each pound of her weight.

The young usually appear in March and April, swimming separately near the surface, and soon seeking deep water to feed and to escape their enemies. Their first food consists mainly of the smaller *Entomostraca* of the plankton, the capture of which is facilitated by the presence, on the lower jaw of the young fish, of four sharp strong teeth, the two anterior ones curved backwards and slightly inwards, and the posterior pair much smaller and directed almost exactly inwards. These teeth disappear as the fish grows up, the food changing likewise until, in the adult, it consists mainly of small mollusks and crustaceans, with larvæ of insects and other animal forms. The gill-rakers of the adult are of a size and number to enable it to separate from the water organisms as small as *Entomostraca*, and where these are abundant they make a large percentage of the food. The general character of the contents of the stomach indicates, however, that the fish feeds habitually at the bottom, as might indeed be inferred from the character of its mouth. In aquaria it has been forced to feed on small fish in winter, and has learned to pursue and seize its prey much as a trout would do.

It is caught mainly in gill- and pound-nets from April to the end of December. It is not properly an angler's fish, although where abundant it may be taken on the hook with a bait of worms or insect larvæ. Fortunately for the future of the species, this valuable and popular food-fish is one of those best adapted to artificial propagation. Females are adult in three or four years, and 75 to 95 per cent. of their eggs yield the young in the hatchery.

A single other species of the genus *Coregonus* (*C. quadrilateralis*, the round or Menominee whitefish) is taken in Lake Michigan, though much more rarely than the common whitefish. A sufficient characterization of this species will be found in the key to the species of *Coregonus* preceding.

Genus **ARGYROSOMUS** Agassiz

CISCOES

Close to *Coregonus*, from which it differs chiefly in the larger mouth and more produced jaws, the premaxillaries being placed nearly horizontally, and the lower jaw projecting decidedly beyond them; gill-rakers very long and slender; dorsal fin of 9 to 12 rays; caudal forked; scales, etc., as in *Coregonus*; vertebræ 55. Fresh waters of northern Europe, Asia, and North America. Species numerous; about 6 known from the Great Lake region of the United States.

KEY TO SPECIES OF **ARGYROSOMUS** FOUND IN LAKE MICHIGAN

a. Body elongate, herring-shaped, depth usually considerably more than 3½ (3½ to 4½); scales 73 to 90 in longitudinal series, uniform in shape and size, the free edges convex.

b. Lower fins pale or merely tipped with dusky; scales punctulate with dark specks.

c. Eye large, not much, if any, shorter than snout, its length 3½ to 4½ in head.

d. Maxillary 3¼ to 3⅜ in head; lower jaw projecting beyond upper; gill-rakers long and numerous, usually about 47 on first gill-arch (15 to 19 + 30 to 38) .... **artedi.**

dd. Maxillary 2⅜ to 3 in head; lower jaw scarcely projecting or not at all; gill-rakers usually not more than 39 or 40 on first gill-arch (14 + 25 or 26)... **hoyi.**

cc. Eye small, shorter than snout, about 5 in head; maxillary very long, 2½ in head; mandible reaching usually to posterior edge of orbit, half as long as head .... **prognathus.**

bb. Lower fins all blue-black; body stout; mouth large; gill-rakers at least 50 on the first arch (17 + 33).......... **nigripinnis.**

aa. Body short, deep, and compressed, the curve of the back similar to that of the belly; depth 3 to 3⅕ in length; scales 67 to 74, larger forward and closely imbricated, the free margin often concave or notched......... **tullibee.**

ARGYROSOMUS ARTEDI (LE SUEUR)

LAKE HERRING; CISCO

Le Sueur, Journ. Ac. Nat. Sci. Phila., I, 1818, 231 (**Coregonus**).
G., VI, 198 and 199 (**Coregonus harengus** and **clupeiformis**); J. & G., 301 (**Coregonus**); M. V., 78 (**Coregonus**); J. & E., I, 468; N., 44 (**clupeiformis**); J., 54 (**Coregonus**); F., 73 (**Coregonus**); F. F., II. 7, 436 (**Coregonus**); L., 20.

Length 12 inches; body elongate, compressed, not elevated; depth 4½ in length. Color bluish black or greenish above; sides silvery, scales with dark specks; fins mostly pale, the lower dusky-tinged. Head 4½ in length, compressed, somewhat pointed and rather long, the distance from occiput to tip of snout usually a little less than half the distance from occiput to dorsal fin; interorbital space 3⅓ in head; eye 4 to 4½; nose 4; mouth rather large, the maxillary reaching not quite to the middle of the pupil, 3¼ to 3½ in head; the mandible 2⅛ in head, slightly projecting; gill-rakers very long and slender, 15 to 17+28 to 34, the longest 1⅖ in eye. Dorsal rays 10; anal 12. Scales 8–75 to 90–7, 10 rows under base of dorsal; lateral line continuous.

Great Lakes and neighboring waters, including Lake Champlain; north to James Bay, but not in Alaska or Arctic America; abundant in Lake Michigan.

This is by far the most abundant food-fish of the Great Lakes, the catch of 1899 aggregating nearly sixty million pounds, about a third of it from Lake Michigan. The commonest name of the species, it scarcely need be said, is a misnomer, as this is properly a whitefish and not a herring. It should be generally known by the much more distinctive name of cisco, already frequently used for it but now commonly limited to a variety of the species found in the smaller lakes of Wisconsin and of Indiana, but not in those of Illinois.

In food and habits it is similar to the common whitefish, although it is notorious for its enormous destruction of the spawn of the latter, upon whose multiplication, in view of its own greater abundance and the rapidly decreasing supply of whitefish, it must place a serious check. Like the whitefish it spends the summer and the winter in the deeper water of its habitat, moving shorewards in spring evidently in search of food, and again in fall for the deposit of its spawn, which takes place chiefly in November. Its eggs are laid in shallow water, preferably upon a sandy bottom, although it sometimes spawns on the mud along the borders of the shallower waters of the lakes and in the mouths of their tributary streams.

It is caught with gill-nets in shallow water from April to the last of May, but the larger part of the catch is obtained by pound-nets. Up to 1899 it seems to have withstood successfully the enormous drain of our fisheries, the yield of that year being more than double that of 1885, while the catch of whitefish, on the other hand, had diminished to less than a third.

In addition to the common lake herring, four other species of the genus *Argyrosomus* (*A. hoyi*, the mooneye cisco; *A. prognathus*, the longjaw; *A. nigripinnis*, the bluefin; and *A. tullibee*, the tullibee) are more or less commonly taken in Lake Michigan. None of these species is as abundant as the lake herring (*A. artedi*), however, and none, unless the bluefin, is taken at all frequently in southern Lake Michigan, within the limits of this state. For purposes of the present report all of these species are sufficiently characterized in the key to the species of *Argyrosomus* preceding.

Genus **CRISTIVOMER** Gill & Jordan

GREAT LAKE TROUT

Body moderately elongate; mouth large; hyoid with a band of strong teeth; vomer boat-shaped, with a raised crest behind the head and free from its shaft, this crest being armed with teeth; caudal little forked; scales very small.

CRISTIVOMER NAMAYCUSH (Walbaum)

GREAT LAKE TROUT

Walbaum, 1792, Artedi Piscium, 68 (**Salmo**).
G., VI, 123 (**Salmo**); J. & G., 317 (**Salvelinus**); M. V., 80 (**Salvelinus**); J. & E., I, 504; N., 44 (**Salmo**); J., 54; F., 73 (**Salvelinus**); L., 21.

Length 3 feet; body elongate, depth 4 in length. General coloration dark grayish green to brownish, sometimes paler, sometimes almost black; everywhere with rounded paler spots, which are often yellowish or reddish tinged; head usually vermiculate above; dorsal and caudal reticulate with darker, the anal faintly so. Head 4¼ long, and its upper surface flattened; eye 4½ in head; interorbital space 3⅕; nose 3⅕; mouth very large, the maxillary extending much beyond eye, nearly half length of head; teeth very strong. Dorsal rays 11; anal 11; caudal well forked. Scales very small, 185 to 210 in longitudinal series; lateral line continuous, pores about 100.

This magnificent species, one of the three most important fishes of our Great Lakes is, like the whitefish, a species of northern distribution. It is found throughout the Great Lake region, and in the lakes of New York, New Hampshire, and Maine, thence to the headwaters of the Columbia and Fraser rivers and the streams of Vancouver Island, and northward to the arctic circle. It is common in the northern part of Lake Michigan, but rarer to the southward. In our Illinois markets it is known almost wholly by the name of lake trout, but farther north the names of Mackinaw trout, salmon-trout, and namaycush are sometimes used. It is extremely variable in size, form, and color, particularly under the influence of local conditions, and hence has received many local names.

Although the usual weight of specimens taken in large-meshed gill-nets is about eight pounds, and of those captured with lines and seines not more than two pounds, the species is said by Goode to attain a weight of a hundred and twenty pounds, which is eight times the maximum size of the closely allied brook trout. "This is due, perhaps," he says, "to the greater ease with which, for hundreds of generations, the lake trout have obtained their food. They are almost always found in the same lakes with one or more kinds of whitefish, whose slow helpless movements render them an easy prey, and upon whose tender luscious flesh the lake trout feeds voraciously." This trout is a fish of highly predaceous habit, living especially upon lake herring of all sizes, but eating, in an emergency, almost any animal food which comes in its way.

A lake trout twenty-three inches long has been known to swallow a burbot of a length of seventeen inches, and whitefish of two or three pounds weight are not infrequently taken from the stomachs of large trout. A twenty-pound trout caught off Beaver Island, in northern Lake Michigan, had thirteen herring in its stomach. "They are as omnivorous," says Goode, "as codfish, and among the articles which have been found in their stomachs may be mentioned an open jack-knife seven inches long, tin cans, rags, raw potatoes, chicken and ham bones, salt pork, corn-cobs, spoons, silver dollars, a watch and chain, and, in one instance, a piece of tarred rope two feet long." Most of this debris was doubtless taken while the fish were following steamers.

The greater part of the year is spent by this fish in deep water, but in the spawning season it approaches the shore, depositing its eggs late in October, usually on rocky bottoms, at depths varying from seven feet to fifteen fathoms. Mr. Milner found nearly fifteen thousand eggs in a lake trout of twenty-four pounds weight. The young appear in late winter or early spring.

Lake trout are taken chiefly in pound- and gill-nets during their spawning season—that is, in September, October, and November—but they are also caught in deep water from the time the ice breaks up until late fall. They may be readily taken with a hook baited with a piece of fish, but they are not sufficiently "game" to reward the patient angler with a "first-class fight."

The value of the lake-trout fishery is second only to that of the whitefish in the Great Lake region. The product of Lake Michigan alone in 1899, was five and a half million pounds. The species has been propagated artificially to a considerable extent, particularly in Michigan, where the Northville hatchery recently handled over eleven million eggs in a single year, about 70 per cent. of them successfully.

Order **APODES**

THE EELS

Body eel-shaped; skeleton bony; vertebræ numerous, the anterior ones distinct, without Weberian ossicles; ventral fins absent; all fins without spines; pectoral arch, if present, not connected with, and remote from, the skull; mesocoracoid absent; opercular bones small and concealed; premaxillaries absent maxillaries persistent in some forms (*Anguillidæ*); air-bladder, if present, communicating with œsophagus by an open duct.

The eels are elongate serpentine fishes, mostly with naked skin, or with extremely small imbedded scales. Their origin is unknown. They show some kinship with the *Isospondyli* (shad- and herring-like forms), from which they may have sprung by degradation, though this is by no means certain. The forms without paired fins are mostly marine. There are several families, of which one is represented in American fresh waters.

Family **ANGUILLIDÆ**

THE TRUE EELS

Body serpentine, or eel-shaped, covered with very fine scales which are deeply imbedded in the skin; head naked; lateral line present; skeleton osseous; vertebræ numerous, the anterior ones not modified; ventral fins absent; no spines in fins; dorsal and anal continuous with caudal around tail, which is isocercal (i. e., with the caudal vertebræ decreasing in size in a straight line backwards, as in the *Anacanthini*); mesocoracoid absent; gill-openings much restricted, about as wide as the base of the pectorals; operculum small, concealed beneath skin; mouth terminal; jaws about equal; premaxillaries absent; maxillaries lateral, separated on median line by the coalesced ethmoid and vomer; maxillary, mandible, and vomer with cardiform teeth; air-bladder with open duct; young passing through a larval stage, the ribbon-shaped larva being known as *Leptocephalus* (a name first used to designate these forms as a distinct genus of fishes).

Fresh and brackish waters of most parts of the world, but not found on Pacific coast of North America or in islands of the Pacific. A single genus known.

FRESH-WATER EEL, *Anguilla chrysypa* (Rafinesque)

GENUS **ANGUILLA** SHAW

EELS

Characters included in description of the family. Species not numerous and those known not very well distinguished from each other, *A. anguilla* of Europe, *A. chrysypa* of the eastern United States, and *A. japonica* of east Asia being very closely allied.

ANGUILLA CHRYSYPA RAFINESQUE

AMERICAN EEL; FRESH-WATER EEL

Rafinesque, 1817, Amer. Month. Mag. & Crit. Rev., 120.
G., VIII, 31 (**bostoniensis**); J. & G., 361 (**rostrata**); M. V., 90 (**anguilla**); J. & E., I, 348; N., 51 (**vulgaris** var. **rostrata**); J., 68 (**rostrata**); F., 71 (**rostrata**); L., 20.

Length 3 to 4 feet, weight 5 to 8 ℔; body serpentine, subcylindrical anteriorly, compressed behind; depth in length 12 to 17. Color variable, usually nearly plain greenish brown, often more or less tinged with yellowish; belly paler, greenish gray. Head 7 or 8 in length, 2 to 2.5 in trunk (distance from gill-openings to front of anal); interorbital space 5 to 7 in head; eye 2 to 2.8; a single pair of short nasal barbels; mouth wide, maxillary past orbit, lips thin, and lower jaw projecting; gill-membranes very broadly joined across isthmus, the gill-openings confined to the sides of the neck below top of pectoral basis; jaws with bands of cardiform teeth; vomer toothed. Dorsal fin inserted about head's length in front of anal, its distance from snout about 3 in length; dorso-caudal with about 60 rays to tip of tail; pectorals very short, 3 in head; no ventrals. Scales minute*, oblong, slender, and deeply imbedded, the oblique rows taking a zigzag direction; lateral line developed, nearly straight.

Atlantic and Gulf coasts and West Indies, ascending rivers; not in the Pacific; found throughout the Mississippi Valley; in all the larger streams of Illinois. Taken regularly in small numbers from the Illinois River at Havana from deep water.

The eel reaches a length of 3 to 4 feet and a weight of 4 to 6 ℔. A majority of those taken are between 2½ and 3 feet long. A specimen 34 inches long recently caught at Havana weighed 3¾ pounds.

Eels prefer deep water with mud bottom. They are often found in the mouths of shallow sloughs at night, and in such places may be taken along with bullheads on trot-lines. They are powerful and rapid swimmers, and can travel rapidly over the ground, like snakes. They have been known to come up

* In a specimen 2½ feet long 150 scales were counted on one square inch of surface of side of body, half way between tip of tail and vent.

out of the water into damp meadows, where they are sometimes found hiding under stones near springs.

They are among the most voracious of all carnivorous fishes, but are chiefly scavengers in their feeding habits, eating all manner of refuse, preferring, however, dead fish or other animal matter. They sometimes devour fishes caught in gill-nets, and on the Atlantic coast frequently mutilate shad, caught in the net, to get at their roe. It is said by Jordan and Evermann that it frequently happens that the greater part of a gill-net catch may consist, when it is removed, simply of the heads and backbones of fishes, the remainder having been devoured by myriads of eels. They are nocturnal feeders, "poking their noses into every imaginable hole in their search for food." An eel in our aquarium at Ottawa, sought its food only at night, and hid by day under a stone on the bottom of the tank.

The flesh of the eel is highly esteemed by many, and it always brings a good price. In the Great Lake region and in the East eels are often salted and smoked. They are also put up in tins with jellies or a spiced sauce of vinegar. Their skins are used in England for binding books and making whips. Eels are caught in traps and eel-pots and on set-lines, and sometimes also with seines.

The mode of reproduction and the development of their young were unsolved riddles from the time of Aristotle to near the end of the nineteenth century, but all essential facts in the life history of the species are now well understood. The principal difficulty arose from the fact that the eel, although a fresh-water fish during the greater part of its life, migrates to the sea to propagate, spawning in salt water, usually on muddy banks off the mouths of rivers. The young develop within two or three months, but they are so unlike the adults that they were not recognized as belonging even to the same genus. Spawning occurs in fall, and at the beginning of the second spring the young find their way to the mouths of rivers, which they ascend in considerable numbers, remaining in fresh water until full grown, when they return to the sea. During this migration, eels, like salmon and shad, do not take any food. Their sexual organs do not mature until they have been some weeks in salt water. After spawning both sexes die, neither males nor females ever returning to fresh water the second time. The eel is remarkably prolific, a single female 32 inches long having been estimated to produce 10,700,000 eggs.

ORDER **EVENTOGNATHI**

THE CARP-LIKE FISHES

Skeleton osseous; anterior vertebræ modified, with Weberian apparatus; fins without spines in typical forms; ventral fins abdominal; pectoral arch suspended from the skull; a mesocoracoid present; opercular bones all present; branchiostegals few, usually 3 or 4; air-bladder with open duct; jaws without teeth. Species exceedingly numerous, in all of the streams and lakes of the northern hemisphere.

KEY TO FAMILIES OF **EVENTOGNATHI** FOUND IN ILLINOIS

a. Dorsal fins of more than 25 rays, or shorter and the lips thickened and covered with plicate or papillose skin; pharyngeal teeth numerous and comb-like .... **Catostomidæ.**

aa. Dorsal fin of not more than 10 rays; lips usually thin, never plicate or papillose; pharyngeal teeth fewer than 8 on a side, in 1 to 3 rows......**Cyprinidæ.**

FAMILY **CATOSTOMIDÆ**

THE SUCKERS

Body oblong or elongate, usually more or less compressed, covered with large or small cycloid scales; head naked; lateral line usually present; belly not serrated; skeleton osseous; anterior 4 vertebræ modified and provided with Weberian apparatus or *ossicula auditus*; fins without spines; ventrals abdominal; no adipose fin; tail more or less forked; a mesocoracoid arch present; gill-membranes more or less united to the isthmus, restricting the gill-openings to the sides; pseudobranchiæ present; branchiostegals 3; margin of upper jaw formed in the middle by the small premaxillaries, and on the sides by the maxillaries; jaws toothless; lower pharyngeal bones falciform, armed with a sing e row of numerous comb-like teeth; mouth usually protractile and with fleshy lips (sucker-like); alimentary canal long; stomach simple; no pyloric cæca; air-bladder large, divided into 2 or 3 parts by transverse constrictions, not surrounded by a bony capsule, communicating with œsophagus by a slender open duct.

One of the most striking characteristics of the fish fauna of Illinois, and indeed of the whole Mississippi Valley, is the prominence of the sucker family, which includes, within the limits of this state, eight genera and fifteen recognized species, several of them among the most abundant and most generally distributed of our larger fishes.

The family is found in the fresh waters of North America at large, in which about 15 genera and 60 species occur; and there are 2 species also in eastern Asia. They range in length from 6 inches to 3 feet. The suckers have usually been regarded by European writers as a subfamily of *Cyprinidæ*, from which they differ chiefly in the structure of the mouth and the lower pharyngeal bones. They are generally of sluggish habit and, as a rule, prefer water of good depth and little current, but some of them may be found in almost every stream and pond within their range. Their spring migration is familiar to all fishermen, and to many who do not fish, all of our species running up the smaller streams in May or June to deposit their eggs. The males of most species develop black or red pigment on the body and fins in spring, and in many kinds peculiar wart-like tubercles, called pearl organs, appear at this season on the head, fins, and caudal peduncle.

The suckers are, on the whole, an unusually homogeneous group as represented in Illinois, not only agreeing in the character of their feeding structures which gives them their common name, but unusually similar also in their movements, habits, modes of life, and places of most frequent resort. They feed, without exception, on the bottom of the waters they inhabit, and commonly on substantially the same kinds of food, differing somewhat in respect to the places in which they seek it. The buffalo-fishes, for example, are from 2¼ to 3 times as abundant in our collections from the bottom-land lakes as they would be if they had been equally distributed throughout all waters. In other words, the frequency coefficient of one of the two buffaloes is 2.26 for lowland lakes and that of the other is 2.93. On the other hand, the common sucker, the chub-sucker, and the striped sucker show a decided preference for the smaller streams, their coefficients of frequency in creeks being 4.27, 3.41, and 3.17 for the three species respectively. The most marked departure from the average habit of the family is made by the hogsucker, or stone-roller (*Catostomus nigricans*), which especially frequents swift water on rocky stretches of the larger streams, filling there the place which the darters occupy in creeks and brooks.

Notwithstanding these divergencies in local distribution, the family as a whole forms a rather definite ecological group, as is shown especially by the frequency with which representatives of the several species are found in company in the same situations and appear together, consequently, in our collections. The average frequency of this joint occurrence of the species of suckers and buffaloes in collections is decidedly greater, according to our experience, than the corresponding average for the darters or the sunfish, being represented, for suckers, by the general coefficient of 2.45, for darters by 2.02, and for sunfish—that is, the *Centrarchidæ* exclusive of the black bass—by 1.87.

When full grown, the majority of the species are safe from any enemies of their kind which the water contains, but their survival to adult age is dependent on their fortune in escaping from a host of predaceous and voracious fishes against which they have no defense, and to whose depredations their haunts and habits freely expose them. In the food of 1,221 Illinois fishes, representing 87 species, studied by the senior author during the dozen years preceding 1888, suckers and buffalo-fish were found most frequently in the food of the pike, but occurred also in that of dogfish, bullheads, sheepsheads, and sunfish. The sucker family would evidently suffer much more severely, however, if it were not for the presence in the waters they inhabit of the gizzard-shad, more abundant, and probably more accessible to pike and other predaceous fishes, than are either suckers or young buffaloes. It is an interesting illustration of the way in which companion species having little or nothing to do with each other directly may nevertheless greatly influence each others' welfare, that while 20 pike out of 37 had eaten gizzard-shad, which made, in fact, nearly half the food of the entire number, only 3 per cent. of their food came from the sucker family, and this had been eaten only by three of the pike.

Examining the other side of the food relation, we find that the food of this family itself, as illustrated by a careful study of the stomach contents of 109 specimens, belonging to five genera and eleven species, consisted mainly of the smaller mollusks living in the mud and larvæ of aquatic insects, the two being about equal in ratio and together making more than three fourths of the entire food. Vegetation contributed less than 10 per cent. to the mass examined, and no element of this class was especially prominent.

The structures of alimentation vary noticeably in definite directions as one passes along the series from the most cylindrical suckers to the thin and deep-bodied buffalo and carp. In the former the pharyngeal bones are heavy, and the lower teeth are thick and strong, usually with a well-developed grinding surface, while the gill-rakers are short, thick, and few, and the intestine is comparatively short and large. As the body deepens, the pharyngeal bones become longer, the pharyngeal teeth smaller and more numerous, with diminished grinding surface; the gill-rakers are longer and more numerous, making a more effective straining apparatus, and the intestines become longer and smaller. Corresponding to these differences of structure, mollusks form a larger percentage of the food of the cylindrical suckers, and *Entomostraca* and vegetable food a very much greater part of that of the deep-bodied species. All the species commonly swallow much mud, since they collect most of their food from the bottom by suction, to which their protractile mouths and fleshy lips are peculiarly adapted.

As food fishes they do not hold a high place, the flesh being rather coarse, dry, and either flavorless or strong, and always provokingly full of small bones. The buffalo and sucker fishery is nevertheless an important one in the Mississippi Valley and the Great Lake region. (See under *Ictiobus*.) Of the 15 species found in the waters of the Illinois alone, about one third have a greater or less commercial value.

Key to the Genera of CATOSTOMIDÆ found in Illinois

a. Dorsal fin elongate, with 25 to 40 developed rays.

b. Posterior fontanelle almost obliterated by the union of the parietals; head small and slender, its length 6 to 7 times in body; lips with several series of tubercle-like papillæ..**Cycleptus.**

bb. Posterior fontanelle well developed, extending forward between frontals a distance equal to more than ⅓ of their length; head 3½ to 5 times in body; lips plicate, striate, or smooth......................................

c. No anterior fontanelle, the frontals being closely joined with the ethmoid; cheek somewhat shallow and foreshortened, distance from eye to lower posterior angle of preopercle about ¾ of that to upper corner of gill-cleft; subopercle broadest at its middle, subsemicircular..................**Ictiobus.**

cc. Anterior fontanelle well developed, separating anterior edges of frontals and notching ethmoid; cheek relatively deep and long, eye about equidistant between upper corner of gill-cleft and infra-posterior angle of preopercle; subopercle broadest below its middle, subtriangular.............**Carpiodes.**

aa. Dorsal fin short, with 10 to 18 developed rays.

d. Lateral line more or less incomplete or wholly wanting; scales large and uniformly distributed, 30 to 50 in lateral line.

e. Lateral line entirely wanting at all ages...........................**Erimyzon.**

ee. Lateral line more or less developed in adults......................**Minytrema.**

dd. Lateral line complete and continuous.

f. Scales small and crowded anteriorly, the number in the lateral line 55 to 110 (except in *C. nigricans*, for which see below **ff**)...............**Catostomus.**

ff. Scales large and nearly equal all over the body, 40 to 55 in the lateral line.

g. Air-bladder in two parts; scales 48 to 55 in lateral line...**Catostomus (Hypentelium) nigricans.**

gg. Air-bladder in three parts; scales larger, 40 to 50 in lateral line.

h. Upper lip protractile, lower entire or incised only part way to anterior margin.

i. Pharyngeal teeth compressed; mouth wholly inferior................**Moxostoma.**

ii. Lower pharyngeal teeth much enlarged, subcylindrical and truncate; mouth somewhat oblique, lips very thick...........................**Placopharynx.**

hh. Upper lip not protractile; lower lip in two separate lobes...........**Lagochila.**

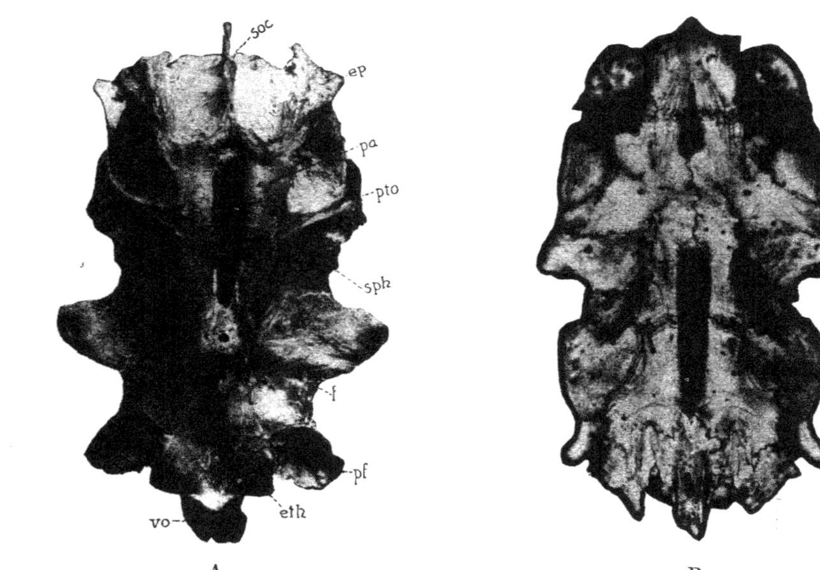

Dorsal view of skull of (A) *Ictiobus bubalus* (Rafinesque) and of (B) *Carpiodes carpio* (Rafinesque): *ep*, epiotic; *eth*, ethmoid; *f*, frontal; *pa*, parietal; *pf*, prefrontal; *pto*, pterotic; *sph*, sphenotic; *soc*, supraoccipital; *vo*, vomer.

Genus CYCLEPTUS Rafinesque

Body elongate, little compressed, caudal peduncle very long; head very small, short and slender; mouth small, inferior; lips tuberculate. The skeleton is remarkable for deficiencies of ossification and other features which may indicate affinity with a primitive catostomoid stock. Forward portion of chondrocranium strongly developed, the trabeculæ fusing anteriorly into a broad and thick ethmoid plate, which is continuous in front with the bulbular cartilages of the end of the vomer, and above with the broad girdle-like *tegmen cranii*; bones of skull somewhat heavy, their exposed surfaces more or less rough; prefrontals, meso- and ento-pterygoids very spongy, and other bones subject in varying degrees to incompleteness of ossification; sutures very distinct, never close and strongly joined, with cartilage between the edges of the articulating elements in many instances; configuration of roofing bones of brain case and orbits much as in *Ictiobus*; nasal foramen closed externally by a sieve-like plate; a small supraorbital bone intervening between lateral wings of prefrontal and frontal; posterior fontanelle represented by a small opening at intercalation of supraoccipital and frontals; anterior fontanelle present, notching ethmoid and extending a short distance backward between frontals; sub- and inter-operculum and branchiostegals rather small; pharyngeal bones narrow and spongy, the teeth from 25 to 35 in number, the lower ones somewhat compressed but strong, the remaining teeth weak, diminishing rapidly in size upward; vertebræ 49 in number, rather heavy and poorly sculptured; ribs 13, short and weak; floating pairs 14, very slender and thread-like, their parapophyses (vertebræ 17 to 30) short and stout and similar in form and size, with distal extremities expanded and their free margins crenate; air-bladder in two parts, the posterior very long and slender and much tapered behind, furnished interiorly with a spiral band of supporting cartilage; dorsal rays about 30, the first rays elongated, about half the length of the fin; scales elongate, with a broad membranous posterior border; lateral line complete, a peculiar and conspicuous membranous area about the posterior terminus of each tube. Mississippi Valley; one species known.

CYCLEPTUS ELONGATUS (Le Sueur)

MISSOURI SUCKER; BLACK-HORSE

Le Sueur, 1817, J. Ac. Nat. Sci. Phila., I, 103 (**Catostomus**).
G., VII, 23 (**Sclerognathus**); J. & G., 121; M. V., 46; J. & E., I, 168; N., 50; J., 64; F., 81; L., 12.

Body elongate, little compressed and the back little elevated, depth 4 to 5 in length. Size large; length 2½ feet. Color dark, bluish black about head; fins dusky to black; spring males almost black, the head covered with small tubercles. Head very small and slender, conic, its length 5.8 to 6.4, width 8.2 to 8.8, depth 8.1 to 8.5 in length of body; snout fleshy, tapering to the bluntly pointed muzzle, which extends considerably beyond the decidedly inferior mouth; distance from eye to muzzle 2 to 2.2 in head; mouth small, its width from 5.8 to 6 in head; lips rather thick, protractile almost directly downward, each furnished with 5 or 6 rows of strongly developed tubercle-like papillæ; lower lip incised behind; eye very small, located a little back of center of head, 6 to 8.3 in its length; interorbital space convex, about 2 in head. Dorsal rays 31 to 32, the first two developed rays elevated to about ½ the length of base of fin, the succeeding rays rapidly shortened to about the eighth, the remaining rays all low and of about equal height; position of dorsal well forward, the distance from insertion of fin to muzzle 2.2 to 2.4 in length of body; caudal deeply forked, the lobes about equal. Scales 9 or 10, 55–58, 8–10, much longer than broad, much crowded on nape, breast, and belly, and at base of dorsal fin; lateral line complete.

This peculiar species, the only one of its genus, is confined to the Ohio and the Mississippi rivers. It is reported abundant at Pittsburgh, but is not common in the Mississippi above the latitude of Quincy. It is frequently taken in spring at Cairo and at Grafton, on the Mississippi, and in the lower part of Rock River, but it disappears from the product of the fisheries, except for an occasional specimen, about the last of June, as soon as the spring run is over. It is also caught in spring in considerable quantities in the Illinois River, but much less abundantly now than in former years. To Illinois and Mississippi River fishermen in this state it is commonly known as the Missouri sucker, or occasionally as the black sucker. The name "black-horse" we have not found in current use.

It reaches a length of 2 or 2½ feet, and Ashlock reports specimens taken at Alton of a weight of 16 pounds. As a food fish it is the best of the suckers. It is caught on set-lines as well as in fyke-nets and with seines. Its habits are but little known, but it apparently lives in the deeper water of the river channels, except during the spawning migration. Eggs are deposited in May and June.

Genus **ICTIOBUS** Rafinesque

Body robust, compressed, both dorsal and ventral outlines curved; head rather large; mouth terminal or slightly inferior; lips thin, plain or more or less strongly plicate, the upper protractile, the lower lobed at corners of mouth, plicate. The generally heavier bones, with more or less roughened surfaces, and the different configuration of certain cranial elements (see key to genera of *Catostomidæ*) in *Ictiobus* furnish the most reliable means of distinction between this genus and *Carpiodes*. Frontals joined closely with ethmoid, obliterating anterior fontanelle, posterior fontanelle large, somewhat narrowed forward, its posterior margin formed by the supraoccipital; a supraorbital bone present; suboperculum symmetrically rounded, subsemicircular, broadest at its middle; cheek shorter and not so deep as in *Carpiodes*, the lower posterior border of the preopercle a gentle curve, the eye evidently closer to the angle of the preopercle than to the upper corner of the gill-cleft; pharyngeal bones broad, but thin and weak, the teeth short and compressed; vertebræ 36; air-bladder in two parts; dorsal fin long, with from 25 to 30 rays, the anterior rays produced, about ½ the length of base of fin, scales roundish; lateral line complete; color rather dark, never silvery; sexual differences slight.

Mississippi and Ohio rivers and their larger tributaries; three species known, all of them common to our larger streams. These fishes are the largest in size of the *Catostomidæ*, not infrequently reaching a length of 3 feet and a weight of 50 pounds. The name "buffalo-fish" refers to the bull-like hump at the nape in old individuals. The relationships of these fishes with the carp are remote. The view, not uncommon among fishermen, that carp and buffalo interbreed is not supported by any facts in our knowledge, and is probably based solely on the superficial* resemblance of the buffalo and the carp in the form of the body and of the dorsal fin.

The species are gregarious and nocturnal, coming out at night on bars not frequented by them by day, and where they may be readily reached by the seine. Fishermen report that they move into lakes in cold weather, spending the winter as much as possible in weedy water. They are said to dig holes in the bottom, like the European carp. This genus includes closely related species of identical general distribution in Illinois, but differing noticeably in respect to the structures of food selection, and likewise to some extent in situations preferred, one of the more abundant species especially (*bubalus*) habitually occurring in deeper water than the other. In the red-mouth buffalo (*cyprinella*) the pharyngeal jaws are lighter than in *bubalus*, their teeth have a smaller grinding surface, and the gill-rakers are longer and more numerous.

The feeding habits of the buffaloes, like those of all the fishes inhabiting the muddy waters of central Illinois, are difficult of observation, but several fishermen and other river men have reported to us that these fishes have the habit of whirling around in shallow water, or plowing steadily along with their heads buried in the mud, their bodies in an oblique position, and their tails occasionally showing above the surface. These operations have nothing to do with the act of spawning, and probably indicate a search for small mollusks and insect larvæ living in the mud. Buffaloes breed in the spring, depositing their eggs in great num-

* The presence of the conspicuous maxillary barbels in the carp, entirely wanting in the buffalo and the heavy serrated dorsal spine of the carp—all fins of the buffalo being spineless—are sufficient marks of distinction.

bers near the edges of sloughs. Fishermen on the Illinois say that their set-nets become coated with eggs when spawning is in progress. All species spawn early, ordinarily in April. Mosher (Bull. U. S. Fish Comm., 1885, p. 190) has described their spawning behavior. They proceed shoreward in shallow water to deposit their eggs, each female forming the center of a bunch of 3 to 8 males. The oviposition is attended with a tremendous splashing, which on a still evening may be heard a mile. The people call it tumbling; in fact it is a sight which once seen will never be forgotten.

Buffaloes form a large part of the fish catch in the Mississippi Valley, 11,491,000 ℔ having been taken from the Mississippi and its tributaries in 1903. The annual product of the Illinois River and its tributary streams, although decreasing considerably during the past twenty years, is now about 3,000,000 ℔. The flesh of the buffalo, while perhaps superior to that of the carp, is not much more esteemed, and brings a low price.

Key to the Species of **ICTIOBUS** found in Illinois

a. Mouth large, oblique, upper lip about on level with lower margin of orbit, angle of mandible with horizontal more than 40°; maxillary as long as snout; lips thin and nearly smooth...**cyprinella.**

aa. Mouth smaller, little oblique, level of upper lip about midway between chin and lower margin of orbit, angle of mandible with horizontal slight, less than 20°; maxillary not more than ¾ length of snout; lips more or less coarsely striate.

b. Back scarcely elevated, depth 3 to 3¼ in length...........................**urus.**

bb. Back elevated and compressed, depth 2½ to 2¾ in length.............**bubalus.**

ICTIOBUS CYPRINELLA (Cuvier & Valenciennes)

RED-MOUTH BUFFALO; BIG-MOUTH BUFFALO

(Map IX)

Cuvier & Valenciennes, 1844, XVII, 477 (**Sclerognathus**).
G., VII, 24 (**Sclerognathus**); J. & G., 114 (**bubalus**); M. V., 44; J. & E., I, 163; N., 49 (**bubalus**); J., 65 (**bubalus**); F., 82; F. F., I. 2, 81 (**bubalus**), II. 7, 451 (**cyprinellus**); L., 11.

Body elliptical, robust, dorsal outline but little more curved than ventral; body compressed somewhat more above than below median axis, but nowhere keeled, being rather broadly rounded at belly and nape; greatest depth from 2.8 to 3.3 in length, usually 3. Size large, reaching a length of 2½ feet and a weight of 40 ℔. General coloration a dull brownish olive, never silvery, fins dusky. In breeding dress top of head slate with a tinge of greenish, cheeks and opercles olive-green; upper part of body, except in front of dorsal, of a coppery tint; region of median axis a pale green; ventral

RED-MOUTH BUFFALO, *Ictiobus cyprinella* (Cuvier & Valenciennes)

Red-mouth Buffalo, *Ictiobus cyprinella* (Cuvier & Valenciennes)

region white dulled with bluish; predorsal region and upper part of caudal peduncle slate; dorsal and caudal fins drab-gray; anal dusky olive; ventrals lighter; pectorals dull white under olive. Head large and heavy, its length from 3.3 to 3.7, depth 3.9 to 4.2, width 4.8 to 5.2 in length of body; snout blunt and broadly rounded; interorbital space convex, 2 to 2.4 in head; snout separated from frontal region of head by a slight transverse depression in front of orbits, giving it a turned-up appearance; mouth large and wide, terminal, protractile forward, very oblique, upper edge of mandible about reaching level of median axis, upper lip almost on a level with lower margin of orbit; mandibles strong and broad, forming a wide protruding angle at their union with the quadrate; lips thinner and smoother than in other species of *Ictiobus*, upper very thin and nearly smooth, lower thicker and somewhat lobed at corners, rather faintly and finely striate; eye 5.6 to 7 in head, situated well forward; opercle strongly striated and very broad. Dorsal rays 24 to 28, longest ray a little more than half the base of fin; caudal not deeply forked; anal short, inserted under last rays of dorsal; ventrals falling about as short of vent as pectorals do of ventrals. Scales large, uniform in size and evenly distributed, rather loosely imbricated, their number 7 or 8, 37 to 40, 6 or 7; lateral line complete, rather flexuose posteriorly and somewhat abruptly elevated in front of dorsal fin.

FIG. 14

Sexual differences slight, the males averaging a little smaller in size and darker in color than the females; spring males without tubercles.

Distributed throughout the Mississippi Valley, in rivers, lakes, ponds, and larger creeks; also in the Red River of the North to Winnipeg. It does not occur east of the Alleghanies, nor in the Great Lakes.

This is a very abundant fish in our larger streams and in the lakes of the river bottoms, being one of the three species most commonly shipped from the Illinois and the Mississippi under the name of "buffalo-fish." It is taken abundantly in the latter river at Cairo, Grafton, and Quincy, and is one of the important commercial species of the Illinois, from which it is caught in large numbers as far north as Henry. It is much less abundant now, however, than some years ago. It is the common "buffalo-fish" of the fishermen, and generally receives no more distinctive name. It grows to a large size, sometimes reaching a weight of

50 pounds. Although its flesh is of poor quality, it is used everywhere as food.

Its structures of food prehension and appropriation—the mouth, the gill-rakers, and the pharyngeal jaws and teeth—are so constructed as to enable it to collect its food readily from a muddy bottom, to strain away the greater part of the mud, retaining objects large enough to serve as food, and to crush and masticate hard or shell-covered objects, unfit for digestion entire. Its pharyngeal jaws are not so strong as those of *bubalus*, the thickness being about a fourth the depth. The teeth are some seventy-five in number on each jaw, minute above, gradually but not greatly thickened below, the ten lowest occupying nearly a fifth of the length of the arch. The gills are compactly disposed in a rather small branchial chamber, the upper ends of the arches being decurved and the lower elevated so that each gill forms about three fourths of a circle. There are seventy-five gill-rakers in the anterior row, the longer of which are fully equal in length to the corresponding gill-filaments, and eight or ten of the lower rakers are fused in the form of thick oblique ridges.

About a third of the food of seventeen specimens examined, consisted of algæ, seeds of aquatic plants, and distillery slops, the last obtained off the Peoria city front where the wastes from distilleries were emptied into the stream. Of the remaining two thirds, nearly half consisted of *Entomostraca*, and more than half of aquatic insects, very largely *Chironomus* larvæ and larvæ of day-flies.

The species breeds in early spring, ordinarily between the 10th and 20th of April (Capt. Schulte). In 1898 the red-mouth spawned between the 15th and the 30th of that month.

ICTIOBUS URUS (Agassiz)

MONGREL BUFFALO; ROUND BUFFALO

(Pl., p. 71; Map X)

Agassiz, 1854, Amer. J. Sci. Arts (Silliman's Journal), XVII, 355 (**Carpiodes**).
J. & G. (**Bubalichthys**), 116; M. V., 44; J. & E., I, 164; N., 50 (**Bubalichthys niger**); J., 65 (**Bubalichthys**); F., 82; F. F., I. 2, 81 (**Bubalichthys niger**), II. 7, 452; L., 11.

Body robust, elliptical, the dorsal and ventral outlines nearly equally curved, the general form being much as in *cyprinella* except that the body is somewhat more elongate and the back more broadly rounded in front of dorsal; depth 3 to 3.4 in length. Size large, about as in last species. Color usually darker than in *cyprinella*, a dark slaty gray, shading to almost black

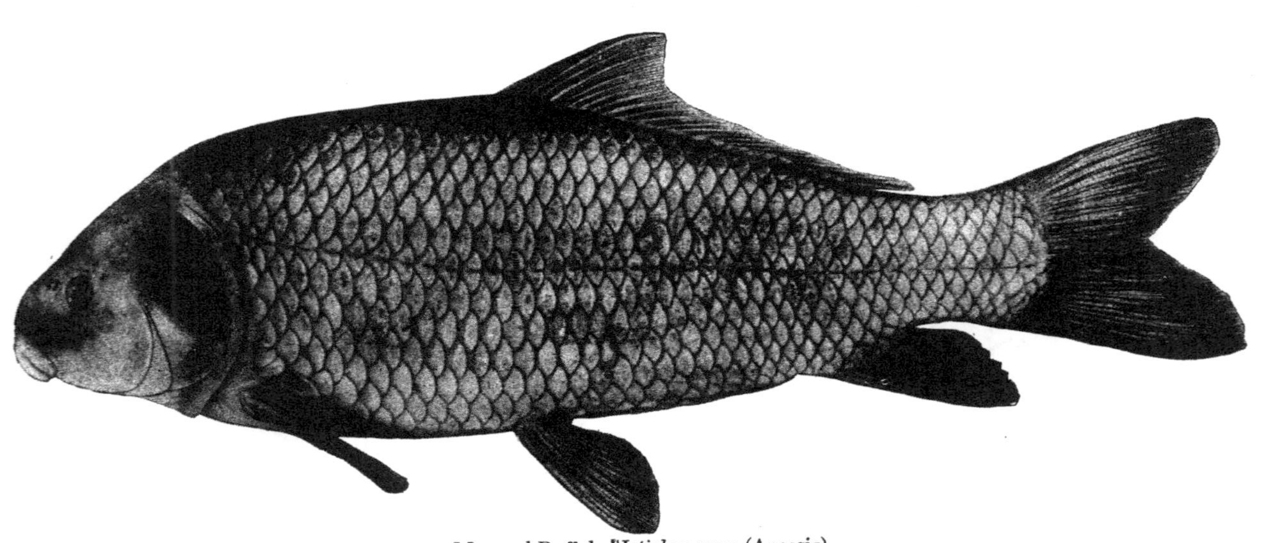

Mongrel Buffalo, *Ictiobus urus* (Agassiz)

when taken from clear water; all fins dark. Head thick and heavy, its length 3.7 to 4, depth 4 to 4.8, width 4.9 to 5.6 in length of body; snout very blunt and broadly rounded, its profile continuous with that of frontal region; interorbital space 2 to 2.3 in head; mouth moderate, considerably smaller than in last species, and but slightly larger than in next species, subterminal, protractile forward and downward, as a rule but little oblique, the edge of the mandible falling considerably below median axis, level of upper lip about midway between chin and lower margin of orbit; angle formed by articulation of mandible with quadrate evident, but less prominent than in *cyprinella*; lips rather thin, but less so than in last species, the upper faintly, the lower rather coarsely, striated; eye 5.1 to 6.6 in head, situated well upward and forward; opercles not so broad as in the last. Dorsal rays 29 or 30, the longest considerably less than ½ base of fin; other fins about as in the preceding species, the caudal not quite so deeply forked. Scales 7 or 8, 36–40, 6 to 8; lateral line complete, less flexuose posteriorly and not so abruptly elevated in front of dorsal as in *cyprinella*.

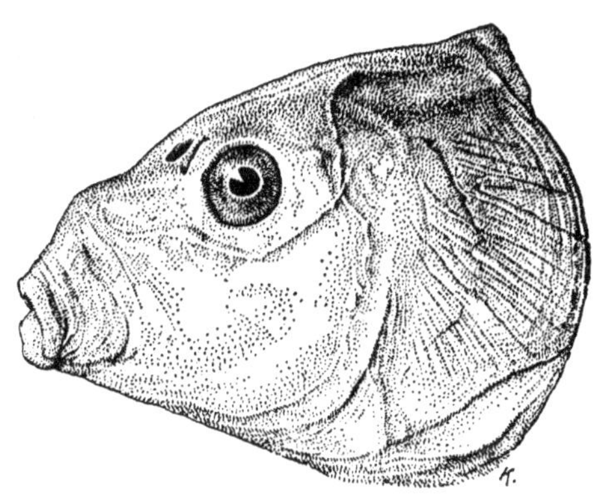

Fig. 15

Spring males without tubercles.

The mongrel buffalo appears to vary somewhat more than either *I. cyprinella* or *bubalus*, but we have met with no cases which appear to show intergradation with either. This species seems to be always distinguishable from the former by its much smaller and less oblique mouth, the upper lip falling far below the level of the lower margin of the orbit, and by the coarsely striate lower lips; from the latter by the more elongate and less compressed body, and by the broad rounding of the frontal region and of the back in front of the dorsal fin.

Distributed throughout the Mississippi Valley practically as the red-mouth is, but less abundantly.

This is a large species, sometimes exceeding 50 pounds in weight, though commonly less than 20. It resembles the red-mouth in habits and value.

The same may be said with respect to its food, our 17 specimens, well distributed as to time and place of capture, having taken ratios of animal and vegetable food almost identical with those of *cyprinella*—67 per cent. and 33 per cent. respectively. There was a larger ratio of mollusks and of insects—the latter

42 per cent.—but the principal species of each were the same as in *cyprinella*. The *Crustacea* (13 per cent.) were almost all *Entomostraca*, a young crawfish taken by one of the buffaloes being the only exception. This species had likewise eaten distillery slops and various forms of aquatic plants, including duckweeds and unicellular algæ.

This buffalo spawned at Havana in 1898 between the 15th and the 30th of April, but ripe females were caught the following year as late as May 29.

ICTIOBUS BUBALUS (RAFINESQUE)

SMALL-MOUTH BUFFALO; RAZOR-BACKED BUFFALO; QUILLBACK BUFFALO

(MAP XI)

Rafinesque, 1818, J. Phys., 421 (**Amblodon**).
G., VII, 22 (**Sclerognathus urus**); J. & G., 116 (**Bubalichthys altus**); M. V., 44; J. & E., I, 164; N., 49, (**cyanellus**); J., 66 (**Bubalichthys cyanellus**); F., 82; F. F., II. 7, 448; L., 11.

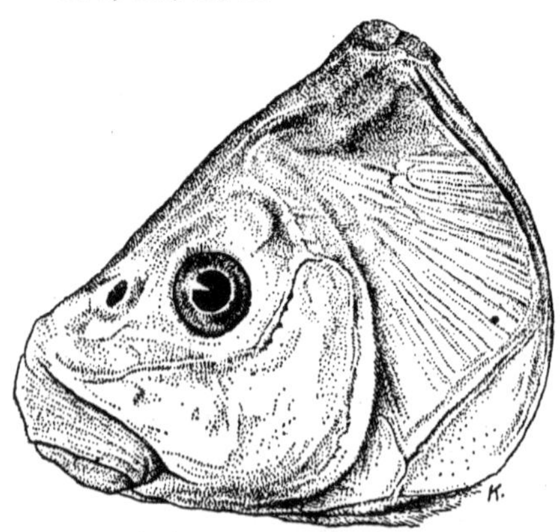

FIG. 16

Body compressed, back much elevated; ventral line not much decurved; back in front of dorsal fin compressed into a keel; depth from 2.5 to 2.9 in length of body. Size somewhat smaller than in the two preceding species. General coloration much as in *cyprinella*, but becoming paler in adults, sometimes exceedingly so, old specimens usually a muddy whitish, with but faint traces of blue and coppery about head and anterior half of body; young specimens usually quite dark, the head dark bluish gray below; all fins more or less dusky. Head smaller, more compressed, and more pointed than in the foregoing species, the occipital region high and sharply arched transversely, length of head 3.6 to 4.1, depth 4.4 to 5, width 5.1 to 5.8 in body; interorbital space 2.1 to 2.6 in head; snout pointed; mouth small, inferior, protractile downward and forward, in size and form sometimes scarcely distinguishable from that of the last species; lips rather coarsely and brokenly plicate; mandibles nearly horizontal, scarcely forming an evident angle at the articulation with the quadrate; eye 4.4 to 6.2 in head, rather larger than in either of the preceding species; opercle about as in last. Dorsal rays 27 to 30, the longest a little less than half base of fin; caudal somewhat more deeply forked than in *cyprinella* or *urus*. Scales 7 or 8, 37–39, 5 to 7; lateral line complete, gently flexuose.

Head and snout of males finely tuberculate in spring.

SMALL-MOUTH BUFFALO, *Ictiobus bubalus* (Rafinesque)

Small-mouth Buffalo, *Ictiobus bubalus* (Rafinesque)

Distributed throughout the Mississippi Valley much as the other buffalo are, but tending more generally to deep water, according to the reports of fishermen.

It is common in the Mississippi and the Illinois rivers, and in the principal streams of the state at large. It is not so frequently taken in shallow water as the other species, and it is said to have a stronger preference for flowing streams. Nevertheless, it must be said that more than two thirds of the specimens in our collections came from lakes and sloughs, the greater part of the remainder being from rivers of the larger size.

This buffalo does not average as large as the preceding species, its maximum weight in the Mississippi being, according to Mr. Ashlock, of Alton, less than 40 ℔.

About a fifth of the food of the specimens examined, consisted of vegetation, mainly duckweed, but with an occasional admixture of terrestrial rubbish. The animal food was divided, with approximate equality, between mollusks, insects, and *Entomostraca*, the latter taken chiefly in spring when they are present in the greatest abundance. The food of the young of this buffalo consists largely of the minuter forms of the plankton, including especially *Protozoa*, rotifers, and unicellular algæ.

The gill-rakers of this species are less numerous than those of *cyprinella* and scarcely so long, and seem to form a less efficient straining apparatus. The pharyngeal jaws are heavier, triangular in section, and about as thick as high. Seventeen specimens of this species, collected from the Illinois and the Mississippi in various months from April to October, contained aquatic vegetation amounting to about a third of the total food, the principal element being a small duckweed (*Wolffia*) especially abundant where a part of the fishes were taken, and amounting in some cases to 95 per cent. of the contents of the stomach. A larger duckweed, fragments of hornwort (*Ceratophyllum*), diatoms, and other unicellular algæ had also been eaten. Animal food (80 per cent.) was fairly equally divided between mollusks, insects, and *Crustacea*, the first (30 per cent.) being mainly a thin-shelled bivalve (*Sphærium*) common in the mud. Several specimens had eaten nothing but this mollusk. *Chironomus* larvæ and *Entomostraca* were the principal other elements, each making practically a fifth of the entire food.

GENUS **CARPIODES** RAFINESQUE

CARP-SUCKERS

Body more or less thin and compressed, becoming deeper and more arched above with age; ventral line almost straight or but slightly curved downward; head small, short, somewhat compressed; lips thin and slightly striate; bones of skull with generally smoother surfaces and not so heavy as in *Ictiobus*; a well-developed anterior fontanelle at intercalation of frontals and ethmoid; a supraorbital bone present; posterior fontanelle narrowest behind, its posterior margin formed by the converging parietals; suboperculum very broad, subtriangular, its greatest breadth below middle; cheek deep and long, the lower posterior border of the preopercle somewhat angled, the center of orbit equidistant between its infraposterior angle and the upper corner of the gill-cleft; pharyngeal bones broad but very thin, the teeth very much compressed, weaker than in *Ictiobus*; vertebræ 35 or 36; air-bladder in two parts; dorsal fin long, rays 23 to 30, the anterior rays sometimes produced into a long filament that may reach almost to the caudal; scales large; lateral line complete; color light, usually more or less silvery; snout tuberculate in spring males of some species (*difformis* and *velifer*).

Four species of these fishes are known in Illinois, mostly of small size, seldom over 12 inches long, and of little or no commercial value. The name of carp was applied to them by the early settlers of Virginia, although they bear only a general resemblance to the European species of that name. Since the latter was introduced into our waters the native species have been called "American carp." Since they belong to a different family from the foreign species, to which the name was originally given, the common name of carp-sucker, already considerably used, is much to be preferred.

In Illinois they are distributed throughout the greater rivers of the state and their larger tributaries, and occur also in Lake Michigan and the smaller lakes of northern Illinois. They are extremely common in the lakes and ponds of the river bottoms.

The carp-suckers are rather filthy feeders, swallowing a greater quantity of mud than the nearly related buffalo-fish. The structures of food prehension carry to its extreme a development of the gill-rakers and a correlative degradation of the pharyngeal jaws and teeth. The pharyngeal bones are very thin and brittle, each with about 200 teeth, minute above and gradually enlarging downwards, but not thickening or lengthening greatly on the lower part of the arch. The intestine is very slender, and about four times as long as the head and body taken together. The gills are remarkably compacted, the upper

QUILLBACK, *Carpiodes velifer* (Rafinesque)

and lower ends nearly meeting when the mouth is closed, and the longest of the anterior series are a little longer than the corresponding filaments.

Nineteen specimens, representing 13 localities from extreme northern to extreme southern Illinois, and various dates from April to October, indicate that our native carp differ from their near allies, the buffalo-fishes, in the smaller amount of vegetation eaten, in the greater quantity of mud mingled with the food, and in a deficiency of the larger insect larvæ. The vegetable food of these specimens was only 8 per cent., mostly the small duckweed, *Wolffia*. Mollusks made about a fourth of the food, all the thin-shelled bivalve *Sphœrium*. Insects averaged about a third, the greater part larvæ of *Chironomus*. *Entomostraca* made nearly a fourth, and included a considerable list and variety of our more abundant species.

Key to the Species of **CARPIODES** found in Illinois

a. Snout short, 3½ to 4½ in head; nostrils well forward, the distance from anterior nostril to end of snout considerably less than diameter of eye; tip of lower jaw little in advance of nostrils.

b. Body robust, subfusiform, depth 2⅔ to 3 in length; snout obtusely pointed; eye moderate, 4½ to 5 in head; anterior rays of dorsal scarcely elevated, osseous at base; large species, reaching over 5 ℔ in weight........... **carpio.**

bb. Body thin and compressed, the back much elevated in adults, depth 2¼ to 2¾ in length; snout very blunt, squarish at tip; eye large, 3¾ to 4½ in head; anterior rays of dorsal much lengthened, sometimes equaling length of base of fin; small species, not over 12 inches in length.............. **difformis.**

aa. Snout longer, 3 to 3½ in head; nostrils situated well back, the distance from anterior nostril to end of snout usually greater than diameter of eye; tip of lower jaw far in advance of nostrils.

c. Body robust, subfusiform, depth 2⅔ to 3½ in length; anterior rays of dorsal scarcely elevated, about ½ length of base of fin; halves of lower tip meeting at a wide angle; large species, reaching a weight of 5℔........... **thompsoni.**

cc. Body compressed, the back more or less arched, depth 2½ to 3 in length; anterior rays of dorsal much elevated, nearly or more than equaling length of base of fin; halves of lower lip meeting at a sharp angle; species of small size, not exceeding 12 inches.. **velifer.**

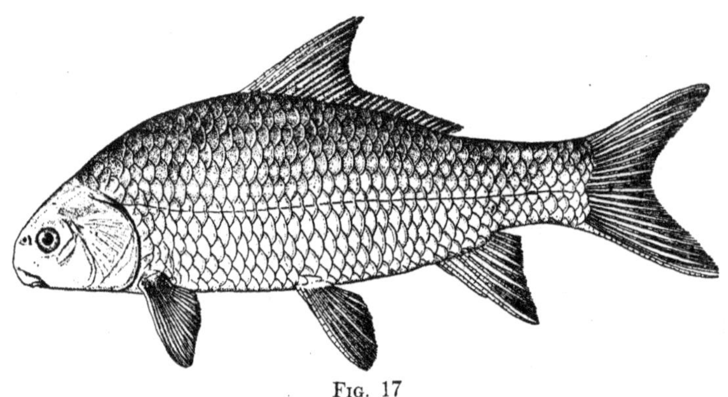

Fig. 17

CARPIODES CARPIO (Rafinesque)

COMMON RIVER CARP

(Map XII)

Rafinesque, 1820, Ichth. Oh., 56 (**Catostomus**).
J. & G., 118; M. V., 45 (**Ictiobus**); J. & E., I, 166; N., 49 (**Ichthyobus carpio** and (?) **bison**); J., 65 (**carpio** and (?) **bison**); F., 81 (**Ictiobus cyprinus**, part); L., 11,

Body elongate, subelliptical, somewhat compressed, but more fusiform than in the next species, the back not greatly arched and the ventral line nearly straight; depth 2.9 to 3.3 in length. Size large, frequently taken weighing 3 or 4 ℔ and said sometimes to reach a weight of 7 or 8 ℔. Color smoky to olivaceous over silvery, lighter below. Head short, deep and heavy, its length 4 to 4.4, depth 4.9 to 5.4, width 6 to 6.8 in length of body; snout short, somewhat pointed, 3.3 to 4.1 in head; the nostrils well forward, but not quite so much so as in the next species, the distance from the anterior nostril to end of snout 3/5 to 4/5 of diameter of eye; mouth wide and short, wholly inferior, the tip of lower lip very slightly in advance of nostrils; lips thin, the halves of lower meeting at a very wide angle or open curve; interorbital space 2.2 to 2.6 in head; eye moderate, 4.4 to 5.1 in head. Dorsal rays 23 to 27, the first rays notably osseous at base, little elongated, about 1/2 length of base of fin. Scales large, 6, 35–37, 6, usually 35 or 36 in longitudinal series; lateral line complete, almost straight; scales (as in *difformis*) somewhat thinner and less closely imbricated than in *thompsoni* and *velifer*.

Occurs throughout the Ohio and Mississippi valleys, ranging southwest to central Texas. It seldoms ascends the smaller streams, and our collections have come mainly from the Illinois at Meredosia and Havana, and from the Mississippi at Grafton. We have not found it anywhere abundant. It is said by Mississippi River fishermen sometimes to reach a weight of 10 ℔.

It is sold for food, but is flavorless and soft. It breeds in spring, but the time of spawning is not indicated by our notes.

This fish is closely related to *C. difformis*, from which it may be distinguished by the more pointed snout, smaller eye, and more robust, subfusiform body. It and the next species agree in the shortness of the snout, 3⅓ to 4½ in head, and in the anterior position of the nostrils, and both are by these marks readily distinguishable, except in the case of very young specimens, from *thompsoni* and *velifer*, in which species the snout is notably longer, 3 to 3½ in head, and the nostrils are situated far back from the end of the snout, the distance from the anterior nostril to the end of the muzzle being greater than the diameter of the eye.

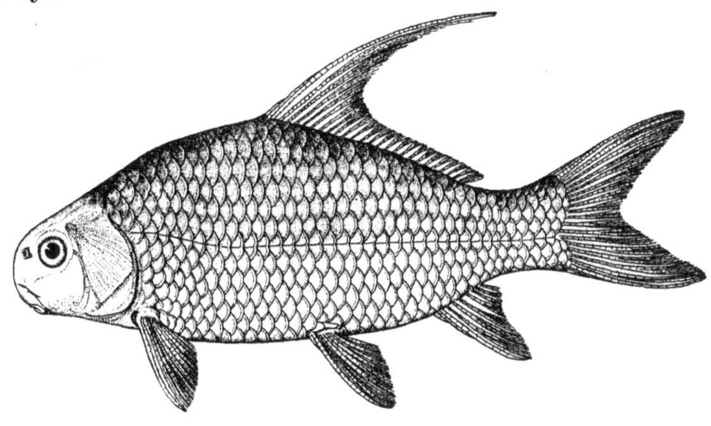

FIG. 18

CARPIODES DIFFORMIS COPE

BLUNT-NOSED RIVER CARP

(MAP XIII)

Cope, 1870, P. Amer. Phil. Soc., 480.

J. & G., 120; M. V., 45 (**Ictiobus**); J. & E., I, 166; N., 49 (**Ichthyobus**); J., 65 (**difformis** and (?) **cutisanserinus**); F., 81 (**Ictiobus cyprinus**, part); L., 12.

Body short, compressed, the back much arched, ventral surface broad and nearly straight; depth 2.4 to 2.7 in length. Size small, seldom over 12 inches in length. Color silvery, obscured above by smoky olive, much as in the preceding species. Head small, short and deep, its length 3.9 to 4.3, depth 4.5 to 4.9, width 5.7 to 6.4 in length of body, snout short, very blunt, the muzzle squarish, distance from eye to tip 3.9 to 4.5 in head, usually greater than 4; nostrils near tip of snout, distance from anterior nostril to end of snout being ⅓ to ⅗ diameter of orbit; mouth wholly inferior, not quite so wide as in the last species, the lips somewhat thicker, weakly plicate, the halves of lower meeting at a rather sharp angle; tip of lower lip scarcely in advance of nostrils; interorbital space 2.2 to 2.5 in head; eye larger than in other species of *Carpiodes*, 3.9 to 4.6 in head, usually but little more than 4. Dorsal rays 24 to 25, the first rays rather osseous at base, but not so robust as in *carpio*, and as a rule much elongated, sometimes exceeding in length the base of the fin. Scales large, 6–7, 35–37, 6, usually 35 or 36, rather loosely imbricated; lateral line complete, nearly straight.

Males with snout tuberculate in spring.

Ohio Valley and westward; generally common. Common in our collections, seeming to prefer the shallow waters of the smaller streams, where the young are often found in large numbers; adults taken sparingly in the Illinois and Rock rivers.

Represented in 102 of our collections, more than half of which are from creeks. We have found it less frequent in the larger than in the smaller rivers, and still less so in lakes and ponds. The size is small and the species is of little value as food. It is abundantly distributed throughout central Illinois, but has occurred less commonly in our southern Illinois collections, and is absent from the most of those made in the extreme northern part of the state. It apparently avoids in great measure the lower Illinoisan glaciation, having been taken but five times by us within that area.

CARPIODES VELIFER (Rafinesque)

QUILLBACK; SILVER CARP

(Pl., p. 74; Map XIV)

Rafinesque, 1820, Ichth. Oh., 56 (**Catostomus**).

J. & G., 118 (**tumidus**), 119 (**cyprinus**); M. V., 45 (**Ictiobus**); J. & E., I, 167; N., 49 (**Ichthyobus**); J., 65; F., 81 (**Ictiobus cyprinus**, part); L., 12.

Body ovate, compressed, back much arched in adults; ventral line lmost straight; depth 2.7 to 3 in length. Size small, seldom exceeding 12 inches. Color light olive above, sides silvery, fins pale. Head moderate, its length 3.6 to 4, depth 4.3 to 5.2, width 6 to 6.7 in length of body; snout long, bluntly pointed, as in last species, 2.9 to 3.5 in head, usually less than 3.2; nostrils well back, distance from anterior opening to end of snout greater than diameter of eye; mouth rather narrow, slightly oblique, tip of lower lip far in advance of nostrils; lips weakly plicate, rather thick, the lower halves meeting in a sharp angle; interorbital space 2.3 to 2.5 in head; eye small, 4.8 to 5.5 in head. Dorsal rays 27 to 30, usually 27, the anterior rays slender and elongate, sometimes longer than base of fin. Scales 7, 39–40, 6; lateral line complete, usually somewhat flexuose.

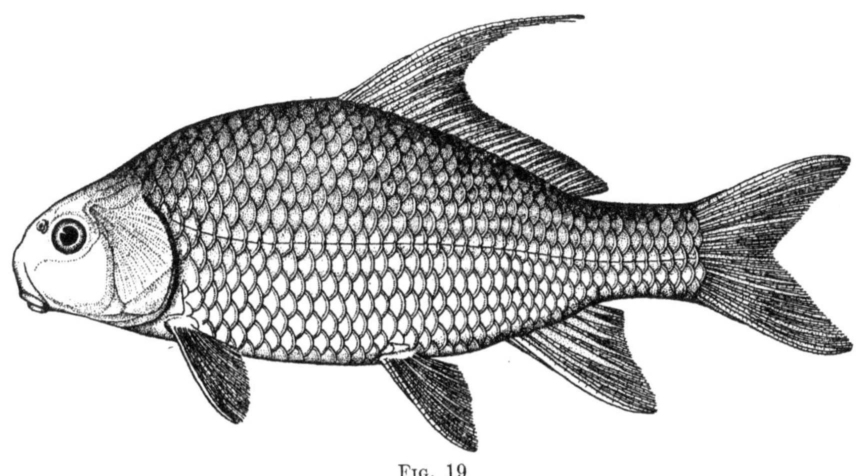

Fig. 19

This species, unlike the others of its genus, is most abundant in northern Illinois and least so in the southern part of the state. It is almost wholly wanting from our southern Illinois collections made within the area of the lower Illinoisan glaciation. Like the preceding species, however, it is found chiefly in the smaller rivers and creeks, nearly twice as frequently in the latter as in the rivers of larger size. It ascends small streams freely at the time of the spring floods. In 1898 it spawned at Havana about April 15. The snout of the male is tuberculate in the spawning season.

CARPIODES THOMPSONI Agassiz

LAKE CARP

(Map XV)

Agassiz, 1855, Amer. J. Sci. Arts, XIX, 76.

J. & G., 119; M. V., 45 (**Ictiobus**); J. & E., I, 167; N., 49 (**Ichthyobus**); J., 65 (**thompsoni** and (?) **selene**); F., 81 (**Ictiobus cyprinus**, part).

Body elongate, subfusiform, the back little arched and the ventral line nearly straight, in general form and proportions very close to *C. carpio*, depth 2.8 to 3.2 in length. Larger than *difformis* and *velifer*, known to reach a weight of 3 to 5 ℔, and said by lake fishermen to grow much larger. Color not different from that of *carpio*. Head moderate, its length 3.7 to 4, depth 4.5 to 5.1, width 5.7 to 6.4 in length of body; snout long, bluntly pointed, 3 to 3.4 in head; nostrils situated well back from end of snout, distance from anterior opening to tip of muzzle greater than diameter of eye; mouth narrower and longer than in the two preceding species, subterminal and somewhat oblique, the tip of the lower lip far in advance of the nostrils; lips evidently plicate, not very thin, the halves of the lower one meeting at a rather wide angle; interorbital space 2.4 to 2.7 in head; eye small, 5 to 6.4, usually more than 5.5. Dorsal rays 25 to 30, usually nearer 30, anterior rays slender, little elevated; scarcely more than half the length of base of fin. Scales somewhat smaller and more closely imbricated than in the two preceding species, 7, 38 to 40, 6, usually 39 in longitudinal series; lateral line complete, nearly straight.

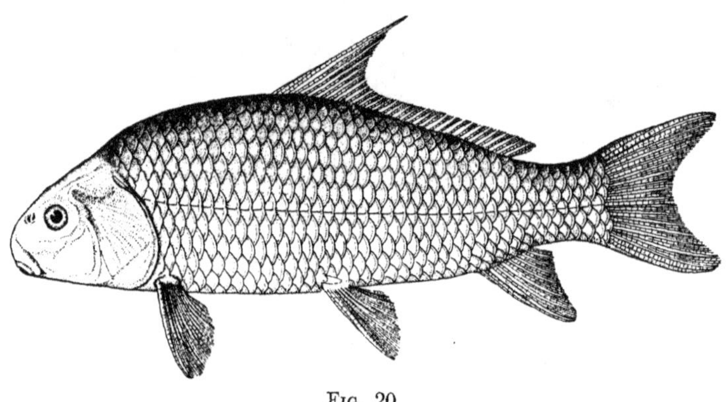

FIG. 20

This species can be separated with readiness from both the preceding by its longer nose, more oblique mouth, and more posterior nostrils; it is easily distinguished from the next when adult by its larger size and by the differences in general proportions, and by the shortness of the first dorsal rays. The young of these two species can not be separated with any certainty.

This carp-sucker belongs to the fauna of the Great Lake region and is but rarely taken in the inland waters of Illinois, our adult specimens numbering a very few from the Illinois river at Ottawa, Henry, Havana, and Meredosia. It is too rare in our waters to be commercially important. Its special habits are unknown.

GENUS **ERIMYZON** JORDAN

CHUB-SUCKERS

Body oblong, more or less compressed; mouth subinferior; upper lip protractile; lower lip plicate, infolded, forming an acute angle in front; no anterior fontanelle; posterior fontanelle well developed; no supraorbital bone, suborbital bones well developed, not much narrower than the fleshy

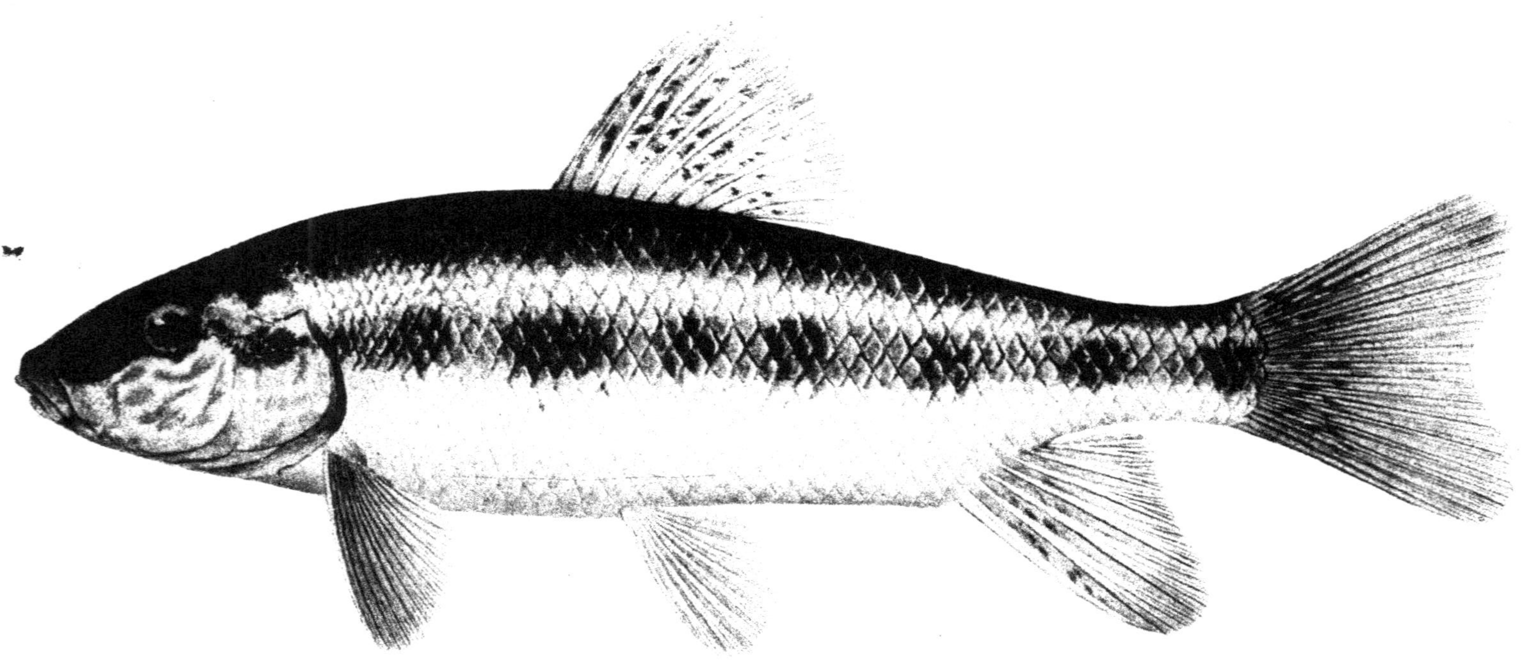

CHUB-SUCKER, *Erimyzon sucetta oblongus* (Mitchill)

portion of the cheeks below; pharyngeal bones weak, the teeth small and slender, rapidly diminishing in length upward; vertebræ 34; ribs 13; dorsal rays 11 or 12; scales large; lateral line wanting at all ages; air-bladder with two chambers. Fresh waters of the United States; one species, widely distributed.

ERIMYZON SUCETTA OBLONGUS (MITCHILL)

CHUB-SUCKER; SWEET SUCKER.

(MAP XVI)

Mitchill, 1815, T. Lit. & Phil. Soc. N. Y., 1 (**Cyprinus oblongus**).
G., VII, 21 (**Moxostoma oblongum**); J. & G., 133; M. V., 46; J. & E., I, 186; N., 48 (**Erimyzon oblongus**); J., 64; F., 80; F. F., II, 7, 447; L., 12.

Body oblong, compressed, the depth increasing with age; predorsal region often more or less elevated and profile angled at nape in old specimens; depth 3.1 to 3.9 in length. Size small, length about 10 inches. Coloration varying considerably with age; in adults a nearly uniform brownish olive, intermixed with pinkish anteriorly, and everywhere with more or less of a coppery luster; paler below; fins dusky, ventrals and anal most so. In young specimens the sides are marked by four distinct bands of color: a dark band extending from occiput backward on each side of dorsal fin to middle of caudal peduncle, covering 4 upper rows of scales; below this a band of light color, extending from just above upper corner of gill-cleft to upper part of base of caudal; next, and most prominent, a narrow band of purplish black, extending from center of base of caudal forward along sides and through eye to end of snout; and beneath this dark lateral band the sides pale to the whitish or silvery belly. Adults are found which retain to a greater or less extent the markings of the young, specimens from 6 to 8 inches in length sometimes showing more or less plainly the dark lateral stripe, as well as the apportionment of color in bands above and below; the black lateral band may break up into indistinct bars with age, various stages between the barred condition and a uniform dusky coloration being found. Head short, compressed, considerably tapered, its length 3.5 to 4.1, width 5.1 to 6.5, depth 4.6 to 5.6 in length of body; interorbital space weakly convex, 2.2 to 2.6 in head; snout (usually) 2.5 to 3.2 in head; mouth subterminal, rather small, mandibles more or less obliquely set, tip of upper lip in old specimens sometimes not far below level of lower rim of orbit; lower lip strongly plicate, its halves meeting in a rather acute angle; eye large, 3.8 to 5.8 in head. Dorsal fin a little higher than long, its developed rays 9 to 12. Scales large, 36 to 45 in longitudinal series, transverse rows 13 to 15; scales more or less crowded anteriorly and somewhat irregularly arranged on posterior half of body; lateral line as a rule entirely wanting at all ages; specimens occasionally found with one or two imperfectly developed pores.

Head of spring males with three large tubercles on each side of snout, two in longitudinal series in front of eye, one lower down, near corner of mouth.

This species, with its two varieties, extends throughout the Great Lake region; northeast to the St. Lawrence and the Connecticut rivers, and to the St. Johns River, in New Brunswick; southeast to Georgia, South Carolina, and Florida; southward to the Gulf, southwest to the Rio Grande, and northward to the Dakotas. The northern representatives of the species belong to the variety *oblongus* and the southern to *sucetta*.

In this state it is widely distributed in large and small streams, and in the small lakes of McHenry county, in northeastern Illinois; but it is much the most abundant in the eastern part of the state in the drainage of the Wabash and the Ohio rivers, and in the headwaters of the Sangamon and of the Kaskaskia adjacent to these. A line drawn through the middle of the state from north to south but swerving slightly to the west below central Illinois, has 101 of our localities for this species to the east of it and but 8 to the west. It is essentially a creek species, occurring proportionally five times as frequently in our collections from creeks as from rivers, large or small, and eight times as frequently as from lakes and ponds.

The chub-sucker is a bottom feeder, and has the habit of supporting itself on the bottom, like the darter, by means of its paired fins. In ordinary seasons it spawns in central Illinois in April and May. Ripe males were taken at Havana April 10, 1899, and females with ripe ovaries from March 20 to April 15. This fish bites readily at a small hook, but its flesh is bony and without flavor, and owing to its small size the species has no commercial value.

Genus **MINYTREMA** Jordan

SPOTTED SUCKERS

Body elongate, compressed; mouth inferior; upper lip freely protractile; lower lip plicate, forming an angle posteriorly; posterior fontanelle large; supraorbital bone present; suborbital bones well developed; pharyngeal bones as in *Erimyzon*, but the teeth somewhat coarser; vertebræ 39; thoracic ribs 17; dorsal rays about 12; scales rather large, nearly equal all over the body; lateral line interrupted in adults, more or less imperfect in half-grown specimens and entirely obsolete in the young; air-bladder with two chambers. Fresh waters of the United States; one species known.

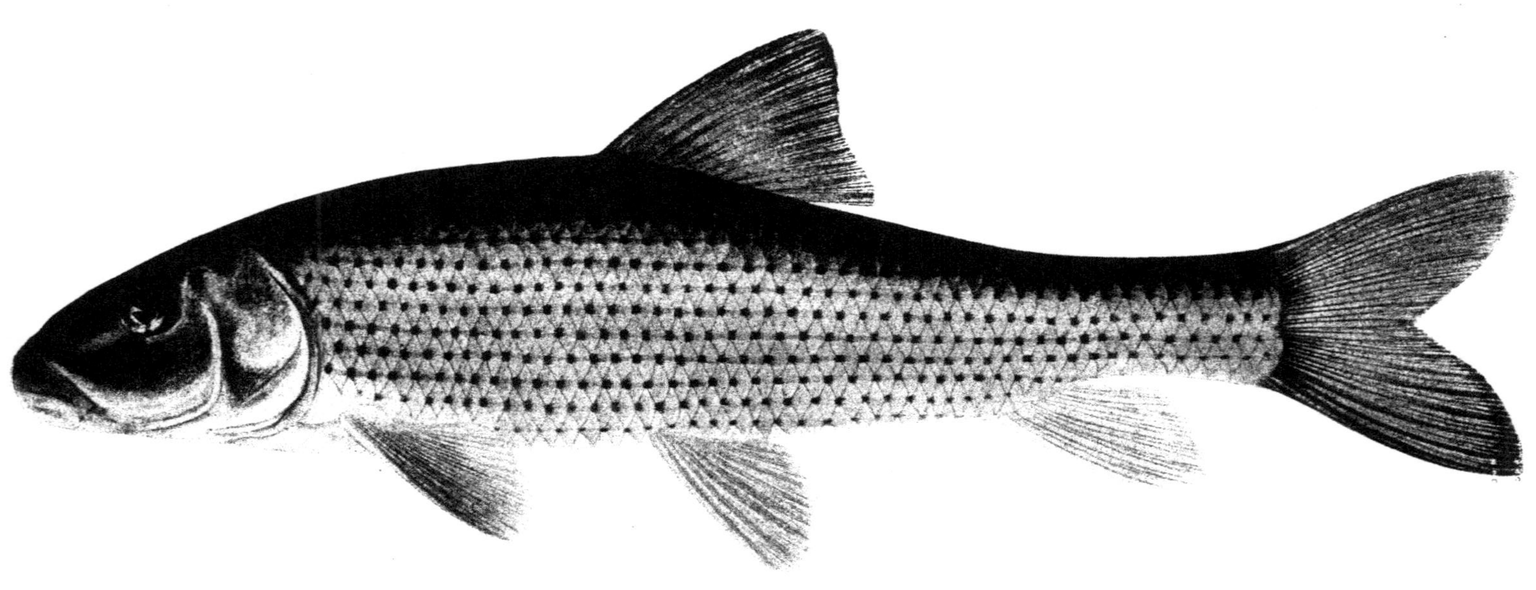

SPOTTED SUCKER, *Minytrema melanops* (Rafinesque)

MINYTREMA MELANOPS (Rafinesque)

SPOTTED SUCKER; STRIPED SUCKER

(Map XVII)

Rafinesque, 1820, Ichth. Oh., 57 (**Catostomus**).
G., VII, 19 (**Catostomus fasciatus**); J. & G., 136; M. V., 47; J. & E., I, 187; N., 48 (**Erimyzon**); J., 64; F., 80; F. F., II. 7, 444; L., 12.

Body oblong, little compressed, adults becoming deeper, depth 3.9 to 4.5 in length. Size rather large, reaching a length of 18 inches. Head olivaceous above, lighter olive to silvery on cheeks and opercles, with some coppery; sides coppery above, greenish gray to silvery below; each scale along sides with a quadrate spot of very dark greenish at base, the spots forming rows lengthwise of body; belly greenish to silvery, with suggestions of coppery luster; fins scarcely dusky, the membranes light greenish. Head 3.9 to 4.6 in length of body, its width 5.9 to 6.8, depth 5.3 to 6, rather flattened above but not depressed; snout 2.3 to 2.7 in head, bluntly pointed; upper lip with faint plicæ, lower evidently plicate, its halves meeting at a rather sharp angle; interorbital space 2.2 to 2.5 in head; eye small, 4.4 to 6.9 in head, placed high, about midway of length of head. Dorsal rays 11 to 12, not including rudiments, the fin higher than long, its position about midway, usually a very little forward. Scales large, 6 or 7, 42–46, 5 to 7, regularly imbricated, not crowded forward; lateral line incomplete in adults, in young specimens imperfect or wanting.

Head of old males covered with small tubercles in spring.

This species is found in the Great Lake region, the upper Mississippi Valley as far north as the Yellowstone, southward and southwestward to the Gulf and to Texas, and on the Atlantic slope from New Jersey to North Carolina. In Illinois it has been taken in all our stream systems, including the Lake Michigan drainage, but most abundantly in the Wabash and the Kaskaskia basins. In proportion to the number of collections made, it has been found in central Illinois twice as frequently as in northern, and in southern Illinois twice as frequently as in central. It is mainly a species of creeks and the smaller rivers—twice as abundant in the former as in the latter—and is comparatively rare in lakes and ponds. It grows to a length of 18 inches, but is not abundant enough in Illinois to have any noticeable value. From the little that is known of its food we may surmise that it lives largely on mollusks and insect larvæ.

Genus **CATOSTOMUS** Le Sueur

FINE-SCALED SUCKERS

Head more or less elongate; mouth inferior, the upper lip thick, protractile, papillose; lower lip greatly developed, incised behind so as to form two lobes; posterior fontanelle large; supraorbital bone wanting, as in *Erimyzon* and *Moxostoma*; suborbital bones narrow; pharyngeal teeth shortish; vertebræ (*commersonii*) 44; ribs 17; dorsal rays 9 to 14; scales usually small, 50 to 115 in the lateral series; lateral line well developed; air-bladder with two chambers. Species numerous; fresh waters of the United States and Canada, east and west of the Rockies; one species (*C. rostratus* Tilesius) found in Siberia; two species found in Illinois. Breeding males of most species with a rosy lateral band, with median fins higher than in female, and with anal swollen and tuberculate.

Key to the Species of **CATOSTOMUS** found in Illinois

a. Head transversely convex above, the orbital rim not elevated; scales in lateral line 60 or more, crowded and smaller anteriorly.

b. Scales in lateral line 95–115 .... **catostomus.**

bb. Scales in lateral line 68–80 .... **commersonii.**

aa. Head broad, depressed, transversely concave between the orbits; scales nearly equal all over the body, not crowded anteriorly, 48 to 55 in the lateral line .... **nigricans.**

CATOSTOMUS CATOSTOMUS (Forster)

LONG-NOSED SUCKER; NORTHERN SUCKER; RED SUCKER

Forster, 1773, Phil. Trans., 155 (**Cyprinus**).

Body elongate, subterete, the depth 4¼ to 4¾ in length. Head quite long and slender, 4¼ to 4⅔ in length, depressed and flattened above, broad at base, but tapering into a long snout, which considerably overhangs the large mouth. Lips thick, coarsely tuberculate, the upper lip narrow, with 2 or 3, rarely 4, rows of tubercles; lower lip deeply incised, the lobes shorter than in *C. griseus*, and the mouth narrower. Lower jaw with a short cartilaginous sheath. Eye rather small, behind the middle of the head. Scales very small, much crowded forward, 95 to 114 in the lateral line, and about 29 (26 to 31) in a cross-row from dorsal to ventrals. Dorsal rays 10 to 11. Males in spring with the head and anal fin profusely tuberculate, the tubercles on the head small; the sides at that season with a broad rosy band. Size large. Length 2½ feet. Great Lakes, upper Missouri river, upper Columbia, and northwestward to Alaska; very abundant northward, but not coming south of lat. 40°.—Jordan and Evermann (Bull. U. S. Nat. Mus., No. 47, I., p. 176).

Found in lower Lake Michigan at Miller, Indiana, and doubtless occurring in the lake within the limits of Illinois.

COMMON SUCKER, *Catostomus commersonii* (Lacépède)

CATOSTOMUS COMMERSONII (Lacépède)

COMMON SUCKER; FINE-SCALED SUCKER

(Map XVIII)

Lacépède, 1803, Hist. Nat. Poiss., V. 502 (**Cyprinus**).
G., VII, 15 (**teres**); J. & G., 129; M. V., 46 (**teres**); J. & E., I, 178; N., 48 (**teres**); J., 64; F., 81 (**teres**); F. F., II. 7, 444 (**teres**); L., 12.

Body elongate, subterete, rather heavy forward, depth 4.3 to 5.3 in length, usually 4.5 to 5. Length 18 inches. Color olivaceous on back and sides, with more or less golden luster; belly whitish; vertical fins with some dusky on rays, membranes paler, those of ventrals and pectorals orange, becoming deeper in spring males, which also have a faint rosy lateral band. Young brownish with blackish blotches and mottlings which are more or less confluent, sometimes forming an indistinct lateral band. Head rather stout, subconical, flattish above, its length 4 to 4.8, width 5.5 to 7, depth 5.5 to 6.6 in body; interorbital space nearly flat, 2.1 to 2.6 in head; snout blunt, decurved, squarish at tip; mouth inferior, rather large, the lips strongly papillose, the upper rather thick, with 3 or 4 rows of papillæ; eye moderate, 4.5 to 6.2 in head, more than 5 in adults. Dorsal fin with 11 to 13, usually 12, rays, its height scarcely, if at all, exceeding the length of the fin's base. Scales 10–11, 63–80, 9–11, crowded anteriorly and below; lateral line complete in adults, pores wanting on some scales in young.

The fin-scaled sucker occurs in streams and ponds from the Great Lakes to New Brunswick and Labrador, in the Hudson River, on the Atlantic slope from New Jersey to South Carolina, and northward to Great Bear Lake and Hudson's Bay. It is abundant throughout the central part of the eastern United States from Massachusetts to Kansas, and is common in the northern third of Illinois, especially in the smaller rivers and larger creeks. It occurs but rarely in the Illinois River as far south as Peoria, and has not been taken by us south of Alton except in the streams of extreme southern Illinois below the Illinoisan glaciation. It is with us essentially a species of creeks and small rivers, nearly four times as common, according to our data, in the former as in the latter. It has been taken but four times in our 293 collections from rivers of the larger size, and but twice from 591 collections made from lakes, ponds, and sloughs. It is common, however, in Lake Michigan. Our collection data show that it is much more likely to be abundant on bottoms with more or less rock and sand than on a completely muddy bottom, and that it has also a decided preference for clear, swift waters. The species reaches a length of 22 inches and a weight of 5 ℔.

The food of this sucker has not been carefully studied, but the strong, thick pharyngeal jaws, nearly twice as wide as high, and the relatively small number of pharyngeal teeth, the lower of which are very much thickened, with expanded crowns, constitute a crushing and grinding apparatus which strongly suggests a prevailing molluscan diet. The gill-rakers are less effective than those of the red-horse, indicating a smaller ratio of crustacean food.

The species spawns in April or May, preferring for the purpose riffles or swift-flowing water to quiet pools.

Though bony, these fishes have a sweet, firm, and flaky flesh, and furnish a food of considerable importance in many parts of the country. They are frequently salted for winter use, and are sometimes sold in our local markets under the name of "family whitefish." They are taken with seines, traps, and gill-nets, bite readily at the hook baited with worms or bits of crawfish, and are sometimes caught by boys in spring with snares fastened to poles.

CATOSTOMUS NIGRICANS Le Sueur

HOGSUCKER; HOGMOLLY; STONE-ROLLER

(Map XIX)

Le Sueur, 1817, J. Ac. Nat. Sci. Phila., 102.

G., VII, 17; J. & G., 130; M. V., 46; J. & E., I, 181; N., 48 (**Hypentelium**); J., 64; F., 81; F. F., II. 7, 445 (**Hypentelium**); L., 12.

Body moderately elongate, subcylindrical, heavy forward, much tapered posteriorly, depth 4.6 to 5.1 in length. Size rather large, reaching a length of 2 feet. Color olivaceous, with brassy luster on sides; belly satiny white; back and sides in younger specimens with 4 rather broad and distinct oblique bars of dark color, one half way between occiput and dorsal, one just behind fin, and one half way between back of dorsal and base of caudal, these bars becoming faint or obsolete in adults; lower fins reddish, with some dusky shading, appearing as faint mottlings on pectorals and ventrals. Head very large, the frontal region broad and foreshortened, length of head 3.6 to 4.5, width 4.7 to 5.8, depth 5.9 to 6.6 in body; interorbital space transversely concave, 1.9 to 2.5 in head; snout long and strongly decurved, 1.8 to 2.2 in head; mouth wholly inferior, the lips very thick and strongly papillose, the upper almost as thick as the lower, with 8 to 10 series of papillæ; lower lip less incised behind than in *Catostomus* proper; eye moderate, 4.8 to 6 in head, over 5 in adults. Dorsal fin with 10 or 11 rays, rather low, the longest ray scarcely equaling the length of the base of the fin; pectorals very long, reaching ⅔ to ¾ of distance to ventrals. Scales rather large, 7, 46–51, 6, somewhat smaller on breast and belly, but not crowded forward on sides or in predorsal region; lateral line complete, almost straight.

This peculiar sucker is distributed throughout the Great Lake region and along the Atlantic slope as far as the Carolinas,

HOGSUCKER, *Catostomus nigricans* Le Sueur

westward to Minnesota and Kansas, north to the Lake of the Woods, and south to Arkansas. It is especially abundant in swift and rapid streams, and is rarely found in muddy water. Its avoidance of muddy situations is illustrated especially by its distribution in Illinois, not a single collection of this species having been made by us from the persistently turbid water of the lower Illinoisan glaciation. It is rare in the southern third of the state, and was taken by us but once from any locality of extreme southern Illinois. It has occurred in our collections most abundantly in the headwaters and smaller tributaries of the Illinois, the Kaskaskia, the Embarras, and the Big Vermilion, in the northern and eastern parts of the state.

The most striking peculiarities of this fish are related to its haunts and feeding habits. The large bony head and the unusually developed pectoral fins, together with the full lips and the papillose mouth, are all related to the fact that it seeks its food in the more rapid parts of streams, pushing about the stones upon the bottoms and sucking up the ooze and slime thus exposed, together with the insect larvæ upon which it mainly depends for food. The slender body, the large pectoral fins, and the comparatively high coloration of this species give it the aspect of a darter among the suckers, and its active habit and the peculiar character of its food resources is another point of affinity with that interesting group. It has also, like the darters, the habit of resting quietly on the bottom, supported by its paired fins, where its coarsely mottled colors serve well to conceal it among the surrounding stones.

Proportionately to the number of collections made by us, this species was about three times as abundant in central Illinois as in southern, and three and a half times so in northern Illinois as in central. It was much commonest in the smaller rivers and about half as abundant in creeks, although not wholly wanting in either the larger rivers or in the glaciated lakes of northeastern Illinois. It was not taken by us at all off really muddy bottoms.

Widely different as are the food and feeding habits of this species and those of the common sucker, its nearest ally in our waters, their alimentary structures are not remarkably unlike. The pharyngeals of the present species are somewhat lighter, the pharyngeal teeth more slender and more prominently hooked, and the gill-rakers somewhat stouter, thus affording a better apparatus for the retention of the relatively large insect larvæ upon which this species chiefly feeds. It is, in short, a molluscan feeder which has become especially adapted to the search for insect larvæ occurring in rapid water under stones. It feeds, so far as our observations go, almost wholly upon aquatic larvæ, mainly those of day-flies, more than half of the food of the specimens examined consisting of a single form (*Cœnis*) abundant under stones.

A few aquatic larvæ of a gnat (*Chironomus*), and some other insect remains, with an insignificant ratio of small bivalve mollusks, were the other elements of its food.

It ascends the swifter brooks in spring, no doubt for spawning, although its habits of reproduction are not known. It is sometimes used for food, but has virtually no economic value.

Genus **MOXOSTOMA** Rafinesque

RED-HORSE

Body more or less elongate, usually more or less compressed; mouth inferior; lips with transverse plicæ, the folds rarely so broken up as to form papillæ; posterior fontanelle always well open; supraorbital bone wanting; suborbitals very narrow; pharyngeal bones weak, the teeth rather coarser than in *Erimyzon* and *Catostomus*; vertebræ (*aureolum, breviceps*) 39 to 41; ribs 15 to 17; dorsal rays 11 to 17, usually about 13; scales large, usually about 44 in the median lateral series; lateral line well developed; air-bladder with 3 chambers. Males in spring with lower fins reddened (whence the common name), and with anal rays swollen and tuberculate.

United States, east of the Rocky Mountains; species numerous; 3 species found in Illinois.

The gill-rakers of the red-horse are largely modified into transverse leaf-like plates with notched edges projecting in triangular outline only a little beyond the margin of the thick, strong arch. Those of the anterior gill are more elongate, but stout and triangular, and about three fourths as long as the gill-filaments, the whole branchial apparatus being thus coarse and strong, better adapted to hold hard and somewhat bulky objects than to strain from the water small and delicate ones. The pharyngeal jaws are moderately heavy, with strong teeth, and the intestine is small and about one and a fourth times the length of the head and body. Quite in correspondence with these features of the feeding apparatus, the main food of the red-horse consists of water-snails of various species, and small bivalve mollusks belonging to the genus *Sphærium*. About a third of the food of specimens examined by us consisted of insects, practically all aquatic larvæ. The vegetable matter present in the food of specimens taken from the Illinois River at Peoria was mainly distillery slops entering the streams from the adjacent distilleries. The latter element was insignificant, however, in total amount, insects and mollusks making fully 95 per cent. of the stomach contents studied, mollusks being nearly twice as abundant as insects. In consequence of the manner in which the food is collected from the bottom, considerable quantities of mud are, of course, swallowed with it.

These fishes are caught mainly with seines and pound-nets, but they also bite readily at the hook.

Key to the Species of **MOXOSTOMA** found in Illinois

a. Folds of lower lip more or less broken up into papillæ.
b. Head short, 4½ to 5½ in body; lower lip truncate behind, mouth small; developed dorsal rays 12 or 13.......................................**breviceps.**
bb. Head longer, 3½ to 4⅓ in body; halves of lower lip meeting in a sharp angle, mouth large; developed dorsal rays 14 to 16.......................**anisurum.**
aa. Lips strongly plicate.
c. Head 4 to 4½ in body; halves of lower lip meeting in a rather wide angle, mouth large; developed dorsal rays 12 to 14.......................**aureolum.**

MOXOSTOMA ANISURUM (Rafinesque)

WHITE-NOSED SUCKER

(Map XX)

Rafinesque, 1820, Ichth. Oh., 54 (**Catostomus**).
G., VII, 20 (**Catostomus carpio**); J. & G., 139 (**carpio**); M. V., 47; J. & E., I, 190; N., 49 (**Teretulus carpio**); J., 63 (**Myxostoma carpio**); F., 80 (**carpio**).

Body stout, heavy forward, deep and compressed, the back elevated, rather humped in front of dorsal in old specimens; depth 3.3 to 4.1 in length. Size large, reaching a weight of 5 to 10 ℔. Color pale, silvery, darker above, nose and chin whitish; dorsal and caudal with some dusky, lower fins white or light reddish. Head broad and short, squarish in cross-section in region of orbit, its length 3.5 to 4.3, width 5.2 to 6.5, depth 4.6 to 5.5 in head; interorbital space flat, 2.2 to 2.6 in head; snout rather long, 2.1 to 2.6 in head; its tip squarish, little decurved, the profile nearly straight to its tip when the mouth is closed; mouth rather large, the upper lip thin, plicate-papillose, the lower thicker, its folds broken into evident papillæ, the halves meeting at a sharp angle; eye rather large, slightly back of middle of head, 4 to 6.4 in its length. Dorsal fin long, its rays about 15 (14 to 17), the longest about ⅚ length of base of fin, the free margin straight; lower fins long, pectorals reaching ¾ of distance from pectoral to ventral basis; upper lobe of caudal a little longer than lower. Scales 6, 42–45, 6; lateral line complete, somewhat flexuose, but nearly straight.

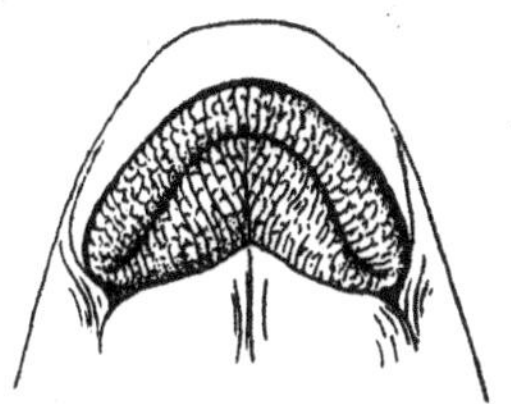

Fig. 21
Lips of *Moxostoma anisurum*

Found in the Great Lake region and the Ohio Valley, including Pennsylvania and New York; also ranging down the St. Lawrence and into the streams of the Atlantic coast as far south as North Carolina. Northward its range extends to Lake Winnipeg and the Assiniboin River.

This is the so-called white-nosed sucker of the Great Lakes. It is distributed throughout Illinois, but in rather moderate numbers, and mainly in the larger streams—the Illinois, the Rock, the Mississippi, the Ohio, and the Wabash. The species reaches a large size, varying in length from one to two feet, and it is a somewhat acceptable, though not abundant, food fish. At some points on Lake Michigan it contributes a considerable percentage to the catch of suckers, although the fine-scaled sucker and the short-nosed red-horse commonly outnumber it.

MOXOSTOMA AUREOLUM (Le Sueur)

COMMON RED-HORSE

(Map XXI)

Le Sueur, 1817, J. Ac. Nat. Sci. Phila., I, 95 (**Catostomus**).
G., VII, 18 (**Catostomus duquesni**); J. & G., 140 (**macrolepidotum**, part); M. V., 47 (**macrolepidotum duquesnei** and (?) **aureolum**); J. & E., I, 192; N., 49 (**Teretulus duquesnii** and **macrolepidotum**); J., 63 (**Myxostoma macrolepidotum** var. **duquesnii**); F., 80 (**macrolepidotum**); F. F., II. 7, 442 (**macrolepidotum**).

Body elongate, heavier forward, considerably compressed, the back little elevated; depth 4 to 4.4 in length. Size rather large, attaining a weight of 5 or 6 ℔. Color of back and sides an almost uniform olivaceous, very little darker above, taking on a faint silvery tinge lower down; faint tints of salmon or yellowish along sides in front of dorsal; belly smoky white; dorsal quite dusky, without pale edge; caudal grayish olive; lower fins with some orange near base, the broad outer margins faintly dusky. Head moderate, 3.9 to 4.5 in length, its width 5.7 to 6.8, depth 5.2 to 5.9, not strongly tapered, rather flattened above, the cheeks nearly vertical; interorbital space nearly flat, 2.2 to 2.6 in head; snout 2.3 to 2.8 in head, its tip squarish, little decurved; mouth large, both upper and lower lips thick, strongly and coarsely plicate, halves of lower lip meeting at a rather wide angle; eye large, 4 to 5 in head. Dorsal rays 12–14, the fin a little higher than long, last ray more than half the length of longest anterior ray; free margin of dorsal straight; lower fins rather longer than in the next species, longest in the males, pectorals reaching 2/3 to 3/4 of distance from pectoral to ventral basis; upper lobe of caudal a little longer than lower. Scales 6, 41–48, 5–7; lateral line complete, faintly flexuose.

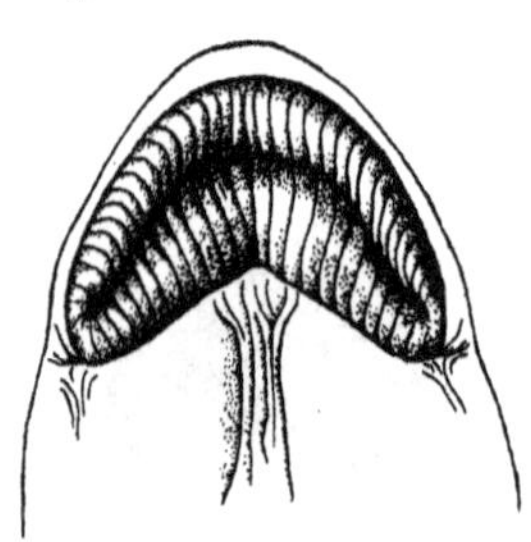

Fig. 22
Lips of *Moxostoma aureolum*

This species, much the most abundant of the Illinois red-horse, occurs outside our limits from the St. Lawrence and the Hudson rivers through the Great Lakes to the Missouri River, north to Winnipeg and the Assiniboin, and southward to Arkansas and Georgia. In this state it is much the commonest in the northern and eastern two-thirds of our area, showing a tendency, like the preceding species, to avoid the turbid waters of southern Illinois, although present in the clearer waters south of the lower Illinoisan glaciation. It occurs in 148 of our collections, most abundantly, in proportion to the number made, in the Rock River and the northwest basins, and in the Kaskaskia and Wabash systems. It has been taken by us, however, in all the other stream systems except that of the Big Muddy. It is much the commonest in creeks and the smaller rivers, the numbers found in the larger rivers being only half the normal ratio for the species, and those in lakes and sloughs a fourth that ratio. Its preference for swiftly flowing streams and its avoidance of a mud bottom are also conspicuously shown by our data of ecological distribution.

This red-horse is not tenacious of life, but dies quickly in the aquarium if the water is in the least impure. It also readily succumbs to impure conditions of its native waters such as are likely to occur in midsummer, sometimes perishing in vast numbers and stranding along the banks when violent summer rains, following long periods of drought, overload the streams with mud and decomposing vegetation.

It spawns in April and May, ascending the smaller streams for the purpose. Females taken from the Illinois River at Meredosia May 5, 1899, were already spent.

MOXOSTOMA BREVICEPS (Cope)

SHORT-HEADED RED-HORSE

(Pl., p. 92; Map XXII)

Cope, 1870, P. Am. Phil. Soc., 478 (**Ptychostomus**).

J. & G., 141 (**anisurum** and (?) **aureolum**); M. V., 48 (**crassilabre**); J. & E., I, 196; N., 49 (**Teretulus aureolum**); J., 63 (**Myxostoma aureolum**); F., 80 (**aureolum**); F. F., II. 7, 444 (**aureolum**); L., 12 (**macrolepidotum**).

Body subfusiform, moderately compressed, rather deep under front of dorsal, in form much like a *Coregonus*; depth 3.8 to 4.4 in length. Size moderate, our largest specimens about 15 inches in length. Color pale yellowish olive, with a faint coppery tint on sides in predorsal region; rest of sides and caudal peduncle very light pea-green, grading to whitish or dull silvery lower down and on belly; dorsal very pale olive, scarcely dusky;

caudal light reddish outward, olive near base; lower fins salmon with paler, greenish margins. Head extremely short, subconical, tapering both above and below to the tip of the pointed snout; length of head 4.6 to 5.4 in body, usually more than 5 in adults, width 6.6 to 7.6, depth 5.7 to 6.7; interorbital space 1.9 to 2.4 in head, noticeably convex; chin convex; cheeks shallow, not vertically continuous to a flat chin as in *aureolum* and *anisurum*, a cross-section of the head in the orbital region not being squarish as in those species; snout 2.3 to 2.9 in head, not at all decurved; mouth small, upper lip rather coarsely plicate, the folds shallow and not continued back to the inside of the lip; lower lip truncate behind, the two halves scarcely separated at the shallow incision, the coarse but shallow plicæ evident in front, but breaking up into irregular papillæ posteriorly; eye small in comparison with length of body, but contained 4 to 5 times in the very short head. Dorsal rays 12 or 13, the fin notably higher in front than behind, the last ray being less than half the length of the longest anterior ray, which is usually considerably longer than the base of the fin; free margin of dorsal concave; pectorals longer than the short head, but relatively shorter than in the two preceding species, scarcely reaching ⅔ of the distance from pectoral to ventral basis; upper lobe of caudal falcate, usually, though not always, longer than lower. Scales 6, 43–45, 5 or 6; lateral line complete, nearly straight.

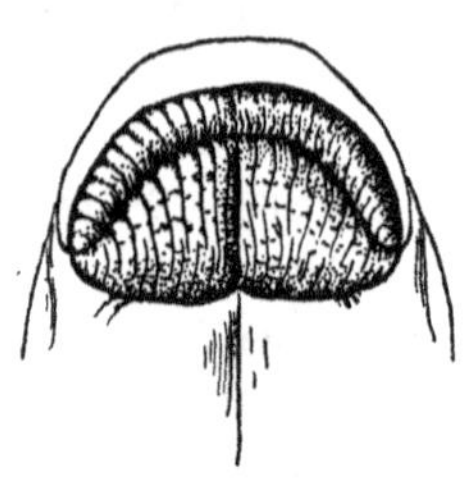

Fig. 23
Lips of *Moxostoma breviceps*

This species occurs in the Ohio Valley and the Great Lake region, being especially abundant in Lake Erie. In the Mississippi Valley it ranges up the Missouri to Cheyenne Falls. It is especially a northern Illinois fish, only one of our collections made in the southern part of the state containing it, and this falling outside the area of the lower Illinoisan glaciation. It is about equally common in central and northern Illinois, and has been more uniformly distributed, according to our observations, than the other species of its genus, occurring in about equal frequency, relatively to the number of collections made, in the larger rivers and in creeks and lakes, but about twice as abundantly in the smaller rivers. It shows also considerably less marked preference than the preceding species for clear and swiftly flowing waters.

Genus **PLACOPHARYNX** Cope

PAVEMENT-TOOTHED RED-HORSE

Suckers like *Moxostoma* in all respects, except that the pharyngeal bones are much more developed and the teeth reduced in number, those on the lower half of the bone very large, 6 to 10 in number, nearly cylindrical in form, but little compressed and with a broad and more or less flattened

SHORT-HEADED RED-HORSE. *Moxostoma breviceps* (Cope)

Placopharynx duquesnei (Le Sueur)

grinding surface; mouth larger and more oblique, and lips thicker than in most species of *Moxostoma*. Fresh waters of southeastern United States; one species known.

PLACOPHARYNX DUQUESNEI (Le Sueur)

Le Sueur, 1817, J. Ac. Nat. Sci. Phila., I, 105 (**Catostomus**).
J. & G., 143 (**carinatus**); M. V., 48 (**carinatus**); J. & E., I, 198; N., 49 (**carinatus**); J., 63 (**carinatus**); F., 80 (**carinatus**); F. F., II. 7, 441 (**carinatus**); L., 13.

Body elongate, heavier forward, the form much as in *Moxostoma aureolum*, but the back less elevated and the body somewhat less compressed; depth 3.8 to 4.5 in length. Length 15 to 30 inches. "Color dark olive-green, the sides brassy, not silvery; lower fins and caudal orange-red" (Jordan & Evermann). Head broad, flattish above, but less so than in *M. aureolum*, cheeks vertical, chin flat; length of head 4.2 to 4.5, width 6.2 to 6.7, depth 5.3 to 6 in body; interorbital space slightly convex, 2.1 to 2.3 in head; snout blunt, squarish at tip, scarcely decurved, 2.3 to 2.4 in head; mouth very large, the lower jaw oblique when the mouth is closed; lips very thick and coarsely plicate, the folds broken in places into very fine papillæ in old specimens; lower lip very large, protruding when mouth is closed, its halves meeting behind in an almost straight line; eye large, 4.3 to 5 in head. Dorsal fin with 12 or 13 rays, higher than long, its free margin weakly concave, last ray half length of longest anterior ray; pectorals short, reaching but about ⅖ of distance from pectoral to ventral basis; ventrals short, their tips 5 or 6 scales from vent. Scales 6, 43–47, 6 or 7; lateral line complete, almost straight.

This fish has not ordinarily been separated readily from specimens of *Moxostoma* without removal and examination of the characteristic pharyngeal bones, but, as it seems to us, its very large mouth and subtruncate lower lip, and its shorter lower fins should enable one to distinguish it with ease from both *Moxostoma anisurum* and *M. aureolum*—the only species found in its range, so far as is known, that resemble it at all closely.

Its branchial apparatus is not notably different from that of *Moxostoma*, the gill-rakers being short and few, and effective only on the upper part of the arch, the lower arm being, like that of *Moxostoma*, covered by a rigid pad. The species is very remarkably distinguished, however, by its heavy pharyngeal jaws and its thick and strong pharyngeal teeth with conspicuous grinding surface. These number about 30 on each pharyngeal, the upper ones minute and useless rudiments, and the lower 10 very large, occupying about two thirds the length of the arch—the lower 6, in fact, about half of it. It is probable that this apparatus is related to a preference for mollusks as food, but the number of specimens available for our examination has been too small to test this supposition. In two examples taken from the Illinois River at Havana in October, the food was about a third mollusks and two thirds insects, the latter largely larvæ of May-flies and of large water-beetles (*Hydrophillidæ*).

Michigan to Tennessee, Georgia, and Arkansas; especially abundant in the Ozark region and in the French Broad River basin. Rare in Illinois; one specimen from the Wabash; two specimens from the Illinois; and two or three others from localities unknown.

Genus **LAGOCHILA** Jordan & Brayton

RABBIT-MOUTH SUCKER

Suckers in all respects like *Moxostoma* except for the singular structure of the mouth; upper lip not protractile, greatly prolonged and closely plicate; lower lip much reduced, divided into two distinct lobes, which are weakly papillose, the split between the lobes extending backward to the edge of the dentary bones; lower lip entirely separated from upper at angles by a deep fissure, which is mostly covered by the skin of the cheeks. Ozark region, Wabash, Clinch, Scioto, Cumberland, Chickamauga, and White (Arkansas) rivers. One species known, *L. lacera* Jordan & Brayton, not at present known from Illinois, although not unlooked for in collections from the Wabash basin. (For description see Jordan & Evermann, Bull. U. S. Nat. Mus., No. 47, I., p. 199.)

Family **CYPRINIDÆ**

THE MINNOWS AND THE CARP

Form varied, elongate and subfusiform, more or less compressed, or sometimes thin and deep; head naked; body scaly, except in a few forms not occurring in the United States; scales cycloid; skeleton osseous; anterior vertebræ modified and provided with Weberian apparatus; fins typically without spines; ventrals abdominal; no adipose fin; a mesocoracoid arch present; gill-membranes broadly joined to isthmus; pseudobranchiæ usually present; branchiostegals 3; margin of upper jaw formed by premaxillaries alone; jaws toothless; lower pharyngeal bones well developed, falciform, and nearly parallel with the gill-arches, each armed with 1 to 3 series of teeth, 4 to 7 in the main row, and a less number in the others, if more rows are present; stomach without appendages, being a simple enlargement of the intestine; intestinal canal short or long, usually less than twice length of body in species partly or wholly carnivorous (see key), but often very much longer in herbivorous and limophagous forms; air-bladder typically present and with open duct, commonly divided into 2 more or less distinct chambers.

The minnow family, much the largest and most complex of the fish families of the state, has become variously differentiated in respect to habits, ecological relations, and some of its more important structures, in a way to adjust the group with considerable exactness to the various features of its environment. In respect to territorial distribution, we may distinguish among the minnows a group distributed mainly through the Mississippi drainage, another mainly through the Ohio drainage, and a third which is generally distributed throughout the state. We may also distinguish a group of species which does not enter or remain in the persistently turbid waters of the southern Illinois region covered by the fine-grained drift of the lower Illinoisan glaciation; another group which is common in the lowland lakes, and a much larger group which is rarely found in lakes of any kind; a group of minnows which prefer large rivers, and another which is most abundant in the smaller streams; one more than normally common over a mud bottom, and another evidently most at home over a bottom of rock and sand; one which prefers a swift current, and another which seeks quiet waters.

The various species of the family show also considerable differences of preference in respect to the kinds of food which they choose from the general supply offered to them. They are mainly carnivorous, on the whole, in this country, although we have found fishes and mollusks only rarely in the food of our native species. Insects and crustaceans, including *Entomostraca*, are their principal dependence, except for a few which eat largely of vegetation and a few others which feed almost wholly on the highly organic mud of the bottoms of our ponds and streams. The special structures of alimentation correspond in their variations, in the several divisions of the family, to these differences of their food.

Fishes so small as most of our minnows, are, as a rule, in no need of a specially developed set of gill-rakers, since the gill-arches themselves are so small and the spaces between them so narrow that any object large enough to be useful for food is little likely to be carried out through the gills with the respiratory current. In two of our species, however (*Abramis crysoleucas* and *Notropis heterodon*), the gill-rakers are considerably developed, and in these species *Entomostraca* appear more largely in the food than in any other minnows. Even *Protozoa* and unicellular algæ have been found common in the stomachs of *N. heterodon*.

The intestine varies greatly in length, being longest in the mud-eating minnows and shortest in those dependent wholly or mainly on animal food. In *Campostoma*, a typical mud-eater, it is five to nine and a half times the length of the head and body, and is wound spirally about the air-bladder, while in the more strictly insectivorous genera it is only two thirds to five sixths as long as the head and body taken together. The mud-eating forms also differ from the others in the fact that the pharyngeal teeth have a large grinding surface at the free end, and are without the terminal hook-like processes with which those species are provided which feed mainly on insects.

Although the cyprinoids are mostly of small size, the European carp and a few native species, some of which are abundant on the Pacific slope in America, attain a considerable weight.

There are some two hundred genera in the world and about a thousand species. In Illinois there are fourteen genera and thirty-six species known, seventeen of the latter belonging to the single genus *Notropis*. All our native species are small and commercially insignificant except as they are used for bait and serve as a valuable food resource for other fishes. The top of the head in spring males, and often also the fins and sides—particularly the sides of the caudal peduncle—are covered with small tubercles called pearl organs, and the fins and lower parts of the body are, in the breeding season, often highly colored with bright pigments, either red, satiny-white, yellow to orange, or black. The young of the deeper-bodied species are much more slender than the adults and have much larger eyes. They may also show color markings not found in adults of the same species, such as a caudal spot or a black lateral stripe.

Taken as a group the minnows are, on the whole, fishes especially of the creeks and smaller rivers, and they show, in these situations, a decided preference for a more or less rapid current and for a clean bottom rather than one of mud. There are notable exceptions, as already said, but the general fact is well shown by our data of frequency of occurrence in the various ecological situations, drawn from the 24 Illinois species of which we have collections numerous enough to make them available for this study. Of these 24 species, 6 are more than usually abundant in the larger rivers, 20 are extraordinarily so in rivers of the second class and 19 in creeks, 5 are more numerous than the average in lowland lakes, and only 1 is unusually so in upland lakes of glacial orgin.

Only two of these 24 species were *most* abundant in the larger rivers, and 6 in the smaller rivers. Fourteen species were found *most* frequently in creeks, 1 was most abundant in lakes, another in the bottom-lands, and another in clear upland lakes. If we may take our miscellaneous collections to have been fairly distributed as to varieties of situation and to proportionate extent of each variety, we may further infer from our data that minnows will generally be found over a relatively hard and clean bottom about two and a half times as abundantly as over a bottom of mud.

In the general scheme of aquatic life, the native members of this family, taken together as a group, play a multiple role. They operate, to some extent, as a check on the increase of the aquatic insects, from which they draw a large part of their food supply; they make indirectly available, as food for their own most destructive enemies, these aquatic insects, many terrestrial insects also, which fall into the water and are greedily devoured by them, and the mere mud and slime and confervoid algæ gathered up from the bottom of the waters they inhabit; and they rival the young of all larger fishes, their own worst enemies included, by living continuously, to a great degree, on the *Entomostraca* and insect life which these fishes must have, at one period of their lives, in order to get their growth. They also offer a considerable means of subsistence to certain aquatic birds, such as kingfishers, and members of the heron family; and, through their contributions to the support of the best food fishes, they form an important link in the chain of agencies by which our waters are made productive in the interest of man.

Among the enemies of *Cyprinidæ* disclosed by our study of 1,221 Illinois fishes, already referred to, are practically all our most predaceous fishes, including the dogfish, both our common species of gar, the wall-eyed pike, both our species of pickerel, both species of black bass, the yellow perch, the mud-cat, the bullheads, the crappies, the green sunfish, and, finally, one of their own family, the horned dace. That this list might be considerably enlarged by more extensive studies of the food of fishes is beyond a doubt, and it is safe to say that no fish-eating fish would, if hungry for fish, refuse a minnow of any kind unless it seemed too small to be worth the trouble of capturing.

From the standpoint of the predaceous species, minnows are young fishes which never grow up, and thus keep up the supply of edible fishes of a size to make them available to the smaller carnivorous kinds when the young of the larger species have grown too large to be captured or eaten. They thus not only furnish the necessary food to the smaller aquatic *Carnivora*, but they ease the way of growth to the largest kinds, all of which pass through a period when they need fish food, but are not yet large enough to capture the prey upon which they chiefly depend when they are themselves adult. Moreover, by their great numbers, by their various adaptations and correspondingly general ecological distribution, and by their permanently small size, the minnows must distract in great measure the attention of carnivorous fishes from the young of the larger species, upon which, without them, the adults of these larger species would fall with the full force of their voracious appetites. By offering themselves, no doubt as unconscious, but sufficient substitutes, they thus help to preserve—for their own future destruction, however, be it noticed—the young of many species which would otherwise be forced to feed on each other's progeny. It is not too much to say, consequently, that the number of game fishes which any waters can maintain is largely conditioned upon its permanent stock of minnows.

Owing to their abundance in all situations, the number and variety of their species and genera, and the ease with which they may be collected and preserved, minnows are an admirable group for a study of local distribution and ecological relationship, and the data of our collections applicable to such a study have been assembled, for convenient inspection and comparison, in the following tables and lists.

TABLE I

Relative Abundance of Principal Species of Cyprinidæ in Principal Classes of Situations

TABLE OF COEFFICIENTS OF FREQUENCY

Species	No. of collections	Large rivers	Small rivers	Creeks	Lowland lakes	Upland lakes	No. of available collections	Rapid current	Quiet water	No. of available collections	Clean bottom	Mud bottom
Campostoma anomalum	195	.21	2.22	3.28	.05	......	65	1.70	.59	105	3.26	.31
Hybognathus nuchalis	183	.75	2.18	1.91	.43	......	48	.72	1.38	49	.59	1.68
Pimpephales promelas	95	.85	1.82	2.68	.23	......	22	.73	1.37	34	.48	2.08
P. notatus	377	.31	2.03	2.57	.05	.67	108	.92	1.09	202	.92	1.09
Semotilus atromaculatus	151	.22	1.67	3.77	.11	......	42	.83	1.20	81	1.11	.90
Opsopœodus emiliæ	80	.82	.36	2.16	1.97	......	7	......	......	17	......	......
Abramis crysoleucas	303	.71	1.04	1.76	1.36	.59	28	.36	2.79	82	.29	3.79
Cliola vigilax	194	1.04	1.85	1.67	.42	......	36	2.46	.41	72	2.04	.49
Notropis cayuga	30	......	.79	1.59	3.29	.17	13	......	......	15	......	......
N. heterodon	93	.98	.17	.63	1.44	2.68	1	......	......	14	......	......
N. blennius	195	.41	2.65	2.23	.17	......	73	1.18	.85	103	2.00	.50
N. gilberti	30	.15	2.95	2.57	.10	......	7	......	......	18	......	......
N. hudsonius	147	1.80	.29	.14	1.76	.60	......	......	......	10	......	......
N. lutrensis	163	1.43	1.33	1.82	.82	......	13	......	......	55	.59	1.69
N. whipplii	270	.35	2.35	2.41	.11	.14	65	1.30	.77	126	1.60	.62
N. cornutus	189	.11	2.45	3.00	.02	.20	76	.79	1.27	102	2.20	.45
N. jejunus	51	1.63	1.12	80	.67	......	2	......	......	12	......	......
N. atherinoides	206	1.21	2.14	.93	.66	......	23	1.19	.84	48	1.22	.82
N. umbratilis	208	.16	1.90	3.91	.02	......	69	.57	1.76	109	1.01	.99
Ericymba buccata	74	.09	1.06	4.85	......	......	14	......	......	38	3.20	.31
Phenacobius mirabilis	159	.32	2.19	3.18	.05	......	53	1.32	.76	92	1.36	.73
Hybopsis amblops	51	.29	1.72	3.97	......	......	13	......	......	20	.67	1.50
H. storerianus	28	1.28	1.93	.70	.64	......	2	......	......	4	......	......
H. kentuckiensis	137	.26	2.47	3.08	.05	......	55	1.38	.72	74	2.24	.40

TABLE II

MINNOWS AND THE ENVIRONMENT

RELATIONS TO CURRENT

SPECIES AND FREQUENCY COEFFICIENTS

Swift-water minnows		Still-water minnows	
Species	Coefficients	Species	Coefficients
Cliola vigilax	2.46	Abramis crysoleucas	2.79
Campostoma anomalum	1.70	Notropis umbratilis	1.76
Hybopsis kentuckiensis	1.38	Hybognathus nuchalis	1.38
Phenacobius mirabilis	1.32	Pimephales promelas	1.37
Notropis whipplii	1.30	Notropis cornutus	1.27
N. atherinoides	1.19	Semotilus atromaculatus	1.20
N. blennius	1.18	Pimephales notatus	1.09

TABLE III

RELATIONS TO BOTTOM

SPECIES AND FREQUENCY COEFFICIENTS

Preferring clean bottom		Preferring mud bottom	
Species	Coefficients	Species	Coefficients
Campostoma anomalum	3.26	Abramis crysoleucas	3.79
Ericymba buccata	3.20	Pimephales promelas	2.08
Hybopsis kentuckiensis	2.24	Notropis lutrensis	1.69
Notropis cornutus	2.20	Hybognathus nuchalis	1.68
Cliola vigilax	2.04	Hybopsis amblops	1.50
Notropis blennius	2.00	Pimephales notatus	1.09
N. whipplii	1.60		
Phenacobius mirabilis	1.36		
Notropis atherinoides	1.22		
Semotilus atromaculatus	1.11		
Notropis umbratilis	1.01		

TABLE IV

PRINCIPAL CYPRINIDÆ OF LARGE RIVERS

Species	No. of collections	Frequency coefficients
Cliola vigilax	194	1.04
Notropis heterodon	93	.98
N. hudsonius	147	1.80
N. lutrensis	163	1.43
N. jejunus	51	1.63
N. atherinoides	206	1.21
Hybopsis storerianus	28	1.28

TABLE V

PRINCIPAL CYPRINIDÆ OF INTERIOR LAKES

Species	No. of collections	Frequency coefficients	
		Lowland lakes	Upland lakes
Opsopœodus emiliæ	80	1.97	
Abramis crysoleucas	303	1.36	.59
Notropis cayuga	30	3.29	.17
N. heterodon	93	1.44	2.68
N. hudsonius	147	1.76	.60

TABLE VI

GEOGRAPHICAL GROUPS, ILLINOIS MINNOWS

PREFERRING THE OHIO DRAINAGE

Notropis illecebrosus
Ericymba buccata
Hybopsis amblops

PREFERRING THE MISSISSIPPI DRAINAGE

Chrosomus erythrogaster
Hybognathus nubila
Pimephales promelas
Notropis gilberti
N. hudsonius
N. lutrensis

EVIDENTLY AVOIDING LOWER ILLINOISAN GLACIATION

Campostoma anomalum
Notropis blennius
N. cornutus
Ericymba buccata
Hybopsis kentuckiensis

FREELY ENTERING LOWER ILLINOISAN GLACIATION

Hybognathus nuchalis
Pimephales notatus
Abramis crysoleucas
Cliola vigilax
Notropis whipplii
N. atherinoides
N. rubrifrons
Hybopsis amblops

The first table, relating to the twenty-four most abundant species, shows the relative frequencies of occurrence of each species in our collections from each class of situations indicated by the headings of the columns. The figures of these columns, called coefficients of frequency, when larger than 1 indicate a greater than average frequency in the situation named, and, when smaller than 1, a lesser frequency. That is to say, if all the species of minnows had been equally and uniformly distributed through all classes of situations, the coefficients of this table would all have been 1. Referring, for example, to *Campostoma anomalum*, in the first line of the table, it will be seen that 195 of our collections contained this species. The number of collections from larger rivers containing this minnow, as shown by the figures in the second column of the table, were

.21 of the number which would have contained it if it had been uniformly distributed. From the entry in the third column it will be seen that in small rivers the abundance of *Campostoma anomalum* was a little more than 2⅕ times as great as if the species had been uniformly distributed; and from the fourth column, that in creeks it was a little more than 3¼ times as abundant. The number of its occurrences in lowland lakes was but .05 of the normal average, and in upland lakes the species has not been taken by us at all.

The seventh and tenth columns of these figures give the numbers of collections for each species concerning which data were recorded available for computing their relative frequencies in rapid and quiet waters, and on clean and soft bottoms. From the figures in the last six columns of the table we learn, concerning *Campostoma*, that 65 collections give us a coefficient of 1.7 for a rapid current as compared with .59 for quiet water, equal frequency in the two situations being, as before, represented by 1. The strong preference of the species for a clean bottom over one of mud is shown by the last two numbers, applying to 105 collections, the two coefficients being respectively 3.26 for a clean bottom and .31 for one of mud.

In Tables II. to V., relating to minnows and the environment, the species most characteristic of each situation are brought together in lists arranged in the order of the size of their coefficients of frequency. The remaining lists refer to peculiarities of territorial distribution within the state.

The following keys and descriptions of *Cyprinidæ* have been designed for use with a minimum of attention to obscure characters and to those difficult of access. However, it will be necessary in all cases for beginners in ichthyology to ascertain by dissection whether their specimen belongs to the long- or the short-intestined class of minnows (see key to genera of *Cyprinidæ*). It is possible, however, to dispose entirely with the use of dental characters in the indentification of minnows, and our keys have been constructed with that fact in view; although, for the purpose of completeness and for the aid of those who may wish to carry their studies further than the simplest artificial key will take them, we have in every case included a reference to the number and form of the pharyngeal teeth.*

* In Illinois *Cyprinidæ* the main row of teeth on each pharyngeal bone contains 4 or 5 teeth; inside of this main row is a so-called "lesser row" which may contain 1 or 2 teeth or be unrepresented altogether, in the latter case being designated "0" in the formula. For example,

KEY TO THE GENERA OF NATIVE **CYPRINIDÆ** FOUND IN ILLINOIS

(Not including the European carp, *Cyprinus carpio* Linnæus, which, with the goldfish, *Carassius auratus* Linnæus, is sufficiently distinguished from all native American *Cyprinidæ* by the presence of a serrated spine in dorsal and anal fins.)

a. Intestine more than twice length of body; peritoneum usually black, brown, or very dark gray; species generally mud-eaters.

b. Intestine spirally wound around air-bladder; teeth 4–4 or 1, 4–4, 0............ .... **Campostoma.**

bb. Intestine not wound around air-bladder.

c. Scales very small, 65 to 90 in longitudinal series; teeth 5–5, or 4–5........... .... **Chrosomus.**

cc. Scales larger, about 35 to 50 in lateral line; teeth 4–4.

d. Scales before dorsal 12 to 16 in number, not crowded; first (rudimentary) ray of dorsal fin slender, bony, and closely attached to second.......... .... **Hybognathus.**

dd. Scales before dorsal small and considerably crowded, 22 to 25 in number; first (rudimentary) dorsal ray more or less club-shaped, inclosed in thick skin, and separated from second ray by a distinct membrane...**Pimephales.**

aa. Intestine less than twice the length of body; peritoneum usually pale; species generally carnivorous, or partly so.

e. Maxillary without barbel*.

f. Mouth extremely small and upturned, the angle with vertical formed by its cleft less than 40°.

g. Peritoneum pale; teeth 4–5 or 5–5.............................**Opsopœodus.**

gg. Peritoneum black; teeth 4–4. **Notropis** (**anogenus** only; for main division of genus see k, below).

ff. Mouth horizontal or more or less oblique, the angle with vertical formed by its cleft usually much more than 40°.

h. Abdomen behind ventral fins with a sharp keel-like edge over which the scales do not pass; body much compressed; anal fin long, its rays 12 to 14; teeth 5–5...**Abramis.**

hh. Abdomen behind ventrals never sharply keeled, but rounded and fully scaled; form various, elongate or fusiform, or more or less compressed.

i. First (rudimentary) ray of dorsal club-like, covered with thick skin, and separated from second ray by a distinct membrane; teeth 4–4......**Cliola.**

ii. First (rudimentary) ray of dorsal slender and bony and closely attached to second.

j. Lips normal, nowhere conspicuously thickened; the mouth subterminal, more or less oblique.

k. Lower portion of head rounded, not swollen, and without externally visible mucus channels; teeth in the main row normally 4–4, the lesser row often wanting ....**Notropis.**

"teeth 2, 4–4, 2" means 4 teeth in each main (outer) row, and 2 in each lesser (inner) row; "teeth 4–4" means that there is but a single row on each pharyngeal bone; while "1, 4–4, 0" would indicate that the lesser row is represented on one side but not on the other. The teeth may be removed for study in the smaller species by the use of a needle or small hook, or fine forceps, which should be inserted through the gill-opening *at the back of the opercular cavity* and directly under the shoulder girdle. A convenient mode of removal consists in grasping the shoulder of the pharyngeal arch with the forceps and pulling forwards after first taking care to cut loose the attachments of the upper and lower limbs. The whole operation may be performed without removing the opercle, which may be merely lifted up to allow room for insertion of the forceps.

* Care should be exercised here as a barbel may be present but concealed.

kk. Lower portion of head with an appearance of being swollen, the suborbitals, interopercles, and dentaries with greatly distended mucus cavities, appearing externally as transverse vitreous streaks; teeth 4–4 or 1, 4–4, 1.. **Ericymba.**

jj. Lower lip with two lateral fleshy lobes, separated at the middle by the more or less horny and knob-like chin; scales rather small, 40 to 60 in lateral line; teeth 4–4.. **Phenacobius.**

ee. Maxillary with a barbel* at or near its extremity (sometimes quite small and difficult to make out, especially in preserved specimens).

l. Barbel on upper side of maxillary and distinctly in front of its posterior tip; mouth exceptionally large, maxillary 2.4 to 2.8 in head; scales 50 to 60; teeth 4 or 5 in main row, 1, 2, or 0 in lesser row................ **Semotilus.**

ll. Barbel terminal on the maxillary, situated in the axil formed at meeting of upper and lower lip-grooves; maxillary more than 2.8 in head.

m. Premaxillaries not protractile; scales small, 60 to 70; dorsal fin posterior; teeth 2, 4–4, 2.. **Rhinichthys.**

mm. Premaxillaries protractile.

n. Scales 35 to 45 in lateral line; teeth 4–4, or 1, 4–4, 1 or 0........... **Hybopsis.**

nn. Scales small, 50 to 60 in lateral line; head much depressed and flattened above; teeth usually 2, 4–4, 2................................ **Platygobio.**

Genus **CYPRINUS** (Artedi) Linnæus

THE CARP

Mouth with four long barbels; teeth molar, broad and truncate, 1, 1, 3–3, 1, 1; dorsal fin very long, with a stout spine which is serrated behind; anal fin with a serrated spine. Native to fresh waters of Asia; introduced into ponds and streams of both Europe and America, where they are now abundant.

CYPRINUS CARPIO Linnæus

EUROPEAN CARP

(3 Plates)

Linnæus, 1758, Syst. Nat., Ed. X, 320.
G., VII, 25; J. & G., 254; M. V., 50; J. & E., I, 201; L., 13.

Length 2 feet or over; body robust, compressed; back considerably elevated; general form resembling that of the buffalo-fishes (*Ictiobus*); depth in length 2.75 to 3.4 (as a rule less than 3); depth caudal peduncle 1.2 to 1.4 in its length. Color olivaceous, upper parts dusky to bluish; lower part of sides and belly more or less yellowish. Head conical, tapering rapidly from above to the tip of the pointed snout, 3 to 4 in length; width of head 1.4 to 1.6 in its length; interorbital space nearly flat, 2.3 to 2.7 in head; eye 5.5 to 6.8 in head; nose bluntly pointed, 2.6 to 3.3 in head; mouth rather small, anterior, oblique, the maxillary not reaching past anterior nostril, 3.3 to 3.9 (usually about 3.5) in head; two pairs of maxillary barbels, the upper shorter, the lower longer than eye; teeth broad and truncate with molar surfaces, in three rows, 1, 1 or 2, 3–3, 1 or 2, 1; intestine longer than body; peritoneum gray, often more or less specked. Dorsal and anal fins each with a large

* Read l and ll for exact indication of location of barbel.

EUROPEAN CARP, *Cyprinus carpio* Linnaeus
Commoner scaled form from river and muddier lakes

strong posteriorly serrated spine; dorsal rays 17 to 21, the base of the fin longer than the head, the spine and first three rays higher than the posterior part of the fin, as in the buffaloes, insertion of dorsal slightly in front of ventrals; anal rays 5 or 6; pectorals reaching nearly to front of ventrals, 1.3 to 1.5 in head; ventrals scarcely ⅔ to vent. Scales 5 or 6, 35 to 37, 5 or 6; lateral line continuous, usually somewhat flexuose.

The above description is based on specimens of scale-carp only; the mirror and leather varieties, differing from the scaled forms chiefly in the squamation, are comparatively rare in the waters of this state.

The carp, which is native in China, was introduced into Europe as early as 1227 (Hessel), and was first brought to England at the beginning of the sixteenth century. The first successful introduction of carp into the United States was made in 1877, when R. Hessel, for the U. S. Fish Commission, brought 345 carp to this country. Of these, 227 were of the mirror and leather varieties, and 118 were scale-carp. All were put into ponds at Washington, D. C., and multiplied rapidly, more than 12,000 young being distributed in 1879 to more than 300 persons in 25 states and territories. From that time distribution rapidly increased until a few years before its final discontinuance in 1897.

The introduction of carp into the waters of Illinois began with the first distribution (1879), and in 1880 scaled carp to the number of 800 were received from the U. S. Fish Commission. In 1881 and 1882 a total of 2,500 more carp were received and distributed by the Illinois Fish Commission, the distribution being mostly made in lots of only ten to a single person. In 1885 the first carp were planted in public waters, a total of 30,900 being set free in the Illinois, Fox, Sangamon, Des Plaines, Kaskaskia, Little Wabash, Big Muddy, and a few other streams. In 1886 the first large carp was caught in the Illinois River, a specimen 30 inches long being taken at Meredosia—probably escaped from some pond which had received a consignment from one of the early distributions. In 1887 about 16,000 more carp were planted in the public waters of the state. Between 1888 and 1890 reports of the capture of carp of considerable size increased in number, particularly from points along the Illinois River, and by 1892 this fish had multiplied to such an extent in the waters about Havana that more than 3,000 ℔ were taken from Clear Lake in a single haul. A year earlier Bowles had begun to ship carp from Meredosia. By 1898 the multiplication and utilization of carp had increased to such an extent in this state that Captain John A. Schulte, of Havana, wrote: "From the information I can get as an official of the Illinois Fishermen's Association from all points along the Illinois River, the carp have brought more money than the catch of all the other fish combined. Long live the carp!" Carp are now found very generally distributed over the state, being most common, however, in the Illinois River and in our other larger and more sluggish streams and lakes and bayous connecting with them. They are not yet very abundant in southern Illinois. The carp catch of the Illinois River alone now reaches six to eight million pounds a year, valued at more than $200,000.

Three races of carp are distinguishable: (1) the regularly-scaled form, which is nearest to the native type of the domesticated races; (2) the mirror-carp, which has the body partly bare, with but two or three irregular rows of large scales along the back; and (3) the leather-carp, which is scaleless, with a thick, soft, velvety skin. Many local German races of carp, of no interest here, have been described. Although the first importation of carp by the U. S. Fish Commission contained a greater proportion of the mirror and leather races than of the scaled carp, the former did not thrive except under domestication, and to-day there are few mirror or leather carp living in a wild state in American waters.*

Carp prefer moderately warm water, not too deep, and with plenty of aquatic vegetation. They will live in almost any situation, thriving in waters of all degrees of turbidity and contamination. They are very hardy under extremes of temperature, and are easily resuscitated after freezing. Carp shipped from Havana, Ill., to New York City by freight arrive alive provided the gills are kept moist by melting ice. Although of lazy habit, resting much of the time on the bottom, they are wary, and are particularly quick to find a way out of a net, or to jump over it. They are omnivorous feeders, taking principally vegetable matter, but insect larvæ, crustaceans and mollusks, and other small aquatic animals as well. They often pull up the roots of tender aquatic plants while feeding. Cole (1905) found them feeding at all times of day. They apparently seek deeper water in winter, where they remain semi-torpid, taking little or no food.

* Cole (1905) found that over 91 per cent. of 3,000 carp counted at Lake Erie were scaled carp. In half a carload of carp looked over as they were unloaded from skiffs at Havana in August, 1905, I was unable to detect a single specimen of the mirror or leather varieties.—R. E. R.

EUROPEAN CARP, *Cyprinus carpio* Linnaeus

Darker-colored scaled form from cleaner waters with vegetation

Carp spawn in the northern United States in May and June. The eggs are small and exceedingly numerous, 400,000 to 500,000 being a common number in a 4- or 5-lb female. They spawn most frequently during the early hours of the morning One large female is ordinarily accompanied by four or five males. Five or six hundred eggs are emitted at a time, the oviposition being accompanied by much splashing on the part of both sexes. The eggs are scattered about, according to Cole, adhering to roots and stems and other objects. In moderately warm weather the young hatch, in this latitude, in about twelve days. The young carp reach a length of 4 to 6 inches by the end of the first summer, and attain a weight of about 1 lb in twelve months. By the end of the second summer a weight of about 3 lb may be reached, this depending upon their nourishment. They first spawn in the spring of their third year. Carp in our waters do not ordinarily reach more than 5 to 10 lb weight, although occasional specimens have been taken weighing as much as 30 lb. In Europe double the latter weight is said to have been reached in one or two instances.

The carp lends itself more readily perhaps than any other fish to the requirements of artificial culture. The rearing of carp is a very ancient practice, a treatise on the subject by a Chinese dating from the third century. In this country it has practically been discontinued since the species has multiplied on such a vast scale in our natural waters. However, the adaptability of the carp to confinement is still taken advantage of in certain localities, especially in the Great Lake region, in the use of retention ponds, in which large numbers of the summer catch are held over to get the advantage of the winter market.

Carp bite readily on such baits as worms, liver, paste, and bread crumbs, and in fact will take nearly any except live bait, and they are not lacking in game qualities when hooked. They have long been valued by English anglers, but are not much thought of by the American sportsman of the newer school.

The carp does not hold a very high place as an edible fish. As a cheap flesh food it compares favorably in price with any of the products of either fresh or salt water. Various efforts have been made to devise means of preparing carp in a way both simple and acceptable to palates accustomed to better fish. The Germans in order to get rid of the muddy flavor, have in some instances adopted the plan of placing the carp in fresh running water for a short time before cooking. Such a measure is not generally practicable in this country, where the resources of cultural establishments are lacking, and the sole recourse is to parboiling and spicing and other subterfuges of the cuisine. Experiments recently made in this country in smoking and salting carp have not been very successful. Carp caviar is known to have been used in former centuries by the Jews of Italy, but its red color is objectionable to the American purchaser. Owing to the low price which carp bring in springtime—often not more than a third of a cent per pound—many of these fish in the Great Lake region are used for fertilizing, although the more progressive firms are more and more holding the spring and summer catches for the better winter price—two to two and a half cents per pound.

Among fishermen and anglers in America the carp has both its partisans and its enemies. However, it is coming more and more to be believed that its good qualities more than overbalance the other side of the account, the most serious of the charges against it appearing to rest on uncertain or gratuitously assumed premises. These charges have been, in brief, that carp roil the water and spoil the breeding and feeding grounds of other fish; that they eat the spawn of other fish and prevent the nesting of such species as bass and sunfishes; that they spoil the feeding grounds of water-birds by eating and rooting up the wild rice and other aquatic plants; and, that they are of no value either as a food or a game fish. With regard to the first charge it appears doubtful if the damage is serious in waters already as muddy as those of the Illinois and Mississippi rivers. Carp do not naturally seek out clear and cold waters to defile them, and they would probably in no case be serious competitors of such fish as trout and small-mouthed bass.

The second charge, if true, is a much more serious one; but few direct observations bearing on this point have been made. The common form of the argument, that "*carp eat spawn, as shown* by the simultaneous rapid increase of carp and decrease of fine fish," is not supported by the statistics of the fisheries of the Illinois River. These show, on the contrary, that during the five years between 1894 and 1899, when the carp catch increased from ½ to 8⅓ million pounds, the black bass, instead of decreasing, increased from 70,000 to 102,000 ℔. The decrease in black bass between 1899 and 1903 to 45,000 ℔ was accompanied by a corresponding decrease in carp to 6,000,000

EUROPEAN CARP (MIRROR CARP), *Cyprinus carpio* Linnaeus

lb. It is shown also that catfish gradually increased from 700,-000 to 990,000 lb between 1894 and 1903; that crappie increased from 138,000 to 210,000 lb; that sunfish increased from 175,000 to 507,000 lb between 1894 and 1899, falling off somewhat in 1903; and that suckers, although falling off from 155,000 to 67,000 lb between 1894 and 1899, rose again to 199,999 lb in 1903. The sole important commercial species that have fallen off steadily since 1894 are buffalo and drum, the first declining from 3⅓ million pounds to about half that amount in 1903; and drum from 348,000 to less than 100,000 lb in the year last mentioned. If these records show anything at all it would seem to be that the competition of the carp as spawn-eater and water-soiler has not seriously affected many of our Illinois River species. It is by no means improbable that causes entirely apart from depredations and competition of carp may have had a large influence in producing the recent decrease of buffalo and drum. Among such causes may be mentioned increased contamination of waters from municipal and industrial sources; the obliteration, by drainage and diking, of backwaters used as spawning grounds; and the increased rapidity of run-off from the prairie and upland, as a result of tiling and the cutting of the forests, affecting the extent and duration of the spawning havens afforded by both swampy areas and small streams. To these causes is to be assigned the decrease and approximate disappearance of such minor species as pickerel and lake sturgeon, which were never very abundant in the rivers in question, and which began to fall off in numbers long before the carp entered the field.

It is not denied that carp will eat fish spawn; but it has not yet been shown that they seek out spawn for the purpose of consuming it. Black bass, crappie, and sunfish are doubtless able to defend their nests against carp in any case. Certainly the devouring of spawn has not affected the multiplication, as shown by the output, of any of these three species, or of suckers or catfish. That even a favorable effect of the multiplication of the carp is not impossible is evident when it is remembered that the myriads of young carp offer an almost inexhaustible supply of food to the growing bass, crappies, and sunfish. The drum and buffalo, which have decreased, are in their food habits more directly in competition with the carp—being chiefly bottom feeders, utilizing mollusks, crustaceans, and insect larvæ.

Of the third charge little can be said. While it is admitted by all competent to judge that carp do uproot vegetation in large quantities, no means are at hand for comparing the effect of this destruction on the decrease of water-birds with the effects of the operations of the hunters themselves. Since 1900 the problem has been complicated in the case of the Illinois River by the effect of the increased flow from Lake Michigan, which has diminished vegetation in many areas.

GENUS **CAMPOSTOMA** AGASSIZ

STONE-ROLLERS

Body elongate, little compressed; jaws with thick lips; premaxillaries protractile; no barbel; teeth 4–4 or 1, 4–4, 0, with oblique grinding surface and a slight hook on one or two teeth; intestine 6 to 9 times length of body, wound in many coils about the air-bladder, which is suspended in the abdominal cavity, this condition being unique in *Campostoma* among all known fishes; peritoneum black; dorsal rays 8; anal rays 7 or 8; scales 46 to 75; lateral line present. Size moderate, not over 6 or 8 inches. Four species known.

CAMPOSTOMA ANOMALUM (RAFINESQUE)

STONE-ROLLER; DOUGH-BELLY; GREASED CHUB

(MAP XXIII)

Rafinesque, 1820, Ichth. Oh., 52 (**Rutilus**).
G., VII, 183 (**dubium**); J. & G., 149, 150 (**prolixum**); M. V., 52; J. & E., I, 205; N. 44; J., 55; F., 79; F. F., I. 6, 77; L., 14.

Distinguishable from all other Illinois *Cyprinidæ* by the peculiar disposition of the very long intestine, which is wound many times in a transverse spiral about the air-bladder in the species of this genus, in which alone of all fishes this arrangement is known to occur. Length 6 inches; body stoutish, subfusiform, only moderately compressed; depth 3.9 to 4.8 in length, usually more than 4.3 in adults; caudal peduncle as a rule somewhat longer than head, its depth 2 to 2.5 in its length; old males heavy forward, the predorsal region swollen and the back more or less elevated. Color brownish olive, the upper parts with brassy luster; sides and caudal peduncle irregularly blotched or mottled with blackish; belly satiny whitish; a dusky vertical bar behind opercle; males with a dark cross-bar through middle of dorsal and anal and a vertical bar at base of caudal, especially conspicuous in spring, when the rest of each fin is fiery red and the snout and sometimes almost the entire body covered with tubercles; females sometimes with a faint dusky cross-bar on dorsal, the anal and caudal plain; young with more or less pinkish to purplish on body. Head subconic, little compressed, 4 to 4.6 in length, its width in its length 1.7 to 2; interorbital space very little convex, 2.5 to 3.3 in head, usually less than 3; eye small, circular, 4.2 to 5.2 in head, situated forward of middle of head and nearer its upper than under

STONE-ROLLER, *Campostoma anomalum* (Rafinesque)

surface; nose 2.3 to 2.8, the muzzle moderately decurved, overhanging the rather large and horizontal mouth; maxillary 3.3 to 4.6 in head, reaching scarcely back of vertical from posterior nostril; lower jaw wholly included; upper lip quite fleshy; breadth of isthmus 1.3 to 1.5 times diameter of orbit. Teeth 4–4 or 1, 4–4, 0, with oblique grinding surface without terminal hooks, or with only a slight one on one or two teeth; intestine 5 to 9.5 times length of head and body; peritoneum black. Dorsal fin with 8 rays, set slightly behind ventrals and nearly midway between muzzle and base of caudal; longest dorsal ray 1.2 to 1.6 in head; anal rays 7; pectorals about ⅔ to ventrals, 1.2 to 1.4 in head, ventrals falling quite short of vent in males, reaching or almost reaching it in females. Scales rather small, 6–8, 46–53, 6–8, more or less crowded forward, the crowding scarcely noticeable in females but very evident and often conspicuous in old males; scales on breast very small, about 15 transverse series between pectorals; scales before dorsal 15 to 26; lateral line complete.

This is a species of wide distribution occurring in the Great Lake region, along the south Atlantic slope to the Gulf, and in the valley of the Mississippi from Wyoming to Indiana, Ohio, and Texas.

It is a fish of the creeks and the smaller rivers, its ratios of preference, according to our collections, being 3¼ for the former and 2¼ for the latter. It has been taken only occasionally by us from rivers of a large size, and but rarely from lakes and ponds. Indeed, the notable preference of the species for rocky or sandy streams as shown by its frequency coefficient of 3.26, and for swift water over still water (coefficients respectively, 1.70 and .59) would tend to exclude it from stagnant or muddy waters of any description. In accordance with these preferences, it has not once occurred in our collections from the streams of the lower Illinoisan glaciation, none of our 166 Illinois localities for this species falling within that district. Nine of them are from the hill region of extreme southern Illinois, and one is from the Wabash in Wabash county, but the southernmost points for the remaining 156 localities are in Montgomery county in the western part of the state, and in Coles county in the eastern part.

This species is distinguished from all our other minnows by the great length of the intestine, which is wound spirally about the air-bladder. There are about twenty gill-rakers to each gill, but they are so short as to constitute a very inefficient straining apparatus. The pharyngeal teeth have well-developed grinding surfaces, and are practically without terminal hook. Intestines of specimens examined with reference to the food of the species were invariably found filled from end to end with a slime-like matter consisting almost wholly of fine mud from which, with proper treatment, fragments of organic matter could be readily separated. This was nearly all of vegetable origin, chiefly filamentous algæ, with diatoms, and minute fragments of various kinds of plant tissue. Sometimes the intestine was filled with almost pure mud.

Dr. Jordan says of this species that "it spawns early in spring, and it ascends in great numbers all the running streams even the very smallest. Later it retires to the deeper places in the creeks, where it may be readily recognized by its quick motions and dusky colors. Most of the specimens seen are comparatively small, but occasionally an old male may be noticed in the spring with its entire body rough and gray with tubercles, and with its vertical fins gaily variegated with black and orange. Such individuals appear to have exhausted their vitality and die quickly in confinement, and are often found dead. Young individuals are active and hardy in the aquarium, where they feed on confervæ and diatoms."

This minnow is unusually tenacious of life, being among the hardiest of the aquarium fishes and extremely persistent on the hook. It is regarded by anglers as one of the best of live baits for black-bass fishing. Males in breeding dress and females apparently near spawning have been found by us from November 15 to December 15 in fall, and from May 1 to June 15 in spring. Breeding males often have the head and almost the entire body tuberculate. According to Dr. Reighard, an excavation is made by the male in sand or gravel in advance of spawning.

Genus **CHROSOMUS** Rafinesque

Body moderately elongate; not much compressed; no barbel; jaws normal; premaxillaries protractile; teeth 5–5 or 4–5, moderately hooked, with well-marked grinding surface; alimentary canal twice length of body; peritoneum black; dorsal rays 7 or 8; anal rays 9; scales small, 67 to 85 in lateral series; lateral line imperfect or wanting; size small, not over 3 inches. Three species; New England to the Dakotas, chiefly northward.

CHROSOMUS ERYTHROGASTER Rafinesque

RED-BELLIED DACE

(Map XXIV)

Rafinesque, 1820, Ichth. Oh., 47 (**Luxilus**), 48.

G., VII, 247 (**Leuciscus**); J. & G., 153; M. V., 53; J. & E., I, 209; N., 47; J., 61; F., 79; F. F., I. 6, 80; L., 14.

The minute scales, 77 to 91, in the lateral line, and the two longitudinal stripes of dark color upon the sides, will readily distinguish the present species

RED-BELLIED DACE, *Chrosomus erythrogaster* Rafinesque

from all other species of *Cyprinidæ* found within our range. Length 2 to 3 inches; body oblong, moderately compressed, tapering about equally each way from middle of body; depth 4.4 to 4.9 in length; depth of caudal peduncle 2.1 to 2.4 in its length. Color above brownish olive, with a broad vertebral streak of dusky and dark spots forming an indistinct row on upper part of each side; sides marked with two black stripes (faint in females), the upper and narrower one extending from upper corner of gill-cleft nearly straight backward to base of caudal, sometimes breaking up into spots or oblique bars on caudal peduncle; the lower stripe broader, extending from snout through eye and along lower portion of sides to end of caudal peduncle, followed by a black spot at base of caudal rays; the interspace between lateral bands a bright silvery or satiny cream, tinged with brassy to crimson in males; belly white, overlaid with silvery; females much more obsurely marked than males which in spring coloration have the belly, breast, and chin bright scarlet, and the fins a bright lemon-yellow, the dorsal with a large blotch of bright scarlet at its base and the body everywhere minutely tuberculate. Head rather pointed, 4 to 4.2 in length, its width 1.8 to 2; interorbital space nearly flat, 2.6 to 3 in head; eye 3.3 to 3.8; nose 2.9 to 3.5, short, pointed, longer than the small eye; mouth moderate, terminal, oblique, the tip of upper lip nearly at level of middle of pupil; maxillary 3.2 to 4 in head (usually greater than 3.4), reaching but slightly past anterior nostril-opening; jaws about equal; isthmus less than width of eye. Teeth 4–4, 4–5, or 5–5, long, slender, and compressed, with a long and narrow masticatory groove, and with tips slightly hooked; intestine 2.4 to 3.5 times length of head and body; peritoneum black. Dorsal fin with rays usually 7, in occasional instances 6, placed behind ventrals and about equidistant between snout and base of caudal; longest dorsal ray 1.1 to 1.3 in head; anal rays 7 or 8, usually 8; pectorals 1.2 to 1.5 in head; ventrals reaching vent. Scales very small, 17–20, 77–91, 9–12 (not usually over 85 in Illinois specimens), of uniform size everywhere, the exposed surfaces scarcely deeper than long; lateral line incomplete, there being usually no pores present on posterior half of body; scales before dorsal 35 or 40.

This beautiful species, one of the most showy in our waters, occurs rarely in our collections from the northern half of the state and from extreme southern Illinois. None of our twenty-two localities of its occurrence falls within the lower glaciation, and all but three of them are in northern Illinois. We have not taken the species from Lake Michigan or from any part of the lake drainage. Outside the state it has been reported from Maine and New Brunswick to North Carolina, from Michigan, and from the Ohio Valley generally to the streams of Kansas tributary to the Missouri, and to northern Alabama. It is commonly found only in small clear streams, and has not once been taken by us from any of the larger rivers.

Its food is evidently obtained by nibbling or sucking the surface slime from stones and other objects on the bottom. It consists, in all the cases examined by us, mainly of mud containing algæ with an occasional trace of *Entomostraca*.

The breeding season falls in May and June, at which time the colors of the male reach their most gorgeous development. While not especially hardy, this species lives well in the aquarium, where it is indeed a most beautiful object.

Genus **HYBOGNATHUS** Agassiz

Body elongate, somewhat compressed; jaws normal, sharp-edged, the lower in some species with a slight hard protuberance in front; premaxillaries protractile; no barbel; teeth 4–4, with oblique grinding surface and little if any hook; alimentary canal 3 to 10 times length of body; peritoneum black; dorsal rays 8; anal rays 7 to 9, scales large, usually 32 to 41 in lateral series; lateral line complete. Size moderate, 2½ to 6 inches. Described species numerous, though most are imperfectly known, and doubtless many synonyms. Ventral and southwestern United States into northern Mexico; two species found in Illinois.

Key to the Species of **HYBOGNATHUS** found in Illinois

a. Silvery species, with a prominent hard protuberance at tip of inside of lower jaw and with teeth long and scarcely hooked; length 6 inches.......**nuchalis.**

aa. Olivaceous, with dark lateral band continued through eye to end of snout; no symphysial protuberance; teeth short and distinctly hooked; length 2½ inches ....**nubila.**

HYBOGNATHUS NUCHALIS Agassiz

SILVERY MINNOW

(Map XXV)

Agassiz, 1855, Am Jour. Sci. Arts (Silliman's Journal), XIX, 224.

G., VII, 184; J. & G., 156; M. V., 53; J. & E., I, 213; N., 45 (also **argyritis**), J., 56 (also **argyritis**); F., 79; F. F., I. 6, 79; L., 14.

A large silvery minnow, with large and loosely imbricated scales, spindle-shaped body and pointed head, the lower jaw thin and hard and furnished with a small hard lump just inside the mouth in front. Length 6 inches, body subfusiform, not much compressed, deepest at front of dorsal and tapering about equally backward to base of caudal and forward to the pointed snout; depth 3.9 to 4.5 in length; caudal peduncle rather stout, shorter than head, its depth 1.7 to 2.3 (usually less than 2) in its length. Color olivaceous green above, translucent in life; sides clear silvery, with bright reflections; fins unspotted; scales not distinctly dark-edged, their entire surface being about equally specked. Head small, slender, subconical, its length 4 to 4.6, its width 1.8 to 2.1 in its length; interorbital space gently convex, 2.5 to 2.9 in head; eye small, circular, 3.8 to 4.5 in head; nose 2.9 to 3.5 in head, pointed and considerably longer than the small eye; mouth small, terminal, oblique, tip of upper lip not far below level of middle of pupil; maxillary 3.6 to 4.3 in head, its length but little greater than diameter of eye; back of maxillary falling far short of orbit, scarcely exceeding as a rule the vertical from anterior nostril-opening; lower jaw with a hard sharp edge and a noticeable protuberance just inside the mouth at the symphysis of the mandibles; jaws about equal; isthmus less than pupil. Teeth 4–4, narrow, with little grinding surface and very little hook; intestine extremely variable in length, from 3.7 to 8 times length of head and body, being as a rule over 5; peritoneum dusky. Dorsal fin with usually 8 rays, occasionally 7, set slightly in front of ventrals, usually a little nearer muzzle than base of caudal; longest dorsal ray 1 to 1.2 in head; anal rays 8 (rarely 7); pectorals 1.1 to 1.4 in head; ventrals falling far short of vent in adults. Scales 5, 37–39, 4, large and rounded, the exposed surfaces little deeper than long; lateral line complete, and nearly straight except for a slight downward curve in front of ventrals; scales before dorsal 13 to 16.

This species is generally distributed throughout the state, occurring in all our stream systems, including those of the Michigan drainage, but most abundantly in those of southern Illinois. It is essentially a river species—one of the few Illinois minnows occurring in larger ratio in rivers than in creeks. It is most abundant in rivers of the second class (coefficient, 2.18), and next in creeks (1.91), but we have also found it not very infrequent in the lakes and ponds of the river bottoms (.43).

In general distribution it ranges from Delaware to Georgia and Alabama, and from thence southwest to the Rio Grande, north to the tributaries of the Missouri in the Dakotas, and to the Red River of the North. In this state it is often found in deep and muddy waters, and less frequently than most minnows in swift and gravelly streams. It is one of the five Illinois species found most generally over a mud bottom, its frequency coefficient being 1.68. It has the long intestine, the simple pharyngeal teeth with a well-developed grinding surface, and the few and short gill-rakers characteristic of the mud-eating minnows, and its food corresponds to these structural peculiarities. According to our observations the intestine is always filled with fine mud, containing only filamentous algæ, diatoms, and other vegetable forms likely to be found on a mud bottom. It is frequently seen in large schools of from fifty to one hundred in deep and quiet water, always lying nearer the bottom than the top, or moving slowly along the bottom as it feeds. The chisel-shaped lower jaw tipped with cartilage is probably used for scraping up the mud and ooze.

The sexual differences of this species are not striking, although the spring males have the nuchal region somewhat swollen, and the top and sides of the head beset with very minute tubercles. Females greatly distended with eggs have been taken by us early in June. This minnow is not hardy, and is consequently an undersirable live bait. It is said by Dr. Bean to be much used for food.

HYBOGNATHUS NUBILA (FORBES)

(MAP XXVI)

Forbes, 1878, Bull. Ill. State Lab. Nat. Hist., I. 2, 56 (**Alburnops**). J. & G., 167 (**Cliola**); M. V., 53; J. & E., I, 215; F., 79; L., 14.

Length 2 to 2½ inches; form much as in the last, the body subfusiform, moderately compressed, and evenly tapered in both directions from the rather deep middle-body region; depth 4 to 4.5 in length; caudal peduncle as long as head or a little longer; readily distinguished from *H. nuchalis* by smaller size, absence of a symphysial protuberance, and by the prominent dark lateral band, which passes around snout. Color usually rather dusky; sides dull silvery, belly yellow; a dark band along the lateral line and the row of scales above, extending from a faint caudal spot forward through the eye and around the snout, tipping the chin; black vertebral line before the dorsal; dorsal scales thickly specked with black, those of belly plain; none of the scales distinctly dark-edged; fins plain. Head 3.5 to 4.8 in length, slender, conic, depressed above, being nearly quadrate in transverse section behind orbits; interorbital space nearly flat, 2.8 to 3.5; eye large, high, nearly circular, 2.8 to 3.1 in head; nose scarcely longer than eye, 3.5 to 4.5; mouth larger than in the last species, terminal, oblique, the maxillary 3.5 to 4 in head, extending back of posterior nostril, and almost in front of orbit; jaws about equal, the lower lacking the hard sharp edge and the symphysial protuberance found in the last species; isthmus less than pupil. Teeth 4–4, only slightly hooked, with long though narrow grinding surfaces; intestine 2.8 to 3.5 times the length of head and body; peritoneum black. Dorsal fin with 8 rays, over ventrals and farther from muzzle than base of caudal; anal rays 8; pectorals reaching ⅔ to ventrals; ventrals short of vent in females, exceeding it in males. Scales 5 or 6, 36–38, 3 or 4, of uniform size and distribution on all parts of body; lateral line complete, very slightly decurved anteriorly; scales before dorsal 13 or 14.

Males in breeding dress with head somewhat sparsely studded with small but hard and sharp tubercles; smaller tubercles sprinkled over scales of predorsal region. Tuberculate males and females distended with eggs taken from the Kiswaukee at Belvidere on May 12.

This species, which was described by the senior author from specimens collected from Rock River, at Oregon, Ill., has since been taken only rarely in this state, principally in the extreme northwestern part. Our later collections number 2 from Jo Daviess and Stephenson counties, 2 from the Kishwaukee at Belvidere, 1 from Sand creek, Warsaw, and 1 from the Ohio at Cairo. It seems to be essentially a western species, occurring abundantly in the tributaries of the Missouri River in Missouri, and in the streams of the Ozark region in northern Arkansas. It is also reported from the Northwest as far as Wyoming.

Genus PIMEPHALES Rafinesque

FATHEADS

Body robust or elongate, little compressed; head short and rounded; mouth small, inferior; upper jaw protractile; no barbel; teeth 4–4, with oblique grinding surface, usually but one of the teeth hooked; intestinal canal more than twice length of body; peritoneum black; dorsal rays 7 or 8; anal rays 7; the first (rudimentary) dorsal ray in males evidently separated by membrane from the second, and not adnate to it as usually in minnows; scales rather small, 43 to 47 in lateral series; lateral line complete or imperfect. Size small, 2½ to 4 inches. Two species, generally distributed throughout the United States east of the Rockies.

Key ro the Species of PIMEPHALES found in Illinois

a. Body short and stout, depth 3 to 4 in length; lateral line more or less incomplete .... **promelas.**
aa. Body moderately elongate, depth 4 to 5 in length; lateral line complete.... .... **notatus.**

PIMEPHALES PROMELAS Rafinesque

BLACK-HEAD MINNOW; FATHEAD

(Pl., p. 128; Map XXVII)

Rafinesque, 1820, Ichth. Oh., 53.
G., VII, 181; J. & G., 158; M. V., 55; J. & E., I, 217; N., 45; J., 55; F., 79; F. F., I. 6, 78; L., 14.

Length 2½ inches; body robust, short, thick and deep, much heavier forward, not notably compressed; depth 3.2 to 4 in length; caudal peduncle stout, its length about same as head, its depth usually less than 2 in its length. Color rather dark olive, with a tinge of coppery or purplish forward; dorsal fin with a dusky cross-bar about the middle, faint in females and young, but appearing as a large jet-black blotch covering most of the lower two thirds of the fin in spring males; other fins plain in females, in males all more or less dusky, pectorals and anal most so; spring males often found in which almost the entire body is dusky, the head in such instances being a jet-black.* Head 3.6 to 4 in length, very broad, short, and blunt, sometimes appearing almost globular in breeding males; width of head usually great (see *Cliola vigilax*), 1.4 to 1.7 in its length; interorbital space broad and nearly flat (except in spring males, in which it is swollen), 2 to 2.5 in head; eye 4.1 to 4.8 in head; nose longer than eye, 3 to 3.5 in head; mouth rather small, subterminal and quite oblique in females, in which the tip of the upper lip is nearly on a level with the upper margin of the pupil—less oblique in males,

* Males taken from Kickapoo Creek at Elmwood in June, 1900, have the head jet-black, and all the rest of the body an extreme dusky with the exception of a broad transverse bar of lighter color just back of and tipping the opercle and a similar bar which passes around the sides directly beneath the dorsal fin.

in which level of upper lip is scarcely above that of lower margin of orbit; maxillary a little longer than eye, reaching very little past anterior nostril, 3.5 to 4.5 in head; jaws about equal; isthmus comparatively broad, its width greater than diameter of eye. Teeth 4–4 or 4–5; intestine 2 to 3 times the length of head and body; peritoneum black. Dorsal fin I,* 8, low, placed directly over ventrals and a little farther from muzzle than base of caudal; longest dorsal ray 1.2 to 1.6 in head, usually greater than 1.4, anal rays I,* 7; pectorals ⅔ to ventrals, 1.2 to 1.5 in head; ventrals past front of anal in males, scarcely reaching vent in females. Scales 8 or 9, 42–48, 5 or 6, much crowded in front of dorsal fin, before which there are about 25–30 rows; lateral line incomplete, sometimes almost wanting; when present, with a noticeable downward curve anteriorly.

This species has a general range from the northeast to the southwest, but is not reported from the southeastern part of the United States. It occurs throughout the Great Lake basin to Lake Champlain, throughout the Ohio basin and up the Mississippi to the headwaters of the Missouri, and thence northward to the Red River of the North and the Saskatchewan, and southwest to the Rio Grande. Its distribution in Illinois is a miniature copy of its general range, being limited to the northern and western three fourths of the state, leaving the southeastern part with no representation of this species in our collections. It is, in fact, one of the fishes already frequently mentioned, which are practically limited to the Mississippi drainage in this state, and occurs in our collections from the tributaries of the Ohio only from one group of four localities on the headwaters of the Embarras where these approach most closely to the upper tributaries of the Kaskaskia. Notwithstanding the general exclusion of a large part of southern Illinois from its range, it enters the lower Illinoisan glaciation in the branches of the Kaskaskia. It frequents muddy waters freely, occurring there, indeed, in disproportionate frequency, our ninety-five collections of the species giving us a frequency coefficient of 2.08. Like most of our minnows, it is relatively more abundant in creeks than in other waters (coefficient 2.68) and, next to these, in the smaller rivers (1.82). It is fairly well represented, however, in rivers of the first class (.85), and occurs not infrequently in lowland lakes and ponds (.23). It has not been taken by us from our northeastern lakes of glacial orgin nor from Lake Michigan or from the drainage of its basin.

We have found it commonest in the short muddy creeks connected with the larger rivers, and especially abundant in the

* See key to genera of *Cyprinidæ*.

muddy parts of a short stream near Warsaw, in Hamilton county, running down from the bluffs to the Mississippi River, where it was associated with *Cliola vigilax*, a species of somewhat similar distribution.

Its tolerance of muddy waters is shown by our frequency coefficient of 2.08 for those with a mud bottom; and we have found it with less than the average preference of minnows for a rapidly moving stream (coefficient, .73; still water, 1.37).

It belongs to the mud-eating group of minnows, and its alimentary structures correspond to this fact, the intestine being from two to three times the length of the head and body, and the pharyngeal teeth not hooked but with well-developed grinding surface. Our only knowledge of its food is derived from a study of four specimens from muddy streams in northern and central Illinois. The intestines of these were largely filled with mud containing some algæ and a considerable number of insects, partly of terrestrial species and partly aquatic larvæ of *Diptera*.

Females greatly distended with eggs, and males in full breeding color, have been taken by our collectors in May and June. The snout of the breeding male bears three rows of very large tubercles, one on a level with the nostrils and the others between this and the upper lip. Dr Kirtland reports that these fishes make shallow excavations in the breeding season under stones and the ends of logs in still water, and that, after depositing their eggs, they defend them bravely against all intruders. The species is not a good live bait, although often sold as such.

PIMEPHALES NOTATUS (Rafinesque)

BLUNT-NOSED MINNOW

(Map XXVIII)

Rafinesque, 1820, Ichth. Oh., 47 (**Minnilus**).
G., VII, 182 (**Hyborhynchus**); J. & G., 159 (**Hyborhynchus**); M. V., 54; J. & E., I, 218; N., 45 (**Hyborhynchus**); J., 55 (**Hyborhynchus**); F. F., I. 6, 79 (**Hyborhynchus**); F., 78; L., 14.

Length 2 to 3½ inches; body elongate, little compressed, the back broad and rather flat; depth 4.3 to 4.8 in length; caudal peduncle rather slender, longer than head, its depth 2.1 to 2.6 in its length, as a rule greater than 2.3. Color pale olivaceous above, all the scales of upper part of body with dark edgings prominent; sides a dull silvery bluish, under which is a plumbeous lateral stripe, extending across opercle and through eye to end of snout; no dark vertebral streak; a prominent dark spot at base of caudal; belly whitish; dorsal fin with a dark blotch in front on first 3 rays, a little less than half way up from base of fin; other fins plain, except for faint dusky lines crossing dorsal and caudal; breeding males with the head jet-black, except for a light transverse bar at back of opercle, the dorsal blotch enlarged and extending as a broad bar from front to back of fin; other fins and entire body more or less dusky. Head 4 to 4.4 in length, small, but rather broad and flat above; the muzzle very blunt; width of head 1.6 1.8 in its length; interorbital space 2.2 to 2.5; eye 3.5 to 4.4 in head; nose 3.1 to 3.4, longer than eye; mouth small, inferior, nearly or wholly horizontal, the tip of the upper lip below level of lower margin of orbit; maxillary scarcely longer than eye, 3.8 to 4.3 in head, reaching to posterior nostril; lower jaw included; isthmus not quite so broad as in the last species, its width about $^7/_{10}$ diameter of orbit. Teeth 4–4; intestine about twice the length of head and body; peritoneum black. Dorsal fin I–8 (rarely I–7), placed a little behind ventrals and about equidistant between front of eye and base of caudal; longest dorsal ray 1.4 to 1.7 in head; anal rays 7; pectorals short, reaching little more than half way to ventrals, no difference in this respect being noticeable between males and females; ventrals in both males and females falling short of vent. Scales 6 or 7, 41 to 44, 4, rather crowded before dorsal, but not so much so as in the last species, rows before dorsal about 23; lateral line usually complete, with a slight downward curve in front of ventrals.

FIG. 24

This is by far the most abundant and widely distributed minnow in Illinois. It appeared in 377 of our collections, and is abundant in all of our river basins, in the glacial lakes of the northeastern part of the state, and in the streams of the Lake basin. Generally speaking, it ranges from Winnipeg and Lake Champlain through the Great Lake basin and the north Atlantic region as far as New Jersey, and down the Mississippi Valley to the Alabama and the Rio Colorado of Texas. It passes freely into the lower Illinoisan glaciation, occurs abundantly in small streams along the bluffs of the Mississippi, and seems to find a satisfactory place of residence in streams of any size or lakes or ponds of any description. It is most abundant in creeks (coefficient, 2.57), and scarcely less so in the smaller rivers (2.03), but is rather rare in the larger rivers, from which it has been taken by us but 23 times in 293 collections.

It is one of the mud-eating group, the alimentary canal being commonly packed from end to end with mud containing filamentous algæ and miscellaneous vegetable debris. Occasionally fragments of insects or a specimen of the mud-loving *Entomostraca* may be found in the general mixture, and individual specimens have been reported to eat decayed fish in the aquarium.

Its spawning season, if we may judge from our collections, is from May 15 to June 15 in central Illinois. Dr. Eigenmann reports that the eggs are sometimes laid on the under surface of various objects submerged in shallow water. He found them throughout June and a part of July, one of the parents being, as a rule, on guard about the nest. The snout of the male in the breeding season bears three rows of large tubercles, seven in one row at the margin of the upper lip, five in a row directly above this, and four in an upper row, two of them between the nostrils and one on each side between the nostril and the eye.

Genus **SEMOTILUS** Rafinesque

FALLFISHES

Body robust; mouth terminal; upper jaw protractile; a small barbel on the upper side of the maxillary just in front of its extremity (not at its tip as in most American minnows); teeth 2, 5–4, 2, hooked, without grinding surface; intestine short; peritoneum pale; dorsal rays 7 or 8; anal rays 8; scales 45 to 60 in lateral series; lateral line continuous. Size large, 6 to 18 inches. Two species, *S. atromaculatus* being found from Maine to Wyoming, and *S. corporalis*, the large chub or fallfish of the Eastern creeks, being confined to the east of the Alleghanies.

Fig. 25

SEMOTILUS ATROMACULATUS (Mitchill)

HORNED DACE; CREEK CHUB

(Map XXIX)

Mitchill, 1818, Am. Month. Mag., II, 324 (**Cyprinus**).

G., VII., 269 (**Leucosomus corporalis**); J. & G., 221 (**corporalis**); M. V., 66; J. & E., I, 222; N., 45 (**corporalis**); J., 62 (**corporalis**); F., 75 (**corporalis**); F. F., I. 6, 88 (**corporalis**); L., 15.

Length usually 6 to 8 inches, sometimes reaching a length of a foot; body rather elongate, but robust, heavy forward, the back gently arched in front of the dorsal fin; depth 4.1 to 4.6 in length, caudal peduncle shorter than head, its depth 2 to 2.5 in its length. Color dusky bluish-olive above; tinges of light purplish on sides as far down as lateral line; a faint plumbeous lateral band, somewhat more distinct towards end of caudal peduncle; a faint vertebral streak and a dark bar behind opercle; sides below lateral line greenish gray to silvery; belly silvery; dorsal fin with a distinct black blotch at base, between first and third rays; in breeding males there is sometimes a broad but indistinct transverse bar of dusky color crossing the fin about midway; other fins plain, or, at most, with slight traces of dusky in spring males. Head large, everywhere convex, broadly rounded above, 3.5 to 3.9 in length; width of head 1.6 to 1.8 in its length; interorbital space 2.4 to 2.7; eye 4.8 to 7.1 in head, usually more than 6 in adults; nose long, broadly and bluntly rounded, 2.7 to 3.3 in head; mouth very large, terminal, oblique, tip of upper lip at level of lower margin of pupil; maxillary about 2½ times eye, reaching beyond anterior margin of orbit; jaws about equal; isthmus less

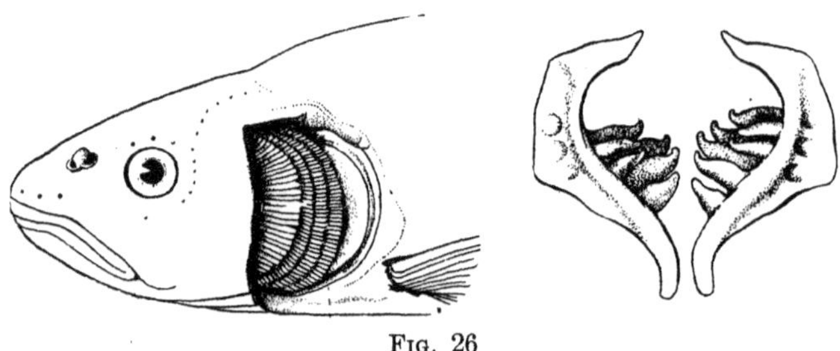

FIG. 26

Left branchial cavity of *Semotilus atromaculatus*, with opercle removed to show left pharyngeal arch *in situ*; also pharyngeal jaws removed and viewed from front.

than eye. Teeth extremely variable,—4,1–0,4, 4,1–0,5, 4,2–1,5, 4,2–2,5, 5,2–1,5, 4,2–2,4, in nine specimens examined by us; intestine .9 to 1.1 times length of head and body; peritoneum pale, a very little dusky forward. Dorsal fin with 8 rays, situated behind ventrals, equidistant between front of eye and base of caudal; longest dorsal ray 1.6 to 1.8 in head; anal rays 8; pectorals short, reaching ½ to ⅔ to ventrals, 1.5 to 1.9 in head; ventrals short of vent in adults. Scales 10 or 11, rarely 9, 55 to 69, 5 to 7, considerably crowded in predorsal and scapular regions, about 35 rows before dorsal fin; lateral line complete, with a strong downward curve in front of ventrals.

This is essentially a creek species, our frequency coefficient for creeks being 3.77, and for the smaller rivers 1.67. In lakes and ponds we have taken it but 5 times in 591 collections, and in the larger rivers but 5 times in 293 collections. Its preference for creeks is also reported by R. C. Osburn, who says that in seining up stream an increase in its numbers is very noticeable as the headwaters are approached. Within these limits its distribution in Illinois has been quite general, including all our hydrographic divisions except the Michigan drainage and showing no marked preponderance in any. Outside this state it ranges far and wide throughout the central and western United States, excepting, however, the Great Lakes and the extreme southern and southwestern part of our area. From the St. Lawrence and its tributaries in Canada, and from New Brunswick, Maine, and Vermont, it is found westward and southward through the Hudson valley to the Potomac and the Roanoke, through the Ohio and the Mississippi valleys to the Alabama River, and northwestward to Wyoming.

It is an active swimmer and exceedingly voracious, and with an unusually varied diet for a minnow, including considerable quantities of vegetable food on the one hand, and small fishes on the other. A fourth of the food of twenty-two specimens consisted of algæ and of miscellaneous vegetable debris. Four of these specimens had eaten little else than filamentous algæ, and three had captured small fishes. Grasshoppers, caterpillars, ants, chrysomelid and scarabæid beetles and various other terrestrial insects, together with *Corisa*, dipterous larvæ, and other aquatic forms, were the insects represented, and three of our twenty-two specimens had eaten only crawfishes.

This species is reported by Jordan to reach a length of a foot, and to be an excellent bait, when of the proper size, for bass, wall-eyed pike, and pickerel. With the possible exception of *Hybopsis kentuckiensis*, it is decidedly our gamiest minnow. It is always ready to bite at a grasshopper, and will even rise to the fly. It thrives in the aquarium, and with good treatment soon becomes so tame as to feed from the hand*.

Males in full breeding dress have been taken in our May collections. There are, in spring males, two large tubercles on each side of the upper lip just below the nostrils, a row of four other large ones on each side of the eye, a cluster of minute tubercles on the lower part of each opercle, and a row on the margin of most of the scales on the upper part of the caudal peduncle. Reighard has seen a male of this species preparing a nest by excavating the sand and gravel in advance of spawning, but this is abandoned after the eggs have been laid.

* The eastern chub (*Semotilus corporalis*) does not occur west of the Alleghanies. It is said by Atkins to spawn in May. It builds great heaps of gravel in running water, but avoids eddies and ripples when spawning. The males build the nest, carrying pebbles in their mouths.

GENUS **OPSOPŒODUS** HAY

Body fusiform, somewhat compressed; mouth extremely small, terminal; upper jaw protractile; no barbels; teeth 5–5 or 4–5, with edges serrated and no grinding surface, the tips hooked; intestine short; peritoneum white; dorsal rays 7 to 10; anal rays 7 or 8; scales 37 to 42; lateral line complete or imperfect. Size very small, 2½ inches. Species 3 or 4; confined to the Mississippi Valley and the eastern United States.

FIG. 27

OPSOPŒODUS EMILIÆ HAY

(MAP XXX)

Hay, 1880, Proc. U. S. Nat. Mus., 507.
Forbes in J. & G., 247 (**Trycherodon megalops**); M. V., 68; J. & E., I, 248 (**megalops**); F., 74; L., 15 (**emiliæ and megalops**).

The very small and upturned mouth, the black spot on the posterior rays of the dorsal fin, and the incomplete lateral line of this species serve to distinguish it readily from all other minnows found in our range. Length usually less than 2¼ inches; body moderately elongate, compressed, the back perceptibly elevated, the profile a more or less even incline from a point over the tips of the reflexed pectorals; depth 4.1 to 4.8 in length; caudal peduncle slender, longer than head, its depth 2.2 to 3.2 in its length, not usually, however, over 2.5. Color light olive, yellowish, the scales except on and very near belly conspicuously dark-edged;* a narrow dark lateral band, extending forward across opercle and through eye to end of snout, becoming faint anteriorly; no distinct caudal spot, but sometimes, in highly colored males, an indistinct vertical bar at base of caudal; fins of females plain, or, at most, the dorsal with faint traces of dusky on anterior third; breeding males with the snout and chin thickly studded with minute tubercles, and with a large blotch of dusky covering almost entire dorsal fin except a patch at base and another at tip of fin; a second blotch of dusky at back of fin in some males, situated about half way up from base and crossing last three rays; other fins plain. Head small, 4.2 to 4.5 in length; width of head

* No other species of *Cyprinidæ* found in this state has the cross-hatching more distinct or extending farther below the lateral line, typical specimens having almost the entire body so marked.

1.7 to 1.9 in its length; interorbital space little convex, 2.3 to 2.6 in head; eye 3.1 to 3.7, a little longer than the snout, but less than the interorbital space; nose short and blunt, 3.2 to 3.8 in head, the extremely oblique mouth giving it a turned-up or "snubbed" appearance; mouth extremely small and very oblique, making an angle of less than 30° with the vertical; maxillary 3.7 to 4.6 in head, shorter than the eye and scarcely reaching anterior nostril; upper lip almost or quite on a level with upper margin of pupil; jaws about equal; isthmus less than pupil. Teeth 5–5 or 4–5, very slender, strongly hooked, and sharply and irregularly crenate; intestine about .9 of length of head and body; peritoneum very lightly specked with dusky. Dorsal fin with 8 or 9 rays, inserted a little behind front of ventrals, but nearer muzzle than base of caudal; longest dorsal ray 1 to 1.3 in head; anal rays 8; pectorals ⅔, or more, to ventrals; ventrals to or slightly past vent. Scales 6, 38–40, 4; lateral line variously imperfect, sometimes present only on the first 4 or 5 scales, sometimes extending, with numerous interruptions, to the middle of the caudal peduncle; slightly decurved anteriorly; 15–18 scales before dorsal.

This is a southern species in general range, distributed from Ohio through Indiana and Illinois to Georgia, Arkansas, and Oklahoma, and in our collections is relatively much the most abundant from southern Illinois. Northward it has been taken almost wholly along the larger rivers—the Illinois, the Mississippi, and the Rock. It is mainly a species of creeks and ponds with us, however, although more than usually abundant from the larger rivers also. Females greatly distended with eggs, and tuberculate males in high spring color, have been taken by us about Meredosia between the 10th and the 20th of June.

Genus **ABRAMIS** Cuvier

BREAMS

Body deep and strongly compressed; belly before ventrals forming a keel over which the scales do not pass; mouth oblique or horizontal; premaxillary protractile; no barbels; teeth 5–5, hooked and with grinding surface; alimentary canal short; peritoneum (in American species) pale; dorsal rays 8 to 10; anal typically long, with 20 to 40 rays in the European species; American forms with anal shorter, the rays 9 to 18; scales 39 to 55; lateral line developed. Size rather large,* the American bream reaching a length of 12 inches. Species numerous, inhabiting both Europe and North America; American forms 1 (or 2); distributed from Nova Scotia to Texas.

* The common bream of Europe (*Abramis brama*) has been known to attain a weight of 12 lb in some of the Irish lakes.

ABRAMIS CRYSOLEUCAS (MITCHILL)

GOLDEN SHINER; ROACH; BREAM

(MAP XXXI)

Mitchill, 1814, Rep. Fish. N. Y., 23 (**Cyprinus**).
G., VII, 305 (**americanus**), 306 (**leptosomus**); J. & G., 249 (**Notemigonus leptosomus**), 250 (**N. chrysoleucus**); M. V., 68 (**Notemigonus**); J. & E., I, 250; N., 48 (**Notemigonus americanus**); J., 61 (**Notemigonus**); F. F., I. 6, 81 (**Notemigonus chrysoleucus**); F., 74 (**Notemigonus**); L., 15.

The small, pointed head, greatly compressed form, strongly decurved lateral line, and the sharp keel on the belly behind the ventral fins, will as a rule distinguish this species with readiness from all other Illinois species of its family. Length 6 to 8 inches; body moderately elongate in the young, in adults becoming very deep and strongly compressed, the thickness in the predorsal region contained sometimes nearly three times in the greatest depth in fully adult specimens; depth 3 to 3.6 in length; caudal peduncle short, its greatest depth 1.4 to 1.7 in its length. Color a clear dark greenish olive above, becoming steel-blue in some lights; sides silvery, with bright golden reflections; a half-diamond-shaped or triangular spot of dark color more or less evident at base of exposed portion of each scale; dorsal and anal fins tipped with dusky; lower fins yellow, the ventrals bright orange at tips in breeding individuals of boths sexes; young with a faint vertebral streak and a distinct dark band along sides. Head small, subconic, flattened on the sides, 4 to 4.5 in length; width of head 1.7 to 1.9 in its length; interorbital space, 2.4 to 2.7 in head, markedly convex; eye 3.4 to 4.4 in head, within the anterior half of the head, and rather low, about as near chin as crown; nose sharply pointed, appreciably longer than eye, 3.2 to 3.8 in head; mouth rather small, terminal, oblique, tip of upper lip even with top of pupil; maxillary not reaching past anterior nostril; 3.5 to 3.9 in head; jaws about equal; isthmus less than pupil. Teeth 5–5 to 4–4, constricted at base and sometimes slightly hooked; intestine from 1 to 1.8 times length of head and body; peritoneum lightly specked with dusky. Dorsal fin with 8 rays, set distinctly behind ventrals, its first ray about equidistant between upper corner of gill-opening and base of caudal; longest dorsal ray 1 to 1.3 in head; anal rays 11 to 14; pectorals 1.1 to 1.3 in head, reaching about ⅔ to ventrals; ventrals falling short of vent in adults. Scales 9 to 11, 45 to 52, 3; lateral line complete, broadly and deeply decurved, and often flexuose from back of opercle to a point about midway of caudal peduncle, its distance from the back in the middle of the body 2½ times the interval below.

This extremely abundant species occurs from New Brunswick and the Province of Quebec southward to St. Johns River and the lakes of Orange county, Florida, westward to the branches of the Missouri in the Dakotas, and southwest to the Nueces River in Texas. It is not reported from the Great Lakes. Professor Hay says that it prefers slow streams and grassy ponds, and is sometimes found in large numbers in the muddiest and most uninviting holes. In Ohio, Osburn found it chiefly in ponds, quiet pools, and weedy bayous. According to Dr. Bean,

GOLDEN SHINER, *Abramis crysoleucas* (Mitchill)

it is one of the commonest fishes of Pennsylvania, frequenting sluggish waters and abounding in bayous and weedy ponds where it grows to a length of a foot and a weight of a pound and a half. According to Dr. Jordan, "it is especially characteristic of sluggish waters in either lake, pond, or bayou. In Ohio it is extremely abundant, in the weedy bayous most of all. The yellow pond-lily is its favorite shelter."

It has been taken by us in 303 collections, more frequently than any other fish except the blunt-nosed minnow(*Pimephales notatus*), which has appeared in 377. The most notable peculiarities of its local and ecological distribution in Illinois are its frequency in lowland lakes and ponds (coefficient, 1.36), and over a muddy bottom (3.79). Our map of the distribution of the Illinois collections of this species shows that, although it is widely distributed throughout the state, occurring in many localities in each of our stream systems, there is a notable difference in the size of the streams which it chiefly inhabits in the southern and eastern parts of the state, where it is essentially a creek species, and in the remainder of the state, where it has been taken chiefly along our larger rivers. It is also very much more abundant in the Wabash basin, the Big Muddy, and the tributaries of the Ohio than in any other part of Illinois, appearing there three and four times as frequently to the hundred collections as in the Illinois valley or the streams of northwestern Illinois.

It has a more efficient equipment of alimentary structures than any other of our common minnows, and a correspondingly wide range of food resources. Its intestine is rather long—one and a third times the length of the head and body together; the gill-rakers are long, fine, and numerous; and the pharyngeal teeth are provided both with terminal hooks and grinding surfaces. We find its food varying, consequently, according to situation, from a mere mass of mud, to mollusks, insects, *Entomostraca*, and vegetable substances. Where mollusks are abundant, it sometimes feeds on nothing else; and in ponds containing many minute *Crustacea*, these may be its sole food One specimen taken from Nippersink.Lake, in the northern part of the state, had filled itself with wild rice. Insects, mainly terrestrial, were also eaten by several, and some of the specimens studied, had devoured quantities of algæ.

The golden shiner is said to be an excellent pan-fish, if of sufficient size. It is active all winter, and can be taken through the ice. It lives well in the aquarium, and makes a good bait for black bass.

Spawning females, with eggs running from the vent, have been taken by us from the first to the last of May, and occasional specimens were found full of eggs as late as July 30. The eggs are extremely adhesive, and contain no oil globule. The males average smaller in size than the females, and have the back sonewhat more swollen at the nape. Their sides are rough with minute tubercles, but the head and snout are not tuberculate.

GENUS **CLIOLA** GIRARD

Fishes with the form and appearance of *Pimephales*, but with the alimentary canal shorter than the body, the peritoneum pale, and the teeth more hooked—allying them rather with *Notropis*; mouth inferior; premaxillary protractile; teeth 4–4; dorsal rays 8, the anterior ray club-shaped and separated from the second by membrane, as in *Pimephales;* anal rays 7; scales 42 to 48; lateral line developed. Size small, 2½ to 3 inches. Two species known; central and southwestern United States.

FIG. 28

CLIOLA VIGILAX (BAIRD & GIRARD)

BULLHEAD MINNOW; FATHEAD

(MAP XXXII)

Baird & Girard, 1853, Proc. Ac. Nat. Sci. Phila., 391 (**Ceratichthys**).
G., VII, 259 (**Leuciscus tuditanus**); J. & G., 165 (**tuditana**), 166 (**taurocephala**), 169; M. V., 54; J. & E., I, 253; J., 56 (**Alburnops tuditanus**); F., 78; L., 15.

Length 2 to 3 inches; body stout, only moderately elongate, not much compressed, the thickness of the body in the predorsal region contained about 1⅓ times in its depth; depth 4.1 to 4.5 in length; caudal peduncle stout, shorter than head, its depth 1.5 to 2.2 in its length. Color dusky olive or yellowish above; sides silvery, with but a faint suggestion of a dark lateral band; a small jet-black caudal spot, and a prominent black spot on the anterior 3 or 4 rays of the dorsal fin about half way up; spring males with head leaden to blackish, and entire body more or less dusky. Head 3.7

BLACK-HEAD MINNOW, *Pimephales promelas* Rafinesque

BULLHEAD MINNOW (Male), *Cliola vigilax* (Baird & Girard)

BULLHEAD MINNOW (Female), *Cliola vigilax* (Baird & Girard)

Notropis cayuga Meek

to 4.1 in length, broad and flat above and little tapered forward, the muzzle very blunt; width of head 1.5 to 1.7 in its length; interorbital space 2.3 to 2.8, nearly flat; eye small, circular, entirely within upper half of head, 3.2 to 4; nose longer than eye, 2.9 to 3.3 in head; mouth rather small, terminal, oblique, tip of upper lip about on a level with inferior margin of orbit; maxillary 2.9 to 3.6 in head, not reaching orbit; jaws equal; isthmus about half diameter of eye. Teeth 4–4, with grinding surface and slight hook; intestine about equal to length of head and body; peritoneum silvery with a few small and scattering dark specks. Dorsal fin low, its longest ray 1.4 to 1.9 in head, usually less than the head's width; dorsal rays I–8, the first little more than half the length of the second, thickly covered with flesh in spring males; insertion of dorsal nearly directly over ventrals and about equidistant between snout and base of caudal; anal rays 7; pectorals reaching little more than ⅔ to ventrals; ventrals in both males and females usually reaching to vent, but always falling short of anal. Scales 6 to 8, 39 to 44, 4 or 5, usually 7–4 above and below; 21 to 27 rows before dorsal; lateral line complete, but slightly decurved in front of ventrals.

This fish, though often confounded with *Pimephales notatus*, differs sharply from it in its more oblique mouth and in the distribution of the dark punctulations on the scales, the entire surface of the scales of the upper half of the body being more or less dusted with dark specks in *Cliola*, while in *P. notatus* the scales are very distinctly dark-edged. It will scarcely be confused with *P. promelas*, which has the mouth smaller and lips (except in males) thinner, and the lateral line to a greater or less degree imperfect. If at any time external differences fail, it may be separated with ease from either species by its generic characters.

This little species, although one of our minor minnows, only two or three inches long, is one of the most abundant in the larger rivers of the state—the fifth on our list in order of frequency in rivers of the first class. This feature of its distribution is derivable also from our map of the state showing the distribution of the 116 localities from which our 194 collections of the species have been made. It occurs with still greater frequency in the smaller rivers and the creeks, more abundantly in the former, however, than in the latter. From lakes and ponds it has been taken by us only 28 times in 591 collections. Its preference for a rapid current (coefficient, 2.46) and a clean bottom (2.04) is also especially pronounced. Professor Hay likewise reports, in his list of the lampreys and fishes of Indiana, that this species appears to prefer clear streams. It is generally distributed from Ohio to Georgia, the Dakotas, Iowa, Arkansas and Texas, and the Rio Grande. It has occurred to us much the most abundantly in the streams of the Kaskaskia and the Wabash basins, its frequency coefficients for those stream systems (3.31 and 2.27 respectively) being many times those for any others in the state. It is an exception to the general rule in the fact that it enters freely the lower Illinoisan glaciation, notwithstanding its evident preference for clear water.

Gravid females occur in our June collections, and in others taken as early as the 21st of May. Females are uniformly smaller than males, and the latter are further distinguished in spring by nine large tubercles on the snout, five of them in a row just above the upper lip, two additional ones between the nostrils, and one on each side between the nostril and the eye.

Genus **NOTROPIS** Rafinesque

Body oblong or elongate, either more or less compressed; mouth mostly terminal and oblique, sometimes subinferior; premaxillaries protractile; no barbels; teeth in 1 or 2 rows, the main row always 4–4; peritoneum as a rule pale, though often dusky, and in some species black (*anogenus*); dorsal rays usually 7 or 8; anal rays ordinarily 7 or 8 (or 9), in a few species 11 or 12; scales usually rather large, as a rule less than 40 in lateral series; lateral line complete or imperfect. Size usually small, most species not exceeding 3 or 4 inches. A very large group, embracing about 100 species, all confined to the fresh waters of America east of the Rocky Mountains; 17 species in Illinois.

Key to the Species of **NOTROPIS** found in Illinois

a. Anal rays typically 7 or 8; occasionally 9 in two compressed forms (see **bb**, below), in which, however, scales before dorsal are not over 17, and no black spot is present at base of first dorsal rays; teeth 4–4; 1, 4–4, 1; or 1 or 2, 4–4, 1 or 2.

b. Eye moderate, 2⅓ to 2⅔ in head, always less than 4; body not usually much compressed, the back gently and broadly rounded in front of dorsal fin; scales not closely imbricated; teeth 4–4; 1, 4–4, 1; or 1 or 2, 4–4, 1 or 2.

c. Small species, seldom over 2½ inches in length; with (1) a black lateral stripe along sides and through eye to end of snout, or (2) a conspicuous dark spot above and below each pore of lateral line anteriorly, or (3) pale species, with no vertebral streak and the spots above lateral pores inconspicuous; teeth 4–4 or 1, 4–4, 1 (except *heterodon*).

d. Eye 3 or more in head (sometimes under 3 in *heterodon*, in which dark lateral stripe extends through eye to end of snout, tipping chin); small, usually less than 2½ inches.

e. Scales before dorsal large, 12 to 15 in number; teeth 4–4 (except *heterodon*).

f. A black stripe along sides through eye to end of snout.

g. Chin white; mouth small, nearly horizontal, the upper lip below level of lower margin of pupil.......................................**cayuga**.

gg. Chin black at tip; mouth moderate or very small, oblique, tip of upper lip at level of upper margin of pupil.

h. Maxillary reaching posterior nostril; mouth moderately oblique, making 40° to 60° with vertical; teeth 0, or 1, or 2, 4–4, 0, or 1, or 2; peritoneum silvery ....**heterodon.**

hh. Mouth extremely small and upturned, the maxillary scarcely reaching anterior nostril, and making an angle of 20° to 30° with vertical when mouth is closed; teeth 4–4; peritoneum black....................**anogenus.**

ff. Black lateral stripe, if present, developed only posteriorly (not continued forward through eye to end of snout).

i. Mouth more or less oblique, jaws subequal; lateral line distinctly decurved anteriorly. A dark vertebral streak, and a plumbeous lateral band more or less distinct posteriorly; scales of lateral line of average depth; length 2½ inches ....**blennius.**

ii. Mouth little, if any, oblique, tip of upper lip below level of lower margin of orbit; lower jaw distinctly shorter than upper; lateral line nearly straight. .... **phenacobius.**

ee. Scales before dorsal smaller, 17 to 19 in number; mouth inferior, lips rather thick; teeth 1, 4–4, 1..**gilberti.**

dd. Eye very large, 2⅓ to 2¾ in head; dark lateral stripe not developed anteriorly; some dusky color on chin at tip; teeth 1, 4–4, 1; length 3 inches.. .... **illecebrosus.**

cc. Large species, 4 to 6 inches in length when adult; plumbeous lateral stripe not continued to head; course of lateral line not anywhere marked out by conspicuous dark spots above and below each pore; a broad vertebral streak always present; teeth 1 or 2, 4–4, 1 or 2.

j. A prominent black spot at base of caudal fin; scales before dorsal 18 to 20. .... **hudsonius.**

jj. No black spot at base of caudal; scales before dorsal 15 or 16........**jejunus.**

bb. Eye small, 4 to 5 in head in adults; body more or less distinctly compressed, the back sharply rounded in front of dorsal fin; scales closely imbricated; teeth 4–4 or 1, 4–4, 1.

k. Body very short and deep, the depth 3 to 3.3 in length; usually no dark color on posterior membranes of dorsal fin, teeth as a rule 4–4, sometimes 1, 4–4, 1 or 0..**lutrensis.**

kk. Body more elongate, depth 3½ to 4 in adults; a more or less distinct black blotch on last membranes of dorsal; teeth 1, 4–4, 1...............**whipplii.**

aa. Anal rays 9, 10, 11, or 12; teeth 2, 4–4, 2.

l. Dorsal fin in front of or over ventrals; exposed portions of scales of flanks notably deeper than long; a broad dark vertebral streak; anal rays 9 or 10, usually 10..**cornutus.**

ll. Dorsal fin behind ventrals; scales roundish, the exposed portions not notably deeper than long.

m. Scales loosely imbricated, those before dorsal in 15 to 17 series; no black spot at base of dorsal.

n. A dark vertebral streak; anal rays 9 or 10..........................**pilsbryi.**

nn. Vertebral streak very narrow and usually faint.

o. Eye equal to or longer than snout; maxillary equal to eye; snout blunt; anal rays 9, 10, or 11 (usually 10)............................**atherinoides.**

oo. Eye shorter than snout; maxillary 1⅓ times eye; snout sharp; anal rays 9 or 10..**rubrifrons.**

mm. Scales closely imbricated, about 30 series in front of dorsal; a black spot usually evident at front of base of dorsal; anal rays 10 to 12, usually 11 ....**umbratilis.**

FIG. 29

NOTROPIS ANOGENUS Forbes

Forbes, 1885, Bull. Ill. State Lab. Nat. Hist., II. 2, 138.
M. V., 55; J. & E., I, 259; L., 16.

A small, weak species, very similar in general appearance to *N. heterodon*, but with complete lateral line, and always clearly distinguishable from that species by its black peritoneum and its very small and extremely oblique mouth, the maxillary standing at an angle of no more than 40° with the vertical. Length 1⅘ inches; body moderately elongate, considerably compressed, the depth 4.3 to 4.5 in length; caudal peduncle rather slender and longer than head. Color dark above, yellowish beneath; sides silvery with a distinct plumbeous to blackish lateral band, extending from a small dark spot at base of caudal along sides and through eye to end of snout, tipping the chin; scales of back quite thickly specked with black over most of their surfaces; the third row above lateral line only narrowly edged with dusky; the two rows covered by the lateral band rather densely dusted with fine specks among which are occasional much larger ones; fins faintly dusky. Head small, 4.3 to 4.5 in length, bluntly conic, its width 1⅗ in its length; interorbital space 2.6 to 2.9; eye 3.1 to 3.3; nose short and blunt, 4.5 to 4.8 in head; mouth very small, terminal, extremely oblique, the tip of the upper lip at about same level as upper margin of pupil; maxillary 4.5 to 5.1 in head, scarcely twice diameter of pupil, not reaching back of anterior nostril; isthmus less than pupil. Teeth 4–4, with well developed grinding surfaces, sometimes plain, sometimes crenate; teeth more or less hooked at tip; intestine 1.2 to 1.3 times length of head and body; peritoneum black. Dorsal fin with 8 rays; about one scale behind ventrals, a little nearer base of caudal than muzzle; longest dorsal ray somewhat more than head; and rays 7; pectorals less than ⅔ to ventrals; ventrals reaching vent. Scales 5 or 6, 34 to 37, 3 or 4; rows before dorsal 13 or 14.

This well-marked species was described by the senior author in 1885 from 24 specimens collected in the upper Fox River at McHenry, Ill. It has since been taken in the state but once. A well-marked specimen was found in Fourth Lake in 1892. Dr. Meek found the species in Cayuga Lake, N. Y., in 1888, and has recently obtained a number of excellent specimens from northern

Indiana. It has been taken in Orchard Lake, Oakland county, Mich., by Mr. T. L. Hankinson during the present summer (1906).

A female taken June 12, was full of eggs, as were some of the types, taken from the 8th to the 10th of May.

NOTROPIS CAYUGA Meek

(Pl., p. 128; Map XXXIII)

Meek, 1888, Ann. Ac. Nat. Hist., N. Y., 305.
J. & E., I, 260; L., 16.

Length 2½ inches; body moderately elongate, depth 4.5 to 5.2 in length; caudal peduncle about equal to head, rather slender, its depth 2.3 to 2.8 in its length. Color olivaceous, the scales above dark edged, their outlines sharply defined; a black lateral stripe along sides and through eye to end of snout; a faint caudal spot; the base of each scale of lateral line marked out by a conspicuous crescentic band* of black, these bands crossing the lateral stripe and breaking it up into bars posteriorly, extending below it on anterior portion of body; vertebral streak almost obsolete. Head bluntly conic, proportionately longer than in the variety next described, 3.7 to 4.1 (average of 10 specimens 3.84) in length, width of head 1.9 to 2.2; interorbital space 2.9 to 3.5 in head; eye large, equal to snout, 3.1 to 3.5 in head; nose 3.2 to 3.8 in head; mouth very small, subterminal, very slightly oblique, the upper lip below level of lower margin of pupil; back of maxillary under first nostril; its length less than eye, 4.2 to 4.9 in head (average of 10 specimens 4.47); jaws subequal; isthmus less than pupil. Teeth 4–4, hooked, the grinding surface narrow; intestine 1 to 1.2 times length of head and body; peritoneum silvery. Dorsal fin with 8 rays, inserted distinctly behind ventrals and farther from muzzle than from base of caudal; longest dorsal ray a little less than head, in which it is contained 1.1 to 1.2; anal rays 7 or 8, usually 8; pectorals ¾ to ventrals, 1.3 to 1.5 in head; ventrals to vent or front of anal. Scales 5, 34 to 36, 3 or 4; 12 to 15 rows before dorsal; lateral pores wanting on some scales.

This species is distributed from Lake Champlain and the St. Lawrence River to the Dakotas and Assiniboia, Nebraska, Kansas, Arkansas, and the Neches and Comal rivers in Texas. It is not abundant in Illinois, having been taken by us in only 30 collections, nearly all of them from the northern half of the state. It is most abundant in creeks, although it occurs in the northeast glacial lakes and has been taken once by us from the Michigan drainage.

Females apparently near spawning have been captured as early as June 5 and as late as August 1.

* Compare description of *N. heterolepis* Eig. & Eig., Amer. Nat. Feb. '93, p. 152.

NOTROPIS CAYUGA ATROCAUDALIS Evermann

Evermann, 1891, Bull. U. S. Fish Comm., XI, 76.

Length 2½ inches; body comparatively shorter and deeper than in the last species, the depth 4 to 4.6 in the length; caudal peduncle slender, its depth 2.2 to 2.7 in its length. Color as in the last, except that the dark lateral stripe is solid, there being no transverse crescentic bars at bases of scales of lateral line. Head short, 3.8 to 4.2, its width 1.7 to 1.9 in its length; interorbital space 2.6 to 3.1; eye 2.8 to 3.3; nose 3 to 3.7; mouth very small, but relatively larger than in the last species, the maxillary 3.6 to 4.3 (average 3.83 for 10 specimens). Teeth, intestine, and peritoneum as in last species. Dorsal fin with 8 rays, inserted distinctly in frónt of ventrals and closer to the muzzle than to the base of the caudal. Scales 5, 33–38, 3 or 4; 12 to 14 before dorsal; lateral line sometimes wanting on a few scales.

Females distended with eggs taken in June; snout, cheeks, chin, and top of head of breeding males quite thickly covered with evident though small tubercles. (Tubercles not observed in males of *N. cayuga*.)

We have ten collections of this minnow, containing thirteen specimens from the Illinois and adjacent waters, near Meredosia, and one from the main river at Havana. A specimen from Mackinaw creek in Woodford county, one from Anderson's branch, in Union county, and one from the Little Fox River at Phillipstown may be referred with some uncertainty to this variety. Specimens taken at Greenway, Arkansas, by Dr. Meek are, without much question, identical with the form here described. The uncertainty arises from the difference between the published figure of *N. cayuga atrocaudalis* and the specific description, the figure showing the lateral stripe solid and the dorsal fin inserted in front of the ventrals, and the description stating that the dorsal is slightly behind the ventrals.

NOTROPIS HETERODON (Cope)

(Map XXXIV)

Cope, 1864, Proc. Ac. Nat. Sci. Phila., 281 (**Alburnops**).
G., VII, 261 (**Leuciscus**); J. & G., 163 (**Hemitremia**); M. V., 55; J. & E., I, 261; N., 47 (**Hemitremia**); J. 62 (**Hemitremia**); F. F., I. 6, 85 (**Hemitremia**); F., 78; L., 16.

This small species, distinguished from *N. anogenus* by its larger and less oblique mouth and pale peritoneum, agrees with it in the general form of its body and in having a dark lateral stripe from the tip of the snout to the base of the caudal. It is sharply enough separated from *N. cayuga* by its larger mouth and black-tipped chin. Care is sometimes required to separate it from *Hybognathus nubila*, although that species differs from it radically in its generic characters. Length 2 inches; body moderately compressed and back as a rule noticeably elevated in adults; depth 4.1 to 4.6 in length; caudal peduncle slender, its depth 2.3 to 3 in its length. Color olivaceous, rather dusky above, the dark punctulations on the scales confined mostly to the edges; sides leaden silvery, with a black stripe extending forward through eye to end of snout; belly with an orange tint; fins plain. Head small, conic, 3.9 to 4.2 in length; width of head 1.8 to 2 in its length; interorbital space 2.6 to 3.1; eye quite large, 2.7 to 3 in head, being usually about ⅓ longer than the snout, the distance from the tip of which to the anterior rim of the pupil is about equal to the diameter of the orbit; nose short and rather sharp, 3.5 to 3.8 in head; mouth moderate, oblique, the upper lip as a rule on a level with the upper margin of the pupil; cleft of mouth making an angle of 40° to 60° with the vertical; maxillary scarcely reaching front of orbit, its length about ¾ the diameter of the very large eye; jaws subequal, the isthmus less than pupil. Teeth as a rule 1, 4–4, 1, in occasional instances 1, 4-4, 0, 0, 4–4, 1, or 4–4; the first three teeth of the outer row usually strongly hooked and with a well-developed groove whose edges are somewhat crenate; intestine shorter than body and head; peritoneum silvery. Dorsal fin with 8 rays, slightly nearer snout than base of caudal, set almost directly over ventrals; longest dorsal ray somewhat less than head (1.1); anal rays 8, occasionally 7; pectorals short, less than ⅔ to ventrals, 1.3 to 1.6 in head; ventrals reaching vent. Scales 5, 35–38, 3; 12 to 14 scales before dorsal; lateral line as a rule developed only anteriorly; some specimens met with, however, in which not more than 2 or 3 pores were lacking on posterior half of body.

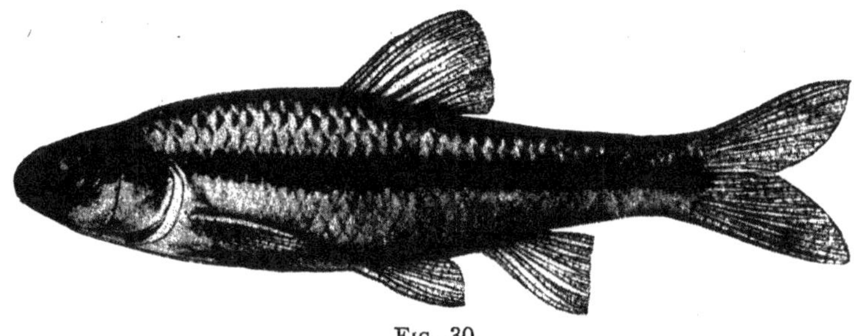

Fig. 30

The typical form of this species appears to be confined, with us, to the northern part of Illinois, being most abundant in the small glacial lakes of Lake and McHenry counties, where it is found in clear, cool water among weeds and over sand along shore. Specimens taken from the headwaters of the Fox, Des Plaines, and Du Page rivers, and some from the upper Rock and its tributaries (Yellow creek, Stephenson county, Kiswaukee River at Sycamore, Rock River at Oregon, and Green River at Geneseo) have the teeth 0, 4–4, 1, or 1. 4–4, 1, though the body is somewhat slender and the eye is hardly so large as in the lake form. From farther southward we have about 80 collections, chiefly from the sluggish waters of the Illinois River and tributary lakes at Havana and Meredosia, in which the dentition is more usually 2, 4–4, 2, and the lateral line is nearly always complete. Collections of the same form, which may be identical with the unnamed* variety of *N. heterodon* described some years ago from Switz City swamp, Indiana, and localities in southern Illinois, have also been taken in lowland streams of the Wabash, Ohio, and Big Muddy valleys.

New York to Michigan, Minnesota, and Kansas, including Lakes Michigan and Huron and the Ohio basin. Distributed sparingly throughout the state, mainly in the lowland and glacial lakes, and in a way to indicate an avoidance of the lower Illinoisan glaciation. Our 93 collections, from 21 localities, were derived in extraordinarily small proportion from either creeks or rivers of the smaller size. The order of relative abundance in our waters is as follows: glacial lakes, 2.68; lowland lakes, 1.44; the larger rivers, .98; creeks, .63; and the smaller rivers, .17. It is about equally abundant from northern and from central Illinois, but is considerably less common in the waters of the southern part of the state.

The food of eighteen specimens studied, was peculiar in respect to the large percentage of *Entomostraca* included— a fact perhaps to be accounted for by the small size of the species and the somewhat unusual development of the gill-rakers, although many of the specimens examined were taken where *Entomostraca* were very abundant at the time. Aquatic insect larvæ, mainly *Chironomus*, an amphipod crustacean (*Allorchestes*), and flowers and seeds, with filamentous algæ, were the other principal elements of the food.

The species spawns in May and June in central Illinois. The snout and top of the head of the male are finely tuberculate.

* *Notropis heterodon*, var., Gilbert Proc. U. S. Nat. Mus. 1884 p. 207.

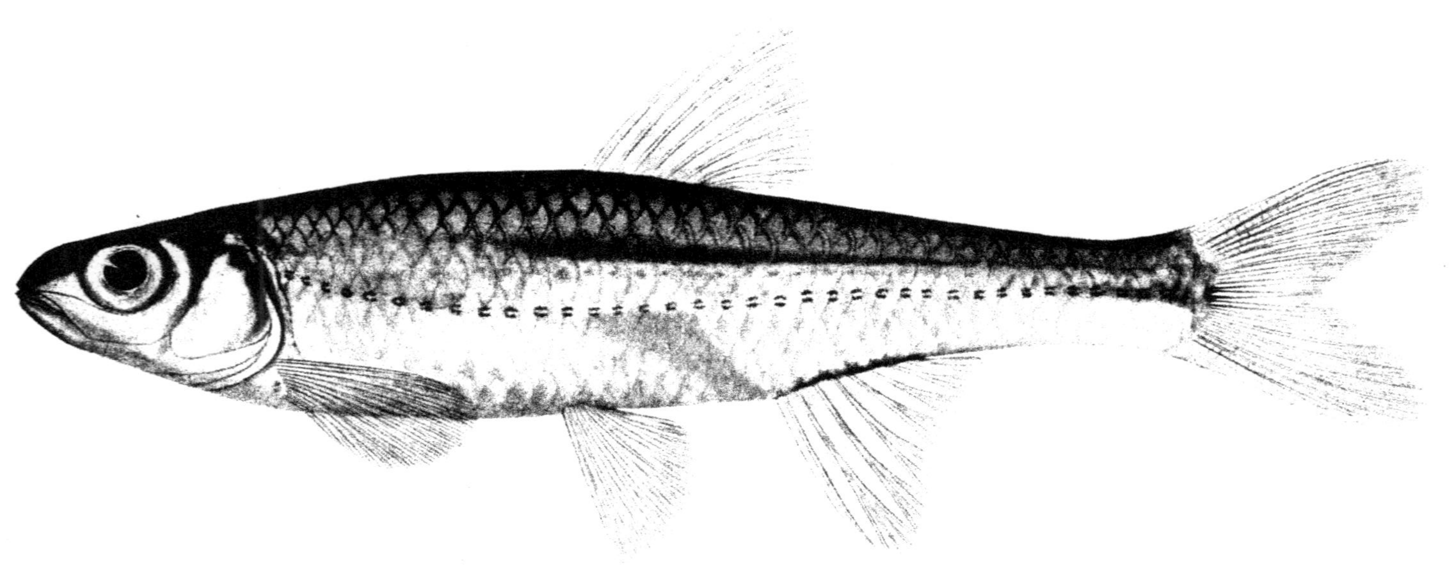

STRAW-COLORED MINNOW, *Notropis blennius* (Girard)

FIG. 31

NOTROPIS BLENNIUS (GIRARD)

STRAW-COLORED MINNOW

(MAP XXXV)

Girard, 1856, Proc. Ac. Nat. Sci. Phila., 194 (**Alburnops**).
M. V., 56 (**deliciosus**); J. & E., I, 261; N., 46 (**Hybopsis stramineus**); J., 57 (**Alburnops stramineus**); F. F., I. 6, 84 (**Luxilus cornutus**); F. 78 (**stramineus**); L., 17.

A small pale species of rather indefinite characters, almost entirely without marked distinctions of either form or color. Length $2\frac{1}{2}$ inches; body about equally tapered both forward and backward from its deepest point, which is a little in front of a line connecting first dorsal and ventral rays; moderately compressed; depth 4.2 to 4.8; caudal peduncle rather slender, its depth 2 to 3.1 in its length. Color very light olive above, paler below; sides silvery, with an indistinct light-leaden stripe above lateral line, above and below each pore of which is a black spot; belly silvery; a faint vertebral streak, broadening into an evident blackish blotch at front of dorsal; caudal spot faint or but a trace; head olivaceous above, the cheeks and opercles silvery; dorsal and caudal often with some dusky; other fins pale. Head small, conic, 3.8 to 4.2 in length of head and body; width of head 1.7 to 2 in its length; interorbital space 3 to 3.6 in head; eye 2.9 to 3.4, usually over 3.2 in full-grown specimens; nose bluntly conic, scarcely decurved, its length equal to diameter of eye in adults, 3.3 to 3.8 in head, usually about 3.5; mouth rather small, terminal, slightly or moderately oblique, the tip of the upper lip seeming to vary in position from quite on a level with the inferior margin of the pupil to even with the lower margin of the orbit; maxillary 3.3 to 3.7 in head, about reaching vertical from front of orbit; jaws about equal; isthmus less than pupil. Teeth 4–4, rather strongly hooked, with grinding surfaces developed on at least two or three teeth; intestine .9 to 1.2 times length of head and body; peritoneum more or less densely sprinkled with rather large and coarse black specks. Dorsal fin with 8 rays (rarely 7), inserted almost directly over, or slightly in advance of, ventrals, and usually almost exactly equidistant between muzzle and base of caudal; longest dorsal ray 1.1 to 1.3 in head; anal rays 7 (rarely 6); pectorals

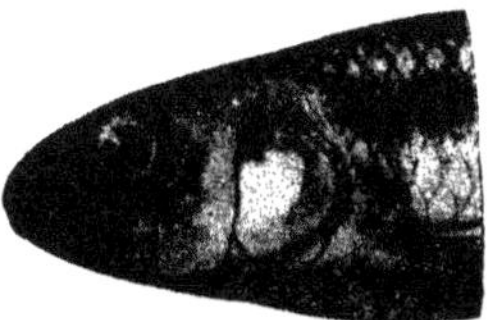

FIG. 32

about ⅔ to ventrals, 1.2 to 1.4 in head; ventrals reaching vent or front of anal. Scales 5, 32–36, 4; 12 or 14 before dorsal; lateral line complete, generally noticeably decurved on anterior half of body.

This abundant but rather insignificant and indefinite species belongs to the group which apparently avoid the streams of the southern Illinoisan glaciation. Although distributed throughout the state from the Ohio and Saline rivers on the south to the extreme northern boundary, and represented in our records by 128 collection localities, but five of these are within that area, and these are on its northern borders where its peculiarities are least pronounced. It is consistent with this limitation to its distribution in this state that it should show a decided preference, according to our collection records, for clean swift waters over muddy and stagnant ones. Its frequency coefficient for waters over a bottom of rock or sand is 2.00, and the corresponding frequency ratio for a swift current is 1.18. It is essentially a species of small rivers and creeks, our frequencies for these two classes of streams being 2.65 and 2.23 respectively, while that for the larger rivers is only .41 and that for lakes and ponds but .17. In general distribution it is limited to a region extending from the Great Lake basin, Lake Champlain, and the streams of the St. Lawrence system, by way of the Missouri River to Wyoming, northward to the Lake of the Woods and the Red River of the North, and southward through the Ohio and the Mississippi basins to the San Antonio River in Texas.

From the little that is known of its feeding habits, its food is no more peculiar than its general appearance, consisting of a mixture of aquatic insects, crustaceans, and chance vegetation.

NOTROPIS PHENACOBIUS Forbes

Forbes, 1885, Bull. Ill. State Lab. Nat. Hist., II. 2; 137.

This fish unites with a strong general resemblance to *Phenacobius* the characters of *Notropis*. The body of the adult is short and deep, the head square, the nose long, and the eye unusually large. Length 2½ inches; depth 3.5 to 4; caudal peduncle 4 to 4.75. Color in alcohol indefinite; sides somewhat silvery, scales along and above the lateral line slightly specked with black. The head is quadrate in transverse section, flat above, 3.75 to 4; nose decurved, 3.4 to 3.5; interorbital space 2.9 to 3.1. The mouth is inferior, horizontal, rather small, lips fleshy, not lobed, lower jaw much the shorter, 2.75 to 3.1 in head, upper lip opposite the lower margin of the pupil, upper jaw to posterior margin of nostrils, 3.33 to 3.9

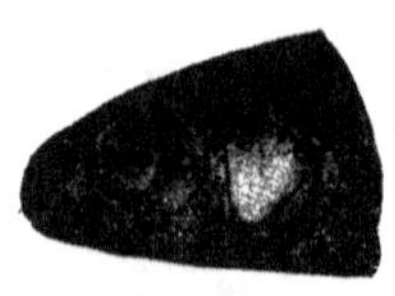

Fig 33

in head. Teeth 4–4. Intestine about equal to head and body, .97 to 1.17. Eye very large, circular, placed high up, 3.4 to 3.5 in head. Branchiostegals free from isthmus. Dorsal I–8, decidedly before ventrals, its length 7 to 8 in body; anal low, I–8; paired fins rather broad and short; ventrals not reaching vent, and pectorals falling far short of ventrals, the former 6.25 to 6.4 in head and body. The scales are thin, large, crowded anteriorly upon the sides, breast wholly naked in all the specimens seen. Lateral line 35 to 36, longitudinal rows 7 to 9, 13 to 14 before dorsal. Described from 10 specimens, the only ones seen, all taken at Peoria.

This species is retained with some hesitation, owing to the fact that the ten type specimens obtained many years ago are the only ones of it ever seen, and through some unaccountable misadventure all but one of these types have disappeared from the State Laboratory collection. Concerning this species Dr. Evermann writes me, under date of March 8, 1908, after an examination of this type: "In some respects this specimen resembles *N. blennius*, but is much deeper and more arched, and the head is slightly longer. We have compared it with the type of '*Cliola chlora* Jordan,' which is considered a synonym of *N. scylla*, but it is not that species. * * * If you have any reason for believing that this specimen is the type of your *N. phenacobius*, I would be disposed to accept it as such and let the species stand as good."

FIG 34

NOTROPIS GILBERTI JORDAN & MEEK

(MAP XXXVI)

Jordan & Meek, 1885, Proc. U. S. Nat. Mus., 4.
M. V., 57; J. & E., I, 266; L., 17.

The long, broad, and flat head, comparatively inferior mouth, and rather thick lips of this species distinguish it sufficiently from all other Illinois species of the genus *Notropis*. Length 2½ inches; form much as in *Ericymba buccata*, the body subfusiform, usually rather long and slender, and the back gently and broadly elevated; depth 4.3 to 5; caudal peduncle usually longer than head, slender, its depth 2.1 to 2.9 in its length. Color light olive above; sides silvery; a conspicuous median dorsal stripe and a plumbeous lateral streak; scales above dark-edged, those below lateral line on posterior half of body and caudal peduncle rather sparsely specked with black; top of head and muzzle darkish; fins all plain; dorsal, caudal, and pectorals pale rosy in spring males, in which also the head is covered with very fine tubercles that suggest a sprinkling of white dust. Head long, broad, flattish above, 3.5 to 4 in length; its width 1.8 to 2.1 in its length; interorbital space 3 to 3.6; eye 3 to 3.8; nose long and muzzle decurved, the snout usually greater than eye, 2.8 to 3.3 in head; mouth rather large, nearly horizontal and inferior, the tip of the upper lip below the level of the lower margin of the orbit; lower jaw included; isthmus less than pupil. Teeth 1, 4–4, 1; intestine a little less than head and body; peritoneum silvery, with sometimes a very few dark specks. Dorsal fin with 8 rays (sometimes 9) quite uniformly set slightly behind ventrals; longest dorsal ray 5/7 of head in adults, 1.1 to 1.4; anal rays 8 (occasionally 9); pectorals about 2/3 to ventrals, 1.3 to 1.6 in head; ventrals to or past vent. Scales 6, 34–37, 4, smaller and crowded anteriorly, 16 to 18 rows before dorsal; lateral line complete, decurved anteriorly.

This is a western species, the range of which to the eastward terminates in Illinois. It extends westward through Iowa to eastern Colorado, being most abundant, so far as known, in muddy streams of the plains from the Des Moines to the Platte. It occurs also in tributaries of the Missouri in Missouri and Iowa. Only 2 of the 32 localities from which it has been recognized in this state lie outside the Mississippi drainage, and both of these are in the Wabash Valley, one near the mouth of that stream and the other on the extreme headwaters of the Embarras. It seems to be essentially a species of small rivers and creeks, our ratios of occurrence in the larger rivers and in lakes and ponds being quite insignificant.

Gravid females have been found by us in the latter part of June.

NOTROPIS ILLECEBROSUS (GIRARD)

(MAP XXXVII)

Girard, 1856, Proc. Ac. Nat. Sci. Phila., 194 (**Alburnops**).
J. & E., I, 268 (**illecebrosus**); L., 17 (**shumardi**).

The very large eye, large oblique mouth, and broad head of this species distinguish it from all other Illinois minnows of its genus. Length 3 inches, body moderately compressed, the back little elevated; depth 4.5 to 5.4 in length; caudal peduncle rather slender, its depth 2.1 to 2.7 in its length. Color olivaceous or straw, the sides little silvery; a dark lateral band, continued forward through eye to end of snout, tipping the chin; fins all plain. Head broad and flat above, 3.8 to 4.1 in length; width of head 1.8 to 2.1; interorbital space 2.8 to 3.2; eye very large, 1/5 to 1/4 longer than nose or maxillary, 2.4 to 2.8 in head; nose 2.9 to 3.6, blunt and shorter than the very large eye; muzzle not decurved; mouth large and quite oblique, the tip of upper lip above level of lower margin of pupil; maxillary reaching front of orbit; lower jaw slightly shorter than upper; isthmus less than pupil. Teeth 1, 4–4, 1; intestine about 1.15 times length of head and body; peritoneum a very dark brown to almost solid black. Dorsal fin with 8 rays, inserted a little behind ventrals, about equidistant between muzzle and base of caudal; longest dorsal ray usually a little less than head, 1 to 1.2; anal rays 8 (occasionally 7); pectorals ⅔ to ⅘ to ventrals, 1.1 to 1.3 in head; ventrals to vent, not reaching anal in any of our specimens. Scales 5 or 6 (usually 5), 35–37, 3; 13 to 15 in front of dorsal fin; lateral line complete, somewhat decurved anteriorly.

Fig. 35

This species, rather rare in Illinois, is closely limited in the main to the tributaries of the Wabash in the eastern part of the state, from which it is recorded in our collections at 17 localities, the only other places of its occurrence in this state being Cedar Lake, in northeastern Illinois, Mazon creek, a branch of the Illinois River near its origin, and a small bluff stream of the Mississippi, in Hancock county. Its general range is from the Lake Erie basin and the Ohio River westward to Arkansas and Missouri.

Females with fully developed eggs, and breeding males with muzzle and chin tuberculate, have been taken by us in the latter part of May.

NOTROPIS HUDSONIUS (DeWitt Clinton)

SPOT-TAILED MINNOW

(Map XXXVIII)

DeWitt Clinton, 1824, Ann. Lyc. Nat. Hist. N. Y., I, 49 (**Clupea**).
G., VII, 251 (**Leuciscus**); M. V., 57; J. & E., I, 269; N., 46 (**Hybopsis**); J., 56 (**Alburnops**); F. F., I. 6, 82 (**Hybopsis**); F., 77; L., 17.

The usually large and conspicuous black caudal spot of this minnow, rarely absent in western specimens of the species, will commonly serve to call attention to it when found, and will serve to separate it from the other larger and paler species of Illinois *Cyprinidæ*. Length 4 to 6 inches; body moderately robust, not much elongate, considerably compressed, the sides vertical at their middle; depth 4 to 4.5 in length; caudal peduncle shorter than head, its depth 1.9 to 2.3 in its length. Color very pale olive; sides with a very broad silvery to plumbeous band; commonly a large black spot at base of caudal fin; scales faintly cross-hatched on upper part of body and for a little distance below lateral line forward; spots above and below pores of lateral line faint or wanting; fins pale. Head short, 4.1 to 4.7 in length of head and body; width of head 1.8 to 2.1; interorbital space 2.5 to 2.9; eye moderate, 2.8 to 3.5 in head, equal to nose or slightly shorter or longer in adults; nose blunt, usually somewhat decurved, 3.2 to 3.5 in head; mouth rather small, nearly horizontal, the tip of upper lip below level of lower margin of pupil; maxillary usually not quite reaching orbit, 3.7 to 4.5 in head; lower jaw shorter than upper; isthmus less than pupil. Teeth variable: 0, 4–4, 1; 1, 4–4, 1; 1, 4–4, 2; or 2, 4–4, 2; teeth of main row more or less hooked, and generally quite compressed, the grinding surface developed as a quite narrow groove whose edges are smooth; intestine .9 to 1.4 times length of head and body; peritoneum silvery, finely but not densely specked with dark. Dorsal fin with 8 rays, set usually a trifle in advance of the ventrals and nearer snout than base of caudal; longest dorsal ray about equal to the length of the short head; anal rays 8; pectorals scarcely ⅔ to ventrals; ventrals usually short of vent. Scales 5 or 6, 36 to 39, 4; 15 to 18 before dorsal; longitudinal rows of scales above lateral line with the appearance of "running out" behind dorsal fin, as in *N. cornutus;* lateral line usually complete, not much decurved anteriorly.

FIG. 36

This abundant, graceful, and well-known species, essentially a northern minnow in this state, is much the most abundant in our largest rivers and in lakes, its frequency ratio in the former being 1.8, and in the latter 1.76. In small rivers and in creeks it has been taken only occasionally, the corresponding ratios being .29 and .14. It is abundant in its favorite localities, and appears in 147 of our collections. In Illinois it is limited to the Mississippi and Lake Michigan drainage, and has occurred but twice south of the central part of the state, once in Union county and once from the Ohio at Cairo. We have found it most frequently in the Illinois River and its adjacent waters at Havana and Meredosia, from which two places 119 of our collections have come. It is also one of the commonest longshore minnows in southern Lake Michigan, swarming especially about the piers off Chicago, where it is caught in quantities and sold for bait.

RED-FIN MINNOW, *Notropis lutrensis* (Baird & Girard)

Although reported from South Carolina, it is essentially a northern species, ranging from New England, Quebec, and the Lake of the Woods through the Hudson and Great Lake basin to the streams of the Missouri in Minnesota and the Dakotas. It is abundant in the Great Lakes and at the mouths of the rivers opening into them. In Ohio and in Indiana, as in Illinois, it is generally confined to the northern parts of the state.

It is a typical minnow in its food, depending on insects, crustaceans, and vegetation, the latter partly algæ of the filamentous forms and partly fragments of aquatic plants. This general statement does not indicate the variety of its resources or the seeming indifference with which it will fill itself with one or the other kind of food which it finds most abundant. One of our specimens, for example, had eaten nothing but algæ, and these plants made three fourths of the food of another. Three had eaten only insects, and these were 90 per cent., or more, of the food of three others. Two had taken nothing but *Entomostraca*, all a species of *Cypris* feeding upon the bottom. Four had filled themselves with various vegetable structures, and 90 per cent., or more, of the food of three others consisted of like material. Three out of four of these minnows, taken at Nippersink Lake in May, had eaten only terrestrial snout-beetles (*Rhynchophora*), whose occurrence in the water was a matter of chance. The larvæ of day-flies (*Ephemerida*) made more than three fourths of the food of three other specimens. One had eaten a small fish, and traces of like food were found in another.

NOTROPIS LUTRENSIS (Baird & Girard)

REDFIN

(Map XXXIX)

Baird & Girard, 1853, Proc. Ac. Nat. Sci. Phila., 397 (**Leuciscus**).

G., VII, 258 (**Leuciscus**); J. & G., 172 (**Cliola iris** and **C. jugalis**), 174 (**C. gibbosa** and **C. forbesi**), 175 (**C. lutrensis**), 176 (**C. suavis**), 177 (**billingsiana**); M. V., 57; J. & E., I, 271; J., 57 (**Cyprinella forbesi**); F., 77; L., 17.

This little fish is especially distinguished among Illinois *Cyprinidæ* by the brilliancy of its color and by the depth and thinness of its body, fully grown specimens not seldom having the depth in length less than 2¾. It is very nearly allied to the next species, *N. whipplii*, compared with which it seems to be merely a more specialized form, the two sometimes intergrading in an obscure and very puzzling way. It may, however, be distinguished from the next species, as a rule, by its greater depth when adult, by the greater thickness at the nape, the more elevated back and steeper profile, and by the absence, in most specimens, of the black spot on the posterior part of the dorsal fin. Length 2¾ inches; depth 2.7 to 3.2 in length in adults, the young more slender; caudal peduncle shorter than head, its depth 1.7 to 2.1 in its length. Color of females and postnuptial males olivaceous under iridescent steel above, pale greenish to greenish gray and silvery lower down and on belly; a faint purplish wedge-shaped bar behind opercles; fins plain (in typical specimens), tinged with reddish or orange in males. Spring males with the upper parts a brilliant iridescent steel-blue, the sides and belly orange-red to crimson, and the top of head, cheeks, and opercles flushed with rose; gill-opening bordered with red; the postopercular bar a brilliant purplish violet, behind which is a broad vertical band of faint crimson; all the fins reddish, the dorsal dusky with greenish at base; pectorals plain red; ventrals blood-red tipped with a narrow margin of orange; caudal dusky near base, crimson outward, tipped with darker. Head 3.6 to 4 in length, stout and deep, depressed but not flat above, the profile angled at the nape, most so in males; width of head 1.8 to 2.2 in its length; interorbital space 2.5 to 2.8, nearly twice the small eye; eye 4 to 4.5, less than nose; nose 3.1 to 3.6 in head, conic, sharper and upturned in males; mouth oblique, the tip of upper lip above level of lower margin of pupil; maxillary 3 to 3.6 in head, reaching to vertical from back of posterior nostril, but not to orbit; lower jaw included, the upper considerably projecting in males (in females the jaws are usually very nearly equal); isthmus less than pupil. Teeth variable, usually 4–4, though 0, 4–4, 1, 1, 4–4, 0, and 1, 4–4, 1 are not uncommonly met with in our collections; the supernumerary teeth are usually weak and much less developed than in the next species, in which the number is normally 1, 4–4, 1; intestine shorter than head and body, in which it is contained .8 to .9 times; peritoneum silvery, finely but not densely specked with black. Dorsal fin with 8 rays, set a little behind or over the ventrals; longest dorsal ray 1.1 to 1.3 in head; anal rays usually 8, sometimes 7 or 9; pectorals ⅔ to ventrals, 1.2 to 1.4 in head; ventrals to vent in females, to front of anal in males. Scales 6, 34–37, 3–4; rows before dorsal 14 to 17; lateral line complete, strongly decurved, being approximately parallel with the lower outline.

This little redfin, one of the most beautiful, in its breeding colors, of any of our minnows, is essentially a western species; and all our 163 collections have been made from the streams of the Mississippi drainage. Outside this state the species ranges from South Dakota and Wyoming to Nebraska, Kansas, Missouri, and Arkansas, and the tributaries of the Rio Grande. It is a minnow of the streams, present in about equal ratio in creeks and the larger and the smaller rivers, but found in lowland lakes with only about half the frequency of its occurrence in running waters. It tolerates muddy waters, as is shown by its frequency coefficient of 1.69, and it enters the lower Illinoisan glaciation in the branches of the Big Muddy. It is closely allied to *N. whipplii*, and appears, in fact, to intergrade with that species, of which it is the representative to the south and west.

This active minnow loves to play in the swift ripples of rocky streams, where its presence may be betrayed to the watchful observer by flashes of rainbow color from a fish not otherwise visible. It spawns from the middle of May to the last of June. The breeding males are excessively tuberculate, with a double row of tubercles bordering the upper lip, a triangular or crescentic patch about each eye, two longitudinal rows along the middle of the top of the head, and several shorter ones upon the sides. The scales of the nape and those of the sides of the body are also tuberculate, especially those on the caudal peduncle between the anal fin and the lateral line. Sometimes all the scales are tuberculate, with the exception of a few in front of the ventrals, on the lower part of the sides and belly. We have even seen females with small tubercles upon the head.

NOTROPIS WHIPPLII (GIRARD)

STEEL-COLORED MINNOW; SILVERFIN; LEMON-FIN

(MAP XL)

Girard, 1856, Proc. Ac. Nat. Sci. Phila., 198 (**Cyprinella**).
G., VII, 254 (**Leuciscus spilopterus**); J. & G., 178 (**Cliola**), 179 (**C. analostoma**); M. V., 58; J. & E., I. 278; N., 47 (**Cyprinella galacturus**); J., 57 (**Photogenis analostanus**); F., F., I. 6, 87 (**Photogenis analostanus**); F., 77; L., 17.

This species, which presents a general resemblance to *N. lutrensis*, is generally distinguishable from that species by its more elongate, lanceolate form; by its longer and more pointed head, and, in most cases, by the black spot on the posterior membranes of the dorsal fin (a mark absent in typical specimens of *lutrensis*). Length 3 to 4 inches; depth 3.3 to 4 in length in adults; females and young more slender, the depth 4.3 to 5; caudal peduncle slightly shorter than head, its depth 1.7 to 2.2 in its length. Color leaden silvery over olive in females, somewhat bluish forward and above. Males bright steel-blue to purplish above, dull silvery white or greenish on lower part of sides and on belly; steel color most prominent behind and above opercles and above lateral line backward along sides to tip of caudal peduncle; cheeks and opercles metallic purplish blue; iris brassy, purplish outward above; scales of sides with dusky bluish lines parallel to their edges, producing the appearance of a very regular and sharply defined lozenge-blocked reticulation* over the entire side, this appearance being aided by the great uniformity in size of the scales; a rather broad but faint vertebral streak; two black blotches on the posterior membranes of the dorsal (fainter in females); paired fins, lower part of belly, tips of anal and caudal, and the

* These lozenges of darker blue outline on a purplish or steel-blue ground form one of the most noticeable features of the coloration of this species distinguishing it ordinarily with readiness from *N. lutrensis*, in which, except in some specimens from the more northward part of its range, the cross-hatching on the scales is indistinct.

front and upper margin of the dorsal charged with clear satin-white pigment in males in the spring; basal half of dorsal in full breeding dress light green; lower fins lemon-yellow, except tips of ventrals and anal. Head small, subconic, not so stout as in the last species, 3.9 to 4.2 in length; profile scarcely angled at nape; width of head 1.9 to 2.2; interorbital space 2.5 to 2.7 in head, very convex; eye small, 3.9 to 4.8 in head; nose somewhat longer than in the last species, 2.8 to 3.2 in head, conic and usually more or less upturned, especially in males; mouth slightly less oblique than in the last, the tip of the upper lip scarcely above level of lower margin of orbit; maxillary longer than eye, reaching to back of posterior nostril-opening, but not to orbit, 3.1 to 3.6 in head; lower jaw shorter than upper; isthmus less than pupil. Teeth usually 1, 4–4, 1*, the edges of the grinding surface often more or less crenate, intestine .8 to .9 times length of head and body; peritoneum silvery, finely specked with black. Dorsal fin with 8 rays, set a little behind the ventrals, its longest ray usually a little less than head, in which it is contained 1.9 to 1.2; anal rays 8 or 9; pectorals 1.2 to 1.4 in head, about ⅗ to ventrals in fully grown specimens, about ⅘ in young but sexually mature males; ventrals to vent in females, past front of anal in males. Scales 6, 36-39, 3; 14 to 16 before dorsal, where they are scarcely crowded; lateral line decurved anteriorly to about parallel with lower outline.

Extremely abundant in Illinois, especially in the smaller streams of the central part of the state, and taken in 270 of our collections. A species of the creeks and smaller rivers in this state, its frequency ratios for those streams being approximately 2½, while those for lakes and the larger rivers are but .11 and .35 respectively. It shows a marked preference for swift water and for a clean bottom, our coefficients for these situations being 1.3 and 1.6 respectively. It is generally distributed from Lake Champlain and the St. Lawrence River through the lakes of central New York and the Great Lake basin to Minnesota, Pennsylvania, Virginia, northern Alabama, and Arkansas.

Two thirds of the entire food of 33 specimens examined, consisted of insects, nearly half of which were terrestrial. Three of our specimens had eaten small fishes, and a mixture of vegetable elements derived from both aquatic and terrestrial plants had been eaten mainly by four, one of which had fed only on algæ, while three others had taken some 90 per cent. of their food from miscellaneous plant structures, including seeds, anthers, and pollen, and fragments of grass-like vegetation.

Females apparently about to spawn have been taken by us from May 21 to June 12, but others which had not yet deposited their eggs occur in our collections occasionally up to the middle

* Cases of apparent *N. whipplii* in which the teeth are 4–4 or 1, 4–4, 1 occur in a few collections from localities in which *N. lutrensis* and *N. whipplii* seem to intergrade. In general our collections show, however, that little variation need be looked for in this species.

COMMON SHINER, *Notropis cornutus* (Mitchill)

BLACKFIN, *Notropis umbratilis atripes* (Jordan)

of August. Breeding males have the head largely tuberculate, together with a pad-like tuberosity, closely set with tubercles, on the snout. The scales of the upper part of the sides in front of the dorsal fin are likewise tuberculate.

NOTROPIS CORNUTUS (MITCHILL)

COMMON SHINER

(MAP XLI)

Mitchill, 1817, Am. Month. Mag., I, 289 (**Cyprinus**).

G., VII, 249 (**Leuciscus**); J. & G., 186 (**Minnilus**), 192 (**M. plumbeolus**); M. V., 58 (**megalops**); J. & E., I, 281; N., 47 (**Luxilus**); J., 57 (**Luxilus**) F., 77 (**megalops**); L., 17.

This species, in size one of the largest of our minnows, is distinguished especially by the great depth of the exposed portions of the scales and (in spring males) by the brilliant and more or less mottled salmon-pink coloration. Length 5 to 8 inches; body elongate in the young; adults shorter and much compressed, the sides nearly vertical; depth 3.3 to 4.4 in length; anterior dorsal region gibbous and rather swollen in adult males; caudal peduncle rather deep, its depth 1.6 to 2.3, usually less than 2.1, in its length. Color of midsummer males olivaceous above with steel-blue luster; belly and lower part of sides silvery; a broad dark vertebral streak and a faint plumbeous lateral band, showing as gilt when seen through water; scales above lateral line thickly specked with dusky, with narrow edges of darker; scales along middle of each side partly with the most of the exposed surface unspecked bright silvery with dusky bases, and partly wholly dusky, giving rise to a mottled appearance which is most accentuated in the breeding season; dorsal and caudal fins somewhat dusky, other fins plain; coloration of spring males very brilliant, the upper parts greenish and the sides a rich salmon-pink over silvery, with mottlings of dusky emerald; females and young are plain olivaceous above and silvery below. Head 3.8 to 4.2 in length, rather large and heavy, compressed, rounded between the eyes, the muzzle bluntish; width of head 1.9 to 2.1; interorbital space 2.6 to 3.1 in head; eye rather small, 3.1 to 4.7 in head, usually over 4 in adults; nose much longer than eye in adults, 2.8 to 3.3 in head; mouth moderately large and oblique, the tip of the upper lip usually very little above level of lower margin of orbit; maxillary ⅓ longer than eye in fully grown specimens, 2.9 to 3.2 in head, scarcely reaching front of orbit; lower jaw slightly shorter than upper; isthmus less than pupil. Teeth 2, 4–4, 2, with rather narrow grinding surface; intestine .9 to 1.5 times length of head and body; peritoneum dusky to solid brown. Dorsal fin with 8 rays, set usually a little in advance of the ventrals and closer to muzzle than base of caudal; longest dorsal ray 1 to 1.3 in head; anal rays 9 or 10, usually 9; pectorals ⅔ to ¾ to ventrals, 1.2 to 1.5 in head; ventrals usually not reaching vent. Scales 6, rarely 7, 37–40, 3, rows before dorsal 16 to 25; always much deeper than long on the flanks, becoming exceedingly so in adults; longitudinal rows with an appearance of "running out" behind the dorsal fin; lateral line complete, decurved anteriorly.

This common, large, and well-known minnow, one of the most conspicuous in our series, is unequally distributed throughout the state, very abundantly so in its northern two thirds. It occurs also in the hill streams of southern Illinois, but is nearly absent from the lower Illinoisan glaciation, whence we have taken it indeed but three times—from two localities on the Little Wabash and from one on the headwaters of the Kaskaskia at the northern boundary of this area. It is especially a minnow of creeks and the smaller rivers—our coefficients for which are 3 and 2.45 respectively—scarcely ever occurring in either lakes or the larger streams. It shows also a marked preference for clear waters, which corresponds to its avoidance of the lower Illinoisan glaciation. Its coefficient of preference for a clean bottom is 2.2. Outside our territory it is reported from the entire eastern United States (including the Great Lakes) from the Rocky Mountains to the Atlantic, with the exception of Texas and the southeastern region from the Neuse River on the north to the Alabama on the west. It also ranges into Canada, from New Brunswick and the River St. Lawrence and its tributary streams in Quebec to the Assiniboin in Manitoba.

Somewhat more than a third of the food of 21 specimens examined by us consisted of vegetable objects, a large percentage of which were algæ, and the greater part of the remainder was insects, both aquatic and terrestrial, the former, however, largely preponderant. A single specimen had eaten only fishes. The crustacean ratio was, as usual, insignificant. A single aquatic worm (*Lumbriculus*) was observed in one. The individuals of this little collection varied widely in respect to the food they had last taken, five, for example, having eaten insects only, while two had eaten little or nothing but algæ and other vegetable objects.

Its spawning season begins about May 1 and continues to the last of June. Spring males have the top of the head, the tip of the snout, and the predorsal region covered with rather large tubercles. This minnow takes a worm or a grasshopper readily, and is one of the fishes most likely to be found on a boy's string. Although it sometimes grows to a length of eight inches, it is usually too small to be of importance as a pan-fish, but Dr. Henshaw recommends it as the best live bait for black bass.

NOTROPIS PILSBRYI Fowler

Fowler, 1904, Proc. Acad. Nat. Sci. Phila., LVI, 245-247.

Fishes intermediate between those forms typified in Illinois by *N. cornutus* on the one hand and *N. atherinoides* and *rubrifrons* on the other, and possessing resemblances to both. Readily distinguished from the first by the rounded and loosely imbricated scales of the sides and by the backward insertion of the dorsal fin, and from the latter by the difference in general proportions (the present species being much shorter and deeper), and by the presence (as in *N. cornutus*) of a broad dark streak along the mid-dorsal line.

Length 2¾ inches; form robust, the body deep in front of dorsal and moderately compressed; back elevated, the upper and lower outlines tapered evenly to the tip of the pointed snout, much as in *Hybognathus nuchalis*; depth 4 to 4.4 in length; caudal peduncle but little shorter than head, more slender than in *N. cornutus*, its depth 2.3 to 2.5 in its length. Color in life not known; in spirits, a dusky olive above, the scales rather densely specked over their entire surface and not distinctly dark-edged; sides below lateral line and belly silvery, unspecked; a broad dusky band along side, interrupted on opercle and in eye (in preserved specimens), but faintly apparent before eye to end of snout, tipping chin; a broad and distinct dark vertebral streak; dorsal and lower fins pale; caudal somewhat dusky. Head conical, 4 to 4.3 in length, the muzzle pointed and profile slightly angled at nape; width of head 2 to 2.1 in its length; interorbital space nearly flat, 2.9 to 3.1 in head; eye 3.4 to 3.5 in head, slightly less than snout; nose 3.3; mouth rather large, oblique, tip of upper lip above lower margin of orbit; maxillary longer than eye, 2.8 in head, barely reaching front of orbit; jaws subequal; isthmus less than pupil. Teeth 2, 4-4, 2, compressed and hooked, the grinding surface developed as an extremely narrow groove on at least two of the teeth; peritoneum densely and coarsely specked with brown. Dorsal fin with 8 rays, inserted distinctly behind ventrals, its first ray farther from muzzle than base of caudal; longest dorsal ray 1.3 to 1.5 in head; anal rays 9 or 10; pectorals ⅔ to ventrals, 1.3 in head; ventrals quite reaching vent. Scales 6, 37 or 38, 3 or 4, large, cycloid and loosely imbricated, not notably deeper than long on sides and not crowded anteriorly; the rows appearing to "run out" on back behind dorsal as in *N. cornutus*; lateral line decurved anteriorly, complete; 15 scales before dorsal fin.

Sexual differences not known, the three specimens from Illinois which were taken on May 30 (1901; Ac. No. 28174) being males with sexual organs considerably developed but without tubercles.

Found in this state only from the East Fork of the Mazon River, near Gardner. The identity of this species with *N. pilsbryi* Fowler, which was described in 1904 from the White River basin in Arkansas, seems open to no question.

FIG. 37

NOTROPIS JEJUNUS (FORBES)

(MAP XLII)

Forbes, 1878, Bull. Ill. State Lab. Nat. Hist., I. 2, 60 (**Episema**).
J & G., 194 (**Minnilus**); M. V., 60; J. & E., I, 290; F., 77; L., 18.

A pale silvery minnow of rather indefinite characters, in form resembling *Hybognathus nuchalis*, the outline being fusiform, with dorsal and ventral contours similar, but lacking the long intestine and maxillary protuberance of that species and with the head rather blunter. Length 2 to 2½ inches; depth 3.8 to 5 in length, the body deepest just in front of the dorsal fin; body considerably compressed, the greatest width about ½ the greatest depth; caudal peduncle somewhat shorter than head, its depth 1.9 to 2.4 in its length. Color pale, the sides silvery with a broad plumbeous band; lateral scales rather coarsely specked with black, those of back more finely specked over their entire surfaces; cross-hatching most evident along lateral line and below it, where the scales are pale except at outer edges; a dark vertebral streak but no caudal spot; cheeks and opercles silvery below, steel-blue to cerulean above; a conspicuous splash of emerald on lateral aspect of occiput—just behind eye; iris silvery with some lavender; fins all plain. Head 3.8 to 4.5 in length, squarish in transverse section at orbits, being only slightly rounded above; width of head 1.7 to 2.2 in its length; interorbital space 2.5 to 2.9 in head; eye very little shorter than snout in adults, 3.2 to 3.8 in head; nose bluntly conic, 3.1 to 3.6; mouth moderately large, very little oblique, the tip of the upper lip little above level of lower rim of pupil; maxillary 2.8 to 3.4 in head, extending hardly to front of orbit; lower jaw slightly shorter than upper; isthmus less than pupil. Teeth usually 2, 4–4, 2; sometimes 1, 4–4, 1 or various intermediate combinations; grinding surface, if present, narrow and irregular; intestine .9 to 1.2 times length of head and body; peritoneum silvery, with a few small specks of dark color. Dorsal fin with 8 rays, occasionally 7, set as a rule almost directly over ventrals and about equidistant between muzzle and base of caudal; longest dorsal ray 1.1 to 1.4 in head; anal rays usually 7, occasionally 6 or 8; pectorals short, 1.1 to 1.4 in head, as a rule less than ⅔ to ventrals; ventrals falling distinctly short of vent. Scales 5, 34–37, 3 or 4; rows before dorsal 13 to 15; scales rather large, thin, and round; lateral line little decurved.

Notropis jejunus (Forbes)

This is a small and insignificant species, without marked specific characters, obviously limited by preference to the larger rivers (coefficient, 1.63) and apparently avoiding the lower Illinoisan glaciation. It occurs also in considerable numbers in the smaller rivers (1.12), but is usually scarce in creeks and only moderately abundant in the lowland lakes. In Illinois it has occurred in 51 collections, rather sparingly distributed along the main streams and in their neighborhood, from the northern boundary to Cairo and from the Wabash and Ohio to the Mississippi. It is reported from the northern Mississippi Valley at large, and from the Ohio basin, ranging from Kansas and western Pennsylvania to Wyoming and Winnipeg. In Pennsylvania it occurs only in the Ohio basin.

The species is too small to be of any importance except as food for larger fishes.

Its breeding season is apparently late, no females with swollen ovaries occurring in our collections until the last of June, and specimens loaded with eggs being found by us as late as August 27. The sexual differences are not noticeable.

NOTROPIS ATHERINOIDES Rafinesque

SHINER

(Pl., p. 158; Map XLIII)

Rafinesque, 1818, Am. Month. Mag., 204.
G., VII, 254 (**Leuciscus rubellus**), 255 (**L. copii**); J. & G., 202 (**Minnilus rubellus** and **M. dinemus**); M. V., 61; J. & E., I, 293; N., 47 (**Minnilus dilectus** and **amabilis**), 48 (**M. rubellus** and **M. dinemus**); J., 60; F. F., I. 6, 86 (**Minnilus**); F., 76 (**dinemus,** part); L., 18 (also **arge** and **dilectus**).

A common slender silvery minnow of the larger rivers, known especially by its bright silvery color and by the posterior insertion of the dorsal fin. Length 2½ to 4½ inches; general form slender, moderately compressed, both back and belly about equally and very little arched, the body deepest in front of dorsal fin; profile from dorsal to muzzle a gentle convex curve; depth in length in typical specimens 4.9 to 5.5*. Color translucent green above (olivaceous); sides bright silvery, the iridescent emerald, lavender, and cerulean, common in other silvery minnows, being scarcely noticeable in this species; scales above faintly specked, but not blotched or prominently dark-edged; a narrow and rather faint dark vertebral line, and a faint plumbeous lateral band from opercle to caudal; no caudal spot; cheeks and opercles

* Specimens in some collections from Illinois have the depth as low as 4 to 4.25 in length, these shorter and deeper forms seeming to grade insensibly into the typical slender *atherinoides*.

pure silvery, having the sheen of fine silver-leaf; iris almost pure silvery; fins all pale, transparent; well called "shiner" or "silvery minnow". Head short and very bluntly conic, 4.1 to 4.8 in length, usually about 4.5; width of head 2.1 to 2.4 in its length; interorbital space 2.9 to 3.3; eye about equal to snout (larger in younger specimens), 3 to 3.4 in head; nose 3.3 to 3.6; mouth moderate, terminal, oblique, tip of upper lip even with middle of pupil; maxillary 3 to 3.4 in head, scarcely longer than eye, nearly reaching front of orbit; jaws subequal; isthmus less than pupil. Teeth 2, 4–4, 2, occasionally 1, 4–4, 2 or 2, 4–4, 1; the masticatory surface a very narrow groove; intestine commonly less than length of head and body; peritoneum rather densely specked with black. Dorsal fin with 8 rays, set well behind ventrals, the distance from dorsal to caudal not more than 78 to 85 per cent. of that from snout to dorsal; longest dorsal ray 1.1 to 1.2 in head; anal rays 9, 10, or 11, usually 10; pectorals short, about ⅔ to ventrals, 1.2 to 1.4 in head; ventrals not reaching vent. Scales rather large and very thin, 6, 36–40, 3, rows before dorsal 18 to 21; lateral line decurved.

Extremely variable, having been described under various names even from our own state. No attempt is made here to separate the forms *atherinoides, arge*, and *dilectus*, the two latter of which should probably be regarded as synonyms of the present species. It appears to be distinct in our collections from *N. rubrifrons*, from which it differs in its shorter head, shorter maxillary, larger eye, and blunter snout, as well as in its coloration and faintly developed secondary sexual characters.

This graceful and attractive species, distinguished by a golden lateral stripe on a clear green ground, is an excessively abundant and active minnow, occurring throughout the state, but almost strictly confined everywhere to the larger lakes and rivers. Among our collections from the smaller lakes of northeastern Illinois we have not obtained a single specimen of this species, while the waters of Lake Michigan, but a few miles away, were swarming with them along the shore, and especially about the wharfs. There they are captured in great numbers, together with the most abundant of the lake species, the spot-tailed minnow, and sold for bait. Of our 206 collections, the greater part are from rivers, 2.14 being the coefficient for rivers of the second class, and 1.21 for those of the first class. The coefficient for creeks is .93, and that for lowland lakes is .66, our Lake Michigan collections not being represented in this series. The distribution map of the state, for this species, shows a curious difference between southern Illinois, where this minnow occurs mainly in the creeks and smaller rivers, and the remainder of the state, in which the larger streams are its principal resort. It appears to have a moderate preference for a good current (1.19) and for a clean bottom (1.22). but it is nevertheless one of the species which enters the lower Illinoisan glaciation freely. It is distributed throughout the state in fairly equal ratio, although less abundant in the Illinois, the Kaskaskia, and the Big Muddy than in the other stream systems. It is one of the small number of species which we have found present in the Michigan drainage in larger ratio (1.96) than in any other section. In its continental distribution it is, on the whole, a northern species, its general area extending from the St. Lawrence and Lake Champlain through the Great Lakes to the northern shore of Lake Superior, the Red River of the North, and the Saskatchewan, and through the Ohio Valley to Tennessee and the Washita River in Kansas, and up the tributaries of the Missouri.

It moves and feeds in large schools, thousands being frequently seen together near the surface. The food of those examined by us (18 specimens, all from the northern part of the state) consisted principally of insects, nearly two thirds of which were terrestrial species, and the remainder chiefly case-worms and larvæ of day-flies. Six of the specimens had, indeed, eaten insects only, and these made 90 per cent. of the food of two others. Three taken from Peoria Lake in October had eaten only *Entomostraca*, which amounted, in fact, to the unusual ratio of 22 per cent. of the food of the whole group. A single specimen had taken about 40 per cent. of its food from the thread algæ, and a minute fish had been eaten by another.

Females greatly distended with eggs and apparently about to spawn have been collected by us from the middle of May to the first of June. The sexual differences are slight, and we have seen no tuberculate males.

NOTROPIS RUBRIFRONS (Cope)

ROSY-FACED MINNOW

(Map XLIV)

Cope, 1865, Proc. Ac. Nat. Sci. Phila., 85 (**Alburnus**).
G., VII, 255 (**Leuciscus**); J. & G., 202 (**Minnilus rubrifrons** and **M. percobromus**); M. V., 61 (**dilectus**); J. & E., I., 295; N., 47 (**Minnilus**); J., 60; F., 76 (**dinemus**, part); L., 18.

The smaller size, darker and less silvery coloration, shorter and deeper body, longer head, longer snout and maxillary, and smaller eye, as well as the dense tuberculation and flushed color of the head and predorsal region in spring males of this species, will serve to distinguish this from the last species described. Length 2¾ inches; body moderately elongate, back little elevated; caudal peduncle slender, its depth 2.4 to 2.8 in its length; depth in length 4.8 to 5.8. Color of upper parts rather dark olive, the scales dark-edged; sides silvery above and below the dark, to almost black, lateral band;

a faint and narrow dark vertebral streak; fins plain; forehead, opercles, and predorsal region flushed with red in spring males. Head long, conic, pointed, 3.8 to 4.3 in length, its width 2.3 to 2.6 in its length; interorbital space little convex, 3 to 3.6 in head; eye smaller than in the last species, 3.2 to 3.6 in head in adults, in which it is distinctly less than the maxillary; nose 3 to 3.4 in head; mouth rather large, oblique, tip of upper lip almost at top of pupil; maxillary distinctly longer than eye, 2.7 to 3.1 in head, reaching vertical from front of orbit; jaws subequal; isthmus less than pupil. Teeth 2, 4–4, 2, the grinding surface slight and present on few teeth; intestine .8 to .9 of length of head and body; peritoneum dusted with coarse brown specks. Dorsal fin with 8 rays (occasionally 7), set well behind ventrals, so that distance from dorsal to caudal is 74 to 81 per cent. of that from muzzle to dorsal; longest dorsal ray 1.3 to 1.5 in head; anal rays usually 10, sometimes 9 or 11; pectorals scarcely ⅔ to ventrals, 1.2 to 1.5 in head; ventrals usually short of vent. Scales 6 (or 7), 36–40, 3; rows before dorsal 17 to 21; lateral line decurved anteriorly.

The rosy-faced minnow is a bright-colored species which delights in the clear waters of rapid streams. It has been rare in our work, occurring only in the Mississippi drainage of the northern third of the state, in the tributaries of the Illinois, the Rock, and the Mississippi, and only once from the main stream. It is a species of northern distribution, ranging from the lower St. Lawrence and Lake Champlain to the Lake of the Woods, thence southward to the headwaters of the James, through the Ohio Valley to the Alleghany River, and to the tributaries of the Missouri in Kansas and Missouri. In Ohio it is reported by Osburn as occasionally occurring in large schools over clean gravelly places in ripples, the females ready to spawn during the latter part of May—a date which agrees with our own observations in Illinois. The spring males have the head and fore part of the body excessively tuberculate, and there are sometimes weak tubercles on the same parts of the breeding females also.

NOTROPIS UMBRATILIS ATRIPES (Jordan)

BLACKFIN

(Pl., p. 147; Map XLV)

Jordan, 1878, Bull. Ill. St. Lab. Nat. Hist., I. 2, 59, (**Lythrurus atripes**).

J. & G., 197 (**Minnilus atripes**); M. V., 61 (**umbratilis**); J. & E., I, 300, also (?) 301 (**umbratilis fasciolaris**); N., 47 (**Lythrurus diplæmius**); J., 59 (**Lythrurus atripes** and **diplæmius**); F., 76 (also **macrolepidotus**) and Bull. Ill. St. Lab. Nat. Hist., II. 2, 138 (**macrolepidotus**); L., 18 (**umbratilis**).

Fishes with the dentition and the elongate anal fin of *Notropis* (e. g., *atherinoides* and *rubrifrons*), but with the form of body (deep and compressed) of *Cyprinella* (e. g., *N. whipplii*) or *Moniana* (*N. lutrensis*); most easily distinguished from the fishes of the first subgenus mentioned by the deeper and more compressed body, and from the latter by the smaller scales, which are much crowded anteriorly. Length 3 inches; body as a rule rather deep and compressed, the depth 3.2 to 4.2 in length; profile usually angled at nape in adults; caudal peduncle less than head, its depth 1.7 to 2.4 in its length. Color dark purplish blue above, greenish blue, not silvery, on middle part of sides, and greenish lower down and on belly; a dusky lateral band on caudal peduncle, becoming obsolete forward; scales, except on belly, dusted with dark specks but not prominently dark-edged; dorsal fin with a more or less prominent black spot at its base in front*; anal tipped with dusky in males; dorsal with or without a dusky bar mesially; spring males with the dorsal and caudal fins greenish at base and bright brick- to blood-red outward; lower fins nearly uniform red, the pectorals less brilliant, pinkish or rose; females pale olive, plain. Head conic, comparatively pointed, 4 to 4.1 in length; width of head 1.8 to 2.1; interorbital space quite convex, 2.2 to 3 in head; eye small, shorter than snout, 3.4 to 4.2 in head; nose 2.8 to 3.3; mouth moderate, oblique, tip of upper lip above lower margin of pupil; maxillary 2.7 to 3.2 in head, reaching front of orbit; jaws about equal; isthmus less than pupil. Teeth 2, 4–4, 2, with more or less developed grinding surfaces on the median teeth of the outer row, this surface narrow and either plane or concave; intestine .8 to .9 of length of head and body; peritoneum silvery, rather sparsely and coarsely specked with brown. Dorsal rays 8, the fin set well back of ventrals; longest dorsal ray 1 to 1.1 in head; anal rays 10, 11, or 12, usually 11; pectorals more than ⅔ to ventrals; ventrals to or past vent. Scales 9 or 10, 41 to 48, 4, crowded anteriorly, the rows in front of dorsal fin 26 to 30, lateral line deeply decurved.

This is an exceedingly handsome species, especially during the breeding season. It is commonly said to be most frequently seen in clear, swift streams. Our frequency coefficient for creeks reaches, in fact, the extraordinary number of 3.9, while that for the smaller rivers is 1.9, and for the larger rivers, .16. In lowland lakes we have found it but once in 549 collections, and in glacial lakes not at all. On the other hand, 109 collections for which we have the necessary data give us a frequency coefficient of 1.76 for still-water situations as compared with those with a rapid current—from which we may infer that in Illinois, at any rate, the species is more frequently to be found in quiet waters than in those with a rapid flow. Our similar data concerning cleanness or muddiness of bottom, drawn from 69 collections only, give us no evidence of any definite choice, the corresponding coefficient being 1.01. The species has been

* Great variation in color is found in our specimens, making it extremely difficult to distinguish varieties. We have included all Illinois specimens accordingly under the oldest name for this portion of the range of this wide-spread and variable species. Most of our specimens have the dark blotch at base of dorsal prominent and anal dusky in males (*atripes*); others, but much fewer in number, have the spot faint or obsolete (*macrolepidotus*); in some specimens there are distinct traces of 3 to 5 vertical bars of dusky on back portion of sides and fore part of caudal peduncle (*fasciolaris*?).

taken by us 208 times, from 136 Illinois localities. Outside the state it is distributed far and wide, from the Great Lakes and the smaller lakes of New York to the Roanoke River on the Atlantic coast and to the Tombigbee in Alabama, and westward through the Ohio Valley to the Arkansas and the tributaries of the Missouri in Kansas and Missouri. Notwithstanding this wide-spread general occurrence, its distribution in this state is somewhat peculiar, as shown by the fact that, although we have collected it throughout the state, our records of its occurrence are several times more numerous from the eastern half of Illinois than from the western. It is one of the species which enters freely the lower Illinoisan glaciation, and is, indeed, much more abundant southward than in the northern parts of the state. Its area of greatest proportionate abundance in our collections is that containing the Big Muddy, the tributaries of the Wabash, and the small rivers and creeks of extreme southern Illinois.

Females bursting with eggs have been taken about the first of June, together with spring males with heads profusely covered with small tubercles of a peculiar whitish tint. Tuberculate males have occurred, indeed, in our collections from the middle of May to August 1.

Genus **ERICYMBA** Cope

Body elongate, little compressed; muzzle broad; interorbitals, suborbitals, and dentaries containing greatly developed mucus channels, which appear externally as distinct transverse vitreous streaks; no barbel; premaxillaries protractile; teeth 1, 4–4, 1 or 4–4, without grinding surface, hooked; intestine short; peritoneum silvery; dorsal rays 8; anal 8; scales about 35; lateral line continuous. Size small. One species known.

ERICYMBA BUCCATA Cope

SILVER-MOUTHED MINNOW.

(Map XLVI)

Cope, 1865, Proc. Ac. Nat. Sci. Phila., 88.
G., VII, 185; J. & G., 204; M. V., 62; J. & E., I, 302; N., 45; J., 61; F., 76; L., 18.

Small, pale silvery to straw-colored fishes with an elongate and decurved snout, sufficiently distinguished from all other Illinois *Cyprinidæ* by the externally visible mucus channels in the infraorbital and lower jaw-bones. Length 3 to 4 inches; body fusiform, rather elongate and little compressed, and the back not much elevated; profile not angled at nape, being a gentle convex curve from base of dorsal to tip of snout; depth 4.1 to 5.2 in length;

caudal peduncle as a rule about 4/5 length of head, slender, its depth contained 2.2 to 2.9 in its length. Color pale olive above, the scales rather narrowly and indistinctly dark-edged; sides pale silvery with bluish reflections; a dark dorsal streak and an indistinct plumbeous lateral band developed posteriorly; no caudal spot; fins all plain; cheeks and opercles bright silvery; iris silvery below, with some dusky above; spring males without bright colors. Head long for its depth, depressed above, with prominently decurved muzzle; chin broad and flat; length of head 3.5 to 3.7 in body and head, its width 1.9 to 2.4 in its length; interorbital space nearly flat and quite narrow, 3.5 to 3.9 in head; eye 3.3 to to 3.6 in head; suborbitals, interopercles, and lower jaw-bones with greatly developed mucus channels, appearing externally as vitreous streaks; nose 2.6 to 3 in head, always distinctly longer than eye; mouth small, horizontal, subinferior, tip of upper lip below level of lower margin of orbit; maxillary 3.5 to 4 in head, not reaching past anterior nostril-opening; lower jaw much shorter than upper; isthmus less than pupil. Teeth 4–4, or 1, 4–4, 1, rather strongly hooked, the grinding surface somewhat weakly developed as a narrow groove whose edges are smooth; intestine .9 to 1.0 times length of head and body; peritoneum bright silvery, with a very few scattered dark specks. Dorsal fin with 8 rays, set nearly directly over ventrals, but distinctly nearer tip of snout than base of caudal; longest dorsal ray 1.1 to 1.2 in head; anal rays 8, sometimes 7; pectorals long, reaching nearly to ventrals; ventrals past vent but not quite to front of anal. Scales 5, 32–35, 3; 13 to 15 rows before dorsal; breast without scales; lateral line nearly straight.

FIG. 38

This interesting little fish is especially peculiar because of the tubular cavities, the so-called mucus canals, in the bones of the side of the head and the lower jaw. It has, on the whole, an easterly distribution, ranging, according to Jordan and Evermann, from Michigan and western Pennsylvania to Kansas and southward to western Florida. In our collections it has been limited almost wholly to the central eastern part of the state, occurring chiefly in the headwaters of the minor tributaries of the Wabash and in the upper course of the Kaskaskia River, and in the tributaries of the Iroquois and of the Sangamon. The distribution map of the state for this species suggests a relation to an eastern center, and an extension past the watersheds from the tributaries of the Wabash to the headwaters of adjacent streams. Our 74 collections came in so large a proportion from the smaller streams that the coefficient of frequency for creeks is 4.85, and that for the smaller rivers is 1.06. It has occurred to us from first-class rivers but once in 293 collections, and not at all from stagnant waters of any description. It has a very decided preference for a clean bottom, it we may judge from the 38 collections of the species made for which data of this description were recorded, its frequency coefficient for this class of situations being 3.2. It is a noticeable fact, however, that the species nevertheless occurs within the lower Illinoisan glaciation, particularly in the headwaters of the Kaskaskia in the northern part.

Females apparently near spawning condition have been taken by us in late May and early June. The sexual differences are not well marked, and the males have neither tubercles nor brilliant colors in spring.

Genus **PHENACOBIUS** Cope

SUCKER-MOUTHED MINNOWS

Body elongate, little compressed; mouth inferior, the lower lip thin mesially and enlarged on each side into a fleshy lobe; upper jaw protractile; no barbel; teeth 4–4, hooked and with grinding surface; intestine short; peritoneum silvery; dorsal rays 8; anal 7; scales 45 to 60; lateral line complete. Length 3 to 4 inches, the adults having much the appearance of young suckers. About 5 species known, confined chiefly to the central and southeastern United States.

PHENACOBIUS MIRABILIS (Girard)

SUCKER-MOUTHED MINNOW

(Map XLVII)

Girard, 1856, Proc. Ac. Nat. Sci. Phila., 191 (**Exoglossum**).
J. & G., 205; M. V., 63; J. & E., I, 303; N., 46 (**teretulus liosternus**); J., 61 (**scopiferus**); F. F., I. 6, 88 (**scopiferus**); F., 76; L., 18.

The inferior sucker-like mouth, thick lips, small scales, and black spot at base of caudal fin in this species will, taken together, distinguish it from all other minnows found in Illinois. Length 3½ inches; form of body much as in the common red-horse (*Moxostoma aureolum*),—the inferior mouth and fleshy lips adding to the resemblance,—fusiform, the back moderately elevated, depth 4.6 to 5 in length; caudal peduncle about equal to head, its depth 2 to 2.2 in its length. Color olivaceous, the sides with a dull silvery luster overlying a dusky lateral shade; a distinct black caudal spot and a narrow vertebral streak, golden in life, when the

Fig. 39

SUCKER-MOUTHED MINNOW, *Phenacobius mirabilis* (Girard)

SHINER, *Notropis atherinoides* (Rafinesque)

shoulders are also dusted with gold specks; belly silvery; all scales except those of belly sprinkled with minute black specks which become denser at edges of scales; cheeks and opercles silvery with some greenish; pupil brilliant black; iris with a wide inner rim of gold above and silvery below, the outer portion being variegated light or dark green and gold with some silvery below; fins all pale. Head subquadrate in transverse section and flat above, short, 3.9 to 4.5 in length; width of head 1.6 to 1.9 in its length; interorbital space flat, 2.7 to 3.3 in head; eye small, 3.6 to 4.8; nose nearly twice length of eye, 2.3 to 2.6 in head; mouth very small, wholly inferior and horizontal, the tip of the upper lip on level of chin and breast; maxillary 3.7 to 4.3 in head, not reaching to orbit; lower jaw included; upper jaw provided with a fleshy lip which is continuous on each side with the lower lip, forming laterally a somewhat prominently projecting lobe; the two lobes of the lower lip separated at the middle by a narrow and projecting horny frenum, not separated from the chin by either a groove or a fold; isthmus less than pupil. Teeth 4–4, hooked, one of them occasionally with a narrow grinding surface; intestine about equal to length of head and body; peritoneum plain silvery. Dorsal fin with usually 8 rays, sometimes 7 or 9, always set distinctly in front of ventrals and nearer muzzle than base of caudal; longest dorsal ray 1 to 1.4 in head; anal rays 7; pectorals short, reaching little more than half way to ventrals in fully grown specimens; ventrals a little short of vent in adults. Scales 6, 43–51, 5; rows before dorsal 18 to 22; lateral line complete and little decurved.

Owing to the range of variation in size of scales in this species, we have found it impossible to separate this and *P. scopifer* in our collections, and have therefore included the latter species in the synonymy of *P. mirabilis.*

This little fish is, in Illinois, upon the eastern border of its range, doubtless extending into Indiana, although not hitherto reported from that state. It is distributed mainly west and south through Iowa to South Dakota and through Missouri to the Sabine and Trinity rivers emptying into the west Gulf. In this state it is of general distribution, occurring in all our river basins, but mainly in the smaller streams. It is most abundant with us in creeks—where its frequency coefficient rises to 3.18—and in the smaller rivers—2.19. In the larger rivers its coefficient falls to .32, and in lowland lakes to .05. Although we have taken it in 159 Illinois collections, it has not occurred once in the upland glacial lakes. It is also most abundant here in swift streams, particularly in those with a sandy bottom, or in the more rapid and rocky portions of somewhat sluggish creeks. The corresponding coefficients are 1.32 for waters with a rapid flow, and 1.36 for those with a clean bottom.

Nine of our specimens studied with reference to their food were found to have eaten little but the aquatic larvæ of a gnat-like fly (*Chironomus*), which is abundant on the bottom and under stones. A few case-worms (*Phyrganeidæ*) occurring in some similar situations were the only other important element of the food, of which insects made practically 98 per cent. Its small inferior mouth, provided with fleshy lips something like those of a sucker, enables this minnow to collect readily its peculiar food, in respect to which, as well as in its favorite haunts, it bears a considerable resemblance to the darters. In the aquarium it rests, like a darter, upon the sand, supported by its pectoral fins, the head moving gently up and down with the opening and closing of the gills.

Females greatly distended with eggs were taken by us in late May and early June. Spring males are profusely but rather minutely tuberculate on the top of the head, on the opercles, and on the back and upper part of the sides to the posterior end of the dorsal fin.

GENUS **RHINICHTHYS** AGASSIZ

Body elongate, little compressed; mouth small, subinferior; upper jaw not protractile, the upper mesially continuous with the skin of the forehead; a small barbel at tip of maxillary; teeth 1 or 2, 4–4, 1 or 2, hooked and without grinding surface; intestine short; peritoneum dusky; dorsal rays 7 to 9; anal 6 or 7; scales 60 to 70; lateral line continuous. Size small, 3 to 5 inches. Species few, 2 in Illinois. Active fishes, inhabiting mountain springs of the east and west and the swifter and cooler brooks of the central United States.

KEY TO THE SPECIES OF **RHINICHTHYS** FOUND IN ILLINOIS

a. Snout long and prominent, projecting far beyond the inferior mouth, less than 2½ in head and more than twice length of eye in adults......... **cataractæ.**

aa. Snout moderate, projecting little beyond the mouth (which is subterminal), more than 2½ in head, and not over 1½ times length of eye in adults....... .... **atronasus.**

RHINICHTHYS CATARACTÆ (CUVIER & VALENCIENNES)

LONG-NOSED DACE

Cuvier & Valenciennes, 1842, XVI, 315 (**Gobio**).

G., VII, 176 (**Ceratichthys**) and 189 (**Rhinichthys marmoratus** and **R. nasutus**); J. & G., 207; M. V., 63; J. & E., I, 306; N., 45 (**nasutus** and **maxillosus**); J., 62; F., 75 (**atronasus,** part).

Distinguished from the next species by its longer snout, longer and much projecting upper jaw, more elongate body, and less coarsely mottled coloration. Length 2½ inches; depth 4.8 to 5.2 in length; caudal peduncle as long as or longer than head, its depth 2.1 to 2.6 in its length. Coloration olivaceous, paler below; sides with some spots and splotches of dark color, but the mottling less prominent than in *R. atronasus*; back, sides, cheeks and opercles, and caudal peduncle more or less densely punctulate with dusky; lateral band indistinct; a black spot on opercle; fins all plain, no spot at middle of base of dorsal fin. (Spring males with lips, cheeks, and lower fins crimson.—Jordan & Evermann.) Head long and greatly narrowed, the pointed muzzle very prominent, 4 to 4.1 in length; width of head 1.8 to 2.2; interorbital space 3.2 to 3.3 in head; eye 4.8 to 5.6; nose long and pointed, twice the length of the eye, 2.2 to 2.5 in head; mouth wholly inferior and horizontal, tip of upper lip half way between lower margin of orbit and chin; maxillary 2.9 to 3.1, extending a little past anterior nostril; lower jaw much shorter than upper, the muzzle projecting beyond tip of chin for a distance nearly equal to half length of snout; a small maxillary barbel; isthmus twice diameter of orbit. Teeth, 2, 4–4, 2; peritoneum finely but not very densely punctulate with brown. Dorsal fin with 8 rays, set behind ventrals, its distance from muzzle 15 to 20 per cent. greater than to base of caudal; longest dorsal ray 1.2 in head; anal rays 7; pectorals about ⅔ to ventrals, 1.1 to 1.3 in head; ventrals short of front of anal, passing vent. Scales very small, 7 to 10, 63–70, 7 or 8; lateral line little decurved.

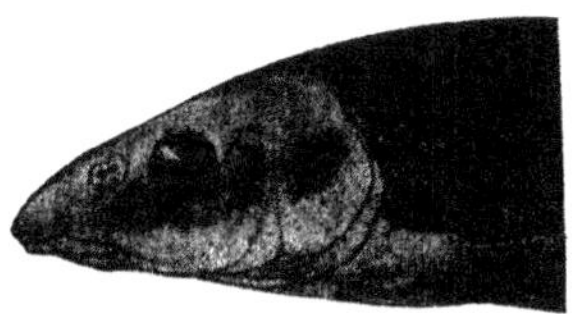

Fig. 40

This species, although very wide-spread and abundant under its preferred conditions, has been very rare with us, being represented in all our collections by only four specimens, one obtained near Waukegan, in northeastern Illinois, and three from Big creek, near the town of Anna, in Union county, in the extreme southern part of the state. It generally prefers clear, cold streams—a fact sufficient to account for its scarcity within our limits. It ranges very widely north, south, east, and west, from New Brunswick and the Province of Quebec through the Great Lakes to the headwaters of the Missouri in Montana, northward to the Saskatchewan, and across the mountains to the Columbia River, southward along the Atlantic coast to the Potomac and the James, and by way of the Mississippi Valley to the Rio Grande. It is said to occur also in the Great Salt Lake basin of Utah.

RHINICHTHYS ATRONASUS (MITCHILL)

BLACK-NOSED DACE

Mitchill, 1815, Trans. Lit. and Phil. Soc. N. Y., I, 460 (**Cyprinus**).
G., VII, 191; J. & G., 208; M. V., 63; J. & E., I, 307; N., 45, also 46 (**lunatus** and **meleagris**); J., 63 (**obtusus** and **meleagris**); F., 75 (part); L., 18.

Length 2¼ inches; body moderately elongate, very little compressed; depth 4.5 to 5 in length; caudal peduncle rather short and deep, less than head, its depth 1.7 to 2.1 in its length. Color dusky to blackish above, the back and sides variously mottled with darker; a black band along sides, through eye to end of snout, below which is a paler streak; belly silvery; a distinct black blotch at base of dorsal behind; dorsal otherwise and all other fins plain; spring males with the lower fins and often almost entire body more or less blood-red, this color becoming obsolescent by midsummer. Head pyramidal, subquadrate in transverse section, being a little wider than deep; length of head 3.6 to 4.2 in head and body, its width 1.7 to 2 in its length; interorbital space flat, 2.8 to 3.1; eye small, 4.3 to 4.9; nose long and projecting, but not decurved, both nostrils lying well in upper half of head; length of nose 2.7 to 3 in head; mouth rather small, subterminal, slightly oblique, tip of upper lip as high as lower margin of orbit; maxillary shorter than in the last species, 3.3 to 4 in head, usually over 3.6, reaching scarcely past anterior nostril; a minute maxillary barbel; lower jaw included; isthmus twice width of orbit. Teeth 2, 4–4, 2; peritoneum silvery except high up, where it is dusky. Dorsal fin with 8 rays, set distinctly behind ventrals, 15 to 20 per cent. farther from muzzle than base of caudal; longest dorsal ray 1.3 to 1.4 in head; anal rays 7; pectorals about ⅔ to ventrals, 1.3 to 1.5 in head; ventrals past base of anal in adult males. Scales 9 to 11, 62–71, 8 to 10; lateral line complete, little decurved.

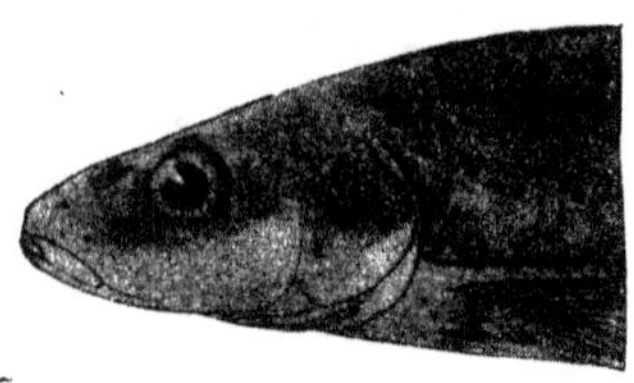

FIG. 41

This species, widely distributed like the preceding, extends from New Brunswick and the rivers of northeastern Quebec through the Hudson and the Great Lakes to the James and the Roanoke, to the Dakotas in the northwest, and through the Ohio basin to Iowa and northern Alabama. We have found it in only six Illinois collections, all but one in the clear swift brooks of the northern part of the state. The northern Illinois localities reported are Oregon, Ogle county, Bailey's creek and other streams of La Salle county, Big Rock creek and Little Rock creek, near Plano, in Kendall county, the lakes about Henry, in Marshall county, and Farm creek, near Peoria. We have also two specimens from Big creek, near Anna, in Union county, in extreme southern Illinois.

This is an active fish, decidedly preferring clear rocky streams. Breeding males were taken about Ottawa in June. It has been seen to spawn in shallow running water, piling pebbles up about the nest after the eggs are deposited. Spring males have the front of the head and the occipital region finely tuberculate.

Genus **HYBOPSIS** Agassiz

Body robust or elongate; mouth terminal or inferior; a barbel always present, terminal on the maxillary (in one species there are 2 barbels on each side); premaxillary protractile; teeth 4–4, or 1, 4–4, 1 or 0, hooked and with grinding surface narrow or obsolete; intestine short; peritoneum pale, dusky, or black; dorsal rays 7 or 8; anal 6 to 8; scales 35 to 60; lateral line continuous. Species numerous, about 17; 5 in Illinois. A large and varied group, embracing both small species from 2½ to 5 inches in length and larger forms up to a length of 10 or 12 inches. United States east of the Rockies; one species from California.

HYBOPSIS HYOSTOMUS (Gilbert)

Gilbert, 1884, Proc. U. S. Nat. Mus., 203 (**Nocomis**).
M. V., 64; J. & E., I, 316; L., 19 (part).

Very small minnows with an inferior mouth, and with barbel ⅓ to ½ as long as snout, easily distinguished among Illinois *Cyprinidæ* by their small size, elongate eye, posteriorly placed mouth (tip of lower lip under first nostril), and rusty- to blackish-punctulate coloration. Length of our largest specimens 1¾ inches; body moderately elongate, subfusiform, little compressed, heaviest forward of dorsal fin; depth 4.9 to 6.2 in length; caudal peduncle slender, its depth 2.5 to 2.8 in its length. Color silvery, everywhere more or less dusted with brownish specks; similar but larger specks, suggesting rust-spots in preserved material, found on nose, suborbitals, and opercles; fins all pale. Head rather long, 3.7 to 4, its width 2 to 2.1 in its length; interorbital space nearly flat, 3.5 to 4 in head; eye 2.8 to 3.4, elliptical, its long diameter 1⅓ to 1½ times its short; nose 2.7 to 3.1, about as long as eye, broad, bluntly pointed and decurved, projecting nearly half its length beyond the mouth; mouth wholly inferior and horizontal, tip of lower lip directly under first nostril; maxillary 3.3 to 3.8 in head, reaching past front of orbit; barbel long, 2 to 3 in snout; isthmus less than pupil. Teeth 4–4, rather strongly hooked, the grinding surface extremely narrow or not at all developed; peritoneum silvery, with some rather coarse specks upward. Dorsal fin with 8 rays, rarely 7, set about over ventrals and equidistant between muzzle and base of caudal; longest dorsal ray 1.1 to 1.3 in head; anal rays 7 or 8, usually 7; pectorals more than ⅔ to ventrals; ventrals past vent. Scales 5, 34–36, 4; 14 before dorsal; lateral line decurved.

Sexual differences not noted, our specimens being few and probably not fully grown.

Taken by us in only three collections—from the Rock River at Erie, from Green River at Cleveland, and from the Illinois River at Naples. The first two came from fairly swift water running over rock and gravel. The species is said to be rather common in sandy river channels from Iowa and southern Illinois southward to the Alabama River. It ranges also westward and northward in the Missouri to Nebraska and Minnesota.

HYBOPSIS DISSIMILIS (KIRTLAND)

SPOTTED SHINER

(MAP XLVIII)

Kirtland, 1840, Bost. Jour. Nat. Hist., III, 341 (**Luxilus**).
G., VII, 177 (**Ceratichthys**); J. & G., 215 (**Ceratichthys**); M. V., 64; J. & E., I, 318; N., 45 (**Ceratichthys**); J., 62 (**Ceratichthys**); F., 74 (**Semotilus**); L., 19.

Known from *H. amblops*, which, of our species, it most resembles, by its more slender body, smaller eye, and more or less mottled coloration. Length 3 inches; body long and slender, subfusiform, little compressed, depth 4.7 to 5.3 in length; caudal peduncle slender, about equal to the head, its depth 2.3 to 2.8 in its length. Color olivaceous, the sides silvery; a more or less distinct bluish lateral band, most evident posteriorly, in places widened or broken into blotches; back and sides marked with irregularly X-shaped splotches formed by dark punctulations on the scales; a dusky band through eye to end of snout; fins plain. Head somewhat long flattish above, 3.9 to 4.2 in length, its width 1.9 to 2.2 in its length; interorbital space 3.3 to 3.9; eye 3.1 to 3.8, little elliptical; nose 2.4 to 2.7 in head, bluntly pointed and somewhat decurved, projecting little beyond the mouth; mouth horizontal, inferior, tip of lower jaw as far in front of anterior nostril as that is in front of eye; length of maxillary 3.6 to 4.3 in head, reaching to anterior nostril; barbel usually rather less than diameter of pupil; isthmus wide, its breadth equal to diameter of orbit. Teeth 4–4, with very narrow grinding surface; intestine 1 to 1.5 times length of head and body; peritoneum black. Dorsal fin with 8 rays, set distinctly in front of ventrals, and about equidistant between tip of snout and base of caudal; longest dorsal ray 1.1 to 1.3 in head; anal rays 7; pectorals about ¾ to ventrals; ventrals to vent. Scales 5 or 6, 38–47, 4 or 5; 14 to 17 rows before dorsal; lateral line complete, nearly straight.

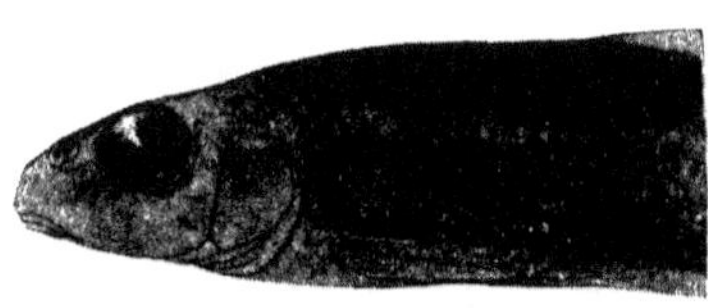

FIG. 42

No females with eggs found in our collections, which are few, and mostly taken in midsummer or after. Males with organs apparently well developed, but without tubercles, taken in the middle of June.

An uncommon species in this state, its known localities being one on the lower Kaskaskia, one on the upper Embarras in Coles county, one on the Sangamon in Macon county, one on the Kickapoo in Logan county, one on Spoon River in Fulton county, and four on Rock River, in Lee and Winnebago counties. In northern Illinois it has been taken chiefly in swift water flowing over sand. Outside the state it is to be found from Lake Erie to the headwaters of the Tennessee, west to Arkansas and Iowa, and north to the Saskatchewan River and to Calgary.

HYBOPSIS AMBLOPS (Rafinesque)

BIG-EYED CHUB; SILVER CHUB

(Map XLIX)

Rafinesque, 1820, Ichth. Oh., 51 (**Rutilus**).
G., VII, 179 (**Ceratichthys hyalinus**); J. & G., 214 (**Ceratichthys**); M. V., 64; J. & E., I, 320; J., 62 (**Ceratichthys**); F., 75 (**Semotilus**); L., 19.

Length 2 to 3 inches; a small but rather robust species, the body less slender and more compressed and the eye larger than in *H. dissimilis;* depth 4.6 to 5.2 in length, being greatest in the predorsal region; caudal peduncle rather slender, its depth 2.2 to 2.5 in its length. Color olivaceous, overlaid above with translucent greenish and with silvery on sides; scales above lateral line everywhere finely punctulate, only indistinctly dark-edged; a dusky to blackish lateral stripe continued forward through eye to end of snout; no vertebral streak or caudal spot; fins all plain; males and females similarly colored. Head 3.6 to 3.9, broad and flattened above; width of head 1.9 to 2 in its length; interorbital space 3 to 3.9 in head; eye large, usually longer than interorbital space or snout, 2.8 to 3.1 in head; muzzle bluntly decurved, the nose 2.9 to 3.4 in head, projecting sometimes as much as width of pupil beyond mouth; mouth small, horizontal, inferior, the tip of the lower jaw little in advance of first nostril; maxillary 3.6 to 4.6 in head, usually reaching to vertical from front of orbit; barbel variable, usually rather small, sometimes scarcely discernible, and as a rule not projecting below cheek; isthmus less than pupil. Teeth 1, 4–4, 1, occasionally 4–4 or with the supernumerary tooth absent on one side; teeth stoutish towards base, with a very small and sharp hook; grinding surface not much developed; intestine shorter than head and body; peritoneum coarsely specked with brown. Dorsal fin with 8 rays, set as a rule almost directly over ventrals about equidistant between muzzle and base of caudal; longest dorsal ray 1.1 to 1.3 in head; anal rays 7 or 8; pectorals about ¾ to ventrals; ventrals to vent. Scales 5, 35–38, 4 or 5; 12 to 15 rows in front of dorsal; lateral line nearly straight.

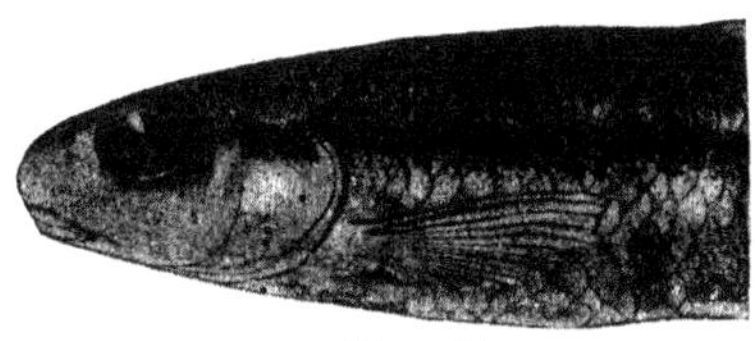

Fig. 43

Males without tubercles or flushed coloration in spring. Females much distended with eggs taken about first of June.

This is one of our Illinois species whose distribution in the state presents an ecological problem which we have no present means of solving. Ranging from Lake Erie to the Black Warrior and the Alabama southward, and to Iowa and Arkansas on the west, it occurs abundantly in southeastern Illinois, but has been taken by us in only two neighboring localities additional, one on the upper Kankakee and the other on the Mackinaw. It is one of the species, in fact, which has the appearance of spreading over the state from the south and east mainly by the branches of the Wabash, but reaching adjacent waters as if by overland migration. It is notably a species of creeks, for which its frequency coefficient rises to the unusual figure of 3.97. We have found it relatively about half as abundant in the smaller rivers, and of only occasional occurrence in rivers of the larger class. None of our 51 collections has been taken from stagnant waters of any kind.

HYBOPSIS STORERIANUS (Kirtland)

STORER'S CHUB

(Map L)

Kirtland, 1842, Proc. Bost. Soc. Nat. Hist., I, 71 (**Rutilus**).
J. & G., 213 (**Ceratichthys lucens**); M. V., 65; J. & E., I, 321; N., 46; J., 56 (**Alburnops**); L., 19.

A large species, known at once from our other species of *Hybopsis* by the double-rowed dark edging of the scales above the lateral line. Length 5 or 6 inches; body elongate, considerably compressed; back often somewhat elevated; depth 4.3 to 5.3 in length; caudal peduncle rather slender, its depth 2.2 to 2.6 in head. Color translucent greenish above, with purplish reflections; brilliantly silvery on sides and below; an indistinct plumbeous lateral band, overlaid in life with emerald, below which is a band of silvery to bluish blending with the silvery of belly; no caudal spot and no vertebral streak; scales above lateral line, except a few along middle of back in front of dorsal fin, each with two subparallel rows of dark dots near posterior border, between which is a crescentic lighter space; cheeks and opercles bright silvery; fins plain, the dorsal and caudal sometimes slightly dusky. Head 4.3 to 5.3 in length, comparatively short and compressed, cheeks nearly vertical; width of head 1.8 to 2; interorbital space entirely flat or somewhat concave, 3.3 to 3.5; eye 2.9 to 3.4 in head; preorbital bone especially prominent, large, oblong, and silvery; nose 2.8 to 3.1, a little longer than eye, moderately decurved, the tip of the muzzle somewhat thickened and pad-like, though not projecting much beyond mouth; mouth rather small,

STEEL-COLORED MINNOW, *Notropis whipplii* (Girard)
STORER'S CHUB, *Hybopsis storerianus* (Kirtland)

inferior and horizontal, tip of upper lip far below level of lower margin of orbit; maxillary 3.2 to 3.7 in head, barely reaching front of orbit; barbel evident, though scarcely projecting; isthmus less than pupil. Teeth 1, 4–4, 1 or 0, stout and little hooked, with grinding surface usually not much developed; intestine about .9 of length of head and body; peritoneum silvery. Dorsal fin with 8 rays, occasionally 9, more or less falcate, set a little in advance of ventrals, and distinctly closer to muzzle than base of caudal; longest dorsal ray 1 to 1.2 in head; anal rays usually 8, sometimes 7 or 9; pectorals ⅔ or less to ventrals; ventrals to vent in young only. Scales 6, 37 to 40, 4; 14 to 16 rows in front of dorsal; upper longitudinal rows with appearance of running out behind dorsal fin, as in *Notropis cornutus*, this appearance aided by converging longitudinal lines formed by connecting cross-marks of light color on the scales of some of the rows; lateral line gently decurved anteriorly.

Sexual differences slight; upper surface of pectoral rays in spring males with very fine pectinately disposed tubercles; no sexually mature females in our collections; some rather young females with ovaries just beginning to enlarge taken about May 20.

A fish of the larger streams and lowland lakes, widely distributed in Illinois, though rare with us throughout its range. Our 28 collections carry it from Cairo to Jo Daviess county and from the Wabash to the Mississippi. None of them, however, are from the lower Illinoisan glaciation. One collection is from the Rock River near Milan, seven come from the Illinois and its larger tributaries, an equal number are from the Mississippi and its neighboring lakes and bayous, five from the Wabash and its tributaries, three from the Saline River, and two from the Ohio. Outside Illinois it is generally distributed from Lakes Erie and Ontario to Wyoming, Nebraska, and Arkansas, ranging southward also to Tennessee.

HYBOPSIS KENTUCKIENSIS (Rafinesque)

RIVER CHUB; HORNY-HEAD

(Map LI)

Rafinesque, 1820, Ichth. Oh., 48 (**Luxilus**).

G., VII, 178 (**Ceratichthys biguttatus** and **C. cyclotis**) and 179 (**C. stigmaticus** and **C. micropogon**); J. & G., 212 (**Ceratichthys biguttatus** and **C. micropogon**); M. V., 65; J. & E., I, 322; N., 45 (**Ceratichthys biguttatus**); J., 62 (**Ceratichthys biguttatus**); F. F., I. 6, 89 (**Ceratichthys biguttatus**); F. 75 (**Semotilus biguttatus**); L., 19.

A large species, with a general resemblance in form to *Semotilus*, but the snout more pointed, mouth less oblique, and with no caudal spot (except in young). Length 6 to 8 inches; body subfusiform, very little compressed, robust anteriorly, the body deepest in front of the dorsal fin; profile scarcely declined from front of dorsal to occiput in adults, the descent from that point to muzzle rapid; depth 3.9 to 4.5; caudal peduncle less than head, its depth 1.9 to 2.1 in its length. Color of top of head and back a rich green, darkest at edges of scales; below this a narrow and more or less indefinite band of much lighter green, extending forward on iris above pupil and on opercle as yellowish; passing forward through pupil and ending behind in a faint caudal spot, is a more or less indistinct dark lateral band; lower part of sides and belly yellowish to pearly gray; sides everywhere with coppery and greenish reflections; on each side of head behind eye a spot of pale red about size of pupil, most brilliant in spring males; a curved dusky bar behind opercle; dorsal and caudal fins with membranes orange except at tips, the edges being bluish gray; anal orange in the membranes; other fins plain; breeding colors brighter, red spots on sides of head accentuated in males; very young specimens with a prominent black lateral stripe passing around snout forward and ending behind in a pronounced caudal spot. Head 3.6 to 3.8 in length, conical, top of head and cheeks quite rounded; width of

FIG. 44

head 1.8 to 2; interorbital space 2.6 to 2.9; eye very small, 4.1 to 5.6 in head; nose sharp, scarcely decurved, 2.4 to 2.9; mouth rather large, subterminal, not very oblique, the tip of the upper lip about half way between lower margin of orbit and lower edge of cheek; maxillary 3 to 3.6 in head, not quite reaching to front of eye; lower jaw shorter than upper; breadth of isthmus nearly equal to diameter of orbit; barbel as a rule evident, though usually not projecting beyond cheek, occasionally discernible only with difficulty. Teeth variable, usually 4–4 in our specimens, though not infrequently 1, 4–4, 1 or 0; on pharyngeal jaws from eight well-preserved specimens, which were all carefully examined for lost or broken teeth, the following combinations were found; 1, 4–4, 1; 0, 4–4, 1; 1, 4–0, 3; 0, 4–1, 3; 0, 2–1, 4; 0, 2–1, 3; intestine 1.1 to 1.4 in length of head and body; peritoneum dusky. Dorsal fin with 8 rays, placed almost exactly over the ventrals, a little nearer base of caudal than muzzle; longest dorsal ray 1.3 to 1.4 in head; anal rays 7; pectorals somewhat over ⅔ to ventrals; ventrals to vent in males, short of it in females. Scales 6 or 7, 39 to 44, 5; 17 to 22 rows before dorsal fin; lateral line complete or nearly so, gently decurved anteriorly.

This fish is of particular interest to us because of the peculiarity of its distribution in this state. Although it occurs throughout the Great Lakes from Michigan to Ontario, and from Wyoming to Pennsylvania and southward to North Carolina and Alabama, our collections in the state of Illinois are limited to the more recently glaciated areas, only one having been made by us below the southern boundary of the Wisconsin glaciation. Against this single locality in southern Illinois (Union county) we have 122 localities in the northern two thirds of the state, where the species is not only abundant but is generally distributed, mainly in the smaller streams and also in the glacial lakes of the northeastern section. We have taken it from Lake Michigan at Chicago.

According to our 137 collections of the horny-head, it is almost wholly a species of the creeks and smaller rivers, the frequency coefficient for the first being 3.08 and for the second 2.47. It has been so rare in stagnant waters that we have taken it but twice in our 591 collections from lakes and ponds. From the larger rivers we have obtained it 6 times in 293 collections. It seems to be with us especially a fish of swift waters and a hard bottom, the coefficient for the former class of situations being 1.38 and for the latter 2.24. It is consistent with this fact that, although commonly scattered throughout the Wisconsin glaciation, it stops short at the southern boundary of this area, not entering the lower Illinoisan at any point.

The spawning season of this species is late May and early June. In spring males the top of the head is swollen to form a kind of crest, which may be considerably higher than the level of the neck, and is covered with large tubercles.

The length of ten inches which this fish sometimes attains, perhaps accounts for the rather prominent appearance of crawfishes in its food. Thirteen specimens from northern and central Illinois had derived less than half their food from the animal kingdom, about a fourth of it consisting of insects, largely caseworms and other larvæ of *Neuroptera*, another fourth of crawfishes, eaten by two of the specimens. The vegetable food was about equally divided between thread algæ and seeds of grasses. Although insects appear in relatively small ratio, two of these fishes had eaten nothing else, and another had eaten 95 per cent. of aquatic larvæ. Two other specimens had taken only vegetation, which also composed 80 per cent. of the food of three additional. It will be noticed that the alimentary canal of this minnow is of more than average length, a fact probably related to its vegetarian habit. As a game fish, according to Jordan and Evermann, it is the most active and vigorous of its tribe. "Any sort of hook baited with an angleworm or white grub is a lure the hornyhead can seldom resist, and he bites with a vim and energy worthy of a better fish. The fight he makes, though it would not wholly satisfy the veteran black bass angler, is quite enough to fill the youthful Walton with unbounded joy and pride. But as his experiences widen his chief interest in the hornyhead lies in the fact that it is one of the best of live baits for nobler fish. For muskallunge, pickerel, wall-eyed pike, and black bass of either species, as a live bait it is not surpassed; large individuals for muskallunge and increasingly smaller ones for the others, those for the small-mouthed black bass being not over 3 to 5 inches in length. A hardy, active minnow, and of an attractive color, as a live bait it is unsurpassed."

Genus **PLATYGOBIO** Gill

Body elongate, somewhat compressed; head short, broad, and depressed; mouth subterminal; a well-developed barbel at back of maxillary; teeth 2, 4-4, 2, with narrow grinding surface; dorsal 8; anal 8; scales 45 to 50; lateral line continuous. Length 6 to 12 inches. Species few, confined principally to the east slope of the Rocky Mountains; one species found in Illinois.

Fig. 45

PLATYGOBIO GRACILIS (Richardson)

FLAT-HEADED CHUB

Richardson, 1836, Fauna Bor. Amer., Fishes, 120 (**Cyprinus**).
G., VII, 240 (**Leuciscus gracilis**), 267 (**Leucosomus communis**) and 268 (**Leucosomus gulonellus**); J. & G., 219, also 220 (**pallidus Forbes**); M. V., 65; J. & E., 326; F., 75 (**pallidus**); L., 20 (**pallidus**).

A silvery minnow with a broad, flat head, fine scales, and an evident barbel terminal on the maxillary. Length of our largest specimens 3 inches; specimens 10 to 12 inches long known from the waters of the upper Missouri; body rather elongate, the depth 5.1 to 5.4 in the length; adults much more slender than young; caudal peduncle slender, its depth 2.1 to 2.4 in its length.

Color plain silvery, with a plumbeous luster along sides, and traces of a dusky lateral stripe behind dorsal; fins all plain; young with sides more or less punctulate with brown, suggesting the appearance of *Hybopsis hyostomus*. Head 4 to 4.3, broad and depressed and flat above, its width 1.6 to 1.7 in its length; interorbital space 2.2 to 2.5; eye small, 3.9 to 4.6*; nose 2.7 to 3.1 in head, blunt, the muzzle overhanging the inferior mouth; mouth rather large, nearly horizontal, tip of upper lip below level of lower margin of orbit; barbel prominent, as a rule extending below cheek; lower jaw shorter than upper; isthmus narrow, scarcely wider than pupil. Teeth 2, 4–4, 2, hooked and with masticatory surface; peritoneum bright silvery. Dorsal fin with 8 rays, set a little in front of ventrals and nearer muzzle than base of caudal; longest dorsal ray 1 to 1.1 in head; anal rays 8, occasionally 9; pectorals long, pointed, ¾ to ⅘ to ventrals; ventrals nearly to vent. Scales 6, 50–55, 5, crowded forward, 21 to 23 rows before dorsal; lateral line complete, very little decurved.

Sexual differences not well known, probably not strongly marked. A young male taken by us from the Ohio River had the snout tuberculate.

This is a northwestern species whose occurrence once within the limits of this state is to be taken as little more than an accident. Some 20 specimens were collected by us in 1880 from the Ohio River at Cairo, but it has not been otherwise reported from any point east of the Mississippi. Its territory of general distribution extends throughout the Missouri River and its tributaries as far down as Kansas City, and thence to the Saskatchewan, Assiniboin, Athabasca, and McKenzie rivers, in the Dominion of Canada. A careful comparison of *P. pallidus* Forbes with specimens of the present species obtained by Dr. Meek from the Missouri River at Sioux City, Iowa, leads us to conclude that the two are identical, such differences as are manifest being probably due to the immature condition of the Ohio River specimens.

This is said to be a fish of the river channels, and is not known to ascend small streams. It is especially characteristic of the shallow alkaline creeks of the Northwest.

---

* Up to 6 in adults, according to Jordan and Evermann.

Order NEMATOGNATHI

THE CATFISHES

Skeleton bony; four anterior vertebræ coössified, modified, and furnished with a chain of small bones (Weberian ossicles) connecting the air-bladder (if present) with the auditory organ; ventral fins abdominal; dorsal and pectorals each with a single spine; pectoral arch suspended from the skull; a mesocoracoid arch present; suboperculum wanting, or modified into the uppermost branchiostegal; premaxillary forming border of mouth (except in the genus *Diplomystes*, of Chili), the maxillary being often rudimentary and supporting the base of a barbel; air-bladder, if present, with open duct (physostomous). A large group, comprising some 1,200 species and 150 genera, found in the fresh waters of both hemispheres and of all the continents, few species being marine; most abundant in the Amazon region. Most species are naked-skinned, although the numerous small forms of the South American family *Loricariidæ** have the sides and back armored with rough bony plates.

Family SILURIDÆ

THE CATFISHES

Body more or less elongate, naked or covered (in many South American forms) with bony plates; no true scales; lateral line usually present; skeleton osseous; 4 anterior vertebræ modified, and furnished (in forms in which air-bladder is developed) with a chain of small bones (Weberian ossicles) connecting the air-bladder with the ear; ventral fins abdominal; anterior rays of dorsal and pectorals usually spinous; an adipose fin usually present; tail not heterocercal; mesocoracoid present; gill-openings generally wide; suboperculum wanting, or modified into the uppermost branchiostegal; margin of upper jaw formed by premaxillaries only; teeth in jaws in broad bands; lower pharyngeals separate; air-bladder usually present, simple, with open duct, connected (see above) with the organ of hearing by Weberian ossicles.

This family is very large and widely distributed, embracing about 700 species, found chiefly in fresh water, in all parts of the globe. Catfishes are most abundant in tropical and subtropical regions. Some species grow to a very large size, and all except the very small forms are of more or less value as food. The giant "sheatfish," or "wels," of Europe, which is abundant in the Danube, reaches a weight of 300 to 400 ℔, being next after the sturgeons the largest European fish. There are in the United States, Canada, and Mexico upwards of 35 species of catfishes,

* Some tropical *Siluridæ* are imperfectly mailed.

three genera and 12 species of which are found in the waters of the Mississippi Valley. It is a remarkable fact that no catfishes are found indigenous to the waters of the United States west of the Rocky Mountains, although several species have recently been introduced there by the United States Fish Commission. No extinct forms of importance are known. A few remains have been recovered from the lower and middle Eocene and Tertiary. The evidence from paleontology (chiefly the absence of fossils) and from the anatomy of the living forms, indicates that the catfishes are a recent group, derived doubtless from scaly ancestors, and probably related to the *Characinidæ* or *Cyprinidæ*.

The catfishes are mainly dwellers in more or less muddy water, making their home most of the time upon the bottom and chiefly feeding there. Agreeably to this habit, their eyes are small, and their cuticular sensory organs are highly developed. The family, taken together, is nearly omnivorous in habit, and their alimentary structures have a corresponding generalized character. The capacious mouth, the wide œsophagus, and the short, broad stomach admit objects of relatively large size and of almost any shape. The jaws, each armed with a broad pad of fine sharp teeth, are well calculated to grasp both hard and soft bodies. The gill-rakers are of average number and development, and the pharyngeal jaws—broad, stout arches below and oval pads above, with their opposite surfaces covered with minute, pointed denticles—serve well to crush the crusts of insects and the shells of the smaller mollusks. The indifference of several of the species to the past history or the present condition of their food distinguishes them as the most important scavengers among our common fishes. With the eel, they are to be considered among the most destructive enemies of shad in the streams of the Atlantic coast, as is proven by the contents of stomachs of many specimens taken over the spawning grounds of that fish. Most of the species are nocturnal, remaining more or less sluggish throughout the day. In winter they appear to take little or no food. Their extreme tenacity of life and omnivorous habit favor their multiplication in almost any kind of situation, often enabling them to survive through drought or other hardships to which all their neighbors succumb.

All except the smaller catfishes, the stonecats, are used for food, and the best of them rank well among river fishes for edible qualities. The bullheads are mostly consumed locally, as pan-fish. The larger catfish keep well in cold storage and may be shipped great distances in ice alive, frozen in the cake. Small quantities are smoked in Chicago and St. Louis and at other points in the middle Mississippi Valley, as a substitute for the higher-priced smoked sturgeon. The smoked product was 50,-000 ℔ in 1898. The larger species are taken in seines and fyke-nets, while the bullheads are most commonly caught on set-lines. The larger catfishes, as well as the bullheads, will bite readily at the hook. The catfish catch, including bullheads, for the state of Illinois was 1,500,000 ℔ in 1899, while that for the Illinois River and its tributaries in 1903 was 999,000 ℔.* Statistics of the Illinois River Fishermen's Association for 1899 showed a catch of 241.000 ℔ of the larger catfishes (*Ictalurus*) and of 499,100 ℔ of bullheads.

Catfishes are well adapted for stocking ponds and sluggish, muddy streams. Their ready acclimatization has led to their successful introduction into the streams of Europe and the Hawaiian Islands. Local species have been introduced in the streams of the Pacific coast and are now thriving there. The United States Commissioner of Fish and Fisheries has said (Rep. 1903, p. 83) that "both commercial fishermen and anglers throughout the country are showing increased interest in catfishes, and requests for stocking public and private waters have recently been numerous." It is thought that it will not be long before the government undertakes the establishment of a breeding station for the purpose of supplying the need indicated by such requests.

By looking to the numbers, food, habits, endurance, methods of reproduction, and local and ecological distribution of our catfishes and bullheads, and to their means of defense and offense, we may form a more or less definite idea of their place, significance, and efficiency in the general scheme of fresh-water life, and thus be enabled to see something of the consequences which would necessarily follow if they were to be generally destroyed.

By their ability to live contentedly in situations commonly avoided by most other fishes, they organize into their living substance much food material which would otherwise disappear as a mere natural waste, and, in so far as they are themselves eaten by other fishes, they thus increase the general supply of fish food in

* In 1894 the total catch for the interior waters of the United States (23 states) was 14,726,000 ℔, Illinois coming first with nearly two million pounds and Iowa next with 985,000 ℔. The total for the United States (17 states) had fallen to 7,648,000 ℔ in 1899 and to 5,191,000 ℔ in 1903.

the waters they enter and inhabit. By their services as scavengers, they help to protect more sensitive fishes from the effects of the pollution of the water through a decomposition of objects which they are themselves very willing to devour, and in this way also they may convert into a form acceptable to other fishes food substances otherwise useless. As we have found them to be eaten more or less by both our species of black bass, by the sand-pike (*Stizostedion canadense*), and by the yellow bullhead and the mud-cat, their utility in this sense seems appreciable.

On the other hand, it must be noticed that they have appeared very rarely in the food of fishes, in comparison with their numbers and general distribution. Only nine fishes out of more than 1,200 examined had eaten them, while 45 of these same fishes had eaten more or less freely of a *single species* of another family—the gizzard-shad. Reviewing the food of the catfishes themselves, it seems to us clear, from our present data, that they devour other fishes much more generally than others devour them—that whatever tends to their multiplication and continuance tends rather to diminish the number of other species in our waters than to increase them. Their partial immunity is doubtless due in considerable measure to their remarkable defensive apparatus of stiff, acute, projecting, poisoned spines in the pectoral and dorsal fins, weapons capable of inflicting really painful punctures in animals as large as man. These fin-spines are evidently an advantageous substitute for the defensive armor of scales which our catfishes have lost in the course of their evolution.

The nocturnal habits of catfishes must also contribute to their protection from predaceous enemies, and the wide range of their dietary enables them to exist in much larger numbers than would be possible if their choice of food were more restricted. Where one kind fails them for a time they may find an abundance of another. Their power to crush the shells of many mollusks and to reject the fragments gives them access to a means of subsistence very abundant in many of the waters which they inhabit, and available to but few other fishes, and their habit of leading and guarding their young of course greatly increases their chances of survival.

Our catfishes are not by any means all of equal habit, or of similar distribution and geological relationship. The stonecats remain the size of minnows and the channel-cats are among the heaviest of the fishes of our great rivers. The former lurk, like darters, under stones in small streams, and the latter spend their time in the deeper waters of the Mississippi and the Illinois. The species of *Ictalurus* prefer clear water and a strong current, while certain of the bullheads thrive in stagnant pools, exposed to the vicissitudes of the overflow and retreat of the waters upon the river bottoms, and liable, indeed, to destruction by the complete drying out of the ponds in which they often become imprisoned. If they succeed in living there, however, until the next overflow, they add by so much to the average catfish population of the streams. Even these bullheads, so like that the species can be distinguished with difficulty, diminish mutual competition by difference of ecological preference, and a consequent different local distribution. The yellow and black bullheads, for example, are commonest in creeks (frequencies, 2.22 and 2.25), and the brown bullhead in lakes and ponds (frequency, 1.36); and the first two, notwithstanding their similar situations, have been taken together by us less frequently than either of the other two pairs, indicating some difference of local preference within the limits of their like more general distribution. The three more abundant stonecats also plainly evade each other, *Noturus flavus* and *Schilbeodes miurus* by a different general distribution within the state, and both of these avoiding *S. gyrinus* by a difference of ecological preference, being most abundant in clear swift waters, while *gyrinus* is found most frequently in quiet waters over a mud bottom. By all these various characteristics of structure, habit, preference, and capacity, the family is remarkably adapted to life in our interior waters, and its predominance in them is thus easily understood.

Key to the Genera of **SILURIDÆ** found in Illinois

a. Adipose fin with its posterior margin free.

b. Premaxillary band of teeth without lateral backward extensions; anal rays 17 to 35, including rudiments.

c. Bony bridge from occiput to dorsal fin complete; tail deeply forked... **Ictalurus.**

cc. Bony bridge from occiput to dorsal fin broken; caudal fin typically rounded, truncate or slightly emarginate (forked in **A. lacustris**)........... **Ameiurus.**

bb. Premaxillary band of teeth with a backward extension on each side; anal rays 12 to 15, including rudiments.................................... **Leptops.**

aa. Adipose fin adnate to the back, continuous with the caudal and separated from it only by a notch.

d. Premaxillary band of teeth with lateral backward extensions, as in *Leptops;* skin thick, tough, and villose, not translucent...................... **Noturus.**

dd. Premaxillary band of teeth truncate at the ends, as in **Ameiurus**; skin thinner than in **d**, smooth or very finely villose, sometimes translucent......... .... **Schilbeodes.**

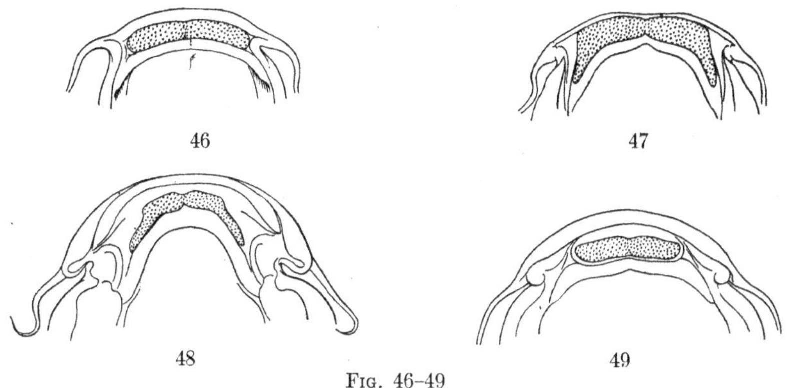

FIG. 46–49

Premaxillary teeth of (46) *Ameiurus melas* (47) *Leptops olivaris*, (48) *Noturus flavus*, and (49) *Schilbeodes gyrinus*.

GENUS **ICTALURUS** RAFINESQUE

CHANNEL-CATS

Body elongate, slender, compressed posteriorly. Head typically slender and conical; broad in a single species, *anguilla*, which approaches the genus *Ameiurus*. Supraoccipital process produced backward, its emarginated end receiving the acuminate anterior point of the second interspinal, thus forming a continuous bony bridge from the head to the dorsal spine. Mouth small, terminal, the upper jaw longer. Teeth subulate, in a short band on each jaw. Anal fin long, with 25 to 35 rays. Caudal fin elongate, more or less deeply forked, the lobes pointed. Coloration usually pale, bluish olive to silvery.

Fresh waters of North America; 4 species known, all being large, more or less active, species of the river channels.* These are the true "catfishes," in distinction from the bullheads (*Ameiurus*) and the mud-cat (*Leptops*). They are the best of the family as food.

KEY TO THE SPECIES OF **ICTALURUS** FOUND IN ILLINOIS

a. Anal fin of from 30 to 35 rays, including rudiments, its free margin nearly straight; eye low, nearer lower than upper surface of head; color bluish or silvery, usually without specks.................................... **furcatus.**

aa. Anal fin shorter, of 24 to 29 rays, including rudiments, its free margin rounded; eye above median axis of body, nearer upper than lower surface of head.

b. Head small, slender, subconic, its greatest width about 7/10 of its length; dorsal fin high and pointed, the longest ray about 5/6 of head; color bluish olive to silvery, always more or less spotted with darker........ **punctatus.**

bb. Head large, broad and heavy, its greatest width nearly 8/10 of its length; dorsal fin low and more or less rounded, its longest ray little more than 1/2 of head; color slaty olive to yellowish.......................... **anguilla.**

* This statement is not well known to apply to *I. anguilla*.

ICTALURUS FURCATUS (Le Sueur)

BLUE CAT; CHUCKLE-HEADED CAT; FULTON CAT

Le Sueur, 1840, in Cuv. & Val., XV, 136 (**Pimelodus**).
G., V, 103 (**Amiurus**); J. & G., 109; M. V., 39; J. & E., I, 134; N., 50; J., 66 (**Ichthælurus furcatus, Amiurus nigricans** [part]; F., 82 and 83, (**furcatus, ponderosus, nigricans** [part]; F. F., II. 7, 456; L., 9.

Body slender, somewhat compressed, the back elevated, depth 4 to 4.5 in length; profile long, steeper than in the next species, the elevation 18° to 23° and the contour broken at the nape (the elevation from that point to dorsal being greater than from snout to nape). Size large, reaching a weight of over 40 pounds. Color bluish or slaty gray above, shading to silvery below and almost white on belly; fins, especially the anal, frequently edged with dusky; spots very few or entirely absent. Head small, wedge-shaped, more angular than in the next species, its length 4 to 4.4, its greatest depth 5.2 to 5.6 in body; top of head and nape prominently convex, the back subcarinate in front of dorsal, the skin thin and fitted closely over the bones; mouth small, inferior, the lower jaw wholly included; lips thin; maxillary barbels reaching past gill-opening; eye small, oval, lying on the median axis of the body and nearer lower than upper surface of head; diameter of orbit 7.2 to 7.8 in head. Dorsal fin high, nearer snout than adipose, its distance from snout 3 to 3.5 in length; the spine rather longer and more slender than in *I. punctatus*, its length 1.5 to 1.7 in head; the posterior edge usually furnished with well-developed retrorse teeth. Caudal deeply forked, the lobes about equal. Anal fin long, of 30 to 35 rays, including rudiments, its base about ⅓ length of body, the free margin straight or very slightly rounded. Pectoral spine a little shorter than that of dorsal; humeral process 1.3 to 1.6 in length of spine.

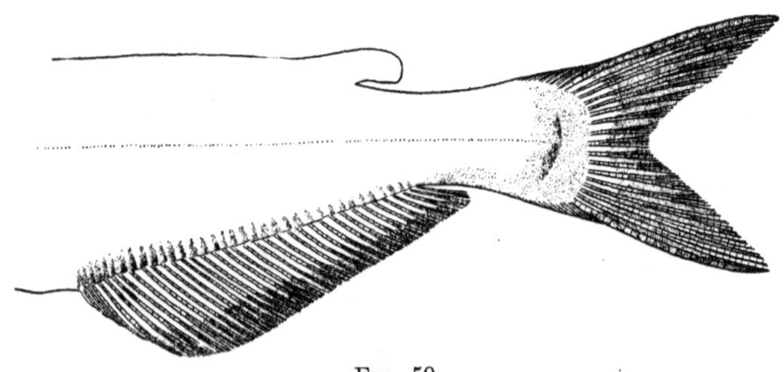

Fig. 50

Anal and caudal fins of *Ictalurus furcatus*.

This species is found throughout the Mississippi Valley and the Gulf states, being most abundant southward, and especially so in the Atchafalaya in Louisiana, where one to two million pounds are taken annually. It forms a large per cent. of the

Ictalurus anguilla Evermann & Kendall

catch of catfishes at Alton, where the smaller channel-cat (*I. punctatus*) is known as "fiddler," and fished for with special small nets. It is rare in the Illinois River and the smaller tributaries of the Mississippi in this state. It grows to a great size, specimens weighing as much as 150 ℔* being occasionally caught, although the average size of the larger ones taken is only 15 to 20 ℔. It is commonly known as the "Fulton" or "blue cat" by Mississippi River fishermen. It is called "white Fulton" by those who apply to the smaller species (*I. punctatus*) the name "blue Fulton"; and "Mississippi cat" is the name given it by some Illinois River fishermen.

It frequents the deeper waters of the river channels, coming out into the shallower sloughs and backwaters in spring. A specimen examined by Dr. Kofoid had eaten fragments of bark (twenty per cent.), insect fragments and larvæ (fifty per cent.), and miscellaneous organic debris. The senior author found fishes only in the stomach of a specimen taken in 1887. The breeding habits of the species are not known. It is caught on trot-lines baited with hickory-shad, mooneye, or crawfish (Louisiana), and in fykes and bait nets. In the words of Dr. Jordan: "The flesh is of excellent quality, firm and flaky, of very delicious flavor, nutritious in a high degree, and always commanding a high price. * * * It is of all the catfishes the one most deserving of cultivation and popular favor, and which could with profit be introduced into other countries."

ICTALURUS ANGUILLA Evermann & Kendall

Evermann & Kendall, 1897, Bull. U. S. Fish Comm., 125.
J. & E., III, 2788.

Body robust, head broad, the back little elevated, the contour from occiput to adipose fin being almost straight and parallel with median axis; depth 4.7 in length; profile steep from snout to postorbital region, from which point the elevation to dorsal is slight and gradual. Length of single specimen obtained 24 inches; others of somewhat larger size, weighing 10 to 12 pounds, reported by fishermen about Henry, Illinois. Color slaty olive, darker above, yellowish on sides; anal and caudal dark-edged. Head large, broad, and heavy, much as in species of *Ameiurus*, the cheeks and postocular portion unusually prominent; length of head 4.1; width 4.7 in length of body; interorbital space somewhat concave, a deep groove extending backward to front of dorsal; bones of top of head covered heavily with flesh and thick skin; mouth broad, upper jaw longer than lower; maxillary

* These large specimens were formerly thought to belong to another species (*Ameiurus nigricans*, *ponderosus*, etc.), but have recently been shown by Dr. Evermann not to be distinct.

barbels scarcely reaching gill-opening, other barbels short; eye small, 8 in head, situated near upper surface of skull. Dorsal fin low, its longest ray little more than ½ of head; the spine short and robust, about 3 in head; dorsal distance 3 in body. Caudal moderately forked, the lobes not much pointed. Anal fin with 25 rays, its free margin symmetrically rounded. Pectoral spine short and robust, with strong retrorse teeth on its posterior edge; humeral process about 2½ in pectoral spine.

This species is here described from a single specimen, obtained in Senachwine Lake, near Henry, in August, 1903. Since then, several specimens have been seen by us at Alton and Grafton, where it is not rare in fyke-net catches made in May and June. H. L. Ashlock, of Alton, says that fishes of this species weighing 26 ℔ are taken at Alton and Grafton, where it is sometimes called "nigger-lips" by the fishermen. Its flesh is said by Dr. Evermann to be firm and of excellent flavor.

ICTALURUS PUNCTATUS (Rafinesque)

CHANNEL-CAT; FIDDLER

(Map LII)

Rafinesque, 1818, Amer. Month. Mag., 359, (**Silurus**).
G., V, 102 (**Amiurus caudafurcatus**); J. & G., 108; M. V., 39; J. & E., I, 134; N., 50; J., 66 (**Ichthælurus punctatus and robustus**); F., 82; F. F., II. 7, 456; L., 9.

Body slender, scarcely compressed, and the back very little elevated, depth 4.2 to 5 in length, usually nearer 5 than 4; profile long and almost straight, very slightly convex, the elevation 16° to 18°, that from nape to dorsal somewhat less than elevation from snout to nape. One of the larger catfishes, reaching a weight of 20 to 25 pounds. Head and upper parts of body dark to lighter olive, with coppery luster on cheeks and sides above lateral line; sides below lateral line light olive with much silvery luster and with small spots of darker; belly pearl-gray in region of ventrals, more yellowish forward; maxillary barbels black, chin barbels whitish or ashen; fins, except ventrals and pectorals, greenish, the anal with a silvery band at base; ventrals and pectorals a smoky greenish gray. Head small, slender, subconic, its length 3.6 to 4 in body, its greatest depth less than in *I. anguilla*, 4.9 to 5.2 in body; interorbital space flat or slightly convex; occipital region and shoulders gently rounded and covered with thin, close-fitting skin; mouth more nearly terminal than in *anguilla*, the upper jaw only slightly longer than the lower; lips somewhat thicker than in preceding species; maxillary barbels long and slender, reaching past gill-opening; eye oval, lying above median axis of body and nearer upper than lower surface of head; diameter of orbit 4 to 8 in head. Dorsal fin high, placed a little nearer snout than adipose, distance from snout to dorsal 2.5 to 2.7 in length; dorsal spine usually rather more robust and shorter than in *I. furcatus*, 1.4 to 2.2 in head, its posterior edge usually almost smooth. Caudal fin deeply forked, the upper lobe longer and more slender than the lower. Anal fin short, composed of 24 to 29 rays, including rudiments, its base from 3.4 to 3.7 in length of body,

MUDCAT, *Leptops olivaris* (Rafinesque).

CHANNEL-CAT, *Ictalurus Punctatus* (Rafinesque)

the free margin rounded. Pectoral spine about equal in length to dorsal; humeral process one half length of pectoral spine.

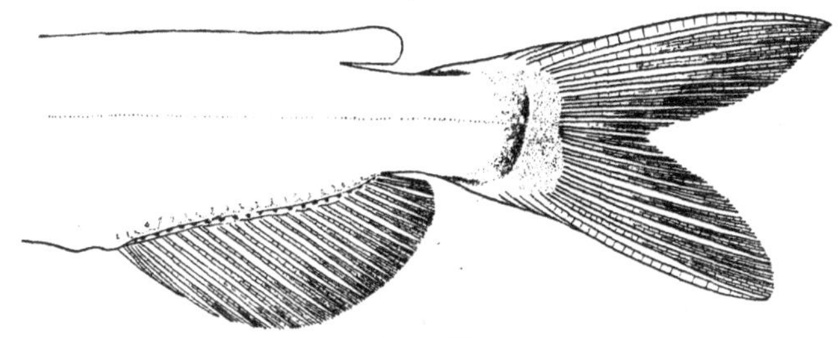

FIG. 51
Anal and caudal fins of *Ictalurus punctatus.*

This is the most abundant of our true catfishes. It is commonly distributed throughout the state, occurring in 171 of our collections, in all our river basins, and in all our principal classes of situation except the glacial lakes of northeastern Illinois. The young of this species have, however, a much wider range than the adults, and are frequently abundant in headwater streams and creeks in which full-grown individuals are never taken.

The channel-cat is about equally common in the three sections of the state, and approximately so in the three classes of our streams. The frequency coefficients for rivers of the first and second classes and for creeks are 1.02, 1.6, and 1.37 respectively. In lakes and sloughs it is much less abundant, its frequency ratio in 549 collections from such situations being but .39. It has a decided preference for clear swift waters, but not so general or so strong as to exclude it to any appreciable degree from the lower Illinoisan glaciation.

It is found throughout the Mississippi Valley, the Gulf and Great Lake regions, and northward to Ontario and Winnipeg, being especially abundant in the Red River at the latter place. Southward it extends to the Alabama River and the Florida peninsula, Louisiana, Texas, and the rivers of northern Mexico.

This fish is often known by fishermen as the "fiddler" or "blue Fulton," but anglers on the upper Illinois and the Fox usually refer to it as the "channel-cat." It is seldom taken of more than five pounds weight, although specimens are occasionally seen weighing from fifteen to twenty pounds. It is "a trimmer, more active fish than any of the related species, * * * living in clearer, more swiftly flowing water," for these reasons being well esteemed by anglers in many localities. Its flesh is likewise firmer, and perhaps more flaky and better flavored than that of any of the other catfishes.

Our knowledge of its food is based upon an examination of 43 specimens taken from the Illinois and the Mississippi rivers during the spring, summer, and autumn months of 1878, 1880, and 1887. About a fourth of the food consisted of vegetable matter, much of it miscellaneous and accidental. Three specimens, however, had eaten nothing but algæ, and fragments of pondweed (*Potamogeton*) made 20 per cent. of the food of another three. A single fish had fed on still-house slops; and a dead rat, pieces of ham, and other animal debris attested the easy-going appetite of this thrifty species. Pieces of fish were found in all of this group, commonly, however, of so large a size as to make it certain that they were the debris of the fishing boats. Occasionally fishes evidently taken alive composed the whole food. Mollusks, about equally large water-snails and large thin clams (probably in most cases *Anodonta*), were a decidedly important element, being found in 15 of the 43 fishes. They amounted to 15 per cent. of the food of the group, and several specimens had taken little or nothing else. Notwithstanding the number of bivalves eaten by this fish, no fragment of a shell was ever found in their stomachs, but the bodies of the mollusks seem to have been separated, while yet living, from the shells, as indicated by their fresh condition and by the fact that the shell muscles were scarcely ever present. Fishermen say that they are often first notified of the presence of catfishes in their seines by seeing the fragments of clams floating on the surface, disgorged by the struggling captives. Still more interesting and curious is the fact that the spiral-shelled mollusks found in the stomachs of these fishes were almost invariably naked, the more or less mutilated bodies having only the opercles attached. The shells are evidently cracked in the jaws of the fish and rejected before the food is swallowed. As many as 120 bodies and opercles of water-snails (*Melantho* and *Vivipara*) were by us taken from the stomach of a single Illinois River cat-fish. Insects were, however, a principal food of the specimens studied, making 44 per cent. of all, and eaten by 28 of the fishes. Five, in fact, had eaten nothing else, and others had taken 90 per cent., or more, of insects, mostly aquatic, although now and then a fish had filled itself with terrestrial specimens. Most of the aquatic insects were larvæ of day-flies, dragon-flies, and gnats, to be found only on the bottom. Our records indicate that this fish spawned in May in 1898 (Craig). The spawning season in the Wabash is said by Dr. Jordan to begin in June.

The channel-cat is taken very frequently in bait nets and baskets, the former being called by the fishermen "fiddler-nets." These are baited usually with "dough-balls," made by mixing flour and water, allowing the paste to sour, and then baking it; or, in summer, with "roasting ears" of corn which become sour after soaking in water for a day or so. The sour smell of either the dough or the corn is said to be especially attractive to this fish. Separate statistics of the fisheries of this species are not available, although it may be said to constitute the bulk of the catfishes (not including bullheads) of the annual Illinois River catch, which was 241,000 lb in 1899.*

GENUS **AMEIURUS** RAFINESQUE

BULLHEADS; HORNED POUT

Body moderately elongate, robust anteriorly, the caudal peduncle much compressed. Head large, wide. Supraoccipital bone extended backward, terminating in a more or less acute point, which is entirely separate from the second interspinal buckler, leaving a gap in the bony bridge from occiput to dorsal fin. Mouth large, the upper jaw in most species the longer. Teeth on premaxillaries and dentaries in broad bands, of equal breadth and without backward prolongations at the angles. Anal fin of varying length, its rays 17 to 35. Caudal fin short, truncate, or only slightly emarginate in typical species, more or less deeply forked in those species (as *A. lacustris*) which approach the genus *Ictalurus*. Color various, usually darker than in *Ictalurus*, species found in Illinois being yellow, brown, black, or mottled.

Species numerous, swarming in every pond and sluggish stream in the central and eastern United States; one species found in China. All of the local species except the one first described (*A. lacustris*) are smaller than the channel-cats, not often exceeding 12 inches in length. All are of value as food fishes.

KEY TO THE SPECIES OF **AMEIURUS** FOUND IN ILLINOIS

a. Caudal fin deeply forked.. **lacustris.**

aa. Caudal fin rounded, truncate or slightly emarginate.

b. Anal rays 24 to 27, including rudiments, usually 25 or 26; caudal fin rounded posteriorly; color waxy yellow to greenish, sometimes blackish above.... .... **natalis.**

* Statistics of the Illinois Fishermen's Association.

bb. Anal rays 17 to 24, including rudiments, seldom more than 23; caudal fin always evidently emarginate.

c. Anal rays 21 to 24, usually 22 or 23, including rudiments; pectoral spine in young with 5 to 10 well-developed strong and sharp teeth on its posterior edge, their length more than half the diameter of the spine, becoming more numerous and relatively much reduced in size in adults, in which they range from 10 to 25; black pigment on anal fin typically densest on membranes near their free margin, in spots forming an obscure longitudinal bar near base of fin, or in faint mottlings irregularly distributed on both membranes and rays; in pale unmottled specimens both the membranes and the rays about equally pigmented.................. **nebulosus.**

cc. Anal rays 17 to 20, usually 18 or 19, including rudiments; pectoral spine at all ages entire or only slightly roughened behind, or (rarely) in adults with 5 to 10 obscure weak and blunt teeth on its posterior edge; outer ⅔ of anal membranes uniformly pigmented, always darker than the rays, the fin never mottled or barred or uniformly pigmented on both membranes and rays as in **c**....................................... **melas.**

AMEIURUS LACUSTRIS (WALBAUM)

CATFISH OF THE LAKES*

Walbaum, 1792, Artedi Pisc., 144 (**Gadus**).
G., V, 100 (**borealis**); J. & G., 108 and 882 (**Ictalurus lacustris, I. nigricans,** [part]); M. V., 39 (**nigricans,** part); J. & E., I, 137; J., 66 (**nigricans,** part); F., 83 (**Ictalurus nigricans,** part); L., 9.

Large fishes with the tail forked as in *Ictalurus* and with the occipito-dorsal bridge nearly complete, but with the dark coloration and broad, depressed head of *Ameiurus*; weight ordinarily 5 to 15 pounds, sometimes 40 pounds.† Depth 4.5 in length; caudal peduncle stout, its depth 1.6 in its length. Color dark slaty to bluish black above, paler below; without dusky spots; anal dusky-edged. Head broad and depressed, 3.8 in length; width of head 1.2 in its length; interorbital space flat, 1.8 in head; eye 8.3 in head, 4.6 in interorbital distance; nose 2.5; upper jaw longer than lower; maxillary barbels to gill-opening. Dorsal fin I–6, inserted nearer snout than adipose; dorsal distance 2.7 in length; spine short and bluntly pointed, about as long as nose, its posterior edge not serrate; caudal deeply forked; anal rays 24; pectoral spine about same length as dorsal, weakly serrate behind; humeral process about ⅓ pectoral spine.

Described from a single specimen taken at Green Bay, Wis., in 1904.

This species is peculiar to the Great Lake basin, being common in the Great Lakes and the St. Lawrence River. It was long confused by American ichthyologists with the great blue cat (*Ictalurus furcatus*) of the Mississippi River. Little is

* Recent studies by Dr. Evermann (Bull. U. S. Nat. Mus. No. 47, III, 2788) have shown that this species is probably confined to the Great Lakes and the St. Lawrence basin, the specimens of "Great Mississippi Catfish" hitherto described from the Mississippi under the names *nigricans*, *ponderosus*, and *lacustris* belonging to *Ictalurus furcatus*.

† The large size, 150 ℔, assigned to the species by Jordan & Evermann (Bull. 47) and by Bean, l. c., is due to inclusion with it of Bean's *A. ponderosus*. Jordan and Evermann in the appendix to Pt. III. of Bulletin 47 state that the skeleton of *A. ponderosus* is that of an *Ictalurus*.

known distinctively of its habits, commercial value, or edible qualities. M. Montpetit, writing of the fishes of Canada, speaks enthusiastically of it as a food species, and describes the methods of catching it in the St. Lawrence.

AMEIURUS NATALIS (Le Sueur)

YELLOW BULLHEAD

(Pl., p. 187; Map LIII)

Le Sueur, 1819, Mém. Mus., V, 154 (**Pimelodus**).

G., V, 101 (**Amiurus**); J. & G., 105 and 881 (**bolli**); M. V., 40; J. & E., I, 139; N., 50 (**cupreus**); J., 66 (**Amiurus**); F., 83 (**Ictalurus**); F, F.. II. 7, 459 (**Ictalurus**); L., 9.

Body stout, sometimes obese, rather short and thick and tapering but little from dorsal to adipose fin, depth 3.5 to 3.9 in length; profile low, the elevation from snout to dorsal fin 10° to 14°; caudal peduncle deep, 1.7 to 2.2 in head; skin thick, the epidermis of belly very coarse; fleshy prominences covered with thick and loose skin on either side of a median groove through occipital region to base of dorsal. Length 12 to 18 inches, not often found over 12 inches. Color of upper parts yellowish green to blackish, the sides lighter, yellowish brown or waxy yellow; belly yellow; nasal and maxillary barbels light brownish, lower barbels pinkish buff; fin membranes very weakly pigmented, the rays lighter. Head large, broad, and somewhat depressed, its length 3.1 to 3.5 in body, its greatest width through the cheeks, the breadth here about same as depth of body at front of dorsal; nose short and broadly rounded; mouth wide, horizontal, upper jaw usually slightly longer than lower, maxillary barbels reaching about to posterior edge of opercles; eye small, 7.2 to 8.5 in head. Dorsal fin small and low; the spine rather short, 2.2 to 2.6 in body. Caudal rather short, rounded posteriorly. Anal fin of 24 to 27 rays, including rudiments, usually 25 or 26, the longest rays somewhat less than depth of caudal peduncle; base of fin 3.5 to 4 in length of body, the free margin but slightly rounded, almost straight from the fifth to the twentieth ray. Pectoral spine strong, its length about same as dorsal spine, usually smooth, but sometimes weakly serrate near tip; humeral process 1.8 to 2.2 in pectoral spine.

An abundant species throughout the state, but much less so than the black bullhead (*Ameiurus melas*). Taken in 122 of our collections. It is commonest in creeks, and next in lowland lakes, the coefficients for these two situations being 2.22 and 1.18 respectively. In local distribution it contrasts in an interesting way with the brown bullhead, which is much the commonest in lakes and ponds, and comparatively scarce in creeks, where its frequency coefficient is only .28. These species resemble each other so closely that they are not often distinguished by fishermen, and their food and habits are virtually identical.

Their mutual rivalries might hence result to their common disadvantage except for a partial avoidance of competition by a difference of local and ecological preference. Our collection data indicate for this species a strong preference for muddy water, its frequency coefficient for streams with a mud bottom being 1.72. Consistent with this fact is its distribution in the lower Illinoisan glaciation. We have found it in all our river basins, including the Michigan drainage area and the north-eastern glacial lakes, but have not taken it in the extreme north-western part of the state. It has also been absent in our collections from the main streams of the Wabash, the Ohio, and the Mississippi, and from the short creeks of the Mississippi bluffs. It seems with us to be more abundant southward, and has occurred with the greatest frequency in the streams of the Wabash Valley.

It is generally distributed from Lakes Erie and Huron and the smaller lakes of Ontario to North Carolina and the Florida peninsula, the Alabama River, and Texas. It occurs also in the Arkansas River and up the Missouri to South Dakota. It is one of the commonest and best known bullheads throughout its range.

As illustrated by the food of a dozen specimens, this species has the habits of a scavenger. One of these fishes had gorged itself with the waste of a fish boat, and one had made the greater part of its last meal from the remnants of a dead cat. Three of these specimens had eaten fishes taken alive, and four others had eaten crawfishes. May-fly larvæ and a few water-snails were the only other objects worth mentioning. Seven young specimens, from two to three and a half inches long, had fed principally on *Entomostraca*, the remainder of their food being chiefly small mollusks and insect larvæ.

This fish is distinguished from the brown bullhead (*A. nebulosus*) only by the more observant of our fishermen, some of whom call it "greaser" or "slick bullhead," its skin being very thin, and the fish, in consequence, particularly hard to dress. Its maximum weight is 1½ to 2 ℔.

The yellow bullhead spawned at Havana in May in 1898 (Craig). Females with ripe spawn were seen in market at Meredosia on May 24, 1900 (Large). In the words of Dr. Jordan these fishes are "small, but good eating," as we have ourselves proven.

YELLOW BULLHEAD, *Ameiurus natalis* (Le Sueur)

AMEIURUS NEBULOSUS (Le Sueur)

SPECKLED BULLHEAD; COMMON BULLHEAD; BROWN BULLHEAD

(Map LIV)

Le Sueur, 1819, Mém. Mus., V, 149 (**Pimelodus**).
J. & G., 104 (**catus**); M. V., 40; J. & E., I, 140; N., 50 (**albidus, atrarius, vulgaris**); J., 66 and 67 (**catus, xanthocephalus** (?), **marmoratus, vulgaris**); F., 83 (**Ictalurus nebulosus**, part); F, F., II. 7, 460 (**Ictalurus**); L., 10.

Body typically elongate, never more than moderately robust, rather more compressed than in *A. melas*; depth from 3.5 to 4.3 in length, usually nearly or a little more than 4; profile long and almost straight, the shoulders never prominent and no groove before dorsal; skin thin, fitting closely over top of head and nape, that of belly consisting of a very thin and delicate epidermal layer over a thick layer of unpigmented connective tissue. Size ranging larger than in the next species, reaching 18 inches. Color variable, usually a rather dark yellowish brown faintly clouded, more strongly mottled with darker in the nominal variety *marmoratus*, sometimes nearly black; under parts, including chin, breast, and belly, pale gray, pinkish, or satiny whitish; nasal and maxillary barbels of same shade as top of head; lower barbels slaty to pinkish white, sometimes faintly marbled with darker; fin membranes less strongly pigmented than in *A. melas*, the black on anal typically densest in the membranes near their free margin, in spots which form a more or less faint longitudinal bar near base of fin, or in faint mottlings irregularly distributed on both membranes and rays; in pale unmottled specimens both the rays and membranes weakly, but about equally pigmented. Head 3.2 to 3.6 in body, subconic, rather narrower and more slender than in the next species and somewhat more depressed, its length always considerably greater than its width, which is contained 1.2 to 1.3 in length of head in adults, in length of body from 3.9 to 4.7; nose longer and the snout more sharply rounded than in *A. melas*; upper jaw usually distinctly longer than lower; maxillary barbel usually reaching considerably beyond gill-opening, often beyond humeral process. Dorsal spine variable, 1.8 to 2.5 in head, as a rule rather long. Caudal typically somewhat more deeply emarginate than in the next species. Anal fin of 21 to 24 rays, including rudiments, usually 22 or 23, its base from 3.2 to 4.1 in length of body; free margin of fin from about the eighth to the fifteenth ray but little rounded, sometimes almost straight, the rays rather slender and split usually less than a third of the way to base. Pectoral spine as a rule rather long, curved, and sharply pointed, its length 1.8 to 2.4 in head, usually less than 2; the posterior edge in the young furnished with 6 to 10 well-developed retrorse teeth, whose length

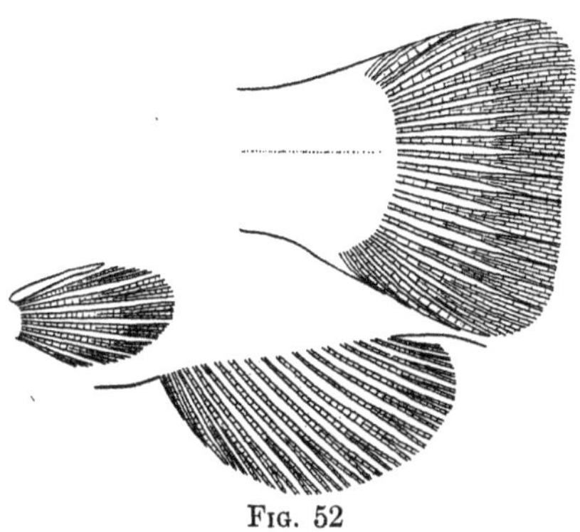

Fig. 52

Caudal, anal, and pectoral fins of *Ameiurus nebulosus.*

is half, or almost equal to, diameter of spine, the teeth relatively much smaller and more numerous in adults, in which their number ranges from 10 to 25; humeral process longer and sharper than in *A. melas*.

The brown bullhead, distributed throughout the length of the state, is nevertheless the least abundant of our common horned pouts. As remarked under the preceding species, it is peculiar in its preference for stagnant waters, of both lowland and upland lakes and ponds, and it is next commonest in the larger streams. Our frequency coefficients are 1.46 for glacial lakes, 1.25 for lowland lakes, and .94 for the larger rivers. We have found it most frequently in the immediate course of the Illinois River, and have not taken it at all in the northwestern part of the state, nor at any point within the lower Illinoisan glaciation.

Outside our area it is reported from lakes of New Brunswick to those of the Saskatchewan system, including the Great Lakes in general, and from thence southward to the Florida peninsula and to Texas. It has been introduced also into many rivers of the Pacific states, and into the small lakes of southern Oregon, in all of which it has become excessively abundant. It is said by Bean to be the commonest catfish in Lake Erie and its tributaries. It is the common bullhead or horned pout of New England and New York, but in this state these names are much more likely to be applied to the more abundant black bullhead (*A. melas*), the commonest of its kind in the smaller creeks. The present species is the principal bullhead of the market catches from the larger rivers.

The food of 13 specimens examined by us was unusually simple for that of a catfish, consisting chiefly of small bivalve mollusks, larvæ of insects taken upon the bottom, distillery slops, and accidental rubbish. One of the specimens had eaten eighteen leeches, leeches appearing in the food of four others, and a few had taken terrestrial insects and univalve mollusks.

The adults are almost always more or less blotched or mottled, all gradations between the well-mottled form (*marmoratus*) and the typical brown *nebulosus* being found regularly in the same market catches. These fishes have thick skin, and are easier to dress than the yellow bullheads (*A. natalis*). We have found both the mottled and the brown forms, with occasional specimens of the black bullhead (*A. melas*), indiscriminately referred to as "bullpouts" or "speckled bullheads" by the fishermen who were dressing them.

The horned pout are "dull and blundering fellows," fond of the mud, and growing best in weedy ponds and rivers without current. They stay near the bottom, moving slowly about with their barbels widely spread, watching for anything eatable. They will take any kind of bait from an angleworm to a piece of tomato can, without hesitation or coquetry, and they seldom fail to swallow the hook. They are very tenacious of life, opening and shutting their mouths for half an hour after their heads have been taken off. They spawn in spring, and the old fishes lead the young in great schools near the shore, caring for them as a hen cares for her chickens. "A bloodthirsty and bullying set of rangers, with ever a lance at rest and ready to do battle with their nearest neighbor."—THOREAU.

It is known that many pond-stocking experiments with this species in France failed at first owing to the failure to select the proper kind of situations.

These fishes will live where no others can survive, and when the air supply is bad far past the point of supporting life in ordinary fishes, they have merely to come leisurely to the surface and renew the supply in their swim-bladders. In the late fall they become sluggish and cease feeding, often "mudding up," or burying themselves more or less in soft leafy ooze along shore.* They will lie dormant in the mud at the bottom of dried-out shallows for weeks at a time without harm, and have even been found, according to some (Dean), in cocoon-like clods of nearly dried mud, still alive. In pond culture experiments in Georgia (Bull. U. S. Fish Comm., 1884, p. 32) they were found to relish apples, persimmons, watermelons, and even corn, wheat, and sorghum seed. They will take almost any kind of bait. The charge of spawn-eating has frequently been preferred against this fish, as well as its near relatives, especially by the whitefish and shad culturists. The evidence for such a view is, however, scanty.†

The brown bullhead spawns in spring, the time having been May in 1898 at Havana (Craig). Their nests were found by Professor Birge in shallow bays with sandy bottom, six inches to two feet deep. The eggs are laid in masses similar to those of the frog, and are of a beautiful cream-color. In aquarium

* Shallow lakes in Vermont are mowed in the spring by the farmers to allow seining for them.—Evermann and Kendall, Rep. U. S. Fish Comm., 1894.

† It is interesting in this connection to note that Herr Fuhrmann, writing of recent experiments carried out in France (Bull. Soc. Acclim., Vol. 51, p. 351, Nov., 1904), states that this species does not eat the eggs of *Coregonus* except when they are *very fresh*, that is before they are hardened by the water, which occurs very quickly after they are deposited.

experiments by Smith and Harron (Bull. U. S. Fish Comm., 1902, p. 150) the eggs hatched in 5 days, during which time both parents constantly watched them, fanning them with their fins. At times the male will take masses of eggs into his mouth, possibly to clean them, as they are ordinarily soon ejected. The young are watched by the male and are sometimes mouthed as are the eggs.

This species is of fair food quality, being perhaps somewhat inferior to the yellow bullhead. It was successfully introduced about twenty years ago into Germany, France, the Netherlands, and England, and, in the continental countries especially, its flesh is much esteemed. It has multiplied very rapidly since its introduction into California, being in fact one of the readiest of fresh-water species to undergo acclimatization. Separate statistics of the Illinois product of this catfish are not available, though it may probably safely be said that it forms by far the major part of the total bullhead catch, which was 499,100 ℔ for the Illinois River in 1899.

AMEIURUS MELAS (Rafinesque)

BLACK BULLHEAD

(Map LV)

Rafinesque, 1820, Q. J. Sci. Lit. Arts, Lond., 51 (**Silurus**).

J. & G., 104 and 881 (**Silurus xanthocephalus** and **A. brachyacanthus**); M. V., 41; J. & E., I, 141; N., 50 (**confinis, pullus**); J., 67; F., 83 (**Ictalurus nebulosus**, part); L., 10.

Body typically robust, shorter and deeper than in the preceding species, but sometimes quite elongate, the depth 3.1 to 3.5 in length of body in adults; profile slightly convex and hardly so long as in *nebulosus*; top of head and occipital region covered with thick and rather loose skin; shoulders rather prominent on each side of a median groove in well nourished adults; skin noticeably thicker and tougher than in the last species, that of belly consisting of a thick and coarsely cellular epidermal layer over a thin layer of pigmentless connective tissue. Size rather small, not often over 12 inches in length. Color as a rule very dark brown or green to black above, the sides with more or less luster of green or gold; under parts of head and body greenish, plumbeous, or yellowish as far back as anal fin, never satiny white; fin membranes dusky to black, the rays usually much lighter, the contrast in color quite evident in the anal fin,

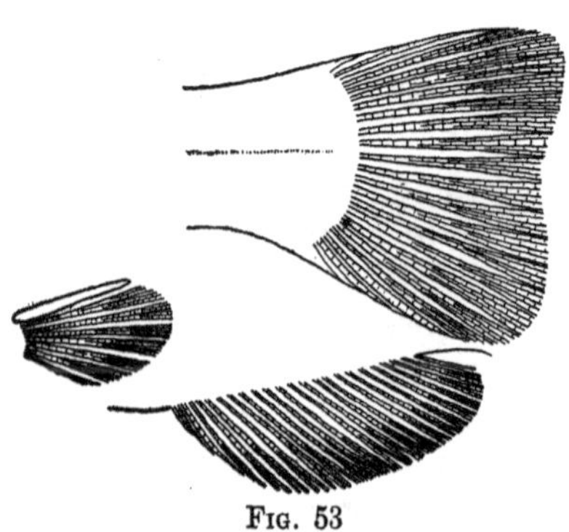

Fig. 53

Caudal, anal, and pectoral fins of *Ameiurus melas*.

BLACK BULLHEAD, *Ameiurus melas* (Rafinesque)

which is never marbled or equally pigmented on both membranes and rays as in *A. nebulosus*. Head heavy, 3.1 to 3.5 in length, rather short and much broadened behind, its greatest breadth 3.5 to 4 in length of body, usually about 3.7 and sometimes almost equaling its length, in which the width is contained 1.1 to 1.2, usually less than 1.2; mouth wide, the snout short and broadly rounded; jaws about equal; maxillary barbels reaching to or only slightly beyond opercular opening, seldom to tip of humeral process. Dorsal spine variable, in typical specimens rather short and robust and quite or nearly straight, but sometimes long and slender and considerably curved. Caudal slightly emarginate. Anal fin short, of 17 to 20 rays, including rudiments, usually 18 or 19, its base from 3.9 to 4.4 in length of body, the free margin distinctly rounded; anal rays rather stout, those about middle of fin split almost half way to base. Pectoral spine rather shorter and blunter than in *A. nebulosus*, usually not much curved, its length 2.4 to 3.6 in head, usually a little less than 3; the posterior edge usually entire or only slightly roughened, or, more rarely (in adults) with 5 to 10 indistinct weak and short teeth; humeral process rather short, rugose, and bluntly pointed. This species much resembles *A. nebulosus*, and is quite variable, but may usually be distinguished by its smaller size, shorter and deeper anal fin, and shorter pectoral spines.

This, the common bullhead of the Illinois boy, abundant everywhere in our smaller streams, is distributed throughout the entire length and breadth of the state. In the main features of its distribution it agrees with the yellow bullhead, being, like that species, decidedly the most abundant in creeks, and least so in the larger rivers. Its frequency coefficients for our 247 collections containing it are as follows, in the order of their size: creeks, 2.25; the smaller rivers, 1.26; lowland lakes, 1.00; glacial lakes, .55; the larger rivers, .47. This species also shows a notable preference for the more quiet and muddier parts of the streams it inhabits, as shown by our ratios of 1.58 for a muddy bottom and 2.37 for stagnant water or a quiet current. Notwithstanding the similar ecological distribution of the black and yellow bullheads, they show an observable tendency to a local separation, as illustrated by a study of our collections of the species in detail, 247 of the black bullhead and 122 of the yellow. These represent 319 separate collections of fishes, only 50 of which contain examples of the two species together, the less numerous species, *natalis*, occurring in 72 of these collections without the more numerous one.* With reference to the

* Recurring to our detailed collection records, bringing into comparison as to frequency of associate occurrence *natalis* and *nebulosus* on the one hand and *natalis* and *melas* on the other, and computing the coefficients of association for each of these two pairs of species, we get for the first pair a larger coefficient (3.07) than for the second pair (2.12). Since the species of the first pair differ widely in the kinds of water bodies which they principally inhabit and those of the second pair agree closely in this respect, we see in the distribution of these species

different sections of the state, we find this bullhead most abundant in the creeks of the Mississippi bluffs and in the valleys of the Wabash and the Kaskaskia, where its ratios of frequency, mentioned in the above-named order, are 1.23, 1.58, and 1.71. We have found it least abundant in the streams of the Michigan drainage.

Generally speaking, it is not distributed so far to the northward or eastward as our other abundant bullheads. Its range extends from the Genesee River in New York through the Great Lakes of Ontario, Erie, and Michigan to the Missouri basin, which it seems to occupy thoughout, and thence southward to Kansas, Alabama, and Texas. It is especially abundant west of the Mississippi. It is said by Jordan to thrive in small ponds, particularly in those with a mud bottom.

When the studies on the food of fishes from which our information on that subject is chiefly drawn, were made by the senior writer in 1888, this species was not clearly distinguished from the brown bullhead, *nebulosus*, and the statements made under the latter head relate in part to the present species. The food of 36 specimens, doubtless composed of these two species commingled, is distinguished by the fact that nearly a fourth of it consisted of aquatic vegetation of various kinds, including distillery refuse eaten by one of the fishes. Two of these bullheads had filled themselves with other fish, a sunfish and a perch among them. Small bivalve mollusks made a fifth of the food, and river snails and aquatic insects—the latter somewhat more than a fourth of the entire quantity—together with crawfishes and other crustaceans, were the other more important elements.

The habits of the species are, so far as known, very similar to those of the brown bullhead. It is of smaller size, and, owing to its local distribution, is not very common in the market catches, which are usually made from the larger streams.

This fish was spawning at Meredosia May 4, 1899.

---

evidence of two methods of avoiding competition over the same territory, one by a difference of preference as to size and kinds of waters inhabited (*natalis* and *nebulosus*) and the other by a difference in the kinds of situations chiefly frequented (*natalis* and *melas*). A similar computation for *natalis* and *nebulosus* gives us a still smaller associative coefficient (1.9). In other words, of these three pairs of species, the yellow and the brown bullheads are found least frequently in the same kinds of waters, and least frequently also in the same situations; the black and the yellow bullheads are found most frequently in the same kinds of waters, but with medium frequency in the same situations; and the yellow and the brown species are found least frequently in the same waters, but most frequently associated in the same situations.

Genus **LEPTOPS** Rafinesque

Body elongate, and much depressed anteriorly. Head large, wide and depressed; skull covered with thick skin; supraoccipital bone entirely free from head of second interspinal. Teeth in broad bands on premaxillaries and dentaries, the band of teeth on upper jaw continued backward on each side in an elongated triangular extension. Lower jaw longer than upper. Dorsal spine enveloped in thick skin. Anal rays about 13. Caudal oblong, subtruncate, with numerous accessory rays. One species known; a large catfish, living in the muddy bottoms of deep rivers.

LEPTOPS OLIVARIS (Rafinesque)

MUD-CAT; YELLOW CAT; GOUJON; MORGAN CAT

(Map LVI)

Rafinesque, 1818, Amer. Month. Mag., 355 (**Silurus**).

G., V, 101 (**Pimelodus punctulatus**); J. & G., 102 and 881 (**Pilodictis**); M. V., 41; J. & E., I, 143; N., 50 (**Hopladelus**); J., 67 (**Pelodicthys**); F., 83; F. F., II. 7, 462; L., 10.

Body elongate, depth 4.4 to 5.2 in length, back broad and flattened as far back as origin of ventrals, the region between ventrals and front of adipose very nearly cylindrical; caudal peduncle narrow and compressed, 2.5 to 3.1 in head; profile straight as far as nape, the elevation from nape to dorsal somewhat abrupt. Size large, reaching a weight of 50 to 75 pounds. Color usually dark olive, variously mottled in the young, the mottling tending to become obsolete in adults; upper parts darker, belly yellowish or grayish; fins colored about as adjacent parts of body, usually darker near margins; dorsal and adipose fins marbled with darker in young specimens. Head long and very broad, much depressed and exceedingly flattened above, its length 3.2 to 4, its width 3.7 to 4.4 in length of body; interorbital space very wide and almost flat, 2 to 2.4 in head; lower jaw longer than upper, lips rather thin; barbels short and slender, the maxillary pair falling much short of gill-opening; eye very small, 8 to 14 in head, situated far forward and high up on head and directed obliquely upward. Dorsal spine very slender, its length about ½ height of fin; distance from snout 2.3 to 2.5 in length. Caudal very little emarginate. Anal short, its rays 12 to 15. Pectoral spine short and robust, 3 to 4.4 in head, much flattened dorso-ventrally, its anterior and posterior edges roughened or weakly serrate; humeral process short, its length less than ⅓ of pectoral spine.

This huge catfish, one of the largest of our river species, is common in the Illinois and the Mississippi rivers, and occurs in our collections from the Rock and the Wabash. We have it also from a branch of the Little Wabash, in Wayne county; from Crooked creek, in Brown county; and from Spoon and Green rivers. Our frequency coefficients are 3.25 for the larger rivers, 1.29 for the smaller, .5 for lowland lakes, and .34 for creeks. It is perhaps best known to the fishermen of the Mississippi River as the "Morgan cat," and less often referred to as the "cushawn," a corruption of the French *goujon*. Other local names are mud-cat, flat-belly, and nigger-belly.

This fish frequently reaches a weight of 50 to 75 pounds, and is said by Dr. Evermann occasionally to weigh as much as a hundred pounds. It lives and feeds on or near the bottom, and fishermen at Havana say that they frequently find it in hollow logs. Fishes are, so far as known, its principal food. Among those eaten by it we have observed a common river sunfish (*Lepomis*), several minnows, and a bullhead. In the Southern States, fresh hickory-shad is greatly valued as a live bait for the mud-cat, and crawfishes and cut bait made from eels are also used. This fish is caught both on set-lines and in fyke-nets, and is often taken by jugging, the bait being attached to a jug filled with air, the effect of which is finally to bring the worn-out fish to the surface. It is commonly regarded as one of the very best of the catfishes for food, the flesh being of a fine texture and an excellent flavor. The spawning time in Illinois is in May or later, according to Havana fishermen. The species is found in all suitable waters throughout the Mississippi Valley, and in the Gulf states, from Alabama west and south to Mexico. It is most abundant in the lower courses of the larger streams, and in the bayous and overflow ponds of the lower Mississippi Valley.

Genus **NOTURUS** (Rafinesque)

Form more or less elongate, the head broad and much flattened above, the body behind dorsal nearly cylindrical. Skin thick and tough and appreciably villose. Band of teeth in upper jaw with a backward prolongation on each side, as in *Leptops*. Adipose fin adnate to the back, separated from the caudal by a notch, as in *Schilbeodes*. A poison gland present at base of pectoral fin. The single species belonging to this genus is similar in appearance and habit to the species of *Schilbeodes*, though it grows to a much greater size and frequents large streams rather than brooks. The broad flat skull of *Noturus*, the dentition, and the thick and villose skin, are characters which ally the genus closely with *Leptops*.

NOTURUS FLAVUS Rafinesque

STONECAT

(Map LVII)

Rafinesque, 1818, Amer. Month. Mag., 41.
G., V, 104 (also **platycephalus**); J. & G., 100; M. V., 41; J. & E., I, 144; N., 50; J., 67; F., 84; L., 10.

Body moderately elongate, broad and flattened in front of dorsal, subcylindrical behind it, the tail compressed; depth 4 to 5 in length. Length 9 inches.* Color above almost uniform olive-green, sometimes blackish; sides of head and body shading to yellowish brown or yellow, belly whitish; a saddle-like or crescentic blotch of yellowish or gray behind dorsal and usually a large but fainter squarish one in front of it; lips, chin, and lower barbels yellow; fins of about same shade as adjacent parts, with edges paler. Head very broad, much flattened above, its length 3.6 to 3.9, its width 4 to 5 in length of body; upper jaw projecting, lips thick and coarsely striate; maxillary barbels short, about half length of head; eye 4.6 to 6 in head, placed high and directed well upward. Dorsal fin small, its distance 2.4 to 2.8 in body, the spine very short, but little more than ⅓ the height of fin. Caudal not quite symmetrically rounded, the upper posterior margin usually truncate; notch between adipose and caudal deep. Anal fin of about 16 rays. Pectoral spine with a few weak retrorse teeth on its anterior edge near tip, the posterior edge entire or very little roughened; humeral process very short.

This interesting little fish, commonest under stones in swift waters in the larger creeks and smaller rivers, is rather abundant and widely distributed throughout the northern half of the state, but has not been once taken by us south of Douglas county. It is hence wholly absent from the lower Illinoisan glaciation, and is confined to the Mississippi drainage, in our experience, except for three localities on the headwaters of the Big Vermilion and the Kaskaskia. The frequency ratios of our 40 collections are 3.19 for the smaller rivers, 2.06 for creeks, and .58 for the largest streams. It has not once appeared from stagnant waters of either highland or lowland lakes. Its decided preference for a swift current and a clean bottom is shown by our coefficients of 5.31 for the latter situation and 2.75 for the former.

The peculiar limitation of the range of this fish in Illinois seems entirely independent of its general distribution, which includes the territory from Canada through the Great Lakes to Virginia and Tennessee, and thence west and southwest to Montana, Wyoming, Nebraska, and Texas. In Indiana it occurs, according to Hay, in the Wabash and its tributaries, in the Kaskaskia, and in Lake Michigan, the St. Joseph River, and the small lakes of northern Indiana.

The species has very little value as food on account of its small size, which seldom exceeds a length of twelve inches. It is much dreaded by fishermen because of the pain produced by the punctures of its poisoned pectoral spines. It seems to have no common name, being doubtless usually mistaken for a young bullhead. Together with the other stonecats it may be easily distinguished from the bullheads (*Ameiurus*) by the fact

* Largest one in our Laboratory collections. Jordan says it sometimes reaches 12 inches.

that the long and low adipose fin is continuous with the caudal except for a shallow notch, while these fins are wholly separate in the other catfishes. According to Dr. Jordan, it lurks habitually under stones and logs. Dr. Eigenmann reports that the eggs of this species were laid, in Turkey creek, Indiana, in the latter half of June, in depressions under boards, and that they were apparently watched by the adult. The young remain for some time in the nest after hatching.

Genus **SCHILBEODES** Bleeker

Body more or less elongate, subcylindrical anteriorly, the tail compressed. Head less depressed than in *Noturus*. Skin rather thin, very finely villose or almost smooth. Supraoccipital bone free from head of second interspinal. Teeth subulate, in broad bands, the band of upper jaw abruptly truncated at each end as in *Ameiurus* (without lateral backward extensions as in *Leptops* and *Noturus*). Adipose fin long and low, connected with the accessory rays of the caudal, from which it may or may not be separated by a notch. Caudal fin obliquely truncated or rounded, with numerous rudimentary or accessory rays both above and below caudal peduncle. Anal fin short, its rays 12 to 23. Ventrals much rounded. A poison gland present beneath the epidermis surrounding base of pectoral spine.

Key to the Species of **SCHILBEODES** found in Illinois

a. Pectoral spine entire behind or only slightly roughened near base;* adipose fin continuous with caudal, the notch being absent or faint, never acute.

b. Jaws equal; anterior and posterior edges of pectoral spine entire, or the anterior edge very slightly roughened near tip; color purplish olive to dark brownish, without noticeable specking; three dark streaks on sides............ **gyrinus.**

bb. Lower jaw included; pectoral spine entire in front or with 1 or 2 obscure points near tip, entire or weakly toothed near base behind; color dark brown to blackish, flecked rather coarsely with darker; dorsal, anal, and caudal fins pale-edged.......... **nocturnus.**

aa. Pectoral spine with distinct posterior serræ, which are recurved and in length more than ⅓ the diameter of spine; notch between adipose and caudal fins always more or less acute.

c. Pectoral spine short, 3 in head, the posterior serræ not ½ diameter of spine; notch between caudal and adipose fins usually shallow; color light brown, sometimes faintly mottled; a large squarish spot of lighter color on back before dorsal and a smaller crescentic one behind it.......... **exilis.**

cc. Pectoral spine longer, less than 2 in head, its posterior serræ strong and in length nearly equaling diameter of spine; notch between adipose and caudal fins deep and acute; color grayish with black specks and larger blotches; 4 saddle-like blotches on back, the last but one extending upon adipose fin to its edge.......... **miurus.**

---

* Arkansas specimens of *S. nocturnus* have a few short sharp teeth near base behind (Jordan).

Tadpole Cat, *Schilbeodes gyrinus* (Mitchill)

Freckled Stonecat, *Schilbeodes nocturnus* (Jordan & Gilbert)

Slender Stonecat, *Schilbcodes exilis* (Nelson)

Brindled Stonecat, *Schilbeodes miurus* (Jordan)

TADPOLE CAT. *Schilbeodes gyrinus* (Mitchill)

STONECAT. *Noturus flavus* Rafinesque

SCHILBEODES GYRINUS (MITCHILL)

TADPOLE CAT

(MAP LVIII)

Mitchill, 1818, Amer. Month. Mag., 322 (**Silurus**).
J. & G., 98 (**Noturus**); M. V., 42 (**Noturus**); J. & E., I, 146; J., 68 (**Noturus sialis**); F., 84 (**Noturus**); F. F. II, 7, 462 (**Noturus**); L., 10.

Form robust, the body shorter and deeper than in other species; depth 3.8 to 4.4 in length. Length of adults 3 to 5 inches. Color olivaceous to almost blackish, top of head darker; translucence of skin giving rise to a marked light purplish or flesh color on sides in strong light; a dark median lateral streak on side extending to base of caudal, a similar fainter one near belly, and two higher up on side, the upper one extending along base of adipose fin; belly, breast, and chin yellowish; pupil dull dark blue, iris bluish, tinged with gold or coppery; fins plain, all except ventrals and pectorals a rather dusky olive. Head large and fleshy, broad forward, short and flat, the contour from snout to dorsal steep and almost straight; length of head 3.2 to 3.9, width 3.6 to 4.9 in length of body; interorbital space 1.6 to 2.1 in head, eye 6.3 to 7.6; jaws about equal; barbels barely reaching gill-opening. Dorsal fin placed well forward, its distance 2.5 to 2.9 in length; the spine rather long, more than ½ the height of fin, 2.4 to 2.9 in head. Caudal rather long, broadened mesially and tapering slightly to its truncate end. Anal short, its rays 13 to 15. Pectoral spine strong, its length 1.9 to 2.4 in head, tapering evenly from the base to the sharply pointed tip, its upper surface strongly ridged and grooved diagonally, not flattened as in *S. nocturnus*; the anterior edge entirely smooth or with 2 or 3 obscure points near tip; posterior edge smooth; humeral process moderate, its length less than 4 in pectoral spine. Lateral line developed anteriorly, much interrupted or altogether wanting on posterior half of body.

This fish, although distributed throughout the state, is most abundant in our collections to the southward and eastward in the branches of the Kaskaskia and the Wabash. The species enters with special freedom the lower Illinoisan glaciation, avoided by *Noturus flavus*. We have found it about equally common in large rivers, creeks, and lowland and upland lakes, but for some unexplained reason only three of our 193 collections have come from the smaller rivers. It is more abundant, relatively to the number of collections made, in still and muddy waters than in those with a rapid current and a clean bottom, our frequency coefficients for the first and second of these situations being 1.47 and 1.45 respectively. According to Professor Hay, it is accustomed to hide under stones and logs.

Generally speaking, it is a species of wide range, from the Hudson River on the east through the Great Lakes to the Dakotas and Montana, and from this line southward to the

Florida peninsula and through the valleys of the Missouri and Ohio to the Tombigbee River in Alabama.

Though the commonest of the stonecats in Illinois, it is nevertheless not usually distinguished by fishermen, and has no generally accepted common name. Like the other species of this name, it is provided with poison glands, placed just beneath the epidermis surrounding the spines of the pectoral and dorsal fins, and the wound from either of these spines is little less painful than a bee's sting. These glands are ductless, and the poison which they secrete is only liberated when the epidermis of the spine is torn.

The food of 13 specimens examined, consisted almost wholly of amphipod and isopod *Crustacea*, of various forms of *Entomostraca*, and of insect larvæ (case-worms, day-flies, and gnats) of kinds likely to be found on the bottom. A single specimen had eaten a small fish, and another a planarian worm.

Males and females taken by us June 8 were already spent, and the spawning season probably falls in May.

This little fish is too small to be used for any purpose except as bait. It is said to be very tenacious of life, and to serve as an excellent bait for black bass, against which its formidable defensive apparatus evidently does not protect it.

SCHILBEODES NOCTURNUS (Jordan & Gilbert)

FRECKLED STONECAT

(Pl., p. 196)

Jordan & Gilbert, 1886, Proc. U. S. Nat. Mus., 6 (**Noturus**).
J. & E., I, 146; L., 10.

Moderately robust, but less so than in *S. gyrinus*, the head narrower forward and the profile less steep than in that species; depth 4.8 to 5.1 in length. Size small, not found over 3 inches. Color a uniform dark brown, thickly and rather coarsely flecked with black, except on breast and belly; dorsal, adipose, caudal, and anal fins specked with black much as body, but with narrow edgings of pale. Head short and moderately broad, its length 3.8 to 4.1 in body, its greatest width in opercular region, narrower forward, 4.3 to 4.6 in body; interorbital space 1.9 to 2.4 in head; eye moderate, 4.8 to 6 in head; upper jaw longer than lower; barbels short and robust, the maxillary pair falling considerably short of gill-openings. Distance from snout to dorsal 2.8 to 3 in length; dorsal spine short, scarcely half the height of fin, 2.4 to 3.4 in head. Caudal long and somewhat tapered terminally. Anal fin short, of 15 to 16 rays, Pectoral spine moderate, its length 2 to 2.1 in head, slender towards base and widening outward, the tip acute; the upper surface comparatively flat and the diagonal grooves inconspicuous; the anterior edge with 2 or 3 obscure points near tip, posterior edge smooth or with a few weak teeth near base (not found in Illinois specimens); humeral process about 4 in pectoral spine. Lateral line usually complete.

This little species is rare in Illinois, having been taken by us but eight times—twice from creeks near Havana, three times from creeks near Lincoln, twice from tributaries of the Kaskaskia in Clinton and Shelby counties, and once from Camp creek in Henderson county. Outside our limits it is reported from sandy streams of the lower Wabash basin in Indiana, from the Poteau, Washita, and Saline rivers in Arkansas, and from the Sabine, Trinity, and Lampasas rivers in Texas. It appears to be nowhere common, and we have no information concerning its natural relations or special habits.

SCHILBEODES EXILIS (Nelson)

SLENDER STONECAT

(Pl., p. 196)

Nelson, 1876, Bull. Ill. State Lab. Nat. Hist., I. 1, 51 (**Noturus**).
J. & G., 100 (**Noturus**); M. V., 42 (**Noturus**); J. & E., I, 147; J., 67 (**Noturus**); F., 84 (**Noturus**); L., 10.

Elongate, the slenderest of our stonecats, the body almost cylindrical in region of dorsal, depth 4.9 to 6 in length, diminishing but slightly to caudal peduncle; profile low. Length 3 to 4 inches. Color yellowish brown, uniform on sides, but darker above, with a crescentic spot of lighter color on back behind dorsal and a larger squarish one on occiput; median fins pale or slightly dusky with darker margins, the contrast in color most marked in the dorsal. Head small, narrow and depressed, its length 3.9 to 4.3 in body, its width 4.8 to 5.8; interorbital space 2.2 to 2.9 in head; jaws nearly equal, the upper very slightly longer than lower; maxillary barbels not reaching gill-openings; eye 5.3 to 7.3 in head. Dorsal fin small and low, placed well forward, its distance from snout 2.9 to 3.1 in length; the spine short and sharp, scarcely half the height of fin. Caudal symmetrically rounded posteriorly; its accessory rays numerous and well developed; the notch between adipose and caudal variable, usually obscure, sometimes acute. Anal fin with 14 to 17 rays. Pectoral spine short and sharp, 2.7 to 3.1 in head, weakly serrate anteriorly near tip, the basal ⅔ of the posterior margin furnished with about 6 slender teeth, whose length is about ⅓ the diameter of the spine; humeral process obscure.

This little stonecat was originally described in the first volume of the Bulletin of the Illinois State Laboratory of Natural History, from specimens found in the Illinois River. We have since taken it from the Pecatonica at Freeport, in Stephenson county; from the Du Page River in Will county; from Honey creek in Henderson county; and from two creeks in Union county, in extreme southern Illinois. It is also reported from Wisconsin, from the Tippecanoe River in Indiana, from the Arkansas River, and from the streams of the lower part of the Missouri basin as far west as Kansas.

SCHILBEODES MIURUS (JORDAN)

BRINDLED STONECAT

(PL., P. 196; MAP LIX)

Jordan, 1877, Ann. Lyc. Nat. Hist. N. Y., Vol. XI, 371 (**Noturus**).

J. & G., 99 (**Noturus**); M. V., 42 (**Noturus**); J. & E., I, 148; N., 50 (**Noturus marginatus**); J., 68 (**Noturus**); F., 84 (**Noturus**); L., 10.

Body broad anteriorly, though scarcely robust; slender and compressed posteriorly; depth 4.6 to 5.6 in length; profile rather steep and nearly straight. Length 3½ inches. Color grayish with black specks and larger blotches; the back crossed by more or less definite saddle-like blotches of black, one before dorsal, one behind it, one on adipose, and a fainter one at base of caudal, the last blotch but one extending into adipose fin to its edge; tip of dorsal, caudal, and anal blackish. Head wide and extremely depressed anteriorly, much higher behind; interorbital space flat, 2.1 to 2.5 in head; length of head 3.5 to 3.9 in body, width 3.9 to 4.3; upper jaw a little longer than lower; maxillary barbels hardly reaching gill-openings; eye large, 4.3 to 5 in head. Dorsal fin higher than long, its distance from snout 2.6 to 2.8 in length; the spine long, more than half the height of the fin. Notch between adipose and caudal usually deep and acute, the caudal tapering terminally. Anal short, the rays 13 to 15. Pectoral spines long, 1.5 to 1.8 in head, much curved; the basal ⅔ of anterior edge very finely serrate, the posterior margin with 6 to 8 strong hooks, whose length is more than half the diameter of the spine; humeral process short.

In our Illinois collections this species has been taken but 30 times, and, with a single exception, from localities in the eastern part of the state on the tributaries of the Wabash and the Ohio. It has occurred once in the extreme headwaters of the Kaskaskia, in close proximity to upper branches of the Embarras, in which we have found it several times. It contrasts, however, in distribution with *Noturus flavus*, occupying those parts of the state which the former does not penetrate. Indeed, these two species have been taken together in only one of our collections. It agrees closely with *flavus* in its ecological preferences, being, like that species, found only in running streams (but most abundantly in creeks) and absent, so far as our observations go, from standing waters. It likewise agrees with *flavus* in its preference for a clean bottom and a swift current. The relations of these two species to each other, and of both to *Schilbeodes gyrinus*, offer an interesting example of the methods by which closely related species may avoid disadvantageous competition with each other, *flavus* and *miurus* occupying similar situations in similar waters, but mainly distributed in different parts of the state, while *gyrinus*, with its general distribution covering the area of both the other species, is related differently from these both to water bodies and to situations in them. Like both the other species mentioned, *miurus* has a wide general range which offers no explanation of its limited distribution in Illinois.

From the tributaries of Lake Michigan on the north it ranges south to Louisiana and west to the lower part of the Missouri basin. Hay, in his list of Indiana fishes, mentions its occurrence in Minnesota and North Carolina.

Order HAPLOMI

PIKE-LIKE FISHES

Skeleton bony; anterior vertebræ distinct, without Weberian ossicles; ventral fins abdominal, rarely wanting; all fins soft-rayed, although the first dorsal ray is in a few forms somewhat stiffened and spine-like; no adipose fin; pectoral arch suspended from the skull; mesocoracoid wanting (this character constituting the only important distinction between these fishes and the *Isospondyli*); opercular bones well developed; air-bladder with a distinct duct. Four families; species numerous and widely distributed, chiefly inhabiting fresh or brackish waters of both hemispheres.

Key to Families of HAPLOMI found in Illinois

a. Vent normal, not far in front of anal fin; eyes normal.
b. Lateral line present; jaws duck-bill-like .... **Esocidæ.**
bb. Lateral line wanting.
c. Upper jaw not protractile .... **Umbridæ.**
cc. Upper jaw protractile (the upper lip separated from the skin of the forehead by an evident groove, which passes wholly across the muzzle) .... **Pœciliidæ.**
aa. Vent jugular, in front of pectorals and close behind gill-openings; eyes more or less concealed by thick skin; ventrals ordinarily wanting, or much reduced .... **Amblyopsidæ.**

Family UMBRIDÆ

THE MUDFISHES

Body oblong, broad anteriorly and compressed behind; head somewhat flattened; scales cycloid, covering head and body; lateral line wanting; skeleton osseous; anterior vertebræ simple; no spines in fins; ventrals abdominal; dorsal fin posterior; caudal rounded; no mesocoracoid; gill-membranes little connected; branchiostegals 6 to 8; pseudobranchiæ hidden, glandular; gill-rakers little developed; mouth moderate, premaxillary not protractile; lateral margin of upper jaw formed by the maxillaries, which are toothless and without distinct supplemental bone; premaxillaries, lower jaw, vomer, and palatines with bands of villiform or cardiform teeth, stomach without blind sac; no pyloric cæca; air-bladder simple, with distinct duct; oviparous fishes.

Fishes of small size and carnivorous habit, inhabiting muddy weedy bottoms of fresh-water streams and ponds; very tenacious of life. One genus, with three species, one European and two American, one of the latter inhabiting local waters. The *Umbridæ* represent an archaic type, older than the *Esocidæ*, and evidently characteristic of an earlier fish fauna. Their survival in forms so widely separated geographically is interestingly suggestive to the student of distribution and descent.

GENUS **UMBRA** (KRÄMER) MÜLLER

MUDFISHES

Generic characters included in description of family. Size small; species 3, inhabiting fresh waters of the United States and Austria; one species known from Illinois.

UMBRA LIMI (KIRTLAND)

MUD-MINNOW; MUDFISH

(PL., P. 211; MAP LX)

Kirtland, 1840, Bost. J. Nat. Hist., Ill, 277 (**Hydrargira**).

G., VI, 232; J. & G., 350; M. V., 87; J. & E., I, 623; N., 43 (**Melanura**); J., 52 (**Melanura**); F., 71; F. F., I. 6, 73; L., 21.

Length 4 inches; body oblong, compressed, caudal peduncle deep; depth in length 3.9 to 5 3; greatest width of body about ⅔ its greatest depth; depth caudal peduncle 1.3 to 1.6 in its length. Color of upper parts dull brownish olive mottled with black; sides with about 14 indefinite narrow transverse bars of dark color, the interspaces bluish forward; breast, belly, and under sides of head yellowish; a large black blotch-like bar at end of caudal peduncle; a black stripe across cheek and through eye to end of snout; fins plain olive-green, the caudal somewhat darker at center. Head 3.3 to 3.8; width of head 1.7 to 1.9 in its length; interorbital space nearly flat, 4.3 to 5.4; eye 3.8 to 5.2; nose 3.9 to 5; mouth rather large, maxillary reaching to middle of orbit, 2.8 to 3.8 (usually about 3) in head; teeth on premaxillary, lower jaw, vomer, and palatines; gill-membranes free from isthmus. Dorsal fin 14, sometimes 15, inserted behind ventrals and behind middle of body; anal 8 or 9; caudal rounded; pectorals short, broad and round, 1.6 to 2 in head. Scales 35, transverse series 13 or 14; no lateral line; opercles with large scales; scales on opercles embedded.

Mud-minnows are small fishes, few individuals exceeding five or six inches in length. They are frequently mistaken by fishermen for the young of the dogfish, from which, however, they are very readily distinguished by the short dorsal fin. They rest quietly upon the bottom much of the time, and when disturbed first dart away to a little distance, and then bury themselves, tail downwards, in the mud with one or two quick twists of the body. They have also the singular habit of burrowing into the mud when the water evaporates from a pond. Professor Baird says that a locality which, with the water perfectly clear, will appear destitute of fish, will perhaps yield a number of mudfish on stirring up the mud at the bottom and drawing a seine through it. Ditches on the plains of Wisconsin, or mere bog-holes containing nothing else beyond tadpoles, may thus be found full of mudfish.

The intestine is short, less than the body in length, the gill-rakers are thick and rather long, about half the length of the filaments, and the pharyngeal apparatus is insignificant. The food of ten specimens taken from six localities consisted largely of minute duckweed (*Wolffia*) and unicellular algæ, insects and crustaceans making, however, more than a fourth of the food. The latter were mainly *Entomostraca.* Thin-shelled univalve mollusks (*Physa*) were taken from two of the specimens, and amphipod *Crustacea* (*Crangonyx*) from one. Dr. Abbott reports that he has seen mud-minnows leap out of the water a distance greater than their length to catch insects resting on blades of grass.

They apparently spawn in early spring, and Abbott reports that in New Jersey he has found them apparently ripe on the 16th of March, and that even earlier than this they were making their way up stream in small brooks, leaping from eddy to eddy, evidently on their way to their spawning beds. We have found ripe females during the first week of April at Havana. Dr. Ryder says that their adhesive eggs are laid singly upon the leaves of aquatic plants. Those observed by him hatched on the sixth day.

This little fish is rather peculiarly distributed in Illinois, occurring in our collections almost entirely in the extreme northern and the extreme southern parts of the state. We have elsewhere taken it only at Havana and Meredosia, on the Illinois River, where it has occurred ten times in nearly eleven hundred collections. Its frequency coefficients are correspondingly unequal for the three sections of the state, those for southern and northern Illinois being 1.48 and 1.28 respectively, while that for central Illinois is but .23. We have found it most frequently in lakes and ponds, and next in the smaller rivers.

It is a northern species, on the whole, ranging from Quebec and Ontario throughout the basin of the Great Lakes to the Ohio, and southward along the Atlantic as far as New Jersey, and northward to the Minnesota River. We have found no record of its occurrence in the Missouri basin. It is usually taken from grassy ponds and clear creeks with a soft mud bottom.

Family **ESOCIDÆ**

THE PIKES

Body elongate, more or less compressed posteriorly; scales cycloid, covering body and portions of head, which is always naked above; lateral line weakly developed; skeleton osseous; anterior vertebræ simple; no spines in fins; ventral fins abdominal; dorsal posterior; caudal emarginate; no mesocoracoid; gill-membranes separate; branchiostegals 12 to 20; pseudobranchiæ glandular, hidden; gill-rakers tubercle-like, toothed; mouth very large, its cleft half of head; premaxillaries not protractile, most of margin of upper jaw formed by maxillary, which is furnished with supplemental bone; premaxillaries, vomer, and palatines with bands of strong cardiform teeth; lower jaw with strong teeth of different sizes; tongue with a band of small teeth; stomach not cæcal, without pyloric appendages; air-bladder simple, with distinct duct; oviparous.

Fresh waters of northern parts of Europe, Asia, and North America. Size moderate or large. One genus with six species, all but one confined to North America; fossil remains found in Oligocene of Europe. All are of carnivorous habit, being voracious and gamy. The flesh is flaky and of good flavor.

Genus **ESOX** (Artedi) Linnæus

PIKES

Characters of the genus included above.

Key to the Species of **ESOX** found in Illinois

a. Cheeks entirely scaly; branchiostegals 11 to 16.

b. Opercles entirely scaly; dorsal rays 11 or 12; scales 105; color greenish, barred or reticulated with darker; fins without black spots; length 12 inches .... **vermiculatus.**

bb. Opercles with the lower half bare of scales; dorsal rays 14 to 16; scales 125; color purplish gray to greenish, with many small whitish or yellowish spots; dorsal, anal, and caudal spotted with black; length 3 feet.......... **lucius.**

aa. Lower half of both cheeks and opercles naked; branchiostegals 17 to 19; dorsal rays 17; scales 150; color dark gray, sides usually with scattered round black spots, sometimes without spots, sometimes banded with dark; fins spotted with black; length 4 to 8 feet.......... **masquinongy.**

ESOX VERMICULATUS Le Sueur

LITTLE PICKEREL; GRASS PIKE

(Map LXI)

Le Sueur, 1846, in Cuv. & Val., Hist. Nat. Poiss., XVIII, 333.
G., VI, 230 (cypho); J. & G., 352 (salmoneus); M. V., 88; J. & E., I, 627 (Lucius); N., 43 (salmoneus, cypho, and umbrosus); J., 53 (salmoneus, cypho, and ravenelli?); F., 71 (Lucius); E. F., II. 7, 435; L., 21 (Lucius).

Length 12 inches; body elongate, compressed, caudal peduncle slender; depth 5 to 7 (5.2 to 6.7) in length; greatest width of body about 3/5 its greatest depth; depth caudal peduncle 2 to 2.6 in its length. Color typically grassy to grayish green, with darker streaks, bars, and reticulations, the lighter colored interspaces worm-track-like (hence *vermiculatus*); color variable, sometimes nearly plain; centers of scales (sides) brassy, blue, or green; a yellowish streak along middle of back; belly white; head dark olive with light patches; a dark slaty streak below eye; opercles grassy green; a dusky streak from eye across cheek and opercle; pupil dull bluish black; iris with narrow inner ring of burnt golden, rest brownish to blue and purplish; caudal mottled near base; other fins dusky in the rays, otherwise plain. Head 3 to 3.4 (usually greater than 3.2); width of head 2.8 to 3.2; interorbital concave, 5 to 6.2; eye 5.5 to 6.8, midway of head; nose long, duck-bill-like, shorter than in the next species, 2.4 to 2.7 in head; mouth large, maxillary past front of orbit, 2 to 2.4 in head. Dorsal rays 12; anal 12; caudal well forked; ventrals less than half to vent; pectorals short 2.8 to 3.3 in head. Scales 103 to 108; cheeks and opercles fully scaled; no supplementary lateral line.

This little pike, never over 12 inches in length, but frequently mistaken for the young of a larger species, is distributed throughout Illinois, most abundantly, however, according to our experience, in the southern part of the state, where its frequency coefficient rises to 1.73 as compared with .69 for central Illinois and .88 for northern. It is most abundant in creeks, but is also quite common in ponds and the smaller rivers. It has a noticeable preference for quiet and muddy waters, and the greater part of our collections have come from the weedy branches of the Embarras, Little Wabash, and Big Muddy, in eastern and central Illinois. It has also occurred occasionally in the main stream of the Illinois, or in the muddy overflow ponds of the bottoms. Indeed, large numbers of this fish are annually destroyed by the drying up of such ponds after the overflow.

Its general range includes the tributaries of Lake Erie and Lake Michigan, extending thence southward to the Tennessee, Escanaba, and White rivers, and, according to Evermann and Cox, to the Neuse River on the Atlantic slope. From the fact that it is not contained in Evermann and Goldsborough's list

Common Pike, *Esox lucius* Linnæus

of the fresh-water fishes of Canada, we infer that it is not to be found north of the Great Lakes.

In its feeding structures, this little species is a reduced copy of the destructive and voracious common pike, and its food, as illustrated by eighteen specimens, seems to be purely animal. Two of these had eaten frog tadpoles, and eight had taken fishes, one of which was a cyprinoid minnow, one a sunfish, and the other a common top-minnow (*Gambusia*) of the southern part of the state. The remaining food was mostly composed of the larger aquatic insects. Amphipod and isopod crustaceans have been found in the stomachs of other specimens, taken from Quiver Lake, near Havana.

The species apparently spawns early, and ripe individuals of both sexes have been seen by us in March.

ESOX LUCIUS Linnæus

COMMON PIKE; PICKEREL

(Map LXII)

Linnæus, 1758, Syst. Nat., Ed. X, 314.

G., VI, 228 & 229 (**estor** and **depraudus**); J. & G., 353; M. V., 89; J. & E., I, 628 (**Lucius**); N., 43 (**lucius** var. **estor**, and ? **boreus**); J., 53; F., 71; F. F., II. 7, 435; L., 21 (**Lucius**).

Length 3 feet; elongate and compressed; depth 5 to 7; greatest width about 3/5 greatest depth; depth caudal peduncle 1.7 to 2.2 in its length. Color of back and sides bluish or greenish gray with more or less of purplish luster; yellowish below and white on belly; sides with irregular rows of small roundish spots of yellowish or gold; single scales of side each with a broad V-shaped golden spot; top of head plain dark olive-green; cheeks and opercles bluish gray or heliotrope with pale greenish spots; iris light drab below with golden margin, brassy yellow above pupil and forward; all fins wax-yellow in the rays; dorsal with 3 to 5 rows of roundish black spots equal in length to the width of three membranes; caudal and anal similarly marked; ventrals with faint traces of spots; pectorals plain. Head 2.9 to 3.6 (usually less than 3.4); width of head about 3; interorbital 4.3 to 6.2; eye 5.8 to 9.5, midway of head; nose 1.9 to 2.4; mouth very large, maxillary past front of orbit, 2 to 2.2 in head. Dorsal rays 15 or 16; anal 14 or 15; ventrals half way to front of anal; pectorals 2/5 to ventrals, 2.2 to 2.6 in head in adults. Scales 122 to 125; cheeks fully scaled; lower half of opercles naked; lateral line irregular, supplementary lateral pores in short and broken series above and below it, especially on caudal peduncle.

This noble fish, completely and almost ideally equipped for the predatory life, has now nearly disappeared from the larger and muddier streams of Illinois, but is still found in abundance in the headwaters of the Kankakee and in the small glacial lakes of the northeastern part of the state. It is also occasionally caught in the clearer sloughs and lakes (usually fed by springs) of the Illinois, Rock, and Green rivers. Several specimens of good size have recently been taken by us from the lock pond at Henry, on the Illinois.

It is a cosmopolitan species of the northern hemisphere, found in the fresh waters of northern Europe, Asia, and North America, and ranging as far south in Europe as Italy and Greece. In this country it is abundant in suitable situations from Alaska southward through Canada, and through the upper Mississippi Valley and the eastern United States to the Potomac on the Atlantic slope and to the Missouri and its branches in Iowa and Nebraska.

The average weight of the pike taken from our region is not over 5 ℔, but a specimen weighing 26½ pounds is reported by Dr. Jordan to have been caught in the Kankakee. The record weight for Europe is 145 ℔—that of a specimen taken at Bregenty in 1862.

This fish is commonly called pickerel in Illinois, although its more appropriate name of pike is also sometimes used. It prefers clean, clear, cool water of a sluggish current, in which it remains generally quiet by day. It is a strong and active swimmer, extremely voracious, and with senses remarkably acute. It launches itself like an arrow upon its prey, seldom missing its aim, and fighting courageously with others of its kind. It is purely carnivorous, its food consisting of fishes among which we have noticed sunfish and black bass, together with frogs, crawfishes, and the larger insects. Mice, reptiles, and young ducks have been reported by various authors to have been taken from the stomachs of pike.

It spawns in March in our latitude, selecting shore water about a foot and a half in depth. Professor Benecke of Konigsberg says of this species, as quoted by Goode, that "it lives a hermit life, only consorting in pairs during the spawning season. The pairs of fish then resort to shallow places upon meadows and banks which have been overflowed, and, rubbing violently upon each other, deposit their spawn in the midst of powerful blows of their tails." The spawning time in east Prussia falls in the months from February to April, occasionally beginning before the departure of the ice. A single female may deposit as many as a hundred thousand eggs. The young hatch in about fourteen days, and may reach a length of a foot by the end of the first year.

The flesh of the pike is of fairly good flavor, but is full of small bones. It is not much prized in this country, but is generally more esteemed in Europe. The voracity of this fish and its inferior quality as food have led to attempts at its destruction in Europe and in parts of Canada. It is readily captured with minnow bait, or with a trolling-spoon, and will also take a fly. It is often caught with a hook through holes in the ice in winter, and affords a valuable food to many an Indian hunter in the Canadian woods.

This destructive fish has greatly decreased in numbers in this state during the last twenty-five years. The older fishermen at Havana remember when a thousand pounds were caught at a time, while now scarcely as many will be taken during an entire year. In 1899, according to the report of the United States Fish Commission, 21,000 pounds of pike were taken in the Mississippi and Illinois rivers within the state of Illinois. The total catch from the Mississippi Valley was 216,952 pounds, having fallen to that figure from 809,134 pounds in 1894.

ESOX MASQUINONGY Mitchill

MUSKALLUNGE

Mitchill, "Mirror, 297, 1824".*

The muskallunge is sufficiently distinguished from other species of the genus *Esox* in the key preceding.

This giant fish, reported to reach a weight of a hundred pounds and to average three feet in length—specimens six feet feet long and weighing eighty pounds have been caught—has not been taken by us in Illinois, although it occurs in Lake Michigan and rarely in the smaller lakes in the northeastern part of the state. It is said by Jordan to be native to all the Great Lakes and the upper St. Lawrence, to certain streams and lakes tributary to the Great Lakes, and to a few of the lakes in the upper Mississippi Valley. It occurs also in Canada to the northward. In Ohio, according to R. C. Osburn, a variety of the species, *ohiensis*, distinguished by narrow irregular crossbars formed by the coalescing of spots upon the sides, is found in the Ohio River and its tributary streams. It is equally esteemed for its game and food qualities.

* Reference on authority of De Kay.

Family **PŒCILIIDÆ**

THE KILLIFISHES

Body oblong or moderately elongate, compressed behind; head broad and depressed; scales cycloid, rather large, adherent; head scaly, at least above; lateral line wanting or represented by a few imperfect pores; skeleton bony; anterior vertebræ simple; fins without spines, or (rarely) a rudimentary spinous dorsal, or a single spine (not in Illinois forms); ventrals abdominal, rarely wanting; dorsal inserted posteriorly, about over anal; caudal not forked; no mesocoracoid; gill-membranes somewhat connected, free from isthmus; branchiostegals 4 to 6; pseudobranchiæ wanting; gill-rakers very short; mouth terminal, small, the lower jaw usually projecting; premaxillary extremely protractile; margin of upper jaw formed by premaxillaries; teeth incisor-like or villiform, sometimes present on vomer, but usually on jaws only; stomach siphonal, without pyloric appendages; air-bladder simple, often wanting; most species oviparous; some forms ovoviviparous, the young well developed at time of birth.

Fresh-water fishes of small size, widely distributed in Southern Europe, Asia, Africa, and America. Some species occur in bays and arms of the sea, in more or less brackish water. Genera about 35; species about 200; 2 genera and 4 species found in Illinois.

Many of the species of this family are surface swimmers, "top-minnows," inhabiting canals, ponds, swamps, and sluggish or stagnant streams, where they feed on insects and other life found swimming or floating at the surface of the water. Other forms (not found in Illinois) are free swimmers in the river channels, and still others dwell in the mud of stream bottoms. Certain species are especially valuable as mosquito destroyers.

Key to Genera and Species of **PŒCILIIDÆ** Found in Illinois

Fundulus.—Anal fin of the male similar to that of the female, not modified into an intromittent organ; species oviparous.

a. Dorsal rays 13 or 14; scales 43–45; color olivaceous with numerous dusky cross-bars .... **diaphanus.**

aa. Dorsal rays 7 to 9; scales 28 to 36.

b. Scales 33 to 36.

c. Sides with numerous narrow lengthwise streaks or rows of dots of dark color, the males with dark cross-bars .... **dispar.**

cc. A single black lateral stripe from head to tail; males with obscure cross-bars. .... **notatus.**

Gambusia.—Anal fin of males modified into a sword-shaped intromittent organ; species viviparous.

bb. Scales 28 to 30; no evident stripes or cross-bars .... **affinis.**

MUD-MINNOW, *Umbra limi* (Kirtland)

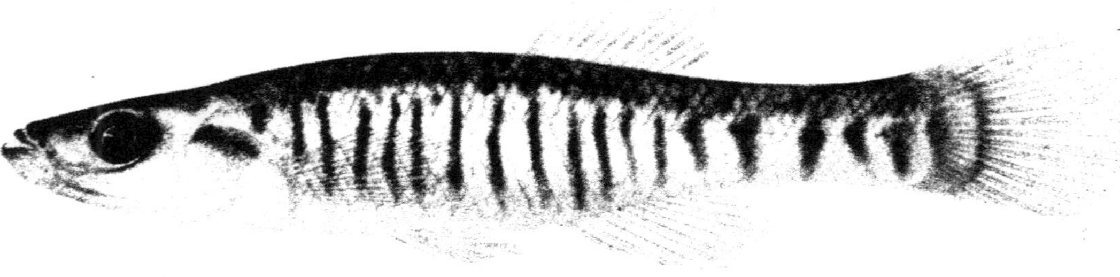

MENONA TOP-MINNOW (Male), *Fundulus diaphanus menona* (Jordan & Copeland)

GENUS **FUNDULUS** LACÉPÈDE

KILLIFISHES

Body rather elongate, little elevated, compressed behind head broad and flat above; mouth moderate, lower jaw projecting; jaws each with 2, or more, series of pointed teeth; preopercle, preorbital, and mandible with conspicuous mucus pores; dorsal and anal fins rather similar in size, either large or small, the anal slightly higher in males of some species than in females, but not developed as an intromittent organ; scales moderate.

Species very numerous, mostly American, inhabiting the fresh waters of the interior and the arms of the sea, on both coasts. All are oviparous. They are all carnivorous in greater or less degree. The three species found in Illinois* are typical "top-minnows," feeding on surface-swimming insects, etc.

FUNDULUS DIAPHANUS MENONA (JORDAN & COPELAND)

MENONA TOP-MINNOW

(MAP LXIII)

Le Sueur, 1817, J. Ac. Nat. Sci. Phila., 130 (**Hydrargira diaphana**).
Jordan & Copeland, 1877, P. Ac. Nat. Sci. Phila., 68 (**menona**).
J. & G., 335 (**menona**); M. V., 85; J. & E., I, 645; N., 42 (**diaphanus**); J., 52 (**menona**); F., 72 (**diaphanus**); F. F., I. 6, 71 (**diaphanus**); L., 21.

Length 3 inches; body rather slender and not much compressed, caudal peduncle long; depth 4.5 to 5.3; greatest width about ¾ of greatest depth; depth caudal peduncle 2.2 to 2.4 in its length. Color (males) light olivaceous, spotted with dusky on back and on sides above lateral line; 15 to 20 dark transverse bars on each side, reaching from back to belly, broader than the silvery interspaces; belly silvery white; opercles emerald, dusted with dark specks; an emerald-green spot behind opercle; iris mingled iridescent emerald to lavender, with a narrow inner rim of gold next to pupil; fins pale, dorsal with a faint longitudinal bar of dusky near base; base of caudal with a squarish golden spot. Females have dark bars shorter and narrower than in males, and the interspaces wider than the bars, olivaceous, without silvery luster; dorsal fin without dark bar. Head quite flat above, 3.5 to 3.9; width of head 1.9 to 2.2 in its length; interorbital space 2.8 to 3.1 in head; eye 3 to 3.5; nose 2.9 to 3.7, usually more than 3.3; mouth small, maxillary 3.6 to 4 in head, mandible equal to eye, lower jaw slightly projecting; teeth pointed, curved, the outer ones scarcely enlarged. Dorsal inserted in front of ventrals, its rays 13 or 14; anal rays 11; ventrals short of vent; pectorals 1.7 to 1.9 in head. Scales 43 to 45; transverse series 14 or 15; no lateral line; cheeks and opercles covered with large scales.

* For key to species, see key to genera and species of *Pœciliidæ*, preceding.

This little top-minnow, rare in Illinois and taken by us but twenty times, all in the northern half of the state, is, in fact, a northern species in the United States, found outside Illinois in the lakes and ponds of Ohio, Indiana, Michigan, and Wisconsin, and in the Missouri basin as far south as the Kansas River. The typical form (*Fundulus diaphanus*) occurs from the headwaters to the brackish mouths of coastwise streams from Quebec, New Brunswick, and Maine to Cape Hatteras, and in the lakes of New York State. Our Illinois examples of *menona* have been mainly taken from upland lakes of the headwaters of the Fox and Des Plaines, from the headwaters of the Rock River, from the lakes of the Calumet series, and from pools near Bloomington, in McLean county. In Wolf and Calumet lakes it was most frequent near shore among weeds and rushes, in clear water and over a bottom of sand.

The food of eight specimens from the northeastern lakes comprised insects, both aquatic and terrestrial, amphipod *Crustacea* (*Allorchestes*), various *Entomstraca*, especially those living upon the bottom, a few thin-shelled univalves (*Planorbis*), and the seeds of plants which had fallen into the water, these last taken in quantity too large to have been accidental.

Females moderately distended with large eggs were taken by us in Sand Lake Aug. 3, 1887, a fact which indicates a late spawning period. Dr. Eigenmann, however, found the eggs of this species in grassy bottoms of Indiana lakes June 24.

FUNDULUS DISPAR Agassiz

(Map LXIV)

Agassiz, 1854, Amer. J. Sci. and Arts, 353 (**Zygonectes**).
J. & G., 341 (**Zygonectes**); M. V., 86 (**Zygonectes**); J. & E., I, 658; N., 42 (**Zygonectes**); J., 52 (**Zygonectes**); F., 72 (**Zygonectes**); F. F., I. 6, 72 (**Zygonectes**); L., 21.

Length, 2½ inches; body rather short and deep, compressed, caudal peduncle short; depth 3.5 to 4.3; greatest width about ⅗ of greatest depth; depth caudal peduncle 1.5 to 1.9 in its length. Color (females) light olive, with 9 or 10 wavy longitudinal lines of brown traversing each side along the lower edges of the rows of scales; no distinct* transverse bars; dorsal and anal with a few faint dusky spots; caudal plain; adult males and females with a triangular bluish blotch below eye, and a smaller blotch above and in front of it, the two blotches more or less confluent with similar color in the eye itself. Males with irregular longitudinal rows of reddish brown

* Females 1½ inches long taken in Wolf Lake South Chicago, in August, 1903, had faint vertical bars. These disappeared at times and on one occasion when apparent in direct side view disappeared at other angles. These females were in all other respects typical.

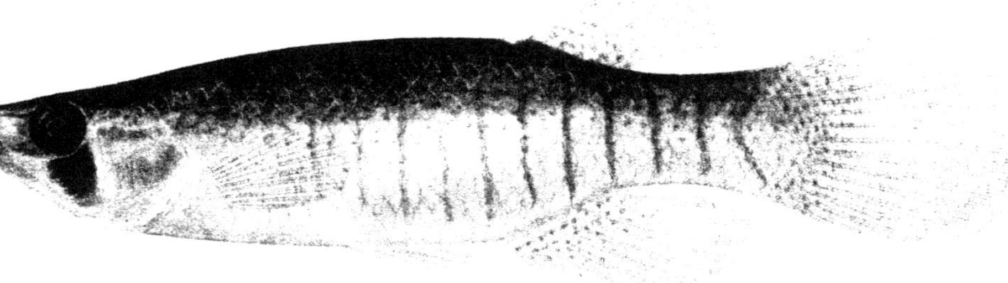

Fundulus dispar (Agassiz), male

Fundulus dispar (Agassiz), female

dots on sides, not connected in wavy lines as in females, and with about 10 narrow transverse bars of dusky olive; conspicuous reddish brown spots on proximal half of caudal and fainter ones on dorsal and anal. Head 3.5 to 4.3, broad and flat above; width of head 1.5 to 1.7 in its length; interorbital space 1.9 to 2.3 (usually about 2); eye 2.8 to 3.4; nose 2.8 to 3.7; mouth small, maxillary 2.8 to 3.3, mandible less than diameter of eye; lower jaw scarcely projecting; teeth pointed, those on lower jaw rather short and weak. Dorsal inserted behind ventrals, its rays 7; anal rays 9 or 10, the fin much longer in males than in females; ventrals to vent; pectorals nearly to ventrals, 1.5 to 1.8 in head. Scales 34 to 36; transverse series 11; no lateral line; cheeks and opercles covered with large scales.

This little killifish although occurring in all parts of the state, is peculiarly distributed. Nearly all our collections of it have been made along the course of the larger rivers—not from the streams themselves, however, but rather from the weedy lakes and ponds of the river bottoms and the upland lakes of northeastern Illinois. Consistently with this statement, the frequency coefficient of this species is 2.17 for lakes and sloughs, and but .22 for creeks, and .67 for the larger rivers. None of our 83 collections has been taken in rivers of the second class.

The known general distribution of the species is rather limited, extending from lakes and sluggish streams of northern Ohio westward to Missouri and southward to the Pearl and Big Black rivers in Mississippi.

This minnow swims habitually at the surface with the head and back showing, in which position it may be easily identified by a bright silvery spot on the top of the head. About half the food of the specimens studied by us consisted of insects, fully half of these land insects which had fallen into the water. Mollusks and crustaceans, with a small amount of the more delicate aquatic vegetation, were the other objects of the food.

Ripe fishes of both sexes were obtained by us at Havana on the 29th of May, 1896.

FUNDULUS NOTATUS (Rafinesque)

TOP-MINNOW

(Map LXV)

Rafinesque, 1820, Ichth. Oh., 86 (**Semotilus**).

G., VI, 314 and 315 (**Haplochilus pulchellus** and **aureus**); J. & G., 339 (**Zygonectes**); M. V., 86 (**Zygonectes**); J. & E., I, 659; N., 42 (**Zygonectes**); J., 52 (**Zygonectes**); F., 72 (**Zygonectes**); F. F., I. 6, 71 (**Zygonectes**); L., 22.

Length 2½ to 3 inches; body moderately elongate, flattened above, little compressed anteriorly; depth in length 4.4 to 5.3; greatest width more than ¾ greatest depth; depth caudal peduncle 1.5 to 2.1 in its length. Color (females) brownish olive with a purplish black lateral band continued forward across cheek and opercle and through eye to end of snout; belly pinkish white; median fins more or less specked with dusky, anal faintly so and only near base; males with sides crossed by 16 or 17 rather obscure bars of dusky, and with edges of lateral band somewhat serrate; anal with two or three rows of prominent dark specks. Head much depressed and rather elongate, 3.5 to 3.9 in length; width of head 1.6 to 2; interorbital space 2.2 to 2.5; eye 3.3 to 3.9; nose 2.8 to 3.4, noticeably longer than eye; maxillary 2.8 to 3.3 in head, mandible greater than eye; jaws subequal, the lower scarcely so long as upper; "teeth in a broad band, the outer series considerably enlarged, canine-like" (J. & E.). Dorsal inserted behind ventrals, its rays 9; anal rays 11, the fin noticeably longer in males (longer than head) than in females (about 4/5 head); ventrals to vent; pectorals almost or quite to ventrals, 1.4 to 1.9 in head. Scales 33 to 34; transverse series 11; cheeks and opercles and top of head covered with large scales.

This is much the most abundant Illinois species of its family, and is the one to which the name of top-minnow has been most generally attached. It occurs in great abundance throughout the state in waters of all descriptions, most frequently, however, in the smaller streams and headwaters of southern and eastern Illinois. Its condensation southward is illustrated by our frequency coefficients for the three sections of the state—2.13 for southern Illinois and .42 and .44 for central and northern Illinois respectively. By far the greater part of our collections have been taken from the basins of the Kaskaskia and the Wabash, and the ponds and creeks of the extreme southern part of the state.

Outside Illinois it occurs from Michigan, and Wisconsin southward throughout the entire lower Mississippi Valley to Louisiana and the rivers of Texas. It is reported by collectors to be most abundant in ponds, creeks, and canals, and along the margins of sluggish streams. It is a surface swimmer, as its common name implies, and, like *Fundulus dispar*, it is easily distinguished in the water by a silvery occipital spot.

Nearly the whole food of the species consists of insects, as illustrated by our examination of 17 specimens taken from various places in central and southern Illinois. The 10 per cent. of vegetation eaten by these fishes was almost wholly filamentous algæ, taken in such quantities by some as to make it certain that their presence in the food was not a matter of accident. In one fish, for example, the entire intestine was crammed with these algæ, and in three others they made more than half the food. Insects were the major part of the remainder, although *Entomostraca* and amphipod *Crustacea* (*Crangonyx*) were likewise common.

Dr. Eigenmann found ripe females in Turkey creek, Indiana June 27; and we have taken specimens greatly distended with eggs between the 16th and the 27th of the same month.

Genus **GAMBUSIA** Poey

Body moderately elongate, becoming deep in the adult female; head flat above; mouth moderate; lower jaw projecting; both jaws with bands of pointed teeth; dorsal and anal fins rather short and small, the anal more or less in advance of the dorsal and in the male much advanced and modified into a long intromittent organ; scales as in *Fundulus*.

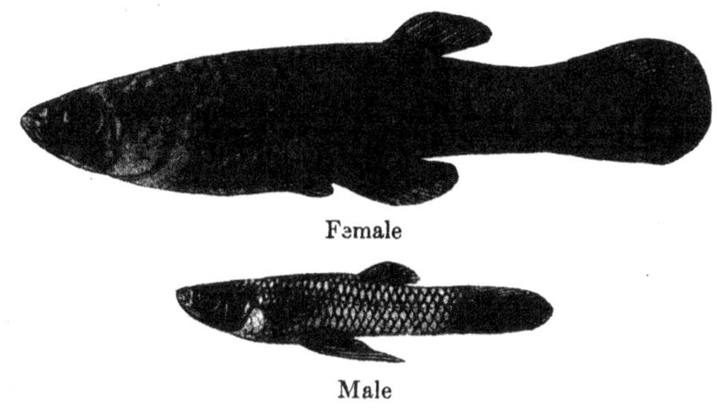

Female

Male

Fig. 54

GAMBUSIA AFFINIS (Baird & Girard)

VIVIPAROUS TOP-MINNOW

(Map LXVI)

Baird and Girard, 1853, Proc. Ac. Nat. Sci. Phila., 390 (**Heterandria**).
G., VI, 334, 335, 336 (**holbrooki, humilis,** and **affinis**); J. & G., 345, 346 (**patruelis, humilis, affinis**), 340, 341, 892 (**Zygonectes atrilatus, brachypterus, inurus**); M. V., 87 (**patruelis**); J. & E., I, 680; J., 52 (**Zygonectes menalops**); F., 71 (**patruelis**); L., 22.

Length 1½ to 2 inches; body robust and not much elongate, considerably compressed; depth 3.7 to 4.3 in length; greatest width of body about 3/5 of its depth; depth of caudal peduncle 2.1 to 2.4 in its length. Color "light olive, each scale edged with darker; a very narrow dark streak* along sides; top of head dusky; a more or less distinct triangular bluish-black bar below eye; sides and belly anteriorly dusky with dark dots; a black blotch on each side of belly, caused by the black internal organs showing through the skin; young specimens often uniformly yellowish; fins dusky; the caudal usually with cross series of dots". Head short, broad, and flat above, 3.7 to 4 in length; width of head 1.4 to 1.6 in its length; interorbital space 2 to 2.5 in head; eye 2.6 to 3.2; nose 2.8 to 3.6; maxillary 2.8 to 3.4; mandible equal to eye; lower jaw slightly longer than upper; teeth in broad villiform bands.

* Not evident in our preserved material.—R. E. R.

Dorsal rays 6 or 7, the fin inserted behind ventrals; anal rays 8 (females) or 6 (males); anal fin of males inserted nearer muzzle than base of caudal (vice versa in females), its anterior rays modified into a long, blade-like intromittent organ; ventrals reaching to vent; pectorals past front of ventrals, 1.2 in head. Scales 28 to 30; transverse series 8 or 9; top and sides of head covered with large scales.

G. affinis lives along the southern coasts, in brackish as well as in fresh water, from the Potomac and Delaware to the St. Johns and the Escambia rivers in Florida, and down the Mississippi to New Orleans and thence to the rivers of Texas and Mexico.

Specimens examined by Dr. H. M. Smith were found to have fed on algæ, diatoms, and fragments of mosquitoes.

Sexual dimorphism is strongly manifested in this species, the males being very small in comparison with the females and furnished with a long intromittent organ, the modified first ray of the anal fin. The males are much fewer than the females, 68 out of 69 specimens counted by Dr. Smith having been females. The species is viviparous, and a specimen taken by us in Running Lake, Union county, July 15, 1883, contained embryos with prominent eye-spots. Dr. Smith found females with large eggs July 1 in Maryland, and Aug. 11 obtained others containing young apparently ready for extrusion. Dr. Evermann found specimens containing well-developed embryos at San Antonio, Texas, in November and December, and observations by A. A. Duly, reported by Dr. J. A. Ryder, indicate that more than one brood may be produced in a season.

This little top-minnow, fairly common in extreme southern Illinois, has been taken by us outside that region only from Quincy, Meredosia, and Pekin. Our 18 collections are too few to give us data of local distribution, but when treated with reference to the joint occurrence of this species with others more abundant and more widely scattered through the state, they disclose an interesting situation, illustrating the methods by which closely related species occupying the same territory come to evade an injurious competition with each other. Bringing into comparison the collection records for the four species of this family, and taking note of the relative frequency with which the same species have been taken together in the same collection, we find that *Gambusia affinis* occurs with our most abundant and most widely distributed top-minnow (*Fundulus notatus*) with nearly three times the relative frequency of the joint occurrence of *F. notatus* and *F. dispar*, and that it occurs jointly with the less abundant species, *F. dispar*, with one and a third times that frequency—facts which are to be understood only when the general distribution of all these species is taken into account. *G. affinis* finds in southern Illinois the northern limit of its range, its occurrences beyond that boundary being evidently merely accidental. In its general distribution it goes southeast to Florida and southwest to Mexico, while the three other species are so distributed that Illinois is in the midst of the area occupied by them. These general occupants of our area have come to avoid each other locally in great measure, as shown by their relatively small coefficients of association—an adjustment forced upon them by the competitive relations in which they otherwise would live—while *G. affinis*, entering the territory of these three species only at its southern border, has not become ecologically adjusted to them, and is consequently to be found in their favorite haunts more frequently than they are in those of each other. These various relations may be more clearly shown by the following table.

Table of Associate Relations of Fundulus dispar, F. notatus, and Gambusia affins

Species	Collections	Joint occurrences	Frequency coefficients
F. dispar F. notatus	83 210	17	1.47
F. dispar G. affinis	83 18	2	2.01
F. notatus G. affinis	210 18	11	4.37

Family **AMBLYOPSIDÆ**

THE BLINDFISHES

Body moderately elongate, compressed behind; head long and depressed; body with small cycloid scales, irregularly placed, and more or less imbedded, so that the body appears naked; head naked, the surface sometimes crossed by papillary ridges; lateral line wanting; skeleton osseous; anterior vertebræ simple; ventral fins small or wanting, abdominal; no spines in fins; dorsal nearly opposite anal; caudal truncate or rounded; no mesocoracoid; gill-membranes more or less completely joined to isthmus; branchiostegals about 6; pseudobranchiæ concealed; gill-rakers very short; eyes in typical genera very rudimentary and hidden under the skin, in such forms the body being translucent and colorless; mouth rather large; lower jaw projecting; premaxillaries scarcely protractile, forming entire margin of upper jaw; jaws and palatines with bands of slender villiform teeth; stomach cæcal, with one or two pyloric appendages; air-bladder present; ovary single; some (and probably all) of the species ovoviviparous; vent jugular.

Fishes of small size, living in or about subterranean streams, caves, and swamps of the southern United States. Four genera and six species known, the majority being blind, with pale, almost pigmentless, bodies, and with the eyes covered with thick skin, inhabiting the cave region of southern Indiana, Kentucky, and Missouri. The single species found in Illinois retains the use of its eyes, and has the color of ordinary fishes. The group *Amblyopsidæ* is a very ancient one, as indicated by many points in their anatomy. The forward position of the vent, though not peculiar to these fishes, is found in only one other fresh-water family (*Aphredoderidæ*), likewise a relict of a family all but extinct.

Genus **CHOLOGASTER** Agassiz

Eyes well developed; ventral fins wanting; body not translucent, the skin having more or less pigment, and the color being much as in ordinary fishes; pyloric cæca 4; character otherwise those of the family. Swamps of the southern United States; a single species found in Illinois, at the mouths of caves in Union and Pope counties.

CHOLOGASTER PAPILLIFERUS Forbes

SPRING CAVE-FISH

(Pl., p. 220)

Forbes, Amer. Nat., 1882, 2.
J. & G., 325, 890 (**papillifer**); M. V., 83; J. & E., I, 704; F., 72; L., 22.

Length 2.4 inches; elongate, little compressed, caudal peduncle deep; head with rows of tactile papillæ, as in the true blindfishes (*Amblyopsis* and *Typhlichthys*); depth 5 to 6; greatest width ⅚ of depth; depth caudal peduncle 2 in its length. Color dark brown above, paler below; sides with 3 narrow longitudinal stripes, the upper and lower ones black, and the middle one of the ground color or paler (not black, as in *C. cornutus*); caudal fin dark brown, with several vertical rows of white specks running across the rays; anterior portion of dorsal similar in color but paler. Head short, broad, and exceedingly depressed, 4 in length; width of head 1.5 in its length; interorbital space flat, 3.4 in head; eyes 2.8 in head, mostly on its upper surface; nose broadly rounded, 3.5; mouth rather large, maxillary not reaching eye; lower jaw projecting; sides and top of head with numerous mostly short and broken and chiefly single rows of small sensory papillæ; a prominent double row on outside of each lower jaw, sunk in a groove extending from back to front of mandible, and within this a parallel irregular row of smaller papillæ on the lower surface of the jaw; especially conspicuous papillæ about the nostrils; the latter conspicuous, tubular, projecting forward, with expanded openings. Dorsal and anal fins thick and fleshy, their height about equal to their length; developed dorsal rays 6, the fin inserted behind the middle of the body and slightly in front of the anal; developed anal rays 5; caudal broadly rounded; ventrals wanting; pectorals 1.7 in head. Scales very small, cycloid, covered with thick skin.

Known at present only from a cave spring in Union county coming from the foot of a Mississippi River bluff, and from a cave on the Ohio River near Golconda, in Pope county. This species was originally described from material sent the senior author in 1879 and again in 1881 by F. S. Earle, of Cobden, Ill., and specimens have since been repeatedly taken from the Union county spring by various assistants of the State Laboratory. The occurrence of the species in Pope county was reported to me by Dr. Meek in 1908.

Especial interest attaches to this little fish as intermediate between the true blindfishes of the caves (*Amblyopsis* and *Typhlichthyus*) and earlier described species of *Chologaster*. The sensory structures of *C. papilliferus* correspond in character to its situation as a partially subterranean species. Studies recently made by Dr. Eigenmann show that the optic nerve and all of the important elements of the eye are present, but that the choroid is very thin and its pigment scanty, and that the retina is much degenerated.

The food and feeding habits of this species have not been especially studied, although it is known to be carnivorous. Dr. Shufeldt, quoting a note from Eigenmann, says that it detects its prey by its cutaneous sense-organs and not by its eyes, illustrating this statement by Eigenmann's observation of the behavior of a fish in capturing, by an instantaneous movement, a *Gammarus* which was approaching it from behind and below, where it could not have been seen by its captor. This does not, however, preclude the usefulness under other conditions of such eyesight as it has retained, especially when the fish is lurking under stones in the neighborhood of the outlet of its subterranean resort.

ORDER **ACANTHOPTERI**

THE SPINY-RAYED FISHES

Skeleton bony; the anterior vertebræ unmodified and without Weberian ossicles; ventral fins more or less anterior (thoracic) in nearly all forms, being abdominal in a few of the more archaic families; ventrals typically with 1 spine and 5 soft rays; anterior rays of dorsal and anal typically simple (unsegmented) and spinous; shoulder girdle attached to the skull by a post-temporal; no mesocoracoid, so far as known; hypercoracoid usually perforate; opercular apparatus complete; border of mouth formed by the premaxillaries alone, which are usually dentigerous; maxillary always present and toothless, normally distinct from the premaxillary; air-bladder typically without duct in adult; scales usually, though not always, ctenoid.

To this group belong the great majority of existing marine fishes, as well as numerous families more or less peculiar to fresh water. At least 5 more or less distinct suborders of *Acanthopteri* are represented in the waters of Illinois, by far the greater number of the species belonging to the perch-like or bass-like families of the group *Percoidei*.

KEY TO FAMILIES OF **ACANTHOPTERI** FOUND IN ILLINOIS

a. Ventral fins abdominal, i. e., inserted nearer first (soft) rays of anal than to the angle under throat formed by the union of the free gill-membranes (which definition does not include some members of the families *Gasterosteidæ* and *Percopsidæ* found outside of Illinois).

b. Dorsal fin with a single spine or preceded by 4 or more free spines.

Suborder Hemibranchii.

c. No adipose fin; dorsal fin preceded by 4 or more free spines. . **Gasterosteidæ.**

Suborder Salmopercæ.

cc. An adipose fin; dorsal, anal, and ventral fins each with a weak and rather indistinct spine .... **Percopsidæ.**

Suborder Percesoces.

bb. Dorsal fin preceded by a finlet of 3 to 8 slender spines.......... **Atherinidæ.**

aa. Ventral fins thoracic, i. e., inserted nearer to angle of gill-membranes than to the first anal spine, except in the deep-bodied genera *Centrachidæ* (which have dorsal spines 6 to 13 and anal spines 3 to 9 and ventrals nearer to throat than to first soft ray of anal).

Group Percoidei.

d. Ventral rays usually I, 7 (I, 6 or 7), never I, 5; vent jugular. . **Aphredoderidæ.**

dd. Ventral rays I, 3 to I, 5, typically I, 5.

e. Chin without barbel.

f. Body scaled.

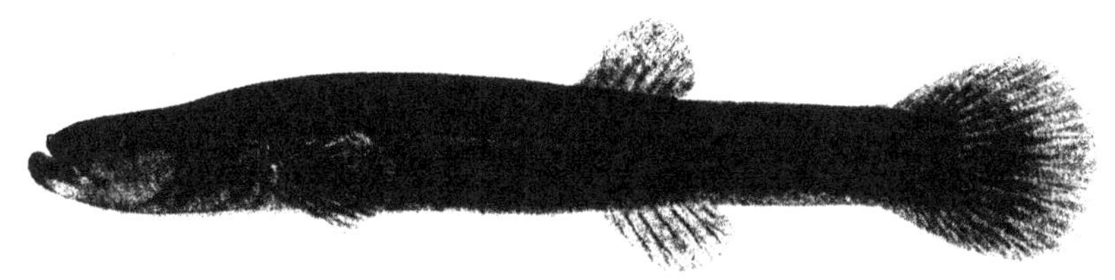

CAVE-FISH, *Chologaster papilliferus* Forbes

BROOK STICKLEBACK, *Eucalia inconstans* (Kirtland)

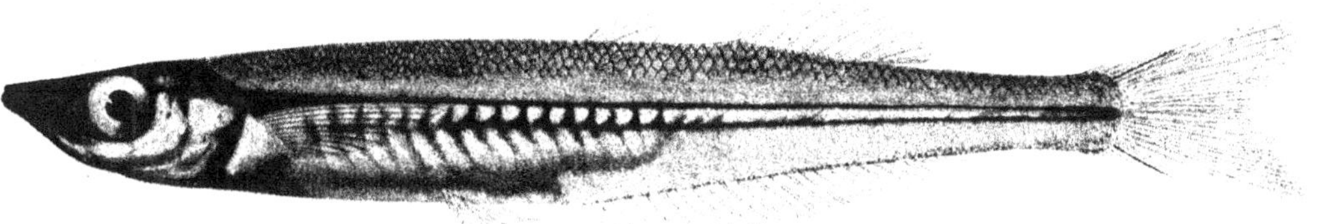

BROOK SILVERSIDE, *Labidesthes sicculus* (Cope)

g. Anal spines 3 to 10.

h. Lateral line wanting.. **Elassomidæ.**

hh. Lateral line present.

i. Dorsal fins confluent, the spinous portion low or high; in forms with the notch deep, approaching separation, the highest dorsal spine is but little more than ½ height of the highest ray.................... **Centrarchidæ.**

ii. Dorsal fins either (1) separate and with soft and spinous portions about equally high, or (2) barely confluent, with the notch very deep and with the highest dorsal spine as high or higher than the highest soft ray (which definition does not include marine genera).................... **Serranidæ.**

gg. Anal spines 1 or 2, never more than 2.

h. Lateral line not extending on rays of caudal fin.................. **Percidæ.**

hh. Lateral line extending on rays of caudal fin...................... **Sciænidæ.**

Suborder Loricati.

ff. Body naked, or variously armed with prickles or bony plates...... **Cottidæ.**

Family **GASTEROSTEIDÆ**

THE STICKLEBACKS

Body more or less fusiform, somewhat compressed, tapering behind to a slender caudal peduncle; skin naked or with vertically oblong bony plates; no true scales; skeleton osseous; four anterior vertebræ more or less enlarged; middle and sides of belly shielded by the pubic bones; ventral fins abdominal or subabdominal, consisting of a stout spine and one or two rudimentary rays; dorsal fin preceded by 2 or more free spines; caudal lunate; no mesocoracoid; gill-membranes broadly joined, free from isthmus or not free; branchiostegals 3; gill-rakers moderate or rather long; mouth-cleft oblique; premaxillaries protractile; maxillary bent at r ght angles and overlapping premaxillary at corner of mouth; teeth sharp, in a narrow band on each jaw; no teeth on vomer or palatines; pyloric cæca present, few in number; air-bladder simple.

These are small fishes, inhabiting fresh waters and arms of the sea in northern Europe and America. Genera 5, species about 12; two species, representing two genera, found in Illinois.

The fresh-water sticklebacks are very similar in their habits. All are active, pugnacious, and greedy, and, in spite of their small size, they are known to be very destructive to the fry of other fishes. In certain localities along the Atlantic coast they occur so abundantly as to be a nuisance to the fishermen, clogging the nets used for smelt. Certain European species will bear with impunity transplantation from fresh water into salt water, and vice versa.

Most or all of the sticklebacks build nests, constructing them out of sticks which they fasten together by silk-like threads formed from the secretion of a gland, found only in the males. The substance* secreted by this gland, which is in reality the

* See Möbius Arch. f. Mikr. Anat. Vol. 25 p. 554.

kidney, is much like the mucin secreted by the vineyard snail, *Helix pomatia*. The nest is built, by the exertions of the male alone, among the stems of aquatic plants where there is some current.* It has two openings, which are "as smooth and symmetrical as the hole leading into a wren's nest, and not unlike it." The male induces the female to enter the nest and lay her eggs, after which he enters and deposits his milt. The holes in the nest are in the direction of the current, so that a stream of water passes through it continually. The pugnacious male watches the nest and wards off all intruders.

KEY TO THE GENERA OF **GASTEROSTEIDÆ** FOUND IN ILLINOIS

a. Pubic bones firmly united, forming a lanceolate plate with a single strong median keel; tail without keel, deeper than broad; dorsal spines 4 or 5, the spines in a right line, non-divergent........................**Eucalia.**

aa. Pubic bones weak and feebly united to form an elongate plate with a median longitudinal groove, on each side of which is a raised edge; tail broader than deep, with lateral bony keel; dorsal spines 8 to 11, divergent from right to left at various angles..........................**Pygosteus.**

GENUS **EUCALIA** JORDAN

FIVE-SPINED STICKLEBACKS

Sticklebacks of typical form, feebly armed, the skin not mailed, and the dorsal spines few (not more than 5) and non-divergent; tail deeper than broad, without keel; pubic bones firmly united, forming a lanceolate plate with a single strong median carina. Fresh waters of North America; one species known.

EUCALIA INCONSTANS (KIRTLAND)

BROOK STICKLEBACK

(PL., P. 220)

Kirtland, 1841, Bost. Journ. Nat. Hist., III, 273 (**Gasterosteus**).
J. & G., 394 (**Gasterosteus**); M. V., 97; J. & E., I, 744; N., 42 (**inconstans** and **pygmæa**); J., 51; F., 70 (**Gasterosteus**); F. F., I. 6, 68; L., 22.

Length 2½ inches; body rather deep and moderately compressed; caudal peduncle rather stout and not keeled; depth 3.8 to 4.4; greatest width about ⅗ of greatest depth; depth of caudal peduncle 1.8 to 2.9 in its length. Color (females and young) olivaceous, with faint lighter mottlings and with many fine dots of black; upper part of sides and caudal peduncle with about 10 dark cross-bar-like bands more or less confluent in ring-like pattern; lower

* For full description of nest-building of *Gasterosteus cataphractus* see J. K. Lord as quoted by Dr. Jordan in "Guide to the Study of Fishes," Vol. II. p. 230.

parts silvery; upper part of cheek and opercle crossed by a splash of bright green; median fins more or less dusky; spring males said to be jet-black, tinged with red anteriorly. Head 3.2 to 3.8; width of head 1.9 to 2.3 in its length; interorbital space 4.6 to 5.7; eye 3.2 to 3.4; nose 4 to 5; mouth small and very oblique, the maxillary considerably short of front of orbit, 4 to 4.8 in head. Dorsal V (or VI), 9–10, the spines in a right line, not divergent; caudal subtruncate (scarcely lunate in our specimens); anal rather large, I, 9 or 10, the spine shorter than the anterior rays; ventrals with a short but strong and sharp spine with minute serratures, its length 3.5 to 4 in head; pectorals 1.7 to 2 in head; post-pectoral plate present; thoracic processes slender and covered with skin, widely separated; pubic bones firmly united, forming a lanceolate, keeled process which extends backward from between ventrals. Skin smooth, destitute of dermal plates.

This little stickleback, one of the hardiest, most combative, and most individual of our smaller fishes, has been confined, in our collections, to the lakes of northeastern Illinois, the Calumet River at South Chicago, and clear brooks in LaSalle county. It is a northern species, ranging through the Dominion of Canada from New Brunswick to Calgary on the branches of the Saskatchewan, and thence through the St. Lawrence, Lake Champlain, and the Great Lakes from Ontario to Superior, to central Ohio and the basin of the Missouri as far south as Kansas. It is confined to fresh waters, and prefers clear cool brooks. This species builds nests, like the others of its family. In the aquarium it is quarrelsome, and destructive even to fishes of larger size.

Its mouth is small, its gill-rakers are long and slender, about half the length of the corresponding filaments, and its pharyngeal apparatus is insignificant. The intestine is short and simple, not longer than the head and body together. Notwithstanding this equipment for a carnivorous life, five specimens examined by us were found to have fed on plants and animals in equal quantities—the former wholly filamentous algæ, which had been taken by four of the specimens in quantities to make it certain that they were purposely eaten. The animal food was about equally insects and crustaceans, the latter chiefly *Entomostraca* and the former largely *Chironomus* larvæ. These and specimens of *Cypris* taken by one of these fishes are evidence that it feeds, in part at least, upon the bottom.

GENUS **PYGOSTEUS** BREVOORT

NINE-SPINED STICKLEBACKS

Dorsal spine 9 to 11, divergent from right to left at various angles; tail broader than deep, with a lateral bony keel; pubic bones weak and feebly united, forming an elongate plate with a median longitudinal groove, on each side of which is a raised edge*; characters otherwise as in *Eucalia*. Species two, in the waters of northern regions, one of them native in China; a single species, cosmopolitan in distribution, found in the waters of Illinois.

PYGOSTEUS PUNGITIUS (LINNÆUS)

NINE-SPINED STICKLEBACK

Linnæus, 1758, Syst. Nat., Ed. X, 296 (**Gasterosteus**).
G., I, 6 (**Gasterosteus**); J. & G., 393 (**Gasterosteus**); M. V., 97; J. & E., I, 745; N., 42 (**nebulosus**); J., 51 (**occidentalis** var. **nebulosus**); F. F., I. 6, 69.

Length 3 inches; body quite slender, considerably compressed, the caudal peduncle very long, slender and tapering, broader than deep, and with lateral bony keel; depth 5.1 to 5.6; greatest width about 3/5 of greatest depth; depth of caudal peduncle 4.3 to 6.2 in its length. "Color olivaceous above, profusely punctulate, irregularly barred with darker; silvery below" (J. & E.). Head 3.3 to 3 7; width 2.4 to 3; interorbital space 4.5 to 5.1 in head; eye 3; nose 3.3 to 3.8; mouth somewhat less oblique than in the last species, the maxillary nearly to orbit, 3.3 to 4.4 in head. Dorsal IX (or X), 9 or 10, the spines promiscuously divergent to right and left at various angles; caudal scarcely lunate; anal rather low, the spine nearly as long as anterior rays; ventrals with a long finely serrated spine, which is less than 3 in head; pectorals 1.7 to 1.9 in head; post-pectoral plate well developed; thoracic processes prominent, forming a U-shaped figure; pubic bones thin and feebly united, lanceolate, with a median groove between two raised edges. Skin naked except for small bony plates along bases of dorsal and anal and on caudal keel.

This little species has been taken by us but once, and then from the lower Calumet River and from Lake Michigan near the mouth of that stream. It inhabits both fresh and brackish water, and is found throughout northern Europe, and in North America as far southward as the Great Lake region. It is thus a strictly northern species.

Our only hint of its food was given us by the examination of two specimens which had fed wholly on the larvæ of gnats (*Chironomus* and *Simulium*) and on various *Entomostraca*.

* Not verified for *P. sinensis* of China.

FAMILY PERCOPSIDÆ

THE TROUT-PERCHES

Body moderately elongate, somewhat compressed; caudal peduncle rather long and slender; scales with edges strongly ctenoid; head naked; lateral line developed; skeleton bony; anterior vertebræ simple; ventral fins abdominal, somewhat anterior; dorsal fin with 2 spines; ventrals with 1 rudimentary spine and about 8 rays; anal with 1 or 2 spines; caudal forked; an adipose fin present; no mesocoracoid; gill-membranes separate, free from isthmus; branchiostegals 6; pseudobranchiæ present; gill-rakers short, tubercle-like; opercle with entire edges; mouth small, horizontal; premaxillaries not protractile; teeth very small, villiform, on premaxillaries and lower jaw only; stomach siphonal, with about 10 well-developed pyloric cæca; air-bladder present; with an open duct (Boulenger); ova large, not falling into the abdominal cavity before extrusion.

Small fishes of the fresh waters of North America; 2 genera known, each containing a single species; one species found in Illinois.

This family "shows the remarkable combination of true fin-spines, ctenoid scales, and a percoid mouth, with the adipose fin, abdominal ventrals, and naked head of the *Isospondyli*" (herring-like forms). It is doubtless a surviving remnant of a fauna which marked the transition from the soft-rayed herring-like forms to the later-appearing groups of acanthopterygian fishes.

GENUS PERCOPSIS AGASSIZ

TROUT-PERCH

Characters in the main as above, differing from the single other known genus of the family (*Columbia* Eigenmann, recently described from the Pacific slope) in the weaker dorsal spines, the more translucent body, and the relative absence of serration of the preopercle. Atlantic slope and Great Lake region, in clear cold waters; one species.

PERCOPSIS GUTTATUS AGASSIZ

TROUT-PERCH

(MAP LXVII)

Agassiz, 1850, Lake Superior, 286.
G., VI, 207; J. & G., 322; M. V., 82; J. & E., I, 784; N., 43; J., 53; F., 72; L., 22.

Length 6 inches; body elongate, not much compressed, strongly tapered posteriorly, the caudal peduncle slender; depth 3.9 to 4.5; greatest width ⅔ greatest depth; depth caudal peduncle 2.7 to 3.2 in its length. Color of upper parts pale olive-buff, the scales with faint edgings of black; 8 or 9 black spots on each side anterior to adipose fin and above lateral line; a dusky median lateral band, more or less broken into spots; lower portion of sides and belly silvery; entire fish translucent; the cerebral membranes showing olive underneath skin of head; peritoneum silvery; cheeks, opercles, jaws, and chin silvery with emerald luster; iris silvery white with faint luster of rose; fins plain, transparent. Head slender, conical, 3.2 to 3.7; width of head 1.8 to 2 in its length; interorbital space 3.5 to 4 in head; eye .9 to 1.2 in interorbital space, 3.3 to 4 in head; nose 2.4 to 3; mouth moderate, subinferior, maxillary short of orbit, 3 to 4 in head; lower jaw included. Dorsal I (occasionally II), 9–11; the spine very weak, the fin inserted much nearer muzzle than base of caudal, almost exactly over ventrals; caudal deeply forked; anal I, 5–7; ventrals abdominal, nearer anal than angle of union of gill-membranes; pectorals reaching past front of ventrals, 1.2 to 1.5 in head. Scale 6, 47–54, 7, ctenoid, being most distinctly so on caudal peduncle; lateral line developed, nearly straight.

This interesting and graceful little fish, a distinctly northern species in its main range, has been found by us chiefly in clear spring waters at various points along the Illinois River from Meredosia to Hennepin. We have taken it also once from a small stream near Lincoln, in Logan county, and once from Lake Michigan, off Chicago. It is a wide-ranging species, known from the streams of New England and Quebec, thence west to Kansas and northward to Hudson Bay and the Saskatchewan Valley near Medicine Hat. It is common in the Great Lakes, but rare south of them.

It spawns in spring, and females greatly distended with eggs were caught by us at Havana on the 10th of March. Surface says that in Cayuga Lake, New York, females captured in May were in ripe condition.

FAMILY ATHERINIDÆ

THE SILVERSIDES

Body rather elongate, somewhat compressed; scales generally cycloid; head usually scaly; lateral line absent or represented by only a few rudimentary tubes; skeleton osseous; anterior vertebræ simple; ventral fins abdominal; two dorsal fins, well separated, the first consisting of 3 to 8 slender flexible spines, and the second of soft rays; anal with a weak spine; no mesocoracoid; gill-membranes not connected, free from isthmus; branchiostegals 5 or 6; pseudobranchiæ present; gill-rakers usually long and slender; opercular bones without spines or serrature; premaxillaries protractile or not; teeth usually present on jaws, sometimes on vomer and palatines; no pyloric cæca; air-bladder present.

"Carnivorous fishes, mostly of small size, living in great schools near the shore in temperate and tropical seas; a few species in fresh water." A single genus and species found in Illinois waters. The presence in all the species of a silvery band along the side, often underlaid by black pigment, gives the common name to the family.

Genus **LABIDESTHES** Cope

BROOK SILVERSIDES

Body elongate, more or less compressed; belly rounded before ventrals; head oblong, compressed; mouth small, the cleft curved, oblique, the jaws being prolonged into a short depressed beak; premaxillaries freely protractile, broad behind; lower jaw longer than upper; no teeth on vomer or palatines; both dorsals short; scales with entire edges. Eastern North America to Texas; confined to fresh waters; a single species known.

LABIDESTHES SICCULUS (Cope)

BROOK SILVERSIDE

(Pl., p. 220; Map LXVIII)

Cope, 1865, Proc. Ac. Nat. Sci. Phila., 81 (**Chirostoma**).
J. & G., 406; M. V., 100; J. & E., I, 805; N., 42; J., 51; F., 70; F. F., I. 6, 69; L., 22.

Length 3 inches; body quite slender and elongate and considerably compressed; depth 6 to 8; greatest width about ⅗ in greatest depth; depth of caudal peduncle 2.3 to 3 in its length. 'Color pale olive-green, translucent; a very distinct lateral silvery band, scarcely broader than pupil, bounded above by a dark line; back dotted with black' (J. & E., slightly emended); dorsal of males tipped with black. Head long and pointed, flattened, and broader above than below, 4.1 to 4.6; width of head 2.1 to 2.5; interorbital space 3.5 to 4; eye 3.5 to 4; nose long and slender, the jaws prolonged into a short depressed beak, whose length is nearly twice the eye; mouth large, maxillary to front of orbit, cleft 2.2 to 2.6; jaws equal, edge of upper jaw strongly concave. Dorsal IV–I, 9 to 11; first dorsal inserted slightly behind front of anal; caudal forked; anal I, 21 to 24; ventrals abdominal, much nearer front of anal than throat; pectorals nearly to ventrals, 1.3 to 1.6 in head. Scales cycloid, 15–16, 75–79; lateral line represented by a few isolated pores (as a rule only on caudal peduncle); cheeks and opercles scaled.

This delicate and exquisite little fish, slender as a pike, semi-translucent, and decorated with lateral stripes of brilliant silver, is distributed through the northern, central, and eastern parts of the state, but is wanting in all our collections from the Kaskaskia, the Big Muddy, the Saline, and the waters of extreme southern Illinois. It evidently avoids the lower Illinoisan glaciation. It is more abundant north than south, the frequency ratios of our 121 collections of it being approximately as 1, 2, and 3, for southern, central, and northern Illinois respectively.

It occurs in a great variety of waters from Lake Michigan and the northeastern glacial lakes of Illinois to the borders of the main stream of the Illinois River and the muddy lakes of the Illinois bottoms, commonest, however, in the quieter and clearer parts of the waters which it inhabits. We have found it somewhat most abundant in the smaller rivers (coefficient 1.67), and next in the glacial lakes (1.13) and in lowland lakes and sloughs (1.01). It is not infrequent, however, in our collections from creeks and the larger rivers (.76 and .77).

Outside the state, it is present in all the Great Lakes, and ranges thence southward to Florida and southwestward to Missouri, Arkansas, and Texas.

It seems to live wholly on the animal plankton, apparently catching its minute prey one by one, as a pike captures fish. Its mouth, though small, is well equipped with teeth, and its gill-rakers are unusually well developed, being numerous, slender, armed with minute denticles, and longer than the gill-filaments. Corresponding to its predaceous habit, its intestine is uncommonly short, the whole alimentary canal being considerably shorter than the body without the head. The food of twenty-five specimens, obtained from widely scattered localities, was wholly animal, and consisted mostly of minute larvæ of gnats (*Chironomus*) and many species of *Entomostraca*, both copepods and *Cladocera*. Land insects and spiders, washed or fallen into the water, were also frequent in its food, including forms as small as plant-lice, chalcids, springtails, and thrips. One specimen had taken a very small unrecognizable minnow.

Family **APHREDODERIDÆ**

THE PIRATE-PERCHES

Body oblong, elevated at base of dorsal, compressed behind; caudal peduncle thick; scales strongly ctenoid; sides of head scaly; lateral line imperfect; skeleton osseous; anterior vertebræ simple; ventrals thoracic, with a small spine and more than 5 soft rays; dorsal fin single, with 3 or 4 small spines; anal with two slender spines; caudal rounded; no mesocoracoid; gill-membranes slightly joined to isthmus anteriorly; branchiostegals 6; pseudobranchiæ obsolete; gill-rakers tubercle-like, dentate; preopercle and preorbital with free edges sharply serrate; opercle with a spine; mouth somewhat oblique; premaxillary not protractile; maxillary without evident supplemental bone; teeth in villiform bands on jaws, vomer, palatines, and pterygoids; pyloric cæca about 12; intestinal canal ending at throat in the adult, the vent more posterior in the young, migrating forward, with growth, from just behind the ventral fins; air-bladder simple, large, adherent, the duct probably obsolete.

Fresh waters of the United States; a single living genus and species; several fossil genera While the structure of the skeleton is essentially that of percoid fishes, the character of the forward position of the vent leaves the *Aphredoderidæ* singularly isolated, without close relationships with the true perch-like forms.

Genus **APHREDODERUS** Le Sueur

PIRATE-PERCHES

Characters of the genus included above.

Fig. 55

APHREDODERUS SAYANUS (Gilliams)

PIRATE-PERCH

(Map LXIX)

Gilliams, 1824, J. Ac. Nat. Sci. Phila., IV, 81 (**Scolopsis**).
J. & G., 460; M. V., 113; J. & E., I, 786; N., 39 (**A. sayanus** and **Sternotremia isolepis**); J., 48; (**Aphododerus isolepis**); F., 70; L., 22.

Length 2 to 4 inches; body robust, rather deep and considerably compressed, the caudal peduncle stout; depth 3.1 to 3.5; greatest width scarcely more than ½ greatest depth; depth caudal peduncle 1.6 to 1.9 in its length. Color dark olivaceous over transparent pinkish to lavender, the head and body everywhere profusely specked with black, appearing bluish over the ground-color; under side of head and sometimes fore part of breast and belly yellowish; two blackish bars at base of caudal; fins, except ventrals, dusky with a more deeply pigmented band around bases; ventrals yellowish; median fins with a narrow marginal fringe of white. Breeding males and females show much iridescent color, the predominating lusters being violet and purple;

light coppery, green, and silvery sometimes visible; the entire bodies of breeding males often almost black. Head broad below, depressed, the profile concave, 2.8 to 3.2; width of head 1.5 to 1.8 in its length; interorbital space 3.3 to 4; eye 1.4 to 1.8 in interorbital, 4.5 to 5.3 in head; nose 2.8 to 3.4 (usually less than 3.2); mouth moderate, oblique, maxillary nearly to front of orbit, 2.7 to 2.9; lower jaw projecting; sides and top of head, chin, and lower jaw with rows of sensory papillæ, as in *Amblyopsidæ*. Dorsal III, 9–12 (usually 10 or 11), the fin nearer muzzle than base of caudal, behind ventrals; caudal fin broadly rounded, with a slight notch; anal II, 6; ventrals jugular in adult*, nearer angle of gill-membranes than front of anal; pectorals 1.4 to 1.8 in head, reaching more than half way to anal. Scales 9–13 (usually 11–12), 49–59, 12–14, strongly ctenoid; lateral line developed anteriorly; cheeks and opercles fully scaled.

This obscure but peculiar little fish has been found by us in muddy pools and streams throughout Illinois, much the most abundantly southward. It is indeed so rare in northern Illinois that only one of our hundred collections of it has been taken in that part of the state, giving us a frequency coefficient of less than 5 per cent., while that for central Illinois is .72 and that for southern Illinois is 2.23. We have found it most abundant in creeks (coefficient, 2.51), and about half as common in large rivers (1.1) and in lowland lakes (1.24). The streams and situations it most affects are those in which there is little or no current and a muddy bottom, our coefficient of the species for quiet water being 3.26, and that for a muddy bottom, 3.26.

The general distribution of the pirate-perch carries it from Long Island around the coasts of the Atlantic and the Gulf to Texas, and northward up the Mississippi basin to South Dakota and Minnesota and through the Great Lakes at least as far east as Lake Erie. It has not been reported from Canada.

It was named the "pirate-perch" by Dr. C. C. Abbott, because it ate only fishes when confined in his aquarium. Studies made by us in Illinois show, however, that fishes form only a small part of its normal food. The intestine is short and simple, less than the length of the head and body without the tail; the gill-rakers are short, thick, blunt, and few, and covered with short spinules; and the pharyngeal jaws are small plates covered with short, sharp, minute teeth, similar to those of the sunfishes. The mouth is large, but not remarkably protractile. Judging from 19 specimens dissected, the food is virtually all animal. Small fishes had been eaten by but two, the only one recognizable being a minnow (*Cyprinidæ*). Insects formed the major

* On variability in position of vent with age, see Jordan (Bull. Ill. State Lab. Nat. Hist., No. 2. 1878, p. 48), and Jordan and Evermann (Bull. 47, U. S. Nat. Mus., Pt. I., p. 787).

part of the food, all of them of aquatic species except a few gnats, accidental in the water. Nearly half of the food consisted of larvæ of gnat-like insects (*Chironomus* and *Corethra*), and the remainder was mostly larvæ of May-flies, water-bugs, and larvæ of aquatic beetles, together with a few amphipod and isopod crustaceans. One of these fish had eaten a water-worm (*Lumbriculus*) allied to the earthworms, and *Entomostraca* had been taken by a few. A comparison of the food of specimens of various ages, beginning with those in which the vent was just in front of the ventral fins and ending with those in which it had moved far forward on the throat, gave no hint of the reasons for this extraordinary step in development, these fishes all having eaten substantially the same food.

Dr. Abbott says that the pirate-perch builds a nest which is guarded by both parents, who likewise protect the young until they are about a third of an inch long. The species spawned in the hatchery troughs at Meredosia May 1, 1899, and males running with milt were taken in Meredosia Bay on May 23.

Family **ELASSOMIDÆ**

THE PIGMY SUNFISHES

Body oblong, compressed, covered with large cycloid scales; head scaly; lateral line obsolete; skeleton osseous; anterior vertebræ simple, ventrals thoracic, I, 5; dorsal fin single, with 4 or 5 spines; anal with 3 spines; caudal rounded; no mesocoracoid; gill-membranes broadly united, free from isthmus; branchiostegals 5; pseudobranchiæ small, glandular, covered by skin; gill-rakers tubercle-like; preopercles, preorbitals, and opercles with edges entire; mouth terminal; upper jaw protractile; each jaw with strong conical teeth, in few series; vomer with a few weak teeth; palatines toot less; no pyloric cæca; vent normally placed; air-bladder without duct, so far as known.

Very small fishes, inhabiting the swamps of the southern United States. A single genus, with 2 species. The *Elassomidæ* differ from the *Centrarchidæ* chiefly in their small size. Cycloid scales, while not normal to *Centrarchidae*, are found in some forms.

Genus **ELASSOMA** Jordan

PIGMY SUNFISHES

Characters of the genus included above.

Two species: *E. zonatum*, widely distributed in the southern United States; and *E. evergladei;* confined to the swamps of southern Georgia and of Florida.

ELASSOMA ZONATUM Jordan

PIGMY SUNFISH

Jordan, 1877, Bull. U. S. Nat. Mus., X, 50.
J. & G., 461; M. V., 113; B., I, 34; J. & E., I, 982; J., 47; F., 70; L., 23.

Length 1½ inches; body oblong, deep and compressed, the profile convex; depth 3.3 to 3.6; greatest width about ½ greatest depth; depth caudal peduncle 1.8 to 2 in its length. "Color olive-green, everywhere finely punctulate; sides with about 11 parallel vertical bands of dark olive, about equal in width, narrower than the eye, about as wide as the pale interspaces; a conspicuous roundish black spot, nearly as large as the eye, on the sides just above the axis of the body, under the beginning of the dorsal; soft fins faintly barred; a blackish bar at base of caudal. Head 2.9 to 3, its width in its length 1.8 to 1.9; interorbital space 4 to 4.3 in head; eye 3 to 3.5; nose short, blunt, 5.3 to 5.8; mouth terminal, oblique, maxillary past front of orbit; jaws equal. Dorsal IV to V, 9 to 10; caudal rounded; anal III, 5; ventrals past vent; pectorals 1.8 to 1.9 in head. Scales 18–19, 37–39, cycloid; no lateral line; cheeks and opercles scaled.

This little fish, rare in our waters and not abundant anywhere, has been taken by us in only six collections, all from southern Illinois, four of them from the Wabash Valley, one from Running Lake, and one from a bluff spring in Union county. The Wabash localities are Little Fox River at Phillipstown, Wabash River at Wabash station, Drew pond in White county, and Swan pond near St. Francisville. It is a southern fish, reported from North and South Carolina, Alabama, Louisiana, and Texas.

Family CENTRARCHIDÆ

THE SUNFISHES

Body more or less shortened and compressed, the regions above and below the horizontal axis about equally developed; scales usually not very strongly ctenoid, in rare cases cycloid; sides of head scaly; lateral line present; skeleton osseous, anterior vertebræ simple; abdominal vertebræ from 3d or 4th to last with transverse processes; ventral fins thoracic, typically with 1 spine and 5 rays; dorsal fins confluent, the spines 6 to 13 (usually 10); anal spines 3 to 9; caudal slightly emarginate or weakly furcate; no mesocoracoid; gill-membranes separate from isthmus; branchiostegals 6, rarely 7; pseudobranchiæ small, nearly or quite covered by skin; gill-rakers variously formed, always armed with small teeth; preopercle entire or somewhat serrate; opercle ending behind in two flat points or prolonged in a black or partially black flap at the angle; mouth terminal; premaxillaries protractile; maxillary typically with a supplemental bone, which is obsolescent or wanting in some small-mouthed forms; teeth in villiform bands on premaxillaries, lower jaw, and vomer, and usually on palatines; tongue sometimes with teeth; no canine teeth; lower pharyngeal bones separate, with conic or paved teeth; intestinal canal short; pyloric cæca 5 to 10; air-bladder without duct in adult; coloration usually brilliant; the young more slender than the adults and in most species marked by broad transverse bars.

Fresh waters of North America; genera about 12, species about 30. Seven genera and 13 species found in the waters of Illinois.

This family includes the crappies and black bass in addition to the smaller forms more commonly referred to under the name of "sunfishes." The species range in size from the smaller sunfishes, some of which seldom exceed 3½ inches in length, to the rock bass and the crappie, which reach a weight of more than 1 ℔, and the black bass, the large-mouth form of which occasionally weighs 12 to 14 ℔.

The typical deep-bodied sunfishes, taken together as a group of species, are about equally frequent in lowland lakes, creeks, and the smaller rivers, and about half as common in upland lakes and in rivers of the larger size, our general coefficients being 1.13 for each of the first three situations and .6 and .55 respectively for the last two.

All the family are spring spawners so far as known. Most of the species build nests, which consist of holes scooped out in alluvial, leafy, or sandy bottom about the margins of the waters they inhabit. Sexual differences in form or coloration are not much developed.

All except the very small species are valued as food, the sunfishes and crappies being among the best of pan-fishes. The output of sunfishes, not including crappie and bass, for the states of the Mississippi Valley in 1899 was 910,963 ℔. Of the total, 507,680 ℔ were furnished by the Illinois River alone.

The sunfishes proper—that is, the *Centrarchidæ* exclusive of the black bass—are a well-marked and homogeneous group of species as to form and external structure, but a diverse assemblage as to ecological relationships. Some of the species, for example, prefer running water, and others quiet; some a clean hard bottom, and others a bottom of mud; some turbid water, and others clear; some creeks and rivulets, and others the larger rivers. They also form a diverse group in respect to the disposition of the several species to avoid each others' company, some of the species having been found together in our collections with more than twice the average frequency, and others with less than a third that average. The family affords, indeed, an excellent illustration of the disposition of species closely allied in structure and in classification and inhabiting the same area to evade the mutually injurious competition to which their similar natural endowments expose them, by avoiding each others' company—by choosing, as a rule, different feeding grounds and different places of resort. If we compare, for example, the proportionate frequency with which the closely similar species of the genus *Lepomis* have been taken together in our collections—in the same haul of the net, or from the same situation at the same time—with the frequency of associate occurrence of the widely dissimilar species of the other genera of the family, we find that the unlike species have been taken together much more frequently than the like—in a ratio of 1½ to 1; that the species of *Lepomis* have, indeed, been taken in company with species of other genera considerably more frequently than with each other. The sunfishes, consequently, are not an associate group, but tend to disperse themselves over a large variety of ecological situations, those least like each other being most likely to meet on common ground, where their unlike capacities enable them to live together in a non-competitive way.

Of our fifteen species of sunfishes proper, including the crappies in this number, eleven are abundant enough in this state to play a significant part in the life of the family. Three of these species have a more or less limited general distribution within the state. The round sunfish (*Centrarchus macropterus*) is confined to extreme southern Illinois; the pumpkinseed (*Eupomotis gibbosus*) is found almost wholly in the northern half of the state, and, except in northern Illinois proper, only along the main streams of the largest rivers; and the long-eared sunfish (*Lepomis megalotis*), which is distributed throughout the state, is so concentrated in southern and eastern Illinois that its competitive relations are strongly affected by this fact. The warmouth (*Chaenobryttus gulosus*) is, indeed, somewhat similarly distributed, the contrast being, however, less marked than in *megalotis*. The rock bass (*Ambloplites rupestris*) is sharply separated from most of the other sunfishes by its strong preference for swift, clear streams; the bluegill (*Lepomis pallidus*), the warmouth, and *Lepomis miniatus* are rather strongly distinguished by their greater frequency in lakes and ponds; while the warmouth and *Lepomis humilis* are especially noticeable because of their high frequencies over a muddy bottom. The principal species of the larger rivers are the two crappies (especially *sparoides*) and the bluegill; those of the smaller rivers and creeks are the rock bass, the long-eared sunfish and *Lepomis humilis;* and a special creek species is the green sunfish (*L. cyanellus*), the usual sunfish of the smaller prairie streams of central Illinois.

These differences of local situation and affiliation are most evident in our miscellaneous collections distributed over the minor waters of the state, and such distinctions diappear largely in the Illinois River, which seems to serve as a kind of reservoir or metropolis for the fish population of the country, in which its various elements unite and mingle in a relatively indiscriminate way. This fact appears especially on a comparison of the data of the collections made at Meredosia and at Havana—about a third of our whole number—with those made outside. Thus, 76 of our 170 collections of the pale crappie were made at either Havana or Meredosia, and 94 of them came from other places. Fifty-five per cent. of these 76 Illinois River collections contained also the bluegill, while only 27 per cent. of the 94 collections outside these points contained both species. That is, local differences of distribution, signifying ecological distinctions, were twice as evident in the collections made from the smaller waters as from those made from the Illinois.

In addition to these distinguishable differences of local preference, the sunfishes are more strongly differentiated than usual with respect to their feeding structures—the mouth, the gill-rakers and the pharyngeal teeth. Those with large mouths have a large ratio of fishes and crawfishes in the food, those with long gill-rakers take more *Entomostraca,* and those with broad and heavy pharyngeal bones, bearing stout blunt teeth, live more largely on mollusks. Additional details on this topic will be found in the discussion of the several genera and species.

Key to Genera of CENTRARCHIDÆ found in Illinois

a. Dorsal fin little longer than anal, if any, its length 1 to 1.4 times length of anal base; anal spines 5 to 8 in number.

b. Dorsal spines 5 to 8 (occasionally 9 or even 10).................... **Pomoxis.**

bb. Dorsal spines 11 to 13.

c. Anal spines 7 or 8 (occasionally 6), the rays 13 to 15........... **Centrarchus.**

cc. Anal spines 6, rays 10 or 11................................ **Ambloplites.**

aa. Dorsal more than twice length of anal; anal spines 3.

d. Body comparatively short and deep, depth in adults as a rule more than ⅖ of length; dorsal fin not deeply emarginate, the shortest spine behind middle of fin more than ⅔ height of longest; operculum entire behind, not emarginate, more or less prolonged in a bony process or flap with a rounded posterior margin.

e. Tongue and pterygoids* with teeth; maxillary reaching past pupil.......... ....**Chænobryttus.**

ee. Tongue and pterygoids toothless; maxillary in most species short of middle of orbit (to middle in *L. cyanellus*).

f. Lower pharyngeals (Fig. 64 and 65) narrow, the width in the length of toothed portion about 3, outer margin straight or weakly concave, the teeth long, slender, and acuminate; pectorals never reaching beyond vertical from base of anal; opercular flap without red, or if red is present, with the color forming a border and not a roundish spot.........**Lepomis.**

ff. Lower pharyngeals (Fig. 66 and 67) broad, the width in the length of the toothed portion about 2, the outer margin a double curve; teeth short, bluntly rounded or paved; opercular flap with a conspicuous roundish red spot on its lower posterior corner or (in case the red spot is wanting) the pectorals reaching past front of anal (to a vertical from last anal ray). ....**Eupomotis.**

dd. Body comparatively elongate, depth about ⅓ length; dorsal fin deeply emarginate, the shortest spine behind middle of fin from ⅓ to ½ height of longest; operculum ending in two flat points.................**Micropterus.**

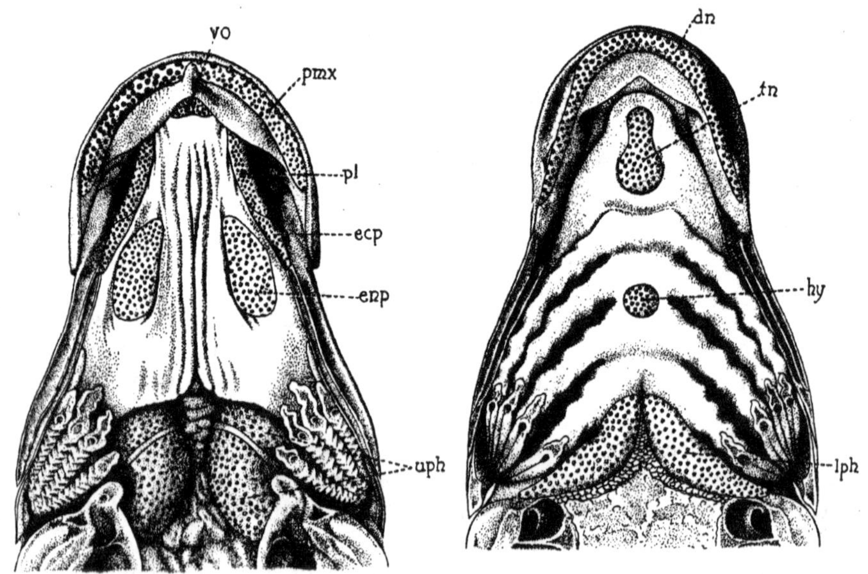

Fig. 56 Fig. 57

Roof (56) and floor (57) of mouth of *Ambloplites rupestris* to show dentition of a typical sunfish. *dn*, dentary; *ecp*, ectopterygoid; *enp*, entopterygoid; *hy*, hyoid; *lph*, lower pharyngeal; *pl*, palatine; *pmx*, premaxillary; *tn*, tongue; *uph*, upper pharyngeal; *vo*, vomer.

* See Fig. 56 and 57 for illustration of full dentition of a sunfish.

Genus **POMOXIS** Rafinesque

CRAPPIES

Body moderately elongate, deep and strongly compressed; opercle emarginate behind; preopercle and preorbital finely serrated; mouth large; maxillary with a large supplemental bone; teeth on vomer, palatines, entopterygoids, and tongue; lower pharyngeals narrow, with sharp teeth; gill-rakers long and slender, numerous; dorsal spines 6 to 8; anal spines 6; caudal emarginate; scales feebly ctenoid.

Eastern United States and Canada; two species, which are very similar in habit, ecological relationship, and food, scarcely avoiding competition, on the whole, in any way clearly discernible in our data. A tendency to geographical separation is shown by the fact that *annularis* is the more abundant southward in the general area of the genus, and *sparoides* northward,—the latter, indeed, also ranging somewhat the farther to the north. That these two species are similarly related ecologically, and thus drawn into each others' company by their relations to their environment instead of being separated as competitors, is shown by a comparison of the coefficients of association of the two crappies, on the one hand, and of one of these crappies and the common bluegill (*Lepomis pallidus*) on the other. With 167 available collections of *Pomoxis annularis* and 178 of *sparoides*, we find 66 joint occurrences, giving us a frequency of association of 2.53. Comparing, on the other hand, *Pomoxis annularis* and its 167 collections with the widely and similarly distributed bluegill, taken 220 times, we find them taken together in the same collections 56 times, equivalent to a coefficient of association of 2.13. The larger number of collections of the two unlike species gives us a relative frequency of joint occurrence distinctly less than that of the smaller numbers of collections of the closely similar crappies.

The species of this genus diverge from the other sunfishes in respect especially to their numerous, long, and finely-toothed gill-rakers, which make the most effective straining apparatus to be found among the sunfishes, excepting only the comparatively rare round sunfish (*Centrarchus macropterus*). The mouth is also large for a sunfish, its opening being considerably increased by the unusual length of the lower jaw. These characters of the feeding structures are represented in the food by the presence of fishes, and by the quantities of *Entomostraca* taken in spring.

Key to Species of POMOXIS found in Illinois

a. Dorsal spines typically VI, rarely V or VII; dorsal distance 1.7 to 1.9 in length, a line drawn from back tip of maxillary at right angles with anterior margin of premaxillary crossing back in front of first dorsal spine; body more slender and profile more strongly S-shaped than in *P. sparoides;* color light, the dark markings tending to form rings...........**annularis.**

aa. Dorsal spines typically VII or VIII, rarely VI, or IX, or X; dorsal distance 1.8 to 2, the line from back of maxillary crossing behind third or fourth, or even fifth or sixth, to last dorsal spine; color dark, spotted, the dark markings not forming rings..............................**sparoides.**

POMOXIS ANNULARIS Rafinesque

WHITE CRAPPIE

(Map LXX)

Rafinesque, 1818, Amer. Month. Mag., 41.

J. & G., 464; M. V., 115; B., I. 7 (**sparoides,** part); J. & E., I, 987; N., 37; J., 47; F., 69; F. F., I. 3, 56; L., 23.

Length 12 inches; body elongate, compressed, and back elevated; the profile long and quite strongly S-shaped; depth 2.2 to 2.6 in length; greatest width about 2.75 in greatest depth; depth caudal peduncle 1.1 to 1.3 in its length. 'Color silvery olive, mottled with dark green, the dark marks chiefly on the upper part of the body and having a tendency to form narrow vertical bars; general color much lighter than in the next species; dorsal and caudal fins marked with green (rather than blackish, as in the next species); anal pale, nearly plain; a dusky opercular spot' (J. & E. with emendations). Head long, 2.8 to 2.9; width of head 2.5 to 2.8 in its length; interorbital space 4.3 to 5.6, convex; eye 4.5 to 5 in head; nose 3.2 to 4.2, noticeably longer than in the next species and also visibly longer than eye; mouth large, oblique, maxillary past middle of orbit, 2.1 to 2.3 in head. Dorsal typically* VI, 15, the fin inserted further from muzzle than in the next species, the dorsal distance† in the present species being 1.68 to 1.88 in the length; caudal lunate; anal VI (occasionally V), 17–19; ventrals past first anal spine; pectorals 1.3 to 1.7 in head. Scales 6, 43–48, 12; lateral line developed on most or all scales.

The white crappie and the species following are commonly regarded in this state as the best for food of the sunfish family, with the exception of the black bass. The present species occurs in all parts of the state, most abundantly in lakes, ponds, and bayous, but commonly also in the smaller rivers and in creeks. It seems to have no marked local or ecological preferences to embarrass its entrance upon any waters containing its means of subsistence. It enters freely, for example, upon the lower Illinoisan glaciation, is found in the clean glacial lakes of the

* Of 337 specimens of the present species examined, 318 had VI dorsal spines, 15 had V, and 4 had VII; of 315 specimens of *Pomoxis sparoides,* 266 had VII spines, 46 had VIII, 2 had VI, 1 had IX, and 2 had X.

† In two typical specimens of exactly the same length (6 inches), one *annularis* and one *sparoides,* the dorsal distance differed 8 tenths of one centimeter. This difference may be said to be due to difference in *length* of fins, the dorsals in both species terminating at the same distance from the end of the last vertebra.

WHITE CRAPPIE, *Pomoxis annularis* Rafinesque

northeastern part of the state, and is reported from every river basin of our entire area.

From the Great Lakes, excepting Ontario, it ranges southward through the Mississippi Valley to Alabama and Texas, and westward to Kansas and Nebraska. It has reached the Potomac by way of connecting canals, has entered the Erie canal in New York, and is reported also from Pamlico and Great Pedee rivers, on the south Atlantic coast. It is said by Jordan to be generally abundant in ponds, lagoons, bayous, and all sluggish waters, and to be much more common in the southern parts of its range. "In the lower Mississippi Valley the young of this species literally swarm in the overflow ponds and bayous, and vast numbers perish every year when these waters dry up."

A fish of so wide a range has, of course, many local names. In Illinois the name of crappie is commonly applied indiscriminately to this fish and the one next described. When separately mentioned, the present species is often called the pale crappie, or the white crappie, or the ringed crappie, the last by reason of the more conspicuous vertical bars upon the sides.

The maximum weight of the fish is about 2¾ pounds, but the average of the Illinois River market specimens weigh less than a pound.

This crappie is strictly carnivorous, living mainly on insects, crustaceans, and fishes. Four fifths of the food of fifteen specimens examined by us consisted of various aquatic insect larvæ, while fishes made but 11 per cent. of the entire food.

Observations made on market specimens at Havana indicate that the species spawns in May.

This is an excellent fish with which to stock artificial ponds. It was introduced into the Potomac in 1894, and has now become abundant there. It takes the hook well, and is held in high esteem as a game fish in the Southern States and in some parts of Illinois. Dr. Jordan says that it will take a minnow bait as promptly as will a black bass, but that it is not very pugnacious, and, owing to its tender mouth, requires considerable skill in handling the tackle. The State and the United States Fish Commissions are doing much to maintain the supply of this fish in this state by collecting the young from overflow ponds along the Illinois and the Mississippi, and transplanting them into other waters.

The annual catch of crappie, including the next species with the present, varies from 800,000 to 1,300,000 pounds for the

Mississippi Valley. The Illinois River alone furnished 294,000 pounds in 1899.

POMOXIS SPAROIDES (LACÉPÈDE)

BLACK CRAPPIE; CALICO BASS

(MAP LXXI)

Lacépède, 1802, Hist. Nat. Poiss., III, 517 (**Labrus**).
J. & G., 465; M. V., 115; B., I, 7 (part); J. & E., I, 987; N., 37 (**hexacanthus**); J., 47 (**nigromaculatus**); F. F., I. 3, 56 (**nigromaculatus**); F., 69; L., 23.

Length 12 inches; body oblong, less elongate than in the last species, deep and compressed; profile shorter and less prominently S-shaped than in *P. annularis*; depth 2.1 to 2.4; greatest width 2.75 in greatest length; depth caudal peduncle 1.1 to 1.4 in its length. Color of upper parts olivaceous, silvery whitish to yellowish below and on belly; body everywhere spotted with very dark green or blackish; much iridescent color everywhere, chiefly emerald and bluish; cheeks and opercles slaty; a dark spot at back of opercle above and a smaller one, looking like a spinous extension of opercle, below it; pupil a bright deep blue; iris brown, lavender, and purplish with a narrow inner ring of gold; median fins reticulated (or barred unevenly) with dusky to black, when partly folded having the appearance of dark fins spotted with lighter. Head 2.8 to 3; width of head 2.3 to 2.7 in its length; interorbital space 3.8 to 4.4, convex; eye 4 to 4.5 in head; nose 3.7 to 4.3, little longer than eye; mouth oblique, maxillary 2.1 to 2.5. Dorsal typically* VII (or VIII), 15, the fin inserted nearer muzzle than in last species, the dorsal distance 1.8 to 2; caudal lunate; anal VI, 16–18; ventrals past second anal spine; pectorals 1.4 to 2.1 in head. Scales 6, 38–44, 12; lateral line complete.

This crappie is a darker, deeper, and more handsome fish than the preceding one, and, like it, is highly valued for food, especially as a pan-fish, if taken where the water is not too muddy or too warm. It is found throughout the state, frequently in company with the preceding species of the same genus, from which it scarcely differs appreciably in local distribution, in habits, or in food. According to our data, derived from 183 collections, it is less common than *annularis* in creeks, and has perhaps a noticeably stronger preference for water with a hard bottom. We have also found it more abundant in the glacial lakes of northeastern Illinois, from some of which, indeed, we have not taken *annularis* at all.

Its general range carries it northward beyond the preceding species, and it is reported from the Ottawa River, in Canada, and from the Lake of the Woods.

Its food, according to our observations, is substantially identical with that of *annularis*, except that 11 specimens ex-

* See note on preceding species.

BLACK CRAPPIE, *Pomoxis sparoides* (Lacépède)

amined had taken a larger percentage of both *Entomostraca* and of fishes, and a smaller one of aquatic insects. These differences of ratio are, however, very likely local and seasonal.

The common names of this species most used in Illinois are black crappie, calico bass, and strawberry bass, the first in central Illinois and the others in the northern part of the state.

It does not reach as large a size as the white crappie, the largest specimens taken weighing not much over 1¼ pounds.

The species spawned in May at Havana in 1898, and specimens taken as early as April 19 yielded eggs and milt under pressure.

This crappie has been successfully introduced into France. Its hardy endurance of both heat and cold, and also of foul water, is especially favorable to its transportation and acclimatization. The statistics of the catch of the black crappie from the Mississippi and the Illinois are included under those of the preceding species.

Genus **CENTRARCHUS** Cuvier and Valenciennes

ROUND SUNFISH

Body short and deep, compressed; opercle emarginate behind; mouth large; maxillary with a supplemental bone; teeth on vomer, palatines, entopterygoids, ectopterygoids, and tongue; pharyngeal teeth sharp; gill-rakers setiform, very long and finely dentate, 20 to 30 in the lower angle of the arch; dorsal spines about 12; anal spines about 8; caudal emarginate; scales not strongly ctenoid. Southern and southeastern United States; one species. The genus is closely allied to *Pomoxis*, from which it is separated only by a greater development of the spinous dorsal and anal fins, and by the presence of teeth on the ectopterygoids.

CENTRARCHUS MACROPTERUS (Lacépède)

ROUND SUNFISH; FLIER

(Map LXXII)

Lacépède, 1802, Hist. Nat. Poiss., III, 447 (**Labrus**).

J. & G., 463; M. V., 114; B., I, 8; J. & E., I, 988; N., 37 (**irideus**); J., 47 (**irideus**); F., 70; L., 23; F. F., I. 3, 56 (**irideus**).

Length 4 inches (occasionally 6); body ovate, strongly compressed, profile angled at nape; depth 1.9 to 2.1 in length; greatest width more than 3 in greatest depth; depth caudal peduncle 1 to 1.2 in its length. Color green, with series of dark brown spots on sides below lateral line, forming interrupted longitudinal lines; a dark spot below eye; soft dorsal and anal reticulated; young with a black ocellus at base of soft dorsal. Head rather small, 2.7 to 3.1 in length; width of head 1.9 to 2.1 in its length; interorbital space

2.9 to 3.5, concave; eye 3.3 to 4; nose pointed, scarcely as long as eye, 4 to 4.7 in head; mouth small, oblique, maxillary nearly to middle of orbit, 2.5 to 2.8 in head; opercular flap broad and thin, not prolonged; gill-rakers X + 30, setiform. Dorsal XI or XII (or rarely XIII), 12–14, its longest spine about 2 in head; length of dorsal about 1.2 to 1.3 times length of anal; caudal lunate; anal VII or VIII (occasionally VI), 13–15; ventrals past fourth anal spine; pectorals to 7th or 8th anal spine, 1 to 1.2 in head. Scales 6 or 7, 41–43, 13 or 14; lateral line complete; scales on cheeks in 6 or 7 rows.

Fig. 58

This little fish, found by us only in extreme southern Illinois from Hamilton county southward, is a distinctly southern species, occurring in lowland streams and bayous of the lower Mississippi Valley, and in the south Atlantic region from Florida to Virginia. In this state we have taken it in only thirteen collections, all from creeks and sloughs tributary to the Little Wabash, the Big Muddy, and the Cache.

The species is said by Jordan to reach a length of six inches. Owing to its small size and comparative scarcity, except here and there in the South, it is of no commercial importance.

Genus **AMBLOPLITES** Rafinesque

ROCK BASS

Body oblong, moderately elevated, compressed, but robust; opercle ending in two flat points; preopercle serrate at its angle; mouth large; supplemental maxillary well developed; teeth (Fig. 56) on vomer, palatines, tongue, entopterygoids, and ectopterygoids, a single patch on the tongue (Fig. 57), pharyngeal teeth sharp; gill-rakers rather long and strong, dentate, less than 10 in number; dorsal spines 10 or 11; anal spines normally 6; caudal emarginate; scales somewhat ctenoid. Central, eastern, and southern United States, and Canada; one species.

ROCK BASS, *Ambloplites rupestris* (Rafinesque)

AMBLOPLITES RUPESTRIS (Rafinesque)

ROCK BASS; REDEYE; GOGGLE-EYE

(Map LXXIII)

Rafinesque, 1817, Amer. Month. Mag., 120 (**Bodianus**).
J. & G., 466; M. V., 115; B., I, 10; J. & E., I, 990; N., 37; J., 44; F., 69; F. F., I. 3, 44; L., 23.

Length 8 to 10 inches; body oblong, rather robust and only moderately compressed; profile scarcely angled at nape; depth 2.2 to 2.5; greatest width about 2 in greatest depth; depth caudal peduncle 1.12 to 1.20 in its length. Color of upper parts olive, with black mottlings and brassy reflections; each scale of sides with a central squarish black spot on band, these forming longitudinal stripes traversing length of fish, being most prominent below the lateral line; belly bluish white with darker punctulations, forming a spot on each scale; breast specked with fine black dots and with some blue, green, or reddish; cheeks and opercles with brassy luster; a dark opercular spot; iris maroon before and behind pupil, plum-colored above and below, and edged with gold; median fins amber with brown mottlings (in handsome irregular bars) and faint edgings of black; ventrals opaque whitish with brown specks; pectorals transparent amber, dusky in males; young irregularly barred and blotched with black. Head rather large, 2.6 to 2.8, the profile little angled above eye; width of head 1.9 to 2.13 in its length; interorbital space 3.7 to 4.3 (usually under 4); eye 3.5 to 4; nose 3.4 to 4.1; mouth large, oblique, maxillary past middle of orbit, 2.1 to 2.4 in head; a single patch of teeth on tongue; operculum emarginate, the flap not prolonged; gill-rakers few, 7 to 10, rather long, strong, and stiff. Dorsal XI (occasionally XII), 10–12 (usually 10), rather long and low, its longest spine 3.25 to 3.5 in head; length of base of dorsal about 1.4 times length of anal; caudal emarginate; anal VI, 10–11; ventrals to vent or somewhat past it, sometimes nearly to first anal spine in males; pectorals to first anal spine, 1.8 to 2 in head. Scales 6 or 7, sometimes 8, 39–43, 11 or 12 (or 13); lateral line usually complete; scales on cheeks in 7 or 8 rows.

This large and handsome member of the sunfish family reaches a length of a foot and a weight of a pound to a pound and a half, although its average weight probably does not exceed half a pound. It is, with us, mainly a northern species, having been taken from but four localities in southern Illinois, and not at all in the lower Illinoisan glaciation. This limitation of its range is accounted for by its decided preference for clear rocky streams, its coefficient for swift water (3.66) being the largest in our list of sunfishes. It has occurred to us most abundantly in rivers of medium size (2.96), and about half as frequently in creeks (1.44), its frequencies in other situations being comparatively insignificant. This peculiarity of local preference tends to separate if from the other members of its family generally, with the exception of the small-mouthed black bass, with which it is found more frequently in company than are any other two species of this entire family.

It has been taken, to the northward, from Lakes Huron, Erie and Ontario, from the St. Lawrence River and Lake Champlain, and from northwestern streams and lakes as far as Minnesota and South Dakota. It ranges southward to the James and the Chattaoochee rivers on the Atlantic coast, to the Alabama and the Tombigbee in the Gulf district, and westward to the Des Moines and Kansas rivers. It is said by Jordan and Evermann to occur also in Louisiana and in Texas.

According to Dr. Jordan, it spawns in spring, constructing a nest on a gravel bed where the water is moderately swift, or on a bar if in a lake, the parent fish defending the nest with great vigor. Spent females were taken by us at Havana June 26.

"This species," says Jordan, "is pre-eminently a boy's fish, though it is by no means despised by anglers of maturer years. * * * * As a game-fish it is rather disappointing. It takes the hook with vim and energy, and begins a most vigorous fight which, however, it usually fails to keep up. It can usually be caught at any season and at any time of day; good fishing may be had even at night. Any kind of bait may be used, but small minnows, white grubs, and angleworms are best. It will take the trolling spoon quite readily, and the spinner and the bucktail also are successful lures. Minnows may be used either in still-fishing or in trolling. During the summer grasshoppers are a good bait, and pieces of fresh-water mussel or yellow perch are excellent. In the fall still-fishing with small minnows usually meets with success. Casting with the artificial fly is not a common method for catching the rock bass, yet we have had many good rises and have taken some fine examples in that way; we have also taken it on the artificial frog. Small crawfish also are a tempting bait."

As a pan-fish it is above the average but not among the best, its flesh being somewhat soft and having a muddy flavor. The fish is taken in rather cool clear water.

It feeds, so far as we know, mainly on insects and small crustaceans, with a moderate allowance of fishes. Its food, however, has not been sufficiently studied to give us a fair average for the species.

The rock bass has been used to some extent successfully as a fish for artificial ponds, and it has been successfully introduced into the waters of the Pacific states.

Genus CHÆNOBRYTTUS Gill

WARMOUTH BASS

This genus has the form and dentition of *Ambloplites*, with the opercle convex at the angle as in *Lepomis*, not ending in two points; preopercle entire; mouth large; a supplemental maxillary present; dorsal spines 10 and anal spines 3, as in *Lepomis*; caudal emarginate; scales weakly ctenoid. United States, east of the Rockies; one species.

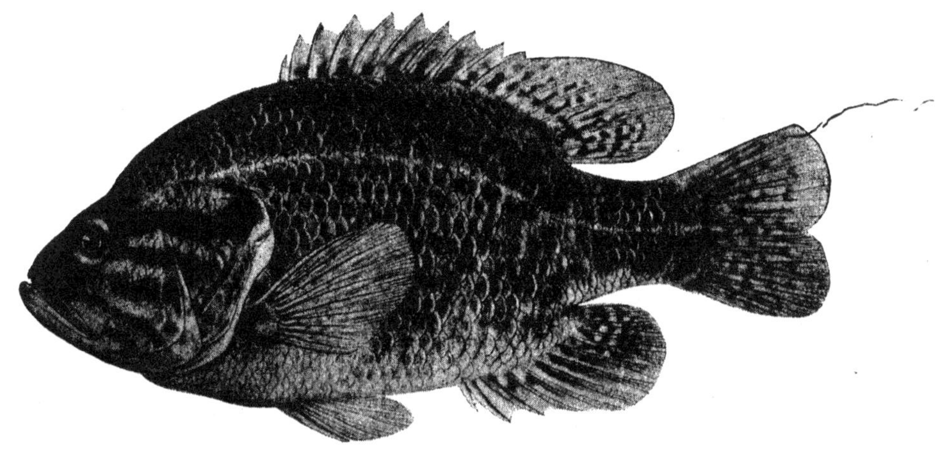

Fig. 59

CHÆNOBRYTTUS GULOSUS (Cuvier and Valenciennes)

WARMOUTH BASS

(Map LXXIV)

Cuvier & Valenciennes, 1829, Hist. Nat. Poiss., III, 498 (**Pomotis**).
J. & G., 468; M. V., 115; B., I, 13; J. & E., I, 992; N., 37; J., 45; F., 69; F. F., I. 3, 44; L., 23.

Length 6 to 8 inches; body robust, elongate, becoming much deeper with age; profile only slightly angled at nape; depth 2 to 2.6; greatest width 2 to 2.5 in greatest depth; depth of caudal peduncle 1.2 to 1.6 in its length. Color olivaceous to grayish, clouded, mottled, and sometimes indistinctly barred, with slate to bluish black; sides with golden and emerald reflections, producing over the ground colors a rich golden brown effect; breast and belly greenish to yellowish, sprinkled with dark dots and finely dusted with gold or emerald; four or five light grayish to lavender streaks (sometimes reddish) running from eye to back of opercle; snout, cheeks, and opercles sprinkled with dusky and finely punctulate with gold; forehead a moldy velvety-slate, characteristic of this fish; bony portion of opercular flap very dark, brownish in front to bluish behind, the membranous portion coppery above to lavender below; a narrow line of crimson about pupil; rest of iris crimson to purplish with streaks of emerald above and below; dorsal and anal fins light grayish to olive, with darker mottlings, the spots forming irregular rows. Head rather large, 2.4 to 2.6; width of head 1.9 to 2.1 in its length; interorbital space 3.9 to 4.3; eye 4 to 5; nose longer than eye, 3.3 to 4.4; mouth very large, maxillary nearly to back of orbit, 2.2 to 2.4 in head; operculum prolonged backward and rounded behind as in *Lepomis* and *Eupomotis*, the membranous flap narrow; gill-rakers 8 or 9 + rudiments, rather long and stiff. Dorsal X (occasionally IX or XI), 9 or 10 (or 11); long and low, longest spine 3.5 to 4 in head; base of dorsal twice length base of anal; caudal lunate; anal III, 8–10; ventrals short of vent in females, to vent in males; pectorals short of front of anal, 1.5 to 1.8 in head. Scales 6 or 7, 39–43, 11 or 12 (occasionally 13); lateral line usually complete; 6 to 8 rows of scales on cheeks.

The warmouth is a heavy, wide-mouthed, red-eyed sunfish, dark and mottled like the rock bass, but with less of bronze or other showy color. This fish, the rock bass, and the green sunfish form a group of abundant Illinois species, all with large mouths, and all feeding almost wholly on fishes and insects. Notwithstanding this similarity of food, they seem to have learned to inhabit the same area without serious mutual competition by establishing different relations to their environment. The rock bass, as already shown, lives by preference in clear waters flowing over a rock bottom, while the present species is the most of a mud lover of all of our sunfishes, as shown by its preference for a muddy bottom, represented in our collections by the surprising coefficient of 7.33. Other factors of this adjustment will be considered in the discussion of the green sunfish.

The warmouth is essentially a species of lakes and ponds and the smaller rivers, occurring also, but less generally, in creeks and in rivers of the largest class. It is distributed throughout the state—in the southern section mainly in the smaller streams, but in the northern half chiefly along the Illinois River. It is abundant in the glacial lakes of northeastern Illinois, and has come to us also from Lake Michigan. In the southern part of the state it is common in the lower Illinoisan glaciation, to an extent to indicate a deliberate preference for muddy water over pure. It is seemingly a southern species by preference in this state, the frequency ratios for the three sections being .44, .78, and 1.78, from north to south.

Lakes Michigan and Erie seem to mark its most northerly distribution, and from these it is found to the Florida peninsula on the southeast, and to Louisiana, Texas, and Kansas on the south and west. It is said to be common in South Carolina, but is most abundant west of the Alleghanies. It is everywhere a fish of the bayous, mud-bottomed ponds and lakes, and lowland streams.

It reaches a length of about 10 inches, and is a fair angler's fish, in that respect something like the rock bass. Owing to the character of the water from which it is most frequently taken, its flesh is apt to taste of mud, and it is not abundant enough on commercial fishing grounds to make it a species of any considerable importance.

Nearly half the food of half a dozen specimens examined by us many years ago was found to consist of fishes, and the remainder of insects—mostly of water-bugs and larvæ of May-flies, with which, however, some terrestrial insects were commingled.

Genus **LEPOMIS** Rafinesque

SUNFISHES

Body oblong, deep and compressed; operculum ending behind in a convex bony or osseo-membranous process or flap; preoperculum entire; mouth large or small; supplemental maxillary developed in large-mouthed forms; teeth on vomer and usually on palatines; none on tongue or pterygoids; lower pharyngeal teeth conical, more or less acute, the bones narrow and weak, flattened or hollowed out underneath, and with the outer margin straight or concave, the width of the toothed portion being about 3 in its length; gill-rakers various, never very long; dorsal spines 10; anal spines 3; caudal emarginate.

Fresh waters of the eastern United States, Canada, and Mexico; species about 15; 8 species found in Illinois.

The genus *Lepomis*, as here understood, includes *Apomotis* of various authors. The forms that have been known under these two names agree in their pharyngeal dentition,* which is remarkably different from that of the genus *Eupomotis* (see Fig. 64–67). The fact that the opercular flap is usually either entirely black or black with a definite border above, behind, and below, serves as a useful distinction of the species of this genus from the single commonly distributed species of *Eupomotis* (*E. gibbosus*), in which there is always a conspicuous roundish spot of red at the lower posterior corner of the opercular flap.

The species of this genus and the next constitute the true sunfishes, as distinguished from the crappies, rock bass, warmouths, and black bass. In the southern half of the state, where

* We have not found the "complete gradation in the character of pharyngeals between *Lepomis* * * * and *Eupomotis* both as to the width and form of the bones themselves and the form of the teeth" that was described by McKay (Proc. U. S. Nat. Mus. 1881 p. 88). (See Richardson 1904 Bull. Ill. State Lab. Nat. Hist. Vol. VII., pp. 27–32.)

the yellow perch (*Perca*) is practically unknown, the name of perch is commonly given to these sunfishes—most frequently, however, under the dialectic form of "pearch."

KEY TO THE SPECIES OF **LEPOMIS** FOUND IN ILLINOIS

a. Black opercular spot borne by the stiff bony upper posterior angle of the operculum, which is plainly distinguished from a flexible (fleshy or membranous) border of different (usually lighter) color. (Fig. 60.)

b. Mouth large and cheek not very deep, the maxillary ⅕ to ¼ longer than the distance from the lower margin of the orbit to the lower posterior corner of the preopercle; in life with blue spots and vertical bars of dusky; margin of ear-flap coppery to purplish; cheeks with wavy blue lines..**cyanellus.**

bb. Mouth smaller and cheek deeper, maxillary about equal to or less than distance from lower margin of orbit to lower posterior corner of preopercle.

c. Sides without longitudinal rows of spots formed by differently colored squarish areas (bronze or purplish in life) at centers of scales.

d. Gill-rakers long, the longest ½ diameter of eye; not mottled.

e. Scales 41 to 49 in lateral line; margin of ear-flap pale blue to pinkish in life ....**ischyrus.**

ee. Scales 32 to 37 in lateral line; in life green, barred with darker; small coffee-colored specks on body and fins..............................**symmetricus.**

dd. Gill-rakers shorter, the longest scarcely more than ⅓ diameter of eye, usually less; mottled, the appearance being much as in the pumkinseed sunfish (*Eupomotis gibbosus*); some red or coppery on ear-flap behind.... ....**euryorus.**

cc. Many scales of sides with squarish light-colored areas (bronze or purplish in life), these forming more or less distinct longitudinal rows; rest of body dusky olive ....**miniatus.**

aa. Portion of opercular flap bearing black spot very thin and flexible.

f. Bony portion of operculum terminating in front of the middle of the black opercular spot, which is confined chiefly to the broad pale (pinkish in life) membranous (not osseous) border; in life olive with orange spots; cheeks and opercles with wavy broken lines of rusty orange; no black blotch at base of last dorsal rays. (Fig. 63)..............................**humilis.**

ff. Bony portion of operculum continued backward as a thin and flexible osseo-membranous flap, which is all or nearly all black, the longitudinal bone-striæ being visible through its ensheathing epidermis. (Fig. 62.)

g. Gill-rakers short and weak, their length not over ⅙ eye; no black spot at base of last dorsal rays; olive with blue and orange spots and wavy vertical streaks of emerald; cheeks with wavy lines of emerald........**megalotis.**

gg. Gill-rakers rather long and slender, their length nearly ⅓ of eye; a black blotch at base of last dorsal rays; life-color olive, with purplish luster..**pallidus.**

LEPOMIS CYANELLUS RAFINESQUE

BLUE-SPOTTED SUNFISH; GREEN SUNFISH

(PL , P. 249)

Rafinesque, 1819, Jour. de Physique, 420.

J. & G., 473; M. V., 117; B., I, 21 (**Apomotis**); J. & E., I, 996; N., 37 (**Telipomis cyanellus** and **T. microps**); J., 45 (**Apomotis**); F. F., I. 3, 47 (**Apomotis**); F., 69; L., 25 (**Apomotis**); R., 27–32.

Length 4 to 7 inches; body elongate, robust, becoming somewhat shorter and deeper with age; dorsal outline rather more curved than ventral; depth 2.1 to 2.5 in length, usually about 2.2. Color olivaceous, taking on a yellowish or coppery tinge below; each scale with a spot of emerald-green, the spots

GREEN SUNFISH, *Lepomis cyanellus* Rafinesque

forming more or less distinct rows, most evident on the caudal peduncle; sides marked with seven or eight vertical bars of dusky, gradually fading backward; two spots of emerald-green in front of eye and one just behind it; three or four wavy lines of same color on cheek below eye, two or three of them continued backward across opercle; iris red; bony portion of gill-flap very dark green to blackish, with posterior edging of darker; membranous margin of flap coppery to purplish, the color strongest on lower posterior portion; fins all dusky, pectorals least so; soft dorsal and anal with large black blotch at base of last rays, the former with a very narrow outer margin of whitish; anal very dark at base, paler outward, and edged below with rich yellow or orange; ventrals dusky near base, paler behind. Head 2.4 to 3 in length, broad and flat above; the profile rather long and usually quite straight, becoming slightly angled above eye in old specimens; eye 3.8 to 5.2 in head, usually about 5 in adults; mouth very large, lower jaw projecting beyond upper; maxillary extending to middle of orbit, 2 to 2.5 in head; supplemental maxillary well developed; teeth present on vomers and palatines; lower pharyngeals narrow but strong, the teeth long and bluntly acuminate; flexible margin of opercular flap fleshy, broad behind and below, narrower above; gill-rakers long and stiff, the longest fully ½ diameter of eye. Dorsal IX or X, 10 to 12, spinous less than half the height of soft portion; longest dorsal spine 3 to 4.2 in head, usually about 4 in adults; anal III, 9 or 10, the spines short and strong; pectorals short, rounded behind, 1.5 to 1.7 in head; ventrals reaching to or a little past vent, never to first anal spines. Scales 6 or 7, 45–49, 15 or 16; those on cheeks in 7 to 10 rows.

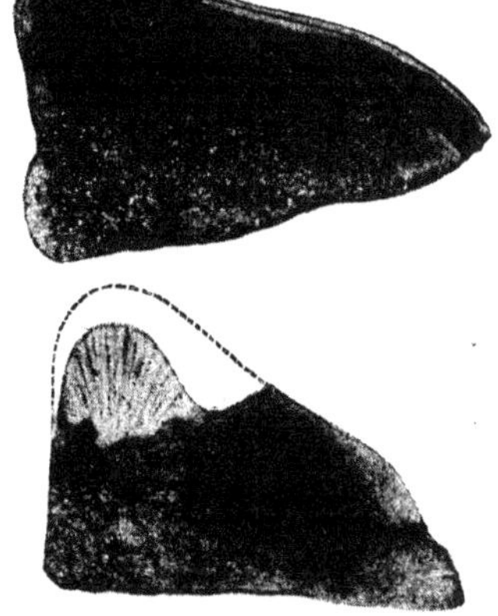

FIG. 60

Opercular flaps of *Lepomis cyanellus*, one figure entire, the other showing flap denuded of epidermis and fleshy or membranous border.

This beautiful little sunfish is much the commonest of its family in our smaller streams, and is, indeed, often almost the sole sunfish product of the net in the prairie creeks. Contrasting with the warmouth, it is most abundant in creeks (1.56), and is next so in the smaller rivers (.76). In the larger rivers and in the lowland lakes it occurs sparingly, but it has not been taken by us at all from the clear upland lakes of the glacial deposits, nor from any of the waters of the Michigan drainage. It has occurred in no less than 315 of our collections; that is, in about a fifth of the whole number made. Its preference is for a quiet current, in which respect it agrees with the next two species. It is evidently not afraid of mud as is shown by its general distribution over the lower glaciation of southern Illinois.

While the warmouth and the rock bass avoid each other in great measure by their strikingly different relations to water and bottom, the former being a mud-loving fish and the latter found mainly in clear rocky waters, the green sunfish avoids the other two by its strong preference for the smaller streams, into which they enter much less freely. The advantage of this avoidance of each other's company is evident when we take into account the similar food habits of these three species—all neglecting mollusks and crustaceans and depending for food on fishes and insects. Owing, however, to their different ecological and local distribution, their coefficients of association are much below the average for their family—1.17 for the rock bass and the warmouth, 1.51 for the rock bass and the green sunfish, and 1.19 for the green sunfish and the warmouth—or a general average of 1.29 for the group, to be compared with a general family average of 1.86.

This sunfish is, according to our data, about twice as abundant in southern Illinois as in either central or northern, our frequency ratio for the first division being 1.5, and .71 and .78 for the other two. In general range it is a fish of the Mississippi Valley, distributed from the Great Lakes to Mexico, and occurring everywhere in small sluggish brooks. It is not reported from Canada and is not found east of the Alleghanies.

It is an excellent pan-fish, although small, weighing usually not more than a quarter of a pound. It takes the hook readily with worm bait, and is a sprightly little fighter for so small a species. The food of the species, as illustrated by that of eight specimens, was more than a third fishes, and the remainder insects and crawfishes.

It was found by Mr. Surface spawning at Meredosia as late as August 14, 1899.

LEPOMIS ISCHYRUS (Jordan & Nelson)

Jordan & Nelson, 1877, Bull. U. S. Nat. Mus., X, 25 (**Lepiopomus**).

J. & G., 474; M. V., 117; B., I, 22 (? **Apomotis cyanellus** [part]); J. & E., I, 997 (**Apomotis**); N., 37 (**Icthelis aquilensis**); J., 45 (**Lepiopomis**); F., 68; L., 24 (**Apomotis cyanellus**); R., 27–32.

Length 5 to 7 inches; robust and rather elongate, the back considerably elevated, the form resembling that of *Lepomis pallidus*; depth $\frac{1}{8}$ to 2 in length. Life colors not known; in spirits dusky olive with mottlings of orange and blue; faint blue bands on cheeks; dorsal and anal fins with dusky spot on last rays; belly and lower fins coppery yellow. Head 2.6 to 2.7 in length, its top short and much flattened; profile conspicuously angled above eye; eye small, 4.7 to 5 in head; mouth large, the lower jaw slightly longer than the upper; maxillary extending to middle of eye, 2.5 to 3 in head; a well-developed supplemental maxillary bone; teeth on palatines; lower pharyngeals narrow but strong, the teeth heavy and bluntly pointed, as in *L. cyanellus*; flexible margin of opercular flap broad and rather thick and fleshy; gill-rakers long, stiff, and rough, ½ diameter of eye. Dorsal X or XI, 12; the spines strong and low, the longest scarcely reaching from snout to middle of orbit, 3.1 to 3.4 in head; anal III, 9 or 10; pectorals short, 1.4 to 1.7 in head; ventrals exceeding vent, not reaching anal. Scales 7 or 8, 43–49, 14 or 15; 6 or 7 rows on cheek.

Described in 1877 from a single specimen, taken in the Illinois River, the exact locality unknown. Not again taken until 1899, when two excellent adult specimens were obtained from the Illinois River at Meredosia. Not known outside of Illinois. Here described from 3 specimens, of which one is the original type.

LEPOMIS SYMMETRICUS Forbes

Forbes, 1883, Jordan and Gilbert's Synopsis, 473.
B., I, 21 (**Apomotis**); J. & E., I, 998 (**Apomotis**); F., 68; L., 24 (**Apomotis**); R., 33.

Length 2½ inches; body robust, rather short and deep; dorsal and ventral outlines about equally curved, giving the fish a distinctively symmetrical appearance; profile almost straight, the angle at nape usually inappreciable; depth 1.9 to 2 in length. Color in life green, with darker bars; in spirits light to darker brown; each scale with a basal spot of darker, the spots appearing as indistinct rows from before backward, 12 or 13 in number; body and fins with numerous small coffee-colored specks; tips of ventrals dusky; a black ocellated spot at base of last dorsal rays in young specimens. Head 2.7 to 2.8 in length; eye 2.8 to 3.3 in head; mouth moderate, maxillary reaching to middle of orbit, 2.4 to 2.6 in head; a well-developed supplemental maxillary bone; teeth on vomers and palatines; lower pharyngeals narrow, as in other species of *Lepomis*, the teeth conical, but rather heavy and bluntly pointed; operculum short, very broadly rounded behind, its membranous margin not very broad; gill-rakers rather long and slender, but firm, the longest more than ½ diameter of eye. Dorsal IX or X, 10 or 11; the spines moderate, not very short, the longest reaching from snout to pupil, 2 to 2.5 in head; anal III, 9 or 10; pectorals 1.1 to 1.3 in head; ventrals short, hardly exceeding vent. Scales large, 5 or 6, 32 to 37, 12 to 14; lateral line incomplete; 4 or 5 rows of scales on cheeks.

This symmetrical little species is rather rare in Illinois, which is the northern boundary of its area of distribution. It has been taken by us, in fact, but nine times, all but two of the collections—made from the Illinois River at Pekin—coming from localities in extreme southern Illinois, as follows: Anderson's branch and Running Lake in Union county; and Drew pond, a pond near Hawthorne, and the Little Wabash River in White county. Elsewhere it is reported from the Mississippi Valley southward as far as New Orleans, and Houston, Texas. Jordan and Evermann say that it is not infrequent in the lower Mississippi Valley, and that in Texas it is a common pan-fish.

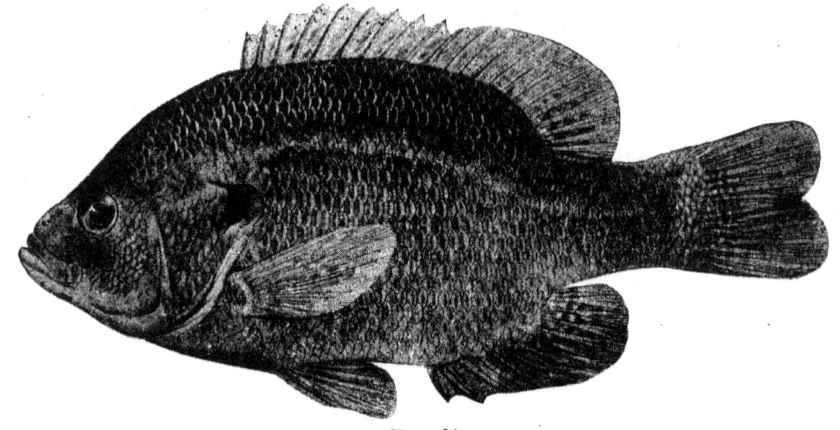

Fig. 61

LEPOMIS EURYORUS McKay

McKay, 1881, Proc. U. S. Nat. Mus., 89.

J. & G., 481; M. V., 119; B., I, 24 (? **Lepomis auritus** [part]); J. & E., I, 1008 (**Eupomotis**); R., 32.

Length 6 to 8 inches; body rather robust and somewhat elongate; depth 2 to 2.3 in length. Color in life not very well known; in spirits dusky olive mottled with darker, the general appearance very much as in *E. gibbosus*; fin-membranes dusky, darker tessellations behind on soft dorsal and anal and near base of caudal; opercular spot black, the margin paler, with some red or coppery behind in life. Head 2.6 to 2.9 in length; eye 3.8 to 4.3 in head; mouth large, oblique, maxillary reaching considerably past front of orbit, 2.6 to 2.9 in head; jaws about equal; supplemental maxillary well developed; teeth on vomers and palatines; lower pharyngeals narrow, but strong, teeth conical, heavy and bluntly pointed; opercle produced backward, sharply rounded posteriorly, the margin wide; gill-rakers well developed, the longest ⅓ diameter of eye, rather stiff and rough. Dorsal X, 11 or 12; the spines low, slightly longer than from snout to eye in young specimens, 2.2 to 2.7 in head; anal III, 9 or 10; pectorals short, 1.3 to 1.4 in head; ventrals reaching slightly past vent. Scales 6 or 7, 43–45, 14 or 15; those on cheeks small, in 6 to 8 rows.

One of the rarest of our sunfishes, and known in this state only by reason of two young specimens taken by us in Crooked creek, near La Harpe, Hancock county, in 1900. It was originally described from the lower part of Lake Huron. It has been taken sparingly in northern Indiana and Ohio, in Minnesota,

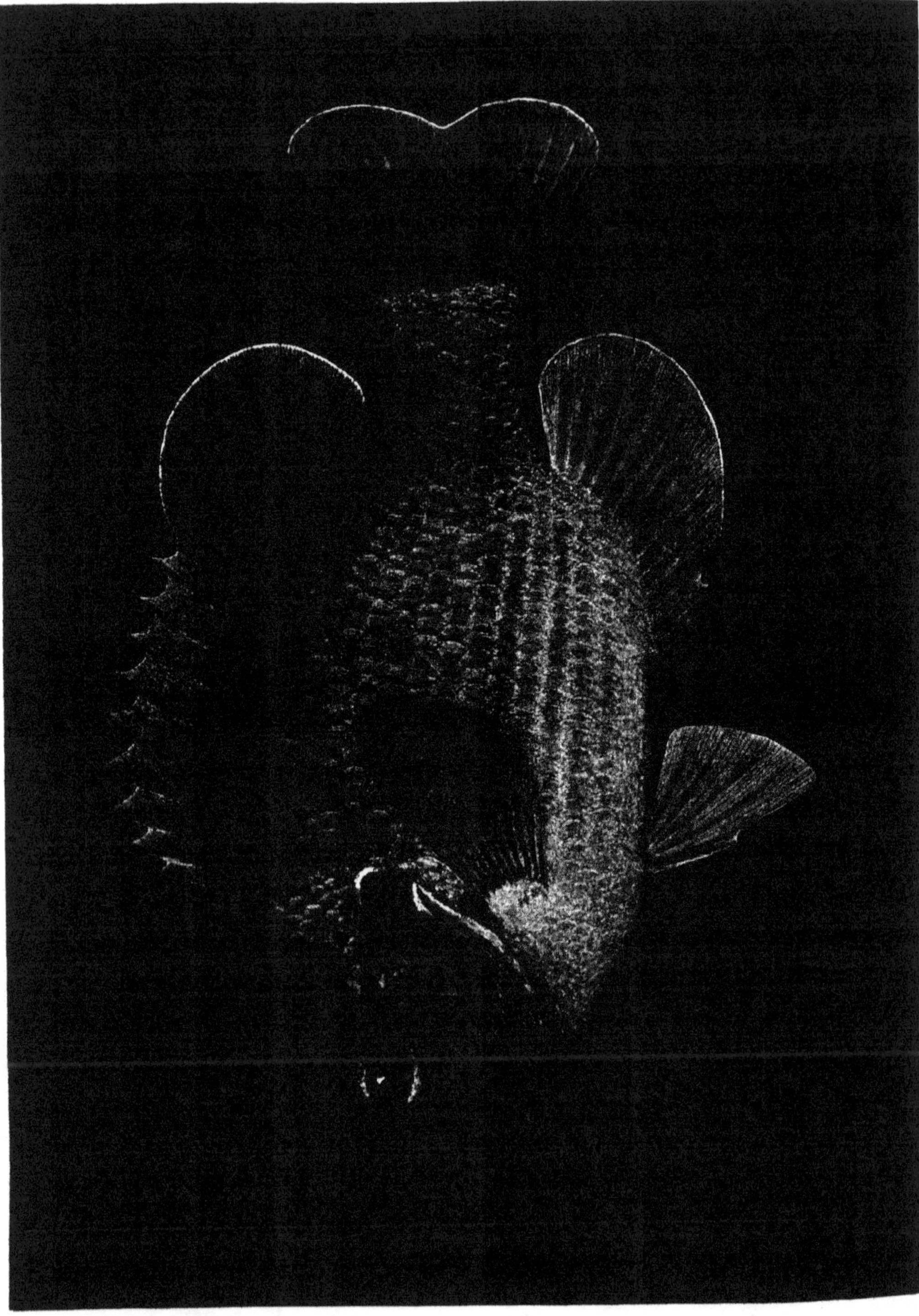

and in southern Michigan. Nothing is on record concerning its habits or its life history.

LEPOMIS MINIATUS Jordan

(Map LXXV)

Jordan, 1877, Bull. U. S. Nat. Mus., X, 26.

J. & G., 476; F. F., II. 2, 135 (garmani); M. V., 119 (garmani); B., I, 24 (auritus [part]), 27 (garmani); J. & E., I, 1002 (also garmani); L., 24 (garmani).

Length 4 inches; body rather short and deep, usually more or less regularly elliptical; variously robust or rather thin; depth 1.8 to 2 in length, usually about 2 in adults. Color dark olive; sides below lateral line striped with rows of bronze or purplish spots, the rows about 7 or 8 in number; under parts light, with some brassy luster; upper part of head almost black; cheeks dark bluish green; ear-flap black, its upper and lower margin silvery, sometimes a posterior edging of pale; outer third of soft dorsal and anal reddish brown with narrow edging of paler; caudal reddish behind, with faint pale edging; iris red before and behind pupil. Head 2.9 to 3.1 in length; profile usually with a more or less decided depression at nape, sometimes almost straight; eye 3.9 to 4.3 in head; mouth smaller than in preceding species, maxillary 2.5 to 3 in head, usually about 2.7 reaching but a little past front of orbit; a small supplemental maxillary bone; teeth present on vomers and palatines; lower pharyngeals narrow but heavy, the teeth long but blunt; operculum short and broadly rounded behind, its membranous margin broad and fleshy; gill-rakers stout and short, about ¼ diameter of eye. Dorsal X, 10 or 11; the spines variable, usually rather low, longest 1.9 to 2.7 in head; anal III, 8 to 10; pectorals variable, always considerably shorter than head, sometimes but slightly longer than to back of cheek in adults; their length 1.2 to 1.6 in length of head; ventrals always extending to vent, sometimes to anal. Scales 5, 34–41, 13 or 14, the number in the lateral line usually nearer 40 than 34; 4 or 5 rows on cheek.

A comparatively rare sunfish, taken by us but twenty-four times, and mostly from the bottom-land lakes and ponds of the Illinois River. We have collected it also from two localities on the Wabash, from one on the Mississippi in Hancock county, and from one on a branch of the Kankakee. It is evidently a southern species, ranging to Florida and Louisiana, and it is not reported by Hay or Osburn in listing the fishes of Indiana or Ohio. It is said to be common in some streams of Texas. Specimens taken by the senior author in 1880 and 1885 from the Little Fox River at Phillipstown, in White county, and from the Wabash River and Drew pond, near Carmi, were described under the name of *Lepomis garmani*.

Females with mature ova, and spawning or about to spawn, were caught by Dr. Kofoid May 18, 1896, and Craig reported it apparently spawning between the 20th and the 30th of May, 1898

LEPOMIS MEGALOTIS (RAFINESQUE)

LONG-EARED SUNFISH

(MAP LXXVI)

Rafinesque, 1820, Ichth. Oh., 29 (**Ichthelis**).

J. & G., 477; M. V., 118; J. & E., I, 1002; B., I, 26; N., 38 (**Ichthelis megalotis** and **sanguinolentus**); J., 46 (**Xenotis megalotis, inscriptus,** and **peltastes**); F. F., I. 3, 53 (**Xenotis peltastes,** etc.); F., 68; L., 24; R., 34.

Length 3½ to 6 inches; body short and deep; back much elevated and profile steep, sometimes excessively so in adults; angle at nape usually rather prominent; depth 1.8 to 2.3 in length. Color light to darker olive; sides irregularly spotted with orange and emerald, spots of latter color often forming somewhat indistinct wavy vertical streaks; belly pale to bright orange; cheeks light olive to orange, with wavy streaks of emerald; opercular flap entirely black or with a very narrow pale margin, pinkish to light crimson behind; iris reddish before and behind pupil; membranes of soft dorsal and anal pale orange; pectorals dusky, usually less so than in females. Head 2.8 to 3.3 in length; eye 3 to 4 in head; mouth moderate, 2.4 to 2.7 in head in adults, maxillary extending almost to middle of orbit; no supplemental maxillary bone and no palatine teeth; lower pharyngeals narrow and weak, the teeth slender and acutely pointed; opercular flap variously developed, in adults generally very long (always much shorter in young), often 1½ times snout, usually rather broadened behind, with or without pale margin; gill-rakers short, not over ⅙ diameter of eye, very soft and weak. Dorsal X, 11, the spines usually low, the longest reaching from snout to middle of eye, 2.1 to 2.8 in head in adults, usually over 2.6; pectorals short, 1 to 1.2 in head; ventrals usually reaching somewhat beyond first anal spine. Scales 5, 37–39, 14, those on cheeks in about 5 rows.

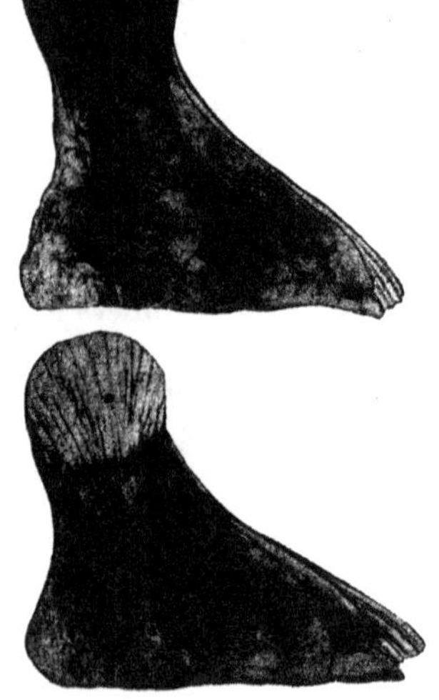

FIG. 62

Opercular flaps of *Lepomis megalotis*, one figure entire the other showing flap denuded of epidermis and fleshy or membranous border.

This is a very showy sunfish, one of the most brilliant, in its breeding colors, of our fresh-water fishes. Its distribution in Illinois is peculiar in the fact that it is extremely abundant in the southern and eastern parts of the state, occurring everywhere in the smaller streams, including those of the lower glaciation, and often likewise in the larger rivers, while in the remainder of the state, although generally distributed, it is comparatively scarce, and is to be found mainly along the principal streams, and

ORANGE-SPOTTED SUNFISH, *Lepomis humilis* (Girard)

not widely distributed through the country at large. Our frequency statistics, derived from 151 collections, show that this is a sunfish of the creeks and smaller rivers, where its coefficients are 2.98 and 2.35 respectively, the corresponding figures for the larger rivers and for lowland lakes being .17 and .14. In the upland lakes we have not taken it at all.

Northward this species grades into a smaller dwarfish variety, probably *Xenotis lythrochloris*, which has been taken only in the clear swift water of the Fox at Ottawa, Lacon, and Algonquin; in the Du Page at Naperville; in the Vermilion at Pontiac and Fairbury; in a small creek in Du Page county; and in Indian creek, La Salle county. These small forms have the ear-flaps red and the scales of the cheek smaller than typical *megalotis*. Their size is alone sufficient to distinguish them, gravid females having been found only 1⅝ inches long, and no specimen exceeding three inches.

Found outside our limits in Lakes Erie, Huron, and Michigan; on the south Atlantic coast in Georgia and the Florida peninsula; through the Ohio and Missouri basins to Iowa and Minnesota, and thence south through Arkansas to the Rio Grande. It is said to avoid muddy water, is especially abundant in small brooks, and frequents deep still places in rivers and clear ponds. It is wanting in the Atlantic drainage of the northern and middle states.

The long-eared sunfish is not ordinarily more than four or five inches long, and has no commercial importance. Our scanty observations indicate that it feeds on aquatic insects, mostly larvæ of gnats and day-flies. Notwithstanding its more limited distribution, it is a frequent companion of the green sunfish (coefficient of association, 2.65), and inhabits similar waters where it is most abundant.

LEPOMIS HUMILIS (GIRARD)

ORANGE-SPOTTED SUNFISH

(MAP LXXVII)

Girard, 1857, Proc. Ac. Nat. Sci. Phila., 201 (**Bryttus**).

J. & G., 479; M. V., 118; J. & E., I, 1004; B., I, 30 (**Eupomotis**); N., 38 (**Ichthelis anagallinus**); J., 45 (**Lepiopomis anagallinus**); F., 68; L., 24; R., 34.

Size small, length not over 3½ inches; body elongate, compressed, the back almost carinate for some distance in front of the dorsal; dorsal outline usually somewhat more curved than ventral; profile long, sloping gradually, usually nearly straight, the angle at the nape in most cases very slight, and greatest in males; depth 2.1 to 2.5 in length, usually about 2.4. Color light olive, the sides sprinkled with fine dots of gold to emerald; belly deep orange, dusted with brown; sides with about 20 to 30 orange spots, somewhat smaller in size than the pupil, irregularly distributed, their color deeper and brighter in males than in females, the spots usually a dull brown in the latter; top of head slaty; a suggestion of wavy lines of emerald on cheeks; black color on the opercular flap mostly confined to the membranous portion, barely tipping the operculum; the pale margin of the membrane quite wide, its color variable—pale lavender, pinkish, or light crimson; spinous dorsal with narrow edging of crimson and soft portion with wide margin of orange in males; ventrals and anal orange, color deeper and approaching crimson in males; distal margin of anal dusky; other fins plain. Head 2.3 to 2.9 in length, its top long, flattened or very little convex; eye 3.7 to 4.5 in head; mouth moderate, maxillary extending past front of orbit, never to its middle, 2.7 to 3 in head; jaws about equal; lower pharyngeals narrow, very weak, the teeth slender and very acutely pointed; opercular bone sharply rounded backward, black only at its tip; the membranous flap long and broad and very thin, not forming a pale edging only, but bearing the most of the black color of the opercular spot; gill-rakers long, rather more than ⅓ diameter of eye. Dorsal X, 10 or 11; spinous and soft portions of about equal height; the spines slender, rather long, the longest 2.4 to 2.6 in head in adults, usually about 2.5; anal III, 9; pectorals 1 to 1.3 in head, usually about 1.1; ventrals reaching to base of first anal spine. Scales 4 or 5, 34–42, 11 to 13; pores lacking on some scales; rows on cheek 5 or 6.

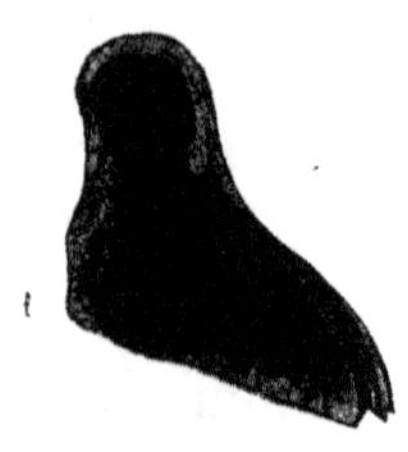

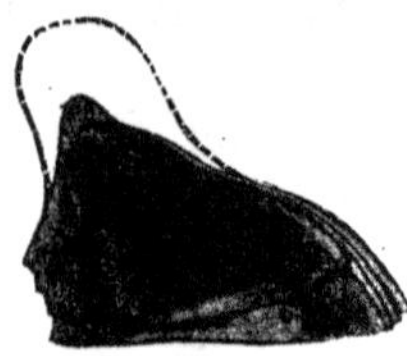

FIG. 63

Opercular flaps of *Lepomis humilis*, one figure entire, the other showing flap denuded of epidermis and fleshy or membranous border.

This is a showy and, indeed, a brilliant little fish, of a size so small that it is ornamental only. Our 177 collections were taken most frequently from creeks (2.06), next from the smaller rivers (1.51), and then from lowland lakes (1.19), none at all coming from upland glacial lakes. They were well distributed through the state, most abundantly, however, in the prairie region of central Illinois, where this species is found in frequent company with the green sunfish. It is often taken along the shore of the Illinois River and in adjacent lakes and sloughs, but has been rare or absent in extreme northern Illinois, occurring in the Fox and Rock river systems only near the mouths of those streams. Its general distribution in the smaller rivers, and in lakes and ponds of the bottom-lands, brings it also into contact with the crappies. Its associative coefficient is 2.35 for the green sunfish and 2.94 for the pale crappie. If one may judge from its feeding structures, it is protected from serious competition with these companion species by differences in its food.

BLUEGILL, *Lepomis pallidus* (Mitchill)

It ranges widely throughout the Mississippi Valley, from Minnesota and South Dakota and the Ohio basin generally, to Kansas, Arkansas, and Texas. We find no mention of it from the Atlantic slope.

Ripe males and females in high coloration, swimming in pairs, were taken by Dr. Kofoid in Meredosia Bay June 8, 1899. The sexes present a notably different appearance in outline as well as in color, the males having the forehead concave, the profile steeper, and the ventrals longer than the females.

LEPOMIS PALLIDUS (MITCHILL)

BLUEGILL; BLUE SUNFISH

(MAP LXXVIII)

Mitchill, 1815, Trans. Lit. and Phil. Soc. N. Y., 407 (**Labrus**).

J. & G., 479; M. V., 118; J. & E., I, 1005; B., I, 29 (**Eupomotis**); N., 37 (**Ichthelis incisor** and **speciosus**); J., 45 (**Lepiopomus**); F. F., I., 3, 48 (**Lepiopomus**); F., 67; L., 25; R., 34.

Length of adults 5 to 8 inches, the body compressed, short and deep, extremely so in adults; the dorsal outline somewhat more curved than the ventral; profile rather steep, not sharply angled at nape but excavate in a shallow curve which continues almost to end of snout, giving the nose an upturned appearance; depth 1.9 to 2.2, usually about 2. Color light to dark olive, with more or less luster of purple to lavender; adults usually very dark; belly yellow or rich yellowish brown, with margins of scales lighter; about six more or less distinct wavy vertical bars of dusky on sides, most apparent below lateral line, usually becoming obsolete in adults; snout dull slate, velvety; chin emerald; cheeks and opercles olive with iridescent gold and emerald; gill-flap deep blue-black behind, velvety, without evident pale margin, the black of the flap sometimes lightening to a dull emerald-green; fins all more or less dusky, ventrals and anal most so; pectorals almost plain, pale; dorsal with a diffuse but usually evident black blotch at base of last rays. Head short, small, 2.9 to 3.4 in length, usually about 3.1 in adults; eye 2.9 to 3.9 in head; mouth small, very oblique, the jaws equal; maxillary scarcely reaching front of orbit, 2.9 to 3.3 in head in adults; supplemental maxillary very rudimentary or wanting; no teeth on

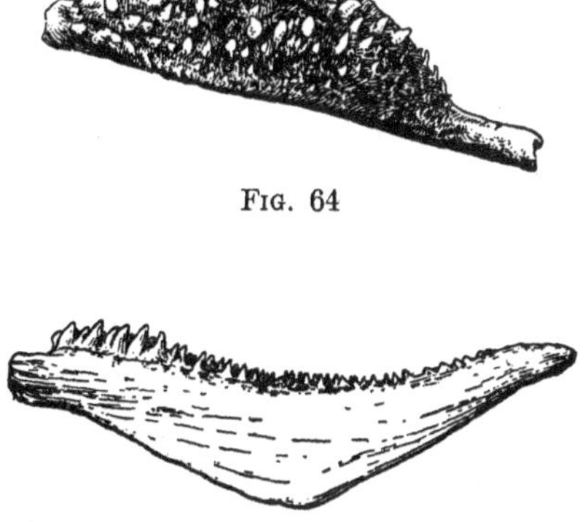

FIG. 64

FIG. 65

Lower left pharyngeal of *Lepomispallidus:* Fig. 64, from above; Fig. 65, from below.

palatines; lower pharyngeals narrow and weak, the teeth slender and sharp; operculum more or less prolonged backward in adults, always rather wide and bluntly rounded posteriorly, usually rather conspicuously striate longitudinally, the membranous margin very narrow or wholly wanting, its color when present very little if any lighter than the black of the osseous portion of the flap; gill-rakers rather long and slender, but firm, the longest almost ⅓ diameter of eye. Dorsal X, 10 to 12, usually X, 11; spines long, the longest 1.3 to 2.4 in head, usually about 2 in adults; anal III, 10 or 12; pectorals long, pointed behind, about equal to head or a little less, .9 to 1 in head, usually about 1 in adults; ventrals reaching anal. Scales 6, 38–48, 13 or 14; those on cheek in 5 rows.

This is the principal sunfish of our larger rivers, and the one appearing most frequently in the large nets of the regular river fishermen. It occurs throughout the state, but is generally limited to the larger streams and their principal tributaries, except that it is common in the northeastern glacial lakes. It has also been taken by us in the Michigan drainage. Judging from our 214 collections, it is primarily a pond species, its frequency ratio in the ponds and lakes being 1.6. In flowing streams it is commonest in the larger rivers, and least common in creeks.

Along the Atlantic coast it is found from New Jersey to the Florida peninsula; in the Great Lakes, from Ontario westward, ranging thence to the south and west through the Ohio and the lower Missouri basins to New Orleans and Texas.

It is said by Jordan and Evermann to be perhaps the best known and certainly the most important of all our true sunfishes, decidedly a lake species everywhere, but more abundant in the smaller lakes. It is the largest of our sunfishes, reaching a length of twelve to twenty-four inches and a weight of nearly a pound, the maximum weight being about a pound and a half.

In the food of twenty-six specimens we have found a trace of fishes—a single darter eaten by one—a moderate percentage of univalve mollusks, a large ratio of insects (45 per cent.), and many of the medium-sized *Crustacea*. The insect food is derived in great measure from larger aquatic larvæ than most of our sunfishes feed upon. The stomachs of some of our specimens were found to contain as much as 24 per cent. of aquatic vegetaton—too large a quantity to have been swallowed accidentally with the animals eaten. Its food differs in detail, however, according to the situation in which it is found.

The bluegill moves in schools, and may be caught with almost any kind of bait or tackle. Its flesh is firm and flaky, and it is not excelled as a pan-fish by any of our species, unless it be the yellow perch. The greater part of the sunfish catch of Illinois, amounting to 200,000 to 500,000 pounds a year, is composed of this species.

It spawns in May, according to our observations at Meredosia, although Dr. Kofoid found a ripe male June 12.

Genus **EUPOMOTIS** Gill & Jordan

PUMPKINSEED SUNFISH

Form as in *Lepomis*; mouth always small; no supplemental maxillary bone and no teeth on palatines; lower pharyngeals deep and broad, with inferior and lateral prominences, the width of the toothed portion about 2 in its length; pharyngeal teeth short with the upper surfaces bluntly rounded or paved (truncate); gill-rakers short; fins rather long; red color on opercular flap in typical species forming a roundish spot. Eastern United States and Canada; 3 species.

Key to Species of **EUPOMOTIS** found in Illinois

a. Pectorals reaching vertical from base of last anal spine; wavy lines on checks faint; border of opercular flap red in male, pale in female............**heros.**

aa. Pectorals scarcely reaching front of anal; evident lines of emerald on cheeks; opercular flap with a blood-red or orange spot at its lower posterior corner (white in preserved specimens)..............................**gibbosus.**

EUPOMOTIS HEROS (Baird & Girard)

Baird & Girard, 1854, Proc. Ac. Nat. Sci. Phila., 25 (**Pomotis**).
J. & G., 480 (**Lepomis**), 482 (**L. notatus**); J. & E., I, 1007; B., I, 32; F., 67 (**Lepomis notatus**); L., 25; R., 35.

Length 6 to 8 inches; depth 2.1 to 2.3 in length. Color pale olive, slightly mottled; opercular flap black with a wide border, which is blood-red in males, pale in females. Head in length 2.7 to 3; profile not angled at nape; eye 3.7 to 4 in head; mouth rather small, the lower jaw but slightly projecting; maxillary 3.1 to 3.3 in head; teeth present on vomer, but not on tongue or palatines; lower pharyngeals broad, with short blunt teeth; flexible margin of opercular flap fleshy; gill-rakers very short, the longest about 1/5 eye. Dorsal X, 11, the longest spine 2/3 height of soft portion; anal III, 10; pectorals very long, reaching past a vertical from base of last anal spine; ventrals past vent. Scales 6, 36–40, 14 or 15; rows on cheeks about 4.

This is a southern fish, and has occurred in our Illinois collections only at a few points in the Wabash basin. It has occurred in Indiana also, in the same stream and its tributaries, and it has been lately taken in Little Eagle Lake in Kosciusko county, by Professor Moenkhaus. It has been reported from the Little Miami in Hamilton county, Ohio. From these more northerly localities it ranges southeastward to west Florida and southwestward to the Rio Grande.

EUPOMOTIS GIBBOSUS (LINNÆUS)

PUMPKINSEED

(MAP LXXIX)

Linnæus, 1758, Syst Nat., Ed. X, 292 (**Perca**).
J. & G., 482 (**Lepomis**); M. V., 119 (**Lepomis**); J. & E., I, 1009; B., I, 32 (**aureus**); N., 38 (**Pomotis auritus**); J., 46 (**aureus**); F., 67 (**Lepomis**); L., 25; R., 35, F. F., I. 3, 53 (**aureus**).

Length of adults 5 to 8 inches; body strongly compressed, short and deep, the back very highly arched in adults, ventral outline less curved than dorsal; profile steep, convex in front of dorsal, the depression at the nape rather slight. Coloration exceedingly brilliant and somewhat variable, olive to grassy greenish, the back and upper portion of body finely dusted with gold or emerald; sides with quite numerous and irregularly distributed large roundish blotches, which are olive to coppery in front and darker behind, or dark all about a roundish coppery-colored central spot; single scales below lateral lines each with a quadrate central spot, these spots forming rows from before backward, alternate ones coppery and forming the central or anterior spot of the large blotches before mentioned, the others bright emerald or turquoise-blue; belly light olive to orange-yellow; cheeks and opercles crossed by four or five wavy lines of emerald, the interspaces with mingled coppery and gold over the ground olive, producing the effect of a rich bronze in well-colored examples; iris variegated blue and greenish with some crimson above pupil; flap of opercle velvety black behind; a definitely bounded roundish spot of orange or turkey-red on the lower posterior portion of the fleshy margin; the margin above and below the spot dark to blackish with some coppery luster; membranes of both portions of dorsal and of caudal and anal somewhat irregularly barred with dull brownish to orange blotches; ventrals dusky in males, paler or entirely pale in females. Head small, short 2.8 to 3.2 in length; the snout with a somewhat snubbed appearance, very short, its length scarcely more than eye; eye 3.5 to 4.2 in head; mouth small, the jaws equal; maxillary reaching but a little past front of orbit, 2.6 to 3.3 in head; no supplemental maxillary and no palatine teeth; lower pharyngeals broad and deep, with inferior and lateral prominences; the teeth short and

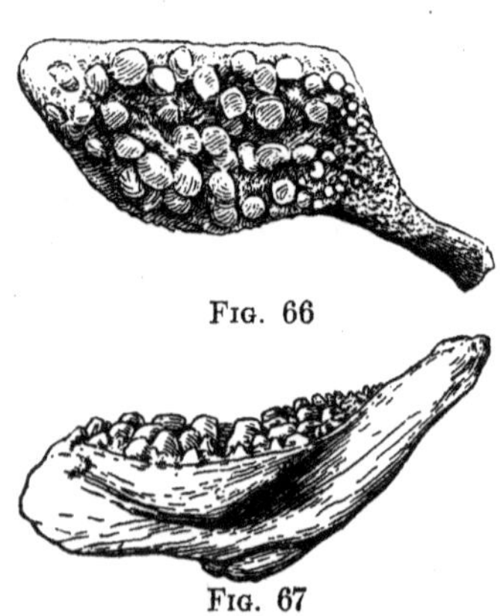

FIG. 66

FIG. 67

Lower left pharyngeal of *Eupomotis gibbosus:* Fig. 66 from above; Fig. 67 from outside.

stout, their upper surfaces bluntly rounded or paved; operculum quite firm behind, the bony portion distinct from a broad paler fleshy margin; gill-rakers short and soft, but little better developed than in *L. megalotis*. Dorsal X, 11 or 12; the spines rather high, the highest 2 to 2.4 in head, about as long as snout and eye. Anal III, 10 or 11; pectorals rather long, 1 to 1.1 in head; ventrals exceeding vent, usually reaching to or a little past first anal spine. Scales 5, 35–40, 13 or 14; 4 or 5 rows on cheek.

This very abundant species of extreme northern Illinois, especially common in the upland lakes of Lake and McHenry counties, is scarcely known south of the center of the state, having occurred, indeed, but twice in all our collections below the latitude of Springfield—once in Clear Lake, across the Ohio from Cairo, and once in Drew pond, near Carmi, on the Little Wabash River. It is essentially a pond species, and is next most abundant in the smaller rivers, our ratios being 2.16 for glacial lakes, 1.24 for lowland lakes, and 1.06 for rivers of the second class. We have taken it only occasionally in the larger rivers and in creeks, its absence in the latter in this state being probably due to its preference for clear streams, in which the greater part of our area is notably deficient. Its local distribution brings it into frequent company with the warmouth (coefficient of association, 3.72), notwithstanding the fact that the pumpkinseed is much the most abundant northward in this state and the warmouth decidedly so southward. Competition is evaded, however, by their widely different food and feeding structures. The pumpkinseed is the best fitted of all our sunfishes to crush and devour mollusks, and we found these making nearly half the food of nine specimens examined by us. Fishes were entirely wanting, insects amounted only to about a fifth, and medum-sized crustaceans (*Allorchestes* and *Asellus*) were represented by another fifth.

Its general range is illustrated by its Illinois distribution, except that it extends down the Atlantic coast, at least as far as the Carolinas. It has, indeed, been attributed to Florida since the days of Holbrook (1855), and Goode reports it as common in all the fresh waters of that state, but we have failed to find any specific account of its capture there or any mention of a precise locality from which it has been taken. Northward it occurs in Ontario, Quebec, and New Brunswick, and in Lakes Huron, Erie, Ontario, and Champlain. In the Mississippi Valley it is found only in the northern portion, abundant as far south as northern Ohio, Indiana, Illinois, and Iowa, and the Osage River in Kansas. Below extreme northern Illinois it is found mainly in lakes and along the Illinois River, this stream serving for this species, as for so many others, as a highway for the dispersal movement.

It is one of the best-known fishes of its area, especially to the small boy. It may reach a weight of six or eight ounces and a length of eight inches, although it is ordinarily much smaller. It is a "very beautiful and compact little fish, perfect in all its parts, looking like a brilliant coin fresh from the mint."

The breeding habits have been described by Dr. Kirtland, who says that the males prepare a circular nest by removing seeds and dead aquatic plants for a space a foot in diameter, excavating to a depth of 3 to 4 inches. The nests are in shallow water, and are encircled by aquatic plants, space being left open for the admission of light. Observations by Dr. Reighard indicate that the male alone is concerned in building the nest. The weight of testimony seems also to the effect that the male guards the nest and young, although the female may be present.* Dr. Reighard says that the male in approaching the female to induce her to enter the nest elevates and puffs out his gill-covers and erects his ear-flaps, so that there is a brilliant display of color to the female in front. He also saw a similar attitude assumed by the male when threatening or attacking other males. The spawning season is May to June.

The pumpkinseed is a good pan-fish, but is not especially important as a commercial product. It is sufficiently hardy to be transported with ease, and has been acclimatized in Europe. It is one of the best of fishes for keeping ponds free from mosquitoes.

Genus **MICROPTERUS** Lacépède

BLACK BASS

Body rather elongate, the back not much elevated; mouth very large; supplemental maxillary well developed; preopercle entire; operculum emarginate behind; teeth on jaws, vomer, and palatines; tongue usually without teeth; gill-rakers long and slender; dorsal spines 10, the spinous and soft dorsals confluent but divided by a deep notch; anal spines 3; caudal emarginate; scales weakly ctenoid.

Key to the Species of **MICROPTERUS**

a. Mouth moderate, the maxillary never extending beyond eye, usually a little short of back of orbit; scales on cheeks in about 17 rows; young more or less barred or spotted, never with a black lateral band .... **dolomieu.**

aa. Mouth very large, the maxillary in the adult extending past back of orbit; scales on cheek large, in about 10 rows; young with a blackish lateral band .... **salmoides.**

* Dr. Smith saw both parents by a nest as a crab approached. The female retired while the male attacked the crab and drove him off, after which he sought the female and returned with her to the nest.

SMALL-MOUTH BLACK BASS, *Micropterus dolomiev* (Lacépède)

MICROPTERUS DOLOMIEU Lacépède

SMALL-MOUTHED BLACK BASS

(Map LXXX)

Lacépède, 1802, Hist. Nat. Poiss., IV, 325.

G., I, 258 (**Centrarchus fasciatus** and **obscurus**); J. & G., 485; M. V., 120; B., I, 15; J. & E., I, 1011; N., 37 (**salmoides**); J., 44 (**salmoides**); F., 67; L., 25; F. F., I. 3, 41 (**salmoides**).

Length 12 to 15 inches; body ovate-fusiform, moderately compressed, becoming deeper with age; profile convex; depth 2.9 to 3.1; greatest width about 3/5 greatest depth; depth of caudal peduncle 1.5 to 1.9 in its length. Color of upper parts silvery to golden green, with faint vermiculations of darker (olive-green) above lateral line and with 10 to 15 more or less indistinct olive-green bars below it; belly and breast pale bluish gray to whitish; cheeks with 5 olive-green bars radiating backward from eye and one forward to end of snout; iris rufous; fins nearly plain in adults, olive to grayish, the caudal dark about margin; young plain, or with dark spots tending to form vertical bars, never with a dark lateral stripe; caudal of young specimens yellowish at base, and with free margin whitish, the region between dusky; color of adults varying* with range, the season, and the mood of the fish. Head 2.9 to 3.7; width head 1.8 to 2.1; interorbital space convex, 3.5 to 3.9; eye 5.6 to 6.9; nose 3 to 3.3; mouth smaller than in the next species, maxillary 2.1 to 2.3, considerably short† of back of orbit; lower jaw projecting; gill-rakers long, X + 6 or 7, + rudiments. Dorsal X (or IX), 13–15, the spinous dorsal long and low and separated by a deep notch from soft dorsal, the fifth (longest) spine about 4 in head and the lowest posterior spine about 1/2 height of fifth; caudal lunate; anal III (rarely IV or II), 10–12; ventrals more than half to vent; pectorals short, little past backward reach of ventrals, 1.9 to 2.1 in head. Scales 10–12, 66–78, 19–22; lateral line complete or nearly so; scales on cheeks in about 17 rows.

This is perhaps the most famous and familiar of our fresh-water fishes, surpassing the brook trout in that respect because of its much more general distribution, and the whitefish and the lake trout both for that reason and because of its surpassing interest as a sportsman's fish. It is far better known to many anglers than to ourselves, and has been written upon so much from the angler's point of view that we shall treat it briefly in this report.

In Illinois it is mainly a northern fish, avoiding the lower Illinoisan glaciation, within whose boundaries it has occurred but once in our 101 collections of the species, owing largely no doubt to its marked preference for clear, swift water. It is much the most abundant in the northern section of the state, its frequency ratio there being 2.35 as compared with .32 for each

* See Reighard, Henshall, et al.

† Old examples sometimes have maxillary nearly to back of orbit, according to Jordan and Evermann.

of the other sections. We have taken it most frequently from the smaller rivers, about half as commonly from creeks, and somewhat less commonly from the clear upland lakes of the northeastern part of the state. It has occurred but rarely in our collections from either the larger rivers or from lowland lakes and sloughs. Its avoidance of such situations is especially illustrated by the fact that it is recorded but five times in 546 collections examined by us from the Illinois River at Havana and Meredosia; that is, only 5 per cent. of the collections of this species have been made from these Illinois River localities, from which 35 per cent. of all our collections came. Its very marked preference for a swift current and a clean bottom is a matter of common observation, and is shown also by the data of our collections, according to which it has come from swift waters more than three times as often as from a quiet current, and from a bottom of rock and sand nearly twelve times as frequently as from one of mud.

These preferences bring about a wide separation between this bass and the closely related species of the same genus—the large-mouthed black bass. These two species inhabit the same general area, may often be found in the same streams, and feed on the same food, differing only, so far as known, in respect to the ratios of the principal elements. Nevertheless, they avoid competition by a difference in the situations preferred. These closely allied species have, according to our data, an associative coefficient of 1.08, while the small-mouthed black bass and the rock bass, differing in characters, habits, and food, have a coefficient of 6.24. In other words, the latter two unlike species are brought by a similarity of local preference into each other's company about three and a half times as frequently as the like species of black bass. The differences of local preference are not so great, however, but that the two species are frequently found together. According to Jordan and Evermann, "Some small lakes that are rather shallow, whose bottoms are chiefly mud and whose water is warm, are found to be well suited to the straw bass [large-mouthed] and to be entirely without the small-mouthed black bass. But small lakes of considerable depth, cool water, and with bottom partly of mud and partly of sand and gravel, such as Lake Maxinkuckee, seem equally well adapted to both species."

The small-mouthed bass is found wide-spread throughout the country, from Lake Champlain and the River St. Lawrence to the Muskoka lakes in Ontario, and southward to Arkansas, northern Mississippi and South Carolina. It is abundant in suitable situations on both sides of the Alleghanies, preferring clear cool streams with moderately swift current, not infrequently being taken in swift riffles. It is not found in warm, muddy, or sluggish water, as is the large-mouthed bass.

Curiously little is known of its food, the literature of the subject containing only general statements apparently based on ordinary observations. But three specimens have been examined by us, and their food consisted wholly of fishes and crawfishes, approximately a third of the first and two thirds of the second. Among the fishes were a stonecat (*Noturus flavus*) and a log-perch (*Percina caprodes*).

The small-mouthed bass reaches a weight of 5 or 6 ℔ (Henshall, Tisdale, et al.). It is always easily distinguished from the large-mouthed species by the shorter maxillary, which never extends to a vertical from the back of the orbit, and by the smaller scales, of which there are 17 rows on the cheeks, and 10 or 11 longitudinal series between the mid-dorsal and the lateral line. In the large-mouthed form the maxillary extends past a vertical from the back of the orbit, and the scales are considerably larger, there being only 9 or 10 rows on the cheeks and 8 or 9 longitudinal series of scales above the lateral line. The young of the small-mouthed bass have a dusky bar crossing the caudal fin, and lack the dark lateral stripe which characterizes the young of the large-mouthed species. This fish is often called "tiger bass" in the East and North.

The small-mouthed bass will take live minnows or any other live bait, and does not disdain the artificial fly. In the words of Dr. Henshall, often quoted, "He is plucky, game, brave and unyielding to the last when hooked. He has the arrowy rush of the trout and bold leap of the salmon, while he has a system of fighting tactics peculiarly his own. * * * I consider him, *inch for inch* and *pound for pound*, the gamest fish that swims."

The small-mouthed bass hibernates in winter, going into deep places under the shelter of rocks and remaining torpid till spring (Tisdale).

This species, like the next, builds a nest,* usually in about three feet of water on a bottom of sand or gravel. The male roots down into the bottom, fanning away the sand with his

* In the account of the nesting habits we follow, except when otherwise stated, Lydell (Bull. U. S. Fish Comm., 1902, pp. 39–44).

tail, until mud is reached, about 3 or 4 inches below the sand. The sand forms a ridge a few inches high around the nest, and a log often forms an additional shelter on one side. The females are not about during the nest-building, which occupies from 4 to 48 hours. When the nest is finished, the male seeks the female to induce her to enter the nest, biting her gently and swimming across beneath her, striking her as he passes. The eggs and milt are deposited with the vents of the two sexes approximated. After the eggs are all laid, in successive ovipositions, the male drives the female away, himself remaining alone to guard the nest. Dr. Reighard has found that in both this and the next species the male cares for the eggs till hatched, and watches over the young till they are well grown. He found the small-mouthed bass spawning in Michigan between the end of April and the end of June. Nest-building was begun at a temperature of 60° Fahr., but the eggs were not laid till the water reached 62° to 65°. Tisdale states that it takes six years for a weight of 3 ℔ to be reached, growth continuing after that at about half a pound a year till a weight of 6 ℔ is attained.

Though practically unexcelled as a fresh-water game fish this species does not take the highest rank as food, being, in the words of Dr. Henshall, "inferior to trout and whitefishes, and perhaps even to pike and channel-cat."

Artificial propagation of this and the next species by taking and impregnating the eggs has not been successful. The eggs are not stripped easily, and it is necessary to kill the male in order to get the milt. Pond culture is resorted to with considerable success, the percentage of natural fertilizations in well-regulated ponds closely approaching the percentage obtained by artificial means for species best adapted to artificial culture. This high ratio is of course due to the fact that the parent guards the eggs. Pond culture has for several years been in successful operation in Missouri and in Michigan, and steps have lately been taken towards the establishment of breeding ponds on the upper Fox River in Illinois. The eggs of the species range in number from 2,000 to 10,000 per individual. The fry will endure shipping long distances in the cool days of spring or autumn or in midwinter.

The small-mouthed bass, while taken in considerable numbers by anglers in the northern part of Illinois, does not figure in the commercial fisheries of this state.

LARGE-MOUTH BLACK BASS (Fingerline and Half-Grown)

Micropterus salmoides (Lacépède)

MICROPTERUS SALMOIDES (Lacépède)

LARGE-MOUTHED BLACK BASS

(Frontispiece; Map LXXXI)

Lacépède, 1802, Hist. Nat. Poiss., 716 (**Labrus**).
J. & G., 484; M. V., 120; B., I, 16; J. & E., I, 1012; N., 36 (**nigricans**); J., 44 (**pallidus**); F. F., I. 3, 39 (**pallidus**); F., 67; L., 25.

Length 15 to 18 inches; form as in last species, depth 2.9 to 3.2; greatest width about ⅗ greatest depth; depth caudal peduncle 1.6 to 1.8 in its length. Color of back and sides above rather dark green, growing lighter toward axis, and everywhere obscurely mottled with darker in ill-defined blotches; middle of side traversed by a dark streak (indistinct in old specimens), which is formed of more or less irregular and discontinuous blotches of dark sage-green; belly opaque greenish white, sometimes with a faint rosy tint; iris sooty green with bronze luster and with a narrow inner rim of gold; fins pale olive-buff, the dorsal and caudal darker than the others; anal opaque whitish toward tip; young with the lateral band conspicuous and as a rule little broken into spots, passing forward through eye to end of snout; caudal of young specimens pale near base and outer margin, between which is a dark band. Head 2.8 to 2.9; width of head 1.9 to 2.4; interorbital space convex, 3.5 to 4.3; eye 5.8 to 7.6; nose 3.5 to 4; mouth very large, maxillary reaching past hinder margin of orbit, 1.9 to 2.1 in head; lower jaw rather more prominently projecting than in *M. dolomieu*; gill-rakers long, 7 or 8 on lower limb of arch, besides rudiments. Dorsal X (occasionally IX), 12–13, the spinous separated from the soft portion by a very deep notch, the last spine scarcely more than ⅓ length of fifth; longest spine about 4 in head; caudal lunate; anal III (or II), 10–11 (or 12); ventrals half way to vent; pectorals short, 2 to 2.4 in head. Scales 8 or 9, 62–68, 14–18; lateral line complete or nearly so; scales on cheeks in 9 or 10 rows.

In marked contrast to the preceding species, the large-mouthed black bass is distributed mainly along the principal streams or the lower courses of their larger tributaries, but it is not by any means confined to these, occurring in lower proportion in the smaller streams as well. It is also more equally distributed throughout the state than the small-mouthed bass, and by passing freely into the lower Illinoisan glaciation illustrates its indifference to warm and muddy water. We have found it relatively commoner, in our 211 collections, in the southern part of the state than in the central, and somewhat more so in central than in northern Illinois, the coefficients of frequency being 1.23, .97 and .80 respectively. Our data show a fairly equal distribution of this species throughout the various situations open to it, the ratios for lowland and upland lakes, for creeks, and the smaller rivers, being approximately equal, and those for the larger rivers about half as large.

The general area of the species extends from Lake Huron, the upper St. Lawrence, and the Red River of the North, southward to Florida, Texas, and northern Mexico. Its western limit is in eastern Nebraska and the Dakotas, and within these boundaries it is everywhere common in rivers, lakes, and bayous, generally preferring still or sluggish waters.

The food of this bass as shown by an examination of fourteen adults, was mainly fishes and crawfishes, the former consisting largely of minnows, but containing likewise catfish, gizzard-shad, and spiny-finned species. The crawfish amounted to only 7 per cent., and the insect food to mere traces.

The color, and other difierential characters of this and the last species have been in as much question among angling enthusiasts as its scientific nomenclature among systematic ichthyologists. Named by Lacépède "*Labrus salmoides,*" and frequently called "trout" in the South, it had the misfortune to be called "black" (*Huro nigricans*) by Cuvier and Valenciennes, and "pale" (*Lepomis pallida*) by Rafinesque, all within the space of a few years at the beginning of the last century. As a matter of fact, both species are variable in color, in the words of Dr. Henshall, "running through all the shades of slate, green, olive and yellow, to almost white." To any one who is acquainted well enough with their anatomical differences to distinguish them certainly without reference to color it will soon be evident that their variability in color leaves little chance for debate as to "which is the black bass and which the green bass," such discussions being idle except for a possible small local value.

Consistently with its habit of living in sluggish or still water, this species is somewhat less active than the last. It will, however, leap five or six feet out of the water to escape a net, and is for that reason called the "jumper" in some localities. It ranks high as a game fish, although it is not so much sought by anglers as its small-mouthed relative. It will take live minnows and other live baits, as grasshoppers, frogs, and helgramites, and is also caught by fly-fishing. It reaches a weight of 8 or 9 ℔ in this latitude, 6 or 8 ℔ usually being the limit, and specimens averaging rather below 4 ℔. In the South the species grows larger, reaching 12 to 14 ℔ (Henshall).

Its breeding habits do not differ greatly from those of the small-mouthed bass. Its nests* are built and protected by the

* In the account of nesting and spawning habits we follow Reighard (Mich. Fish Comm. Rep. 1903–04 Appendix).

males, and are usually placed among fallen leaves or fibrous rootlets, or, perhaps, on plain sand or gravel. The sand, gravel, or leaves are scooped out of the center to form a ridge about the nest a few inches high. The male seeks the female or guards the nest till she appears. The spawning is intermittent, and the process of sexual excitation of the female by the male is similar to that observed in the small-mouthed bass. The spawning season is from May to June. The eggs are viscid, and hatch in eight to ten days. The young are said to remain together in more compact schools than the small-mouthed species, making it easy to seine the fry (Lydell). They reach a length of about 6 inches in the first year after hatching.

This fish always brings a good price in the market, though it is not specially sought. While far superior to the coarse river fishes, it is excelled in flavor and other edible qualities by trout and whitefish.

It bears transportation and acclimatization admirably, and has been introduced successfully into the waters of the Pacific states and of more than one country of Europe. It is propagated by the methods of pond culture, but does not submit to stripping and the ordinary methods of artificial culture used for *Salmonidæ* and other species.

The black-bass fisheries of Illinois, practically consisting altogether of the present species, amounted in 1894 to nearly 90,000 ℔—69,000 ℔ of these coming from the Illinois River alone—and in 1899 to more than 120,000 ℔, of which the Illinois River produced 102,000.

Family **PERCIDÆ**

THE PERCHES

Body more or less elongate, terete or compressed; dorsal and ventral outlines more or less unlike; scales rather small, always ctenoid, adherent; head scaly, or not; lateral line usually present, not extending on the caudal fin; skeleton osseous; vertebræ 30 to 48, the anterior ones without transverse processes; ventral fins thoracic, I, 5; 2 dorsal fins, the first of 6 to 15 spines; anal spines 1 or 2, the usual number 2; caudal fin lunate, truncate, or rounded; no mesococracoid; gill-membranes separate or connected, not joined to isthums; branchiostegals 6 or 7; pseudobranchiæ small, glandular and concealed, or wanting; gill-rakers slender, toothed; preopercle entire or serrate; opercle usually ending in a single flat spine; mouth various, terminal or inferior, large or small; premaxillary protractile, or not; supplemental maxillary not distinct; jaws, vomer, and palatines with bands of teeth, which are usually villiform, but sometimes mixed with canines; vomer or palatines occasionally without teeth; lower pharyngeals separate, with sharp teeth; pyloric cæca few; anal papilla usually more or less developed; air-bladder small and adherent, often wanting.

Fresh waters of cool regions of the northern hemisphere, mostly confined to eastern North America and Europe; genera about 25; species about 125, the majority of them small and belonging to the American subfamily of *Etheostominæ*, or darters. Besides these little-known but unusually interesting and really beautiful small fishes, of which we have 23 species in Illinois, the family contains three of our best known and most highly valued food and game species—the yellow perch, the wall-eyed pike, and the sauger. Taken together, they form a group of highly organized, shapely, powerful, and active fishes, thoroughly equipped for the predatory life, and filling an important place in the ecological system of our inland waters. All are strictly carnivorous, and ranging as they do from a length of an inch or an inch and a half for the least darter to one of three feet for the wall-eyed pike, they are able to inhabit all waters, to search all situations, and to draw their food supplies from every class of aquatic animals, the turtles and the larger and heavier mollusks only excepted. On the other hand, although they are swift swimmers, and well armed for self-defense, we have found them frequently eaten by other predaceous fishes, as well as by numbers of their own family—burbot, black bass, bullheads, yellow perch, sunfish, and crappies being among the species in whose food we have found one or another species of the *Percidæ*.

Key to Illinois Genera of the Family PERCIDÆ

a. Pseudobranchiæ well developed; branchiostegals 7; no anal papilla; fishes growing to a weight of one pound or more; preopercle distinctly serrate below and behind, the lower serræ antrorse.

b. Canine teeth on jaws and palatines; body subcylindrical, elongate, greatest width about ¾ greatest depth.................................**Stizostedion.**

bb. No canine teeth; body moderately compressed, the greatest width about 4/7 of its greatest depth...**Perca.**

aa. Pseudobranchiæ small or wanting; branchiostegals 6; anal papilla usually present; small species, not exceeding 8 or 9 inches, usually much smaller; preopercle entire or nearly so.

c. Premaxillaries not protractile, free only at the sides, connected in front with the skin of the forehead, from which they are not separated by a cross groove.

d. Cranium not compressed or much elevated back of eyes, its elevation* not more than ⅓ of its breadth;* body as a rule more or less slender and little

* Measurement of breadth and elevation is made from a point just behind the eye, situated on the boundary between the top of the cheek (marked by a slight bulge outward from the cranium, by being scaled, or, usually, by a postorbital pore) and the thinly and smooth-skinned parietals.

compressed, subcylindrical or fusiform; depth in length as a rule 6 or more; spring males ordinarily without red or other gaudy coloration.

e. Cranium broad between the eyes, the interorbital space 4 to 4.7 in head; snout pig-like; darters of large size, reaching a length of 6 inches. . **Percina.**

ee. Interorbital space narrower, 5.5 to 9 in head; small fishes, ordinarily not over 4 inches in length.

f. Body moderately slender, the depth as a rule about 6 in length (sometimes 7); scales not often over 70; body not hyaline in life.............. **Hadropterus.**

ff. Body extremely slender, depth 7.8 to 9 in length; scales 89–100; body hyaline in life; back crossed by 4 broad, obliquely-forward-directed dark bands .... **Crystallaria.**

dd. Cranium more or less compressed and elevated back of eyes, ∩-shaped, its elevation as a rule noticeably more than ⅓ (to less than ½) its breadth, (the exceptions being species with spinous dorsal less than 60 per cent. height of soft dorsal, and with a distinct black humeral process or scale); fishes with usually more or less compressed and comparatively shortened bodies, the depth in length as a rule less than 6 (4½ to 6); spring males (except in species with low spinous dorsal) usually with brilliant red, blue, or green coloration.

g. Lateral line present.

h. Lateral line not noticeably flexed upward anteriorly............. **Etheostoma.**

hh. Lateral line conspicuously flexed upward anteriorly, its direction parallel with line of back (least distance between lateral line and middle of back in *B. fusiformis* about ¼ depth of body at same point).......... **Boleichthys.**

gg. Lateral line absent; fins very short, dorsal spines 6; size very small, length not over 1½ inches.. **Microperca.**

cc. Premaxillaries protractile, i. e., a groove separating them from the skin of the forehead (this groove sometimes crossed by a very narrow frenum in *Cottogaster shumardi*, in which also there is a black blotch at front and back of base of spinous dorsal).

i. Groove between skin of forehead and premaxillaries ordinarily, though not always (in Illinois species), crossed by a narrow frenum; a black spot at front and back of base of spinous dorsal..................... **Cottogaster.**

ii. Premaxillaries freely protractile, a frenum never present; no black blotch at back of spinous dorsal fin.

j. Groove separating premaxillaries from forehead inferior, not visible except from below; maxillary adnate to the preorbital for most of its length, nearly immovable; anal spines 2............................... **Diplesion.**

jj. Groove separating premaxillaries from forehead superior, easily visible from in front and above; maxillary separated by a groove from preorbital for its entire length; anal spine single.

k. Anal fin much smaller than soft dorsal; body moderately slender, depth not over 7 in length; not hyaline in life.......................... **Boleosoma.**

kk. Anal fin almost as large as soft dorsal; body extremely slender, depth in length 8 to 10; body hyaline in life........................... **Ammocrypta.**

Genus **STIZOSTEDION** Rafinesque

AMERICAN PIKE-PERCHES

Body elongate, fusiform, back broad; mouth large and premaxillary protractile; preopercle serrated, the serræ below turned forward (antrorse) and spaced rather wide apart; opercle with 1 or more spines; teeth in villiform bands, in addition to which sharp canines are present on jaws and palatines; pseudobranchiæ well developed; pyloric cæca 3; dorsal spines 12 to 15; anal spines 2, slender and closely appressed to the soft rays; scales small, ctenoid.

Large carnivorous fishes of the fresh waters of North America north of Mexico; 2 species known. Highly valued as food, and important as game fishes, but very costly of maintenance if one takes into account the numbers and kinds of other fishes necessary to bring one of these pike-perch to maturity and to keep it in good condition until it is caught.

KEY TO THE SPECIES OF **STIZOSTEDION** FOUND IN ILLINOIS

a. Pyloric cæca 3, subequal, as long as stomach; rays of soft dorsal 19 to 22, usually over 20; cheeks rather sparsely scaled; base of pectorals without distinct black blotch; a black blotch at back of spinous dorsal; soft dorsal obscurely reticulated.................................... **vitreum.**

aa. Pyloric cæca 5 to 8, unequal, the 4 longest much shorter than stomach; rays of soft dorsal 17 to 19; cheeks as a rule closely scaled; a distinct black blotch at base of pectoral; last dorsal spines without black blotch; soft dorsal with rows of dark spots.............................. **canadense.***

STIZOSTEDION VITREUM (MITCHILL)

WALL-EYED PIKE; PIKE-PERCH; JACK-SALMON

(MAP LXXXII)

Mitchill, 1818, Supp. Amer. Month. Mag., II, 247 (**Perca**).
G., I, 74 (**Lucioperca americana**); J. & G., 525; M. V., 135; B., I, 54 (**Lucioperca**); J. & E., I, 1021; N., 36 (**americanum** and var. **salmoneum**); J., 44; F. F., I. 3, 32 (**Stizostethium**); F., 63; L., 26.

Length 3 feet; body slender, only moderately compressed; profile long and straight; depth 4.3 to 5.2; greatest width about ¾ greatest depth; depth caudal peduncle 2.3 to 2.6 in its length. Color a brassy olive-buff ground, shading to olive-yellow in spots, and everywhere mottled with black, mottlings on head, cheeks, and opercles in vermiculate pattern, those on back and sides arranged more or less definitely in five large irregularly-shaped cross-blotches with smaller blotches between; belly whitish, tinged with green; iris chocolate with gold margin next pupil; cornea milky, giving the eye its characteristic muddy or "wall-eye" appearance; spinous dorsal with a narrow inky-black margin and with a large black blotch behind, nearly or quite including posterior two membranes; soft dorsal reticulate or indistinctly barred; base of pectoral without a prominent black blotch, an indistinct and diffused patch of dark color sometimes present; caudal with indefinite bars; ventrals and anal whitish with tinge of green. Head slender and tapered, less depressed than in next species, 3.2 to 3.5 in length; width head 2 to 2.2 in its length; interorbital flat, 5.2 to 5.9; eye 4.6 to 6; nose 3.3 to 3.8; mouth large, terminal, little oblique, maxillary past back of pupil, 2.2 to 2.4 in head; lower jaw slightly shorter than upper; gill-rakers slender; pyloric cæca 3, subequal, as long as stomach. Dorsal XIII or XIV, 19 to 22; longest dorsal spine about 2⅕ in head; caudal lunate; anal II, 12–14; ventrals

* Represented in Illinois by variety *griseum*.

WALL-EYED PIKE, *Stizostedion vitreum* (Mitchill)

half-way to vent; pectorals 1.8 to 2.1 in head. Scales 12–14, 80–89, 19–25; lateral line usually complete, some pores occasionally extending on caudal fin; scales on cheeks as a rule sparse.

Although taken by us but thirty-nine times from sixteen localities, and rare except in a few favorable situations where the water is clear and the current swift, this species is generally distributed in Illinois. It is a far-ranging species, of predominant northern distribution, occurring from Hudson Bay and the Saskatchewan River through New Brunswick and New England to the Potomac and north Georgia, and westward through all the Great Lakes and the Ohio basin to Alabama and Minnesota. It is preferably, however, a lake fish, and is most abundant in the Great Lakes, particularly in Lake Erie.

It is essentially a piscivorous fish, but also feeds, according to Jordan and Evermann, upon crawfishes when in shallow water. Ten specimens examined by us had eaten nothing but fishes, half of them the hickory-shad (*Dorosoma*). Minnows and sunfishes were also noticed. From a single wall-eyed pike caught in Peoria Lake, ten specimens of gizzard-shad were taken, each from three to four inches long. As this is a very thin, high fish, with a serrate belly, these were about as large as a wall-eyed pike can easily swallow, and we may, by a very moderate estimate of its requirements, conclude that at least six hundred fishes of this size would be required for its maintenance during one year. Reckoning the average life of a pike at three years, the smallest reasonable estimate of food for each pike-perch would fall somewhere between eighteen hundred and three thousand fishes, and a hundred pike-perch such as should each year be taken along a few miles of a river like the Illinois would require 180,000 to 300,000 fishes for their food. Probably no fish in our streams is able to meet so tremendous a demand except the hickory-shad—so abundant in the food of this pike—unless the European carp, generally introduced since these observations were made, may be an equally acceptable victim. The wall-eyed pike is a swift and vigorous swimmer, capable of overtaking a black bass.

It reaches a maximum length of about three feet, and a weight of twenty-five pounds, but examples of this size are very rare. According to Jordan and Evermann, it probably does not average more than ten pounds in the Great Lakes. It prefers clear water with a clean and hard bottom, and is not often found in streams or lakes with a bottom of mud. In the

Great Lakes it lives in spring and summer in shallow water near the shore, seeking a greater depth in fall. It is much the largest, and also commercially the most important, of all the American perches, and has but few rivals as a food fish among our fresh-water species. Its flesh is white and firm, and of a flavor to satisfy the most fastidious. It is also a game fish of the first quality, in the opinion of most anglers, and but little inferior to the black bass. It is one of the most important fishes propagated by the United States Fish Commission, and the output in 1900 from a single station, that at Put-in-Bay, was nearly ninety millions.

The catch of this species in the Mississippi Valley has fallen off greatly in recent years, amounting to only 210,000 pounds for seventeen states in 1899, whereas in 1894 Minnesota alone produced 651,000 pounds. The product of the Illinois River in 1899 was 11,000 pounds.

The pike-perch is said to spawn in April in Lake Erie. In 1898 it spawned at Havana, on the Illinois River, between April 1 and 15. The eggs are small, only about half as large as those of the whitefish, and the young begin to practice their carnivorous instincts upon each other when only about ten days old. The species is hardy and prolific, and it is a desirable fish for clean lakes and clear rivers, provided these contain a continuous abundance of otherwise useless fish for its food.

STIZOSTEDION CANADENSE GRISEUM (De Kay)

GRAY PIKE; SAUGER; SAND-PIKE

(Map LXXXIII)

De Kay, 1842, New York Fauna: Fishes, 19 (**Lucioperca grisea**).

J. & G., 526 (**canadense, part**); M. V., 135; B., I, 54 (**Lucioperca canadensis,** part); J. & E., I, 1022; N., 36 (**griseum**); J., 43 (**canadense**) F. F., I. 3, 31, 33 (**Stizostethium**); F., 63 (**canadense**); L., 26 (**canadense**).

Length 1 to 1½ feet; body slender, only moderately compressed, the profile straight or weakly arched predorsally; depth 5.2 to 5.5; greatest width ¾ of greatest depth; depth caudal peduncle 2.4 to 3 in its length. Color olive-gray, the sides brassy to orange, mottled with darker; first dorsal with two or three rows of large, round, inky-black spots as large as pupil; no black blotch at back of spinous dorsal; soft dorsal with 4 or 5 irregular rows of rather indistinct dusky blotches; a large black blotch at base of pectorals; caudal yellowish, barred with dusky. Head tapered and depressed more than in last species, 3.4 to 3.6; width of head 1.9 to 2; interorbital space 4.6 to 5.1; eye 1 to 1.2; nose 3.2 to 3.7; maxillary past back of pupil, 2.1 to 2.2;

gill-rakers slender, pyloric cæca 5 to 8, 4 of them of moderate length, but shorter than stomach, the others mostly rudimentary. Dorsal X to XIII (usually XII or XIII), 17–19; longest dorsal spine about 2⅙ in head; caudal lunate; anal II, 11 or 12; ventrals half way to vent; pectorals 1.7 to 1.8 in head. Scales 9–11, 85–91, 19–24; lateral line usually complete, in some specimens extending on caudal; cheeks fully scaled, the scales very strongly ctenoid, rows about 15.

A much smaller fish than the preceding, seldom exceeding a foot or eighteen inches in length, and a weight of one or two pounds. It has also occurred much less frequently in our collections, which have come mainly from the Mississippi and the Illinois rivers, with a few, also, from the Rock, the Wabash, and the Kaskaskia. It seems to be a species of somewhat more limited range than the wall-eyed pike. The distribution area of our variety (*griseum*) extends from the Red River of the North and the Assiniboin River, through the upper Great Lakes and the upper Mississippi Valley, west to Montana and south to Tennessee and Arkansas. Its habits, so far as known, are similar to those of the preceding species, and it occurs in similar waters, the two having been taken together by us in about the usual ratio for river and lake fishes.

Judging from the results of an examination of fourteen specimens obtained from the Illinois River at different places and times, it feeds wholly, or almost wholly, on fishes. Four of these specimens had eaten gizzard-shad, two had taken catfishes, one of which was a bullhead, two had eaten sheepshead (*Aplodinotus*), and one had taken a black bass and a sunfish. The presence of a medium-sized bullhead in the stomach of one of these fishes, with its dorsal and pectoral poison-spines stiff-set and unbroken, was a striking illustration of the voracity of this species.

It is of much less commercial importance than the wall-eye, the catch from the Mississippi River in 1899 reaching a total of only 39,000 pounds.

Genus **PERCA** (Artedi) Linnæus

RIVER PERCH

Body oblong, considerably compressed, back elevated; mouth moderate; premaxillary protractile; preopercle serrate, the serræ on lower margin antrorse, closely set; opercle with a single spine; teeth in villiform bands on jaws, vomer, and palatines; no canines; pseudobranchiæ small, but perfect;

pyloric cæca 3 to 7; dorsal spines 12 to 16; anal with 2 slender spines, well separated from the soft rays; scales rather small, ctenoid. Fresh waters of northern regions; 3 closely allied species, one each in Europe, Asia, and North America.

PERCA FLAVESCENS (MITCHILL)

YELLOW PERCH; RINGED PERCH; AMERICAN PERCH

(MAP LXXXIV)

Mitchill, 1814, Rep. Fish. N. Y., 18 (**Morone**).
G., I, 59; J. & G., 524 (**americana**); M. V., 134; B., I, 48; J. & E., I, 1023; N., 36; J., 43 (**americana**); F. F., I. 3, 29 (**americana**); F., 63 (**americana**); L., 26.

Length 1 foot; body only moderately elongate, considerably compressed; back elevated, highest in front of spinous dorsal; the profile convex from first dorsal spine to occiput, thence straightish or slightly concave to muzzle; depth 3.3 to 3.8; greatest width of body about 5/7 of its depth; depth caudal peduncle 2 to 2.2 in its length. Color of sides and back brassy green to golden yellow, with seven broad bars of dusky crossing each side from back nearly to belly; belly whitish with reflections of green, salmon, and yellow; iris brassy at edge; spinous dorsal gray, usually with a black spot on last two membranes; soft dorsal and caudal plain green; pectorals transparent grayish green; ventrals and anal variously light grayish green or orange to crimson according to season and habitat. Head 3 to 3.5; width head 1.8 to 2.1 in length; interorbital space nearly flat, 3.8 to 4.3; eye 1.1 to 1.4 in interorbital, 4.5 to 5.5 in head; nose 3.4 to 3.7, longer than eye; maxillary to middle of orbit, 2.4 to 2.8; opercle ending above in several coarse jagged points; preopercle strongly serrate, especially below; gill-rakers X + 15, the longest more than half length of branchial filaments; pyloric cæca 3. Dorsal XII to XIV–II or III, 12 to 13; longest spine a little more than 2 in head; length base of soft dorsal about 3/5 base of spinous; caudal lunate; anal II, 7–8; ventrals more than half-way to vent; pectorals 1.6 to 1.9 in head. Scales 6 or 7, 57–62, 15–18; lateral line nearly or quite complete; cheeks scaled, in about 8 to 10 rows.

This is one of the best-known fishes in the northern part of the state, swarming especially along the piers on the lake front at Chicago, where it is the common game of the local fishermen. It occurs elsewhere in Illinois mainly in the upland lakes of the northeastern part of the state, in the tributary streams flowing into Lake Michigan, and in the Illinois and Mississippi rivers as far south as Meredosia. It is virtually unknown in the southeastern half of the state, and has never once been taken by us in any of the streams of the Wabash or Kaskaskia systems, or from any of those farther south. It is inconstant in its abundance in the Illinois River, and is said to have increased greatly there since the opening of the drainage canal has cooled and cleared the waters of that stream.

YELLOW PERCH, *Perca flavescens* (Mitchill)

Its general distribution is decidedly northerly, except on the Atlantic coast, where it has been found as far south as the Neuse River in North Carolina. It occurs abundantly in the Hudson and in all the Great Lakes, and ranges throughout Quebec and New England to Nova Scotia, westward to Iowa and the Dakotas, and north to the Red River basin. It is unknown from southern Indiana and southern Ohio, as it is from southern Illinois.

It is essentially a lake fish, but occurs also in running streams, most abundantly in the larger rivers and least so in creeks. Our eighty-three collections have been taken with approximately equal frequency from the glacial lakes, the lakes of the bottom-lands, and the rivers of the largest class. It is wholly carnivorous, but differs greatly in its food according to the situation from which it comes. Eighteen river specimens, for example, had made but 6 per cent. of their food of fishes, about a fifth of it of the smaller thin-shelled mollusks, a fourth of it of insect larvæ, and nearly half of it of *Crustacea*—crawfishes, fresh-water shrimps (*Palæmonetes*), amphipods, and isopods—while a dozen lake specimens, on the other hand, had eaten nothing but fishes and crawfishes, the former greatly preponderating. The perch is said by Cole to eat the spawn of other fish. There is a notable difference, also, between the lake and river perch in respect to their coloration, the latter being usually much the more brilliant.

The yellow perch may reach a length of a foot and a weight of more than two pounds, but does not commonly weigh much more than a pound. It spawns in spring, usually during April and May, when the temperature of the water is from 44° to 49° F. Ripe males were taken by Craig at Havana on May 3, 1899. According to Dr. C. C. Abbott, the sexes go in pairs to the spawning beds, which are selected near shore where there is a sandy or pebbly bottom. The eggs are laid in flat bands, and, after fertilization and "water hardening," they increase greatly in size. A single adult deposited in the aquarium of the Washington station of the United States Fish Commission a string of eggs 88 inches long, which, after fertilization, weighed 41 ounces.

This perch is taken in fykes, gill-nets, and traps, or with seines and hooks. It is one of the very best of our fishes for a pan fry, the flesh being white, firm, and of an excellent flavor, better, however, in northern localities than in southern.

The catch of perch from Lake Michigan in 1899 was over three million pounds, of which 677,000 pounds came from the Illinois shore. In the Illinois River it is taken in considerable numbers, but mostly by line-fishing. "As a game fish, the yellow perch can be commended chiefly on account of the fact that anybody can catch it. It can be taken with hook and line any month in the year, and with any sort of bait,—grasshoppers, angleworms, grubs, small minnows, pieces of mussel, or pieces of fish; and it will even rise, and freely, too, on occasion, to the artificial fly; * * * It is easily taken through the ice in winter, when small minnows are the best bait." A State Laboratory assistant some years ago made an experiment at simple and inexpensive fishing for the yellow perch from a pier at South Chicago. With a piece of lath for a pole, a line of cotton twine, a small hook, and a bit of pork for his first bait, he caught a single perch, cut this up as bait for others, and within an hour had a string of seventy-five.

Subfamily **ETHEOSTOMINÆ**

THE DARTERS

The darters have long been a favorite group with students of American fishes. Peculiar to this country,* in which the subfamily has a great development, interesting in their variety, their habits, and their relations to nature, and especially attractive by reason of their graceful forms, their relatively minute size, their brilliant coloration, and the exquisite detail and finish of their structural equipment, they are to the fishes of North America what the hummingbirds are to South American birds. They seem not to be so much dwarfed as concentrated fishes, each embodying in small space all the complexity, spirit, and activity of a perch or a wall-eyed pike.

As a group, they are most likely to be found in comparatively swift and rocky streams, being especially adapted to these situations by their small size, their large paired fins, their pointed heads, and their habit of resting on the bottom or, in some cases, of burying themselves in sand,—all of which are means of maintaining themselves in swift currents, and of securing from among and under stones the insect larvæ and crustaceans on

* Small percoids of Europe belonging to the genus *Aspro* and found in the Danube are of larger size than the American darters, and are thought by most writers to have been independently derived from European percoid stock, and not to be genetically related to the American *Etheostominæ*.

which they mainly depend for food. They swim mainly by means of their pectoral fins, making quick dashes in the current as a bird might make a short, rapid flight against a high wind, and resting in the intervals upon their extended ventral and anal fins. Unlike most of the taxonomic groups we have hitherto discussed, the darters thus form a rather definite ecological assemblage, assimilated by their like adaptive characters and by their similar relations to like situations. There are, nevertheless, well-marked degress of adaptation among the different genera and species; and, likewise, in the strictness of their confinement to the class of situations characteristic of the group. Three of our species, for example, are often found in still or sluggish waters and over a muddy bottom; one, the sand-darter, is much the commonest in streams with a sandy bottom; and another, *Cottogaster shumardi*, is most abundant along the borders of the largest rivers. The species are likewise distinguishable in other features of their local distribution, as may be readily seen by a comparison of the distribution maps of the darters in the atlas accompanying this report. The force of competition is thus more or less broken among them in various ways, no exact analysis of which has ever been attempted. The origin of these species is an interesting and inviting problem, particularly open to solution because of the comparatively restricted range of the family and the fact that there is nothing to suggest an extensive migration from the place of their original differentiation.

The food of the subfamily was studied by the senior author many years ago from the contents of seventy stomachs representing fifteen species, collected in various parts of Illinois in several months of four successive years. These indicated more than their number would imply, since different darters obtained from the same locality and on the same day usually agreed so closely in food that the study of from two to five specimens gave all the facts obtainable from several times as many. Furthermore, the differences between the related species in respect to food are so slight that specific peculiarities were scarcely recognizable. The data obtained, therefore, really apply to the food of the whole subfamily at different seasons in twenty-nine localities within this state. This was, on the whole, remarkably uniform, except that two of the species, the largest and the smallest of the group, were found to differ from the remainder in a way to correspond to a notable difference in their local distribution.

Briefly described, the typical species feed on insect larvæ commonly abundant on the bottoms of streams, under or among stones, and in other similar situations, the smaller species eating mainly dipterous larvæ (most commonly *Chironomus*), together with a smaller proportion of neuropterous larvæ of the smaller sizes; while the larger darters eat essentially the same kinds of food, but in different ratios, the neuropterous larvæ being of larger average size and also making a larger part of the food. The two exceptional species studied, *Percina caprodes* and *Microperca punctulata*, have deserted in great measure the usual situations of the darters, and are frequently found among weeds and algæ in comparatively quiet water with a muddy bottom, the others being much more closely confined to swift and rocky shallows. Consistently with this difference, these two widely unlike species agree in their choice of food, which in both consists largely of *Entomostraca* or other small crustaceans. The larger species had also eaten a few small mollusks (*Ancylus*).

Where a group of species has become assimilated by a similar adaptation to a common class of situations, and has thus become a definite ecological assemblage, those in which the adaptive processes have gone farthest are, of course, most likely to be limited to the characteristic situation—are most likely, consequently, to be taken by the collector in each others' company. By applying this rule to an analysis of the collections of darters made in Illinois, we find that the most typical species obtained by us in any considerable number are the following six, mentioned in the order of the relative frequency of their associate occurrence in our collections: *Hadropterus phoxocephalus*, *Etheostoma zonale*, *Etheostoma flabellare*, *Hadropterus aspro*, *Ammocrypta pellucida*, and *Etheostoma cœruleum*. Apparently the least stringently connected with their kind by the associative relationship are *Diplesion blennioides*, *Etheostoma jessiæ*, *Boleosoma camurum*, and *Boleichthys fusiformis*. The species of the second list will presently be seen to be those which have wandered widely from the common field of the subfamily, and which are consequently found most frequently in situations to which the other species rarely resort. Furthermore, in separating themselves from their fellows in respect to local distribution, they have not, as a rule, approached each other, but remain as loosely affiliated ecologically among themselves as they are with the more typical members of the group. A notable exception to this statement is found in *Boleosoma camurum* and *Boleichthys fusiformis,* which occur in similar waters, and most abundantly also in the same part of the state. In these two common species the coefficient of association each with the other is unusually high, much higher, indeed, than the average coefficient for the most typical species of the subfamily.

The darters are distributed through southern Canada and the United States east of the Rocky Mountains and northern Mexico; as far westward as south Nebraska; and northward to Qu'Appelle, in the basin of the Red River of the North. There are some eighty or ninety species of this subfamily in North America, and in Illinois twenty-three species belonging to ten genera. The majority of them are less than four inches long, and one of them does not exceed an inch and a half. The name of "darter" is given them because of their quick, swift flights through the water, a. fact which also suggested to Rafinesque the technical name of one of the early genera described by him —*Boleosoma,* meaning dart-body. To the fisherman and the ordinary observer these little percoids are usually either wholly unknown or go by the general name of minnow, or, perhaps, by the more appropriate one of "perch minnow." They are, as a rule, brilliantly colored, and sexual color-differences are strongly marked in many species, the females being duller than the males.

The species are much subject to local variation, but they are nevertheless commonly well marked, and the local forms can usually be referred, without much difficulty, to the specific group. All spawn in spring, so far as known.

GENUS **PERCINA** HALDEMAN

LOG-PERCHES

Body elongate, sybcylindrical; mouth small and inferior; premaxillaries not protractile; teeth on vomer and palatines; belly with a median row of enlarged caducous plates; vertebræ (*P. caprodes*) 44 (23 + 21); pyloric cæca (*P. caprodes*) 6; pseudobranchiæ present, rudimentary. In the diagnostic features above noted this genus is scarcely different from *Hadropterus.* On the cranial characters of *Percina,* which in its skull structure more closely resembles *Perca* than do the other etheostomids, Jordan and Eigenmann have said: "As compared with the other darters, the skull of *Percina* is much broader between the eyes; the parietal bones are more strongly ridged, the sutures more distinct, the top of the cranium beyond the eyes more depressed, and the supraoccipital crest more developed than in most of the others."* The largest of the darters; coloration olivaceous, with dark vertical bands on body, more or less broken into spots and reticulations; species 2.

* Proc. U. S. Nat. Mus., Vol. 8, p. 68.

PERCINA CAPRODES (RAFINESQUE)

LOG-PERCH

(MAP LXXXV)

Rafinesque, 1818, Amer. Month. Mag., 534 **(Sciæna).**
J. & G., 499; M. V., 126; B., I, 57; J. & E., 1026; N., 36; J., 39; F., 65; F. F., I. 3, 25; L., 26.

The largest of our darters, length 4 to 6 inches; body cylindrical, elongate; depth 5.4 to 7 in length; greatest width of body about 4/5 of its greatest depth; depth of caudal peduncle 2.6 to 2.9 in its length. Color olive-buff to yellowish; sides of adults crossed by from 30 to 40 bars of dark green color, varying* in width and in extent from above downward, the most usual arrangement being an alternation of short and narrow with wider and longer ones, the merging of bars producing in some older specimens a more or less reticulated pattern on the sides and forming on the back 3 or 4 large saddle-like blotches; fewer bars (15 to 30) in younger specimens, the intermediate narrower and shorter ones being faint or entirely absent in the very young; a small but prominent black spot at base of caudal fin, encircled by a band of yellow; snout dusky; cheeks with iridescent green, blue, and yellow; iris with golden margin; dorsal and caudal fins barred, other fins plain. Head 3.9 to 4.3 in length, long and pointed; width of head 1.9 to 2.2; interorbital space flat or slightly concave, 4·to 4.8 in head; eye high, obliquely set, its long diameter 3.6 to 4.2 in head; snout long, conic, with a pad at its tip, 2.8 to 3.3 in head; mouth small, inferior, overhung by the pig-like snout, maxillary reaching scarcely to posterior nostril-opening; cleft 3.4 to 4 in head; lower jaw much shorter than upper; gill-membranes narrowly connected, distance from tip of snout to their angle scarcely greater than to back of orbit. Dorsal fin XII–15; spinous and soft portions usually very little separated, or not at all; height of first dorsal 2 to 2.3 in head, of second 1.6 to 2.2 (height of first 74 to 94 per cent. of second); caudal truncate; anal II, 10–11 pectorals 1.2 to 1.4 in head; separation of ventrals about equal to their width at base. Scales 9–11, 83–93, 12–14; lateral line usually complete, as many as 1 to 6 pores occasionally lacking; cheeks and opercles fully scaled; nape of typical specimens fully scaled†; breast naked; belly with deeply embedded scales and a median row of rather small pectinate caducous plates.

Sexual differences not marked. The majority of our specimens are young, and no gravid females appear among them. Testes were large and white in males taken on the 12th of June 1901.

The darter is distributed through the state from Cairo to South Chicago and the northeastern glacial lakes, mainly, however, in the larger streams. We have found it relatively most abundant in medium-sized rivers, and next so in creeks, its frequency coefficients for such streams, as represented by our

---

* For an interesting paper on variation in the color pattern of this species see W. J. Moenkhaus, Amer. Nat., Vol. 28, pp. 641-660.

† Naked in var. *zebra* Agassiz (Jordan and Evermann, Bull. U. S. Nat. Mus., No. 47, I., p. 1027). Some apparent specimens of that form were taken in Illinois in early collections by the senior author.

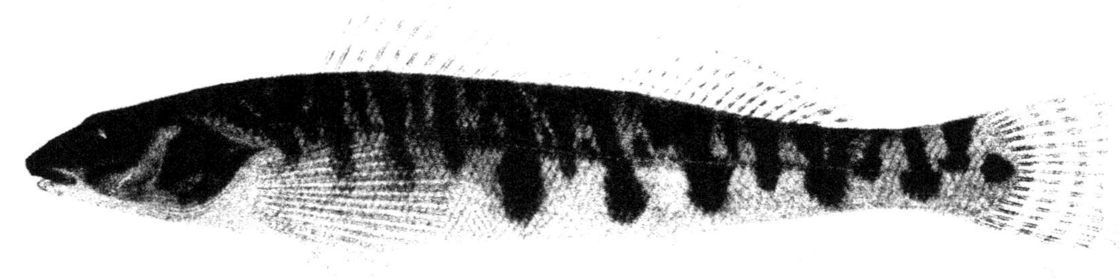

LOG-PERCH, *Percina caprodes* (Rafinesque)

seventy collections of the species, being 2.26 and 1.6 respectively. In the larger rivers, on the other hand, and in lakes, ponds, and sloughs, it is much less common, its ratio for each being .58. It is decidedly more frequent in northern Illinois than in either central or southern. It is not particularly choice of localities, and enters freely the turbid waters of the lower Illinoisan glaciation. It has been taken several times along the banks of the Illinois River, and from bays and bottom-land lakes connected with that stream. It is not a swift-water species, and has but little in its habits, food, or favorite situations, to identify it with the darters at large.

Outside Illinois it occurs in all the Great Lakes, in Lake Champlain, in the St. Lawrence River, and in various smaller streams in Quebec, and thence southward to Virginia and the Ohio basin, westward to Kansas and Missouri, and southwestward to Alabama and Trinity River in Texas.

It is sometimes taken on the hook with a worm bait, and it is probably the only one of our darters definitely known as an angler's fish.

This species is particularly changeable in color, as observed by us in aquarium specimens, the darker tints sometimes deepening to black, and the gold and emerald complexion of the cheeks and opercles becoming extraordinarily bright. It was noticed that the lower part of the transverse bars would sometimes blacken independently of the upper part, giving an appearance of a row of lateral blotches like those of *Hadropterus aspro*.

A third of the food of eleven specimens was found by us to consist of crustaceans (mainly *Entomostraca*), and the remainder of insects, the latter chiefly *Chironomus* larvæ, larvæ of day-flies, and water-bugs (*Corixa*).

Genus **HADROPTERUS** Agassiz

BLACK-SIDED DARTERS

Body rather elongate, compressed or not; mouth rather wide, terminal; premaxillaries not protractile; teeth on vomer and usually on palatines; belly with a median series of enlarged ctenoid plates, which in most species fall off at intervals, but are persistent in some; vertebræ (four species) 39 to 42 (18 or 19 + 20 to 23); pyloric cæca 2 to 4. Darters of more or less slender and graceful form, of active habits, and of moderately brilliant coloration; size various, some species reaching a length of 6 to 8 inches, others much smaller; species 11 or 12.

KEY TO THE SPECIES OF **HADROPTERUS** FOUND IN ILLINOIS

a. Gill-membranes not broadly united at isthmus, distance from tip of snout to angle formed by their union scarcely exceeding that to back of orbit.

b. Color pattern transverse, consisting of (1) bars or bands, or (2) of blotches and transversely rather than longitudinally arranged marblings.

c. Sides with about 15 blotches, some of them extending upward and downward so as to form ill-defined bars; cheeks scaled.............. **evermanni.**

cc. Sides with about 7 broad transverse bars, extending from below lateral line on one side, across back and down on other side; cheeks naked...... **evides.**

bb. Color pattern longitudinal, the sides marked with a median row of blotches or a moniliform band, above which are longitudinally disposed marblings.

d. Scales 8–10, 64–70, 9–11; cheeks scaled.............................. **aspro.**

dd. Scales 6, 52–60, 6; cheeks naked................................. **ouachitæ.**

aa. Gill-membranes united at isthmus in a broad curve, least distance from muzzle to free margin of gill-membranes 1⅕ to 1½ times that from muzzle to back of orbit.

e. Head very slender and snout long and pointed, 1⅓ times eye; interorbital space narrow, its width twice in snout; lateral blotches small and as a rule faint; a very small central caudal spot............... **phoxocephalus.**

ee. Head and snout less slender, the latter equaling eye; interorbital space broader, less than 1½ times in snout; sides with 8 or 9 large and distinct, often more or less confluent, dark blotches; base of caudal with 3 dark blotches, the central and lower spots usually more or less merged.. **sclerus.**

HADROPTERUS EVERMANNI MOENKHAUS

Moenkhaus, 1903, Bull. U. S. Fish. Comm., Vol. 22, 397–398.

Length of single specimen in our collection 3 inches; body stoutish, only moderately elongate, and very little compressed, the cylindrical form suggesting *Percina caprodes*; depth 5.17 in length; greatest width of body about ⅚ of its depth; caudal peduncle short and stout, its depth 2.35 in its length. Color (in preservative) light olive with numerous blotches and marblings; back with about 6 large and more or less quadrate dark blotches; sides with 13 or 14 blotches, some of them extending upward and downward so as to form ill-defined bars, the dark markings above blotches being of a general transverse rather than longitudinal pattern (as in *H. aspro*); first dorsal with membranes dusky at base, especially toward back of fin; tips of last rays and membranes dusky; soft dorsal and caudal faintly barred, other fins plain; head smoky olive, a prominent dark vertical streak below eye. Head rather short, bluntly conic, 4.08 in length; width of head 1.79 in its length; interorbital space flat, 5.76 in head; eye oblique, 3.58; nose 2.97; mouth moderate, the maxillary scarcely reaching to orbit, cleft 3.17 in head, lower jaw included; gill-membranes noticeably but not at all broadly connected at isthmus, the distance from muzzle to angle about 1.1 times that to back of orbit. Dorsal fin XIII, 14; spinous and soft portions scarcely separated; height of first dorsal 1.7 in head, of second 1.6 (height of first 91 per cent. of second); caudal truncate; anal II, 12; pectorals 1.1 in head; separation of ventrals slightly greater than their width at base. Scales 8, 69, 8 [12]*; no pores lacking; cheeks with about 6 rows of rather large scales; opercles and nape fully scaled; breast naked; belly naked anteriorly, a median row of immature caducous plates behind.

* Number in brackets is count to middle line of belly; first count is to front of anal.

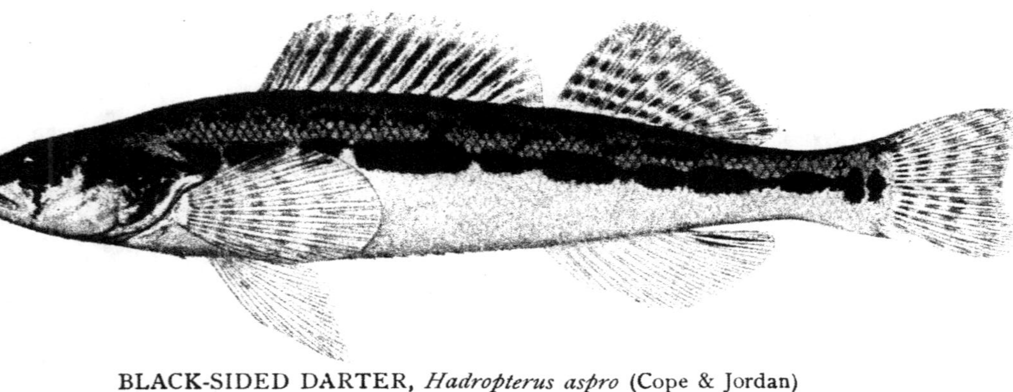

BLACK-SIDED DARTER, *Hadropterus aspro* (Cope & Jordan)

Hadropterus phoxocephalus (Nelson)

Our single specimen of this species was taken at Havana, Illinois, in the summer of 1897. While presenting resemblances to both *H. aspro* and *P. caprodes*, it may be readily distinguished from both by its different color pattern.

Described from Lake Tippecanoe, Indiana.

HADROPTERUS PHOXOCEPHALUS (Nelson)

(Map LXXXVI)

Nelson, 1876, Bull. Ill. State Lab. Nat. Hist., I. 1, 35 (**Etheostoma**).
J. & G., 501 (**Alvordius**); M. V., 127 (**Etheostoma**); B., I, 63 (**Percina**); J. & E., I, 1030; J., 39 (**Alvordius**); F., 65; L. 27.

Length 3 inches; body moderately elongate and compressed; form distinctive among darters for its graceful outlines, the back gently elevated and the anterior portion of the body faultlessly tapered to the end of the slender pointed head; depth 5.4 to 6.2 in length; greatest width of body about 4/5 of its depth; depth caudal peduncle 1.8 to 2.4 in its length. Color yellowish brown, more or less marbled, blotched, and tessellated with darker, but the colors generally duller than in *H. aspro*; sides with about 12 or 13 more or less indefinite dusky blotches, sometimes confluent into a moniliform band, in instances fading so as to become almost imperceptible; back with tessellations and upper portion of sides with marblings of dark color, ordinary examples having a vermiculated appearance; first dorsal with a broad band of orange-red across its middle and with narrow outer edging of pale blue, the hues much more brilliant in males than in females; second dorsal and caudal faintly barred; other fins plain, the anal and ventrals dusky in males; a dark band from front of orbit through nostril to end of snout; vertical streak below eye faint. Head long, slender and quite pointed, 3.6 to 3.9 in length; width of head 2.1 to 2.4; interorbital space extremely narrow, 6.7 to 7.9 in head; eye 3.8 to 4.5; nose pointed, 3.5 to 4 in head; mouth moderate, maxillary reaching a little past front of orbit, the cleft 3.4 to 4 in head; jaws nearly equal; gill-membranes free from isthmus and broadly connected, the distance from muzzle to their free posterior margin 1⅓ to 1½ times that to back of orbit. Dorsal fin XII or XIII, 12–14; spinous and soft portions scarcely separated at base; height of first dorsal 2.2 to 2.9 in head, second 1.7 to 2.1 (height of first 70 to 88 per cent. of second); caudal slightly emarginate; anal II, 8 or 9, rarely 10 or 11; pectorals 1.2 to 1.4 in head; separation of ventrals slightly less than their width at base. Scales 8–10, 64–69, 10–12 [12–18]; usually no pores lacking; cheeks covered with very fine scales, in 14 or 15 rows; opercles and nape scaled; breast naked or with a median large caducous shield; mid-ventral line with small caducous plates.

This modestly colored but shapely darter is distributed much like *Percina caprodes*, except that we have not found it in the northern glacial lakes, and that it is dispersed more widely through the smaller streams. It has occurred in ninety-five of our collections, most abundantly in the Illinois basin, but frequently also in the Rock River and its tributaries. It is commonest in northern Illinois and is least frequently found in the southern part of the state. Like *Percina caprodes*, it has been taken by us most generally from the smaller rivers (3.39) and from creeks (1.59), but only rarely from the largest rivers (.4) or from lakes or sloughs (.2). It is preëminently a species of swift water with a bottom of rock or sand, 94 per cent. of our collections coming from the former situation and 90 per cent. from the latter.

It is further reported from Ohio, Iowa, Kansas, and Missouri to Kentucky, Arkansas, and Oklahoma.

Consistently with the relatively large size of this species, larvæ and pupæ of May-flies were found by us to predominate in its food, including one of the largest larvæ of this family (*Hexagenia*) in our streams. Larvæ of dragon-flies, a small percentage of *Chironomus* larvæ, and water-bugs (*Corixa*), were the other elements of its food.

Females greatly distended with eggs were taken by us June 5, 1901.

FIG. 68

HADROPTERUS ASPRO (COPE & JORDAN)

BLACK-SIDED DARTER

(PL. P. 285; MAP LXXXVII)

Kirtland, 1839, Journ. Bost. Soc. Nat. Hist., 340 (**Etheostoma blennioides**).

Cope & Jordan, 1877, Proc. Ac. Nat. Sci. Phila., 51 (**Alvordius aspro**—substitute for *Etheostoma blennioides* of Kirtland, the name *blennioides* being preoccupied in *Diplesion*).

J. & G., 501 (**Alvordius**); M. V., 127 (**Etheostoma**); B., I, 59 (**Percina**); J. & E., I. 1032; N., 35 (**Etheostoma blennioides**); J. 39 (**Alvordius maculatus**); F., 65; L., 27.

Length 3 to 4 inches; body elongate, fusiform, somewhat compressed, less cylindrical than in *Percina*; one of the most graceful and elegant in form and color of all the darters; depth 5.4 to 6.8 in length; greatest width of body about ¾ of its greatest depth; depth of caudal peduncle 2.5 to 3.3 in its length. Color of midsummer females and immature males yellowish olive or straw, with dark blotches and mottlings; back with about 8 quadrate spots, between which, on upper portion of sides, are dark, longitudinally disposed marblings; a row of 7 or 8 large dark blotches along middle of side, more or less confluent, and sometimes forming a continuous moniliform band, their color dark bluish olive to bluish black; belly grayish in front, darkened with smoky blue posteriorly; head dark olive, with a darker streak before eye, and one below it, directed slightly backward; cheeks and opercles olive, with sprinkling of iridescent coppery and emerald; pupil dead black; iris brownish except for a faint narrow gold rim next to pupil; dorsal and caudal plainly, pectorals faintly, barred. Adult males in breeding color with entire body more or less smoky or dusky, lacking the contrast between blotches and interspaces seen in females; in all adult males the spinous dorsal crossed near its base by a broad dark band and both the caudal and anal dusky. Head pointed, 3.8 to 4 in length; width of head 1.8 to 2.2 in its length; interorbital space flat, narrow, about ⅔ of eye, 5.5 to 6.7 in head; eye nearly round, 3.4 to 4 in head; nose bluntly pointed, 3.6 to 4.1 in head; mouth rather large, the maxillary extending past front of orbit, the cleft 3 to 3.4 in head; lower jaw very little shorter than upper; gill-membranes as a rule not noticeably connected* at isthmus, distance from tip of snout to angle and to back of orbit about equal. Dorsal fin XIII–XV, 11–14; spinous and soft portions as a rule distinctly separated at base; height of first dorsal 1.9 to 2.3 in head, of second 1.7 to 2 (height of first 82 to 94 per cent. of second); caudal noticeably emarginate; anal II, 8–11; pectorals 1.1 to 1.3 in head; separation of ventrals about equal to their width at base. Scales 8–10, 64–70, 9–11; lateral line nearly straight, usually complete, one or two pores sometimes lacking; cheeks and opercles covered with small scales; nape naked or with embedded scales; breast naked; middle line of belly with enlarged caducous plates; scales of body markedly ctenoid, giving this fish a more or less characteristic feeling of roughness.

This darter, of comparatively plain and somber colors, is more abundant in Illinois than *H. phoxocephalus*, but is similarly distributed, differing, however, in the fact that our collections, 168 in number, have come much more generally from the eastern part of the state than from the western, and that it does not occur so frequently as *phoxocephalus* in the larger rivers. It is about equally abundant in the smaller rivers and in creeks, but rarely occurs in the larger rivers or in bottom-land lakes and ponds. In ecological relations it also closely resembles its companion species of the genus, but seemingly has a less decided preference for a rapid current or a clean bottom.

It ranges somewhat farther northward, its area of distribution extending from Manitoba and the Great Lake region to Arkansas. It is especially common in the Ohio Valley. East-

---

* In occasional collections of this species we meet with specimens with gill-membranes more or less broadly connected (e.g., 28187, Salt creek, Logan Co.). These specimens do not have the small mouth and three caudal spots of *H. scierus*.

ward it is reported from the James and the Roanoke, westward from Kansas to Dakota, and northward from Winnipeg and the Assiniboin.

In our studies of its food we were not able to distinguish any differences between this and the related species, and the two have, indeed, occurred together in our collections one and a half times as frequently as is the average for the family.

HADROPTERUS OUACHITÆ (JORDAN & GILBERT)

Jordan & Gilbert, 1887, Proc. U. S. Nat. Mus., 49 (Etheostoma).
J. & E., I, 1035.

Length 2 inches*; body elongate, little compressed; depth in length 7.14; depth caudal peduncle 3.07 in its length. Color (in spirits) strawish olive; back marked with 7 or 8 rather faint roundish to quadrate blotches; upper portion of sides splashed with W- and X-shaped marks; middle of sides with 8 or 9 large, roundish, and more or less confluent dark blotches; dorsals faintly barred; general aspect much as in young of *H. aspro,* from which this species differs markedly only in its larger scales. Head slender, bluntly pointed, 4.38 in length; width of head 1.78 in its length; interorbital space flat, considerably less than eye, 5.71 in head; eye 3.08; nose 3.48; mouth moderate, narrow, and slightly smaller than in *H. aspro,* the maxillary extending to front of orbit; cleft 3.48 in head; lower jaw included; gill-membranes scarcely joined at isthmus, distances from muzzle to angle and to back of orbit equal. Dorsal fin XI, 10; the two portions separated by a space equal to width of eye; height of first dorsal 2.11 in head, second 1.6 (height of first 75 per cent. of second); caudal truncate; anal II, 8; pectorals .96 in head; separation of ventrals same as width of base. Scales 6, 54, 6; lateral line complete; cheeks naked; posterior portion of opercles with 3 or 4 rows of rather large scales; nape and breast naked†; middle line of belly naked.‡

Probably present in Illinois in the Wabash basin, being represented in our collections by a single specimen, 3.5 cm. in length, taken from the Wabash River at New Harmony, Ind., on April 28, 1900. Originally described from the Saline River, a tributary of the Washita, at Benton, Ark.

Here described from one specimen.

HADROPTERUS EVIDES (JORDAN & COPELAND)

Jordan & Copeland, 1877, Proc. Ac. Nat. Sci. Phila., 51 (Alvordius).
J. & G., 503 (Alvordius); M. V., 128 (Etheostoma); J. & E., I, 1036; N., 36 (Etheostoma); J., 39 (Ericosoma); F., 65; L., 27.

Differing from the other species of *Hadropterus* chiefly in squamation and color pattern, the cheeks and nape naked and opercles with caducous

* Specimens 3 inches long have been obtained by Dr. Jordan (Bull. U. S. Fish Comm., 1888, p. 164).
† "Scaled" (Jordan and Evermann).
‡ "Sometimes with caducous plates" (Jordan and Evermann).

scales. "Coloration extremely brilliant; * * * sides with about 7 broad transverse bars extending from below the lateral line on one side, across the back, and down on the other side; these bars wider than the eye and connected along lateral line by a faint black stripe; * * * spinous dorsal with a dusky spot on its posterior rays, and the fins destitute of the dark bars found in related species" (Jordan and Evermann).

Represented in our collections by a single specimen, taken from Rock River in 1877, still identifiable but in poor condition for description. Outside of Illinois taken in the Wabash and Maumee basins in Indiana, and west and southward to central Iowa, Arkansas, Kentucky, and Tennessee, "in the larger clear streams."

FIG. 69

HADROPTERUS SCIERUS Swain

Swain, 1883, Proc. U. S. Nat. Mus., 252.
M. V., 127 (**Etheostoma**); B., I, 80 (**Etheostoma**); J. & E., I, 1037.

Length of our specimens 2 to 2½ inches*; form and appearance of *H. aspro*; depth 6 to 6.7; greatest width ⅘ of depth; depth caudal peduncle 2.9 to 3.1 in its length. Color essentially as in *H. aspro*; yellowish olive, with back and upper part of sides vaguely blotched with black in longitudinal pattern, and with a median lateral row of 8 or 9 large and more or less confluent dark blotches; a faint central caudal spot with a smaller one above it and a larger one below, the central spot more or less merged with the lower one; under side of caudal peduncle with small dark blotches; suborbital bar wanting entirely in our specimens; dorsals, caudal, and pectorals faintly barred. Differs from *H. aspro* in the presence of 3 caudal spots, the lack of the suborbital bar, and in the blotching of under side of caudal peduncle. Head pointed, 4 to 4.2; width of head 2.1 to 2.4 in its length; interorbital space 4.7 to 4.9; eye 3.5 to 4.1; preopercle not serrulate; nose 3.6 to 3.8, short; mouth smaller than in *H. aspro*, the maxillary scarcely reaching front of orbit, the cleft 3.4 to 3.9 in head; lower jaw included; gill-membranes broadly connected, the distance from muzzle to free posterior margin of membranes about 1¼ times that from muzzle to back of orbit. Dorsal fin X or XII, 13; spinous and soft portions separated by a distance equal to width of eye; height of first dorsal 2 to 2.2 in head, second 1.7 (height of first 79 to 85 per cent. of second); caudal lunate; anal II, 9; pectorals 1.1 in head; separation of ventrals equal to or a little greater than their width at base. Scales 7,

* "5 inches" (Jordan and Evermann).

64–67, 11 [15 or 16]; 1 to 13 pores lacking; cheeks and opercles fully scaled; nape scaled; breast naked and belly closely scaled.

These fishes, though bearing a great general resemblance to *H. aspro*, are easily distinguished from it by their much smaller mouth and united gill-membranes*, and by the combination of minor color-marks above mentioned.

Our specimens have the preopercle smooth†, as in *H. aspro*.

Described from 2 specimens taken by T. L. Hankinson from the Embarras River at Charleston, Ill., in 1904. This species was described in 1883 from Bean Blossom creek, Monroe county, Ind., and has since been taken in various localities from northern Indiana to Arkansas.

Genus **COTTOGASTER** Putnam

Body rather robust, not much compressed; mouth moderate or small; forms intermediate between *Hadropterus* and *Boleosoma*, having the premaxillaries typically protractile, or sometimes (in *C. shumardi*) connected with the skin of the forehead by a narrow frenum; teeth on vomer; middle line of belly naked, or with caducous scales; vertebræ (*C. copelandi*) 38 (18+20); pyloric cæca 3; coloration not brilliant. Darters of moderate size, not over 3 inches in length; species few; one known from Illinois.

Fig. 70

COTTOGASTER SHUMARDI (Girard)

(Map LXXXVIII)

Girard, 1859, Proc. Ac. Nat. Sci. Phila., 100 (**Hadropterus**).
J. & G., 498 (**Imostoma**); M. V., 126 (**Etheostoma**); B., I, 92 (**Boleosoma**); J. & E., I, 1046; J., 89 (**Imostoma**); F., 66; L., 27.

Length 2½ to 3 inches; body stout, little compressed except posteriorly; depth 5.2 to 6.9 in length; greatest width of body usually more than ⅚ of

* See note on *H. aspro*.

† "Preopercle finely serrated" (Jordan and Evermann, key to *Hadropterus*); "prepopercle serrulate, at least in young specimens" (Jordan, Bull. U. S. Fish Comm., 1888, p. 165).

its greatest depth; caudal peduncle short and stout, its depth 2.1 to 2.6 in its length. Color (in preservative) straw to brownish olive, densely blotched and marbled with darker; sides with 8 to 15 dark blotches, which are some times obscure, and often extended below lateral line as bar-like bands on anterior portion of body; a faint dark band through nostril to end of snout and a distinct bar below eye; second dorsal and caudal faintly barred in the rays. In breeding males the barring of second dorsal replaced by a more or less uniform dusting of both rays and membranes of lower half of fin; first dorsal with a small black spot in front between first two rays and a second and larger one at the back of the fin, usually between 8th and 10th rays. Head 3.7 to 4 in length, little tapered, muzzle blunt; width of head 1.7 to 2 in its length; interorbital space flat, 5.5 to 6.4 in head, about ⅔ of eye; eye 3.2 to 3.5; nose 2.9 to 3.7; mouth moderate, maxillary to front of orbit, cleft 2.9 to 3.2 in head; premaxillary in Illinois specimens as a rule connected by a narrow frenum with the skin of the forehead; lower jaw slightly shorter than upper; gill-membranes free from isthmus and scarcely connected, distances from muzzle to angle and to back of orbit about equal. Dorsal fin IX, or XI, 13–15; spinous and soft portions as a rule very little separated at base; height of first dorsal 1.7 to 2.2 in head, second 1.6 to 1.7 (height of first 76 to 92 per cent. of second); caudal noticeably emarginate; anal II, 10–12, (usually 10 or 11); pectorals .9 to 1.3 in head; separation of ventrals as a rule nearly equal to their width at base. Scales 6 or 7, 50–56, 7–9; lateral line complete; cheeks, opercles, and nape scaled; breast naked; belly usually naked, sometimes scaled for a short distance in front of vent.

A species of medium size and relatively obscure coloration, notable especially for its extraordinary local distribution, occurring, as it does, almost wholly along the course of our larger streams. It is not common in this state, having been taken but sixteen times from nine localities, six on the Illinois, one on the Wabash, and two on the Kaskaskia. Twice it was taken from the deep water of the river channel at Havana.

It occurs also in the Great Lakes, and has been reported from Erie and Michigan, and elsewhere from the Ohio, the Red, and the Arkansas rivers of the lower Mississippi Valley. Osburn says that it is found in Ohio on sandy bottoms in rivers, but not in small streams.

Females with eggs were taken from the Illinois River on the 18th and the 20th of March, 1899.

GENUS **DIPLESION** RAFINESQUE

Body rather elongate, little compressed; mouth small, inferior, horizontal; premaxillaries protractile downward, the groove not visible from above or in front as in other darters, but only from underneath; known also by the non-protractile maxillary, which is joined for most of its length to the skin of the front of the preorbital; no teeth on vomer or palatines; no enlarged ventral plates; vertebræ 42 (19+23); pyloric cæca 4; coloration largely green. Size moderate, 3 to 5 inches; a single species.

DIPLESION BLENNIOIDES (Rafinesque)

GREEN-SIDED DARTER

(Map LXXXIX)

Rafinesque, 1819, Journ. de Physique, 419 (**Etheostoma** [**Diplesion**]).
J. & G., 497; M. V., 125 (**Etheostoma**); B., I, 100; J. & E., I, 1053; N., 35 (**Etheostoma**); J., 40; F., 66; L., 27.

Length 3 inches; body elongate, neither cylindrical nor (technically) compressed, but narrowed dorsally in front so that a cross-section of the body is roughly triangular; back somewhat elevated in adults and profile very convex; ventral outline straight or slightly concave; depth 5.3 to 6.3; greatest width of body about 4/5 its greatest depth; depth caudal peduncle 2.6 to 3.2 in its length. Color of upper parts light olivaceous, paler beneath, the belly a light creamy white; sides marked with 5 to 8 vertical bars of rich dark grassy green color, these continuous with dark saddle-like back blotches;* below lateral line a row of Y-shaped blotches, sometimes connected so as to form an irregular wavy or zigzag band of rich green; 20 to 50 small rufous-orange spots scattered along sides in irregular zigzag lines, each spot occupying the center of a scale; head dark olive-green, mottled with darker green, a dark green band passing from the eye downward and forward around the upper jaw and a similar one downward to a short distance behind the angle of the mouth; suborbital bar of one side usually extending beneath chin to meet the bar of the other side; cheeks yellowish green, opercles dark green; head pale beneath; pupil black, iris with some gold; spinous dorsal with a band of rufous-orange spots at its base occupying about lower third of fin, which is tipped at outer margin with a narrow edge of pale blue; second dorsal with row of orange spots fainter, and without outer blue edging; other fins paler, greenish; females with orange spots at base of spinous dorsal less brilliant, and with these spots missing on second dorsal. Head short, irregularly pyramidal, flat and broad below, 4 to 4.6 in length; width of head 1.5 to 1.9; interorbital space narrow, flat, 5.2 to 6.8 in head; eye roundish, high, and somewhat protruding, 3.1 to 3.6; nose 3.1 to 3.7, the muzzle much decurved and projecting beyond the inferior mouth; mouth small, inferior, horizontal, maxillary reaching to front of orbit, cleft 3.1 to 3.6 in head; lower jaw much shorter than upper; lips rather more prominent than is usual in darters; gill-membranes connected broadly across isthmus, the distance from tip of snout to free posterior margin of membranes being 1 1/5 to 1 1/4 greater than to back of orbit. Dorsal fin XIII–XIV, 13–14; spinous and soft portions joined or but slightly separated; height of first dorsal 1.6 to 2.3 in head, second 1.4 to 1.6 (height of first 68 to 90 per cent. of second); caudal slightly emarginate; anal II, 8 or 9; pectorals .8 to .9 in head; ventral spines and first 4 or 5 rays rather fleshy and often somewhat

* These blotches are the only part of the bars usually visible in preserved specimens, showing in life as dark pigmented areas under the green of the bars.

GREEN-SIDED DARTER, *Diplesion blennioides* (Rafinesque)

FAN-TAILED DARTER, *Etheostoma flabellare* Rafinesque

knobbed at extremities; separation of ventrals less than their width at base. Scales 6–8, 57–61, 7–9 [10 or 11]; lateral line nearly straight and usually complete, 1 or 2 pores occasionally lacking; cheeks naked or with a few more or less embedded scales; opercles and nape scaled; breast naked; belly with ordinary scales.

This beautiful and peculiar species, distinguishable at a glance by its remarkable head, large prominent eyes, and small inferior mouth, "giving it a decidedly frog-like profile," and by the green or olive zigzag markings on the back, is, in its breeding dress, one of the most beautiful of all fresh-water fishes. "The dorsal fins become bright grass-green, with a scarlet band at the base; the broad anal has a tinge of the deepest emerald; while every spot and line upon the side has turned from an undefined olive to a deep, rich green, scarcely found elsewhere in the animal world except on the backs of frogs. The same tint flashes out on the branching rays of the caudal fin, and may be faintly seen struggling through the white on the belly. The blotches nearest the middle of the back become jet-black, and thickly sprinkled everywhere are little shiny spots of a clear bronze-orange."*

This darter has an almost inexplicable distribution in Illinois, if we may judge by our collections of it. Taken by us in thirty-six localities on the smaller streams of the Wabash system in this state, it has not once occurred elsewhere† in all our sixteen hundred collections, although it has been once taken from the Des Plaines at Joliet, by J. H. Ferris, as reported by Fowler in 1906.‡ Its general distribution is not such as to suggest so limited a range in Illinois, occurring, as it does, from Lakes Ontario and Erie to Pennsylvania, North Carolina, and the lower Alabama basin, and thence to South Dakota, Kansas, and Missouri, and the Red River in Arkansas. It is generally distributed throughout Indiana, as shown by the details of the list of Professor Hay, who reports it as abundant in all suitable streams. This is one of the groups of species occurring, in Illinois, only or mainly in the Wabash drainage, specially discussed in our introductory chapter on geographical distribution. It is found in swift water, oftenest on rocky ripples where there is a

* Jordan and Copeland, American Naturalist, Vol. X., p. 339.

† The indication of its presence at Chicago given on Map VII. of an article on the local distribution of darters (Bull. Ill. State Lab. Nat. Hist., Vol. VII., Art. VIII.) published by the senior author in April, 1907, is due to a clerical error in transferring a record based on the preservation of specimens from collections on exhibition at the World's Fair in 1893.

‡ "Some New and Little Known Percoid Fishes." Proc. Acad. Nat. Sci. Phila., Dec., 1906, p. 522.

vigorous growth of algæ; and it is worthy of note that the peculiar color of this fish seems to assimilate it to its surroundings.

Specimens taken from the Vermilion in Vermilion county were kept by us for several weeks alive in a soft-water aquarium aerated by compressed air. They were very shy and easily frightened, and fell into a panic when disturbed by a sudden movement in the room or by a jar of the aquarium, their actions when frightened—too quick for the eye to follow—stirring up the sand and gravel on the bottom and so clouding the water as to hide their retreat. They seemed very much attached to a mass of algæ placed in the aquarium with them, lying in it by the hour, and they were frequently seen perched on a pebble or stone by means of their ventrals, with the body inclined at an angle of 30 to 45 degrees. When on the bottom, the body was usually curved in a snake-like position, as if prepared for a quick and vigorous stroke.

Genus **BOLEOSOMA** De Kay

TESSELLATED DARTERS

Body moderately elongate, subcylindrical; but slightly translucent; mouth small, horizontal, subinferior; premaxillaries protractile; teeth on vomer; vertebræ (*B. nigrum*) 37 (15 + 22), (*B. camurum*) 38 (17 + 21); pyloric cæca 3 to 6; belly with ordinary scales; plainly colored, usually olivaceous with black or brown specks and with no red or blue; spring males dusky to jet-black. Size small, 2½ inches; species about 5.

Key to Species of **BOLEOSOMA** found in Illinois

a. Lateral line complete or nearly so; pyloric cæca 6; cheeks and breast typically naked, sometimes more or less scaly........................**nigrum.**

aa. Lateral line absent on posterior half of body; pyloric cæca 3; cheeks and opercles, and usually breast, closely scaled......................**camurum.**

BOLEOSOMA NIGRUM (Rafinesque)

JOHNNY DARTER

(Pl., p. 296; Map XC)

Rafinesque, 1820, Ichth. Oh., 37 (**Etheostoma**).
G., I, 77 (**Boleosma maculatum**); J. & G., 492; B., I, 93; J. & E., I, 1056; N., 35 (**brevipinne** and **olmstedi**); J., 40 (**maculatum** and **olmstedi**); F., 66; L., 27.

Length 2½ inches; body typically slender, subfusiform, little compressed; depth 4.7 to 6.9 in length; greatest width of body about ¾ its greatest depth; depth caudal peduncle 2.5 to 3.3 in its length. Color of back and sides a very pale strawish olive, over which are distributed small brownish dots and splashes and more or less vaguely W-, X-, and V-shaped markings, part of the latter forming an indefinite lateral row,—rather aptly called "sandpaper" darter by one of our collectors; back finely tessellated with dark brown in and between 6 or 7 large, but sometimes indistinct, quadrate blotches; sometimes an obscure caudal spot; belly in life translucent pale greenish to dull golden; head olivaceous above, with dark brown specks; a dark streak in front of eye, a rather broad bar-like blotch behind it; lower part of cheek very pale greenish; opercle olivaceous, with dark spots above; pupil dull black; iris with a narrow rim of golden next to pupil; dorsals, caudal, and pectorals barred, the latter only near base; ventrals and anal plain, the anal pale whitish, ventrals of a creamy to strawish hue. Spring males with head, and with first dorsal, anal, and ventral fins a very dark bluish black, and rest of body and fins more or less clouded with same color, the sides being marked with 8 or 9 bars of darker color, the bars indistinct in some specimens and in instances wholly submerged in an almost uniform black coloration; in the less dusky spring males, in which barring is plainest, the spinous dorsal may have dark color mostly confined to the membrane between the first and second spines and to an irregular narrow edging on posterior half of fin. No difference between coloration of late-summer males and females. Head short, 3.5 to 4.2 in length, with decurved snout, protruding eyes, and flat and sloping forehead; width of head 1.6 to 2.1 in its length; interorbital space narrow and concave, 6.5 to 8.5 in head; eye round, protruding above level of cranium, 3.2 to 3.8 in head; nose bluntly pointed, 3.3 to 4.2; mouth rather small, inferior, maxillary reaching past front of orbit; cleft 2.9 to 3.7 in head; lower jaw included; gill-membranes narrowly connected, distance from muzzle to angle and to back of orbit equal. Dorsal fin VIII–X (usually IX), 10–12, the spinous and soft portions often united at base; height of first dorsal 1.7 to 2.1 in head, second 1.4 to 1.8 (height of first 70 to 92 per cent. of second); caudal truncate; anal I, 6 to 9 (usually 7 or 8); pectorals .9 to 1.2 in head; separation of ventrals usually a little less than their width at base. Scales 5–7 (usually 6), 45–52, 6–8 [8–11]; lateral line as a rule complete, but 2 or 3 pores occasionally lacking; cheeks typically* naked or with only a trace of scales on upper portion; opercles covered with small scales; nape either scaled or naked; breast in typical* specimens naked, fully or more or less scaled in many specimens from the Rock, upper Illinois, and upper Wabash basins, in which cheeks also are scaly; belly with ordinary scales.

The Johnny darter, much the most abundant of its subfamily in this state, and taken by us in 243 collections, is not so much a thoroughly typical as a fairly average darter—distinguished, that is, less by a precise adaptation to the special darter environment than by a fairly equal distribution throughout the entire class of situations frequented by the various species of the group.

It occurs virtually everywhere in the state except in the larger streams and in lowland lakes and sloughs, where it is strikingly rare. It has occurred but twice, for example, in over five hundred collections made by us from the Illinois River at

* See table on page 297.

Havana and Meredosia. It is rather disproportionately infrequent in the waters of the lower Illinoisan glaciation, although not by any means excluded from that area, as a glance at the distribution map for the species will show. We have found it most abundant in the small streams of the Wabash and Kaskaskia systems, in which it has occurred in 56 and 66 per cent., respectively, of all collections made.

It is typically a darter of the creeks and small brooks, and 44 per cent. of all our creek collections have contained it. It has come from the smaller rivers with about half this frequency, and from glacial lakes with about a fourth. The *average* character here ascribed to it is illustrated by the fact that it has been taken by us with darters of other species in almost exactly the average frequency of the associate occurrence of one species with another throughout the whole subfamily.

It is usually found among gravel and weeds, although not infrequently on a mud bottom, from which situation some 11 per cent. of our collections came. Its preference for swift waters is not so marked as in the case of the more typical darters, nearly a third of our collections having come from standing or quiet water.

Outside Illinois the species is found from New England and Lake Champlain through the Great Lake region to the Assiniboin River, down the Atlantic slope as far as the Catawba River, and westward throughout the Ohio and Missouri basins to Colorado and Montana.

Its habits are those of its subfamily. It often lies with its head up and its body bent to one side or supported partly by a stone. It can turn its head without moving its body; can roll the eye about in the socket; may rest suspended, as we have seen it do, on the under side of a floating board; and sometimes buries itself, with a whirl, in the soft sand, so that only its eyes are visible.

The food of a dozen specimens was so uniform that they may fairly be taken as representative. Two thirds of it consisted solely of *Chironomus* larvæ, 7 per cent. of other minute larvæ of gnats, and the remaining 12 per cent. of larvæ of small May-flies.

The species spawns in spring, from the last of April to the first of June. Females were depositing their eggs in our aquarium at Meredosia, April 28 and 29, 1899. In the act of spawning the male rode on the back of the female, with ventrals astride,

JOHNNY DARTER, *Boleosoma nigrum* (Rafinesque)

and pectorals and ventrals in active vibration as the pair moved about on the bottom. The eggs are emitted at intervals, and from time to time the female raises a cloud of sand by a vigorous beating with the tail, perhaps for the purpose of covering them. Males in breeding dress have the first dorsal spines more or less swollen, and club-shaped at the tip.

In studying our collections, wide variation was noticed with respect to the scaly covering of the breast and cheeks, ranging from complete nakedness to complete scaliness of both, and also a considerable variation in robustness of build. While, generally speaking, specimens become more scaly northward and more slender southward, it was not possible to make out, even approximately, any line or area of division, either general or local, between the two forms, or to draw any definite dividing line among the variants themselves. This confusion of conditions may be illustrated by the following analysis of a single collection of forty-six specimens (accessions No. 28180) obtained from the north fork of the Vermilion River in Vermilion county June 6, 1901.

VARIATIONS OF BOLEOSOMA NIGRUM (46 SPECIMENS)

Scales on cheeks.	Scales on breast	Males	Females
None	None	2	5
None	Trace	2	2
None	Two thirds covered	0	1
Trace	None	0	1
One third covered	None	1	0
Half covered	None	1	0
Trace	Trace	1	2
Trace	Half covered	2	1
Trace	Fully covered	5	1
One fifth covered	Fully covered	3	1
One third covered	Fully covered	4	1
Half covered	Fully covered	4	2
Fully covered	Fully covered	4	0
Total		29	17

It was also impossible to distinguish any correlation, even approximately constant, between robustness of form and scaliness of cheeks and breasts, both stout and slender forms having these parts sometimes naked and sometimes more or less covered with scales. The larger percentage of specimens with scaly breasts and cheeks came from the Rock River basin, from the northwest district, and from the Lake Michigan drainage; but in all these districts scaly and naked specimens were intermingled, the latter preponderating. In collections from the Kaskaskia, the Saline, the Cache, and the lower Wabash Valley, on the other hand, both cheeks and breasts were almost invariably naked, while in the upper Wabash streams and in the Illinois basin the two forms were indiscriminately commingled. The larger number of the stouter specimens came from the Rock River system and the northwest area, while those from the Kaskaskia, the Cache, and the Saline were of more slender proportions, with the depth usually nearer six times than five times the length. Similar study of specimens from a wider range would probably show that Illinois is in a region of transition between two varieties of this species—the typical *nigrum*, with slender body and naked breast and cheeks, and some scaly-cheeked variety, probably near *olmstedi*, or perhaps identical with it.

Fig. 71

BOLEOSOMA CAMURUM Forbes

(Map XCI)

Forbes, 1878, Bull. Ill. State Lab. Nat. Hist., II. 2, 40.
J. & G., 494 (**Vaillantia camura** and **V. chlorosoma**); M. V., 130 (**Etheostoma**); B., I, 96; J. & E., I, 1060; F., 66; L., 27.

A small species, not reaching more than 1¾ inches in length in our collections; superficially resembling *B. nigrum*, but differing distinctly from it in its less angular head and less pointed snout, less protruding eyes, and widely separated dorsals. The small size, the finely and fully scaled cheeks and breast, and the peculiar ring-like light areas on the back between the quadrate dark blotches will usually serve for its recognization. Length 1¾ inches; body slender, considerably compressed, greatest width of body about ⅔ its greatest depth; depth 6.5 to 7.2 in length; caudal peduncle slender, its depth 3.1 to 3.9 in its length. Color much as in *B. nigrum*, but paler, the side markings less distinctly W-, X-, and V-shaped; color pattern of upper portion of body and back more open, being less densely and finely tessellated than in the preceding species; back with 5 or 6 saddle-like blotches, the corners of which are more or less distinctly connected by dark markings, giving the fish the appearance of being marked dorsally with a chain of rings, which are dark or light according as the eyes are focused on the saddle-like dark blotches and their connecting bands, or on the circular light areas intervening; an evident dark spot on opercles; a conspicuous zigzag streak on nose in front of eye and a very faint suborbital bar; dorsal and caudal faintly barred. Head 3.9 to 4.3, slightly shorter and considerably narrower than in *B. nigrum*, its greatest width 2 to 2.5 in its length; interorbital space flat, 5.2 to 6.6 in head; eye round, 3.3 to 4 in head, not protruding above the cranium; nose bluntly rounded, less decurved than in *B. nigrum*, 3.8 to 4.5; mouth rather small, maxillary to front of pupil, cleft 3.1 to 3.8 in head; lower jaw included; gill-membranes not broadly connected, distances to angle and to back of orbit equal. Dorsal fin VIII–X, 10 or 11 (usually IX–10); spinous and soft portions well apart, separated by a distance about equal to diameter of eye; height of first dorsal 1.7 to 1.9 in head, second 1.4 to 1.7 (height of first 70 to 90 per cent. of second); caudal slightly emarginate; anal I, 7 or 8; pectorals 1 to 1.3; separation of ventrals as a rule considerably less than their width at base. Scales 6, 52–60, 6 or 7 [7–10]; lateral line ordinarily developed on only about half the scales; cheeks, opercles, and breast fully scaled; nape with a median naked strip; belly covered with ordinary scales.

This rather insignificant but interesting little darter is one of the more distinctly southern species of the group. Although it has been taken by us in Illinois as far north as South Chicago on the east and Green River, in Henry county, on the west, our southern Illinois collections preponderate greatly in number over those of central or northern Illinois, the relative frequencies being 2.44, .46, and .10 for these three sections of the state. Like its nearest relative, the Johnny darter, it is essentially a species of creeks and the smaller rivers, it we may judge by our 107 collections; but it is found more frequently than that species in standing water, especially in the lakes and ponds of the river bottoms, and much more frequently also in rivers of the largest class—thirty times, for example, from Havana and Meredosia, where *Boleosoma nigrum* was obtained but twice. It is most abundant in the Big Muddy and the Saline River basins, occurring in the first in seven out of nine collections, and in the second in eleven out of eighteen. It is especially peculiar in the fact that more than two thirds of our material was taken from quiet waters, and about three fifths of it from waters with a muddy bottom. In geographical and local distribution and in ecological preference, this little species thus separates itself notably from its nearest ally.

Described originally from Illinois specimens, it has since been found from Indiana and Iowa to Alabama, and southwest to the Angelina River in Texas.

Females distended with eggs have been taken by us late in May.

GENUS **CRYSTALLARIA** JORDAN & GILBERT

Body slender, elongate, subcylindrical, pellucid in life; mouth small, horizontal; premaxillaries not protractile; teeth on vomer; vertebræ (*C. asprella*) 47 (23 + 24)*; pyloric cæca 3*; belly naked or with a few ordinary scales. In its protractile premaxillaries, as well as in habit, resembling *Hadropterus*, but the body hyaline in life as in *Ammocrypta*. One species known, a darter of rather large size, first obtained by the senior author in Hancock county, Illinois.

GENUS **CRYSTALLARIA ASPRELLA** (JORDAN)

Jordan, 1878, Bull. Ill. State Lab. Nat. Hist., I. 2, 38 (**Pleurolepis**).
J. & G., 490 (**Ammocrypta**); M. V., 123 (**Etheostoma**); B., I, 104; J. & E., I, 1061; F., 66 (**Ammocrypta**); L., 28.

A slender species, with extremely small scales, and pellucid in life. Easily known by these marks and by the peculiar broad saddle-like bands across the back, which are continued obliquely downward and forward to the lateral line in this species. Length 3 to 4 inches; body very long and slender, not at all compressed, being nearly uniformly cylindrical from nape to front of second dorsal; depth 7.8 to 9 in length; caudal peduncle very slender, its depth 3.7 to 4.7 in its length. "Color hyaline-olive with 3 or 4 dark, broad cross-bands meeting over the back, the width of the first 3 about equal to depth of body, the fourth narrower, and all extending somewhat obliquely downward and forward to the lateral line; a dark lateral band along side, made up of about 10 more or less confluent dark quadrate blotches, darkest where it crosses through the cross-bands" (Jordan and Evermann). "In life the oblique bands are of a golden, iridescent color; cheeks below eye bright iridescent silvery; pupil black with brassy rim; iris chiefly dusky; spots on sides dusky with traces of golden between" (H. Garman). Head 3.7 to 4.5, its width 2 to 2.3 in its length; interorbital space very narrow, concave, 8.3 to 9.7; eye somewhat elliptical, 3.3 to 3.9 in head; nose decurved and broadly rounded anteriorly, somewhat shovel-shaped, 2.6 to 3.2 in head; mouth rather broad, subterminal, the maxillary not reaching to front of orbit; cleft 3.5 to 3.9 in head; lower jaw included; gill-membranes only slightly connected, distance from muzzle to angle usually less than to back of orbit. Dorsal fin XII or XIII, 13–15; soft and spinous portions separated by a distance almost equal to diameter of eye; spinous dorsal high in front; height of first dorsal 1.8 to 2.5 in head, second 1.7 to 2.2 (height of first 82 to 105 per cent. of second); caudal lunate; anal I, 13 or 14; pectorals 1.1 to 1.3 in head; sepa-

*In a single specimen (Accessions No. 27670, Ill. State Lab. Nat. Hist.).

Spring Cave-fish *Chologaster papilliferus* Forbes

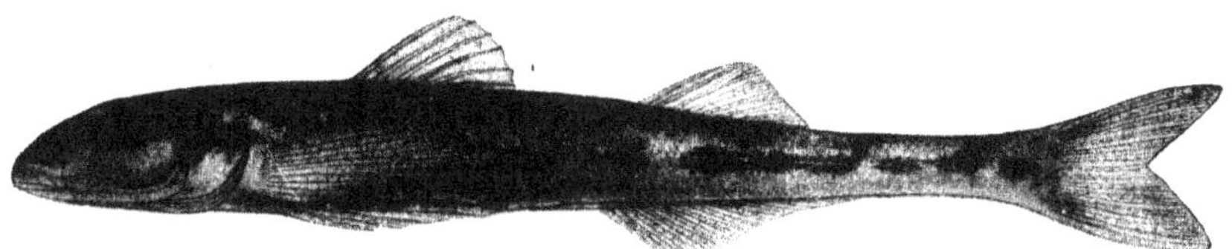

Crystallaria asprella (Jordan)

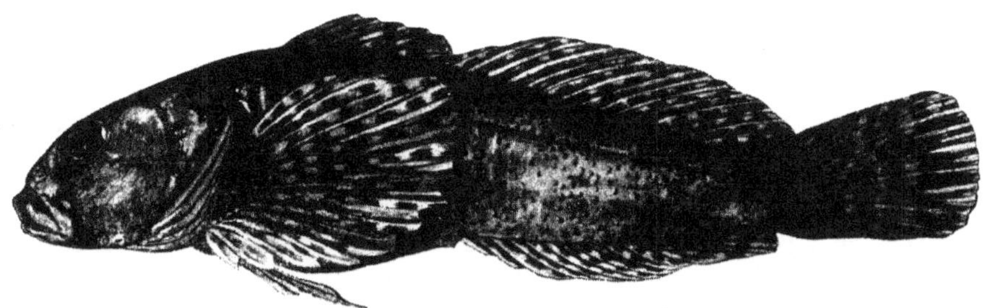

Common Sculpin *Cottus ictalops* (Rafinesque)

ration of ventrals slightly less than their width at base. Scales 8–10, 89–97, 9–11 [12–16]; lateral line nearly straight, 2 to 12 pores usually lacking; cheeks naked or with a trace of scales, or about half covered with very thin scattered scales, a few of which may be pectinate; opercles with a few pectinate scales on upper portion; nape scaled; throat, breast, and belly naked excepting (sometimes) a portion or all of the space in front of the ventral fins directly under pelvic girdle.

A medium-sized and singularly interesting species, first discovered in this state in a rocky creek of the Mississippi bluffs in Hancock county, and since taken from the Rock River at Cleveland, Erie, and Milan, from the Little Wabash at Effingham, and from the Mississippi at East Dubuque, in the northwestern part of the state. Elsewhere it comes from Grosse Isle, Mich., from the Detroit River, from the Ohio River at Rising Sun, from the Wabash as far northward as Terre Haute, and from a few points in Tennessee, Kentucky, Alabama, and Arkansas. It is found chiefly in the swift currents of the larger, clearer streams, but apparently is a rare fish everywhere, and but little known.

AMMOCRYPTA Jordan

SAND DARTERS

Body slender and elongate, subcylindrical; pellucid in life; mouth rather wide, horizontal; premaxillaries protractile; teeth on vomer; vertebræ (*pellucida*) 44 (23 + 21), (*vivax*) 41 (21 + 20); pyloric cæca 4. Extremely slender fishes, with the habit of burying themselves in the sand; size moderate, about 3 inches in length; 2 species known.

AMMOCRYPTA PELLUCIDA (Baird)

SAND DARTER

(Map XCII)

Agassiz, 1863, Bull. Mus. Comp. Zool., I, 5 (**Pleurolepis**).
J. & G., 489; M. V., 122 (**Etheostoma**); B., I, 102; J. & E., I, 1062; N., 35 (**Pleurolepis**); J., 38 (**Pleurolepis**); F., 66; L., 28.

Slender, cylindrical, pellucid fishes, with the premaxillaries protractile and the appearance of *Boleosoma* rather than *Crystallaria* and *Hadropterus*, and probably more nearly related to that genus than to the others. Length 2¼ inches; body subcylindrical, scarcely deeper than wide, the sides slightly flattened along their median line; depth 8.2 to 10.1 in length; caudal peduncle slender, its depth 3.4 to 4.2 in its length. Color "translucent; scales with fine black dots; a series (14 or 15) of small, squarish olive or bluish blotches along the back and another along each side; lateral spots connected by a gill-band" (Jordan and Evermann). Head 4.1 to 4.4 in length, its width 2 to 2.5 in its length, interorbital space narrow, concave, 7.1 to 8.4 in head; eye 3.6 to 4.3; nose decurved, pointed, 3.1 to 3.8 in head; mouth moderate, maxillary extending to front of orbit; cleft 3.1 to 4.4 in head; lower jaw slightly shorter than upper; gill-membranes somewhat connected, but forming a sharp angle, the distance from muzzle to angle about 1¼ times that to back of orbit. Dorsal fin IX–XI, 9–11 (usually IX or X); spinous and soft portions widely separated, the space greater than width of eye; height of first dorsal low, 2.2 to 3.5 (usually less than 3) in head, second 1.8 to 2.1 (height of first 56 to 80 per cent. of second); caudal fin lunate; anal I, 8 or 9 (occasionally 7); pectorals 1 to 1.3 in head; separation of ventrals less than the width at base. Scales 6 or 7, 67–78, 8 or 9+, the upper and lower rows (nearest back and belly) sometimes lacking, body being naked except for a strip along the side of varying width; lateral line usually complete; cheeks and opercles scaled; nape scaled or naked; throat, breast, and belly entirely naked; all scales more or less embedded and with edges little ctenoid.

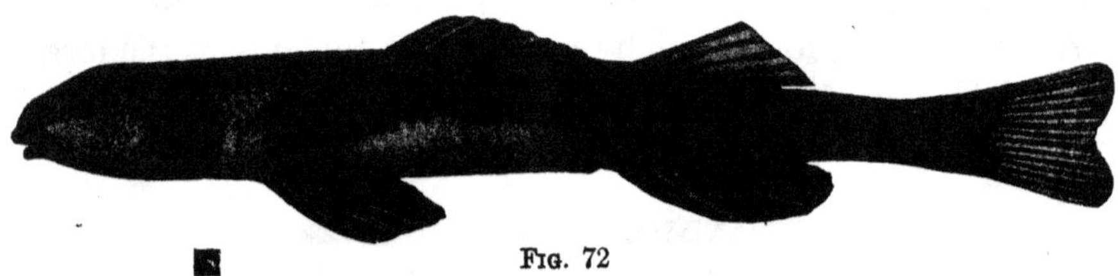

FIG. 72

This extremely interesting fish, peculiar in its very slender form, its semitransparent body, and its habit of living much of the time in the sand, with only its eyes showing at the surface, make it one of the most remarkable cases of special adaptation in this highly adaptive little group. Situations favorable to its habits are so rare in Illinois that its comparative scarcity here was to be expected. It has been found by us twenty-nine times, in localities well distributed—twelve of them from the Wabash Valley, one from the lower Kaskaskia, six on streams of the lower Illinois, one on a creek of the Mississippi bluffs, and three on Rock River or its tributaries. It is reported by Jordan and Evermann from Lake Erie to Minnesota, Kentucky, and Texas, occurring usually in clear sandy streams.

An excellent account of its habits and peculiarities is given in Bulletin 47 of the United States National Museum by Jordan and Copeland. The fish has a very sharp nose with an exceedingly slim and round body, as transparent as jelly but hard and firm to the touch. Its belly and much of its back are quite bare of scales, and those along its sides are small and inconspicuous.

In an aquarium with sand on the bottom, it was seen to bury itself in a few seconds by first stirring up the sand with rapid beats of its tail, as it stood literally upon its head, then lying still as the sand settled again, and quietly putting out its nose and eyes, leaving only these and the front of its head to be seen. Notwithstanding its peculiar habits and its nice adaptation to a special environment, it is among our group of most typical darters, its most frequent associate in our collections being *Hadropterus phoxocephalus*, and next to this, *Hadropterus aspro*.

Its food seems remarkably uniform, consisting, like that of so many other darters, of dipterous larvæ, mainly *Chironomus*, and larvæ of May-flies, the former largely preponderating in the specimens we have studied.

Genus **ETHEOSTOMA** Rafinesque

Body robust or rather elongate, considerably compressed, or greatly so; mouth varying in size, terminal or subinferior; premaxillaries not protractile; teeth usually present on vomer and palatines; vertebræ 33 to 39, usually 36 (15+21); pyloric cæca 3 or 4; belly with ordinary scales. Species numerous, about 30; size small; coloration various, often brilliant.

A large group, difficult to characterize, including a wide range of forms, which, however, agree in having the premaxillaries non-protractile, and differ from all the preceding genera (except possibly *Diplesion*) in having the cranium more elevated behind the eyes—∩-shaped.* These fishes are, as a rule, more or less compressed, and deeper bodied than such forms as *Cottogaster*, *Boleosoma*, and *Hadropterus*. In this group are found our most brilliantly colored darters, bright red and blue in gaudy display on both body and fins prevailing in the dress of many species.

Key to the Species of **ETHEOSTOMA** found in Illinois

a. Lateral line usually complete, occasionally 2 to 6 pores lacking.

b. Gill-membranes joining broadly across the isthmus, distance from muzzle to their angle 40 to 50 per cent. greater than from muzzle to back of orbit .... **zonale.**

bb. Gill-membranes scarcely connected, distances to angle and to back of orbit not far from equal .... **camurum.**

aa. Lateral line always more or less incomplete, the number of pores lacking usually 10 to 30, rarely as low as 5.

* The forms (*flabellare*, *obeyense*, and *squamiceps*) with low dorsal fin and black humeral spot (see key) seem to agree in having the parietals less arched than is usual in *Etheostoma*, and shaped in cross-section more nearly as in *Boleosoma*.

c. Spinous dorsal fin not exceptionally low, its height as a rule 75 to 90 per cent. of height of soft dorsal; no enlarged dark humeral scale.

d. Cheeks and opercles scaled.

e. Rays of second dorsal 9 or 10; scales 55–60; rust-red spots on sides, no bars. .... **iowæ.**

ee. Rays of second dorsal 12 to 13; scales 49–57; brown bars on sides......**jessiæ.**

dd. Cheeks naked; opercles scaled; spring males with alternating red and blue bars ....**cœruleum.**

cc. Spinous dorsal fin as a rule less than 60 per cent. height of soft dorsal; an enlarged dark humeral scale more or less conspicuous.

f. Gill-membranes little connected, distances from muzzle to angle and to back of orbit not far from equal.

g. Cheeks, opercles, nape, and breast naked; chin, cheeks, and opercles sprinkled with fine dark dots; a large black humeral scale, its depth ⅔ diameter of eye ....**obeyense.**

gg. Cheeks, opercles, nape, and breast covered with embedded scales, chin and cheeks with pronounced dark mottlings and vermiculations; humeral scale rather small and not very black.........................**squamiceps.**

ff. Gill-membranes broadly connected, distance from muzzle to their free margin 1⅔ to 1½ times that to back of orbit; dorsal spines each ending in a fleshy knob in the male...**flabellare.**

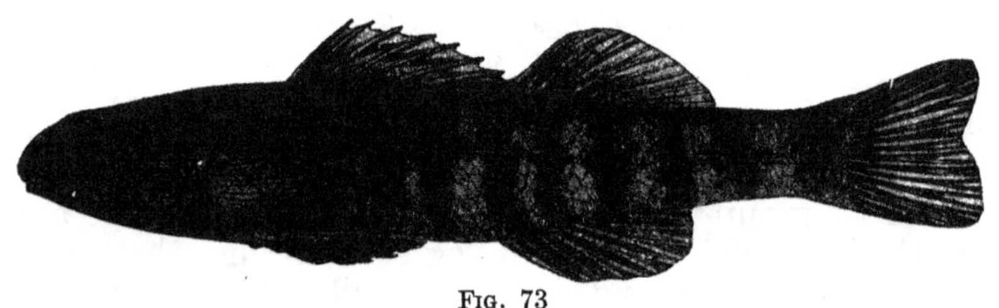

Fig. 73

ETHEOSTOMA ZONALE (Cope)

BANDED DARTER

(Map XCIII)

Cope, 1868, Journ. Ac. Nat. Sci. Phila., 212 (**Pœcilichthys**).
J. & G., 510 (**Nanostoma**); M. V., 130; B., I, 83; J. & E., I, 1075; J., 41 (**Nanostoma**); F., 65; L., 28.

Banded darters which have a superficial resemblance to females of *E. cœruleum*, and may even be confused (especially in preservative) with *E. jessiæ*. From the first this species is easily distinguished by its closely and finely scaled cheeks, and from both, as well as also from all other Illinois species of the genus *Etheostoma* except *flabellare*, it may be readily separated by the broad union of the gill-membranes. Length ordinarily a little less than 2 inches; body moderately elongate, considerably compressed, the depth 4.7 to 6 in length; greatest width of body about ⅔ its greatest depth; depth of caudal peduncle 2.4 to 3.1 in its length. Colors in life "bright olivaceous above, golden below; 6 dark brown quadrate dorsal spots, which connect by alternating spots with a broad, brown lateral band, from which

8 narrower dark bluish bands more or less completely encircle the belly; paired, anal, and caudal fins golden, brown-spotted; middle half of the first dorsal crimson; a series of round crimson spots near the base of the second dorsal; occiput, a band on muzzle, and one below eye, black; a black spot on operculum and one at base of pectoral; females duller and speckled, with ventrals barred and lateral bars feebler" (Jordan and Evermann). Preserved male specimens with whole body and fins more or less dusky, obscuring color pattern; dorsal, anal, pectorals, and ventrals a dark smoky blue, densest in the membranes; bars on body 11 or 12, only the last 7 or 8 (behind tips of reflexed pectorals) distinct; second dorsal, anal, and pectorals (and ventrals of females) barred in the rays; first dorsal with a row of large dark spots in membranes near base, and barred in rays of upper half. Head rather small, short, 4 to 4.9 in length; width of head 1.6 to 1.9 in its length; interorbital space 5.3 to 6.9; eye small, round, not protruding, 2.9 to 3.7 in head; nose short, blunt, and scarcely decurved, 3.2 to 4 in head; mouth small, subinferior, maxillary scarcely past front of orbit; cleft 3.4 to 4.8 in head; jaws nearly equal; gill-membranes connected across isthmus in a broad curve, distance from muzzle to their free margin about 1⅖ to 1½ times that from muzzle to back of orbit. Dorsal fin X or XI, 10–12; spinous and soft portions scarcely separated at base; height of first dorsal 1.7 to 2.1 in head, second 1.4 to 1.7 (height of first 76 to 94 per cent. of second); caudal lunate; anal II, 7 or 8; pectorals .9 to 1 in head; separation of ventrals less than ⅔ their width at base. Scales 6, 46–53, 6 or 7 [8 or 9], weakly ctenoid; lateral line nearly straight and usually complete, 2 to 6 pores occasionally lacking; cheeks, opercles, and nape fully scaled; breast usually fully scaled, sometimes partly naked; belly covered with ordinary scales.

The banded darter is one of the typical members of its subfamily, but with an extraordinary distribution in Illinois. It is limited, according to our experience, to the northern half of the state, with the exception of a single collection from the Wabash, and is distinguished also by its frequency in the smaller rivers rather than in streams which could be classed as creeks. Our thirty-five collections, from almost as many localities, give us a frequency coefficient of 4.42 for small rivers, 1.37 for creeks, and .2 for the larger rivers, the species not having occurred at all in standing water of any description. In the streams which it inhabits, it is found almost wholly in the swifter parts on a bottom of rock or sand.

The general distribution of this darter extends from Lake Erie westward through Ohio, Indiana, and Iowa to Mankato, Mont., southward to the Saline and Washita rivers in Arkansas, to the Black Warrior in Alabama, to the Holston in Virginia, and to the French Broad in North Carolina. It is said by Jordan and Evermann to occur commonly in small clear streams, and to be locally abundant in weedy or gravelly places.

Its food, so far as known, is similar to that of most of the other members of the family, consisting mainly of larvæ of small *Diptera*, *Chironomus* larvæ predominating.

Males and females in breeding colors, the latter greatly distended with eggs, have been taken by us in late May and early June.

ETHEOSTOMA CAMURUM (Cope)

BLUE-BREASTED DARTER

Cope, 1870, Proc. Am. Philos. Soc. Phila., 265 (**Pœcilichthys**).
J. & G., 506 (**Nothonotus**); M. V., 130; B., I, 69; J. & E., I, 1076; N., 34 (**Pœcilichthys niger**); J., 41 (**Nothonotus**); L., 28.

This darter has been taken in the White River basin in Indiana by Dr. Jordan. Although reported by Mr. Thomas Large* from Peoria, from Union county, and from the Saline and lower Wabash basins, it is not now represented in our collections. A single specimen thought to belong to this species was presented to this Laboratory by Mr. J. P. Baur, of the United States Fish Commission, who took it from a pond near Naples, Illinois, but it was unfortunately lost before the preliminary identification could be verified.

The species ranges, so far as known, from Lake Erie to Tennessee in clear swift water.

ETHEOSTOMA IOWÆ Jordan & Meek

Jordan & Meek, 1885, Proc. U. S. Nat. Mus., 10.
M. V., 133; B., I, 72 (**ioæ**); J. & E., I, 1083; L., 28.

Length 2 inches; body rather long, more slender than other Illinois species of *Etheostoma;* depth 5.4 to 6.8, usually not over 6, greatest width of body about ⅔ its greatest depth; depth caudal peduncle 2.3 to 2.8 in its length. Color of sides and upper parts light green, finely blotched with darker; back with 8 or 9 small and rather obscure quadrate blotches of clove-brown color; sides with 9 to 11 clove-brown bars, short and somewhat broken, extending above lateral line half way to back and below it half way to belly (the bars are greenish in pale specimens), squarish blotches of rusty red alternating with the bars; belly greenish yellow to almost white, overlaid between base of pectoral and anal fin with an orange band or a row of blotches of same color; sides and top of head with dark brown vermiculations and bands of brown; a band of brown before eye and one below it; upper half of spinous dorsal, except margin, a brilliant orange, above and below which is clove-brown to light green; pectorals, soft dorsal, and caudal fins barred brown in the rays; ventrals and anal almost plain white. Females and males in

* "A List of the Native Fishes of Illinois, with Keys," by Thomas Large. Rep. Ill. State Fish Comm., Sept. 30, 1900, to Oct. 1, 1902.

Etheostoma jessiæ (Jordan & Brayton)

Etheostoma iowæ Jordan & Meek

late-summer color much lighter, fall specimens often suggesting *Boleosoma nigrum*. The large size and peculiar shade of the rusty-brown to rusty-red blotches will usually serve for the recognition of this species. Head 3.7 to 4, less pointed than *E. jessiæ*, the muzzle rather blunt, scarcely decurved; width of head 1.8 to 2.1 in its length; interorbital space not much wider than half of eye, 6 to 8 in head; eye nearly round, 3.3 to 4.4 in head; mouth rather small, nearly horizontal, subterminal, maxillary reaching to front of orbit; cleft 3.6 to 4; lower jaw included; gill-membranes scarcely connected, distance from muzzle to angle usually less than 1.1 times that to back of orbit. Dorsal fin VIII–XI, 9 or 11; spinous and soft portions separated by a space somewhat greater than diameter of eye; height of first dorsal 2.1 to 2.7 in head, second 1.8 to 2 (height of first 68 to 94 per cent. of second); caudal truncate or very faintly lunate; anal II (occasionally I), 6 to 8 (usually 7); pectorals 1.2 to 1.4 in head; separation of ventrals always less than half, sometimes only ⅓, their width at base. Scales 5 or 6 (occasionally 7), 55–60, 7–9 [10–12], lateral line somewhat flexed upward anteriorly*, as in *E. jessiæ*; about 25 pores usually lacking; cheeks, opercles, and nape fully scaled; breast naked; belly covered with ordinary scales.

A rare species in Illinois, taken by us from eight localities, all in northern Illinois except one from Johnson county. The following are the recorded places: Pistakee Lake, in McHenry county; Wolf Lake, South Chicago; Senachwine Lake, Henry county; Rock River at Milan, Rock Island county; Green River, near Geneseo, in Henry county; Pecunsagan creek, near Utica, La Salle county; Illinois River, at Ottawa; and Dutchman's creek, near Vienna, Johnson county.

Its known general range is northward at least as far as Qu'Appelle River in Assiniboia, westward to Valentine, Neb., and southward to Arkansas.

ETHEOSTOMA JESSIÆ (Jordan & Brayton)

(Pl., p. 306; Map XCIV)

Jordan & Brayton, 1877, Jordan's Man. Vert., 227 (**Pœcilichthys**).
J. & G., 518 (**Pœcilichthys**); M. V., 133; B., I, 72; J. & E., I, 1084; Forbes, in J., 41 (**Pœcilichthys asprigenis**); F., 64 (**asprigene**); L., 29.

Length ordinarily a little less than two inches, though specimens are occasionally found 2½ inches; depth 4.8 to 5.4 in length; body as a rule considerably compressed, its greatest width about ⅗ of its greatest depth; dorsal and ventral outlines usually about equally arched, giving the fish a symmetrical, bass-like form, which appearance is aided by its rather large and oblique mouth; depth of caudal peduncle 2.1 to 2.6 in its length. Color brownish olive, the back with 5 or 6 quadrate saddle-like blotches of blackish

* In *E. jessiæ* and *iowæ* the lateral line is nearly parallel with the line of the back. The difference between these species and *Boleichthys fusiformis* in this feature seems to be in the closeness of lateral line to the back at its highest point rather than in the matter of parallelism.

to greenish brown; 8 or 9 greenish brown bars on sides, becoming obscure in front of caudal peduncle; interspaces between bars rust-red to orange; belly orange; head slaty olive, with dark streak in front of eye and below; cheeks olivaceous, tending to bluish brown or chestnut; opercle olivaceous with sprinklings of iridescent golden green; eye dull, the pupil dull black and iris chestnut; spinous dorsal tipped with a narrow edge of pale blue, under which is a narrow band-like row of orange-red spots; lower half of fin chiefly pale blue; soft dorsal irregularly spotted with rusty orange; pectorals transparent; ventrals dusky at base; anal pale; one of the most elegantly colored of our darters. Females somewhat duller in color, examples in preservative showing less prominently than males the dark bar-like blotch near base of spinous dorsal. Head 3.7 to 4.2, rather large, uniformly tapered above and below to the end of the bluntly pointed muzzle; width of head 1.7 to 2.3; interorbital space about half of eye, 5.4 to 7.4 in head; eye round, 3.3 to 4; nose slightly less than eye, 3.5 to 4.3; mouth rather large, terminal, oblique, upper lip above level of lower margin of orbit; maxillary past front of orbit; cleft 2.8 to 3.3 in head; jaws subequal; gill-membranes narrowly connected, distances from muzzle to angle and to back of orbit about equal. Dorsal fin X–XI (occasionally IX), 12 or 13, the spinous and soft portions scarcely separated; height of first dorsal 1.9 to 2.2 in head, second 1.5 to 2 (height of first 74 to 98 per cent. of second); caudal rounded or slightly emarginate; anal II, 7 or 8; pectorals 1.1 to 1.3 in head; separation of ventrals scarcely more than ⅓ their width at base. Scales 6 (occasionally 5), 49–57, 7–9 [9–11]; lateral line somewhat flexed upward anteriorly, about parallel* with line of back; 3 to 15 pores usually lacking; cheeks, opercles, and nape closely scaled; breast naked; belly covered with ordinary scales.

This little species, very abundant in Illinois, and represented by 161 collections, differs from the remainder of its subfamily in its average distribution. It is consequently among those darters least frequently found in company with others, and our associative coefficient for the species is but 1.47, the general average for the subfamily being 2.02. It seems to prefer the stagnant water of lowland lakes and sloughs, and occurs otherwise most frequently in rivers, large and small, and somewhat less frequently in creeks. Our coefficients for these various waters are 2.02 for bottom-land lakes and ponds, 1.23 for the larger rivers, 1.13 for the smaller rivers, and .99 for the creeks. Its preference for the larger streams and the waters of their neighborhood is indeed plainly evident from the map of its distribution. It is wanting in all our collections from the upland glacial lakes.

Its ecological separateness from its nearest allies, notwithstanding its close resemblance to them, is shown by our coefficients of association of this species with the banded, the rainbow,

* Least distance between lateral line and middle of back equal to ⅓ depth of body. Compare with *Boleichthys fusiformis*.

and the fan-tailed darters, the other relatively abundant species of its genus. These are .37 for the first of the above-named species, .77 for the second, and 1.27 for the third, an average of .8, to be compared with the general subfamily average of 2.02, and with one of 5.54, which is the *mutual* associative coefficient of the three other species of the group. It has, in short, been found by us in company with the three other common species only about one seventh as frequently as they have been found with each other.

The species has occurred nearly three times as frequently in central, and nearly twice as frequently in southern, as in northern Illinois. Notwithstanding this indifferent distribution as to the kinds of waters it inhabits, our data of situation indicate a decided preference for a strong current and a bottom of rock or sand. It is a very common species in the Illinois at Havana and Meredosia, 88 of our collections having come from that situation, usually conspicuous by the absence of other darters.

It is reported outside Illinois from Devil Lake and Tiffin River, Michigan, through Indiana and Iowa to Mississippi, Arkansas, Oklahoma, Texas, and the Rio Grande, and also from the Etowah River in Georgia.

Its food consists of larvæ of May-flies and *Chironomus* larvæ, taken by the specimens studied in about equal quantity.

Females with large eggs were caught in the middle of March, but others captured May 12 had not yet spawned. Craig, however, reports it spawning at Havana in April and May, 1898. Males still retained their breeding colors in August, 1903.

ETHEOSTOMA CŒRULEUM Storer

RAINBOW DARTER; SOLDIER-FISH

(Map XCV)

Storer, 1845, Proc. Bost. Soc. Nat. Hist., 47.

J. & G., 517 (**Pœcilichthys**); M. V., 133; B., I, 71; J. & E., I, 1088; N., 34 (**Pœcilichthys cœruleus** and **spectabilis**); J., 41 (**Pœcilichthys variatus** and **spectabilis**); F., 64; L., 29.

Length 2 inches; robust, rather deep and compressed, and back, especially in males, more or less elevated; depth 4.7 to 5; greatest width about ⅗ greatest depth; depth of caudal peduncle 2.1 to 2.5 in its length. Color dark olive, overlaid with dusky to bluish (or brilliant indigo-blue) bars and blotches; scales of sides each with a dark central spot, these forming more or less longitudinal rows most distinct in females and in the so-called variety *spectabile**; back with 7 or 8 rather obscure quadrate blotches; sides of males

* *E. cœruleum spectabile* (Agassiz), Jordan & Evermann, 1896, Bull. U. S. Nat. Mus., No. 47, Pt. I., p. 1089.

with 11 or 12 bars of dark indigo-blue color, the interspaces between the bars blood-orange, brightest backward, as are also the indigo-bars; head flesh-color, with lavender on chin and yellow to orange on opercles; forehead and top of snout dull bluish black; a blue splash below eye and a dark spot behind it; spinous dorsal crossed at its middle by a row of orange-red spots in an orange band; above and below this a pale to deep indigo-blue band; at base of fin a narrow band of orange with a central row of orange-red spots. Females duller in color than the males, the bars dusky and interspaces olive; spinous dorsal with a narrow outer edging of pale blue, next to which is a straw-colored band with a row of rust-colored spots, in place of the orange of male. Head large, 3.6 to 4 in length, the profile in males a broad and practically continuous curve from front of dorsal to tip of snout; females with nape angled; width of head 1.7 to 2.1 in its length; interorbital space flat, about ⅔ of eye, 5.8 to 7.2 in head; eye nearly round, 3.7 to 4.1; mouth moderate, terminal, somewhat oblique, tip of upper lip nearer to floor of orbit than base of chin; lips rather large, upper with great lateral depth when closed; maxillary reaching to front of orbit; cleft 3 to 3.5; jaws subequal; gill-membranes scarcely connected, distances to angle and to back of orbit about equal. Dorsal fin X (or XI), 12–14; spinous and soft portions scarcely separated, or slightly connected at base; height of first dorsal 2.1 to 2.7 in head, second 1.5 to 1.9 (height of first 67 to 83 per cent. of second); caudal truncate; anal II, 7 or 8 (occasionally 6); pectorals 1 to 1.2 in head; separation of ventrals usually about ⅓ their width at base. Scales 6, 44–51, 7 or 8, occasionally 6 [9 or 10]; lateral line flexed slightly upward anteriorly, 15 to 20 pores usually lacking; cheeks naked; opercles scaled; nape scaled posteriorly, usually naked in a small patch next to occiput; breast naked; belly covered with ordinary scales.

FIG. 74

The rainbow darter, one of the most brilliant of its group and closely allied to *Etheostoma jessiæ*, is less abundant in this state than that species—occurring in 99 of our collections to 161 of the other—and differs widely from it in local distribution also, especially in an avoidance of stagnant waters and the larger streams. Indeed, we have taken it but three times from first-class rivers, and but twice from lakes or sloughs, while the coefficients of frequency for creeks and the smaller rivers are 2.72 and 2.66 respectively. It is also differently distributed throughout the state, being more abundant northward in our collections than *jessiæ*, much less so in the central part of the state, and somewhat more abundant, again, in extreme southern Illinois.* While it occurred three times in the waters of the lower Wabash within the lower Illinoisan glaciation, a comparison of the map of its distribution with that of *jessiæ* indicates unmistakably an avoidance of this area by the present species. It is distinctly a swift-water and clean-bottom species—83 per cent. of our collections bearing ecological data having come from the former and 92 per cent. from the latter situations.

In general distribution it ranges from Lake Superior to Lake Ontario, New Jersey, and western Pennsylvania, and thence throughout the Ohio and the Missouri basins to Missouri and Kansas, and southwest to Texas.

It is a thick-bodied fish, without much grace of appearance or movement, but is very active and alert and always watchful of its surroundings. When alarmed it darts swiftly to the right and left, with confusing rapidity. It is fond of creeping into crevices in the aquarium, and is quite skilful at hiding itself in the sand or gravel by a headlong dive and one or two vigorous flirts of the tail.

We have taken females filled with large eggs and males in breeding color in early June. Their spawning habits are described by Mr. W. P. Seal, who observed them in the aquarium. The eggs were deposited among the pebbles at the bottom of the tank, the female drawing herself along with a quivering motion, and the male pushing up close beside her.

ETHEOSTOMA OBEYENSE Kirsch

Kirsch, 1890 (1892), Bull. U. S. Fish Comm., X, 292.
B., I, 78; J. & E., I, 1092; L., 29.

Length 2 inches; body long and low, depth 5.6 to 6; greatest width about ⅔ greatest depth of body; depth caudal peduncle 2.2 to 2.4 in its length. Color (in preservative) light brownish olive, much and rather finely blotched with darker; back with 6 or 7 ill-defined cross-blotches; sides with 10 or 11 irregularly shaped dark spots along lateral line, often obscure; a dark spot on cheek behind eye; suborbital streak faint or wanting; cheeks, opercles, and

* The frequency ratios for the three sections are, for *E. jessiæ* .53, 1.46, and 1.02 for northern, central, and southern Illinois, and for *E. cœruleum*, 1.30, .42, and 1.28, respectively.

chin rather densely sprinkled with fine dark dots; black humeral scale very large and usually distinct, its depth nearly equal to diameter of eye; spinous dorsal pale below, with a broad outer margin of dusky; soft dorsal faintly barred; caudal with 6 or 7 wavy bars which are continuous for most part on both rays and membranes, as in *E. squamiceps* and *E. flabellare*; pectorals faintly barred; other fins plain. Head 3.36 to 3.46, rather slender and pointed; width of head 2 to 2.3; interorbital space about half of eye, 7.1 to 8.1; eye roundish, somewhat protruding above cranium, 3.2 to 3.7; mouth rather large, subterminal, oblique, tip of upper lip above level of lower margin of orbit; maxillary reaching past front of orbit; cleft 2.9 to 3.2 in head; jaws subequal; gill-membranes scarcely connected, distances to angle and to back of orbit equal. Dorsal fin VI or VIII, 11–12; two fins scarcely separated; first dorsal low, 50 to 59 per cent. of height of second (first 2.7 to 3.8 in head, second 1.6 to 1.9); caudal subtruncate; anal II, 7; pectorals 1.2 in head; separation of ventrals less than half their width at base. Scales 6, 42–45, 6 or 7 [10]; lateral line always incomplete, the pores developed on 15 to 20 scales only; cheeks naked; opercles usually naked, sometimes with a trace of scales; nape and breast naked; belly covered with ordinary scales.

This rare little fish has been taken in this state in only four collections, all from rocky and gravelly creeks in Pope and Hardin counties. It was originally described in 1890 from the tributaries of the Cumberland River in Clinton county, Kentucky, and seems not to have been since reported from any other place.

ETHEOSTOMA SQUAMICEPS Jordan

(Map XCVI)

Jordan, 1877, Bull. U. S. Nat. Mus., No. 10, 11.
J. & G., 514; M. V., 131; B., I, 85; J. & E., I, 1096; L., 29.

Length 2½ to 3 inches; body robust, back low, and caudal peduncle stout; depth 4.9 to 6; greatest width of body about ¾ its greatest depth; depth caudal peduncle 1.6 to 2.3 (usually less than 2) in its length. Color dusky olive, finely and densely mottled and specked with dark brown, lower part of sides and belly scarcely lighter than upper parts; no lateral spots or blotches and no evident cross-bars*; a more or less distinct dark humeral scale, a bar before eye, and a very distinct suborbital streak; chin and cheeks conspicuously vermiculated with dark brown; second dorsal, caudal, and pectorals finely barred, latter faintly. Head 3.7 to 4 in length, nape angled and profile noticeably decurved to end of bluntly pointed snout; interorbital space almost equal to eye, 6 to 7.2 in head; eye round, 3.7 to 4.4; mouth large†, terminal, oblique, the jaws subequal; maxillary reaching past front of pupil; cleft 2.8 to 3.3; gill-membranes scarcely connected‡, distances to angle

* Compare with Jordan and Evermann, Bull. 47, U. S. Nat. Mus., Pt. I., p. 1096.
† "Small" (Jordan and Evermann, l. c.).
‡ "Rather broadly connected" (Jordan and Evermann, l. c.).

and to back of orbit equal. Dorsal fin usually VIII or IX, 12–14 (sometimes VII or X); two portions as a rule scarcely separated at base, sometimes apart a distance equal to about ⅔ of eye; first dorsal very low, its height 48 to 64 per cent. of second; (first 2.6 to 3.7 in head, second 1.8 to 2.1); caudal rounded; anal II, 6 or 7; pectorals 1.15 to 1.27 in head; separation of ventrals about half their width at base. Scales 6–8, 44–57; 7–8 [10–13]; lateral line nearly straight, from 5 to 15 pores usually lacking; cheeks and opercles with more or less closely embedded scales; nape as a rule scaled; breast naked or wholly or partly covered with embedded scales; belly covered with ordinary scales.

Taken by us in ten collections, from eight localities, all but two from southern Illinois, south of the Saline River, the exceptions coming from Robinson creek a branch of the Kaskaskia in Shelby county, and from the Little Wabash River near Carmi, in White county. It is distinctly a southern species, reported from Georgia and Florida to southern Indiana, Kentucky, Tennessee, and the Black Warrior River in Alabama. It is, like *obeyense*, a species of swift clear creeks with a bottom of rock or gravel.

ETHEOSTOMA FLABELLARE Rafinesque

FAN-TAILED DARTER

(Pl., p. 292; Map XCVII)

Rafinesque, 1819, Journ. de Physique, 419.

J. & G., 513; M. V., 131; B., I, 86; J. & E., I, 1097; N., 34 (**Pœcilichthys flabellatus** and **P. lineolatus**); J., 42; F., 64; F. F., I. 3, 24; L., 29.

Length 2 to 2½ inches; body rather slender, compressed, back low, caudal peduncle deep; depth 4.6 to 6.8 in length; greatest width of body about ⅔ its greatest depth; depth caudal peduncle 1.8 to 2.4, usually less than 2, in its length. Color (in preservative) rather dark, with small dark specks and faint cross-bars; each scale of back and sides with a central dark spot, the longitudinal rows formed by these most prominent in females and in the so-called variety *lineolatum**; a rather large and very black humeral spot; a dark streak across opercles and through eye to end of snout; suborbital streak faint or wanting; cheeks and opercles dusted with minute brown specks; males with head and upper parts dark bluish black and with 10 or 12 cross-bars of same color on sides, traces of these bars in females; second dorsal and caudal fins finely barred; pectorals faintly barred, other fins plain; spines of first dorsal in breeding males ending in fleshy pads or knobs of rust-red color, and body and fins all more or less dusky. Head rather long, slender, depressed, 3.6 to 4.2 in length; a distinct but not deep angle at nape, from which profile is almost straight to tip of snout, which is somewhat upturned, especially in males; interorbital space flat, 6.2 to 8.3; eye round, 3.8 to 5; mouth rather large, terminal, oblique, tip of upper lip almost on level with upper margin of pupil;

* *E. flabellare lineolatum* (Agassiz), Jordan and Evermann, 1896, Bull. U. S. Nat. Mus., No. 47, Pt. I., p. 1098.

maxillary past front of orbit; cleft 2.9 to 3.3 in head; lower jaw as long as upper or slightly projecting; gill-membranes broadly connected, the distance from muzzle to their free margin as a rule over 1½ times that to back of orbit. Dorsal fin VII or VIII, 12–14; the two portions very closely approximated or united at base; first dorsal very low, its height 42 to 68 per cent. of height of second (height of first 3.2 to 5.1 in head, second 1.8 to 2.3); caudal rounded; anal II, 7 or 8 (or 9); pectorals 1.2 to 1.3 in head; separation of ventrals about half their width at base. Scales 8 or 9, 51–63, 8–10 [12–16]; lateral line straight, 15 to 25 pores lacking; cheeks and opercles usually naked, the latter with sometimes a trace of scales; nape naked or with very deeply embedded scales; breast naked; belly covered with ordinary scales.

The fan-tailed darter has a distribution in this state very like that of the rainbow darter, although it is a less common inhabitant of our streams. Of the thirty-five localities from which we have taken it, but one falls within the lower Illinoisan glaciation, while two are in Union county in extreme southern Illinois, and the remainder are in the northern two thirds of the state, mostly in northern Illinois proper, for which section the frequency coefficient is 1.92. This is mainly a darter of the smaller streams, usually inhabiting the swifter creeks and brooks, although occasionally taken in rivers and lowland lakes.

It is widely distributed, from Quebec and New England down the Atlantic coast to the Catawba River in South Carolina, westward by way of the Great Lakes and the Ohio basin to Missouri and northeastern Iowa, and southward to northern Alabama.

It stands high on our list of typical darters, and Jordan and Copeland say of it: "The Darter of Darters is the fan-tail, *Etheostoma flabellare.* Hardiest, wiriest, wariest of them all, it is the one which is most expert in catching other creatures, and the one which most surely evades your clutch. * * * It is a slim, narrow, black, pirate-rigged little fish, with a long pointed head, and a projecting, prow-like lower jaw. It carries no flag, but is colored like the rocks among which it lives. * * * The Fan-tailed Darter chooses the coldest and swiftest waters, and in these, as befits his form, he leads an active, predatory life. He is the terror of water-snails and caddis-worms, and the larvæ of mosquitoes."

Six specimens were found by us to have made nearly two thirds of their food from *Chironomus* larvæ, about a fourth from small May-fly larvæ, and the rest from copepod crustaceans.

Females apparently nearly ready to spawn are in our collections obtained the last of May.

Genus BOLEICHTHYS Girard

Darters separated doubtfully from *Etheostoma*, from which genus they differ alone in the more noticeable upward flexure* of the lateral line anteriorly; premaxillaries non-protractile, as in *Etheostoma*, and cranium ∩-shaped, as in that genus; vertebræ (*B. fusiformis*) 36 (16 + 20); pyloric cæca 4†. Species few and variable; size small; colors not brilliant.

Fig. 75

BOLEICHTHYS FUSIFORMIS (Girard)

(Map XCVIII)

Girard, 1854, Proc. Bost. Soc. Nat. Hist., 41 (**Boleosoma**).
J. & G., 519 (**Pœcilichthys barratti**), 520 (**P. fusiformis, P. erochrous** and **P. eos**), 521 (**P. gracilis**); M. V., 134 (**Etheostoma**); B., I, 75 (**Etheostoma**); J. & E., I, 1101; N., 34 (**exilis, eos,** etc.); J., 42 (**eos**), 43 (**elegans**); F., 64 (**Etheostoma eos** and **fusiforme**); L., 29.

Length 2 to 2½ inches; body moderately elongate, compressed, the back more or less elevated; depth 5.8 to 7.1 in length; greatest width of body about ⅗ its greatest depth; caudal peduncle rather slender, its depth 2.9 to 3.3 (3.8) in its length. Color (in preservative) olivaceous, much blotched and dotted with brown, the dark color often in more or less definite W- and X-shaped markings, though more often in vaguely defined zigzag streaks and rusty splotches; a black band in front of eye on snout and a dark blotch behind eye; suborbital streak faint; spinous faintly dusky in membranes near base; soft dorsal and caudal faintly barred. Males are in general darker, with usually 9 or 10 transverse bars of dusky on sides in breeding season; basal third of membranes of spinous dorsal jet-black, and the fin edged with dusky; between these bands on spinous dorsal a row of elongate-roundish pale blotches (crimson‡ in life). Head 3.5 to 4.1 in length, bluntly pointed, the muzzle somewhat decurved; nape scarcely angled, if at all; interorbital space 5.5 to 6.9 in head; eye round, 3.5 to 4; nose 4.3 to 5.2; mouth subterminal, slightly oblique, tip of upper lip scarcely to lower margin of orbit; maxillary past front of orbit; cleft 3.1 to 3.8 in head; jaws subequal; gill-membranes scarcely connected, distances to angle and to back of orbit about equal.

* See preceding description of *Etheostoma jessiæ*; also description of *B. fusiformis*.
† In 3 specimens (Accessions No. 28075, Ill. State Lab. Nat. Hist.).
‡ "Spinous dorsal in life usually bright blue, with a median crimson band" (Jordan and Evermann).

Dorsal fin IX or X, 10–12; the two portions as a rule hardly separated, sometimes apart a distance almost equal to width of orbit; height of first dorsal 1.6 to 2.6 in head, second 1.3 to 1.9 (height of first 71 to 86 per cent. of second); caudal faintly lunate; anal II (or I), 6 or 7; pectorals 1 to 1.3 in head; separation of ventrals about half their width at base. Scales 3 or 4, 48–54, 7–8 [10–12]; lateral line with a marked upward curve anteriorly, where it is parallel with line of back, the least distance between here and middle of back about ¼ depth of body at same point; 25 to 35 lateral pores usually lacking; cheeks and opercles fully scaled; nape usually scaled; breast naked in most of our specimens; belly covered with ordinary scales.

This rather insignificant little fish, with but few of the more characteristic feature of the highly differentiated darters, departs most widely from the rest in ecological situation also. It has consequently the smallest coefficient of subfamily association (1.22) among all our darters—the general average coefficient for the subfamily being 2.02, and the highest general coefficient of any species 2.69 (*Hadropterus phoxocephalus*). It has been obtained by us sixty times, most of our collections coming from the southeastern part of the state, but a few coming from the upland lakes of Lake and McHenry counties and from the upper branches of the Illinois. Several of our localities are on the middle course of the Kaskaskia, and one is on a branch of the Sangamon in Christian county. This is one of the very few species of the subfamily which shows a preference for sluggish or stagnant water and for a mud bottom—78 per cent. of our collections with data coming from the former and 66 per cent. from the latter situation. Next to the glacial lakes we have found it most abundant in creeks, and then in the smaller rivers. It seems to be rare in the larger rivers and in lowland lakes and sloughs.

In general distribution, it is reported from Massachusetts and thence through Lakes Erie and Ontario to Minnesota and Montana, southward to Indian River in Florida, and through the Ohio basin to Mississippi and the Rio Grande. It is everywhere commonest in ponds and lowland streams. Dr. C. C. Abbott, of New Jersey, found it in shallow weedy streams, in water scarcely two inches deep, and caught examples with a baited hook, which, in spite of their small size, they seized with the quickness and voracity of a pike.

Three specimens of this species from southern Illinois had fed, like the darters generally, on larvæ of gnats and May-flies, about two thirds of the latter to one third of the former.

Females containing full-sized eggs were taken by us April 28.

Genus MICROPERCA Putnam

Body short and stout; mouth small, slightly oblique; premaxillaries not protractile; vertebræ (*M. punctulata*) 30 (16 + 20); differing from *Etheostoma* only in the almost or complete absence of the lateral line; the vertebræ and fin rays fewer than in other darters, and the scales larger than in most species. Size extremely small—the smallest of the darters; coloration plain; species few, or perhaps not more than one.

Fig. 76

MICROPERCA PUNCTULATA Putnam

LEAST DARTER

(Map XCIX)

Putnam, 1863, Bull. Mus. Comp. Zool., I, 4.
J. & G., 523; M. V., 134 (**Etheostoma microperca**); B., I, 87 (**Etheostoma microperca**); J. & E., I, 1104; N., 34; J., 43; F., 64; F. F., I. 3, 24; L., 29.

Length 1 to 1½ inches; body not much elongate, compressed, the back moderately arched; depth 4.6 to 5.2; greatest width about 5/7 of greatest depth; depth caudal peduncle 2.6 to 3.1. "Coloration olivaceous, the sides closely speckled and with vague bars and zigzag markings; second dorsal and caudal barred; dark streaks radiating from eye; a dark humeral spot" (Jordan and Evermann). Head bluntly rounded, 3.6 to 4; width of head 1.9 to 2.2 in its length; interorbital space 6.7; eye 3.7 to 4.1; nose 4.8 to 5.5; mouth terminal, oblique, maxillary to middle of orbit, cleft 3.5 to 4 in head; jaws equal; gill-membranes scarcely connected. Dorsal VI, 9; spinous and soft dorsals separated by a space about equal to pupil; anal II, 5 or 6; separation of ventral less than half width of base; pectorals equaling head. Scales large and strongly ctenoid; 33–36, oblique series 9 or 10; lateral line absent; cheeks naked; opercles with a few scales; breast and neck naked.

This, the smallest of the darters and the smallest, indeed, of our spiny-finned fishes, is very rare in our collections outside those from the upland lakes of northeastern Illinois. We have taken it, in fact, but twice south of Joliet, in Will county, the exceptional instances coming from Skillet fork in Wayne county, and from Drury creek in Union county, in the southern part of the state. It has been wanting, it will be seen, in all our central Illinois collections.

This little darter inhabits generally small streams and ponds of the Great Lake region, and ranges thence southwest to Arkansas.

Nine specimens from four localities in northern Illinois had made two thirds of their food from *Crustacea*, mostly *Entomostraca*, but with young specimens of amphipod crustaceans also. The remaining two thirds was essentially all *Chironomus* larvæ, with only a trace of small larvæ of May-flies.

Family **SERRANIDÆ**

THE SEA BASS

Body oblong, more or less compressed; dorsal and ventral outlines usually not perfectly corresponding; scales adherent, usually but not always ctenoid; lateral line present, not extending on caudal fin; skeleton osseous; vertebræ typically $10 + 14 = 24$, never more than 35; anterior vertebræ without transverse processes; ventrals thoracic, usually I, 5; dorsals confluent or not, the spines 2 to 15 in number; anal spines, if present, always 3; caudal variously formed; no mesocoracoid; gill-membranes separate, free from isthmus; branchiostegels normally 7, occasionally 6; pseudobranchiæ present, large; gill-rakers long or short, usually stiff and armed with teeth; preopercle usually more or less serrate; opercles usually ending in 1 or 2 flat spine-like points; mouth not much oblique; premaxillary protractile; supplemental maxillary present or absent; teeth conical or pointed, in bands on jaws, vomer, and palatines; no canines; lower pharyngeals separate (except rarely), with pointed teeth; intestine short; stomach cæcal, with few or many pyloric appendages; air-bladder present, usually small and adherent to wall of abdomen.

Carnivorous fishes, chiefly marine, found in all warm seas; a few genera found in fresh water, 2 in the Mississippi Valley; genera known about 60 to 70, species about 400. Many of the species are of great value for food and game qualities.

Key to Illinois Genera of **SERRANIDÆ**

a. Dorsal fins separate; anal fin III, 11 to 13, the spines graduated, the first about half length of second, and second distinctly shorter than third; lower jaw projecting; base of tongue with teeth.................**Roccus.**

aa. Dorsal fins joined; anal fin III, 10, the spines not graduated, first scarcely ⅓ of second, second and third subequal; jaws almost equal; base of tongue toothless ....**Morone.**

GENUS **ROCCUS** MITCHILL

STRIPED BASS

Body deep and compressed; lower jaw projecting; no supplemental maxillary; lower margin of preopercle simply (not antrorsely) serrate or entire; base of tongue with 1 or 2 patches of teeth; dorsal fins entirely separate; anal spines 3, graduated in size; scales ctenoid. Species 2, American, one inhabiting fresh waters of the Mississippi Valley, the other being the striped bass of the Atlantic (*R. lineatus*).

ROCCUS CHRYSOPS (RAFINESQUE)

WHITE BASS

(MAP C)

Rafinesque, 1820, Ichth. Oh., 22 (**Perca**).

G., I, 67 (**Labrax multilineatus** and **notatus**); J. & G., 529; M. V., 137; B., I, 128 (**Morone multilineata**); J. & E., I, 1132; N. 36; J., J., 44; F., 63; F. F., I. 3, 37; L., 29.

Length 12 to 18 inches; body rather deep and compressed and back elevated; profile angled at nape; depth 2.6 to 2.9; greatest width about ½ greatest depth; depth caudal peduncle 1.2 to 1.3 in its length. "Color silvery, tinged with golden below; sides with narrow dusky lines, about 5 above the lateral line, 1 along it, and a variable number below it, these sometimes more or less interrupted or transposed" (Jordan and Evermann). Head subconic, flattened at sides, 3.1 to 3.4; width of head 1.8 to 2.1; interorbital little convex, 3.4 to 4.1; nose longer than eye, 3.4 to 3.8; mouth terminal, oblique, maxillary to middle of orbit, 2.2 to 2.4 in head; lower jaw strongly projecting; gill-rakers long as gill-filaments, X + 14. Dorsal IX–I, 13 or 14; longest spine about 2 in head; base of soft dorsal 1.25 in base of spinous; caudal forked; anal III, 11 to 13, the spines graduated, first about half as long as second, and second distinctly longer than third; ventrals ⅔ to vent; pectorals 1.6 to 1.9 in head. Scales 8 or 9, 52–57, 13 or 14, very strongly ctenoid; lateral line usually complete and nearly straight; cheeks and opercles fully scaled, rows 10 to 12.

A species, in Illinois, of the larger rivers and bottom-land lakes, but found also in Lake Michigan. It has come to us in fifty-six collections (mainly from seine hauls of the fishermen), made throughout the state from the Mississippi near Cairo to extreme northwest Illinois, and thence to the Calumet River. We have not obtained it, however, in the Wabash or Kaskaskia drainage; and it has been absent also from all our collections in the glacial lakes of northeastern Illinois. It appears to be primarily a lake fish, and secondarily one of the larger rivers, our coefficients for these waters being, respectively, 2.8 and 1.7, and the collections from the smaller streams of insignificant number. It has been much the most abundant with us in the central part of the state (1.7), about half as common in the northern part as in the central, and a fourth as common in southern Illinois.

It is a fish of the lakes and deeper rivers from New Brunswick, the St. Lawrence River, and the Great Lakes through the Ohio basin to Minnesota, Kansas, and Iowa. Its center of abundance is in the Great Lake region, but it is also distributed widely over the Ohio basin and the northern part of the Mississippi Valley.

It ranks well as a food fish, some regarding it as scarcely inferior to the black bass—and it is a game fish of some importance, to be caught with live minnows or even with grubs and angleworms. It will also rise to the fly.

It was formerly much more common than now. We are informed by Mr. H. L. Ashlock that a dozen years ago one could easily get a hundred pounds of it in an afternoon at Alton with a hundred-yard trammel-net, but that it has now almost disappeared. It reaches a weight of one to three pounds and a length of more than a foot.

The little that is known of its food indicates that it is mainly insectivorous, feeding especially upon the large May-fly larvæ to be found in immense numbers at the bottoms of our streams and lakes, but taking also medium-sized crustaceans (*Asellus*), and occasional fishes, among which sunfishes (*Centrarchidæ*) have been recognized.

Its range, local preferences, feeding habits, and food are so similar to those of the brassy bass (*Morone interrupta*) that the two species have been taken together with uncommon frequency in our collections, giving us the unusually high associative coefficient of 5.21. The occurrence of both these species in our territory is, in fact, due to an overlapping of the edges of the areas of their distribution. One being a northern species and the other a southern one, competition is mainly evaded, notwithstanding their like ecological relationships, by their occupancy of different territory. Within this state, however, they are apparently close competitors, with the advantage, in point of numbers at least, in favor of the yellow bass.

Genus **MORONE** Mitchill

Body rather short and deep, compressed; lower jaw scarcely projecting; no supplemental maxillary; lower margin of preopercle simply serrate or entire; base of tongue without teeth; dorsal fins more or less connected by

YELLOW BASS, *Morone interrupta Gil*

membrane; anal spines 3, not graduated; scales ctenoid. Two species, both American, one inhabiting fresh waters of the Mississippi Valley and the other brackish waters and the mouths of rivers of the Atlantic coast.

MORONE INTERRUPTA Gill

YELLOW BASS

(Map CI)

Gill, 1860, Proc. Ac. Nat. Sci. Phila., 118.
J. & G., 530; M. V.,137; B., I, 127 (**mississipiensis**); J. & E., I, 1134; N., 36; J., 44; F., 63 (**Roccus**); F. F., I. 3, 37; L., 29.

Length 12 to 18 inches; body rather deep and compressed and back elevated; profile angled at nape; depth 2.7 to 2.9; greatest width about 2 in greatest depth; depth caudal peduncle 1.4 to 1.6 in its length. Ground color olive-buff, with many small indistinct punctulations of emerald; alternate rows of scales on sides with dark greenish to blackish central bands, these adjoining to form prominent longitudinal stripes, 3 above lateral line, one (which is more or less moniliform) coincident with it, and 3 or 4 below lateral line; stripes below lateral line interrupted on posterior part of body, the breaking point sometimes indicated by irregularly disposed black spots; ventral region lighter than sides but of similar colors; vertical fins with considerable bluish tinge; cheeks and opercles with bluish and emerald iridescence; pupil pale dark blue; iris light greenish above pupil, darker outward. Head subconic, pointed, 3 to 3.2 in length; width of head 2 to 2.1 in its length; interorbital space little convex, 4 to 4.7; nose 3.1 to 3.7; mouth terminal, slightly less oblique than in last species; maxillary barely to middle of orbit, 2.6 to 2.8 in head; lower jaw not sensibly projecting; gill-rakers longer than branchial filaments, X + 13 to 16. Dorsal IX–I, 12; longest spine 1.6 in head; base of soft dorsal about 1.4 in base of spinous; caudal forked; anal III, 10, the spines not graduated, the first usually less than ⅓ of second, the second and third of about equal length; ventrals ⅔ to vent; pectorals 1.5 to 1.6. Scales 7, 51–55, 10–12, strongly ctenoid; lateral line complete or nearly so, scarcely arched anteriorly, somewhat flexuose; cheeks and opercles fully scaled, rows 12.

This species is distributed in Illinois much like the white bass, and although nearly twice as abundant in our collections as that species, it comes everywhere from similar waters—that is, from the large rivers and adjacent lakes. It is primarily a lake species, our one hundred and two collections giving us a frequency coefficient of 3.16 for bottom-land lakes and sloughs, and of 1.82 for rivers of the largest size. But two of these collections were from creeks or the smaller rivers. We have found it, like the preceding species, much more abundant in central Illinois than in either of the other sections, and about equally frequent in the Illinois River and in the Mississippi.

In its general distribution it contrasts strongly with its companion species, the white bass, the latter being northern in its range and the present species southern. It occurs throughout the Mississippi Valley northward to the latitude of Cincinnati and St. Louis, southward to New Orleans, and westward to the Kansas River. Its most northerly localities in this state are Green River in Henry county and the Illinois River at Ottawa, in La Salle county.

This fish reaches a length of twelve to eighteen inches and a weight of one to five pounds, although it does not ordinarily exceed a pound or two. It is common in the market catches at Havana, Meredosia, and Peoria, but hardly ever of a weight of more than half a pound. The catch of the yellow and the white bass together from the Illinois River in 1899, made up, no doubt, mainly of the present species, amounted to 92,931 pounds. It takes live bait readily, and will rise to the fly, and is considered by some anglers as scarcely inferior to the black bass as a game fish. It has been introduced by the State Fish Commission of Pennsylvania into several of the rivers of that state.

What little is known of its food indicates an insectivorous habit, adults feeding on aquatic larvæ, especially those of May-flies, together with small crustaceans and terrestrial insects. The yellow bass spawned in May at Havana in 1899.

Family SCIÆNIDÆ

THE DRUMS

Body compressed, more or less elongate; scales thin, usually ctenoid; head scaled; lateral line continuous, extending on caudal fin; skeleton osseous; vertebræ 22 to 32 (about); ventrals thoracic, I, 5; dorsals confluent or separate, the spines depressible into a more or less perfect groove; anal spines 1 or 2; caudal usually not forked; no mesocoracoid; gill-membranes separate, free from isthmus; branchiostegals 7; pseudobranchiæ usually large, present in most genera; gill-rakers present; preopercle serrate or not; opercle usually ending in 2 flat points; mouth small or large; premaxillary protractile; no supplemental maxillary; chin usually with pores, sometimes with barbels; no teeth on vomer, palatines, pterygoids, or tongue; no incisors; lower pharyngeals separate or united, the teeth conic or molar; ear-bones or otoliths very large; pyloric cæca usually rather few; air-bladder usually large and complicated (occasionally wanting); special drumming muscles developed in abdominal wall of many species, their function being to produce sounds by the impact of their vibrations on the air-bladder.

SHEEPSHEAD, *Aplodinotus grunniens* Rafinesque

Found near sandy shores of all warm seas, none occurring in deep water; a few species confined to fresh water; genera 30; species about 150. Many of them reach a large size and most are valued as food; all are carnivorous.

Genus **APLODINOTUS** Rafinesque

RIVER DRUMS

Body oblong, compressed, back elevated; mouth low, horizontal, the lower jaw included; no barbels; preopercle slightly serrate; teeth in villiform bands; lower pharyngeals very large, fully united, with coarse, blunt, paved teeth; dorsals somewhat connected, the spinous with a scaly sheath at base; second anal spine very strong; caudal double-truncate; air-bladder very large, simple, with no appendages. Fresh waters of the United States; a single species.

APLODINOTUS GRUNNIENS Rafinesque

SHEEPSHEAD; FRESH-WATER DRUM; CROAKER; WHITE PERCH

(Map CII)

Rafinesque, 1819, Journ. de Physique, 88.

G., II. 297 and 298 (**Corvina oscula and richardsoni**); J. & G., 567 (**Haploidonotus**); M. V., 144; J. & E., II, 1484; N., 40 (**Haploidonotus**); J., 50 (**Haploidonotus**); F. F., I. 3, 64 (**Haploidonotus**); F., 62 (**Haploidonotus**); L., 30.

Length 2 to 4 feet; body moderately elongate, robust but considerably compressed, the back strongly arched forward and the profile steep, with almost no angle at nape; depth 2.7 to 3.1; greatest width almost 2 in greatest depth; depth caudal peduncle 2.2 to 2.5 in its length. Color plain silvery gray on sides and back, white on belly; the gray everywhere with a liberal sprinkling of fine black dots; the white iridescent with pearly luster and the gray changeable from light greenish to coppery; lower part of nose white in a broad band plainly marked off from the upper olivaceous portion; iris brownish metallic; fins plain except for dark smoky gray on membranes. Head subconic, with blunt muzzle, 3.3 to 3.6; width of head 1.6 to 1.8; interorbital weakly convex, 3.2 to 3.7, nose 3.1 to 3.7, longer than eye and decurved; mouth subinferior, tip of upper lip below orbit; maxillary past middle of eye, 2.6 to 2.9; lower jaw shorter than upper; opercle emarginate, not ending in sharp points; preopercle serrate; gill-rakers short and stoutish, 6 + 14. Dorsal VIII or IX, I, 25 to 31, spinous continuous with soft portion, the notch gradual and deep, shortest posterior spine ⅓ of longest of spinous dorsal, longest spine a little more than 2 in head; base of soft dorsal 1.4 times base of spinous; caudal rounded or double-truncate; ventrals ⅔ to vent; pectorals rather long, pointed, 1.2 to 1.3 in head. Scales 9–10, 50–56, 11–13, strongly ctenoid; lateral line complete, much arched forward and parallel with the dorsal outline, its pores extending on caudal fin; cheeks and opercles scaled.

This remarkable species, particularly interesting because of its food and feeding structures, and because also of the peculiar grunting noise which it sometimes makes, is one of the more abundant larger species of our principal rivers and lakes. It has been taken by us in 72 collections, ranging from the Ohio at Cairo to the Mississippi at the mouth of Rock River and the Illinois at Ottawa. Two collections have come from the Saline River and from a branch of the Big Muddy in southern Illinois. Most of the others are from the Illinois or the lakes of its bottomlands. Like the two preceding species, this predominates in central Illinois, our frequency coefficient for which is 2.05.

It is generally distributed throughout the Great Lake basin and the Mississippi Valley between the Alleghanies and the western plains, ranging from Lake Champlain to the Red River of the North, and through the Ohio basin to Alabama, Louisiana, Arkansas, Texas, and Mexico.

In the Ohio Valley, in the South, and to some extent on the Illinois River, it is known and marketed as the white perch. In the Great Lake region it is more commonly called the sheepshead, and this is perhaps the name by which it is best known in Illinois. Gaspergou is a name used for it in the southern territories formerly occupied by the French. Thirty years ago the sheepshead was universally rejected by Illinois fishermen as worthless, but at the present time all except the largest are commonly dressed and sold. It reaches a large size, specimens of fifty to sixty pounds' weight being not uncommon. It becomes tough and strong with age, but is at its best when weighing from three quarters of a pound to three pounds. The market catch of sheepshead from the Illinois River in 1899 was 459,580 pounds. This fish is of a sluggish habit, living on the bottom of muddy waters, where it feeds especially on mollusks, the shells first being crushed by the powerful, paved, millstone-like, pharyngeal jaws. Often the stomach contains only the soft bodies and opercula of gastropod mollusks, the crushed shells evidently having been thrown out. Crawfishes are also sometimes found in the food. Half-grown specimens feed largely on aquatic insects, especially the larvæ of May-flies, mingling larger and larger proportions of mollusks with this food as they increase in size, until they come finally to depend almost wholly upon water-snails and the relatively thin-shelled clams.

The peculiar grunting sound made by this fish when caught, and also often heard as it moves about under the water, is probably due to vibrations of the wall of the air-bladder caused by the contraction of special "grunting muscles"—an apparatus demonstrated by Prof. R. W. Tower for the squeteague, a related marine species of drum.*

Judging from the condition of specimens obtained, our sheepshead probably spawns in the latter part of May or the first of June. This is not an angler's fish, but it is sometimes caught with crawfish bait.

The fact that the sheepshead and the white and the yellow bass inhabit the same waters and frequent similar situations, the two bass living on a similar food and the sheepshead on a widely different one, gives to the local distribution of this group of three associate species especial interest as illustrating the competitive relationship among fishes. Comparing our 55 collections of the white bass and our 96 collections of the yellow bass with our 64 collections of the sheepshead, we find that the first two species have been taken together in 20 collections, that the white bass and the sheepshead have also occurred in the same collections 20 times, and that the yellow bass and the sheepshead have been taken together 31 times. The corresponding ratios of associative occurrence are 5.21 for the two species of bass, 7.95 for the white bass and the sheepshead, and 11.91 for the sheepshead and the yellow bass. That is, the species which compete directly for the same food are found far less frequently together in the same situations, proportionately to the abundance of each, than are those which depend on different foods.

Family **COTTIDÆ**

THE SCULPINS

Body moderately elongate, fusiform or compressed, tapering backward from the head, which is broad and depressed; body naked or variously armed with scales, prickles, or bony plates, never uniformly scaled; lateral line present; skeleton osseous; vertebræ 30 to 50; ventrals thoracic, rarely wanting, I, 3 to I, 5; dorsals separate or somewhat connected, the spines 6 to 18, usually slender and sometimes concealed in skin; anal fin without spines; caudal rounded; no mesocoracoid; gills 3½ or 4, the slit behind the last small or obsolete; gill-membranes broadly connected, often joined to the isthmus; pseudobranchiæ present; gill-rakers short, tubercle-like or obsolete; preopercle usually with 1 or more spinous processes at its upper angle; third suborbital connected with preopercle by a bony backward extension or stay; premaxillary protractile; no supplemental maxillary; teeth in villiform or cardiform bands on jaws, and often on vomer and palatines; pyloric cæca usually 4 to 8; air-bladder commonly wanting.

* *Science*, Vol. XXII., p. 376.

The sculpins chiefly inhabit rocky pools and shores of northern regions; many species found in inland waters; genera about 60; species 250. None are valued as food.

Key to Genera and Species of **COTTIDÆ** found in Illinois

a. Ventrals with a concealed spine and four soft rays....................**Cottus.**

b. Preopercular spine short, usually inconspicuous, usually less than ½ eye; interorbital space nearly as wide as or wider than eye, 3.8 to 5.6 in head; depth of caudal peduncle 1.5 to 2 in its length; maxillary to middle of eye; dark cross-bars usually present...........................**ictalops.**

bb. Preopercular spine long, ⅔ to as long as* eye, strongly curved upward, backward, and inward, the skin of the head carried upward by the spine on each side in an ear-like manner; top of head flat, the interorbital space very narrow, little more than half of eye and contained 8 times in head, the eyes directed nearly upward; caudal peduncle very slender, its depth about 3.3 in its length; maxillary scarcely past front of orbit; color spotted or mottled, without distinct cross-bars......................**ricei.**

aa. Ventrals with a concealed spine and three soft rays...............**Uranidea.**

c. Preopercular spine less than ½ eye; interorbital space about half of eye, 7.5 to 8.5 in head; caudal peduncle moderately slender, its depth 2.2 to 2.4 in its length; maxillary to middle of orbit; sides irregularly spotted, without bars ....**kumlienii.**

Genus **COTTUS** (Artedi) Linnæeus

MILLER'S THUMBS

Body fusiform, skin smooth or more or less velvety, prickles, if present, not bony or scale-like; preopercle with a simple spine at its angle, which is usually curved upward, its base more or less covered with skin, rarely obsolete; gill-membranes separated by a wide isthmus, over which the membranes do not form a fold; no slit behind fourth gill; villiform teeth on jaws and vomer, and sometimes on palatines; dorsals nearly or quite separate; ventrals each with a concealed spine and 4 soft rays; lateral line present. These are sculpins of small size, inhabiting clear waters of the northern portions of Europe, Asia, and America; species numerous.

COTTUS ICTALOPS (Rafinesque)

COMMON SCULPIN; MILLER'S THUMB

(Pl. p. 300)

Rafinesque, 1820, Ichth. Oh., 85 (**Pegedictis**).
G., II, 158 (**richardsoni**); J. & G., 696 (**richardsoni**); M. V., 149 (**richardsoni**); J. & E., II, 1950; N., 41 (**Pegedichthys alvordi**); J., 50 (**Potamocottus alvordi, wilsoni, and meridionalis**); F. F., I. 6, 68 (**Potamocottus meridionalis**); F., 62 (**Uranidea richardsoni**); L., 30.

Length 3 to 7 inches; body robust forward, subcylindrical, tapering rapidly back of spinous dorsal; depth 3.7 to 4.3; width about ¾ depth; depth caudal peduncle 1.5 to 2 in its length. Color "olivaceous, more or less barred

* According to Jordan and Evermann; our single specimen with spine ⅔ of eye.

and specked with darker; fins mostly barred or mottled" (Jordan and Evermann). All our specimens have evident oblique dusky bars on posterior half of body. Head 3 to 3.5, convex above, the eyes directed outward as much as upward; width of head almost as great as its length; interorbital space 3.8 to 5.5; nose 2.8 to 3.4; mouth wide and lips very thick, maxillary 1.7 to 2.1 in head, to middle of orbit; upper preopercular spine short, usually less than half eye and rather inconspicuous; lower spines concealed in skin; isthmus 1.3 to 1.5 times eye; palatines with teeth. Dorsal VII to IX, 16 to 18; first dorsal scarcely 3/5 height of second; caudal spatulate; anal 13 to 15; pectorals to vent. Body entirely destitute of scales; a few prickles, often indistinct, behind pectorals; top of head warty; lateral line continuous or interrupted posteriorly.

This species inhabits clear, rocky brooks and lakes of the middle and northern United States, ranging from Kansas and the Dakotas to New York and Virginia. In our collections, which number 10 in all, it has been taken only in northern and southern Illinois: once in McHenry county; once from the Du Page near Joliet; six times from rocky spring branches in Union county; and once each in springs in Calhoun and Jersey counties.

About 25 per cent. of the food of six specimens taken in southern Illinois consisted of small fishes. Aquatic larvæ formed about 40 per cent. of the food, and the rest was mostly *Crustacea* (*Asellus*). In the clear streams and lakes of the north this fish has been found to be extremely destructive to the eggs and fry of trout.

COTTUS RICEI Nelson

Nelson, 1876, Bull. Ill. State Lab. Nat. Hist., I. 1, 40.
J. & G., 694 (**Uranidea spilota**) and 935 (**U. ricei**); M. V., 148; J. & E., II, 1952; J., 50 (**Tauridea spilota**); L., 30.

Length (of our single specimen) 2¼ inches; body rather slender, regularly tapered to the very slender caudal peduncle; depth 4.9; width about same as depth; depth caudal peduncle 3.3 in its length. Color (in spirits) brownish olive, sides irregularly and faintly mottled; faint traces of 2 dusky bars on caudal peduncle; last membranes of second dorsal dusky. Head very flat above, the eyes directed nearly upward; width of head equal to its length; interorbital space flat, very narrow, 8.2 in head; nose 3.6 the posterior nostril with conspicuous raised edges, tube-like; mouth narrow, smaller than in last species, and lips thinner, the maxillary scarcely past front of orbit, 2.9 in head; preopercular spine long, 2/3 of eye*; lower preopercular spines short and mostly concealed; the upper spine hooked backward and upward, carrying with it the skin of the head in an auricular flap-like appendage, giving

* Equal to eye, according to Nelson.

the fish a buffalo-like appearance; isthmus twice eye; palatine teeth obscure (present in Nelson's type). Dorsal VII, 16, the first ⅔ height of second; caudal spatulate; anal rays 13; pectorals to front of anal. Body scaleless, axils and top of head with prominent spinules; lateral line continuous.

Here described from a single specimen taken by the senior author in 1881, from a depth of 600 feet in Grand Traverse Bay, off Old Mission, Mich. Lacking access to Mr. Nelson's type, we refer the present specimen to *C. ricei*, notwithstanding disagreement with Nelson's description in one or two particulars, our specimen lacking the dorsal carination described by Nelson, and having the head smooth.

Genus **URANIDEA** De Kay

Preopercular spines small; usually no trace of teeth on palatines; ventrals reduced to a concealed spine and 3 soft rays; otherwise as in *Cottus*. Cold streams and springs of the United States; species 9 or 10; size small.

URANIDEA KUMLIENII Hoy

Hoy, 1876, in Nelson, Bull. Ill. State Lab. Nat. Hist., I. 1, 41.
J. & E., II, 1967; J., 50; L., 30.

Length 2½ inches; body slender, gradually tapering to the rather slender caudal peduncle; depth 5 to 5.2; width slightly less than depth; depth caudal peduncle 2.2 to 2.4 in its length. Color brownish olive, faintly mottled (in preserved specimens); spinous dorsal with a prominent dusky blotch on anterior and posterior two or three membranes; membranes of soft dorsal dusky toward base; pectorals reticulated with dusky. Head rather flattish above, but more convex than in *Cottus ricei*, 3.1 to 3.4; as wide as long; interorbital space 7.5 to 8.6; nose 3.3 to 3.6; mouth rather narrow, but large, maxillary to middle of orbit, 2.2 to 2.4 in head; preopercular spine about half of eye; lower spines not prominent; isthmus not greater than eye; palatines without exposed teeth. Dorsal VII or VIII, 15-17; first dorsal ¾ height of second; caudal narrow, spatulate; anal 12; pectorals to front of anal. Body nearly smooth; top of head and axils with some prickles; lateral line usually interrupted posteriorly (in one specimen continuous, but the pores on caudal peduncle sunken and inconspicuous).

Described from 3 specimens, taken in deep water in Traverse Bay, off Old Mission, Mich., by the senior author in 1881. Our specimens have not the lower jaw projecting, as called for in original description. Careful comparison with examples of *U. gracilis* from McLean, New York,* has been made, showing

* Courtesy of T. L. Hankinson.

that our specimens differ from that species chiefly in the presence of prickles in the axils—evidently a variable character as shown by our collections—and in the height of the first dorsal, which is 3/4 the length of the head (1/2 the head in specimens of *U. gracilis* examined). It appears not impossible that the present form should be regarded as a variety of *gracilis*.

Order ANACANTHINI

THE COD-LIKE FISHES

Skeleton bony; vertebræ numerous, the anterior simple; no spines in any of the fins; ventrals jugular, below or in front of the pectorals; tail isocercal (i. e., the vertebræ in a right line and becoming progressively smaller backward); pectoral arch suspended from the skull; no mesocoracoid; scapular foramen nearly always between the hypercoracoid and the hypocoracoid, and not in the hypercoracoid as typical in *Acanthopteri*; air-bladder without open duct.

A large group, confined mostly to the cold depths of the ocean and to the northern seas; a few fresh water representatives. Many of the marine species are among our most important food fishes.

Family GADIDÆ

THE CODFISHES

Body more or less elongate; tail tapering, coniform; scales small, cycloid; skeleton osseous; vertebræ numerous; ventrals jugular, the pelvic bones loosely attached to the clavicular symphysis by ligament; dorsal fin extending almost length of back, forming 1, 2, or 3 fins; anal long, single or divided; caudal distinct or confluent with dorsal and anal; no spines in any of the fins, all the rays being articulated; no mesocoracoid; hypercoracoid without foramen; gills 4, a slit behind the fourth; gill-membranes separated or somewhat united, commonly free from the isthmus; no pseudobranchiæ; posterior edge of preopercle usually covered by skin; mouth large, terminal; chin with a barbel; pyloric cæca usually numerous, sometimes few or none; vent submedian; air-bladder generally well developed.

The cods inhabit chiefly the seas of northern regions; a single genus confined to fresh waters. Genera about 25; species about 140. Many of the species are of great value as food fishes.

Genus LOTA (Cuvier) Oken

BURBOTS

Body long and low, compressed behind; head depressed; anterior nostrils each with a small barbel; chin with a long barbel; gill-openings wide, the membranes free from the isthmus; each jaw with broad bands of equal villiform teeth; vomer with a broad crescentic band of villiform teeth; no teeth on palatines; dorsal fins 2, the first short, the second long and similar to the anal; caudal rounded, its outer rays procurrent; scales very small, embedded; vertical fins scaly. One or two species; confined to the fresh waters of northern regions.

LOTA MACULOSA (Le Sueur)

BURBOT; LING; EEL-POUT

Le Sueur, 1817, J. Ac. Nat. Sci. Phila., I, 83 (**Gadus**).
G., IV, 359 (**vulgaris**, part); J. & G., 802; M. V., 162 (**lota**); J. & E., III, 2550; N., 42 (**lacustris**); J., 51 (**lacustris**); F., 62; F. F., II. 7, 433; L., 30.

Length 2 feet; body extremely elongate, not much compressed, except posteriorly, the back low and the profile long and straight; depth 7.6; greatest width of body about .7 to .9 greatest depth. Color "dark olive, thickly marbled and reticulated with blackish, yellowish or dusky beneath; young often sharply marked, the adult becoming dull grayish; vertical fins with dusky margins" (Jordan and Evermann). Head broad and depressed, 4.7 to 5 in length; width head 1.6 in its length; interorbital space flat, 3.4 to 3.6; nose 2½ times eye, 3.4 to 3.5, each nostril with a short barbel (½ eye); mouth horizontal, rather large, maxillary past back of pupil, 2.5 to 2.6; chin with a single median barbel 1½ times length of eye; gill-rakers short, about 3+6. Dorsal 12 or 13, 70 to 75, the second very long and low, its longest rays less than half head; caudal rounded, its outer rays procurrent, the separation between caudal, dorsal, and anal slight; anal rays about 65; ventrals inserted before pectorals; pectorals 1½ in head. Scales very small, embedded, 27 to 30 in an oblique series from front of second dorsal to lateral line; cheeks and opercles with very small embedded scales; all fins more or less scaly.

The range of this species is throughout New England and the Great Lake region and northward to the Arctic zone, in lakes and sluggish streams; occasionally taken in the Ohio and the upper Mississippi. Additional to its occurrence in Lake Michigan, we have specimens on record also from the Illinois River at Peoria, Havana, Meredosia, and Naples, from the Rock River at Milan, and from the Mississippi at Rock Island. These are all cases of the occurrence of a single fish in a place, and there is nothing to indicate any permanent invasion of our rivers by this species.

The burbot lives in deep water, where it lies during the day under the shelter of stones (Brehm). It is exceedingly voracious, not even sparing its own kind. Zadock Thompson* says that he has taken specimens with the abdomen so much distended with food as to give the fish the appearance of a globe-

* Evermann and Kendall, Rep. U. S. Fish Comm., 1894, p. 603.

fish or toadfish. One specimen sixteen inches long, examined by him, contained ten dace, none of which was less than four inches long. Fishes constituted about 80 per cent. of the food of specimens studied by the senior author in 1888, the remainder being crawfishes. Among the fishes recognized was a single whitefish, the remainder being the common yellow perch (*Perca flavescens*).

The flesh of the burbot is coarse and tasteless, and is seldom used for food. It is, in fact, of less value than any other American fresh-water fish of its size unless it be the gar, which it doubtless equals in destructiveness where it is abundant. Its interest to the scientist lies in its being the single fresh-water representative of the cod family in our waters. It is unknown by name to most of our river fishermen. It has been described to us by one of them as a fish "with a skin like a bullhead and a head like a dogfish, with a chin bristle." If the exception be made that very small scales are present, this brief description will suffice very well for the recognition of the species if found astray in our rivers or bottom-land lakes.

SELECTED BIBLIOGRAPHY

General Works on Fishes

Boulenger, G. A.
1895. Catalogue of the fishes in the British Museum. Ed. 2. Vol. 1. Lond., Taylor & Francis.

Brice, J. J.
1898. A manual of fish culture based on the methods of the U. S. Commission of fish and fisheries. Rep. U. S. fish comm., 1897, pp. 1–261, pl.

Bridge, T. W., and Boulenger, G. A.
1904. Fishes. Cambridge natural history, vol. 7, pp. 139–727, illus.

Dean, Bashford.
1895. Fishes, living and fossil. 300 pp. illus. N. Y., Macmillan. (Columbia univ. Biol. ser. 3.)

Goode, G. B.
1888. American fishes; a popular treatise upon the game and food fishes of North America. 496 pp. illus. N. Y., Standard Book Co.

1903. American fishes; a popular treatise upon the game and food fishes of North America. New ed. 562 pp. illus. col. pl. Bost., Dana Estes & Co.

Goode, G. B., and associates.
1884–1887. The fisheries and fishery industries of the United States. 7 vols. text and atlas. Washington, Government.

Günther, A. C. L. G.
1859–1870. Catalogue of the fishes in the collection of the British Museum. 8 vols. Lond., Taylor & Francis.

1880. An introduction to the study of fishes. 720 pp. illus. Edin., Black.

Jordan, D. S.
1888. Manual of the vertebrates of the northern United States. Ed. 5. 375 pp. Chicago, McClurg.

1905. A guide to the study of fishes. 2 vols. illus. N. Y., Holt.

Jordan, D. S., and Evermann, B. W.

1896–1900. The fishes of North and Middle America. Bull. U. S. national museum, no. 47, pts. 1–4, 3313 pp. pl.

1902. American food and game fishes. 573 pp. illus. col. pl. N. Y., Doubleday.

Jordan, D. S., and Gilbert, C. H.

1882. Synopsis of the fishes of North America. Bull. U. S. national museum, no. 16, 1018 pp.

Stevenson, C. H.

1898. The preservation of fishery products for food. Bull. U. S. fish comm., vol. 18, pp. 335–563, pl.

1904. Utilization of the skins of aquatic animals. Rep. U. S. fish comm., 1902, pp. 283–352, pl.

Pearse, A. S.

1915. On the food of the small shore fishes in the waters near Madison, Wisconsin. Bull. Wis. nat. hist. soc., vol. 13, pp. 7–22.

1918. The food of the shore fishes of certain Wisconsin lakes. Bull. U. S. bureau of fisheries, vol. 35, pp. 247–292.

Papers on Illinois Fishes

Kennicott, Robert.

1855. Catalogue of animals observed in Cook county, Illinois. Transactions Ill. agricultural society, vol. 1, pp. 577–595.

Nelson, E. W.

1876. A partial catalogue of the fishes of Illinois. Bull. Ill. state lab. nat. hist., vol. 1, no. 1, pp. 33–52.

1878. Fisheries of Chicago and vicinity. Rep. U. S. fish comm., 1875–76, pp. 783–800.

Jordan, D. S.

1878. A catalogue of the fishes of Illinois. Bull. Ill. state lab. nat. hist., vol. 1, no. 2, pp. 37–70.

Forbes, S. A.

1878. The food of Illinois fishes. Bull. Ill. state lab. nat. hist., vol. 1, no. 2, pp. 71–89.

1879. On some sensory structures of young dog-fishes. Amer. quarterly microscopical journal, vol. 1, no. 4, pp. 257–260, pl.

1880. On the food of young fishes. Bull. Ill. state lab. nat. hist., vol. 1, no. 3, pp. 66–79.

1880. The food of fishes. Bull. Ill. state lab. nat. hist., vol. 1, no. 3, pp. 18–65. Also in Rep. Ill. state fish comm., 1884, pp. 90–127.

Forbes, S. A.—*continued.*

1880. The food of the darters. Amer. naturalist, vol. 14, pp. 697–703.

1881. A rare fish in Illinois [*Chologaster*]. Amer. naturalist, vol. 15, pp. 232–233.

1881. Food of young whitefish—*Coregonus clupeiformis.* Bull. U. S. fish comm., vol. 1, pp. 19–20, 269–270.

1883. The food of the smaller fresh-water fishes. Bull. Ill. state lab. nat. hist., vol. 1, no. 6, pp. 65–94.

1883. The first food of the common whitefish (*Coregonus clupeiformis* Mitch.). Bull. Ill. state lab. nat. hist., vol. 1, no. 6, pp. 95–109. Also in Rep. U. S. fish comm., 1881, pp. 771–782.

——. A catalogue of the native fishes of Illinois. Rep. Ill. state fish comm., 1884, pp. 60–89.

1885. Description of new Illinois fishes. Bull. Ill. state lab. nat. hist., vol. 2, pp. 135–139.

1888. Studies of the food of fresh-water fishes. Bull. Ill. state lab. nat., hist., vol. 2, pp. 443–473.

1888. On the food relations of fresh-water fishes; a summary and discussion. Bull. Ill. state lab. nat. hist., vol. 2, pp. 475–538.

1888. The food of the fishes of the Mississippi Valley. Transactions Amer. fisheries society, vol. 17, pp. 1–17.

Garman, H.

1890. A preliminary report on the animals of the Mississippi bottoms near Quincy, Illinois, in August, 1888. Part 1. Bull. Ill. state lab. nat. hist., vol. 3, art. 9, fishes, pp. 134–148.

Illinois fishermen's association.

1899- ——. Annual reports giving the estimated amount and kinds of fish caught, and value of same. Rep. Ill. state fish comm., Oct. 1, 1896, to Sept. 30, 1898, pp. 5–7; Oct. 1, 1898, to Sept. 30, 1900, pp. 20–21; Sept. 30, 1900, to Oct. 1, 1902, pp. 30–31.

Large, Thomas.

——. A list of the native fishes of Illinois, with keys. Rep. Ill. state fish comm., Sept. 30, 1900, to Oct. 1, 1902. 30 pp. illus.

Richardson, R. E.

1904. A review of the sunfishes of the current genera *Apomotis, Lepomis,* and *Eupomotis,* with particular reference to the species found in Illinois. Bull. Ill. state lab. nat. hist., vol. 7, pp. 27–35.

Forbes, S. A., and Richardson, R. E.

1905. On a new shovelnose sturgeon from the Mississippi river. Bull. Ill. state lab. nat. hist., vol. 7, pp. 37–44, pl.

Miscellaneous Papers

Abbott, C. C.

1861. Notes on the habits of *Aphredoderus sayanus*. Proc. Academy nat. sci. Phil., 1861, pp. 95–96.

1870. Notes on fresh-water fishes of New Jersey. Amer. naturalist, vol. 4, pp. 99–117.

1870. Further notes on New Jersey fishes. Amer. naturalist, vol. 4, pp. 717–720.

1874. Notes on the cyprinoids of central New Jersey. Amer. naturalist, vol. 8, pp. 326–338.

1878. Notes on some fishes of the Delaware river. Rep. U. S. fish comm., 1875–76, pp. 825–845.

Agassiz, Alexander.

1878. The development of *Lepidosteus*. Proc. Amer. academy arts and sciences, vol. 14, pp. 65–76, pl. 1 col. pl.

Agassiz, Louis.

1854. Notice of a collection of fishes from the southern bend of the Tennessee river in the state of Alabama. Amer. journal science and arts, ser. 2, vol. 17, pp. 297–308, 353–369.

Atkins, C. G.

1905. Culture of the fallfish or chub. Amer. fish culturist, vol. 2, p. 189.

Bean, T. H., ed.

1890. Observations upon fish and fish culture. Bull. U. S. fish comm., vol. 10, pp. 49–61.

Berg, L. S.

1904. Zur systematik der Acipenseriden. Zoologischer Anzeiger, vol. 27, pp. 665–667.

Bollman, C. H.

1892. A review of the *Centrarchidæ*, or fresh-water sunfishes, of North America. Rep. U. S. fish comm., 1888, pp. 557–580, pl.

Bridge, T. W.

1878. On the osteology of *Polyodon folium*. Philosophical trans. Royal society Lond., vol. 169, pp. 683–733, 3 pl.

1897. On the presence of ribs in *Polyodon* (*Spatularia*) *folium*. Proc. Zool. society Lond., 1897, pp. 722–724.

Clark, F. N.

1893. History and methods of whitefish culture. Bull. U. S. fish comm., vol. 13, pp. 213–220.

Cole, L. J.
1905. The German carp in the United States. Rep. U. S. fish comm., 1904, pp. 525–641, pl.

Collinge, W. E.
1885. On the presence of scales on the integument of *Polyodon folium.* Journal anatomy and physiology, vol. 19, pp. 485–487.

Cope, E. D.
1866. Synopsis of the *Cyprinidæ* of Pennsylvania. Transactions Amer. philosophical society, n. s. vol. 13, pp. 351–399.

Culbertson, Glenn.
1904. Note on the breeding habits of the common or white sucker. Proc. Indiana academy sci., 1903, pp. 65–66.

Dawson, Jean.
1905. Breathing and feeding mechanism of the lampreys. Biol. bull., vol. 9, pp. 1–21, 91–111.

Dean, Bashford.
1895. Early development of gar-pike and sturgeon. Journal morphology, vol. 11, pp. 1–62, pl.

1896. Early development of *Amia.* Quarterly journal microscopical science, n. s. vol. 38, pp. 413–444, 3 pl.

Dean, Bashford, and Sumner, F. B.
1897. Notes on the spawning habits of the brook lamprey (*Petromyzon wilderi*). Transactions N. Y. academy sci., vol. 16, pp. 321–324, 1 pl.

Eigenmann, C. H.
1896. Fishes, spawning seasons. Proc. Indiana academy sci., 1895, p. 252.

1899. The eyes of the blind vertebrates of North America. 1. The eyes of the *Amblyopsidæ.* Archiv fur Entwicklungsmechanik der Organismen, vol. 8, pp. 545–617, pl.

Evermann, B. W.
1891. A report upon investigations made in Texas in 1891. Bull. U. S. fish comm., vol. 11, pp. 61–90, pl.

1899. Report on investigations by the U. S. fish commission in Mississippi, Louisiana, and Texas in 1897. Rep. U. S. fish comm., 1898, pp. 287–312, pl.

1902. Description of a new species of shad (*Alosa ohiensis*), with notes on other food-fishes of the Ohio river. Rep. U. S. fish comm., 1901, pp. 275–288.

Evermann, B. W., and Kendall, W. C.
1902. Annotated list of the fishes known to occur in the St. Lawrence river. Rep. U. S. fish comm., 1901, pp. 227–240.

Evermann, B. W., and Smith, H. M.
1896. Whitefishes of North America. Rep. U. S. fish comm., 1894, pp. 283–324, pl.

Eycleshymer, A. C.
1901. Observations on the breeding habits of *Ameiurus nebulosus*. Amer. naturalist, vol. 35, pp. 911–918.

Gage, S. H.
1893. Lake and brook lampreys of New York, especially those of Cayuga and Seneca lakes. Wilder quarter-century book, 1868—1893, pp. 421–493, pl.

Gardner, A. P.
1883. Experiments in the pond culture of trout, suckers, and catfish. Bull. U. S. fish comm., vol. 3, pp. 417–420.

Gill, Theodore.
1905. Family of cyprinids and the carp as its type. Smithsonian miscellaneous collections, vol. 48, pp. 195–217, pl.

Goode, G. B.
1882. Notes on the lampreys—*Petromyzontidæ*. Bull. U. S. fish comm., vol. 2, pp. 349–354.

Gurley, R. R.
1902. The habits of fishes. Amer. journal psychology, vol. 13, pp. 408–425.

Heckel, Jacob.
1841. *Scaphirhynchus*, eine neue Fishgattung aus der Ordnung der Chondropterygier mit freien Kiemen. Zoolog. Abhandl. Ann. Wiener Museums Naturgesch., vol. 1–2, pp. 69–78, 1 pl.

Henshall, J. A.
1880. Black bass vs. green bass. Forest and stream, vol. 14, pp. 510–511.

1881. Book of the black bass. 463 pp. illus. Cincinnati, Clarke.

1903. Bass, pike, perch, and others. 410 pp. illus. N. Y., Macmillan.

Hessel, Rudolph.
1878. Carp and its culture in rivers and lakes; and its introduction in America. Rep. U. S. fish comm., 1875–76, pp. 865–900.

Imms, A. D.
1904. Notes on the gill-rakers of the spoonbill sturgeon, *Polyodon spathula*. Proc. Zool. society Lond., 1904, vol. 2, pp. 22–35, 1 pl.

Jordan, D. S.
1878. A synopsis of the family *Catostomidæ*. Bull. U. S. national museum, no. 12, pp. 97–230.

1879. Notes on certain typical specimens of American fishes in the British Museum and in the Museum d'histoire naturelle at Paris. Proc. U. S. national museum, vol. 2, pp. 218–226.

Jordan, D. S., and Copeland, H. E.
1876. Johnny darters. Amer. naturalist, vol. 10, pp. 335–341.

Jordan, D. S., and Fordice, M. W.
1885. Review of the North American species of *Petromyzontidæ*. Annals N. Y. academy sci., vol. 3, pp. 279–296.

Kendall, W. C.
1902. Habits of some of the commercial cat-fishes. Bull. U. S. fish comm., vol. 22, pp. 399–409.

Kirsch, P. H., and Fordice, M. W.
1889. Review of the American species of sturgeons (*Acipenseridæ*). Proc. Academy nat. sci. Phil., 1889, pp. 245–257.

Kirtland, J. P.
1840–1847. Descriptions of the fishes of the Ohio river and its tributaries. Boston journal nat. hist., vol. 3, pp. 338–352, 469–482; vol. 4, pp. 16–26, 231–240, 303–308; vol. 5, pp. 21–32, 265–276, 330–344, pl.

Lydell, Dwight.
1902. The habits and culture of the black bass. Bull. U. S. fish comm., vol. 22, pp. 39–44, 1 pl.

Mark, E. L.
1890. Studies on *Lepidösteus*. Part 1. Bull. Museum comparative zool., Harvard, vol. 19, pp. 1–128, pl.

Marshall, W. S., and Gilbert, N. C.
1905. Notes on the food and parasites of some fresh-water fishes from the lakes at Madison, Wisconsin. Rep. U. S. fish comm., 1904, pp. 513–522.

Milner, J. W.
1874. Report on the fisheries of the Great Lakes and the species of *Coregonus* or whitefish. Rep. U. S. fish comm., 1872–73, app. A, pp. 1–89.

1874. New species of *Argyrosomus* and *Coregonus*. Rep. U. S. fish comm., 1872–73, pp. 86–89.

Moenkhaus, W. J.
1894. Variation of North American fishes. I. The variation of *Etheostoma caprodes* Rafinesque. Amer. naturalist, vol. 28, pp. 641–660, pl.

1896. Variation of North American fishes. II. The variation of *Etheostoma caprodes* Rafinesque in Turkey lake and Tippecanoe lake. Proc. Indiana academy sci., 1895, pp. 278–296.

1898. Material for the study of the variation of *Etheostoma caprodes* Rafinesque and *Etheostoma nigrum* Rafinesque in Turkey lake and Tippecanoe lake. Proc. Indiana academy sci., 1897, pp. 207–228.

Mulertt, Hugo.
1883. Habits of the black-headed minnow. Forest and stream, vol. 20, p. 450.

Page, W. F.
1894. Feeding and rearing fishes, particularly trout, under domestication. Bull. U. S. fish comm., vol. 14, pp. 289–314.

Pappenheim, P.
1905. Ueber die Acipenseriden-gattung Scaphirhynchus. Sitzungsbericht der Gesellsch. naturforsch. Freunde zu Berlin, 1905, pp. 5–7.

Reed, H. D.
1900. The structure of the poison glands of *Schilbeodes gyrinus*. Proc. Amer. ass'n advancement sci., vol. 49, pp. 232–233.

Reese, A. M.
1900. Lampreys in captivity. Biol. bull., vol. 1, pp. 161–162.

Reighard, Jacob.
1900. Breeding habits of the dog-fish, *Amia calva*. Abstract. Rep. Mich. academy sci., vol. 1, 1894–99, pp. 133–157, 1 pl.

1902. Some further notes on the breeding habits of *Amia*. Abstract. Rep. Mich. academy sci., vol. 3, pp. 80–81.

1902. Breeding habits of certain fishes. Science, n. s. vol. 15, pp. 574–575.

1903. Function of the pearl organs of the *Cyprinidæ*. Science, n. s. vol. 17, p. 531.

Reighard, Jacob—*continued*
1903. Natural history of *Amia calva* Linnæus. Mark anniversary vol., pp. 57–109, 1 col. pl.

Ryder, J. A.
1882. The Protozoa and protophytes considered as the primary or indirect source of the food of fishes. Bull. U. S. fish comm., vol. 1, pp. 236–251. Also in Rep. U. S. fish comm., 1881, pp. 755–770.

Seal, W. P.
1890. Observations on the aquaria of the U. S. fish commission at Central station, Washington, D. C. Bull. U. S. fish comm., vol. 10, pp. 1–12, pl.

Shufeldt, R. W.
1900. Notes on the psychology of fishes. Amer. naturalist, vol. 34 pp. 275–281.

Smiley, C. W.
1883. Answers to 118 questions relative to German carp. Bull. U. S. fish comm., vol. 3, pp. 241–248.

Smith, H. M.
1890. Report on an investigation of the fisheries of Lake Ontario. Bull. U. S. fish comm., vol. 10, pp. 177–215, pl.

1893. Statistics of the fisheries of the United States. Bull. U. S. fish comm., vol. 13, pp. 389–417.

1894. The fisheries of the Great Lakes. Rep. U. S. fish comm., 1892, pp. 363–462.

1898. Statistics of the fisheries of the interior waters of the United States. Rep. U. S. fish comm., 1896, pp. 489–574.

1904. The common names of the basses and sun-fishes. Rep. U. S. fish comm., 1902, pp. 355–366.

1905. The drumming of the drum-fishes (*Sciænidæ*). Science, n. s. vol. 22, pp. 376–378.

Smith, H. M., and Snell, M. M., compilers.
1891. Review of the fisheries of the Great Lakes in 1885, with introduction by J. W. Collins. Rep. U. S. fish comm., 1887, pp. 3–333, pl. maps.

Stranahan, J. J.
1897. The methods, limitations, and results of whitefish-culture in Lake Erie. Bull. U. S. fish comm., vol. 17, pp. 315–319.

Surface, H. A.
1897. Lampreys of central New York. Bull. U. S. fish comm., vol. 17, pp. 209–215, pl.

Tisdale, S. T.
1871. Habits of the black bass. Amer. naturalist, vol. 5, pp. 361–364.

Townsend, C. H., ed.
1902. Statistics of the fisheries of the Great Lakes. Rep. U. S. fish comm., 1901, pp. 575–657.

1902. Statistics of the fisheries of the Mississippi river and tributaries. Rep. U. S. fish comm., 1901, pp. 659–740.

Vaillant, Léon.
1873. Sur les affinités des Etheostomata (Agassiz). Comptes rendus Académie des sciences, Paris, vol. 76, pp. 1423–1426.

Wagner, George.
1904. Notes on *Polyodon*. Science, n. s. vol. 19, pp. 554–555.

Wilder, B. G.
1877. Gar-pikes, old and young. Popular science monthly, vol. 11, pp. 1–12.

1878. *Amia calva*. Proc. Boston society nat. hist., vol. 19, p. 337.

Wortman, J. L.
1882. Ichthyological papers by George Powers Dunbar, with a sketch of his life. Amer. naturalist, vol. 16, pp. 371–388.

Young, R. T., and Cole, L. J.
1900. On the nesting habits of the brook lamprey (*Lampetra wilderi*). Amer. naturalist, vol. 34, pp. 617–620.

Zograff, Nicholas.
1887. On some of the affinities between the *Ganoidei Chondrostei* and other fishes. Nature, vol. 37, p. 70.

ERRATA

Page cxxv, line 10 from bottom, for *anguilla* read *Ictalurus anguilla.*
Page 9, delete plate reference under heading.
Page 34, plate facing, as authority for *Lampetra wilderi*, read Gage.
Page 85, line 22, for fin-scaled read fine-scaled.
Page 94, line 5, for *Hydrophillidae* read *Hydrophilidae.*
Page 99, line 3 of table, for *Pimpephales* read *Pimephales.*
Page 145, line 2 of synonymy, for *analostoma* read *analostana.*
Page 160, line 1, for *Phyrganeidae* read *Phryganeidae.*
Page 220, line 8 from bottom, for *Centrachidae* read *Centrarchidae.*
Page 298, last line, for recognization read recognition.
Page 317, line 3, for 30 (16+20) read 30 (14+16).
Insert also the following missing letters, dropped out in printing:—

Page xliv, line 10 from bottom, i in is.
Page lxviii, line 10, i in Pulaski.
Page lxxii, line 13 from bottom, i in insensible.
Page lxxiii, line 19, i in relations; line 8 from bottom, l in called.
Page lxxxiii, under heading, line 4, l in conveniently.
Page xc, sixth-column heading, k in Kaskaskia.
Page xcvii, line 1, d in distinguished; line 2 from bottom, (first column,) *r* in *ricei.*
Page cvi, middle heading, n in glaciation.
Page cvii, line 7, t in turbid.
Page cviii, line 1, i in times.
Page cx, line 10 from bottom, s in Wabash.
Page cxi, line 1, l in miles.
Page cxxvii, line 17 from bottom, i in legislation.
Page cxxx, legend, line 2 from bottom, a in maxillary.
Page cxxxii, first legend, a *semicolon* at end of first line; line 2, *s* in *spl.*
Page 23, line 14 from bottom (not including foot-note), i in interest.
Page 35, line 10 from bottom, l in less.
Page 49, line 3 under first headings, l in dorsal.
Page 58, line 8 from bottom, l in lateral.
Page 61, line 11 from bottom, l in single.
Page 78, line 11 from bottom, a in almost.
Page 231, line 7 above last heading, h in toothless.

INDEX

—31 F

www.ingramcontent.com/pod-product-compliance
Lightning Source LLC
LaVergne TN
LVHW010517100826
845148LV00001B/30

* 9 7 8 1 4 2 5 5 7 3 9 4 2 *